The Canadian Short Story

European Studies in American Literature and Culture

Edited by Reingard M. Nischik
(University of Constance)

The Canadian Short Story

Interpretations

Edited by
Reingard M. Nischik

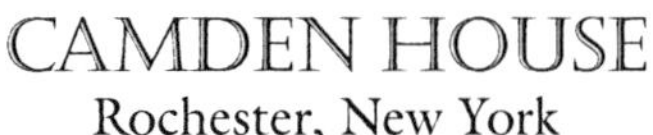

CAMDEN HOUSE
Rochester, New York

First published 2007
by Camden House

Camden House is an imprint of Boydell & Brewer Inc.
668 Mt. Hope Avenue, Rochester, NY 14620, USA
www.camden-house.com
and of Boydell & Brewer Limited
PO Box 9, Woodbridge, Suffolk IP12 3DF, UK
www.boydellandbrewer.com

ISBN-13: 978–1–57113–127–0
ISBN-10: 1–57113–127–2

Library of Congress Cataloging-in-Publication Data

The Canadian short story: interpretations / edited by Reingard M. Nischik.
p. cm. — (European studies in American literature and culture)
Includes bibliographical references and index.
ISBN-13: 978–1–57113–127–0 (alk. paper)
ISBN-10: 1–57113–127–2 (alk. paper)
1. Short stories, Canadian—History and criticism. I. Nischik, Reingard M. II. Title. III. Series.

PR9192.52.C36 2007
813′.010971—dc22

2006035153

A catalogue record for this title is available from the British Library.

This publication is printed on acid-free paper.
Printed in the United States of America.

Contents

Preface

THIS BOOK IS THE PALPABLE RESULT of my longtime love affair with Canadian short fiction, which dates back to the 1980s. Having taught Canadian short fiction and the North American short story off and on and in various contexts over the past two decades, the relative dearth of criticism on this particular body of texts on the Canadian side of the 49th parallel struck me repeatedly. Yet I had to cross the threshold into the twenty-first century before I decided to do my share about this in book form and in English. I hope that this volume will help to contextualize individual writers and their stories and further raise the profile of the Canadian short story, as it so much deserves next to its well-established American counterpart.

I am grateful to everyone who lent a hand to make this undertaking possible: First of all my American publishers at Camden House, who agreed that this book project should see the light of day and who then accompanied the editing and production process with their usual expertise and kindness. I also thank my twenty-six co-authors, who produced enlightening studies of major Canadian short fiction writers and particularly prominent or representative examples of their stories. All the contributors to this book, appearing in the book series European Studies in American Literature and Culture, are or have been affiliated with German, Austrian, and Swiss universities. All of them are engaged, among other things, with Canadian literature. This book, then, is also a tribute to the international involvement with Canadian short fiction, here referring especially to the "Canadophile" German-speaking countries. I made a point of inviting a mixture of senior, established, up-and-coming, and still very young scholars, in order to illustrate the continuing tradition of involvement with CanLit in the German-speaking countries and elsewhere. I find the way the younger contributors have taken up the challenge especially gratifying. Theirs is the future of Canadian studies, and it seems that the field is in very good hands.

I particularly want to thank my highly competent and efficient AmCan team at the University of Constance, without whose conscientious efforts it would not have been possible to complete this daunting project within a manageable period of time: Julia Breitbach and Florian Freitag in particular, but also Eva Gruber and Georgiana Banita were very helpful in editing this volume. Emily Petermann, my American native speaker, who found her way from Wellesley College, Massachusetts, to Constance, promptly and meticulously checked the English of all contributions. Christine Schneider was my constant consolation in the typing and revising process, as the steady flow of MSS in their many versions passed through her conscientious and patient hands at the PC. Anja Ging, finally, conscientiously produced the index.

A few technical comments: with respect to secondary literature, the year given in bibliographical references in parentheses in the articles is from the particular edition used (as shown in the article's works cited list), not the year of first publication. The works cited lists include only titles that are either quoted from or directly referenced in the articles. They do not include novels, poems, or plays mentioned in the articles. All short-story collections referred to are, however, included in the works cited lists (except for the introductory chapter).

R. N.
October 2006

The Canadian Short Story: Status, Criticism, Historical Survey

Reingard M. Nischik

> I incline to find more and more that the short story is one of the trickiest forms.
>
> —Dorothy Livesay

IN ITS MAIN LINE OF DEVELOPMENT, the English-Canadian short story is a relatively recent literary phenomenon, spanning a little more than 100 years by now. It began to coalesce as a national genre in the 1890s, some seventy years after the beginnings of the American short story around 1820. Canadian short stories of the late nineteenth century — by writers like Isabella Valancy Crawford, Susan Frances Harrison, Ernest Thompson Seton, or even Charles G. D. Roberts — could not match the significance and excellence of American short-story writers of the American Renaissance such as Nathaniel Hawthorne, Edgar Allan Poe, or Herman Melville. It was only in the twentieth century, with Morley Callaghan's development of the modernist Canadian short story in the 1920s, that the genre came into its own in Canada and joined the realm of world literature. The crucial ascendancy of the Canadian short story, however, began in the 1960s, raising the quality, diversity, and prominence of the genre in Canada to new levels.

The short story is today generally considered to be a particularly vital genre, if not the flagship genre of Canadian literature. Its continuing success is reflected first of all in the fact that major Canadian writers have almost without exception devoted considerable effort to the form, and have succeeded in producing internationally renowned collections of short stories. Second, several Canadian short-story writers indubitably rank among the world's best — and best-known — contemporary writers of short fiction, such as Alice Munro and Margaret Atwood. These authors have been awarded major international literary prizes for their works, for instance the Booker Prize (Atwood) or the W. H. Smith Award and the National Book Critics Circle Award (Munro). Almost as a matter of course by now, several Canadian writers frequently first publish their short stories in *The New Yorker*, the foremost international forum for the genre. Even apart from such international achievements, the contemporary Canadian short story is a lively and productive genre. Thus the annual Governor General's Award (here: for Fiction), Canada's most important literary prize, has for almost thirty years been granted one out of three times to Canadian short-story collections rather than to novels. Then too, the number of anthologies of Canadian short stories published in Canada is remarkably high.

In contrast to this, surprisingly little literary criticism has been devoted to the Canadian short story. The relatively few helpful contributions (see the bibliography at the end of the book) may be broken down into the categories of historical, generic or subgeneric, literary-sociological, narratological, regional, and didactic approaches. The historical approaches are most numerous, yet so far there are only two systematic and wide-ranging historical surveys (outside the literary histories) of the Canadian short story (Gadpaille 1988, in book form, and Gadpaille 2001, in article form). Students and scholars thus often lack the necessary background information when studying the genre or individual examples of it. The present project attempts to fill this gap — it constitutes the first overview of its topic by way of assembled interpretations of selected major Canadian short stories. The intention is to offer a well-founded survey of the Canadian short story from its beginnings to the present. Since the precursors of the short story proper in Canada go back to the nineteenth century, two texts from the period before the 1920s are included, as well as several classic examples of the modernist Canadian short story of the 1920s through the 1950s. The larger part of the volume, however, is devoted to the Canadian short story from the "Canadian Renaissance" of the 1960s onwards, the two most recent stories included having first been published in 1999.

The selected authors count among the most important Canadian short-story writers. Obviously, many others also deserving attention in a study of the Canadian short story had to be left out, such as Alistair MacLeod, Sandra Birdsell, Rohinton Mistry, Diane Schoemperlen, Bonnie Burnard, Dionne Brand, Timothy Findley, Katherine Govier, Barbara Gowdy, Alden Nowlan, Ray Smith, Austin Clarke, Matt Cohen, Neil Bissoondath, Marian Engel, Eden Robinson, Elisabeth Harvor, and others. In choosing the writers and stories to be included, I avoided a purely subjective selection by basing my choices on a survey of ninety-two Canadian short story anthologies (most published in Canada), selecting writers and — in most cases — stories that have been most frequently anthologized. The stories analyzed in this book, then, are by and large, judging by the choices of a range of editors of Canadian short fiction, the most prominent Canadian examples of the genre. This method of selection is certainly conservative, since it clearly works against newcomers and younger and/or experimental writers, instead privileging older authors and less recent stories (though it does not wholly lose sight of recent developments). Yet it is an appropriate step given the current state of scholarship in the area. For the first time, then, interpretations of prominent Canadian short stories are made available in a single volume.

In order to achieve consistency in the approach throughout the book, the contributors were asked to structure their articles according to the following scheme: brief general information on the author; basic information on and contextualization of the author's short-story production; importance of the author within Canadian short-story history; detailed interpretation of the selected text; conclusion. The volume as a whole is meant to provide not only a collection of interpretations of individual prominent or representative short stories, but at the same time also a historical survey of the Canadian short story.

Precursors of the Short Story in the Nineteenth Century: Early Canadian Short Prose

> At the time of Confederation in 1867, short fiction already filled the magazines of the new country. These early stories, however, differed from the modern short story, often being closer in form and content to other prose genres such as the sketch, anecdote, editorial, and essay. . . . Today's definitions of short fiction must be relaxed when one surveys fiction of these earlier times. . .; much that was then considered excellent writing . . . appears nauseatingly sweet to the twentieth-century reader.

Thus Michelle Gadpaille opens her short survey, "Canadian Short Fiction" (2001, 2898). She then goes on to point out parallels and divergences between early Canadian and American short fiction, American short fiction having been more of a model for the developing genre in Canada than British short fiction. Among the parallels are that in both literatures the sketch and the anecdote were significant antecedents of the short story; that many writers of short fiction worked in journalism as well, which bears on the structure and style of their fiction; and that there were strong local-color traditions in both literatures in the last decades of the nineteenth century, which resulted in the genre moving toward naturalism and realism. Among the divergences between early American and Canadian short fiction Gadpaille mentions the French-Canadian development;[1] the lack of an African-Canadian tradition of storytelling in Canada, such as represented

[1] "Writers in French Canada (Quebec as well as French-speaking parts of Ontario, Manitoba, and New Brunswick) were producing short pieces as early as the 1830's, although recognizable short fiction really began with the Abbé Henri-Raymond Casgrain in the 1860's" (Gadpaille 2001, 2899).

by the works of Charles W. Chesnutt in the USA; the lesser importance of the tall tale, as represented by Mark Twain in the USA; and the lack in Canada of "the detective, supernatural, or scientifically speculative tale" (Gadpaille 2001, 2899) in the line of Edgar Allan Poe. One should add the significant difference that the American short story of the nineteenth century contributed many of the standard representatives of the genre to world literature, whereas in Canada the short story proper, with its tight structure, was only being prepared for in the nineteenth century.

Thomas McCulloch and Thomas Chandler Haliburton introduced the humorous tradition, in a local-color context, to Canadian short prose, later to be picked up and further developed by the Canadian master of humorous prose, Stephen Leacock, at the beginning of the twentieth century. McCulloch's *Letters of Mephibosheth Stepsure* first appeared in the *Acadian Recorder* in 1821 (1862 in book form), Haliburton's Sam Slick stories in *The Novascotian* between 1826 and 1835 (in book form in 1836 as *The Clockmaker: Or, The Sayings and Doings of Samuel Slick of Slickville*). Both texts were originally serialized and thereby forerunners of what later developed into the short-story cycle, still a popular form in Canada. They make use of local color, character sketches, anecdotes, irony, and national stereotyping for their humorous effects.

Other notable Canadian writers of short prose in the nineteenth century include Rosanna Leprohon, Isabella Valancy Crawford, Susan Francis Harrison, Gilbert Parker, and Edward William Thomson. Today they are mainly known for a few of their less formulaic stories reprinted in anthologies of Canadian short fiction. Even these stories nevertheless tend to draw skeptical comments from today's critical perspective:[2] in nineteenth-century Canadian fiction, sentimental romances, plot-driven adventure tales, and formula writing were the order of the day.

The two major original nineteenth-century contributions to Canadian short fiction were the Canadian animal story and Duncan Campbell Scott's story collection *In the Village of Viger*. Ernest Thompson Seton and Charles G. D. Roberts are the main representatives of the animal story. Roberts "invented" the genre in 1892 with "Do Seek Their Meat from God," the first of some 200 animal stories that were to follow from his pen

[2] See e.g. Gadpaille 1988 on Crawford's story "Extradited": "in spite of a ragged narrative and Crawford's infelicitous way with words . . . ," 11–12; or Dean 2000, xiv: "Parker's habit of inventing locales, 'Indian' legends and 'Indian tribes' is stunningly racist as well as frighteningly inaccurate. . . . The traces of racist and masculinist ideologies are clearly identifiable in Roberts' representations of animals, and in Thomson's French Canadians."

and proved very successful at the time — also with an international readership, not least because they fit the image of Canada as a country of wilderness. The animal story became the epitome of the Canadian short story at the time, and was translated into many languages. It brought radical innovation to the time-honored representation of animals in world literature, resulting in the naturalist or realist wild animal story. This new type of story was informed by scientific research such as Darwin's evolutionary theory and offered unsentimental, psychological insight into the struggle for survival from the animals' perspective. The difference between Roberts, who was the more sophisticated storyteller, and Seton, who regarded himself foremost as a naturalist and a painter, was summarized by Alec Lucas: "for Roberts it was art first; for Seton it was science" (1958, vi). With its accurate representation of the Canadian wilderness and wildlife, the animal story took Canadian fiction a decisive step further in the direction of realism.

Duncan Campbell Scott's story collection *In the Village of Viger* (1896) can be seen as a turning point in the development of Canadian short fiction, foreshadowing modernism. Set in Quebec, his stories provide a largely realistic depiction of character and of complex psychological states in the context of a village community. At the beginning of the twentieth century, Sara Jeannette Duncan, influenced by the American realists William Dean Howells and in particular Henry James, formulated the Canadian realist credo: "Life should be represented as it is and not as we should like it to be." Though the author of only one collection of short fiction (*The Pool in the Desert*, 1903), Duncan's sophisticated writing style and handling of theme ushered in the new century, which was to bring tremendous changes to Canadian short fiction.

The Modernist Short Story

The break between premodernist and modernist writing in English-Canadian short fiction could hardly be more evident, with the Canadian short story fully emerging as a distinct literary genre only with the advent of the modernist short story in the 1920s. This is indeed the period when Canadian short stories for the first time correlate with our modern-day definition of the short story, as described, for instance, by Misao Dean:

> The fast pace of "modern" life and the demand of readers for intense experiences seemed to suggest a correspondingly short and intense prose form, leading to the conventional and highly formalized generic definition of the short story as a "fragment of a life": a story unified in place, action and time, whose dramatization of a revelatory and emotionally

> intense moment manages to suggest the outcome of a complete "life story" in a concentrated form. (Dean 2000, xvi)

The modernist development of the Canadian short story is closely connected to the life and works of Raymond Knister (1899–1932).[3] Knister was of fundamental significance for the genre's incipient stage, as well as for the development of Canadian literary modernism in general. His importance in regard to the Canadian short story rests on his contributions to the poetics of the Canadian brand of the genre, on his early attempts, as editor of Canada's first anthology of English-Canadian short stories, to create a canon of the genre, and on his own short-story production.

In "Democracy and the Short Story" (written in 1920, first published in 1975), Knister emphasizes the unrivaled excellence of the contemporary American short story and relates its significance to the high number of short stories published in the USA and their distribution in widely-circulating popular magazines. At the same time he denounces the "Americanization" of the genre, against which he would like the Canadian short story to take a stand ("The Canadian Short Story," 1923). Knister understands "Americanization" to mean the commercialization of short-story writing, fostered by the success of correspondence schools with their stereotypical plot and formula stories that leave no room for innovation. Instead, Knister promotes — as did T. S. Eliot in his seminal essay "Tradition and the Individual Talent" (1919) — individuality and originality as well as a pronounced consciousness of technique and form in order to achieve technical versatility and variation, often in an indirect, concealed manner. Though not using the term explicitly, he thus advocates a "new form" (391), the modernist short story. For Knister (whose equally noteworthy lyrical oeuvre is, significantly, indebted to the imagist movement), short fiction is linked to precise observation, narrative economy, stylistic succinctness, as well as concise, "objectifying" images to indirectly convey feelings and emotions. His sparsely-plotted stories open up to a new, realist dimension, as opposed to the schematically structured plot story.

Knister's influential role in the development of Canadian literature in general and the Canadian short story in particular manifests itself in his editorship of *Canadian Short Stories* (published in 1928 with Macmillan, Toronto), the first anthology of English-Canadian short stories and Knister's first published book. Seven months of intense research and twelve years of extensive reading resulted in a pioneering work. Knister himself wrote about 100 short stories, fifty of which are available in print today. Among his best-known stories are his farm stories (for example "The First

[3] "The name Knister is pronounced with the 'K' sounded and the 'i' long" (Givens 1979–80, 7).

Day of Spring," "Mist Green Oats," "The Strawstack," "The Loading"), set in southwest Ontario and mainly focusing on male protagonists and their experiences of initiation (such as first love), disillusion, guilt and innocence, tensions between family members — in particular between father and son — and death. The vague, hardly realistic hopes and tentative attempts of the protagonists to overcome their sense of confinement on the farm often pivot on their imaginative identification with and spiritualization of nature in all its mythic beauty — in stark contrast to the numbing chores of a monotonous farm life. In his farm stories, Knister introduces the reader to his characters' inner worlds with distinctively modernist narrative techniques such as subjective narrative focalization, allusion, ellipsis, epiphany, and indirect, symbolistic rendering of information. His "state of mind stories" (for instance "Elaine," "The Fate of Mrs. Lucier") reduce the external plot even more than his farm stories, ultimately minimizing it to the function of merely intimating an awareness of their female protagonists' consciousnesses. A third group of stories draws on Knister's brief work experience in the USA: his "Chicago stories" or "crime stories" (for instance "Hackman's Night," "Innocent Man"). Knister's stories smoothed the way for the modernist short story in Canada. They deal with a wide range of themes and employ a variety of narrative styles, demonstrating a general competence in narrative strategies. Once in a while, however, the author's narrative techniques and his use of language betray some of his texts as "beginner's stories," which would have profited from revision at a more mature artistic stage (which he did not experience due to his early death at thirty-three). "Elaine," for example (Knister's fifth story), overuses modernist strategies such as ambiguity, allusion, ellipsis, and the portrayal of consciousness to the point of excessive obscurity; so does "The Loading." Stylistic inconsistencies such as unclear pronoun referents, clumsy sentence rhythms, inadequate vocabulary, or awkward expressions occasionally disturb the quality of Knister's innovative stories.

Frederick Philip Grove (1879–1948), a friend of Knister's and twenty years his senior, had his first short stories published in 1926. Grove is primarily known as the first significant prairie novelist in Canada to write in a realist or naturalist manner. Further, he is the author of semi-autobiographical novels in which the deliberate mingling of fact and fiction anticipates postmodernist strategies, and of literary and cultural criticism. Ever since 1972, when Douglas O. Spettigue exposed Grove's spectacular autobiographical lie (proving Grove to be German writer and translator Felix Paul Greve, who had faked suicide in Germany and established a new identity as Grove in Canada), the interest in Grove's fascinating persona has tended to eclipse the study of his work. But the 1970s also saw the belated rediscovery of Grove as an author of short stories. Like Knister, Grove managed to publish some pieces during his lifetime (mainly in the

Winnipeg Tribune Magazine in 1926 and 1927), yet did not live to see a collection of his stories. *Tales from the Margin: The Selected Stories of Frederick Philip Grove* was not published until 1971, introducing an astonished readership of Grove insiders to a multifaceted short-story oeuvre that is at least on a par with the author's novels. Until then, knowledge of Grove's short stories had been by and large confined to the frequently anthologized story "Snow" (1932), which, in a naturalist manner, reflects key elements of Grove's novelistic oeuvre: the setting in an inhospitable prairie landscape, here in the depths of winter; the overpowering, inevitable influence of the natural or social environment on taciturn characters whose fate appears to have been determined in advance; the detailed, realistic portrayal of setting (particularly the natural surroundings), characters, and plot; the depiction of hardship and privation in the lives of the pioneers, who do not so much act but react — even to the point of downright fatalism at the end of the story. The symbolically coded *in medias res* beginning of "Snow" reveals how vividly Grove's writing used the Canadian prairie as a formative setting for the modernist Canadian short story — a pioneering achievement indeed, which would soon inspire writers such as Sinclair Ross and later W. O. Mitchell, Margaret Laurence, and Rudy Wiebe.

Although Grove's classification as a prairie writer builds on a central aspect of his work, a full appraisal of his short-story oeuvre finds a greater variety than is usually acknowledged. His settings, for example, comprise a diversity of Canadian landscapes and cities, as well as the coastal region of Northern France in the important story "The Boat" or even the indeterminate, allegorical "far-away-country" in the story "In Search of Acirema" (note the anagram of the title: Acirema/America). Grove's protagonists, despite appearing and feeling insignificant in the face of a seemingly omnipotent nature, are far from one-dimensional or repetitive. Grove also commands a broad range of narrative tones, which exceeds what would be expected to accompany the unmitigated tragedy he is usually associated with due to his best-known story "Snow"; he employs irony (for example in "The Sale"), life-affirming optimism (see the ending of "Lazybones"), and even humor (in "The Extra Man").

Thus Grove is a writer whose literary work remains as hard to pin down as his biography, and critics have labeled Grove's style an example of realism (psychological, social, or regional), naturalism, symbolism, and even existentialism. A correlation with "modernism" is missing in this context — and rightfully so. Grove clearly stands in between tradition and modernity. As the first important English-Canadian writer of realist or naturalist stories, publishing about thirty years after Duncan Campbell Scott's and Sara Jeanette Duncan's short-story collections, Grove in fact wrote in the vein of American authors of the last decades of the nineteenth century, such as Bret Harte, Mark Twain, Ambrose Bierce, Stephen Crane, and Jack

London. Thus notwithstanding the importance of Grove's efforts to establish the postromantic, realist short story in Canada, his narrative style in the late 1920s obviously lagged behind the avant-garde modernist writings of his Canadian contemporaries such as Raymond Knister and Morley Callaghan.

With Callaghan (1903–90), the Canadian short story in the late 1920s caught up with world literature, particularly with the American short story. Callaghan's productive period ranges over almost seven decades, until his death in 1990. His first short story, "A Girl with Ambition," appeared in the Paris journal *This Quarter* in 1926, and his main phase of short-story writing stretches from the late 1920s to the early 1950s. Although Callaghan, like Knister and Grove, initially suffered from the still underdeveloped literary infrastructure in Canada at the time, he was already successful in his younger years, especially in the USA and Europe. Callaghan was "Canada's first great internationalist" (Boire 1992, 208), and he soon saw his short prose published in collected form. His first short-story collection, *A Native Argosy*, appeared in 1929 with Scribner's in New York and Macmillan in Toronto. Not counting his novellas, Callaghan wrote more than 100 short stories. They were often first published in *The New Yorker* or *Scribner's Magazine*, and later appeared in four collections. His focus on the short story lay the foundation for the development of the genre in Canada.

Callaghan charted the big city for the Canadian short story: most of his stories are set in his hometown Toronto, but some — particularly in the later collections — are set in New York or Montreal. At the same time, he also features small towns or rural settings, especially in southern Ontario. In his first collection in particular — still heavily influenced by the naturalist tradition — Callaghan shows a preference for characters at the margins of society, isolated outsiders in constant struggle with themselves and with their social environment, whom the author, although displaying an implicitly moralistic tone, nonetheless depicts in their individuality and dignity. In his later stories, too, Callaghan portrays lower-middle-class characters, dealing with their problems in private relationships and questions of social acceptance.

Callaghan's contribution to the further development of the modernist style of writing in the short story is irrefutable. Like Knister, he de-emphasizes plot in favor of fragmentary reflections on his characters' inner worlds rather than extraordinary external events, and points out the significant in the everyday. Further trademarks of his narrative style are the ironic narrative voice, the ambiguity of plot and language, and, above all, the laconic diction, which has time and again spurred associations with Ernest Hemingway. Particularly in his early work, Callaghan's vocabulary and syntax create a deceptively simple and direct, deliberatively repetitive, unadorned style. The combination of narrative techniques that objectify and document while engaging the reader was inspired to a large extent by Callaghan's side job as a journalist for the *Toronto Daily Star* (where he also met Hemingway). Hemingway and Fitzgerald in particular recommended young Callaghan to editors and publishers in Paris and New York and thereby helped him to an early and abiding international success. Thus beginning in 1928 and for the ensuing fourteen years Callaghan's short stories were included in the annual volumes *The Best Short Stories of* . . . [the year] *and The Yearbook of the American Short Story*. The prolific Callaghan brought the Canadian short story not only international standing and praise, but he was also the first to prove the genre profitable on the literary market.

Sinclair Ross (1908–96), on the other hand, who was discovered as an outstanding author only in the 1970s, could not make a living on his writing; he supported himself as a bank clerk. Compared to Callaghan, Ross produced a fairly small oeuvre, which owes its considerable reputation mostly to his early work, his first novel *As for Me and My House* (published 1941 in New York) and his short stories published primarily in the 1930s and 1940s. Ross was the first modern Canadian short-story writer whose stories were mainly published in Canadian magazines, mostly in the Canadian scholarly journal *Queen's Quarterly*. Against the cultural background of the 1930s in Canada, the Canadian literary magazines' acceptance of Ross's, that is, a Canadian writer's, works at the time may be due to his less experimental style in comparison to Knister and Callaghan, a style that in regard to form and narrative technique is rather conventional. His preferred setting, in the early stories in particular, of the Canadian prairie during the Depression era may also have contributed to his early acceptance in Canada. Both form, setting, and theme link Ross to his predecessor Grove. The first collection of his short stories, *The Lamp at Noon*, consists almost exclusively of pieces from this geographical and historical context, thereby introducing Ross as the first native-born prairie writer, who re-creates the Saskatchewan prairie not only as a documentary setting, but as a region of the mind, opening up to the reader the psychological world of the characters. Following the example of the immigrant Grove, Ross turned against the earlier romance-like if not sentimental representation of the prairie (for instance in the works of bestselling author Ralph Connor, 1860–1937), and in the process firmly established the Canadian realist prairie short story.

Among the idiosyncracies of narrative representation in Ross's prairie stories are the close connection between humans and their natural environment, with the prairie farmer repeatedly pitted against an extreme climate and struggling for physical and mental survival in the face of what seems to be an overpowering and indifferently cruel nature; the isolation and alienation of the individual in that environment; the spatial and psychological isolation between husband and wife; the imminence of death.

In a modernist fashion, Ross's stylistic-narrative economy transforms external incidents and images into symbolic, indirect expressions of the characters' inner states (for instance, the "lamp at noon" burning in defiance of the surrounding darkness of the sandstorm). In Ross's classic stories, the desolate conditions in the prairie region in the 1930s, when economic depression and years of drought went hand in hand, are often narrowed down to the emotional and communicative deficits in hopeless relationships between man and woman. Both sexes display a conventionally gendered behavior, outdated from today's point of view: the emotionally repressive, outward-oriented male, who finds his self-esteem in the successful managing of his daily work, in particular the subjugation of nature, versus the lonely housewife confined to the domestic sphere, who feels neglected emotionally as well as sexually and strives in vain to alter her frustrating existence. The manner in which Ross — despite his predominant portrayal of extreme deprivation and human limitations — nevertheless finds meaning in existence and human dignity in his characters raises his stories of the 1930s and 1940s far above their temporal and regional frame in significance.

Ethel Wilson (1888–1980), whose short stories first appeared between 1937 and 1987 (about one-third of them posthumously), took the short story all the way to the Far West of Canada: more than half of Wilson's nearly thirty published stories (the best of which were collected in *Mrs. Golightly and Other Stories* in 1961) are at least partially set in Vancouver, various others in the rural interior regions of British Columbia, Canada's westernmost province. Even stories with locations outside British Columbia frequently feature Vancouverites as protagonists, for instance "Haply the Soul of My Grandmother" or "We Have to Sit Opposite." Although Wilson thus more than any other writer established Vancouver, her place of residence for many years (1898–1980), on the literary map, she is not a "city writer" like her contemporaries Morley Callaghan or Hugh Garner (see below). For even in the stories set in Canada's westernmost metropolis, Wilson underlines the contrast between Vancouver's urban identity on the one hand and the more natural, more rural aspects of both the city itself and the wider region on the other hand. She thereby often divests the picturesquely situated city of all typically metropolitan characteristics (hence preserving the image of Vancouver as a frontier town, a vestige of an earlier phase in the city's history, which Wilson herself experienced after emigrating to Vancouver from England in 1898 at the age of ten). Wilson frequently portrays Vancouver as a liminal space, a space of transition and even escape, but also as the awaited sanctuary from disappointing if not dangerous human relationships (symbolized by the repeatedly described "flying birds"), for example in "The Window" or "Till Death Us Do Part." Echoes of an arcadian contextualization of the big city are continually undercut by the depiction of threats arising from urban and adjoining areas, ranging from juvenile delinquency (in "Fog") to murderous intentions and homicide (in "The Window" and "Hurry, Hurry"). In the final analysis, however, pastoral yearnings are not satisfied by natural settings either (see "On Nimpish Lake"). Even an encroachment of horror upon the beauties of nature can be found in stories like "Hurry, Hurry" or "The Birds." Human existence in both the city and in natural settings in Wilson's stories turns out to be precarious, if not dangerous ground for the protagonists, who are often depicted as lonely and alienated; not without reason does the epigraph to *Mrs. Golightly* by Edwin Muir state: "life '. . . is a difficult country, and our home.' "

With regard to theme, characters, and narrative technique Wilson's stories are very diverse. Among the best-known are "Mrs. Golightly and the First Convention" and "We Have to Sit Opposite" (both 1945), which are set, respectively, in the USA and in Europe — two texts interspersed with irony and comedy, yet conveying a grim level of meaning. The latter story, for example, stages the intercultural confrontation between two cultured Canadian ladies and a lower-class German family in a train compartment en route to Munich in the 1930s, not only parading out common national stereotypes of both countries, but also dealing in retrospect with the then-impending international threat of Nazi Germany. As these stories demonstrate, the polishing of preferably simple words and sentences to a highly concise and elegant style has become the author's trademark.

With the prolific Hugh Garner (1913–79), who published short stories from 1938 through a creative period of four decades, the Canadian short story becomes a popular genre in a wider sense. Garner wrote 100 stories, which were often first published in Canadian popular magazines such as *Chatelaine*, *Canadian Home Journal*, or *National Home Monthly* and were reprinted in five collections during the author's lifetime. Particularly until the early 1960s, Garner professed his interest in reaching a large audience (in 1951 alone, he sold seventeen stories to Canadian magazines). Garner's artistic credo could be said to pander to the reader: "I believe, along with W. Somerset Maugham, that the first duty of a writer of fiction is to entertain" (Garner 1952, n.p.). This approach, together with Garner's undeniably great narrative talent, probably made him the most widely read short-story author in Canada in the 1950s. For the same reason, though, literary critics have often remained skeptical, mistrusting Garner's popular success and the style that he cultivated to achieve it (for instance his stock repertoire of drastic plot elements). His frequent anti-intellectual statements and his candidness, for example in his autobiography *One Damn Thing After Another* (1973), in which he discussed his often hasty creative process under the pressure of deadlines, did not help him with the critics either. Consequently, and also due to some clichéd or formulaic, too "well-made" qualities of some of his most popular stories, Garner is still a disputed and barely studied author among literary scholars. One may well agree with Paul Stuewe's classification of Garner as a "lowbrow," "middlebrow," and "highbrow" writer all in one (Stuewe 1985, 112). Garner is today particularly known for his short-story oeuvre, not least thanks to the frequent anthologization of some of his classic stories (including "One-Two-Three Little Indians," "The Yellow Sweater," and "The Legs of the Lame"). In such pieces, particularly from his early phase, Garner proves his narrative expertise in the tradition of Ernest Hemingway and displays a sure command over the genre's form.

Like Callaghan, Garner is basically a city writer, with a strongly developed sense of place. Most of his stories are set, more or less discernibly, in Toronto, but sometimes also in Montreal or elsewhere in Quebec. Garner adheres to a social realist agenda. What sets him apart from the American realists he takes as examples (such as Theodore Dreiser), however, is the moralistic, even sentimental dimension of some of his stories. In his settings and themes, Garner is a genuinely Canadian writer; in his preface to *The Yellow Sweater* he remarks: "These are Canadian stories; the people in them are all Canadian; the locale is Canada . . ., and they were written in Toronto and . . . Quebec" (Garner 1952, n.p.). Characteristic aspects of Garner's writing can be traced, for example, in his most frequently anthologized story, "One-Two-Three Little Indians" (1950). The story relates the tragic impact of racism on an indigenous family, thereby illustrating the grim situation of Native Canadians trapped between their economic dependence on tourism on the one hand and miserable living conditions on the other.

Joyce Marshall (1913–) has received even less critical attention than Garner, and unjustly so. Yet well-known Canadian novelist and short-story writer Timothy Findley, for one, considers Marshall one of Canada's best short-story writers. She published her first story in 1936, and many of her more than thirty stories were first read on CBC Radio. Her three collections *A Private Place* (1975), *Any Time at All and Other Stories* (1993), and *Blood and Bone / En chair et en os* (bilingual edition, 1995) document her most creative phase, from 1952 through 1995, and explore in various ways the effects of modernity on human consciousness in an often urban setting (Toronto, Montreal). Faced with a world that seems alien and inscrutable to them, Marshall's characters struggle for a sense of identity by projecting their own aspirations and speculations onto their surroundings, thus repeatedly substituting ersatz images for an authentic contact with their environment. In a process of extensive self-reflection, Marshall's almost exclusively female protagonists (who are of all ages) oscillate between feelings of alienation and the insignificance of existence on the one hand and the search for insight on the other hand. In none of Marshall's texts is the unbridgeable gap between human beings as symbolically highlighted as in "The Old Woman" (1952), her most frequently anthologized story. The secluded setting in Northern Quebec and the isolation of the English protagonist Molly, who after three years of separation has joined her Canadian husband Toddy there, mirror the characters' inner worlds and the impossible love between them: years of loneliness in the Canadian wilderness have left Toddy utterly transfixed by the lure of nature and hence incapable of human interaction. The electrical power station where he is employed and which he personifies as "The Old Woman" becomes a substitute for his wife — the end of the story sees him succumbing to complete isolation, to madness, and his wife faced with this gruesome situation to cope with. Timothy Findley describes the story as "the story of a woman's emancipation and a man's enslavement" (Findley in Marshall 1993, 217).

Among Marshall's modernist stylistic techniques are *in medias res*-beginnings, allusions, and experimental narrative forms. A good example is "The Heights" (1993) from *Any Time at All*. Featuring young Martha, who spends her childhood as an Anglophone in French Quebec, the story establishes an internal discourse on Martha's different stages of development right at the beginning of the story by introducing a second narrative consciousness, a "ghost" from the past, to comment in retrospect: "All through this story . . . you'll have to imagine the occasional presence of another person, watching, weighing, adding things up. . . . The strange thing is that I don't remember her . . . though she must often have been in the same place at the same time, since she saw many of the same things. Or so she says" (Marshall 1993, 34). Marshall's stories probe the mental worlds of characters in twentieth-century Canada who find themselves in an acute phase of uncertainty but do not completely lose track of their aim to better understand themselves and their environment. In the course of her career Marshall's narrative style increasingly developed postmodernist traits, as structural and thematic aspects of her third collection *Blood and Bone / En chair et en os* clearly show (see for instance the story "Kat").

Yet it is Sheila Watson (1909–98) who definitively marks the transition from modernist to postmodernist paradigms in English-Canadian literature and in the Canadian short story. Her significance for Canadian literature is therefore larger than her slim oeuvre would suggest (two novels, only five short stories, some essays in literary criticism). Her literary work stems almost exclusively from the 1950s, although some texts were published much later, for instance the story "And the Four Animals" (1980). Watson's long literary silence, which extended from around 1958 to her death in 1998, that is, for about forty years after her most creative decade, remains an enigma in Canadian literary history. Under the title *Five Stories*, Watson's short stories were collected only in 1984, after they had previously appeared as *Four Stories* in 1979 (before the publication of "And the Four Animals").

Watson was particularly interested in narrative aesthetics and its renewal through a turn away from the realist, regional paradigms that had dominated Canadian fiction until then. She expands the suggestive ambiguity of modernist texts towards a hermetic and abstract system of multiple meanings, producing texts of intricate intertextuality and complex intransparency, which are aimed primarily at an academically educated audience. Her allegorical compositions often draw on ancient mythology (four of her five short stories refer to Oedipus; she also mentions for instance Antigone, Ismene, Atlas, and Daedalus), but also on more recent European mythology, for example the Bible, Shakespeare, James Joyce, Gertrude Stein, Freud, and Jung. These extremely dense, impersonal allegories feature fragmentary plots, in which splinters of meaning from the realm of mythology and literature are superimposed in a collage-like fashion on aspects of Canada in the twentieth century, thus creating an abstract, seemingly unreal level of meaning. Watson's texts use a stripped-down plot and imagery, symbols, allusions, and associations, to construct an open, complex framework of meaning, which — in a self-referential and postmodernist manner — engenders literature on literature and emphasizes the text's level of discourse (rather than plot). Watson's elaborate language links her fiction to prose poetry, for instance in "And the Four Animals," the earliest text in *Five Stories*, and the shortest, at only three pages. Shirley Neuman (1982) argues convincingly for an interpretation of this story as "one of the most concise histories of mankind's journey from Creation to Apocalypse ever told" (Neuman 1982, 48). Watson's most frequently anthologized story, "Antigone" (1959), still presents a roughly comprehensible plot, namely the story of Antigone's cousin, in love with Antigone rather than with her sister Ismene. Antigone, outspoken and individualistic, revolts against her father's system of order and discipline by burying a bird on the premises of the mental asylum (Watson grew up in such a place, as the director's daughter). As Shirley Neuman summarizes the story:

> the Provincial Mental Hospital of Watson's childhood and its inmates are transformed and undercut by their allegorical conflation with characters from Greek tragedy. Watson's Antigone is no princess burying a dead brother in the six feet of soil due to him, . . . Creon no longer rules Thebes but a land where Atlas eats dirt, Helen walks naked and all is but a demented inversion of Greek myths and Greek tragedies. . . . This modern parable provides no moral resolution of its dualities. (Neuman, 48)

Stephen Scobie has argued that Watson's fundamental combination of conflicting elements might in itself be considered either modernist, a form of duality, or postmodernist, a form of duplicity — a position that once again emphasizes Watson's watershed function (pointed out by George

Bowering) in contemporary Canadian Fiction. Being a female writer, Watson's position on the threshold between different literary paradigms confirms Barbara Godard's thesis (1984) that women's social eccentricity predisposes them to the role of innovators in literary history: "Women have long been pioneers in new subjects, new forms, new modes of discourse" (qtd. in Legge 1992, 45). The development from Wilson to Marshall to Watson, as it has been traced here, thus anticipates the explosion of female creativity in Canadian writing of the 1960s, also in the genre of the short story.

The Short Story after 1967

As has become clear, the Canadian short story got off to a hesitant start in the twentieth century. To a considerable extent this was due to the lack of appreciation that Canadian literature had to face in its own country at the time and the limited publication facilities in Canada that resulted. Early short-story writers such as Knister, Grove, and Callaghan were thus forced to find their way into print mainly outside the country. The collected stories of all the modernist writers discussed, except for Callaghan and Garner, appeared decades after their conception, in the 1960s, the period known as the Elizabethan Era of Canadian literature or the Canadian Renaissance.

The explosive development of Canadian literature in the 1960s, partly boosted by new supportive cultural policies, had a particular impact on the short story. Due to the fact that short stories typically enjoy multiple publication — a first printing in a magazine, followed by publication in later collections by a single author and/or in anthologies — the genre relies particularly heavily on a flourishing print industry. Indeed, the Canadian Renaissance finally saw the growth of the kind of literary infrastructure that is necessary for a vital national literature: publishing houses specializing in Canadian literature were founded, such as House of Anansi Press, Coach House Press, Talonbooks, and Oberon Press. Several literary magazines were inaugurated as well,[4] providing an essential forum for short-story writing. These periodicals, which had low circulation and are referred to as "little magazines," were kept above water by government subsidies, and still are to some degree: even in the late 1990s, the Canada Council granted a total of $400,000 yearly to some thirty English-language literary

[4] The 1960s saw the establishment of the *University of Windsor Review* (est. 1965), the *Wascana Review* (est. 1966), the *Malahat Review* (est. 1967), and the *Lakehead Review* (1968–1977), all of which also published creative writing.

magazines in Canada. Despite the odd voice of protest, such as John Metcalf's (see below), these cultural measures did much to promote a diverse, competitive literature, including short-story writing. Norman Levine (1923–2005), known primarily as an author of short stories (eight collections between 1961 and 2000), memorialized such literary debuts and the importance of the little magazines in his story "We All Begin in a Little Magazine" (1972).

Another underwriter of Canadian short-story writing was the public Canadian Broadcasting Corporation (CBC) with its various radio programs featuring the reading of Canadian short stories, sometimes by the authors themselves. The internationally unique program *Anthology*, initiated and produced for more than twenty years by Robert Weaver, is of particular interest here, as it broadcast weekly readings of Canadian literature for over thirty years (1953–85). While *The New Yorker* is considered to be the most prestigious American venue for short-story publication, Weaver's *Anthology* was for a long time its Canadian counterpart. Every year about forty stories by well-known and lesser known Canadian writers were broadcast to an average audience of 55,000 listeners per week. Not only did Weaver recognize the affinities between radio and the short-story genre, he also edited important anthologies of Canadian short stories. With Oxford University Press he launched the *Canadian Short Stories* series in 1960, which comprised five volumes by 1991 and documents the evolution of the Canadian short story in one of its very important phases. Moreover, Weaver together with Margaret Atwood edited *The Oxford Book of Canadian Short Stories in English* in 1986 and *The New Oxford Book of Canadian Short Stories in English* in 1995, both of which have become standard works.

With the first volume of his series *Canadian Short Stories* in 1958, Weaver initiated a practice that other editors would later take up, namely the cautious inclusion of French-Canadian short stories in English translation. In his introduction Weaver writes:

> This book is . . . the first comprehensive anthology of Canadian stories to make any attempt to include fiction from both cultures. There have been good reasons for restricting Canadian anthologies to writing in one language, and there is no sense pretending that even today there is a consistent or vital connexion between the literatures of French and English Canada. But in the past few years some short stories from French Canada (and a good deal of poetry) have been published or broadcast in translation, and it seemed worth recognizing this important, if hesitant, meeting of the two cultures by reprinting three of those stories here. (Weaver 1960, x)

The French-Canadian stories (*contes*) in this case are by Ringuet, Anne Hébert, and Roger Lemelin; later collections feature, among others,

Gabrielle Roy, Jacques Ferron, Gilles Vigneault, and Roch Carrier (see Nischik 1994). Regarding the contrast between English- and French-Canadian short-story writing, critical consensus long reigned that "[the] short story is not a major literary form [in French Canada]" (Owen/Wolfe 1978, 7). On the other hand, the less established French-Canadian *conte* is more open to narrative experimentation than the English-Canadian short story, which by and large leans more towards realism and modernism. Moreover, recent developments in French-Canadian short prose in the 1980s and 1990s led critics to speak of the 1980s as the "golden age of short prose" in Quebec, without denying that short prose in Quebec remains a "genre plutôt pour *happy few*" (Michel Lord).[5]

The only one to match Weaver's indefatigable support of the Canadian short story is John Metcalf (1938–). A productive and acknowledged writer of short stories, novellas, novels, and literary and cultural criticism, Metcalf has contributed significantly to the short-story genre not only through his creative work, but also by editing countless anthologies and book series (see Nischik 1987). In his somewhat controversial, sometimes aggressive critical style, Metcalf argues in favor of the traditional realist-modernist strain of the short story, whose representatives are included in his approximately forty anthologies, many of them meant for the classroom (for example, *Sixteen by Twelve: Short Stories by Canadian Writers*, 1970; *Making It New: Contemporary Canadian Stories*, 1982). In addition, he has figured in almost all of the strikingly numerous book series of Canadian short story anthologies, for instance *Best Canadian Short Stories* or *New Canadian Stories.* In *Best Canadian Stories* he repeatedly gave newcomers the chance to publish in an established forum, and thus greatly stimulated up-and-coming generations of writers.

While Weaver and Metcalf prefer the more conventional narrative forms of the Canadian short story, Geoff Hancock, editor of *Canadian Fiction Magazine* between 1975 and 1998, supported experimental, postmodernist short fiction in particular. In various articles and edited anthologies (for example, *Illusion One/Illusion Two: Fables, Fantasies and Metafiction*, 1983; *Moving Off the Map: From "Story" to "Fiction,"* 1986) he encouraged the rejection of the realist-modernist tradition in fiction. As he wrote in the introduction to *Illusion*, with an overstated sideswipe at Sinclair Ross: "Gone at last are those boring fictional depictions of the prairie depression. . . . The illusionists are filling in those blank spaces on the literary map of Canada by uncovering the fantastic." He even states: "Canadian Literature begins again" (Hancock 1983, 9, 8). Hancock's partiality for postrealist narratives also explains his fondness for French-Canadian

[5] See Eibl 2005.

short fiction, which he tried to make accessible to an English-speaking audience in articles as well as book editions (for example *Invisible Fictions*, 1987). However, despite such influential and zealous defenders as Hancock, the postrealist short story did not bloom to the extent in English Canada as it did in the USA (or, for that matter, in French-Canadian literature), not even during postmodernism's heyday in the 1960s and 1970s. Although partly experimental, deconstructive, and self-referential, the Canadian short story was less committed to these features in and of themselves than its American counterpart and more often combined them with the traditional Canadian interest in realist representation. Robert Kroetsch's well-known dictum that Canadian literature skipped the modernist phase and after nineteenth-century Victorianism reached directly into postmodernism therefore becomes questionable in the case of the short-story genre: to this day, the Canadian short story is marked by a clear predominance of modernist and neorealist narratives over outright antirealist, postmodernist styles.

In the past decades an impressive number of collections, book series, and anthologies of Canadian short stories have appeared at an unusual rate even by international standards, which testifies to the prominent position of the short story on the Canadian literary scene (and also to the continued state support of literature in Canada). The stories are collected and grouped according to various criteria: author, quality and representativeness, region, era, ethnicity, gender, etc. Already at the beginning of the 1980s German critic Helmut Bonheim wrote: "the short story has been the most active ambassador of Canadian literature abroad" (Bonheim 1980–81, 659), while Canadian critic David Arnason similarly stated that "the short story has always been a popular literary genre in Canada, and it is the form of Canadian writing that has traditionally had the largest appeal to international audiences" (Arnason 1983, 159). The Canadian editor of a short-story anthology at the turn of the millenium even described the contemporary Canadian short story as "the literary equivalent of a national display of fireworks" (Thomas 1999, vii). The high standing of the short story in Canada is also shown by its popularity with literary prize juries: Since 1978 about one third of the books awarded the most prestigious literary prize in Canada — the Governor General's Award — have been short-story collections, among others by Alice Munro (three times), Mavis Gallant, Guy Vanderhaeghe, and Diane Schoemperlen. The Canadian Giller Prize, in existence since 1994, has also been repeatedly awarded for short-story collections. Demanding stories by prominent Canadian authors such as Margaret Atwood, Alice Munro, Mavis Gallant, Alistair MacLeod, W. D. Valgardson, to name just a few, were often first printed in Canadian magazines of large circulation, such as *Saturday Night*, or in American magazines such as *The New Yorker*, *The Atlantic Review*, or *The Saturday Evening Post*. What Knister had claimed in the 1920s with regard to the contemporary American short story — that strength in the numbers of short stories written and published help to raise the genre's general level of quality — proved true in Canada as well half a century later.

The Montreal Story Tellers

The so-called Montreal Story Tellers contributed notably to the success story of short fiction in Canada. This group of writers living in Montreal at the time was founded by Metcalf in 1970 and included Clark Blaise, Hugh Hood, Ray Smith, and Raymond Fraser. With the exception of the lesser known Fraser, all members remained active in the short-story genre even after the group's dissolution in 1976. Their official denomination, Montreal Story Teller Fiction Performance Group, points out their distinctiveness: Metcalf and company wanted to show that not only poetry, but also the short story lends itself to public reading, perhaps even more so. The readings, as the group members sometimes self-ironically recall in their memoirs (published in Struthers 1985), were intended as performance events and took place before audiences of up to 150 listeners, mostly at universities or colleges, but also in schools and book shops, especially in the Montreal area.

Metcalf was not only the founder but the most important member of this relatively short-lived group. Over the years he developed into an even more active anthologist of Canadian short fiction than Weaver, but also into an acid-tongued, uncompromising critic of the Canadian literary scene. While nationalism and thematic criticism held sway over literary Canada, Metcalf raised his voice against subsidizing mediocre literature, irrespective of its themes, its focus on content related to Canada, or other criteria that he considered ancillary; for him the only acceptable yardstick of a still-budding national literature was literary excellence (see among others Metcalf's controversial works *Kicking Against the Pricks*, 1982; *The Bumper Book*, 1986; *Freedom from Culture: Selected Essays 1982–1992*, 1994; as well as his memoirs, *An Aesthetic Underground*, 1996).

Besides his other merits, Metcalf is counted among Canada's best short-story writers and was dubbed "one of Canada's best-kept literary secrets" by the American *Harper's Bazaar.* He has published six short-story collections (among them *The Teeth of My Father*, 1975; *Selected Stories*, 1982; *Adult Entertainment*, 1986; *Standing Stones: The Best Stories of John Metcalf*, 2004). Some of his longer prose narratives are best described as novellas ("Polly Ongle," "Travelling Northward," "Private Parts: A Memoir," "Girl in Gingham," "The Lady Who Sold Furniture"), as is one of his most recent publications, from 2003, *Forde Abroad: A Novella.* Metcalf the critic once referred to his own narrative style as experimental. But in his literary work he relies on the modernist narrative tradition rather than on postmodernist innovation, which he once dismissed as a frequent excuse for poor, sloppy writing. A good example of Metcalf's style is "Gentle As Flowers Make the Stones" (1975). The story describes the struggles of poet and translator Jim Haine, above all in relation to his creative writing, and his attempts at gaining public recognition in a social context that proves hostile to art. Events such as Haine's poetry reading or the sex scene that follows with a woman from the audience are recounted from Haine's perspective, with Metcalf embracing Joycean stream-of-consciousness and simultaneity in his narrative technique. "Gentle As Flowers Make the Stones" is a satirical turn on the exclusive demand that art makes on a writer's life — Haine reveals himself to be committed to his literary work only.

Considering Metcalf's critical take on Canadian culture and its politics, his particular interest in the satirical artist story comes as no surprise (see also "The Teeth of My Father," "The Years in Exile," or "The Strange Aberration of Mr. Ken Smythe" from 1973, which contrasts different cultures, with a German music group and its conductor Herr Kunst playing a central, parabolic role). A further subcategory of the short story that Metcalf masters in equal measure is the initiation story (see for instance "Early Morning Rabbits" or "Keys and Watercress").[6]

Clark Blaise has so far published six short-story collections, as well as three novels and five partly autobiographical non-fiction works. The thematic content of his story collections is hinted at in their titles: *A North American Education* (1973), *Resident Alien* (1986), or *Man and His World* (1993). Beginning in the year 2000, Porcupine's Quill Press (for which Metcalf is editorial advisor) began publishing a four-volume project, *The Selected Stories of Clark Blaise*, that combines selected, already published stories with some of Blaise's more recent ones, structuring the individual volumes according to the cultural geographies they cover: volume 1, *Southern Stories*, 2000; volume 2, *Pittsburgh Stories*, 2001; volume 3, *Montreal Stories*, 2003; volume 4, *World Body*, 2006. This undertaking testifies to Blaise's cosmopolitanism and cultural mobility, which was predetermined by his childhood: born in 1940 in North Dakota (his first citizenship being American) to an English-Canadian mother and a French-Canadian father, he changed schools twenty-five times due to his parents' nomadic lifestyle, so that even as a child he used to travel between Canada and the USA. Together with his Indian-American wife and fellow writer Bharati Mukherjee he settled in Montreal from 1966 to 1978, which left its mark on his early work in particular (so that he can say even today: "I've always thought of myself as a French Canadian, but . . . I was writing

[6] For a detailed treatment of Metcalf's short stories see Nischik 1988.

in English, not in French," Blaise in Wahl 1997, 51). In 1973 Blaise was granted Canadian citizenship; he regards himself as Canadian but today lives in the USA. Blaise's fiction has also been referred to as a sequential fictional "autobiography," centering on a socially estranged male protagonist whose identity is permanently under threat. This predicament may be considered the epitome of the "North American condition" concerning "rootlessness, homelessness, . . . dislocating contrasts to be found among juxtaposing groups within North American culture" (Davey 1976, 73).

The frequently anthologized short story "A Class of New Canadians" (1970; collected in *A North American Education*) is representative of Blaise's vast short-story oeuvre. Eighteen months before the story opens, protagonist Norman Dyer left the USA upon receiving his Ph.D. and came to Montreal, which has made him feel like a "semi-permanent, semi-political exile." He works as a lecturer in English literature at McGill University and teaches a colorful group of new immigrants from all over the world. His arrogant, self-absorbed attitude towards his students sums up the fragility of the idealized concept of multiculturalism known as the Canadian Mosaic (according to which Canadian society is made up of diverse ethnic groups with equal rights and opportunities). Dyer's positive image of Canada not only seems artificial, but it also fails to win over the immigrants (some of whom regard Canada merely as a stepping stone to the USA), thus uncovering the frequently precarious identities of Blaise's protagonists. The final scene consequently shows Dyer as an insecure and fearful "resident alien."

The thematic and stylistic heterogeneity of the Montreal Story Tellers also shows in the works of Hugh Hood and Ray Smith. Hood prided himself above all on his novelistic work, especially his *roman-fleuve*, the novel series The New Age/Le nouveau siècle, published at regular intervals beginning in 1975 and planned to include twelve volumes, the last of which appeared on schedule in 2000 (shortly before Hood's death). Hood's intention in this ambitious project was to delineate a fictional panorama of contemporary Canadian culture. Set against the vastness of his complete works, Hood's reception by critics and audiences alike seems quite moderate, and he is appreciated above all as a writer of short stories. His collected stories, published over forty years between 1962 (*Flying a Red Kite: Stories*) and 2003 (*After All!: The Collected Stories V*), comprise ten original book publications plus several volumes of reprinted stories, which makes Hood one of the most prolific Canadian short-story writers. Most of his stories are located in Eastern metropolises (Toronto, Montreal); the bilingual Hood was indeed the only one of the Montreal Story Tellers who lived in this city throughout his writing life. His second collection *Around the Mountain: Scenes from Montreal Life*, deliberately published at the time of the EXPO world's fair in Montreal in 1967, conveys an almost documentary attention to detail — Hood's style has in fact often been described as journalistic. A self-professed Catholic and a professor at the University of Montreal for over thirty years, Hood is regarded as one of Canada's most intellectual writers. In his apparently accessible and, in his own phrase, "super-realistic" and often allegorical writing style, he combines realistic elements with supernatural, transcendental aspects, uncovering philosophical and religious questions in the mundane patterns of daily life.

Despite some formal innovations (such as the comatose first-person narrator in "Getting to Williamstown" who supplies the central perspective and thereby lends the plot a dreamlike, surreal touch), Hood's narrative style remains largely traditional. It is Ray Smith who is the most experimental of the Montreal Story Tellers. The fact that he published three short-story collections between 1969 and 1986, and two novels as late as in the 1990s, is evidence of his initial predilections in matters of genre, although clear genre boundaries are difficult to establish with this postmodernist author. His best-known stories include "The Princess, the Boeing, and the Hot Pastrami Sandwich" (from his short-story cycle *Lord Nelson Tavern*, 1974) and "Cape Breton Is the Thought-Control Centre of Canada" from his eponymous first short-story collection (1969). "Cape Breton" belongs unmistakably to the 1960s, an age that questioned conventions also in literary terms: as the text self-referentially proclaims, we are dealing with "compiled fiction," a piecemeal, fragmentary collection of dialogues, reflections, aphorisms, and miniature stories, thirty-one fragments in all. Insofar as thematic threads are still discernible, these fragments deal with the precarious national identity of postcolonial Canada at the time of the Canadian Renaissance, especially in connection with the economic threat posed by the USA, with writing and art, and with love and relationships. The text made up of fragments also rejects any "sense of an ending," to use Frank Kermode's term, and closes instead with the following rather anti-American paragraph: "For Centennial Year, send President Johnson a gift: an American tourist's ear in a matchbox. Even better, don't bother with the postage."

The Three Leading Authors of the English-Canadian Short Story: Alice Munro, Mavis Gallant, Margaret Atwood

While the Montreal Story Tellers, who were so instrumental in the development of the short story as a genre, were all male, the three most highly regarded and at the same time best-known short-story writers in Canada today are female. The first of these is Alice Munro, the master of short fiction in Canada. This judgment derives not least from the fact that Munro writes exclusively short stories, and thereby represents the very rare case of a writer committed to a single literary genre only. Between 1968 and 2006, Munro published twelve collections of short stories as well as four volumes of selected stories, although *Lives of Girls and Women* (1971) and

Who Do You Think You Are? (1979, published as *The Beggar Maid* in the USA and Great Britain) can be described as short-story cycles due to the unifying interconnectedness of the individual stories. Munro often addresses specifically female themes, such as restrictive gender roles in rural and small-town milieus (for example "Boys and Girls" from *Dance of the Happy Shades*, 1968), complex and difficult mother-daughter relationships ("The Peace of Utrecht" from *Dance*), gender-related professional issues ("The Office" from *Dance* or "The Ottawa Valley" from *Something I've Been Meaning to Tell You*, 1974), emotional enslavement in love relations ("Dulse" from *The Moons of Jupiter*, 1982), or problems of aging in female characters ("The Moons of Jupiter" from *Moons* or "What Is Remembered" from *Hateship, Friendship, Courtship, Loveship, Marriage*, 2001). One of Munro's trademarks is her elaborate style, which not only fulfills high aesthetic demands but also attains an unusually complex expressiveness, for instance through its idiosyncratic combining of seemingly paradoxical adjectives (for instance: "People's lives, in Jubilee and elsewhere, were dull, simple, amazing, and unfathomable — deep caves paved with kitchen linoleum," *Lives*, 249). Munro's stories also achieve her self-proclaimed purpose of reaching her readers' emotions.

Munro's writing has had a considerable impact on the literary world (in a recent listing in *Time Magazine*, she was even counted among the 100 most influential personalities alive today, a rare honor for a writer of fiction). Her first short-story collection, *Dance of the Happy Shades*, was awarded the Governor General's Award for Fiction in 1968 (and she has won this coveted prize twice more since then). Since the publication of *Lives of Girls and Women* her new books have regularly topped bestseller lists. The first appearance of many of her stories in *The New Yorker* testifies to the international reception of her work. Munro is also the most frequently anthologized author of short stories in Canada. As with Atwood, Munro's skill is proven in a narrative and linguistic style that never lacks complexity or fails to challenge the reader, yet her stories are still popular with a large readership. Munro is also something of a "writer's writer," who often interweaves poetological questions into her texts (for instance in "Epilogue: The Photographer" from *Lives* or "Material" from *Something*), deftly switches between traditional and non-linear, digressive narratives ("Dulse"; "White Dump" from *The Progress of Love*, 1986), celebrates multiple narrative perspectives ("Fits," also from *Progress*, or "The Albanian Virgin" from *Open Secrets*, 1994) and Joycean epiphany, or subtly blends the mundane with the extraordinary ("Miles City, Montana" from *Progress*). Even the short-story form itself serves one of Munro's central arguments concerning the impenetrability and fragmentariness of the human condition and the episodic, fleeting nature of experience that never coagulates into a consecutive, cumulative sequence (for which the novel form would seem more appropriate): "And what happened, I asked myself, to Marion? . . . Such questions persist, in spite of novels" (*Lives*, 247).

Mavis Gallant, the second most anthologized short-story writer in Canada, grew up bilingual in Montreal, moved to Europe in 1950 at the age of twenty-seven and traveled extensively. Since 1960 she has been living and writing in Paris as the best-known expatriate author of Canadian origin writing in English. Unlike Munro, Gallant has tried her hand at other genres as well, having written two novels and various journalistic essays, but the short story is still closest to her, for poetological reasons similar to Munro's. Due to her emigration to France as well as her frequently European settings, characters, and themes, Gallant belonged for a long time to the ranks of Canada's rather unknown writers, at least with her early collections (*The Other Paris*, 1956; *My Heart Is Broken*, 1964), although she always thought of herself as a Canadian. Her books were first published in the USA and England; the first to appear in Canada was *The End of the World and Other Stories* (1974). It was only with the publication of *From the Fifteenth District* (1979) that Canadian critics and scholars, somewhat belatedly, acknowledged Gallant to be one of the best short-story writers.

Having found brief employment as a journalist, her international literary career began in the early 1950s when she submitted one of her stories to *The New Yorker*. Her second submission, in 1951, made it into print. In 1964 *The New Yorker* negotiated a first-option contract with Gallant, which resulted in the hitherto longest cooperation between a writer and this distinguished magazine: virtually all of Gallant's approximately 100 stories were first published there, a singular achievement, which was, however, a hindrance to Gallant's reception in Canada from the 1950s up to the 1970s.

Gallant's situation as an emigrant has had a lasting effect on her work from a thematic and narrative point of view. Time and again she writes about immigration and exile, outsiders, psychological rootlessness in place and time, socially estranged foreigners in Europe and North America, cultural conflicts and failed communication, multi- and transculturalism (often against the historical background of the Second World War and the postwar period), about political and social rifts reflected in individual destinies and mentalities. The setting of several of her short-story collections is predominantly or even exclusively Paris, her adopted home (see for example *Overhead in a Balloon: Stories of Paris*, 1985). *The Pegnitz Junction* (1973) deals with Germany and the Germans. *Home Truths: Selected Canadian Stories* (1981), the collection for which she received a Governor General's Award for Fiction in Canada, provides Canadian readers with some critical views of their homeland and themselves. The breadth and variety of her settings, characters, and themes make Gallant one of the most flexible, cosmopolitan authors in Canada. Her typically distanced, apparently uninvolved narrative voice has been attributed by scholars to her own personal situation as an emigrant and could partly be responsible for Gallant's modest readership compared to Munro or Atwood. Although her detached narrative voice may be subject for debate ("There is something rather chilling in Gallant," Rooke 1986, 267), what particularly commands respect is her nuanced, polished style, often drenched in wry humor, understatement, or more or less subtle satire.

The thematic and technical breadth and complexity of her narrative art, which also comprises novellas (for example "The Pegnitz Junction"), is reflected in some of the most frequently anthologized of her short stories, such as "The Ice Wagon Going Down the Street," "Acceptance of Their Ways," and "My Heart Is Broken" (from *My Heart Is Broken*), "The Moslem Wife," "The Latehomecomer," and "From the Fifteenth District" (from *From the Fifteenth District*), as well as "In Youth Is Pleasure" (from *Home Truths*). Although herself nationally "dislocated, perhaps forever" — like her character Lottie Benz in "Virus X," one of the stories in *Home Truths*, a young Canadian of German ancestry whose visit to Strasbourg in 1953 unsettles her formerly secure sense of home and belonging — Gallant with her eleven short-story collections published over forty years (including *The Selected Stories of Mavis Gallant*, 1996, which comprises fifty-two of her stories) remains an international flagship figure of the English-Canadian short story, honoring the multicultural, cosmopolitan inclination of contemporary Canadian letters.

Margaret Atwood, the acknowledged figurehead of Canadian literature not only because of the exceptional quality of her writing but also due to the prolificacy and versatility of her output, has placed less emphasis on the short-story genre than Munro and Gallant, concentrating instead on novels and books of poetry. But she has written a considerable body of short stories, in which she is on the whole more experimental than either Munro or Gallant as far as genre conventions are concerned, extending and blending them for instance with those of poetry and the prose poem. Her earlier collections *Dancing Girls* (1977), *Bluebeard's Egg* (1983), and *Wilderness Tips* (1991) contain stories that are in formal terms relatively conventional and still anchored in the tradition of psychological realism. *Dancing Girls* gives a glimpse of the thematic resourcefulness of the author: "The Man from Mars" and "Dancing Girls" shed critical light on Canada's national dream of multiculturalism; "Giving Birth" creates a metapoetical parallel between the human act of conception and creative writing; "A Travel Piece," "Under Glass," and "Polarities" outline psychological problems and pathological developments, in the case of "Polarities" set against the background of an uneven power struggle between Canada and the USA. Other stories in the collection, such as "A Travel Piece," "The Resplendent Quetzal," "The Grave of the Famous Poet," "Hair Jewellery," and "Lives of the Poets," employ motifs of traveling in various contexts, while a central theme of the collection is relationship crises that result in identity conflicts, mostly on a personal, occasionally also on a national level.

Atwood places her stories in a specifically Canadian context, even more so than Munro, which is particularly obvious in stories from *Wilderness Tips* such as "Hairball," "Death by Landscape," "The Age of Lead," or "Wilderness Tips," as they take up Canadian settings (the "wilderness" but also the metropolis of Toronto), Canadian history (the Franklin expedition in search of the Northwest passage), Canadian national challenges (ecological issues, the proximity to and difference from the USA, Canadian identity, multiculturalism), and Canadian myths (Sir John Franklin, the Canadian Mosaic). In addition, and to a greater extent than Gallant and even Munro, Atwood confronts the differences between the sexes and the difficulties of gender relations, not only in her formally more conventional stories (for example "Uglypuss" or "Bluebeard's Egg" from *Bluebeard's Egg*), but especially in the experimental short texts in *Murder in the Dark: Shorter Fictions and Prose Poems* (1983): "Worship," "Iconography," "Liking Men," and "Women's Novels."

Atwood's later short prose collection *Good Bones* (1992) regards gender aspects from an even more critical perspective. The remarkably well-read Atwood thereby makes intertextual use of classic works of world literature, but also of popular culture texts. Her short dramatic monologue "Gertrude Talks Back" rewrites Shakespeare's *Hamlet*, the quasi prose poem "Men at Sea" references Charles Baudelaire's poem "L'homme et la mer," while "The Little Red Hen Tells All" takes up an English children's story, and the delicious "Making a Man" alludes to certain types of texts in women's magazines, especially the recipe format. Atwood's short fiction also reveals her talent of lending a humorous if not comical twist to even the most serious matters, while preserving their intellectual complexity. As a storyteller, Atwood experiments in her short stories with narrative structure (exemplified by the alternating point of view in "The War in the Bathroom," the montage-like composition in "The Age of Lead," or the dense intertextuality in "Bluebeard's Egg"), and thus it is not surprising that 2006 saw the publication of Atwood's first short-story cycle, *Moral Disorder*. Atwood the stylist (and poet) is revealed in the linguistic brilliance of many of her stories.

Regionalism and the Short Story

In its initial stage of development in such a vast country, the modern Canadian short story was closely linked to regional themes, or to rural and urban backgrounds. In contemporary Canadian literature an increasing cosmopolitanism is noticeable, which is often reflected in a much wider and more varied choice of setting (see for example Blaise's fictional geographies). But even in connection with the contemporary short story, one can still distinguish distinct regions spanning literary Canada from coast to coast. There are the large cities in the east (Toronto, Montreal, Ottawa), which serve as backdrops for stories for instance by the Montreal Story Tellers, Atwood, and Austin Clarke. Then there is Vancouver, the western metropolis, often the chosen setting for writers like Audrey Thomas and Jane Rule. And there are the more rural regions, including the prairies, the Pacific coast, and the Atlantic provinces.

The prairie writers W. O. Mitchell, Margaret Laurence, Rudy Wiebe, and Guy Vanderhaeghe, though treading in the footsteps of their forerunners, the prairie realists Grove and Ross, adapt and renew this tradition in various ways. Mitchell (1914–98) was one of the most successful screenwriters in Canada, also a playwright, yet is today mainly well-known for his novels such as *Who Has Seen the Wind* (1947). But also Mitchell's short-story collections *Jake and the Kid* (1961) and *According to Jake and the Kid: A Collection of New Stories* (1989) became bestsellers in Canada, partly because the stories, which began to appear in 1942 in both Canadian and American magazines, were rewritten by Mitchell for a radio format (and aired over about 250 CBC programs between 1950 and 1956) and were finally adapted for television. It was only after they had acquired this media publicity that the texts were released in book form as short-story cycles. Mitchell's writing invests the prairie story with a more cheerful, humorous streak. With their coarse humor, which draws from the oral tradition and tall tales, their emphasis on small-town local color, and their child protagonist and his relationship to a fatherly mentor, Mitchell's texts gave the prairie short story new impulses and twice won him the Stephen Leacock Award for Humour. Their sentimental, leveling, roughly moralizing aspects led Margaret Laurence to conclude in her review of *Jake and the Kid* in 1962 that these stories addressed "a younger audience" in particular.

Margaret Laurence (1926–87) herself delivered one of the best Canadian short-story cycles with *A Bird in the House* (1970) as part of her exceptional Manawaka fiction series, which is set for the most part on the prairie. Written over eight years and according to Laurence "the only semi-autobiographical fiction I have ever written," *A Bird in the House* recounts the making of an artist in a cycle of eight stories. The writer-to-be Vanessa MacLeod grows up in the 1930s in Manawaka, a fictional small town on the prairie, modeled upon the author's own home town Neepawa in Manitoba. The events are described from the perspective of a grown-up, forty-year-old Vanessa, but the focus is nevertheless on the experiences of the growing child. Through her writing, among other things, Vanessa tries to break out of the constricting family and gender roles that are imposed upon her by a patriarchal small-town community. Her purpose is to escape the stifling life script based on family life that her mother had to resign herself to. The text delivers a realistic evocation of small-town life and social structures in the Canadian prairie, subtle character sketches, and a gradual thematic buildup in the manner of a Bildungsroman. Another essential feature is the accessible style and the balanced, consistent tension between the experiencing and the reminiscing Vanessa, the latter learning to reconsider, as a "professional observer," the judgments of her younger self.

Casting off chains of limitation is for Laurence a central theme, which her prairie works mostly address in connection with the empowerment of female characters. Her African stories, inspired by her years in Africa from 1950 through 1957, have been read as a thematic preparation for this, yet most of them were written later than her prairie stories. Collected in *The Tomorrow-Tamer* (1963), these stories — including "The Rain Child," "A Gourdful of Glory," "Godman's Master," and "The Tomorrow-Tamer" — are set against the African struggles for independence and revolve around the topic of freedom, its chances and challenges, from the political to the personal.

Rudy Wiebe (1934–) grew up in the prairie provinces Saskatchewan and Alberta (where he still lives). As a Mennonite he is a member of a religious minority; his parents had been persecuted on religious grounds and emigrated from the Soviet Union to Canada. Wiebe is mainly known as an author of novels in which he recounts the experiences of the Mennonites in the New World, but he also directs his attention towards other minorities such as the Indians, Inuit, and Métis,[7] particularly in the Canadian West. Many of his works recreate landmarks and figures of Canadian history, yet his extremely pronounced authorial voice takes sides with the minorities and reconsiders official historiography. From 1970 onwards Wiebe edited various short-story anthologies, and between 1974 and 1995 he published three collections of his own stories: *Where Is the Voice Coming from?* (1974), *The Angel of the Tar Sands and Other Stories* (1982), and *River of Stone: Fictions and Memories* (1995). The opening sentence of Wiebe's best-known and most complex story, "Where Is the Voice Coming from?," already points to one of his central themes, namely the difficulties of writing and rewriting history and the complexity of perspective and form in fictional (re-)presentation, whereby both themes are often correlated. Although Wiebe's writing leaves behind the limitations of realistic storytelling from a narrative as well as thematic point of view (see for example "The Angel of the Tar Sands") and shares characteristics with a postmodernist style, Wiebe still believes in the meaningfulness of language and existence. He struggles for a better understanding of their complex nature in his highly experimental works, despite occasionally leaning a little too much towards the didactic and the moral. Stories such as "Where Is the Voice Coming from?" or "The Naming of Albert Johnson" (both

[7] The Métis are a nation in Canada whose people are of Cree or Ojibwa and European descent.

based on historical facts) make it clear that Wiebe accords a larger truth value to fiction than to official historiography, not least because the former gives voice to indigenous, that is, marginal aspects in Canadian cultural history. Such epistemological problems trickle down into narrative form, especially in "Where Is the Voice Coming from?" In this metafictional story that exposes history and literature as artificial constructs, the narrator becomes ever more aware of this difficulty of story construction while trying to piece together the story of Almighty Voice, a young Cree Indian, who for his various crimes was tracked down and killed in the nineteenth century by the Canadian Mounted Police. The narrator realizes in the course of a disillusioning narrative process that the numerous but fragmentary historical "facts" are contradictory and that a coherent picture of events, also taking into account the indigenous perspective, is thus quite impossible to achieve. Language itself also threatens to hinder rather than ensure access to truth. Almighty Voice's death cries remain incomprehensible to the storyteller, encoded as they are by intercultural difference — a "wordless cry" that nevertheless reaches beyond the narrative at hand, not least due to the homophony between "Cree" and the French "cri": "I say 'wordless cry' because that is the way it sounds to me. I would be more accurate if I had a reliable interpreter who would make a reliable interpretation. For I do not, of course, understand the Cree myself" (86–87).

Belonging to a younger generation of prairie writers, Guy Vanderhaeghe (1951–) is sometimes referred to next to Wiebe as a "man's writer" (for instance by Aritha van Herk), as he describes the Canadian prairie primarily from a male perspective. Vanderhaeghe received the Governor General's Award for Fiction for his first book, *Man Descending: Selected Stories* (1982). Especially with this first collection, Vanderhaeghe developed the tradition of the Canadian prairie story. There followed *The Trouble with Heroes: And Other Stories* (1983) and *Things as They Are? Short Stories* (1992). These titles are programmatic in that Vanderhaeghe's male protagonists, mentally drained antiheroes, have become ill at ease with conventional male codes of behavior and face up to their weaknesses and their failure to come to terms with life (see especially "Man Descending," "Cages"). A series of stories turns to younger protagonists ("Reunion," "The Watcher," "Drummer").

One of the best-known male writers of the Canadian west coast is Jack Hodgins (1938–). Deeply rooted on Vancouver Island all his life, Hodgins has immortalized this western region of Canada in various novels, but also in his two short-story cycles, *Spit Delaney's Island* (1976) and *The Barclay Family Theatre* (1981). His works characteristically feature hopelessly entwined family relations (the latter volume portrays for example seven sisters and their extended families), eccentric characters, fantastic, burlesque twists and turns, and a hyperbolic style. They convey a "sense of place" in connection with living on an island, the boundaries it creates and those it dissolves. Hodgins regards "the line between water and land as a kind of separation between one kind of reality and another" (in Hancock, 55). His stories also highlight the beauties of nature of the Canadian Pacific Northwest.

Alden Nowlan, who died at the age of fifty in 1983, and David Adams Richards (1950–) are known above all as poets and novelists of the Maritimes, but they also published short-story collections in the tradition of hard realism that delineate what Janice Kulyk Keefer has called an "anatomy of poverty" of the rural inhabitants of the Atlantic provinces (Nowlan, *Miracle at Indian River*, 1968, and *Will Ye Let the Mummers In?*, 1982; Richards, *Dancers at Night*, 1978). This also applies to the main representative of the short story of the Maritimes, Alistair MacLeod (1936–), who has also published an internationally successful and prize-winning novel, *No Great Mischief* (1999). His high reputation in Canada and beyond is mainly based on the sixteen stories that appeared in his two short-story collections, *The Lost Salt Gift of Blood* (1976) and *As Birds Bring Forth the Sun and Other Stories* (1986), as well as in his collected stories (*Island: The Collected Stories*, 2000). Even before his stories had been collected, some of his texts were selected for *Best American Stories*, which considers stories first published in American magazines during the year prior to selection ("The Boat," 1969, and "The Lost Salt Gift of Blood," 1975). Other excellent stories by MacLeod include "The Closing Down of Summer" (1976), "The Road to Rankin's Point" (1976), "As Birds Bring Forth the Sun" (1985), and "Vision" (1986). MacLeod's conventionally structured, highly polished stories describe in an elegiac, occasionally lyrical style his semi-autobiographical narrator's departures from and returns to Cape Breton (MacLeod himself splits his time between Windsor, Ontario, and Cape Breton), the loss but also the maelstrom of local and family bonds. His first-person narratives render an almost palpable impression of the region, with their precise descriptions of ruggedly beautiful landscapes, the hardships of physical work, and the poor economic conditions in the Maritimes. His most frequently anthologized story is "The Boat," a vivid text that is representative of MacLeod's style and proves once again how so-called regional stories can still convey universal meanings.

Female Writers between Compliance, Innovation, and Rebellion

The roughly equal representation of well-known female and male authors that characterizes the whole of Canadian literature also applies to the short story. Not only do the three leading writers of the Canadian short story happen to be female, but such a large number of female authors have written in the genre that this even gender distribution seems self-evident today. It is noteworthy, however, that this state of affairs has partly resulted in a gender-sensitive and gender-oriented writing style not only in Canadian literature in general, but also in Canadian short fiction.

Margaret Laurence is a pioneer of gender-conscious writing from a female perspective in Canada. Her works delineate the psychological, emotional, and intellectual development of female characters in a man's world, her short-story collection *A Bird in the House* (1970) being paradigmatic in this respect. Marian Engel, Jane Rule, Audrey Thomas, and Carol Shields — all born within five to nine years after Laurence (who was born in 1926) — pursued these approaches in various forms. Despite the fact that Marian Engel mainly thought of herself as a novelist (her best-known novel being *Bear*, 1976), she published two remarkable short-story collections, *Inside the Easter Egg* (1975) and *The Tattooed Woman* (1985). In these stories, most of whose protagonists are middle-aged women, Engel addresses typically "female" issues, such as the socialization of girls and women to define "self" in relation to the "other," the consequences of aging, illness, or surgery for women, and the female body ("The Tattooed Woman," "The Confession Tree"). But Engel also finds ways of transcending such limitations through imagination and self-determined writing, whatever code might be chosen for it. A good example is the title story "The Tattooed Woman," first published in 1975: an unnamed forty-two-year-old woman, a housewife, hears her husband's confession about his affair with a twenty-one-year-old colleague. The shocked protagonist responds to this disclosure by carving signs, such as houses, trees, and stars, into her skin, and through this form of "writing" she fashions the body that has been "discarded" by her husband into a work of art. Ironically, this act makes her visible and confident again: "I am an artist, now, she thought, a true artist. My body is my canvas. . . . I am Somebody . . . , and at the same time beautiful and new" (8). Towards the end of her life, Engel gradually shifted from a realistic writing style to a fantastic, surreal, postmodernist style, before her early death in 1985.

Jane Rule, born in the USA in 1936, settled in Vancouver in 1956 and in 1976 moved to Galiano Island, one of the Gulf Islands situated between the mainland and Vancouver Island. Early in her career she became a prominent mouthpiece of the gay and lesbian rights movement after the success of her debut novel *Desert of the Heart* (1964), which describes a homoerotic relationship between two women and was later made into a film (*Desert Hearts*, 1985). In her numerous novels and essays, Rule repeatedly addressed the topic of (mostly female) homoeroticism. Timothy Findley (1930–2002), who sometimes dealt with male homosexuality in his three collections of short stories and more often touched on the broader theme of gender in relation to masculinity, insisted that the significance of his work goes beyond his sexual orientation. The same applies to Rule. In an accessible, transparent, structurally conventional manner, her stories tackle unconventional gender issues in an undogmatic, open-minded, and compassionate way, although her earlier texts in particular do not ignore the difficulties of otherness. Examples of this are the collections

Theme for Diverse Instruments (1975) and especially *Outlander: Short Stories and Essays* (1981), with its stories "Lillian" and "Outlander." A representative example of her even more relaxed later work is "Slogans" from *Inland Passage and Other Stories* (1985). In this story, three women take turns retelling their life stories to each other at their twenty-fifth anniversary class reunion: the long-time couple Nancy and Ann radiate supreme contentment, whereas Jessica, divorced and suffering from cancer, talks of nothing but broken marriages, her own and those of many former classmates. The title story "Inland Passage" is exemplary of the strong regional component of Rule's work, which makes use of the local color and picturesque landscapes of western Canada. Her better-known stories also include "The End of Summer," "Joy," "Brother and Sister," and "My Father's House," which deal with childhood and family issues as well as the past and present lives — and love lives — of elderly female protagonists. Rule has retired from writing after a career of three decades ("I have written what I wanted," qtd. in Klauda 1993, 468).

Like Jane Rule, Audrey Thomas (1935–) and Carol Shields (1935–2003) were also born in the USA and later received Canadian citizenship (both in the 1970s). Particularly the work of the prolific Thomas, who once described herself as a "B.C. writer," has a strong regional component. After her move to Canada in 1958 she settled down in British Columbia, for the first eleven years in Vancouver, then, like Rule, on Galiano Island. Thomas has published as many short-story collections (seven) as novels and has contributed to the development of the Canadian short story over thirty years, both technically and thematically. Her first short-story collection *Ten Green Bottles*, published in 1967, three years ahead of Laurence's *A Bird in the House*, initiated the portrayal of uniquely female modes of experience in a radically new, authentic, and strongly autobiographical way in Canadian literature. For instance, her earliest story, "If One Green Bottle . . ." (first published in *The Atlantic Monthly* in 1965), deals with miscarriage. Written in a consistent stream-of-consciousness technique, the story places Thomas among the formally flexible, experimental postmodernist writers of short fiction in Canada. Thomas foregrounds the level of discourse (for instance, by transcribing lexicon entries and using intertextual references) and self-referentially addresses the topic of writing itself, which she often describes as a liberating act, particularly for female characters. Her strong, playful interest in language sometimes even informs her choice of titles, as in "Initram" ("Martini" spelled backwards). In "The Man with Clam Eyes" from *Goodbye Harold, Good Luck* (1986), the title is based on an unintentional misspelling ("clam" for "calm"), and the self-referential aspect of language and its conditioning of reality, which permeate the entire story, are also reflected in the plot. Like Laurence, Thomas spent some years in Africa, which functioned as a catalyst for her writing and left traces that went beyond her early work (see for instance "Xanadu," "Rapunzel," "Two in the Bush," "Out in the Midday Sun"). Other stories focus on mother-daughter relationships and family bonds in general (see her collection *Real Mothers*, 1981), the critique of the relationship between the sexes, and the reappraisal of female gender roles (see her 1971 Vancouver story "Aquarius," in *Ladies & Escorts*). Thomas also confronts themes such as the liminal space between sanity and madness or, in more general terms, between dreams and reality.

Carol Shields at the time of her death in 2003 could look back on a remarkable literary career, which she only initiated in her forties, after having raised her five children. Particularly well-known are her prize-winning novels *Swann: A Mystery* (1987) and *The Stone Diaries* (1993). But it is particularly in her short-story collections *Various Miracles* (1985), *The Orange Fish* (1989), and *Dressing Up for the Carnival* (2000) that Shields proves herself to be not only a realist-modernist writer, but one also open to postmodernist experimentation, with the publication of her first short-story collection marking a turning point in her oeuvre. The focus on the female experience of a home environment, for which she was initially reproached by male critics, was gradually re-evaluated and finally celebrated as her trademark (this artistic creed of hers is spelled out particularly clearly in her late story "Soup du Jour"). Her writing may indeed record exceptional, even miraculous aspects of everyday life, but the author never looks away from the greater or lesser tragedies of human existence. Her characters belong to the upper middle class. As a result of her long career as a university lecturer and her marriage to a Canadian professor, she often deals with the academic world in an ironic or even parodic tone, for example in "The Metaphor Is Dead — Pass It on" or "Mrs. Turner Cutting the Grass" (both from *Various Miracles*). The latter story sets the eventful life of a simple woman in the outskirts of Winnipeg against episodes from the life of an unpleasant professor at a Massachusetts college. Shields's works often display a joyful, optimistic attitude. Examples of this are stories like "Pardon" (which hyperrealistically and humorously transforms personal relations into gestures of apology), "Various Miracles," or "Absence." Placing great emphasis on family in her personal life, Shields's stories often deal with family issues, such as marriage, mother-daughter relationships, love, as well as the experience of aging (for example "The Orange Fish," "Milk Bread Beer Ice," "Love so Fleeting, Love so Fine," "Flitting Behaviour," and "Chemistry"). The satirical take on academic life in stories like "Our Men and Women," "Ilk," or "A Scarf" proves nevertheless that Shields is capable of reaching outside her familiar field of domestic fiction and addressing larger social issues.

Among the generation of younger female writers, born in the 1940s and 1950s, are Sandra Birdsell, Isabel Huggan, Katherine Govier, and Diane Schoemperlen. Birdsell has resided in Manitoba and Saskatchewan all her life, and the prairie environment and milieu of those provinces has had an impact on the settings and choice of characters in her works (various immigrant groups, but also Mennonites and Métis). Birdsell's first two short-story collections, *Night Travellers* (1982) and *Ladies of the House* (1984), were republished in one volume under the title *Agassiz Stories* in 1987. If slightly misleading, the subtitle of the American edition, *A Novel in Stories*, rightfully points to the cyclic nature of Birdsell's short fiction. Agassiz is the name of a fictional place in Manitoba, which serves as setting for the saga of the Lafreniere clan (with a Métis father and a Mennonite mother) over three generations, with an emphasis on its female family members. The partly self-inflicted marginality and dependence of women as well as the situation of the working-class and ethnic minorities prompt Birdsell to describe larger structures of exclusion, isolation, repression, and discrimination, on the potential change of which she takes a largely pessimistic perspective, particularly in connection with the plight of women. Her better-known stories include "Flowers for Weddings and Funerals," "Keepsakes," "Judgment," and "Night Travellers" (all from the eponymous collection), as well as "The Man from Mars" (from her fourth collection *The Two-Headed Calf*, 1997).

Multicultural Diversity and the Short Story

The contemporary Canadian short story owes its diversity in part to its numerous multicultural voices. The many contributions to the genre from writers of different ethnic backgrounds can only be hinted at here.

The most important representatives of Native short fiction are Thomas King, with so far two short-story collections (see for instance his stories "Borders" and "One Good Story, That One") and Lee Maracle with one collection (see her stories "Yin Chin" and "Bertha"). Caribbean-Canadian literature offers by contrast a more vital literary scene concerning the short story. Its best-known and most prolific representative is Barbados native Austin Clarke (1934–), who published seven collections of short stories between 1965 and 2003 (see for instance *Choosing His Coffin: The Best Stories of Austin Clarke*, 2003). He is joined by two writers from Trinidad: Dionne Brand (*Sans Souci and Other Stories*, 1988, especially "Sans Souci" and "Photograph"), and Neil Bissoondath (*Digging Up the Mountains*, 1986; *On the Eve of Uncertain Tomorrows*, 1990). The foremost representative of the Asian-Canadian short story is Rohinton Mistry, born in Bombay, who mostly writes about his former home India, for example in his 1987 collection *Tales from Firozsha Baag* (see "Condolence Visit" or "Swimming Lessons").

In an immigration country like Canada, not only the so-called minority writers, but also writers with European backgrounds often deal with problems of migration and diaspora, the history and culture of their native countries, and intercultural themes of immigration and assimilation in multicultural Canada. Representative of Icelandic-Canadian literature is Kristjana Gunnars, who emigrated from Iceland in 1968 (*The Axe's Edge*, 1983, and *The Guest House and Other Stories*, 1992). Another writer with an Icelandic background, with three short-story collections to his credit, is Canadian-born W. D. Valgardson (1939–), whose work was shaped by his growing up in Icelandic enclaves in Canada (see his stories "Bloodflowers" and "A Matter of Balance"). Besides radio and television scripts, Valgardson published six short-story collections between *Bloodflowers: Ten Stories* (1973) and *The Divorced Kids Club: And Other Stories* (2002). The versatile Janice Kulyk Keefer, also active in the field of literary criticism as a professor at the University of Guelph, reveals a high awareness of her Ukrainian cultural background in her work, which on a literary level reflects her theoretical concept of "transculturalism." Kulyk Keefer has published three short-story collections (*The Paris-Napoli Express*, 1986; *Transfigurations*, 1987; and *Travelling Ladies*, 1990).

The Contemporary English-Canadian Short Story and the Challenges of Modernism, Realism, Postmodernism, and Neorealism

In a panoramic view of the Canadian short story since the 1960s, several things stand out: first, the diversity and vitality of the genre, partly deriving from the fact that almost all major writers in the fascinating "postnational" literature that is Canadian literature have made contributions to the short story; second, the relative high number of short-story cycles in Canada, a tendency that brings this genre closer to the novel without relinquishing the unity of the individual short story[8] — above-mentioned works by Munro, Gallant, Laurence, Hodgins, Hood, Birdsell, Clarke, Smith, Mitchell, Mistry, as well as Mordecai Richler (*The Street*, 1969) testify to this phenomenon; and finally the primacy of the modernist-realist tradition of storytelling in the English-Canadian short story.

After becoming established as short-story writers, some authors, such as the aforementioned Smith, Thomas, Wiebe, and Engel, as well as some who have not been dealt with here, such as Leon Rooke, George Bowering, Matt Cohen, and Dave Godfrey, have turned away from or outgrown the genre conventions of the realist-modernist short story, redirecting the genre onto an antirealist, surreal, metafictional, postmodernist path (although all of them still produced stories in the realist-modernist

[8] For a possible explanation of this prevalence see Nischik 1992.

vein — see Bowering's "Apples" or Matt Cohen's "Keeping Fit" — and never fully abandoned this writing style). The most prolific and most anthologized among these authors is Rooke (1934–), who has published eleven short-story collections and three volumes of selected stories (most recently *Hitting the Charts: Selected Stories*, 2006). George Bowering, long-time literature professor at Simon Fraser University in Burnaby, British Columbia, and editor of postmodernist stories as well as of critical articles, has published four short-story collections. Best known is his programmatic "A Short Story," a metafictional text that emphasizes the artificiality of writing by giving the individual subsections generic, self-referential titles such as "Setting," "Characters," "Point of View," etc. Matt Cohen (see his story "The Sins of Tomas Benares") had published six short-story collections by the time he died in 1999, as well as a volume of collected stories and *Lives of the Mind: Selected Stories* (1994). It was only at the peak of postmodernism in the 1960s and 1970s that Dave Godfrey made his contribution to fiction in two short-story collections, among them *Death Goes Better with Coca-Cola* (1968; see his stories "River Two Blind Jacks" and "A New Year's Morning on Bloor Street").

Since the 1980s another writing style has developed in the short story alongside the more prominent modernist-realist tradition, one enriched with hyperrealist, surreal elements, indebted to both realist and postmodernist conventions and fully aware of this double heritage. The vast oeuvre of such authors as Atwood or Gallant displays realist, but also metafictional, postmodernist characteristics in one and the same text, to such an extent that the new, "neorealist" variety of the contemporary Canadian short story suggests new labels such as "crossover fiction" (David Lodge).

The individual essays to follow, each focusing on one prominent author and a selected story, will take the reader through representative stories from all periods of the genre and will trace many of the issues dealt with in this surveying article in exemplary detail. Taken together, these essays demonstrate the impressive development and range of the Canadian short story in the twentieth century, particularly since the 1960s.

Works Cited

Arnason, David. "The Historical Development of the Canadian Short Story." *Recherches Anglaises et Américaines* 16 (1983): 159–64.

Blaise, Clark. *A North American Education.* Toronto: General Publishing, 1973.

Boire, Gary. "Morley Callaghan 1903–1990." *Canadian Literature* 133 (Summer 1992): 208–9.

Bonheim, Helmut. "Topoi of the Canadian Short Story." *Dalhousie Review* 60.4 (1980–81): 659–69.

Bowering, George. "Sheila Watson, Trickster." In George Bowering, *The Mask in Place: Essays on Fiction in North America.* Winnipeg: Turnstone, 1982. 97–111.

Davey, Frank. "Impressionable Realism: The Stories of Clark Blaise." *Open Letter* 3 (1976): 65–74.

Dean, Misao. "Introduction." In *Early Canadian Short Stories: Short Stories in English before World War I: A Critical Edition*, ed. Misao Dean. Ottawa: Tecumseh Press, 2000. xi–xvii.

Eibl, Doris. "Die Kurzerzählung." In *Kanadische Literaturgeschichte*, ed. Konrad Groß, Wolfgang Klooß, and Reingard M. Nischik. Stuttgart: Metzler, 2005. 355–59.

Eliot, T. S. "Tradition and the Individual Talent" (1919). Repr. in *The Norton Anthology*, vol. D. Sixth ed. New York: Norton, 2003. 1425–28.

Engel, Marian. *The Tattooed Woman.* Markham, ON: Penguin, 1985.

Gadpaille, Michelle. "Canadian Short Fiction." In *Critical Survey of Short Fiction*, ed. Charles E. May and Frank N. Magill. 2nd rev. ed., vol. 7. Pasadena, CA: Salem Press, 2001. 2898–2907.

———. *The Canadian Short Story.* Toronto: Oxford University Press, 1988.

Garner, Hugh. "Preface." In Hugh Garner, *The Yellow Sweater.* London: Collins, 1952. n.p.

Givens, Imogen. "Raymond Knister — Man or Myth?" *Essays on Canadian Writing* 16 (1979–80): 5–19.

Hancock, Geoff. "An Interview with Jack Hodgins." *Canadian Fiction Magazine* 32/33 (1979–80): 33–63.

Hancock, Geoff, ed. *Illusion One: Fables, Fantasies and Metafictions.* Toronto: Aya Press, 1983.

Klauda, Ann. "Jane Rule (1931–)." In *Contemporary Lesbian Writers of the United States: A Bio-Bibliographical Critical Sourcebook*, ed. Sandra Pollack and Denise D. Knight. Westport: Greenwood, 1993. 468–75.

Knister, Raymond, ed. *Canadian Short Stories.* Toronto: Macmillan, 1928.

———. "The Canadian Short Story." *The Canadian Bookman* 5 (August 1923): 203–4; repr. in Knister, *The First Day of Spring: Stories and Other Prose.* Toronto: University of Toronto Press, 1976. 388–92.

———. "Democracy and the Short Story." *Journal of Canadian Fiction* 4.2 (1975): 146–48.

Legge, Valerie. "Sheila Watson's 'Antigone': Anguished Rituals and Public Disturbances." *Studies in Canadian Literature* 17.2 (1992): 28–46.

Lucas, Alec. "Introduction." In Charles G. D. Roberts, *The Last Barrier and Other Stories.* Toronto: McClelland & Stewart, 1958. v–x.

Marshall, Joyce. *Any Time at All and Other Stories.* Toronto: McClelland & Stewart, 1993.

Munro, Alice. *Lives of Girls and Women*. Harmondsworth: Penguin, 1971.

Neuman, Shirley. "Sheila Watson." In *Profiles in Canadian Literature*. Vol. 4, ed. Jeffrey M. Heath. Toronto: Dundurn, 1982. 45–52.

Nischik, Reingard M., ed. *American and Canadian Short Short Stories*. Paderborn: Schöningh, 1994.

———. "Contrastive Structures in John Metcalf's Artist Stories." *Critique* 29.3 (Spring 1988): 163–78.

———. "'Pen Photographs': Zum Phänomen des (kanadischen) Kurzgeschichtenzyklus." *Deutsche Vierteljahrsschrift für Literaturwissenschaft und Geistesgeschichte* 66.1 (1992): 192–204.

———. "The Short Story in Canada: Metcalf and Others Making It New." *Die Neueren Sprachen* 86.3/4 (1987): 232–46.

Owen, Ivon, and Morris Wolfe, ed. *The Best Modern Canadian Short Stories*. Edmonton: Hurtig, 1978.

Rooke, Constance. "Fear of the Open Heart." In *A Mazing Space: Writing Canadian Women Writing*, ed. Shirley Neuman and Smaro Kamboureli. Edmonton: Longspoon/NeWest, 1986. 256–69.

Spettigue, Douglas O. "The Grove Enigma Resolved." *Queen's Quarterly* 79 (Spring 1972): 1–2.

Struthers, J. R. (Tim). *The Montreal Storytellers: Memoirs, Photographs, Critical Essays*. Montreal: Véhicule Press, 1985.

Stuewe, Paul. "Hugh Garner." In *Canadian Writers and Their Works*, ed. Robert Lecker, Jack David, and Ellen Quigley. Fiction series, vol. 6. Toronto: ECW Press, 1985. 81–127.

Thomas, Joan. "Introduction." In *Turn of the Story: Canadian Short Fiction on the Eve of the Millenium*, ed. Joan Thomas and Heidi Harms. Toronto: Anansi, 1999. vii–xv.

Wahl, Greg. "An Interview with Clark Blaise." In *Speaking of the Short Story: Interviews with Contemporary Writers*, ed. Farhat Iftekharuddin, Mary Rohrberger, and Maurice Lee. Jackson: University Press of Mississippi, 1997. 45–56.

Weaver, Robert. "Introduction." In *Canadian Short Stories*, selected by Robert Weaver. Toronto: Oxford University Press, 1960. ix–xiii.

Wiebe, Rudy. *The Angel of the Tar Sands and Other Stories*. Toronto: McClelland & Stewart, 1982.

Royal Society of Canada in 1890 and national president of the Canadian Authors' Association in 1927, he continued to receive awards and was much praised — some critics say over-praised — during his lifetime. Called by W. A. Deacon a "symbol of Canadian literature" and hailed as the "Father of Canadian Poetry" and "Dean of Canadian Letters," Roberts "assumed the paternal role willingly and proudly" (Adams 1986, 149). In 1926 he was the first recipient of the Lorne Pierce Medal for Literature, and in 1935 he was knighted by George V for his outstanding contributions to Canadian literature.

Roberts's impressive oeuvre consists of more than 1,000 separate pieces, including poems, novels, short stories, romances, travel guides, histories, translations, and essays. Apart from his volumes of poetry, prose, and non-fiction, Roberts also published in newspapers, journals, and magazines, and contributed to many collections. His short-story production makes up a substantial part of his oeuvre: Adams's useful "Preliminary Bibliography" lists 237 stories, published in major American or British magazines, such as *Youth's Companion*, *The Metropolitan*, *McClure's*, or *The Windsor Magazine*. Most of his stories reappeared in subsequent collections of his work. During Roberts's lifetime, nineteen volumes of original short stories, five volumes of stories for young adults, and five selections from previous collections were published, most of which went through four or more editions. The majority of his short stories are animal stories, assembled in such well-known collections as *The Kindred of the Wild* (1902), *The Watchers of the Trails* (1904), *The Haunters of the Silences* (1907), *The House in the Water* (1908), *Kings in Exile (*1909), *Neighbours Unknown* (1911), *Babes of the Wild* (1912), *The Feet of the Furtive* (1912), *Hoof and Claw* (1913), *Wisdom of the Wilderness* (1922), *They Who Walk in the Wild* (1924), or *Eyes of the Wilderness* (1933). Stories from *The Kindred of the Wild* alone — his first book of exclusively animal stories — were published in four separate editions in 1905, which accounts for their spectacular success. From the mid-1890s on, Roberts devoted the largest part of his creativity to this genre, taking advantage of the enormous vogue and new market created by Ernest Thompson Seton's instant bestseller *Wild Animals I Have Known* (1898). Since the 1930s Roberts's stories have gradually disappeared in print, which shows the general decline of interest in the genre. Nevertheless, seven animal story collections were published after the author's death in 1943. Following the pioneering New Canadian Library edition of 1958, *The Last Barrier, and Other Stories* — with a well-known introduction by Alec Lucas — three representative selections of Roberts's short stories were published: *King of Beasts and Other Stories* (1967), *Eyes of the Wilderness and Other Stories* (1980), and *The Lure of the Wild: The Last Three Animal Stories* (1980).

While Seton and Roberts developed the genre concurrently, opinions differ as to who its originator was. Although Roberts admired Seton's work and emphasized his primacy in popularizing the genre, he nevertheless referred to himself as the "father of the animal story." Seton, an excellent artist and naturalist, did not consider himself primarily a writer, and his narrative form inspired by direct observation differs significantly from Roberts's approach. Seton was the more popular writer internationally, but critics have generally agreed upon Roberts's superiority in literary sophistication, stressing that "for Roberts it was art first; for Seton it was science" (Lucas 1958, vi). Both authors regarded the short story as the most suitable genre for their subject. Defined by Roberts as "a psychological romance constructed on a framework of natural science" (*The Kindred of the Wild*, 24), the wild animal story successfully fused seemingly disparate discourses and gave emotional content to a scientific approach (see Dunlap 1987, 116). Written in the spirit of post-Darwinian insights, a keen interest in natural science and animal psychology, and with a deep sympathy for the "kindred of the wild," the wild animal story captivated contemporary readers with the romance of the unknown. With the "Nature Movement" at its height, Roberts's and Seton's stories gained immediate popularity as they spoke to the Zeitgeist of cultural criticism, nature worship, and the rediscovery of the archaic and instinctual. Roberts's stories were sought after by high-paying magazines, enthusiastically reviewed, included in school readers, translated into many languages, and were thus highly influential around the world. Classified as unequaled in their genre, they continue to ensure Roberts's lasting reputation and popularity beyond Canada. In Germany, for instance, Roberts was marketed as a Canadian "hunter, backwoodsman, animal lover and nature worshipper,"[1] and praised exclusively for his animal stories; only a few scattered poems have been translated. In Canada, on the contrary, his poetry was long regarded as his greatest strength, if not his only true artistic accomplishment. Although this perception was fostered by some of his own comments (see Pomeroy 1943, 110; Whalen 1989, 40), he denied that his animal stories were potboilers, declaring that they "grew out of the same emotional urge as his poetry, and that he took meticulous care in writing them" (Adams 1986, 93).[2]

A classic example for the poetic attention Roberts lent to the genre is the very first of his many animal stories, "Do Seek Their Meat from God" (1892), one of the most significant literary products of his prolific Windsor decade. The story juxtaposes a pair of panthers and a man in their respective struggle for the survival of their offspring. The man kills the animals

[1] Translated from a review by Kurt Münzer published in the German edition of Roberts's *The Citadel in the Grass* (*Die Burg im Grase*. Berlin: Universitas, 1927).
[2] Roberts's animal stories gained serious academic attention only in the mid-1960s. Critics like Gold, Keith, Cogswell, and Whalen have since strongly refuted or modified earlier criticism.

to save a child, which turns out to be his own, and leaves the panthers' helpless cubs to starvation. In contrast to his poetry, Roberts's prose focuses on the harsher aspects of nature, here the grim ironies of the food cycle, wherein the life of one creature necessarily means the death of another. The fact that the story was considered too innovative at the time shows in the difficulties Roberts had in placing it. First rejected by editors as "neither fish, flesh, fowl, nor good red herring" (Pomeroy, 107), it was finally accepted by *Harper's Magazine* in 1892 after considerable hesitation and for less than the usual writer's fee. Discouraged by the skeptical reception, Roberts gave up on the genre, and only returned to it after Seton's breakthrough. The story reappeared in his successful first collection of nature stories, *Earth's Enigmas: A Book of Animal and Nature Life* (1896).[3] Thematically united by their occupation with the inexplicable forces of life and death, the fifteen stories in *Earth's Enigmas* fall into different categories; only three of them are animal stories ("Do Seek Their Meat from God," "The Young Ravens that Call upon Him," and "Strayed"). Conway has underlined the remarkable structural and aesthetic integrity of Roberts's story collections and has shown how Roberts had given the 1903 edition of *Earth's Enigmas* a greater thematic unity by exchanging three stories (see Conway 1984, 8–9). The title of the collection also effectively alludes to its general theme. A letter to his cousin Bliss Carman (*Letters*, 182–83) reveals the alternative title considered, *Riddles of Earth*. In choosing *Enigmas* over *Riddles*, Roberts not only indicates his roots in the Romantic tradition but also emphasizes the enigmatic nature of the stories. As he points out in the prefatory note, most of them present "one or another of those problems of life or nature to which . . . there is no adequate solution within sight." "Do Seek Their Meat from God" is a perfect example of this thematic concern.

Roberts opens the story with a seemingly traditional nineteenth-century landscape description. Vivid and evocative depiction of nature is a recurring expository element in Roberts's stories. He usually chooses specific locales as settings, recognizable Canadian landscapes with familiar proper names. Although the scenery hints at a New Brunswick environment, there is also a strikingly universal quality to it. The wilderness is not depicted for its own sake, nor does it merely constitute the backdrop of the ensuing drama, but directly bears on the theme, plot, and frame of the story. Thus, the first sentence, "One side of the ravine was in darkness,"

[3] The story is also available in Roberts's *The Last Barrier, and Other Stories*, and in several short story anthologies, including *The Oxford Book of Canadian Short Stories in English*. A digitized version of the Harper's print is found on the Cornell University website, at http://cdl.library.cornell.edu/cgi-bin/moa/moa-cgi?notisid=ABK4014–0086–13 (date of access 29 December 2005).

maps out the thematic and formal structure of the story as it sets up a world of duality, ambiguity, and conflict. This is in keeping with the duality in Roberts's life during the Windsor period, that is, the tensions caused by his desire for freedom and mobility on the one hand and his social obligations and the stultifying routine of his teaching life on the other. The story evokes its oppositions through a poetic precision of language: While "one side" of the ravine is wrapped in protective darkness and characterized by adjectives with positive connotations ("soft," "rich," "thick," "great," "ancient," "unviolated"), the opposite side, "unlike its fellow," is depicted through negative adjectives ("barren," "rocky," "harsh," "stunted") and a stark imagery of violence ("bossed," "swollen," "obstructed"). Alternating between a variety of pleasant consonants, diphthongs, and round vowels on the one hand, and disturbing sibilants on the other, the rhythm and sound of Roberts's vivid diction echo the opposition of softness and savagery. The reader is presented with both the awesome and sublime side of nature, inspired by Romanticism, and its ugly, grim and merciless counterpart, informed by naturalism. Roberts thus engages in a discourse between what Jack London called "the school of clod" and the school of God (London 1956, 212; see Whalen 1984, 1989). The ravine provides a potent image for these conflicting perceptions of the world, juxtaposing and, at the same time, uniting them: a locus of paradoxical texture. From this dialectic drama, a stream rises, "swollen" and "obstructed": a stream of conflict. That this conflict is fundamental to life and extends beyond the confines of the natural world is made explicit by the formulation "as in a trough," a simile taken from civilization. Roberts employs an anonymous omniscient third-person narrator to direct the gaze of his readers and a technique that anticipates the cinematic mode. Roberts's visually sophisticated eye creates a mysterious atmosphere, making use of light and dark to achieve a painterly chiaroscuro. Interfering with the protective darkness, the moonlight "disclos[es] . . . the other side," the hidden violence: "the bones and antlers of a deer which had been dragged thither and devoured." The "mutable moonlight" with its "transfiguring touch" (*The Watchers of the Trails*, 112) recurs frequently in Roberts's work, evoking a strong Romantic sense of magic and "infinite mystery" (ibid.) in his realistic settings. The "ancient unviolated forest" (11), another leitmotif of Roberts's writing, points to the cultural context of an antimodernist discourse that glorifies the primitive and primeval, the "pre- and under-civilised spaces as realms of emotional and spiritual intensity anterior or adjacent to the materialistic and artificial world of the modern city" (Bentley 2004). Within the narrow boundaries of his five-sentence expository description of nature, Roberts succeeds not only in creating suspense, setting up a narrative frame, and drawing the reader into the setting, but in designing a potent and resonant pictorial composition that signifies the fundamental themes and structure of the story. The realistic depiction conveys transcendental meanings of symbolic significance: "behind every incident, almost behind every phrase, one is aware of a lurking universality, the adumbration of greater things" (Hovey 1972, 6). His technique derives from modern European "symboliste" suggestion (see Bentley) rather than traditional Romantic symbolism as the symbol is not invented, nor divorced from reality, but taken directly from it: "the thing is found to be symbolic" (ibid.).

With the setting of the drama fully realized, Roberts now brings his animal protagonist onto the stage. The male panther emerges "out of a shadowy hollow" from the side of the ravine that represents "nature red in tooth and claw." He is strangely illuminated by the moonrays: while in "common daylight" the animal's coat would have shown a "warm fulvous hue," the "elvish, decolorizing rays" of the "half hidden moon" transform it into a "spectral gray." The diction and imagery create a surreal, ghostly atmosphere that reverberates with the supernatural, the uncanny, and a Romantic sense of universal mystery. The ambiguity found in the expository description of nature continues with that of the panther: his paws step "softly" and his head is "smooth" and "round," but his cry is "shrill" and "terrible," "at once plaintive and menacing." He is both vulnerable and harmful, gentle and rough, endangered and dangerous. A foreboding tone of terror is felt when Roberts compares the animal's cry to "the fierce protestations of a saw beneath the file"; once again, he employs an image from civilization for a creature of the wild, thus eradicating the line between the human and animal world. Reminiscent of biblical diction, the panther's cry, "a summons to his mate," announces that "the hour had come when they should seek their prey." Fusing archetypal quest patterns with the elemental struggle in a Darwinian world, Roberts presents the animals as heroes setting out on a necessary and divinely sanctioned quest for survival. The biblical tone specifically recalls Jesus' words upon realizing his near death (see John 13:1). The call of the panthers is answered by a pair of crows, symbols of death and portents of doom; the fact that they have been nesting in the same spot for three summers, however, stresses the cyclical structure of life and the permanence of nature in contrast to the transience of individual existence. The taut atmosphere is exquisitely handled: the male panther walks "restlessly up and down" as if caged, "impatiently," while he makes no sound. He wanders "along the edge of the shadow" — a tightrope walk, precarious but controlled. The diction of military strategy ("they purposed," "take tribute of the enemies' flocks") highlights Roberts's conviction that animals do not act on instinct alone but with "something akin to reason." For him, "as far, at least, as the mental intelligence is concerned, the gulf dividing the lowest of the human species from the highest of the animals has in these latter days been reduced to a very narrow psychological fissure" (*The Kindred of the Wild*, 23). Roberts's animal heroes are exceptional creatures, "kings" and "masters," with extraordinary grace, dignity, cunning, and physical strength, as many of his books and story titles indicate. Although he portrays a mere representative of the species — unlike Seton, who names his animal heroes and focuses on the life of an individual specimen — they are autonomous protagonists who are neither symbols nor subject to the kind of anthropomorphism imposed on their literary predecessors. Roberts's interest in animal psychology allows him to discern the motives that govern the behavior of the two animals (see *The Kindred of the Wild*, 24). He inserts an explicatory paragraph to stress (for example by using rhetorical questions) that the prime force behind their action is the preservation of their offspring and thus their species. He attributes the panther's desperate situation to the reckless encroachment of civilization on the "world of ancient forest," thereby anticipating an ecocriticism that would become prominent only six decades later (for instance in the works of Farley Mowat and Fred Bodsworth).

As the events unfold in rapid succession, Roberts inserts a number of acoustic details that illustrate that his cinematic technique is not confined to visual impressions. The "vast stillness of the Northern forest," for instance — a recurrent image in Roberts's work — poses a stark contrast to the tense atmosphere and the sudden cry of the child. As a result of the latter, the narrative shifts perspective, adopting the point of view of the panthers to increase suspense: "Soon would they break their bitter fast" (16). However, at the moment of apprehension, Roberts attenuates the tension by taking a long narrative digression in which the omniscient narrator provides background information on the child's plight in the cabin. Once more, Roberts works with stark oppositions when introducing the reader to the settlers: one, a lower class drunkard with a "rickety shed," a "tiny clearing," and a "miserable shanty," the other, "a prosperous pioneer," "master" of a "substantial frame house" in "the midst of a large and well-tilled clearing." In contrast, the cabin of the "shiftless fellow" is placed far outside the settlements, between civilization and the animal realm, and his behavior, which is portrayed in sharp satirical tones, stands in pointed contrast to that of the devoted parents, human and animal alike. However, the righteous patriarchal pioneer is also constructed as an ambiguous figure, his superior attitude caricatured in his use of "unsavoury language" which he despises in the other man. Moreover, had he not forbidden the innocent friendship of his own son with the son of the drunkard, the catastrophe would not have happened; likewise, his extensive settlement has contributed to the starvation of the panthers. Roberts thus sets up interconnecting story lines with innocent and helpless children on each side (the human child is described using similar diction and imagery as the animal offspring) and a perspective that enables the reader's identification with both parties. He then introduces his parallel plot, juxtaposing the panthers with the prosperous settler (who also remains unnamed, i.e. a mere representative of his species). In having both parties stop and listen to the child's wailing at the same time, Roberts suggests the similarity of man's and animal's (primitive) instincts, that is to say, their kinship. That the settler happens to pass by and hear the child's wailing is yet another Hardyesque coincidence in the series of chance occurrences that structure the story. The settler neither knows the severity of the danger nor the true identity of the child, assuming it to be the drunkard's son — and is more than reluctant to redirect his path. His eventual overcoming of primitive drives and selfish instincts and his ability to feel compassion bear witness to man's higher faculties. His altruism is not a moral choice but an emotional response. For Roberts, humans are both inside and outside of nature, both like and unlike animals: humanity harbors the "ambivalent beast" (Gold 1984, 77).

Returning to the first plot line, Roberts interrupts the rising action for a second digression. He abandons his modernist preference of a reticent narrator for a didactic address to the reader whom he explicitly wishes to free from his prejudices of animal barbarity: "It would be thoughtless superstition to say the beasts were cruel. . . . Theirs was no hideous or unnatural rage, as is the custom to describe it" (23). For Roberts, the panthers are but "seeking their meat from God" (Psalm 104:21), with "the strength, the cunning, the deadly swiftness given to them to that end" (23). The biblical quote extols the order of the world as created by God and also provides the story's title. Roberts was well aware of the ambiguities and potential ironies caused by the interaction of title and narrative. That the "food convenient for them" (23) is a human child is mere circumstance, for survival is imperative and has nothing to do with the social conventions of good or evil.

Balancing the reader's sympathies for both sides, Roberts now swiftly moves to the story's climax, joining his parallel plots for the final confrontation at the clearing. The narrator regains his detached composure as an objective observer and recounts the shooting of the female panther with cold-blooded, almost Olympian restraint. Apart from the subordinate role of the female, who is reduced to motherhood (on Roberts's "masculinist discourse" see Dean 1996, 4, 6), her elimination also paves the way for the subsequent "hand-to-paw combat" between the two males, both superior members of their species. The duel of these epic heroes is reported with unflinchingly graphic detail. The panther loses out to the man, who even with his insufficient fowling-piece and after having been severely wounded is still the fitter, or "master animal." The discovery by the settler that he has saved the life of his own son seems overly melodramatic, yet Roberts employs this archetypal motif not for sentimental reasons but to increase the suspense surrounding the settler's hair's-breadth decision and to stress his argument for the higher faculties of man.

The story, however, does not end with the happy reunification of father and child. In an ironic continuance of the kill-or-be-killed pattern, the dénouement has the settler some weeks later, tracking a bear who has killed his sheep, discovering the dead bodies of the two small panther cubs, "now rapidly decaying." Reported with dispassionate candor and complete absence of sentiment, in a chronicle-like, documentary style, the graphic image of these innocent victims is left for the reader to assimilate. The narrator remains impartial, offering neither comment nor lament in order to achieve the desired effect. He holds the puzzled readers at an intellectual distance from which they can contemplate the grim ironies of nature, the frailty of life, the forces that shape the destiny of all beings, the central role of chance and accident, and the ambiguity of human beings in the natural order. After all, the child is saved only at the expense of two other young lives: there is "no adequate solution within sight." Roberts's vision is neither simplistic nor fatalistic, but opts for a transcendent understanding and "something akin to catharsis" (Gold 1965, 26). The animal story, for him, is "a potent emancipator" (*The Kindred of the Wild*, 29) with the therapeutic potential to provide its readers with a "new and clearer vision" (ibid., 23–24) of the complexity of reality and the ultimate order of things. When the perplexed editor called it "neither fish, flesh, fowl, nor good red herring," he was right insofar as Roberts presents no absolutes, no ultimate conclusions, no single-minded either/or. Instead he embraces the ambivalence of nature, torn between the harsh laws of survival and the beauty and mystery of being. He definitely did not depict "a savage and unforgiving natural world inhabited by forces opposed to the order of grace," and gave no "plain and unambiguous portrayal of nature," as James observes (James 2004). Nor does his work reflect the pessimistic notions of victimization and ultimate doom that Margaret Atwood in *Survival* (1972) claims for the Canadian psyche in her animals-as-victims analogy. Roberts rather takes us back to the ravine, closing his narrative frame with an exact reiteration of the diction and imagery employed at the beginning. This rhetorical device (epanalepsis) embodies the cyclical structure of nature and reminds the reader once more of the permanent behind the transitory. Despite destruction, random fate, and undeserved bad luck, death is not futile and life itself persists (see also Roberts's story "The Sentry of the Sedge-Flats"). The ravine, like the "heart of the ancient wood," is not a "heart of darkness" but a "candid and complex centre," "where a balanced perspective on reality is encouraged" (Whalen 1984, 136). This affirmative and universal vision, this celebration of ambiguity, might well be what is most "Canadian" about Roberts's animal stories.

Dubbed "a sketch" by Roberts, "Do Seek Their Meat from God" is a controlled and carefully constructed narrative. It follows the short-story convention of isolating and dramatizing a single incident that contains within it a multitude of implications. Roberts manages, in a very brief space, to compose a consistent imaginative realm and a unity of impression, following the classical structure of exposition, rising action, climax, and dénouement. The techniques of creating suspense and desired atmosphere are exquisitely mastered. Roberts's writing is detailed and vivid, his language concise and polished, and he shows keen attention to sensory detail. His style, at once harshly realistic and allusively poetic, reflects the story's dominant theme, its mixing of Darwinian insight and Romantic sensibilities in an innovative fusion of the scientific and rational with the mysterious and inexplicable. Oppositions, ambiguities, and reconciliation are conveyed in a brilliant interplay of paradigmatic and syntagmatic structures, including diction, imagery, point of view, narrative stance, rhetoric, and a highly symbolic narrative frame. Although structure and narrative progression remain conservative, lending little to the development of the short-story form, Roberts's animal stories mark an important step in the development of realism in Canadian literature. Further, Roberts's innovative use of irony breaks with Romantic nineteenth-century modes of perception and enters the world of twentieth-century literature (see Gadpaille 1988, 6). Yet the story's main appeal and innovation lies in its subject matter. Roberts's animal stories broke with period conventions and rejected Victorian domestication of nature by moving their settings and subjects into the wild outdoors. Subverting conventional man-against-beast narratives, they offered new and exciting visions of wild animals. Their lack of conventional religious sentiment, bearing no relation to moral codes, and the role attributed to chance and accident posed a great challenge for the late Victorian reading public. Yet their enormous success indicates that these stories responded to prevalent discourses and brought readers in touch with their own uncivilized nature. In 1892 Roberts found that he had not "turned the corner in short story writing yet" (*Letters*, 149) and had difficulty placing "Do Seek Their Meat from God." By the end of the decade he could sell every story he wrote. Roberts and Seton had established a genre that became the first international success story in the history of the Canadian short story.

Works Cited

Adams, John Coldwell. "A Preliminary Bibliography." In *The Sir Charles G. D. Roberts Symposium*, ed. and introd. Glenn Clever. Reappraisals: Canadian Writers 10. Ottawa: University of Ottawa Press, 1984. 221–49.

———. *Sir Charles God Damn: The Life of Sir Charles G. D. Roberts.* Toronto: University of Toronto Press, 1986.

Bentley, D. M. R. "'The Thing Is Found to Be Symbolic': Symboliste Elements in the Early Short Stories of Gilbert Parker, Charles G. D. Roberts, and Duncan Campbell Scott." *Canadian Poetry*, 4 September 2004: http://www.uwo.ca/english/canadianpoetry/confederation/roberts/criticism/symboliste.htm.

Conway, Donald. "Actaeon or Odysseus: The Bibliographers of Roberts." In *The Proceedings of the Sir Charles G. D. Roberts Symposium*, ed. and introd. Carrie MacMillan. Sackville/Halifax: Centre for Canadian Studies/Nimbus, 1984. 5–15.

Dean, Misao. "Political Science: Realism in Roberts's Animal Stories." *Studies in Canadian Literature* 21.1 (1996): 1–16.

Dunlap, Thomas R. " 'The Old Kinship of Earth': Science, Man and Nature in the Animal Stories of Charles G. D. Roberts." *Journal of Canadian Studies/Revue d'études canadiennes* 22.1 (1987): 104–20.

Gadpaille, Michelle. *The Canadian Short Story.* Toronto: Oxford University Press, 1988.

Gold, Joseph. "The Ambivalent Beast." In *The Proceedings of the Sir Charles G. D. Roberts Symposium*, ed. and introd. Carrie MacMillan. Sackville/Halifax: Centre for Canadian Studies/Nimbus, 1984. 77–86.

———. "The Precious Speck of Life." *Canadian Literature* 26 (1965): 22–32.

Hovey, Richard. "Modern Symbolism and Maurice Maeterlinck." In Maurice Maeterlinck, *Plays*, trans. Richard Hovey. Chicago: Herbert S. Stone, 1894; New York: Kraus Reprint, 1972. 3–11.

James, William Closson. *Religion and Nature Writing in Canada.* Queen's University, 9 September 2004: http://post.queensu.ca/~jameswc/Design/NatWrtgJan7.htm.

Keith, W. J. *Charles G. D. Roberts.* Toronto: Copp Clark, 1969.

London, Jack. *Martin Eden.* 1908; rpt. New York: Rinehart, 1956.

Lucas, Alec. "Introduction." In Charles G. D. Roberts, *The Last Barrier and Other Stories.* New Canadian Library 7. Toronto: McClelland & Stewart, 1958. v–x.

Pomeroy, Elsie May. *Sir Charles G. D. Roberts: A Biography.* Toronto: Ryerson, 1943.

Roberts, Charles G. D. *Babes of the Wild.* London: Cassell, 1912 [also published as *Children of the Wild.* New York: Macmillan, 1913].

———. *The Collected Letters of Charles G. D. Roberts*, ed. Laurel Boone, introd. Fred Cogswell. Fredericton: Goose Lane Editions, 1989.

———. "Do Seek Their Meat from God." In Roberts, *Earth's Enigmas*, 11–27. [First published in Harper's Monthly Magazine 86 (1892): 120–22.]

———. *Earth's Enigmas: A Book of Animal and Nature Life.* 1896; rpt. (rev.) Boston: Page, 1903.

———. *Eyes of the Wilderness.* Toronto/London: Macmillian/Dent, 1933.

———. *Eyes of the Wilderness and Other Stories.* Toronto: McGraw-Hill Ryerson, 1980.

———. *The Feet of the Furtive.* London: Ward, Lock, 1912.

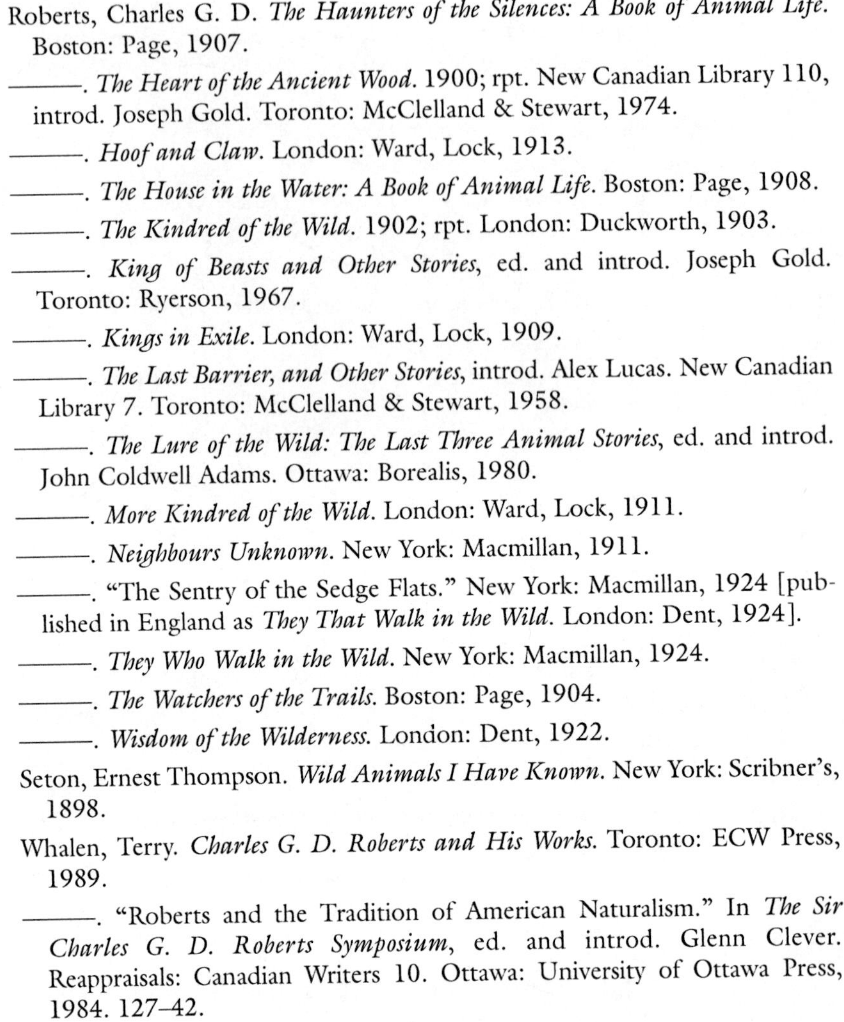

Roberts, Charles G. D. *The Haunters of the Silences: A Book of Animal Life.* Boston: Page, 1907.

———. *The Heart of the Ancient Wood.* 1900; rpt. New Canadian Library 110, introd. Joseph Gold. Toronto: McClelland & Stewart, 1974.

———. *Hoof and Claw.* London: Ward, Lock, 1913.

———. *The House in the Water: A Book of Animal Life.* Boston: Page, 1908.

———. *The Kindred of the Wild.* 1902; rpt. London: Duckworth, 1903.

———. *King of Beasts and Other Stories,* ed. and introd. Joseph Gold. Toronto: Ryerson, 1967.

———. *Kings in Exile.* London: Ward, Lock, 1909.

———. *The Last Barrier, and Other Stories,* introd. Alex Lucas. New Canadian Library 7. Toronto: McClelland & Stewart, 1958.

———. *The Lure of the Wild: The Last Three Animal Stories,* ed. and introd. John Coldwell Adams. Ottawa: Borealis, 1980.

———. *More Kindred of the Wild.* London: Ward, Lock, 1911.

———. *Neighbours Unknown.* New York: Macmillan, 1911.

———. "The Sentry of the Sedge Flats." New York: Macmillan, 1924 [published in England as *They That Walk in the Wild.* London: Dent, 1924].

———. *They Who Walk in the Wild.* New York: Macmillan, 1924.

———. *The Watchers of the Trails.* Boston: Page, 1904.

———. *Wisdom of the Wilderness.* London: Dent, 1922.

Seton, Ernest Thompson. *Wild Animals I Have Known.* New York: Scribner's, 1898.

Whalen, Terry. *Charles G. D. Roberts and His Works.* Toronto: ECW Press, 1989.

———. "Roberts and the Tradition of American Naturalism." In *The Sir Charles G. D. Roberts Symposium,* ed. and introd. Glenn Clever. Reappraisals: Canadian Writers 10. Ottawa: University of Ottawa Press, 1984. 127–42.

2: Tory Humanism, Ironic Humor, and Satire: Stephen Leacock, "The Marine Excursion of the Knights of Pythias" (1912)

Heinz Antor (University of Cologne)

IN 1910, STEPHEN LEACOCK (1869–1944), a one-time schoolmaster who had become a professor of political science at McGill University in Montreal, started a second, complementary career as a creative writer with the publication of *Literary Lapses*, a collection of short and often humorous sketches, anecdotes, and stories he had previously published in various American magazines. Born in Hampshire, England, Stephen Leacock had come to Canada at the age of six. His career as a writer was the first major Canadian literary success story, with Leacock becoming the first Canadian author of world fame.

Leacock made a significant contribution to Canadian literature as a writer of short stories and as a humorist only after he had already published a number of scholarly works. His first book, *Elements of Political Science* (1906), quickly became a standard textbook in its field and was only one of his altogether more than sixty books, which, in addition to studies in political science, included fiction, essays, and literary criticism. Leacock was an exceptionally prolific creative writer. In 1911 he published *Nonsense Novels*, a collection of ten parodic short stories, and one year later what is generally regarded as his masterpiece, *Sunshine Sketches of a Little Town*. With this, as with his subsequent collections of short stories, he took up existing and formed new traditions of the Canadian short story as well as of humorous writing. *Sunshine Sketches of a Little Town* was the book that made Leacock world-famous. This collection of interconnected short stories, all set in the fictitious small Ontario town of Mariposa, is a quintessentially Canadian book that takes up and carries on the Anglo-Canadian tradition of the short-story cycle, which had already been practiced successfully by Duncan Campbell Scott in *The Village of Viger* (1896) and would later also be used by Jessie Georgina Sime, Frederick Philip Grove, Emily Carr, George Elliott, Norman Levine, Margaret Laurence, and Alice Munro, to name but a few. Moreover, Leacock's *Sunshine Sketches* are one of the foremost examples of Canadian literary humor in short fiction, and they continue the tradition of such illustrious forerunners as Thomas Chandler Haliburton and Thomas McCulloch (Rasporich 1982, 227–28, 236–40), a tradition that would later be taken up by such Canadian humorists as Antonine Maillet, Paul Hiebert, Robert Kroetsch, Jack Hodgins, Robertson Davies, Mordecai Richler, and Thomas King. The good-natured ironic portrait of idyllic small-town Canada in *Sunshine Sketches* is supplemented by *Arcadian Adventures of the Idle Rich* (1914), Leacock's second important work of humorous fiction featuring a series of interconnected short stories and sketches satirizing in a harsher, sharper tone the destructive and hypocritical activities of the plutocracy of a big capitalist American city. While in Plutoria, the fictitious urban setting of *Arcadian Adventures*, the idle and manipulative rich and the liberal individualists meet at the Mausoleum Club while the poor work and waste away in slums, *Sunshine Sketches* presents a mellower world of social cohesion and order, and the foibles of the Mariposans can be viewed with ironic amusement. Stephen Leacock's other important books of humorous stories and sketches include *Behind the Beyond, and Other Contributions to Human Knowledge* (1913), *Moonbeams from the Larger Lunacy* (1915), *Further Foolishness: Sketches and Satires on the Follies of the Day* (1916), *The Hohenzollerns in America: With the Bolsheviks in Berlin and Other Impossibilities* (1919), *Over the Footlights* (1923), *Winnowed Wisdom: A New Book of Humour* (1926), *Short Circuits* (1928), *The Iron Man & the Tin Woman, With Other Such Futurities: A Book of Literary Sketches of Today and of Tomorrow* (1929), *The Dry Pickwick and Other Incongruities* (1932), *Funny Pieces: A Book of Random Sketches* (1936), *Model Memoirs and Other Sketches from Simple to Serious* (1938), *My Remarkable Uncle and Other Sketches* (1942), as well as the posthumously published *Last Leaves* (1945) and *My Financial Career and Other Follies* (1993).

Leacock's work as a political scientist and his humorous fiction should not be seen as completely separate aspects of his career. On the contrary, his humor often exposes vices and shortcomings he had analyzed in his academic work. Gerald Lynch has characterized Leacock as a "Tory humanist" (Lynch, 1988, ix). His conservatism was tempered by a gentle understanding of human foibles, but he nevertheless insisted on the importance of order, tradition, a sense of social responsibility, and a sense of home. He saw that self-interest was a driving force in human development but also felt the need to hold unrestrained individualism and materialism in check if human progress were not to be hampered. Such fears were expressed, for example, in *The Unsolved Riddle of Social Justice* (1920), in which he not only criticized the negative social consequences of modern industrial civilization, but also argued in favor of a spiritual renewal of the individual citizen. Similarly, Leacock's humorous fiction was a challenge to the chaotic elements of a commercial age, and it countered these with an emphasis on human values upheld in the face of a wryly and wittily acknowledged human fallibility. As a satirist, Leacock tended to be more of the Horatian kind, viewing his fellow beings' shortcomings with an amused smile of understanding, but, as becomes evident in some of the harsher passages in *Arcadian Adventures*, there is sometimes also a Juvenalian tinge to his satire. The latter, however, never deteriorates into sarcasm because it is softened by pathos and compassion. Like his eighteenth-century literary forebear Henry Fielding, Leacock was enraged by iniquity and cruelty, but he was also able to cast a benevolent eye on the weaknesses that he considered to be part of the human condition and which he thought had to be remedied by human kindness. In this, he also saw himself as heir to his favorite two comic writers, Mark Twain and Charles Dickens, to whom he devoted literary biographies in 1932 (*Mark Twain*) and 1933 (*Charles Dickens, His Life and Work*). In the prefatory note to *Humour and Humanity* (1937), Leacock stated that "the essence of humour is human kindliness" (Leacock 1937, n.p.). This he considered to be necessary in the face of the disillusionments of life. Laughter, to Leacock, was to be taken seriously as "a relief from pain, . . . a consolation against the shortcomings of life itself" (1937, 72). In his essay "American Humour," published in his collected *Essays and Literary Studies*, he defined his idea of "sublime humour," that is, the highest form of humor:

> The final stage of the development of humour is reached when amusement no longer arises from a single "funny" idea, meaningless contrast, or odd play upon words, but rests upon a prolonged and sustained conception of the incongruities of human life itself. The shortcomings of our existence, the sad contrast of our aims and our achievements, the little fretting aspiration of the day that fades into the nothingness of tomorrow, kindle in the mellowed mind a sense of gentle amusement from which all selfish exultation has been chastened by the realization of our common lot of sorrow. On this higher plane humour and pathos mingle and become one. (Leacock 1916, 92–93)

If in *Arcadian Adventures of the Idle Rich* Leacock's emphasis lies more on the negative consequences of the unfeeling acceptance and perpetuation of incongruities and social iniquities in a materialist society, in the much kinder and softer, more nostalgic *Sunshine Sketches of a Little Town* there is a bemused tolerance towards human weaknesses. These weaknesses are foibles rather than vices because they are shared by all of us and because they are embedded in the functioning social microcosm of Mariposa, the small town where everyone knows everyone else and where people still feel responsible for each other. In the twelve stories that make up the book (first published in the *Montreal Star* between 17 February and 22 June 1912 and in book form later that year), the reader is given a portrait of a quintessential Canadian small town, its inhabitants, and their activities. Various characters turn up in several stories and thus become familiar to the reader. Among these very likeable protagonists of the short-story cycle are the scholarly but unworldly Dean Drone, Mariposa's cleric, who is financially inept and constantly struggles with his church's debt (see "The Ministrations of the Rev. Mr. Drone" and "The Whirlwind Campaign in Mariposa"); Jeff Thorpe, the barber, whose financial rise and fall is told in the *Sketches* (see "The Speculations of Jefferson Thorpe"); Peter Pupkin, the bank teller, whose seemingly hopeless passion for Judge Pepperleigh's daughter only comes to fruition after a false rumor about Peter's heroism and supposed death in a bank robbery (see "The Extraordinary Entanglement of Mr. Pupkin," "The Fore-ordained Attachment of Zena Pepperleigh and Peter Pupkin," and "The Mariposa Bank Mystery"); and, of course, Josh Smith, the proprietor of the local hotel, a shrewd pragmatist who sells liquor after hours (see "The Hostelry of Mr. Smith"), solves the Dean's financial problems by setting fire to the heavily over-insured church (see "The Beacon on the Hill"), and finally becomes Mariposa's Conservative candidate in the great Dominion Election (see "The Great Election in Missinaba County" and "The Candidacy of Mr. Smith").

The most popular and most frequently anthologized of the stories in *Sunshine Sketches of a Little Town* is "The Marine Excursion of the Knights of Pythias," which is the third of the twelve sketches and provides a more general introduction to the character of Mariposa and its inhabitants, recognizably modeled upon Orillia, Ontario (Doyle 1992, 55), where Leacock used to spend his summers and where his house can still be visited. This story illustrates in a paradigmatic way the specific kind of gently ironic and "genial humour" (Magee 1976, 268) that is so typical of Leacock's best-known book. It is also representative of the thematic unity of the whole collection, which, throughout the stories, provides an illustration of the meaning of Leacock's Tory humanism.

"The Marine Excursion of the Knights of Pythias" is the story of the "sinking" and subsequent "raising" of the "Mariposa Belle," the local steamer on the fictitious Lake Wissanotti — which is far from the catastrophe it sounds like because there are only six feet of water under the keel of the ship. No one comes to harm, and the whole affair is, in fact, a minor incident in the history of Mariposa and not the only one of its kind. What is significant, however, is the way the reader is told about this "non-event." The narrator begins with a description of Lake Wissanotti in the early morning sun on the day of the annual excursion of the Mariposa Knights of Pythias:

> Half-past six on a July morning! . . . Excursion day! . . . Lake Wissanotti in the morning sunlight! . . . With the boat all decked in flags and all the people in Mariposa on the wharf, and the band in peaked caps with big cornets tied to their bodies ready to play at any minute! I say! Don't tell me about the Carnival of Venice and the Delhi Durbar. Don't! I wouldn't look at them. I'd shut my eyes! For light and colour give me every time

> an excursion out of Mariposa down the lake to the Indian's Island out of sight in the morning mist. Talk of your Papal Zouaves and your Buckingham Palace Guard! I want to see the Mariposa band in uniform and the Mariposa Knights of Pythias with their aprons and their insignia and their picnic baskets and their five-cent cigars! (53–54)

The beginning of the story is characterized by a sense of urgency and enthusiasm produced by a narrator who, evidently a Mariposan himself, cannot wait to see the Mariposa Belle leave the wharf. The number of exclamation marks is indicative not only of the narrator's excitement at what is to come, but also of his enjoyment and appreciation of what apparently is to him an event of enormous importance. The repetition of the narrator's exclamations is symptomatic of a certain loss of control of his enthusiasm, which appears to be magnified by overblown comparisons of provincial Mariposa with world-famous sights and attractions. Here the reader is already confronted with the incongruity at the core of Leacock's humor, and the narrator's verve warns the reader against trusting him too easily. The narrator, seemingly unwittingly, creates a critical distance between himself and the reader, which allows the latter to come up with outside judgments the former cannot pass because he is too closely involved in Mariposan affairs. The reader's double awareness of the narrator's passionate admiration of Mariposa and the small town's real status as a provincial backwater thus embraces the incongruity that triggers the good-natured laughter that is so often elicited in Leacock's stories.

Despite this critical distancing, the narrator immediately establishes a rapport with the reader by directly addressing him/her, a device already used in the introductory sentence of the first of the *Sunshine Sketches*, "The Hostelry of Mr. Smith": "I don't know whether you know Mariposa . . . " (13). This is followed by descriptions and explanations given by a narrator who is supposedly "in the know" about the little town, who is an insider, and very proud of it, too, and who in a good-natured and self-satisfied manner takes the reader into his confidence. The narrator is so engrossed in his enthusiastic admiration and grandiloquent, inflated praise of Mariposa, however, that he neglects to explain, for example, who exactly the Knights of Pythias are, obviously taking it for granted that this must be known to everybody. Apparently, unlike the reader, the narrator is totally unaware of the ludicrous disparity inherent in such comparisons as that between the uniforms of the Buckingham Palace Guard and those of the Mariposa Knights of Pythias. The character of the narrator, then, is constructed in a way that invites both sympathetic understanding and critical distance, which provides the basis for Leacock's kindly humor in *Sunshine Sketches*.

This ironic humor, with which Leacock derides the narrator and his fellow Mariposans, is to be understood as directed not only at the small town and its people, but at Canada and Canadians in general. It is no coincidence that in the initial description of Lake Wissanotti quoted above, the call of the loon, the quintessential Canadian bird, echoes over the lake. For, as we are already told in "The Hostelry of Mr. Smith," after the initial question as to whether we "know Mariposa": "If not, it is of no consequence, for if you know Canada at all, you are probably well acquainted with a dozen towns just like it" (13). In "The Marine Excursion of the Knights of Pythias," the function of Mariposa as "a microcosm of the English-Canadian Nation" (Marshall 1980, 176) becomes obvious again when the Mariposa Belle leaves the wharf with everybody breaking into "Maple Leaf for Ever!" (60) and then returns after her temporary "sinking" with the band playing the Canadian national anthem on the upper deck. Indeed, the very last words of the story — "O CAN-A-DA!" (72) — seem like a well-intentioned but amused comment on the country as a whole.

Canada, then, is associated in *Sunshine Sketches* with the provincial atmosphere of a small town, but this is to be taken not as a criticism of the country, but rather as a positive comment, for — unlike the Plutoria of *Arcadian Adventures* — Mariposa is still what Gerald Lynch has referred to as "an interdependent community" (Lynch, x). The annual excursion of the Knights of Pythias is an all-inclusive social event: as we are told by the narrator, "Why, everybody's here" (54). Mariposa does not yet suffer from the negative effects of the social fragmentation of modernity, and in this context we also learn why the Knights of Pythias have not been clearly defined and introduced. The narrator, in his inimitable, naïve loquaciousness informs us:

> Perhaps I ought to explain that when I speak of the excursion as being of the Knights of Pythias, the thing must not be understood in any narrow sense. In Mariposa practically everybody belongs to the Knights of Pythias just as they do to everything else. That's the great thing about the town and that's what makes it so different from the city. Everybody is in everything. (55)

In Mariposa, the whole community shares woes and joys as an organic whole. The approach of Mariposans to the world is all-embracing rather than exclusive, and so, the reader is told, they all celebrate together, no matter whether the cause for celebration is Irish Home Rule, St. Andrew's Day, St. George's Day, or the Fourth of July: "Oh, it's the most American town imaginable is Mariposa — on the fourth of July" (55). We are thus given the impression of a small town full of likeable people who may have their weaknesses and be a little provincial in some respects, but who also share a strong sense of community.

The various foibles of the Mariposans and, by extension, of Canadians and of human beings in general are the butt of Leacock's ironic humor in *Sunshine Sketches.* Prime among these is their inflated sense of the importance of their little town and of themselves. This, however, does not become the target of a savage Juvenalian attack on human vanity, but rather the object of a gently bemused philosophical contemplation on the effects and the inescapability of perspective, a train of thought that triggers an amused smile in the reader. The description of the Mariposa Belle is a case in point. In the introductory story, "The Hostelry of Mr. Smith," the narrator is still able to take a detached point of view and describe the Mariposa Belle as "a steamer that is tied to the wharf with two ropes of about the same size as they use on the Lusitania" (13). In "The Marine Excursion of the Knights of Pythias," however, this distanced view of the local steamer with its implied humorous criticism of the incongruity between the small boat and its massive ropes is no longer possible, because the narrator becomes so "Mariposan" himself that all he is capable of is a confused meditation on the changeable appearance of things:

> The Mariposa Belle always seems to me to have some of those strange properties that distinguish Mariposa itself. I mean, her size seems to vary so. If you see her there in the winter, frozen in the ice beside the wharf with a snowdrift against the windows of the pilot house, she looks a pathetic little thing the size of a butternut. But in the summer time, especially after you've been in Mariposa for a month or two, and have paddled alongside of her in a canoe, she gets larger and taller, and with a great sweep of black sides, till you see no difference between the Mariposa Belle and the Lusitania. Each one is a big steamer and that's all you can say. (56)

The conflation of the big and the small here creates Leacock's typical humorous effect of incongruity, and it is obviously due to a change of perspective after a long-term stay in Mariposa. What is admirable to Mariposans may seem to be quite normal to an outsider, and what is normal to the inhabitants of the little town may sometimes seem absurd to a stranger. Which of these perspectives is to be preferred is quite clear, at least to the narrator, who in "The Hostelry of Mr. Smith" tries to counter any outsider's possible opinion of Mariposa as a small place with the following remark: "Of course if you come to the place fresh from New York, you are all deceived. Your standard of vision is all astray" (15). The reader is well aware of the fact that the narrator is unreliable because he has fallen victim to the distorting effects of a Mariposan point of view, which, being restricted to the little world of the small town, considers everything there to be of the utmost importance and of enormous size. The very choice of the title "The Marine Excursion of the Knights of Pythias" illustrates this, for there is nothing "marine" about the boat trip at all, Lake Wissanotti being far away from the sea, as we are told on the very first page of *Sunshine Sketches*: "The steamer goes nowhere in particular, for the lake is landlocked and there is no navigation for the Mariposa Belle except to 'run trips' on the first of July and the Queen's Birthday, and to take excursions of the Knights of Pythias and the Sons of Temperance to and from the Local Option Townships" (13).

Mariposans not only exaggerate the size and importance of their little town, they also take themselves very seriously. This is satirized in the descriptions of the passengers' activities on board the Mariposa Belle. There is, for example, Miss Lawson, "the high-school teacher, with a book of German poetry — Gothey I think it was" (61), as the narrator points out, thus revealing the inefficacy of the teacher's pedagogic efforts as well as the limitations of his own learning. Similarly, the bidding match between Dr. Gallagher and Dean Drone as to who is the more learned of the two — with the former trying to impress with his knowledge of early colonial history and the latter countering with Xenophon — is suddenly deflated when Drone offers to show the doctor a map of the invasion of Greece: "Only he [Dr. Gallagher] must come some time between the Infant Class and the Mothers' Auxiliary" (63). This juxtaposition of the high and the low, of the grand and the ordinary, is a device typical of Leacockian humor in *Sunshine Sketches*, both on a thematic and on a stylistic level.

This is also evident in the way in which the narrator presents the whole incident of the "sinking" of the Mariposa Belle. Even before he describes the beginning of the boat trip, he repeatedly comes up with ominous hints about a catastrophic event that is not further defined, so that suspense is created as to what actually happened. This suspense is reinforced by the frequent repetition of the word "accident" (57) as well as by references to "crimson rockets going up against the sky . . . the fire bell ringing" and the Mackinaw lifeboat "plunging out into the lake with seven sweeps to a side" (59). The reader is indirectly warned of the narrator's unreliability by the narrator himself, who briefly becomes aware of having been carried away by his enthusiasm, only to relapse into his old practice:

> But, dear me, I am afraid that this is no way to tell a story. I suppose the true art would have been to have said nothing about the accident till it happened. But when you write about Mariposa, or hear of it, if you know the place, it's all so vivid and real that a thing like the contrast between the excursion crowd in the morning and the scene at night leaps into your mind and you must think of it.
>
> But never mind about the accident — let us turn back again to the morning. (59–60)

The picnic on the Indian's Island, the ensuing speeches, races, and the men's drinking are described only briefly because, as the parochial narrator informs us, "if you've ever been on a Mariposa excursion you know all about these details anyway" (65). This is followed by a dramatic rendering of the long-announced steamboat "accident" and the "rescue" of both the ship and everyone on board. The first news of the calamity reaches the passengers at an auspicious moment: "I think that it was just as they were singing like this: 'O — Can-a-da,' that word went round that the boat was sinking" (66). Once again, the events described can be read as a humorous comment on Canada as a whole. By now, the reader's expectations as to the catastrophe in store may be great, but the reactions of the various passengers are remarkably calm; the narrative bubble of the narrator's disaster story bursts when it turns out that this is not the first time the Mariposa Belle has sunk and when the true dimensions of the incident are exposed:

> You see, the last time but one the steamer had sunk, there had been a man drowned and it made them nervous.
>
> What? Hadn't I explained about the depth of Lake Wissanotti? I had taken it for granted that you knew; and in any case parts of it are deep enough, though I don't suppose in this stretch of it from the big reed beds up to within a mile of the town wharf, you could find six feet of water in it if you tried. Oh, pshaw! I was not talking about a steamer sinking in the ocean and carrying down its screaming crowds of people into the hideous depths of green water. Oh, dear me, no! That kind of thing never happens on Lake Wissanotti. (67)

Not only are the reader's fears dispelled here, but the narrator presents himself as someone who would never even dream of mistaking Lake Wissanotti for the big sea and Mariposa for the wide world. Yet, this is exactly what he has been doing throughout the story and what he will revert to in his description of the "rescue action" that follows. The effect of the passage quoted is one of humorous relief, but the reader's laughter is not only directed at the smallness of the incident described, at the harmlessness of the boat's pseudo-sinking, but also at the narrator and his use of the vocabulary of great maritime disasters. Still, even here, there is a special closeness between reader and narrator because the latter uses a particularly colloquial form of language, with his short questions and exclamations, direct addresses to the reader, and explanatory phrases such as "You see." The result is an inclusion of the reader within the narrator's horizon, and the reader's reaction thus comes more in the form of an understanding, ironic smile than derisive laughter. The "misunderstanding," as the narrator would have it, regarding the size of the accident, like so many incongruities in the story, is due once again to a question of perspective: the narrator is true to his Mariposan self insofar as the idea does not even occur to him that someone might read his story without a thorough knowledge of Mariposa at the back of his or her mind.

Even when he presents himself as a seasoned observer, as in the passage quoted above, the narrator cannot escape the parochial limitations of his Mariposan vision. This also comes out in the description of the "rescue action," during which the narrator presents himself in contradictory terms. On the one hand, having completely forgotten his laid-back pose of the calm witness and relapsing into the Mariposan attitude of inflating all local events, he dramatizes the incident:

> Safe! I'm not sure now that I come to think of it that it isn't worse than sinking in the Atlantic. After all, in the Atlantic there is wireless telegraphy, and a lot of trained sailors and stewards. But out on Lake Wissanotti — . . . — safe? Safe yourself, if you like; as for me, let me once get back into Mariposa again, under the night shadow of the maple trees, and this shall be the last, last time I'll go on Lake Wissanotti. (68)

On the other hand, only a few paragraphs further on, we are confronted again with the experienced sailor and braggart trying to laugh off the incident as a minor affair: "Really, it made one positively laugh! It seemed so queer and, anyway, if a man has a sort of natural courage, danger makes him laugh. Danger! pshaw! fiddlesticks! everybody scouted the idea. Why, it is just the little things like this that give zest to a day on the water" (69).

The ensuing "rescue action," with Mariposa's lifeboat setting out to "save" the passengers on board the supposedly sinking steamer, is also described in dramatic terms. This passage not only takes on a mock-heroic quality in view of the fact that there is no real danger in barely six feet of water, but, in a humorous reversal of the ordinary course of events in a maritime rescue action, here the rescuers need to be rescued themselves by being taken on board the half-sunk Mariposa Belle when their lifeboat takes in water, "and one by one every man was hauled aboard just as the lifeboat sank under their feet . . . Saved! Saved!!" (71). As a consequence of the mock-heroic incongruity between the formal dramatization of the events and their real harmlessness, the narrator, similar to Henry Fielding's, is included in the ironic humor of the story. The satirical effect is thus mellowed and we smile indulgently at the narrator and the Mariposans rather than sneering at them.

At the end of "The Marine Excursion of the Knights of Pythias," the resourceful Josh Smith wins a twenty-five-dollar bet with Mullins by plugging the Mariposa Belle's seams, having the water pumped out of her hull so that the steamer, with Smith at her wheel, can return on her own to the Mariposa wharf, looking quite stately "with all steam up again and with the long train of sparks careering from her funnel" (72). It is significant that Smith only helps the steamer in her plight for his own advantage, since not only does he win the bet, but this feat also prepares for his Conservative candidacy in the great Dominion Election at the end of the short-story cycle. Josh Smith is the one Mariposan who is described more critically than his fellow citizens because in everything he does, his own advantage is always at the fore. Smith comes closest of all Mariposans to the idle rich in Leacock's *Arcadian Adventures.*

Sunshine Sketches of a Little Town is Stephen Leacock's literary masterpiece, and the stories included are typical examples of his art. With their description of a small Anglo-Saxon Protestant community of United Empire Loyalists in rural Ontario, they present a well-ordered interdependent little society that is meant to be taken as a microcosmic representation of Canada by an author whose Tory humanism becomes quite palpable here. Tory humanism has been characterized as "a particularly Canadian stance that Leacock shares to some extent with other Canadian social satirists such as Thomas Chandler Haliburton, Sara Jeannette Duncan, and Robertson Davies, and with philosophers such as Charles Taylor and George Grant" (Pollock 1997, 639). Mariposa is rooted in the humane values of tradition and community, and the little failings of its inhabitants are described as endearing rather than offensive. The resulting ironic humor and mild satire of this collection have contributed to its great success in Canada and beyond. Mariposa, however, also represents a community of the past, while the Plutoria of *Arcadian Adventures*, which is characterized more by a mechanical materialism than by Mariposa's human kindliness, points towards the future, so that the vision of *Sunshine Sketches* is a nostalgic one.

Arcadian Adventures represents the city counterpart to Mariposa's small-town idyll (Bush 1977, 134); Leacock may have felt the tension between the two and that the future would be Plutorian rather than Mariposan when he talked about the ameliorating function of his humor as a civilizing influence and as a respite from the harsher sides of life. This attitude can be felt in the wistful tone of the last of the *Sunshine Sketches*, "L'Envoi: The Train to Mariposa," in which the narrator finds himself in the Mausoleum Club in Plutoria and thinks back to the good old days in Mariposa, imagining himself on the five o'clock train on his way back home to the little town. Once again, he gets carried away as the train, in his imagination, approaches Mariposa, being transformed in the process from a small suburban train into "the fastest train in the whole world" (185). However, when he dreams of finally arriving at his destination, with the brakemen and the porters crying "MARIPOSA! MARIPOSA!" (186), the narrator awakes from his nostalgic reverie, and the disillusionment Leacock sets out to dispel with his humor breaks through once more (Cameron 1965, 41–42). The collection thus ends with words already preparing for the world of the *Arcadian Adventures*: "And as we listen, the cry grows faint and fainter in our ears and we are sitting here again in the leather chairs of the Mausoleum Club, talking of the little Town in the Sunshine that once we knew" (186).

Works Cited

Bush, Douglas. "Stephen Leacock." In *The Canadian Imagination: Dimensions of a Literary Culture*, ed. David Staines. Cambridge, MA: Harvard University Press, 1977. 123–51.

Cameron, D. A. "The Enchanted Houses: Leacock's Irony." *Canadian Literature* 23 (1965): 31–44.

Doyle, James. *Stephen Leacock: The Sage of Orillia.* Toronto: ECW Press, 1992.

Leacock, Stephen. *Arcadian Adventures of the Idle Rich.* New York: John Lane, 1914.

———. *Behind the Beyond, and Other Contributions to Human Knowledge.* London: John Lane, 1913.

———. *The Dry Pickwick and Other Incongruities.* London: John Lane, 1932.

———. *Essays and Literary Studies.* London: John Lane, 1916.

———. *Funny Pieces: A Book of Random Sketches.* New York: Dodd, Mead & Company, 1936.

———. *Further Foolishness: Sketches and Satires on the Follies of the Day.* London: John Lane, 1917.

———. *The Hohenzollerns in America: With the Bolsheviks in Berlin and Other Impossibilities.* London/New York: John Lane, 1919.

———. "The Hostelry of Mr. Smith." In Leacock, *Sunshine Sketches,* 13–35.

———. *Humour and Humanity: An Introduction to the Study of Humour.* London: Butterworth, 1937.

———. *The Iron Man & the Tin Woman. With Other Such Futurities: A Book of Literary Sketches of Today and of Tomorrow.* London: John Lane, 1929.

———. *Last Leaves.* Toronto: McClelland & Stewart, 1945.

———. "The Marine Excursion of the Knights of Pythias." In Leacock, *Sunshine Sketches,* 53–72.

———. *Model Memoirs and Other Sketches from Simple to Serious.* New York: Dodd, Mead & Company, 1938.

———. *Moonbeams from the Larger Lunacy.* Toronto: John Lane, 1915.

———. *My Financial Career and Other Follies.* Toronto: McClelland & Stewart, 1993.

———. *My Remarkable Uncle and Other Sketches.* London: John Lane, 1942.

———. *Nonsense Novels.* London: John Lane, 1911.

———. *Over the Footlights.* London: John Lane, 1923.

———. *Short Circuits.* London: John Lane, 1928.

———. *Sunshine Sketches of a Little Town.* New Canadian Library. Toronto: McClelland & Stewart, 1994.

———. *Winnowed Wisdom: A New Book of Humour.* London: John Lane, 1926.

Lynch, Gerald. *Stephen Leacock: Humour and Humanity.* Kingston/Montreal: McGill-Queen's University Press, 1988.

Magee, William H. "Genial Humour in Stephen Leacock." *Dalhousie Review* 56.2 (1976): 268–82.

Marshall, Tom. "Balance and Perspective in *Sunshine Sketches.*" In *Beginnings: A Critical Anthology,* ed. John Moss. The Canadian Novel 2. Toronto: New Canada Press, 1980. 176–87.

Pollock, Zailig. "Leacock, Stephen." In *The Oxford Companion to Canadian Literature: Second Edition*, ed. Eugene Benson and William Toye. Toronto: Oxford University Press, 1997. 637–40.

Rasporich, Beverly. "The New Eden Dream: The Source of Canadian Humour: McCulloch, Haliburton, and Leacock." *Studies in Canadian Literature* 7.2 (1982): 227–40.

3: The Beginnings of Canadian Modernism: Raymond Knister, "The First Day of Spring" (written 1924/25)

Julia Breitbach (University of Constance)

JOHN RAYMOND KNISTER (with the "k" pronounced and with a long "i") was born in Ruscom, Ontario, on 27 May 1899 to a farming family of partly German ancestry. Helping out on the fields and with his father's pedigree horses, young Knister thus experienced directly the kind of life — its chores and plights but also the compelling, mystical beauty of nature — he would later write about in his farm stories, such as "The First Day of Spring."[1] Alongside his farm poems, these stories (more than his less prominent "state-of-mind stories" and crime/Chicago stories[2]) bear witness to the influence of Knister's rural upbringing on his writing. On the one hand, it provided the author with his major themes and characteristic setting and inspired the development of a modernist-realist style, in defiance of the popular romance/adventure tradition. On the other hand, the numbing hardship of farming infuses many of these stories with a sense of futility, if not tragedy; Knister's own strenuous and unsteady career — a constant struggle between bread-and-butter-jobs and artistic vocation — is certainly a case in point here.[3]

[1] The story was published posthumously in Knister 1976.

[2] Michael Gnarowski distinguishes between "farm stories" and " 'state-of-mind' stories": the former feature sensitive (usually young) male protagonists in trying situations of initiation and individuation, often in conflict with the farming routine and their fathers and in harmony with nature and farm animals; the latter focus on the thoughts and moods of female protagonists, e.g. in moments of embarrassment or fear (Gnarowski 1972). Stevens adds a third category, "Chicago stories," based on Knister's brief work experience (partly as a taxi driver) in Chicago in 1924 (Stevens 1976, xxi).

[3] For a well-informed, concise overview of Knister's life, particularly his struggling between commissioned freelancing, temporary editorial positions, and literary practice in both Canada and the US, see Waddington 1975.

"Mist Green Oats" (1922) — Knister's most frequently anthologized short story — can thus be read as a portrait of the artist as a young man, representing Knister's biography in the truly modernist manner of "objectified pictures" ("The Canadian Short Story," 1976, 389). One of his most explicit engagements with generational and vocational conflict in the farming context,[4] the story features adolescent protagonist Len Brinder, who toils away on his father's farm while daydreaming about the "impossible wonders of the city" (74) and his higher, presumably artistic ("transcendently congenial," 67) ambitions. This unresolved conflict between loyalty and longing, harsh reality and sweet delusion, farm routines and city lure, is potently evoked by the still life in the story's last scene, when the frustrated youth leaves a packed suitcase in the kitchen for his father to discover and for the reader to understand as a portrayal of Knister's closely associated life and works. Note, for example, the way the story draws on Knister's childhood and frequent returns to the countryside, on his restless adult life moving from one job to the next, and on his nonetheless unwavering "determination" to demand nothing but the highest standards from and recognition for Canadian literature. At the end of the story and a hard day, the aspiring artist

> was struck by the triviality of what he allowed to pass as excuses for abandoning the *determination he had so highly taken*. . . .
>
> Then, at the coming of an impulse as he was going out, . . . he stopped a moment and went up the stairs to his room. When he returned it was with a *laden suitcase* in his hand. (75; italics added)

More importantly, consider the allusion to Knister's typically modernist reliance on deceptively simple objects in sophisticated textual arrangements, devised to make the reader locate the meaning his- or herself (to "see it anyway") precisely by moving semantic closure off-center (to "one side") and concealing it from a "plain," familiar view: "He set it *plainly* on the floor before the table, and then thought, 'No, *that's too plain. He'll see it anyway* —' and put it to *one side*" (75; italics added). To literary critics up to today, the "laden suitcase" may foreground the task of fully assembling and assessing a hitherto still uncollected oeuvre, with a substantial part not even having been published yet. Tellingly, no encompassing monograph on Knister's prolific output of prose, poetry, and literary/cultural criticism exists to date — let alone on his journalistic "commercial" work (articles, sketches, and reviews for, among others, the *Toronto Star Weekly*, the Windsor *Border Cities Star*, and Toronto's *Saturday Night*), or on his extensive correspondence with eminent writers and intellectuals of

[4] See also "The Loading" (*The Midland* 1924), listed by the New York *Bookman* among the season's ten best short stories, outranking even Sherwood Anderson and Katherine Mansfield.

his time (Morley Callaghan, Dorothy Livesay, Leo Kennedy, Frederick Philip Grove, and A. J. M. Smith, for example).[5]

In fact, after Knister's (most probably accidental) death by drowning in 1932[6] it took about four decades and the cultural dynamic of the Canadian Renaissance to unearth his multifaceted legacy to Canadian literature in general and the short story in particular. Thus reborn to unprecedented critical attention in the late 1960s and throughout the 1970s, some of the artist's texts that had previously remained unpublished or were out of print by then appeared in various editions, notably three consisting of or including short stories: Michael Gnarowski's *Selected Stories of Raymond Knister* (1972), David Arnason's *Raymond Knister: Poems, Stories, and Essays* (1975; based on his edition of the *Journal of Canadian Fiction's* "Special Knister Issue" in 1975), and Peter Stevens's *The First Day of Spring: Stories and Other Prose* (1976); the 1970s also saw two M.A. theses on Knister's short stories (Everard 1972; Waddington 1977).

Knister's debut in the genre, which would eventually lead to the production of about a hundred stories altogether, had been promising. In 1922, having been rejected by various Canadian magazines, he managed to place his first published piece ever, the short story "The One Thing" (and later also "Mist Green Oats" and "The Loading") with the prestigious American literary magazine *The Midland* (1915–33), where he would also later work briefly as an associate editor from 1923 to 1924. This early affiliation would prove highly significant as it fostered Knister's interest in the new regionalist (midwestern) writers that *The Midland* particularly promoted, such as Sherwood Anderson. More opportunities were to follow when "The Strawstack" (1923) was accepted by the internationally oriented *Canadian Forum* (est. 1920), the only magazine Knister considered

[5] Of Knister's four novels, two have been published, one of them only posthumously: *White Narcissus* (1929; New Canadian Library 32, 1962) and *My Star Predominant* (1934). He did not live to see a collection of his short stories or of his poems; selected poems appeared posthumously in *Collected Poems* (1949) and *Windfalls for Cider* (1983). Anne Burke has compiled ample bibliographical information on both Knister's published and unpublished writing and on secondary literature, reviews etc. (Burke 1979–80, 20–61; Burke and Darling 1981, 281–322).

[6] According to Knister's only daughter Imogen, his death forever confounded "Man and Myth" (Givens 1979–80) by creating the "legend of the romantic artist" (Stevens 1976, xi): a star-crossed and suicidal modernist version of tubercular John Keats, on whom Knister had written the biographical novel *My Star Predominant*. For the origins and perpetuation of the "suicide theory" see Livesay 1949 and Callaghan on the CBC production "The Poet Who Was Farmer Too: A Profile of Raymond Knister" (Wood/Anderson 1964).

as upholding quality writing in his native country at the time (see "Canadian Literati," 166). However, the bulk of the short stories and poems published during his lifetime were printed either in popular Canadian magazines and newspapers (*Toronto Star Weekly*, *Maclean's*, *Chatelaine*, etc.), or outside of Canada, in the avant-garde magazines *The Midland* (Iowa City), *Poetry* (Chicago), and the expatriate *This Quarter* (Paris) — the latter featuring Knister at his most international/"high modernist" with the state-of-mind stories "Elaine" (1925) and "The Fate of Mrs Lucier" (1925), and alongside such literary spearheads as Ezra Pound, James Joyce, and Ernest Hemingway.

Notwithstanding his stint at the University of Toronto in 1919 (to be cut short by a prolonged recovery from pneumonia on his father's farm near Blenheim, Ontario, in 1920–23), Knister's early accomplishments were those of a self-made writer. Encouraged by his mother, a teacher, he had read widely across all periods, nationalities, and genres as a boy, and, significantly, became very knowledgeable about Canadian writing. His life-long extensive reading would not only continuously spur his own artistic development, but also make him a "complete man-of-letters" (George Woodcock, quoted in Nischik 2005, 153), whose tireless educational and promotional efforts on behalf of Canadian literature are unparalleled for his time. He can therefore rightfully be said to prefigure the very upsurge in literary achievement and critical acknowledgement that in the 1960s and 70s belatedly delivered him to prominence. More recently, Joy Kurapatwa has claimed that Knister is "a major Canadian writer — if not the major Canadian writer — of the 1920s" (Kuropatwa 1990, 9); and Knister's oeuvre has also been the subject of a doctoral thesis (Elderkin 1990).

Earlier and recent criticism agrees on the importance of Knister's promotion of the Canadian short story through two main accomplishments (see e.g. Nischik, 151–52): first, his critical assessment of the genre and its Canadian contribution in a predominantly North-American context; and second, his editing of Canada's first, "trend-setting" "benchmark anthology" (New 2002, 586; 1990, 44) *Canadian Short Stories* in 1928, commissioned by Macmillan. The latter in particular can hardly be overestimated, given the paramount role of anthologies in canon formation and generic criticism in Canada. Knister's anthology comprises a rather mixed selection of seventeen authors, rounded off by a "List of Canadian Short Stories in Books and Magazines" (280 stories by 112 writers) and another one comprising all "Books of Short Stories by Canadian Authors" (91 books by 47 writers). On the one hand, Knister includes writers from the last decades of the nineteenth and the early twentieth centuries, such as Duncan Campbell Scott (to whom the book is dedicated for having provided "the most satisfyingly individual contribution to the Canadian short story," "Introduction," 1971, xix), Stephen Leacock, Charles G. D. Roberts, and Edward William Thomson. On the other hand, Knister's anthology features contemporary, more urbane and modernist writing (albeit, surprisingly, not his own), for example, Callaghan's "Last Spring They Came Over" (1927; see the article by Paul Goetsch in this volume).

Moreover, here and elsewhere, Knister seizes the opportunity to review and envision the past, present, and future of Canadian short-story writing. His introduction, "The Canadian Short Story," finds that the genre epitomizes the development, merits, and prospects of Canadian literature and likens the "Canadian spirit" ("Introduction," xix) to the international modernist Zeitgeist of "making it new." Invoking a cultural and literary threshold delineated by the contemporary Canadian writers he considers outstanding, Knister wants to finally overcome Canada's lack of "national consciousness" (xi) and of literary "originality" (xii) precisely in an international, specifically North American (as opposed to transatlantic) context.[7] Unfortunately, Knister finds prose writers still adhering to a deplorable aesthetic of "materialism" (xiii) on the one hand and to an ill-employed, naïve realism on the other ("realism is only a means to an end, the end being a personal projection of the world," xiv). What made the situation even worse in Knister's opinion was the blatant lack of interest of most Canadian editors, who relegated innovative writing to "foreign markets" (xvii) and catered to mass market requirements.

Five years earlier (1923), in an article of the same title which addressed the rather conservative and nationalistically inclined readership of *The Canadian Bookman* (est. 1919), Knister had already lamented the neglect of good short-story writing. He had contrasted the very limited publishing possibilities for quality writing with a commercialized/Americanized mass market that demanded the formulaic "magazine story" taught by correspondence schools ("The Canadian Short Story," 390–91). More importantly, Knister had proposed an alternative kind of poetics, which reads very similarly to that of modernist mastermind T. S. Eliot in his seminal essays, "Hamlet and His Problems" and "Tradition and the Individual Talent" from 1919 (see Nischik). Knister's aforementioned technique of "objectified pictures" ("The Canadian Short Story," 389) can indeed be said to emulate Eliot's famous dictum of the "objective correlative" ("Hamlet"). Both concepts have less to do with authorial neutrality in an "absolute sense" than with the literary conveyance of "emotion" ("Introduction,"

[7] See also his essays "Canadian Literature" (172) and "Democracy and the Short Story" (146) on the close association of American and Canadian modern culture in general and the excellence of modern North-American short-story writing in particular.

xiii).[8] Eliot and Knister further concur on the question of individual originality and its relation to literary tradition. Knister advises the young author aspiring to write authentically about life in his own time and place to study the masters of all ages and schools on an international scale ("The Canadian Short Story," 389, 391). Since a writer's very "consciousness of life" (389) cannot help but be shaped by his cultural, specifically his literary background, he might as well, in fact, he must, learn from his predecessors. In another essay Knister declares, with strong echoes of Eliot, that "every book is the result of all that have gone before; all the books that have hitherto been written will inevitably influence all that are yet to come. . . . Originality is an unknown and indiscoverable quantity" ("Canadian Literature," 172). Compare Eliot in "Tradition": "We shall often find that . . . the most individual parts of his [the poet's] work may be those in which the dead poets, his ancestors, assert their immortality most vigorously" (Eliot 2003, 1425). Of course, there are also crucial divergences between Eliot and Knister — and they usually imply a hierarchical bias: for example, Eliot's taste for poetry of the intellectually coded, elitist kind — in contrast to Knister's praise of the "universal acceptance of and delight in [short stories] by college professors and sales-girls [alike]" ("Democracy and the Short Story," 147); or Eliot's tackling the burden of the entire Western tradition — in contrast to Knister's trying to establish a modern Canadian canon.

More than in his critical writing, the idiosyncracies of Knister's modernist poetics — that is, their similarities but also productive differences in relation to American modernism — may be traced in his literary work. At the onset of Canadian modernism, stories like "The First Day of Spring" provide much more than "case studies" (Gadpaille 1988, 22) of the human condition in modern times, as they strike a delicate balance between authentic individuality and modern character "type": "The task is arduous and heroic of depicting characters which shall square with life. They may transcend the people we see about us, but they must be true to them, *and* true to type" ("The Canadian Girl," 159; italics added). Neither do they simply illustrate universal modernist concerns, but enter a specifically Canadian dialogue that reverberates throughout the twentieth century — a dialogue with a reality of changing times and native locales, with international aesthetics and more traditional national content, with modernist breaks and realist continuities. In Knister's own words, his coming of age as a young artist occurred in the early 1920s (after his hospitalization for

[8] In Eliot's words: "The only way of expressing emotion in the form of art is by finding an 'objective correlative'; in other words, a set of objects, a situation, a chain of events which shall be the formula of that *particular* emotion; such that when the external facts, which must terminate in sensory experience, are given, the emotion is immediately evoked" (Eliot 1964, 100).

pneumonia) with the confluence of his renewed farm experience, his preference for the short story, and his adherence to the "objective":

> When I got back to the farm and recovered my health by dint of working fourteen to sixteen hours in the field until autumn, I began to change my views about writing. There was something about the life that I lived, and all the other farm people round me, something that had to be expressed, though I didn't know just how. But the attempt would have to be made in the form of short stories. . . . Now for a subject; it wouldn't do to start with an autobiographical piece. One must be objective. . . . It was this objectivity which forbade the acceptance of my work in Canadian magazines. My poems and stories were so Canadian and came so directly from the soil that Canadian editors would have nothing to do with them. ("Canadian Literati," 161–62)

Knister's particular notion of "objectivity" thus blends the question of style ("objective pictures"/concise images) with that of subject matter: the artist's faithfulness to his immediate surroundings, his devotion to the "expression of an indigenous mode of life and thought" ("Canadian Literature," 170). A "nascent imagist and modernist" (New 2002, 586), Knister retains a distinctly realist agenda that would characterize much Canadian short-story writing throughout the twentieth century and beyond. "The First Day of Spring" exemplifies Knister's innovative approach to the modern short story in a particularly interesting manner by applying the artist's change in perspective as described above to the theme of initiation — on both the concrete level of plot and on a more abstract, poetological level.

A story of initiation by virtue of its plot, it relates a boy's fall from innocence, ignorance, and romantic illusion through the sudden confrontation with knowledge and truth. Plot in this context is a rather loose term, as a short summary of the text reveals. The story opens in the first two paragraphs with the establishment of a retrospective frame, featuring a conspicuously sovereign and apparently omniscient narrative voice. From his detached position the narrator seems to know it all, namely that the best is already in the past, bliss is to be found only in innocence, and romantic anticipation is preferable to love's consumption: "The new smell [of spring] is there, more potent perhaps than it is ever to be in lush days of blossoms" (3). The narrative tone in the story's first lines suggests some (unspecified) temporal gap between narrative present and narrated past. Significantly though, as we will see later on, Knister neither closes this frame for the reader at the end of the story nor fully discloses the meaning of his unsettling experience to the narrator-as-young-protagonist, a boy of seventeen. Within this lopsided framework, a very limited plot in terms of external action evolves. As the story begins, at the end of yet another tiring day of farm work, not much is going on, and the narrator/protagonist muses about the unruly demeanor of a particular horse, Cherry (she "had led the colts that morning from 'the other farm' a mile away" in a wild "chase," 3). Then, before driving into town with Cherry pulling the buggy, the boy's father tells his son about the disgraceful behavior of a former classmate, Muriel, whom the narrator had always admired "from a distance" as a "complete, demurely perfect creature in her way" (6). However, the father reports, the girl's "foolish" passions eventually "got her in the family way" (5) and very likely into jail, since, not being married, she killed her baby in an act of despair. In stark contrast to the avalanche of drama in the father's account of Muriel, "The First Day of Spring" hardly has a "real" plot to speak of then. But Knister's story is well *plotted*, with its structural composition resembling a Chinese box of ever-increasing action, while simultaneously moving further from the narrative present(s) to the narrated past(s) and from one narrator (the adult boy) to the next (the boy's father). This development can be traced successively. The story opens with the narrator embarking on a lofty, somewhat "lyrical" (New 1987, 65) meditation on nature's cyclic changes and the "intoxicating" effect of springtime on "men and beasts" (3). A giant organism awaking from hibernation, nature grows into a mystic beauty of spiritual proportions here (as it often does in Knister's stories, for example, in "Mist Green Oats" or "The Loading"):

> It had been a mild winter, and yet when March came, and days in which wheels threw the snow like mud in stretches of road where snow still lay, the world was changed. . . . The blue of the sky softens, the air lifts, and it is as though the lightness of a life above the earth were being made ready, an entering spirit to pervade the uncoloured and frost-clogged flesh of the world. (3)

Then the narrator turns to a particular first day of spring in his childhood, introducing rather abruptly the story's first-person perspective in the process: "Perhaps it was the effect of spring on a boy which made me forgetful. Musing in the darkness of the cow-stable after such a day . . . " (3). The events of this particular day, however, provide a mere backdrop for Knister's "true story" of illicit love and scandalous infanticide, and, most importantly, for the boy's attempt at coping with the news. His inner struggle is at the very core of Knister's story, spanning from the love affair through its exposure and tragic ending well into the narrative present, as if, indeed, "his [the father's] words were a long time reaching [him]" (5). Knister's focus is on internal action, namely on the experience of initiation into manhood ("He [the father] spoke as man to man, as though I was old enough, now, for that," 5). Mordecai Marcus has pointed out the origins of the term "initiation" in anthropology, where it denotes the usually ritualized "passage from childhood or adolescence to maturity and full membership in adult society" (Marcus 1960/61, 221). At the same time, he stresses the divergence of initiation *stories* — featuring prominently not least in the modernist context of alienated, isolated individuals (for example, in Hemingway, William Faulkner, or Anderson) — from anthropological models by way of their preoccupation with individual experiences, rather than socially indoctrinated rites:

> An initiation story may be said to show its young protagonist experiencing a significant change of knowledge about the world or himself, or a change of character, or of both, and this change must point or lead him towards an adult world. It may or may not contain some form of ritual, but it should give some evidence that the change is at least likely to have permanent effects. (Marcus, 222)

"The First Day of Spring" shrewdly combines the modernist focus on individual experience with the anthropological tradition of social ritual by employing the typically modernist device of symbolic displacement. Rather than telling directly, it reflects the boy's experience in the image of a colt to be "broken in," that is, through the portrayal of a highly traditional ritual between "men and beasts" (3). In this context, it is important to observe that throughout the story Knister refrains from giving any information on the specific temporal gap between narrative present and narrated past. At times, it appears to be rather large ("I still remember her somehow as one recalls an early love-affair with a woman older than himself," 6); then again, the narrator seems to be present at the very time and place he relates, especially considering the story's long passages of direct speech and the intimate descriptions of the horses' behavior in a given situation ("They crowded about us, snorting trumpets of fog in the thin spring sunshine — turning, shying, shattering films of ice on the puddles," 4). The narrative voice can thus be said to oscillate between the retrospective, knowledgeable tone of an adult and the more immediate, innocent perspective of a child, thereby conveying the very dialectics of experience and interpretation that characterize initiation processes. This in-betweenness of the narrative voice not only manifests itself in its rather tentative rhetoric (note the recurrent use of "seemed," "appeared," "as though") but also contributes significantly to the further classification of the initiation process as "uncompleted" (see Marcus, 224). His first lesson on "true love" leaves the narrator in a certain limbo (as opposed to a clearly matured state), that is, precisely in want of a definite truth. In connection with hearing a strangely disembodied voice singing from across the fields, the narrator implicitly likens this deferral of ultimate knowledge to the infinite cyclic returns of God's creation and the repetitiousness of human behavior, thus interpreting his personal first experience of love's bittersweet nature in the light of a highly archetypal one,[9] which is forever inscribed into humanity's collective memory:

[9] See also Gnarowski's reference to "archetypal elements and psychological significances" in Knister's stories (Gnarowski, 12).

> Some air over the buildings, a new strange echo of our voices, yet one so old I wondered how I could have forgotten it, filled my heart with a mixture of feelings.
>
> A girl's voice came from across the fields, a few words of singing, a voice with something wild and strong in it.
>
> "Hear her? That's the other one. Pretty much alike, for cousins." (7)

> From across the fields the light hidden voice came reaching again, and then it stopped, as though for an answer. The air was chill, and with the darkness winter seemed to be returning. (8)

As mentioned before, the story's end does not tie back in with the aloof narrative voice in the lyrical opening. Rather, Knister only suggests narrative closure — for boy and reader alike — by transferring the completion of the initiation process onto the colt and into the future: "I stroked the warm nose of a colt. 'You're going to be broken in,' I whispered. He was strangely quiet" (8). The animal's silent acquiescence to its fate constitutes a nonverbal answer to the girl's song, expressing the narrator's foreboding of some ultimate "break," which he will only learn to fully understand later in life. Throughout Knister's prose and poetry, farm animals — and particularly horses — epitomize what Stevens describes as Knister's "realistic surface" opening to "symbolic depth" (in the tradition of Anton Chekhov, Henry James, and Anderson; see Stevens, xvii). While for the father the horses are more or less defined by their assigned tasks on the farm, the narrator's rendering of their functional designations in inverted commas ("'driver,'" "'general purpose' mare," 3–4) reveals that he considers them inadequate because non-descriptive. The affection and personalization he instead bestows on them serves as a prerequisite for Knister's symbolic practices: the revelation of psychological processes through the presentation of human character in terms of animal behavior. The analogy between humans and animals carries far in this story. Muriel's character and behavior, too, and her seductive sway over the naïve boy, are more than once paralleled by dear yet stubborn Cherry, the mare's very name clearly reflecting its association with *cherished* Muriel. "A long-haired bay mare with trim legs" (3), striking a "statuesque pose," reckless und unbridled, Cherry leads the colts on just as she does the boy: "I looked up at her large tilted eyes and high-held head . . ., and told her, with a boy's faith: 'Sure, you'd stand, wouldn't you, Cherry. Not run away'" (4). Her ready surrender to "the vicissitude of her fortune" at the end of the day ("as we pulled the shafts over her and fastened the traces, she helped by easing back slightly"), while "still consider[ing] the sound from the road" (4), anticipates the father's account of meeting Muriel the other day, "ducked down" in the very car she and Fred used to make love in by the roadside, now "stuck in the mud" and "burnt . . . out" like the couple's feverish affair (6). Weaving a closely knit imagery of "muddy" motorways

(4) and "slippery" farm lanes (3), steamy window panes (5) and horses "snorting trumpets of fog" (4), exciting yet dangerous automobiles and unfashionable yet functional buggies, Knister condenses the "surface minutiae" (Stevens, xvii) of local-color realism on a symbolical level in order to come to terms with the boy's struggle with sense and sensibility, moral judgment and sexual lure. In fact, symbolical strategies seem to be the only way to assess and express emotional turmoil, in perfect harmony with Eliot's call for "objective correlatives" to save literature from an excess of emotion ("Hamlet," 101–2): "I did not have a word to say, or I had *more than I could say.* It was growing dusk, but a strange new robin called sharply somewhere in the thick jumbled limbs of a crab-apple tree in the garden. A couple of pigeons alighted on the barn ridge, one facing each way, watchfully; we had had a pigeon pie or two lately" (7; italics added). At first glance, the imagery in these lines may appear clichéd and even stale, making use of a basic iconographic arsenal: a robin to connote the devil's work (especially sexual aggression), the sour crab-apple tainting paradisiacal innocence, the pigeon as sacrificial animal. But considering that this passage immediately precedes the aforementioned lines on the singing voice and its evocation of archetypal experiences and collective memories, the conventional imagery seems rather to be quite fitting after all.

For the most part, however, the story displays a distinctively contemporary, modernist mood and tone. William H. New cogently paraphrases: "This story dramatizes the moment when an adolescent farm boy moves from imagining love's pleasures to learning about its possible horrors (a baby's murder, or at least a savage accident), and when his naïveté gives way to a need for order" (New 2002, 586). Clearly, this need pertains to more than the story's plot, that is, to the modernist quest for and creation of new order as such. In his discussion of the modernist short story, Dominic E. Head has slightly yet significantly shifted this well-established critical perspective on modernism by stressing the residual phenomena of imposed order instead, that is, instances of dissonance, contradiction, and disorder. It is precisely in its failure to achieve narrative closure that the modernist short story can be said to assert its aesthetic conclusiveness most effectively (Head 1992). A close reading of "The First Day of Spring" shows that the conflict between order and disorder, meaning and its absence, is at the heart of the story indeed. A father breaks the news and with them his son's world; the son intuitively projects his restorative needs onto the breaking in of a young horse; narrative retrospection leaves him — and the reader — with a new, yet breakable order. Moreover, the conflict opens "The First Day of Spring" to a poetological interpretation of its agricultural locale, in which the farmer's son toiling on the fields and with animal(ist) instincts represents the writer struggling to bring his material and his literary legacy into an adequate new form. Performing but also deliberately undermining this ground-breaking work on form and order,

Knister thus makes this an initiation story for his contemporary readers as well, in two ways. First, he introduces the latter to modernist aesthetics of imposed order on the one hand and impending chaos on the other. Second, he launches the Canadian short story on its trajectory through the twentieth century. It has often been said that "the short story encapsulates the essence of literary modernism" (Head, 1) — if not the modern experience of fragmentation, incoherence, and plurality as such — and, in a specifically Canadian context, that the genre indeed took off in Canada only with the advent of modernism (see Nischik, for example).

Knister's story features a number of modernist devices and themes, such as the use of symbolic images/"objective correlatives," the preoccupation with internal experiences over external plot, the focus on the individual and its relation to society (that is, themes of isolation, alienation, and disintegration). Another good example is the story's focalizing, hence limited perspective, which processes the events through the protagonist's mind. Also worthy of note is the elliptical, episodic, and often unchronological plot, which has the boy and the reader piecing together fragments of information on Muriel's fate. Through the abrupt changes from lyrical to colloquial register in the boy's reminiscent tone and the father's plain talking, Knister foregrounds the modernist preoccupation with "technique [as] not merely an exterior matter" but "essential" to the text ("The Canadian Short Story," 390). Further, the indirect, suggestive, and ambiguous descriptions of characters and events reflect the modernist definition of "great art [as] that which is concealed," 392); a case in point being the disembodied female voice from across the fields, subtly but poignantly expressing the lure and threat of new sexual mores in modern times as a "depersonalized or anonymous force outside the individual that determines his or her actions and reactions" (Isernhagen 1986, 21). In other respects, the story differs from modernist aesthetics, for example, in the hardly economical style of the expository passage and its introductory function (rather than beginning *in medias res*), or the exclusively rural setting and occupations (with the city only being mentioned once and, significantly, as an American locale: "I bet they [Fred and Muriel] were trying to get to Detroit and the other side," 6). Those instances reveal the generic roots of the Canadian short story in a nineteenth-century tradition of rural sketches (which Knister himself would be commissioned to write for the *Star Weekly*), local-color writing, and romance tales.

But if Knister's story is to represent modernist concerns and with them the beginning of the Canadian short-story tradition proper, what can be made of Walter Pache and others' thesis that the "natural mode of the short story in Canada" is realism (Pache 1986, 84)? How should Arnason's statement that the 1920s were the prime time of Canadian realism, explicitly mentioning Knister and Callaghan as representative examples (Arnason 1983, 163), be understood? And finally, how can Knister's own agenda of writing authentically, realistically, "about the life that [he] lived, and all the other farm people round [him]" ("Canadian Literati," 161) be assessed in this context? In order to reconcile seemingly opposing critical claims to either modernist or realist affiliations, one would have to assume their *negotiation* in and through Canadian modernism — similar to the coexistence and mutual influence of modernism and postmodernism in the second half of the century. As Stephen Regan argues, "Just as modernism in Canadian short fiction does not entirely abandon conventional realist narrative, neither does postmodernism entirely reject the preoccupations and techniques of modernism" (Regan 1991, 111). Knister's critical comments explicitly show that this negotiation between an older and a newer model is for him more than simply the inevitable effect of any attempt at breaking with traditions. Rather, he seeks to raise a genuinely Canadian contemporary/modernist voice precisely from the grounds of Canadian reality/realism:

> Let it not be assumed that the only expression I advocate has to do with wheat fields and stock yards. I am only pointing out that we probably will have to come to grips with reality before we shall have a literature, before Canada will mean something to the Canadian besides his own personal experience. ("Canadian Literati," 167–68)

Obviously, Knister is far from emulating the kind of "photographic realism" ("Duncan Campbell Scott," 402) that despite its high surface resolution misses the true picture (such as the complex amorous relations between the men and women photographed for a group portrait in the story/novella "Peaches, Peaches"). He rather challenges naïve documentary realism to go beyond outer appearances and external plots. Similar to the modernist writers of the American Midwest, for example, the admired Anderson, Knister refrains from "too explicit realism" to create a sense of "emotional authenticity" instead ("Democracy and the Short Story," 148). As with Anderson's artistic investment in *Winesburg, Ohio* (1919), he overcomes "quaint regionalism" ("Canadian Literati," 167) with a "provincialism of the right sort," which implies a larger scale all along. While Anderson's portrayal of small-town characters strongly veers towards the grotesqueness of human existence, Knister asks literature to "'body forth' something of the illimitableness of man's destiny" ("Canadian Literature," 172).

"The First Day of Spring" can thus be read as a translation of Knister's poetics and criticism into a fictional text that performs and comments on the vital continuity of realist positions in Canadian modernism and beyond. A case in point for New's stress on the latter's innovativeness and "distinctiveness" in "style," rather than "subject" (New 1987, 68), the story effectively combines a predominantly modernist style with a traditional setting of Canadian realism (the countryside) and the timeless, universal theme of initiation (the fall from innocence into the complexities of love and sexuality). The old world of youthful innocence and clear-cut morality, of coherent characters and omniscient narrators, is still present, yet refracted through the focalizing prism of the narrator/protagonist, thereby infusing the realist tradition with the selectivity of and interpretation through individual experience and the memory thereof. Although the topic of the fallen maiden and the aloof narrative voice in the opening passage speak to a moral and literary era that at the beginning of the twentieth century was fast losing ground, they survive in the narrator's ongoing need to come to terms with reality in the act of recollection. Featuring another one of his alter egos as protagonist, Knister's initiation story encapsulates its author's lifelong "day-dream" (4) of a native literature to join documentary/realist impulse, international/universal impact, and stylistic/modernist perfection in a new writing of excellence. In his own words: "If his [the writer's] eye be true and his emotions universal and directed, he will be one of the artists for which Canada has awaited to heighten the consciousness of portions of her life" ("The Canadian Short Story," 392).

Works Cited

Arnason, David. "The Historical Development of the Canadian Short Story." *RANAM* 16 (1983): 159–64.

Burke, Anne, and Dale Darling. "Raymond Knister: An Annotated Bibliography." In *The Annotated Bibliography of Canada's Major Authors.* Vol. 3, ed. Robert Lecker and Jack David. Downsview, ON: ECW Press, 1981. 281–322.

———. "Raymond Knister: An Annotated Checklist." *Essays on Canadian Writing* 16 (1979–80): 20–61.

Elderkin, Susan Arleen Huntley. *"Passing Beyond Realism": Convention and Experiment in the Works of Raymond Knister.* Ottawa: National Library of Canada, 1990 [Ph.D. Thesis Queen's University, 1989].

Eliot, T. S. "From 'Tradition and the Individual Talent.'" In *The Norton Anthology of American Literature.* Vol. D, ed. Nina Baym et al. New York: Norton, 2003. 1425–28.

———. "Hamlet and His Problems." In *The Sacred Wood: Essays on Poetry and Criticism.* London: Methuen, 1964. 95–103.

Everard, Doris Edna. "Tragic Dimensions in Selected Short Stories of Raymond Knister." M.A. Thesis Sir George Williams, 1972.

Gadpaille, Michelle. *The Canadian Short Story.* Toronto: Oxford University Press, 1988.

Givens, Imogen. "Raymond Knister: Man or Myth?" *Essays on Canadian Writing* 16 (1979–80): 5–19.

Gnarowski, Michael. "Introduction." In Knister 1972, 11–16.

Head, Dominic E. "The Short Story: Theories and Definitions." In *The Modernist Short Story: A Study in Theory and Practice.* Cambridge: Cambridge University Press, 1992. 1–36.

Isernhagen, Hartwig. "Modernism/Postmodernism: Continuities of a 'Split' Repertoire of Narrative Themes and Strategies (a Provisional Restatement of a Traditional View of Twentieth Century Literary Avant-gardism)." In *Critical Angles: European Views of Contemporary American Literature*, ed. Marc Chénetier. Carbondale: Southern Illinois University Press, 1986. 15–28.

Journal of Canadian Fiction 4.2 (1975) [Special Knister Issue].

Knister, Raymond. "The Canadian Girl." *Journal of Canadian Fiction* 4.2 (1975): 154–59.

———. "Canadian Literati." *Journal of Canadian Fiction* 4.2 (1975): 160–68.

———. "Canadian Literature: A General Impression." *Journal of Canadian Fiction* 4.2 (1975): 169–74.

———, ed. and introd. *Canadian Short Stories.* Short Story Index Reprint Series. Freeport, NY: Books for Libraries Press, 1971 [1928].

———. "The Canadian Short Story." In Knister 1976, 388–92 [*The Canadian Bookman* 5 (August 1923): 203–4].

———. "Democracy and the Short Story." *Journal of Canadian Fiction* 4.2 (1975): 146–48.

———. "Duncan Campbell Scott." In Knister 1976, 398–404 [*Willison's Monthly* (Jan. 1927): 295–96].

———. "Elaine." In Knister 1976, 195–201 [*This Quarter* 1.1 (1925): 160–66].

———. "The Fate of Mrs Lucier." In Knister 1976, 178–86 [*This Quarter* 1.2 (1925): 172–81].

———. "The First Day of Spring." In Knister, *The First Day of Spring*, 3–8.

———. *The First Day of Spring: Stories and Other Prose*, select. and introd. Peter Stevens. Literature of Canada: Poetry and Prose in Reprint, vol. 17. Toronto: University of Toronto Press, 1976.

———. "Introduction: The Canadian Short Story." In Knister 1971, xi–xix.

———. "The Loading." In Knister 1976, 13–84 [*The Midland* 10 (Jan. 1924): 1–13].

———. "Mist Green Oats." In Knister 1976, 58–75 [*The Midland* 8 (Aug./Sept. 1922): 254–76].

———. "The One Thing." In Knister 1976, 151–65 [*The Midland* 8 (Jan. 1922): 1–18].

———. "Peaches, Peaches." In Knister 1976, 8–57.

———. *Raymond Knister: Poems, Stories, and Essays*, ed. David Arnason. Montreal: Bellrock, 1975.

Knister, Raymond. *Selected Stories of Raymond Knister*, ed. and introd. Michael Gnaroswki. Ottawa: University of Ottawa Press, 1972.

———. "The Strawstack." In Knister 1976, 186–95 [*The Canadian Forum* (Oct. 1923): 18–22].

Kuropatwa, Joy. *Raymond Knister and His Works.* Toronto: ECW Press, 1990.

Livesay, Dorothy. "Raymond Knister: A Memoir." In *Collected Poems of Raymond Knister*, ed. Dorothy Livesay. Toronto: Ryerson, 1949. xi–xii.

Marcus, Mordecai. "What Is an Initiation Story?" *Journal of Aesthetics and Art Criticism* 19 (1960/61): 221–28.

New, W. H. *Dreams of Speech and Violence: The Art of the Short Story in Canada and New Zealand.* Toronto: University of Toronto Press, 1987.

———. "Knister, John Raymond." In *Encyclopedia of Literature in Canada*, ed. William H. New. Toronto: University of Toronto Press, 2002. 586.

———. "Tense/Present/Narrative: Reflections on English-Language Short Fiction in Canada." In *Studies on Canadian Literature: Introductory and Critical Essays*, ed. Arnold E. Davidson. New York: MLA, 1990. 34–53.

Nischik, Reingard M. "Die modernistische Short Story." In *Kanadische Literaturgeschichte*, ed. Konrad Groß, Wolfgang Klooß, and Reingard M. Nischik. Stuttgart: Metzler, 2005. 151–65.

Pache, Walter. "Narrative Models of the Canadian Short Story." In *Encounters and Explorations: Canadian Writers and European Cities*, ed. Franz K. Stanzl and Waldemar Zacharasiewicz. Würzburg: Königshausen & Neuman, 1986. 82–93.

Regan, Stephen. "'The Presence of the Past': Modernism and Postmodernism in Canadian Short Fiction." In *Narrative Strategies in Canadian Literature: Feminism and Postcolonialism*, ed. Coral Ann Howells and Lynette Hunter. Milton Keynes: Open University Press, 1991. 108–33.

Stevens, Peter. "Introduction." In Knister 1976, xi–xxx.

Waddington, Marcus. "Raymond Knister: A Biographical Note." *Journal of Canadian Fiction* 4.2 (1975): 175–92.

———. "Raymond Knister and the Canadian Short Story." M.A. Thesis Carleton, 1977.

Wood, John and Allan Anderson, prod. "The Poet Who Was Farmer Too: A Profile of Raymond Knister." CBC Radio (19 July 1964).

4: From Old World Aestheticist Immoralist to Prairie Moral Realist: Frederick Philip Grove, "Snow" (1926/1932)

Konrad Groß (University of Kiel)

THE LITERARY STANDING of Frederick Philip Grove, who was born as Felix Paul Greve in Germany in 1879, rests primarily on his novels. An assessment of Grove's novels and short fiction benefits from a closer look both at his life in Germany and his early Canadian writing, for Grove's literary career in Canada can be seen as a moral and aesthetic turning away from his life as a German "immoraliste" (to borrow the title of André Gide's famous novel, which Greve had translated into German in 1905). Grove did indeed have good reason to carefully hide his German past. In his "autobiography" *In Search of Myself* (1946), for which he received the prestigious Governor General's Award for Non-fiction, he spun a new life story complete with a wealthy and cosmopolitan Anglo-Swedish family background. The revelation of his true identity by Douglas O. Spettigue in 1972 came as a big surprise to Canadian readers, who had been misled by the author's masterfully fabricated life story even beyond his death in 1948 (see Spettigue 1972 and 1973; Martens 2001).

The ambitious dream of the young and talented writer Felix Paul Greve to gain renown in Germany ended in disaster. His downfall was brought about not so much by the poor quality of his early literary works (a volume of poems and a verse drama), but rather by his predilection for living in grand style despite modest financial means and by his scandalous love affair with Else Endell, the wife of a well-known art nouveau architect. Following a one-year imprisonment for fraud in Bonn (1903/04), Greve fell into disgrace with the neo-Romantic literary circle of the influential German poet Stefan George, under whose spell he had taken his first steps as a writer. His prison experience weaned him from his earlier aestheticist infatuation, and his satiric treatment of the George circle in his novel *Fanny Essler* (1905) foreshadows the turn towards the kind of realism that would also characterize his Canadian fiction. Greve's vigorous attempts at paying off his debts by translating chiefly modern English and French writers proved abortive. In despair, he faked suicide in 1909 and left Germany via Liverpool for

Montreal and from there traveled on to Pittsburgh, where he was joined by Else. Little is known of his three "American" years. Deserting Else, who would become a member of the Greenwich Village artist community, Greve was apparently determined to break completely with his past. The adoption of a new name, Frederick Philip Grove, as he crossed over the Canadian border into Manitoba in December 1912, may be read as a cathartic act, which symbolizes his transformation from an Old World aestheticist "immoraliste" to a North American moral realist. Grove took up teaching posts in rural schools and settled down to married life with a colleague. For the first time, he probably felt as if embarking on something useful. Arriving in Manitoba near the end of the huge immigration wave to the Canadian West, he encountered children of pioneer farmers who had settled there under extremely severe conditions. Grove could not but note the huge discrepancy between his former aestheticist mannerisms and the harsh reality of his new existence. A whole new world opened up to him, hastening his transformation into a writer who worked in repudiation of his former neo-Romanticist creed. His break with the past sparked a moral and at the same time aesthetic turn that became visible in the moral perceptiveness underlying most of his fiction and in his search for a suitable literary form.

Not surprisingly, Grove experimented with various forms at the beginning of his Canadian literary career. The desire to overcome his cultural and geographical uprooting inspired him to write two nature books, *Over Prairie Trails* (1922) and *The Turn of the Year* (1923). In *Over Prairie Trails* Grove turned his pen to the documentary mode, recalling journeys made in 1917/18 between his school and his home across thirty-four miles of the wild Manitoban landscape. References to the American naturalist John Burroughs suggest that he may have considered nature writing the most appropriate form for capturing the regional specificity of his adopted home. However, Grove would become no Canadian Burroughs, for none of his nature books contains a primarily conservationist message (Stobie 1973, 73–75). The real hero in *Over Prairie Trails* is not nature, but rather Grove, who promotes the image of himself as an observer with the proper physical and intellectual abilities to master the challenges of a dangerous and relentless, though also beautiful, natural world. In addition, he deliberately refrains from indulging in the grandiose descriptions of nature popular in Canadian adventure romances, as the following remark shows: "About halfway up from the northern horizon there lay a belt of faintest luminosity in the atmosphere — no play of northern lights — just an impalpable paling of the dark blue sky. There were stars, too, but they were not very brilliant" (*Over Prairie Trails*, 133). Instead of conjuring the exotic stock-in-trade of numerous adventure novels, Grove downplays the spectacular in nature and turns to its more commonplace appearance.

In a generic sense one can link *Over Prairie Trails* with Grove's short fiction. Critical opinion on the generic classification of *Over Prairie Trails* is split and in that is reminiscent of the beginnings of the American short story. The novelty of the latter was covered by familiar labels such as essay, sketch, and tale, which were applied indiscriminately to what would later come to be known as the short story. While the use of these labels mirrored doubts with regard to the short story's standing in the hierarchy of genres, generic confusion in works by early Canadian practitioners of short prose (best seen in the formal mix of Susanna Moodie's *Roughing It in the Bush*) reflected a quest for appropriate literary forms to capture the New World for European readers (see New 1987, 19–25, 31–35). Grove, like Moodie, was a newcomer to the country, but in contrast to her he wrote for a North American, not a European audience. The mixed generic assortment of *Over Prairie Trails* resulted from his decision to try his hand at what he may have considered as the most genuine North American genre, nature writing, with its combination of essay, sketch, and story. While most critics call the seven chapters of *Over Prairie Trails* sketches or essays (Spettigue 1969, 85; Ross 1970, vii; Gadpaille 1988, 30; Lane 1991, 160), Gerald Lynch describes *Over Prairie Trails* as a "story cycle," whose unity derives from Grove's narration of the speaker's development from a romantic to "a domestic man" (Lynch 2001, 104, 111). For Lynch the chapter "Snow" (not identical with the short story of the same title, which will be discussed below) is the climax and turning-point in this process. After Grove has made it through a blizzard, the ferocity of which is captured in comparisons of snow forms with a boa constrictor, a gorilla, a leopard, and the bomb-proof on a battle field (*Over Prairie Trails*, 79, 82), he arrives home a changed man: " 'You had a hard trip?' asked my wife; and I replied with as much cheer as I could muster, 'I have seen sights to-day that I did not expect to see before my dying day.' And taking her arm, I looked at the westering sun and turned towards the house" (90).

One should take Lynch's label "story cycle" with a grain of salt, however, and rather speak of *Over Prairie Trails* as some sort of life writing, which revolves around the speaker's observations of and reflections on nature. Grove's follow-up book *The Turn of the Year* is less convincing because it still shows remnants of neo-Romantic nature worship. At the same time it marks his final step towards realism. After the discovery of the prairie in his first book, Grove now introduces humans into the prairie landscape. The life story of the farming couple John and Ellen from love to marriage to old age — all captured in three idyllic vignettes that interrupt the nature scenes and link human life to the seasonal cycle — is Grove's last brush with neo-Romanticism. After *The Turn of the Year* his focus shifts radically from nature to the portrayal of human beings. In his first novel *Settlers of the Marsh* (1925) he finally discards the neo-Romantic stance on human tragedy, thus paving the way for realism in Canada.

Grove's work has also to be screened against the cultural background of the 1920s, when literary nationalists and internationalists vied with each other for a greater recognition of Canadian literature. While the nationalists were chiefly preoccupied with Canadian themes, the internationalists were concerned with literary form. With his treatment of the pioneer period on the prairies Grove met the nationalists' expectations for distinct Canadian themes, whereas his choice of the realistic mode was more in line with the internationalists' struggle for the modernization of Canadian literature. It is no accident that in this cultural climate Grove embarked on the short story, which in America was just entering its Golden Age. However, attempts at selling stories to American magazines in 1924 and 1925 were unsuccessful. It is possible that, apart from a lack of interest by American readers in Canadian subjects, American journals may have found the regional focus of Grove's stories too close to the local-color school and hence out of step with the latest developments of the genre, as exemplified in stories by Sherwood Anderson, F. Scott Fitzgerald, or the early Ernest Hemingway.

Surveying Grove's twenty-three short prose pieces in the *Winnipeg Tribune Magazine* from 1926/27, some of them perhaps earlier rejects, one notices a preference for the sketch and the anecdote (Gadpaille, 30; for a list of these texts see Pacey 1970, 200–201). This observation is confirmed by several of the texts assembled in the first collection of Grove's stories, edited as *Tales from the Margin* by Desmond Pacey in 1971, twenty-three years after the author's death. The title *Tales from the Margin*, which can mean stories either coming from the nation's periphery or dealing with marginal lives, had been Grove's idea, but his hopes for a story collection at the end of the 1920s and again in 1945 came to nothing. That no story collection was published during the author's lifetime, although Grove wrote short fiction throughout his Canadian writing career, was partly due to the very small number of periodicals willing to publish stories and partly to the absence of a larger, more sophisticated reading public. A few "better" magazines such as *Canadian Bookman*, *Canadian Forum*, and the university journal *Queen's Quarterly*, which published some of Grove's stories in the 1930s and 40s, had only a limited circulation. The Great Depression with its disastrous impact on the publishing market was an additional hindrance to the advancement of the short story in Canada. An even more important reason for contemporary and also more recent critical neglect, however, may have been the prevailing disregard for Grove's short stories. William H. New in *Dreams of Speech and Violence* (1987) dismisses them in a few sentences for their "Teutonic structures . . . and wooden formal dialogues" (New, 70). Michelle Gadpaille in her short survey of *The Canadian Short Story* (1988) sees a weakness in Grove's "allegiance to an earlier code," that is, first, his belief in the possibility of heroism at a time when such a belief had already been shattered and given way to humans as "the gang of futility" and, second, his inability to fuse "man and prairie in interlocking metaphors"

(Gadpaille, 31, 32). Robert Thacker's article on "Short fiction" in the *Cambridge Companion to Canadian Literature* (2004) mentions Grove only in passing.

According to Desmond Pacey, who traced sixty-eight stories altogether (forty of them unpublished) and tried to save the author's reputation as a short-story writer, Grove himself seemed to have some qualms about the quality of his stories — a number of which should be described more appropriately as scenes from rural life — (Pacey 1971, 2; for a complete list of Grove's published and unpublished stories see Pacey 1971, 313–19). The fact that stories such as "Water" and "The First Day of an Immigrant" may have been discarded scenes from his first novel, *Settlers of the Marsh*, and that some characters appear in more than one story indicate that the author may have seen his real forte in the novel rather than the short story. Grove's stories betray a predilection for character sketches, as demonstrated, for example, by "Lazybones," which portrays a young energetic farming woman who is married to a good-for-nothing lazy "cowboy," by "Saturday Night at the Crossroads," which offers portraits of several prairie characters, among them the money-grubbing store-owner Kalad and his wife, and by "The Teacher," a biographical sketch presenting the protagonist at two stages in life, first as she starts out as a frightened young teacher at a rural school, then thirty years later, when after the mishap of her husband's death she is forced to go back to teaching. "The Lumberjack" is about two brothers, Abe and Alph Standish, whose lives take a horrible turn when Alph, having suffered typhoid fever, develops bouts of insanity, threatens his brother's life, and has to be locked up in an institution. "Riders" tells the story of a promising young man who has become a victim of the Depression. In "The Spendthrift" and "Dead-Beat," Grove portrays the financial downfall of young farmers unable to resist the impulse to spend money recklessly, and in "Relief," a story about the dust bowl on the prairie, a whole farming community, imprudently, goes on a shopping spree with government relief money. Some stories suffer from the intrusion of an explanatory note that bolsters the action with documentary information and moral judgment. In "The House of Many Eyes," for example, an authorial voice describes a pompous house in a prairie town, built by a former speculator and now used to house a poor couple, the crippled Tom Creighton and his bossy wife: "Nearly every western town has some such, if not several, relics of a past prosperity which proclaim both the purse-proud lack of taste and the improvident lavishness of a generation of newly-rich promoters, parasitic upon the pioneer" (*Tales from the Margin*, 65). In "The Spendthrift," the admonitions of the successful farmer John Walker to his improvident brother Norman have the ring of a lecture on economics, whereas Grove in other stories is able to prove that he can also do without sermonizing. In "Salesmanship," his anti-commercial stance, which pervades quite a few of his stories, is implied in the action and expressed modernistically through *showing* rather than telling, as in the selling practices of the crooked traveling salesman Marston and his crony Martha, who fleece unsuspecting and gullible prairie people.

Some of Grove's more memorable pieces are stories in which the author mixes the humorous with the serious. "A Poor Defenceless Widow" is an ironic sketch of an obnoxious yet deplorable woman pestering the mayor of a small Manitoba town to interfere on her behalf with the income tax people in Ottawa. "The Extra Man" tells the witty story of an inexperienced cockney youth fresh from Britain who makes all sorts of hilarious blunders on his first day of work on a farm in Canada. The harsh tragedy in "The Sale," the auctioning off of the farm machinery and implements of the indebted old farmer Altmann, is softened a little by the comedy of the auction, which is first carried out by a bystander as a humorous diversion:

> Cundy raised the pail high over his head. "Ladies and gentlemen," he shouted with the full force of his lungs, ". . . I have a pail here, a good pail, galvanised inside and out . . ." Handling it and showing it about. "I am going to sell it. I am going to sell it to one of you. One of you is going to be the lucky man. Don't think for a moment that this is an ordinary pail. Far from it. It's quite a peculiar pail. Pletz here has told you. It LEAKS. It's like one of them big farms around here. You pour the money in; and you don't need to pour it out. The water in this pail pours out by itself." (151)

The comedy lasts until the professional auctioneer arrives and, with his monotonous voice, kills the show, thus unfortunately reducing the proceeds of the sale for the impoverished old man. Grove's comedy is at its best in "Glenholm Oil Limited," which is reminiscent of the humor in Stephen Leacock's "The Speculations of Jefferson Thorpe" from *Sunshine Sketches of a Little Town* (1912; see the article on Leacock in this volume). In Grove's story, the life spirit of the doting old country doctor Carlton, who has seen better days and now lives in dire financial straits, is revived when three well-meaning former patients set up a hoax company and appoint him as secretary-treasurer in order to provide him with a small salary. In the end the whole undertaking gets out of hand as they have not reckoned with the old doctor's business acumen, a talent that catapults the company into the pool of bigger players on the stock exchange. In contrast to Leacock, whose treatment of Jefferson Thorpe's business gamble is tied to the narrator's nostalgic view of small-town life, Grove casts a more critical glance at the commercial spirit of the age without the intrusion of a moralizing narrative voice. At the end the narrator just wraps up the story and wryly tells the reader that Doctor Carlton, who had sold most of his shares in time, died a rich man, while the company has still found no oil and the "eastern financiers have long since 'unloaded' " (260).

Although readers may consider stories with an admixture of humor the better part of Grove's short fiction, the author himself called "Water" and "Snow," in which the protagonists become victims of either fellow man or nature, his best work (Pacey 1971, 2). In "Water" the pioneer settler Kurtz loses his homestead to the entrepreneur Magnus, who moves across the Manitoba bushland drilling wells for farmers. The more simple-minded Kurtz, who has no water and is forced to drive his cattle several miles to a neighbor's well every day, signs a contract with the shrewd Magnus and falls prey to the complex twists of the legal wording. In "Snow," Grove's most widely anthologized and best-known story, the younger farmer Redcliff freezes to death during a prairie blizzard. Both "Water" and "Snow" are among Grove's early stories and were published in the *Winnipeg Tribune Magazine* in 1926 and 1927. "Snow" was first read in an earlier version by Grove during a public recital in Winnipeg in 1925 and published under the title "Lost" a year later, before it reappeared in a revised form as "Snow" in *Queen's Quarterly* in 1932 (Stobie, 92–93).

"Snow" involves three characters already encountered in other stories: the old farmer Altmann and his son-in-law Redcliff from "The Sale," and Abe Carroll, a competent farmer, who in "Marsh Fire" manages (together with some neighbors) to extinguish a fire threatening several homesteads. While "Marsh Fire" is a sketch about the heroic individual who is able to keep dangerous nature under control, "Snow" shows humans at the mercy of a fierce snow storm. The story line is fairly simple: during a blizzard the horse of the homesteader Redcliff returns home without the sleigh, the other team horse, or its master. Redcliff's young wife, a mother of six children, is alarmed and alerts the neighboring farmer Mike Sobotski. The story begins after the blizzard has died down with Mike calling at Abe Carroll's farmhouse to fetch people for a search party. He, together with Abe and Abe's hired man Bill, sets out for Redcliff's farm, where they examine the returned horse and then search for the lost man, who they eventually find near the sleigh that was caught by snow-covered tree stumps, frozen to death under a snow drift. The tragedy ends on a note of stoic resignation that is witnessed by the helpless Abe, who has brought the news of Redcliff's death to the old parents-in-law:

> The man's big frame seemed to shrink as he sat there. All the unctuousness and the conceit of the handsome man dwindled out of his bearing. The woman's eyes had already filled with tears.
>
> Thus they remained for two, three minutes.
>
> Then the woman folded her fat, pudgy hands; her head sank low on her breast; and she sobbed, "God's will be done!" (270)

This scene illustrates the difference between Grove's story and the popular Canadian adventure tale. The author not only refrains from passing a moral judgment, but also from the sentimentalism and melodramatic characteristics of many romantic frontier stories. The woman's response, her hopeless acceptance of Redcliff's death as an act of providence, demonstrates Grove's confirmation of human dignity in the face of adversity. Grove, who still believes in the possibility of human heroism, furnishes Mrs. Altmann's heroic stance with a sense of the tragic that is very different from the shallow heroism in Canadian wilderness tales by Gilbert Parker, Arthur J. Stringer, Agnes Maule Machar, Theodore Roberts, William McLennan, and Herman Whitaker, popular writers of adventure stories from the turn of the century. The ending of "Snow," with its deliberate avoidance of passionate gestures of grief, is also a far cry from the melodramatic ending of Duncan Campbell Scott's well-known fur-trade story "Vengeance Is Mine" (1923), in which the unfeeling fur trader Ian Forbes gets what he deserves when he freezes to death in the cold of a northern winter.

A popular adventure tale would have certainly exploited the scene of Redcliff desperately fighting his way through the raging blizzard and finally losing his battle. Grove, however, resists the temptation of using nature for the staging of heroic masculinity — the story begins only after the snow storm has abated. When the three men start their search, they carefully try to read nature's signs and reconstruct the fate of the unfortunate Redcliff almost scientifically, as two examples indicate. The first passage shows the men on their way to the Redcliff homestead: "The drifts were six, eight, in places ten feet high; and the snow was once more crawling up their flanks, it was so light and fine. It would fill the tracks in half an hour" (264). In the second scene the search party finds the dead horse:

> The two older men alighted and, with their hands, shovelled the snow away. There lay the horse, stiff and cold, frozen into a rocklike mass.
>
> "Must have been here a long while," Abe said.
>
> Mike nodded. "Five, six hours." Then he added, "Couldn't have had the smell of the yard. Unless the wind has turned."
>
> "It has," Abe answered and pointed to a fold in the flank of the snow-drift which indicated that the present drift had been superimposed on a lower one whose longitudinal axis ran to the north-east. (267)

Michelle Gadpaille praises the realism of such scenes, but complains that Grove's "scientific interest . . . often triumphs over his human interest: in Grove, snow is merely snow after all" (Gadpaille, 32). It is true that Grove hardly ever uses nature as a mirror for the psychic turmoil of a character, as, for example, Sinclair Ross does in his well-known story "The Painted Door." However, several but by no means all nature scenes are presented in the manner of the two examples quoted above, as nature descriptions are also meant to contribute to the mood of the story. The night sky after the blizzard at the beginning of "Snow" is depicted rather matter-of-factly:

"Toward morning the blizzard had died down, though it was still far from daylight. Stars without number blazed in the dark blue sky, which presented that brilliant and uncompromising appearance always characterizing, on the northern plains of America, those nights in the dead of winter when the thermometer dips to its lowest levels" (261). At this stage we do not know what to expect, but the attentive reader, stumbling over the adjective "uncompromising," will sense that there may be something ominous in store. The description of Abe's house a little later does not give the story away yet, but heightens the impression of a world immobilized by the extreme cold: "It [the house], too, looked ice-cold, frozen in the night. Not a breath stirred where it stood; a thin thread of whitish smoke, reaching up to the level of the tree-tops, seemed to be suspended into the chimney rather than to issue from it" (261). It is only now that the reader learns about Redcliff's disappearance in the storm. On three occasions nature descriptions serve to intensify the atmosphere of doom, and the examination of Redcliff's surviving horse results in "gloomy thoughts" of the three searchers, who see how "weird, luminous little clouds issued fitfully from the nostrils of the horse inside" (264). The appearance of nature, as they set out on their search, again adds to the story's dark mood and heightens the curiosity of the reader, who, like the members of the search party, wants to know what really happened: "Nothing was visible anywhere; nothing but the snow in the first grey of dawn. Then, like enormous ghosts, or like evanescent apparitions, the trees of the bluff were adumbrated behind the lingering veils of the night" (267). Finally, the description of the sunrise is also telling. The sun — here metonymous for nature — is presented as an alien rather than a life-giving force, standing aloof from the human sphere: "Clear and glaring, with an almost indifferent air, the sun rose to their left" (268). Immediately after this scene the sunlight leads to the disclosure of the tragedy and directs the searchers' attention to the sleigh. The three examples demonstrate that Grove is no disciple of the local-color movement after all and that he focuses on the universal drama of human life against nature rather than on the specific qualities of the regional setting.

Grove's nature descriptions are in keeping with his character portraits. The scientific orientation of the narrative voice in some nature scenes corresponds to the peculiar emotional detachment of Abe, Bill, and Mike during their search. Margaret R. Stobie finds the fact that the men wait for two hours at the Redcliff home before they begin their search somewhat disconcerting and a flaw in the story (Stobie, 93–94). However, their "leisurely rescue," as she calls it (94), may find its explanation in the sensible behavior of the three, who postpone the search until dawn and then act almost like detectives hunting for clues by attempting to decode the signs in nature. Once they start their job they proceed rationally, drawing the right conclusions from their observations of the returned horse, the carcass of the frozen horse, the direction of the wind, and the lines of snow drifts. Every step in their investigation is taken with the purpose of solving the puzzle of Redcliff's death. Their straight, no-nonsense approach corresponds to Abe's inability to cope with the emotional side of the tragedy. At the Redcliff home he feels sympathy with Redcliff's young wife without being able to "say a word of comfort, of hope" (265). He is equally unable to give the old Altmann couple more than just the news of the terrible accident.

We find a similar emotional detachment in "The Sale," the story in which the germs for the later tragedy are already laid. The young farmer through whose eyes we follow the sale of Altmann's farm equipment is hunting for a bargain and hence does not waste a thought on the bleak future of the impoverished old man. After his successful and cheap bid for a democrat (a large uncovered wagon with two or more seats) and a harness he shrugs off scruples by resorting to the unquestioned moral precept of folk wisdom: "One man's bread is the other man's poison" (155). However, nowhere in the story is there an explicit condemnation of the young man, who is no better or worse than the rest of society. While the tragic cause in "The Sale" is chiefly man-made — Altmann is apparently the victim of his own incompetence, of his unsupportive sons, and of the bidders at the auction — the tragedy in "Snow" is caused by a relentless and indifferent nature. Not only is Redcliff's farm on poor soil, which explains the poverty of his home, but his death in the blizzard is a disaster for the future of both wife and parents-in-law.

The tragic ending of "Snow" does not mean that Grove's characters are generally fated to become victims of nature. True, the tragedy in "Snow" cannot be averted, yet the author places victims side by side with non-victims, that is, Abe, Mike, and Bill, who are able to deal with or "read" nature. This is already suggested in Abe's physical build: "He was himself of medium height or only slightly above it, but of enormous breadth of shoulder: a figure built for lifting loads. By his side the other man [Mike] looked small, weakly, dwarfed" (262). The physical difference between Abe and Mike serves chiefly to give additional emphasis to the former's leadership qualities, not to belittle the latter's competence. For all three men act as observers whose common sense and judgment enable them to cope with perilous nature. In contrast to the many adventure romances set on the Canadian frontier, Grove deliberately refrains from drawing omnipotent victors over nature (Abe Spalding, the progressive conqueror over nature in Grove's 1933 novel *Fruits of the Earth*, has to acknowledge that the prairie finally eludes human control). Instead, the relationship between humans and nature is always a problematic one. Nature may be benevolent to humans, but humans must be constantly on guard against its unpredictable, threatening, and life-destroying force.

Works Cited

Gadpaille, Michelle. *The Canadian Short Story.* Toronto: Oxford University Press, 1988.

Grove, Frederick Philip. *In Search of Myself.* Toronto: Macmillan, 1946.

———. *Over Prairie Trails.* Toronto: McClelland & Stewart, 1970.

———. "Snow." In Grove, *Tales from the Margin*, 261–70.

———. *Tales from the Margin: The Selected Short Stories of Frederick Philip Grove*, ed. and introd. Desmond Pacey. Toronto: Ryerson Press McGraw-Hill, 1971.

———. *The Turn of the Year.* Toronto: Macmillan of Canada, 1929.

Lane, Patrick. "Afterword." In Grove, *Over Prairie Trails.* Toronto: McClelland & Stewart, 1991. 159–64.

Lynch, Gerald. *The One and Many: English-Canadian Short Story Cycles.* Toronto: University of Toronto Press, 2001.

Martens, Klaus. *F. P. Grove in Europe and Canada: Translated Lives.* Edmonton: University of Alberta Press, 2001.

New, William H. *Dreams of Speech and Violence: The Art of the Short Story in Canada and New Zealand.* Toronto: University of Toronto Press, 1987.

Pacey, Desmond, ed. *Frederick Philip Grove.* Toronto: Ryerson, 1970.

———. "Introduction." In Grove 1971, 1–19.

Ross, Malcolm. "Introduction." In Grove 1970, v–xiv.

Spettigue, Douglas O. *FPG: The European Years.* Ottawa: Oberon, 1973.

———. *Frederick Philip Grove.* Toronto: Copp Clarke, 1969.

———. "The Grove Enigma Resolved." *Queen's Quarterly* 79 (Spring 1972): 1–2.

Stobie, Margaret R. *Frederick Philip Grove.* New York: Twayne, 1973.

Thacker, Robert. "Short Fiction." In *The Cambridge Companion to Canadian Literature*, ed. Eva-Marie Kröller. Cambridge: Cambridge University Press, 2004. 177–93.

5: Psychological Realism, Immigration, and City Fiction: Morley Callaghan, "Last Spring They Came Over" (1927)

Paul Goetsch (University of Freiburg, Germany)

MORLEY CALLAGHAN (1903–90) WAS BORN in Toronto to Roman Catholic parents of Irish descent. He attended St. Michael's College at the University of Toronto and the Osgoode Hall Law School. Beginning in 1923, he worked for *The Toronto Daily Star* as a reporter. There he met Ernest Hemingway, who encouraged him to become a writer. While Hemingway, who was five years his senior, left for Europe at the end of 1923 and embarked upon the first important phase of his career, Callaghan continued with his studies, yet also started to publish stories in avant-garde magazines such as *transition* and *This Quarter*, as well as in more popular periodicals such as *Scribner's Magazine*. In 1928 the New York editor Max Perkins accepted for publication Callaghan's first novel *Strange Fugitive* (1928) and his first collection of stories, *A Native Argosy* (1929). After graduation from law school and admission to the Ontario bar, Callaghan — who never practiced as a lawyer — went to Paris in April 1929, at this time the center of the literary and artistic world of the so-called lost generation. There he met Hemingway again and became associated with F. Scott Fitzgerald, James Joyce, and other well-known writers. As he related much later in *That Summer in Paris* (1963), he became somewhat disillusioned as the artists' and writers' jealousies, rivalries, and gossip seemed to reduce Paris to a "small town": "If I didn't want the French culture, then I was there in exile. Could the dream I had for years of being in Paris have been only a necessary fantasy . . . to give me some satisfactory view of myself?" (Callaghan in Morley 1978, 9). He returned to Toronto in the fall of 1929 and became a full-time writer; he also worked for CBC radio and as a columnist for *New World Magazine*. Callaghan wrote eight novels, of which *Such Is My Beloved* (1934), *They Shall Inherit the Earth* (1935), *The Loved and the Lost* (1951), and *The Many Coloured Coat* (1960) are generally considered to be the best. Several of his short stories were reprinted by Edna O'Brien and Martha Foley in their annual edition of *The Best American Short Stories*. Callaghan's reputation as a short-story writer was enhanced by his story collections *A Native Argosy* (1929), *Now That April's Here* (1936), *Morley Callaghan's Stories* (1959), and *The Lost and Found Stories of Morley Callaghan* (1985).

Callaghan's success in the United States was no coincidence. Although many of his works are set in Canada, particularly in rural Ontario or, more often, in the urban centers Toronto and Montreal, Callaghan usually does not emphasize the Canadian setting. Nor does he regularly "Canadianize" his works by addressing specifically Canadian issues in the manner of his contemporary, Hugh MacLennan. His first short-story volume, *A Native Argosy*, collects a number of stories with Canadian settings under the heading "American Made" — Callaghan obviously catered mainly to an American audience. He admired Sherwood Anderson, Hemingway, and other American writers, especially for their use of the vernacular and their rejection of studied literary styles. In 1964 he wrote retrospectively: "I had become aware that the language in which I wanted to write, a North American language which I lived by, had rhythms and nuances and twists and turns quite alien to English speech" (Conron 1966, 17). Apart from the use of the vernacular, he also adopted other methods of American realists and naturalists, at least in the short stories and novels he wrote in the 1920s and 1930s.

This continentalist orientation has irritated some of his readers and critics in Canada, but the fact that Callaghan persistently defined himself as North American (and once even called himself an "American writer") was "perhaps inevitable for a writer of fiction who began his career in Canada in the 1920s" (Morley, 7). Realism, naturalism, and modernism arrived later on the Canadian literary scene than on the American one. Hence, it is small wonder that Callaghan and Canadian writers like Raymond Knister learned primarily from their American predecessors (New 1987, 65). Callaghan called Anderson his "literary father" (Callaghan in Hoar 1969, 1) and was influenced by him as well as by Stephen Crane and Theodore Dreiser. Because he esteemed Hemingway highly and quoted some of Hemingway's statements about art approvingly in *That Summer in Paris*, some critics have exaggerated Hemingway's importance for Callaghan's development (see Sutherland 1972). Callaghan lacks Hemingway's sophistication and sense of style, and where Hemingway is economical, allusive, and suggestive, Callaghan is rather simple and chatty (see Metcalf 1993/94). To call him Hemingway's equal or even his superior has not helped to advance Callaghan's reputation. The following analysis of one of Callaghan's early stories focuses on the writer's realist approach, his treatment of the immigration theme, and the short-story tradition to which his work is indebted.

"Last Spring They Came Over" first appeared in *transition* in 1927. It was Callaghan's third published story and was reprinted two years later in *A Native Argosy*. It is an immigration story and thus belongs to a popular

Canadian short-story genre to which writers such as Frederick Philip Grove ("The First Day of an Immigrant"), Henry Kreisel ("The Broken Globe"), and Sinclair Ross ("The Lamp at Noon"; see the article on Ross in this volume) have contributed. "Last Spring They Came Over" draws upon the author's own experiences as a cub reporter at *The Toronto Daily Star*. The story's protagonists are two brothers from England who represent two types of immigrants Callaghan encountered at the newspaper, as he later revealed in an interview (see Conron, 34). The leitmotif of writing not only characterizes the two brothers but also sheds light on young Callaghan's understanding of realism and the art of writing. The story contrasts two kinds of writing, journalism and letter writing.

The two immigrant brothers, Alfred and Harry Bowles, fail as journalists and eventually lose their jobs with the newspaper, though for different reasons. Alfred is not a good reporter: he wishes to get the facts right, as a journalist should, and tries to be efficient, yet he is lazy, inexperienced, naïve, and somewhat irresponsible. Put on the night beat, he at first feels important and develops some ambition. When Brownson, the assistant city editor, warns him to phone if anything important happens so that someone else can cover the event, Alfred vents his frustration (and amuses himself) by calling Brownson as frequently and as late as possible. Later, still working on the night shift, he regularly leaves the office to join his brother for a couple of drinks. One night, two colleagues from other newspapers take advantage of his credulity and tell him about a big fire that has happened at just about the hour when Alfred usually meets his brother in a bar. Instead of checking the veracity of their story with the police, Alfred writes it up and is fired the next morning for putting a fake story into print. His brother Harry has already lost his job at the same newspaper. Harry Bowles neither likes to write plain copy nor cares about facts and accuracy. He is easily carried away by his imagination: "He liked telling a good tale but it never occurred to him that he was deliberately lying. He imagined a thing and straightaway felt it to be true" (39). This is strikingly illustrated by the episode in which Brophy, a fellow journalist, tells the two brothers of the great temple of the Sikhs at Amritsar. On the basis of this information Harry soon fabricates an account of his own visit to Amritsar: "When he talked that way you actually believed that he had seen the temple" (42).

That the brothers cannot adapt themselves to the "methods" (60) of newspaper work is confirmed by their letter writing. When writing home, they are not obliged to stick to facts. Telling his father about a visit to Niagara Falls, Harry digresses and compares the Falls "favourably with a cataract in the Himalayas and a giant waterfall in Africa, just above the Congo" (38), as if he had been to those places. Writing letters, then, enables the brothers to give free rein to their imagination and to forget about or at least distance themselves from facts. While typing, Alfred occasionally laughs to himself, enjoying his vivid account of "the city room, the fat belly of the city editor, and the hard words the night editor used when speaking of the Orangemen" (37). Later, the two brothers sit side by side in the press gallery, writing "long letters all about the country and the people, anything interesting" (39). They then exchange their letters, and laugh out loud while reading them. The narrator's remark, "Heaven only knows who got the letters in the long run" (39) is apt: the addressees are less interesting than the letter writing itself. Letter writing, Callaghan suggests, mainly helps the two brothers to render their situation bearable.

Callaghan's sympathetic description of the brothers' failure as journalists perhaps reflects the difficulties he himself may have had as a fledgling creative writer attempting to adjust to the discipline of journalism. But it also demonstrates his realist stance and the influence journalism had on the development of his craft. As the story implies, Callaghan avoids romanticizing life and eschews the escapist use of writing. For the author, stories must be grounded in reality and experience. Whereas the two brothers make up facts according to their emotional needs, Callaghan focuses on the observations the brothers' fellow journalists make or might have made and lays special emphasis on typical behavior and reactions.

In the manner of a number of stories in Anderson's *Winesburg, Ohio* (1919), some events — for instance, Harry's funeral — are reported from the perspective of a particular journalist. Usually, however, Callaghan employs a narrator with some degree of omniscience. This narrator chiefly records what an onlooker might see and infer. In addition, he reveals some telling facts and circumstances that are not accessible to a neutral observer, for example, what the brothers say in their letters, how they prepare for the Canadian winter by writing home for Alfred's coat, or what they do on their trip to Niagara Falls. Occasionally, the narrator also affords a glimpse into the characters' minds. Such additional information is needed by the reader because the fact-oriented journalistic or realist observation of external behavior soon comes up against limits. This also holds true for the other journalists at the newspaper: even though they are trained observers, they do not get to know Alfred and Harry very well. For one thing, they are frequently misled by the two brothers' role playing into believing that their situation is tolerable after all. Besides, they are too preoccupied with their own concerns and are contented with stereotyping the immigrants — as potential rivals, bad journalists, Empire-proud immigrants, targets of homophobic jokes, etc. Callaghan characterizes the majority of the journalists as tough and cynical. Even Brophy, who is aware of the men's poverty and loneliness, does not wax sentimental about their situation.

In summary, Callaghan's treatment of the leitmotif of writing suggests that he regards the brothers' retreat from reality into letter writing and their dislike of journalistic discipline as the ultimate causes of their failure.

He himself seems to be more in favor of a kind of realism that acknowledges the objective situation of people while concentrating on their subjective responses to it. *A Native Argosy* has been characterized as follows: "Central . . . is the view that 'man has possibilities to realize himself on a much fuller scale than he does. But the world seems to be full of frustrated people — people who in some mean or desperate way get blocked off from being what they should be'" (Weaver 1958, 23, quoted by Conron, 29). "Last Spring They Came Over" illustrates such a conflict between human possibilities and human failure. It does not, however, dwell upon the disappointments and sufferings of the two immigrants at length. Instead, it focuses on their dreams, their attempts to cope with or forget their problems, their role play, and their pretenses.

This is highly relevant for the direction of sympathies. Whereas the fellow journalists, with the exception of Brophy, dismiss Alfred and Harry as failures and expect that they will soon be fired and forgotten, the reader of the story is encouraged to appreciate Alfred's and Harry's imagination, their endurance, and their refusal to pity themselves. As a result, Callaghan's portraits of the two men are ambivalent, which is especially borne out by his treatment of the immigration theme: Alfred and Harry are not only would-be journalists who fail to adapt themselves to the rules of their chosen profession, they are also would-be immigrants who lack the energy to adjust themselves to the new country.

In Susanna Moodie's *Roughing It in the Bush* (1852), one of the best-known Canadian immigration accounts, English ladies and gentlemen are warned not to emigrate to Canada because they will find life in the new country too hard. Callaghan's much later story does not issue such a general warning, but it subjects certain contemporary English attitudes, those of the imperialist and the dandy, to critical scrutiny and shows that they prevent the brothers from settling down in Canada successfully.

The brothers come from a Baptist parson's home. Poverty forces them to seek a living elsewhere. They are optimistic because they believe that the British Empire, if not the world, is waiting for them. Alfred goes to Toronto and writes home about Canada, typically in such positive terms that he is soon joined by Harry. Both of them are satisfied with little pay and a modest lifestyle. On the other hand, they are not prepared to work hard to lay the foundation for a new existence; instead, they attempt to forget the present by dreaming of going to the Pacific coast of Canada or to India. Though they have never traveled, except to Canada, they pretend to have great knowledge of the world and assume that it is their privilege to discuss the lot of Englishmen in different parts of the Empire: "It was better to take it for granted that the Bowles boys knew all about the ends of the earth and had judged them carefully, for in their eyes was the light of far-away places" (38). Alfred likes to play the expert political commentator:

> Alfred was always willing to talk pompously of the British Empire policing the world and about all Catholics being aliens, and the future of Ireland and Canada resting with the Orangemen. He flung his arms wide and talked in the hoarse voice of a bad actor, but no one would have thought of taking him seriously. He was merely having a dandy time. (37)

Alfred is not aware that Canadians of Irish Catholic descent do not share his prejudices and that he appears to them a caricature of the English Protestant and imperialist.

While such posturing enhances the character's sense of his own importance, it becomes a desperate means to keep up appearances on other occasions. After the two brothers have lost their jobs, Brophy wonders about their financial situation. Alfred again strikes the already familiar pose: "In a grand way, grinning, as if talking about the British Empire" (41), he declares that they have no problems and eagerly explains that they manage to live on five dollars a week. He even asks Brophy to tea, an invitation which Brophy declines because he sees through Alfred's brave façade.

Ultimately, British imperialist ideology fails to support the two brothers. This is highlighted by the leitmotif of home. Alfred and Harry do not succeed in creating a new home for themselves in Canada. Having lost their jobs, the press gallery becomes their surrogate home where they go for warmth and contact of sorts. After Harry's death Alfred lacks the money to stay on, and one day he disappears from the press building forever. As one of the journalists remarks ironically, wherever Alfred has gone, he will probably write home as soon as possible (43). This comment underscores the fact that Alfred possesses a home only in his imagination and memory. The remark also testifies to the journalist's knowledge of Alfred's character, but not necessarily to any real interest in his fate. The story's structure suggests, however, that Alfred may never write letters again. The first part of "Last Spring They Came Over" ends with Harry's disappearance from the press building, the news of his death, and his funeral; the second part climaxes in Alfred's disappearance and, by implication, his death. Such a reading would be in harmony with Callaghan's statement about stories in general: "The story must touch the imagination, and it must go on touching it. It does not finish neatly because life itself does not" (Callaghan in New, 68).

The two brothers not only play at being English imperialists but also act in the manner of dandies in the mode of Oscar Wilde. Alfred sports a cane and light-gray fedora hat to look like a reporter. Harry buys a derby hat, a pair of spats, and a cane from his first paycheck. Later, however, it turns out that they do not have money to buy adequate winter clothes. Like Wildean dandies, both of them enjoy playing roles, making fun of their middle-class colleagues, and trying to steer attention away from serious issues. When Alfred has to admit that he prefers "boys" (40) to women, his colleagues make some nasty remarks about him and his brother. But neither Alfred nor Harry seem to mind because they believe "the fellows were having a little fun" (40). Whether the brothers are actually homosexually inclined or not, they cope with their colleagues' derision by refusing to accept the "importance of being earnest." The fellows in the press room agree that "it was hard to tease him [Alfred] when he wouldn't be serious" (40). This is further illustrated by other episodes. When going to the graveyard for his brother's funeral, Alfred surprises Brophy with the question of whether funerals did not "leave a bad taste in the mouth" (40); he then encourages Brophy to talk about his trip to India. When other journalists express their condolences, Alfred smiles cheerfully and gives them the feeling "that nothing important had really happened" (43).

In the story's final episode, Alfred has reached the end of his tether — and yet he stages his departure from the press building as if his leaving his surrogate home was the equivalent of going Bunburying (in the manner of Oscar Wilde's *The Importance of Being Earnest*) and enjoying himself elsewhere. He sits down in the press gallery, puts his feet up on a desk, and wants to be amused. Asked if a new job had turned up, he says "in a playful, resigned tone, his eye on the big clock" (43) that he has until three to join the Air Force. At three o'clock he disappears. According to the omniscient narrator, he neither joins the Air Force nor returns to the press building. The job offer made by the Air Force is apparently a fiction that enables Alfred to play the nonchalant dandy until the very end and thus hide his despair. Whether he actually commits suicide or not, his acting out of the chosen role is a desperate attempt to remain in emotional control of his hopeless personal situation.

Callaghan presents two English immigrants who fail to make it in Canada. Because of their imperialist and decadent dandy-like poses and their lack of energy, they are not the type of immigrants Canada welcomed. Callaghan reveals the brothers' weaknesses, especially their evasion of reality and their shirking of responsibility. However, he also stresses their human potential as dreamers and imaginative role players. Both brothers are inured to hardships; they neither lament their plight nor wish to become a burden to anyone else. In spite of their implied despair they try hard to keep up appearances. They thus resemble those Englishmen celebrated in imperialist fiction who succeed in keeping their form in an uncomfortable or even dangerous colonial situation (see John Galsworthy's "The Man Who Kept His Form," 1923, and Somerset Maugham's "The Outstation," 1926). Consequently, Callaghan's portraits of his protagonists are infused with some respect and admiration and are more complex than the author's caricaturistic approach to their Englishness might lead to one expect.

As already mentioned, Callaghan's ambivalent characterization of the protagonists suggests his continentalist orientation in that his story bears some resemblance to stories in Anderson's *Winesburg, Ohio.* Anderson's "Hands," to give one example, centers on Wing Biddlebaum, a teacher, who was forced to leave his school because he could not control his urge to touch his students; he has come to Winesburg under an assumed name and has lived there in isolation for a long time. Apart from thematic parallels — the loneliness of newcomers to a community, the protagonist's homosexuality, a failure in one's chosen profession — some formal parallels deserve mention. Both Anderson and Callaghan create round characters by relying on three sources of information, omniscient narration, the observations and reactions of journalists, and the protagonists' self-characterization. Both writers deal with a fairly long time span (Callaghan with roughly a year, Anderson with the past and present of Biddlebaum) and use summary and characteristic short episodes to reveal their characters. They both structure their story with the help of leitmotifs that point to the characters' habitual behavior. And both writers distinguish between prejudiced readings of the protagonists (Callaghan's journalists, Anderson's small-town people) and a more understanding and sympathetic approach. Anderson asserts: "The story of Wing Biddlebaum's hands is worth a book in itself. Sympathetically set forth it would tap many strange beautiful qualities in obscure men" (Anderson 1975, 29). The author of "Last Spring They Came Over" would probably have subscribed to this attitude, too. This is not to say that "Hands" directly influenced "Last Spring They Came Over." All the features mentioned do, however, support the conclusion of many critics that Anderson was one of the American realists from whom the young Callaghan learned.

Like Anderson and other earlier realists, Callaghan eschewed the nineteenth-century plot story, which, following Poe and the story-writing handbooks, relied on external action, surprising twists and catastrophes, and dramatic beginnings and endings to convey its evaluations of human life (see Voss 1973, 183–98). Callaghan and his contemporaries believed that the plot story had been commercialized and reduced to cheap formulaic effects. Turning against the "bag of tricks" recommended by the authors of books on how to write a successful plot story, Anderson wrote:

> Consider for a moment the materials of the . . . teller of tales. His materials are human lives. To him these figures of his fancy, these people who live in his fancy should be as real as living people. He should be no more ready to sell them out than he would sell out his men friends or the woman he loves. To take the lives of these people and bend or twist them to suit the needs of some cleverly thought out plot to give your readers a false emotion is as mean and ignoble as to sell out living men and women. (Anderson in Weber 1975, 124)

The new literary story envisaged by Anderson, Callaghan, and other writers aimed at character revelation. It strove to transform the traditional character sketch and the modern journalistic human interest story into a complex, demanding short work that achieves "psychological depths" and suggests "meanings extending beyond the bare events which carry the story forward" (Patrick 1967, 78). As some stories by Anderson and Callaghan demonstrate, Freudian psychology was a key influence on the new literary story. In any case, unlike Grove and Ross, Callaghan was less interested in a naturalistic study of the impact of the milieu, the economic situation, and other external factors than in his characters' psychology. He concentrated on such recurrent motifs as masks and human illusions and dealt with "strange fugitives in flight from their fears and in search of an elusive goal" (Morley, 13). He thus made an important contribution to the modernization of the Canadian short story.

Works Cited

Anderson, Sherwood. *Winesburg, Ohio: Text and Criticism*, ed. John H. Ferres. New York: Viking, 1975.

Callaghan, Morley. "Last Spring They Came Over." In Callaghan, *Morley Callaghan's Stories*, 36–43.

———. *The Lost and Found Stories of Morley Callaghan*. Toronto: Lester & Orpen Dennys/Exile Editions, 1985.

———. *Morley Callaghan's Stories*. Toronto: Macmillan, 1959.

———. *A Native Argosy*. New York: Scribner, 1929.

———. *Now That April's Here*. Toronto: Macmillan, 1936.

Conron, Brandon. *Morley Callaghan*. New York: Twayne, 1966.

Hoar, Victor. *Morley Callaghan*. Toronto: Copp Clark, 1969.

Metcalf, John. "Winner Take All." *Essays in Canadian Writing* 51/52 (1993/94): 113–45.

Morley, Patricia. *Morley Callaghan*. Toronto: McClelland & Stewart, 1978.

New, W. H. *Dreams of Speech and Violence: The Art of the Short Story in Canada and New Zealand*. Toronto: University of Toronto Press, 1987.

Patrick, W. R. "Poetic Style in the Contemporary Short Story." *College Composition* 18 (1967): 77–84.

Sutherland, Fraser. *The Style of Innocence: A Study of Hemingway and Callaghan*. Toronto: Clarke, Irwin, 1972.

Voss, Arthur. *The American Short Story: A Critical Survey*. Norman: University of Oklahoma Press, 1973.

Weaver, Robert. "A Talk with Morley Callaghan." *Tamarack Review* 7 (Spring 1958): 3–29.

Weber, Alfred. "Eine kleine Quellensammlung amerikanischer Theorien der Kurzgeschichte." In *Studien und Materialien zur Short Story*, ed. Paul Goetsch. Frankfurt: Diesterweg, 1975. 115–33.

and Other Stories (1968), the latter containing nine re-issued and revised stories, all of them rural or small-town in setting. A second collection of nine stories appeared as *The Race and Other Stories* (1982) and ranged from "No Other Way" (1934, his first story) via such excellent pieces as "A Day with Pegasus" (1938) and "The Race" (an excerpt from *Whir of Gold*) to a crime and mystery story, "The Flowers That Killed Him" (1972). Ross's novels and short stories make up a small but exquisite oeuvre and testify to his status as a master of modernist fiction techniques.

His stories are well plotted and rich in symbolic patterns. They incorporate the heritage of prairie realism and a suggestion of naturalism (with farming families victimized by the inclement elements), but are nonetheless documents of modernism, which, as will be shown, emerges as an emphasis on existential conditions. Conflict between husband and wife is the dominant theme in "No Other Way," as well as in such favorites as "A Field of Wheat" and "The Lamp at Noon." A second group of short fiction (showing the author's talent for comedy) consists of initiation stories, usually conveying a boy's experience in the harsh world of the farm, with his battling parents often in the background. The author originally "had *in mind* a group of stories having to do with the same boy" (Ross in McMullen 1982, 19): Ross was attracted to the short-story cycle, a key modernist genre as evidenced by Joyce's *Dubliners,* Hemingway's *In Our Time*, and (pertinently, as a portrayal of a farm boy's maturation process) Steinbeck's *The Red Pony* (see Meindl 1987). "A Day with Pegasus" deals with a boy's wonder at his newborn pony. In "Cornet at Night," the boy protagonist has a transcendent experience of music which sharply contrasts with the piano lessons forced on him by his mother. "The Runaway" focuses on horses again — symbols of freedom and male longing in Ross's work. The stories of married couples typically feature a wheat farmer and his wife, with the latter usually more cultured and sensitive than her often domineering partner, who, in his vulnerability to the weather, may figure "as a slave of the earth-goddess Demeter" (Mitchell 1981, 5), but can also be an easy-going, flashy fellow exploiting his hard-working, fast-aging wife (see "No Other Way" and "Nell"). Natural catastrophes often determine a couple's fate. "Not by Rain Alone" ("Part I: Summer Thunder" and "Part II: September Snow"; originally published as two separate stories) tells of a drought and a snow storm during which the young wife dies in childbirth, unattended by her husband who unnecessarily tries to bring in the cattle. "The Painted Door," for a change, centers on adultery, with the unfaithful wife realizing her husband's worth only after he has become a willing victim to a blizzard. In "A Field of Wheat," the loss of the uninsured wheat harvest by hail damage causes the prescient farmwife Martha to defer criticism of her husband but also hope of betterment for her family. "The Lamp at Noon," with its symbolic dust storm scenario, is arguably Ross's bleakest story about couples at odds.

Given the drought-stricken, dust-ridden condition of Saskatchewan during the Great Depression of the 1930s, Ross may appear a Canadian Steinbeck. However, partly thanks to the parabolic nature of the short-story genre as opposed to the broader canvas of the novel, Ross seems at once more subtle and simpler than Steinbeck. The conflict smouldering between a basically loyal woman and a husband who doggedly clings to what the wife perceives as the hopeless juggernaut of farming (see "A Field of Wheat" and "The Lamp at Noon") makes of her a complex, haunted character and of him an impressive, yet doomed figure: through his protagonists Ross sketches a gendered microcosm of tragic humankind. The stories enact a spiral toward evermore misery, with the elements impacting directly on the man, who, as persistent as deluded in his hope, suffers on his and the family's account, whereas the woman's suffering is compounded by the fact that she regards it as ultimately senseless. At the heart of these texts is the bond and, simultaneously, the chasm between man and woman. In "The Lamp at Noon" wifely endurance reaches its breaking point, with her reason giving way to his tenacity, and marital conflict coming to an irresolvable conclusion in the insularity of a destroyed and thus pacified mind.

In her introduction to the New Canadian Library edition of *The Lamp at Noon and Other Stories*, Margaret Laurence states that "throughout Ross's stories, the outer situation always mirrors the inner" (Laurence 1968, 11). Accordingly, "The Lamp at Noon" synchronizes the couple's quarrel with the dust storm that supplies the text's temporal structure. Storm and quarrel reach their climax and subside on the third day between the lighting of the lamp at noon and its extinction toward evening, that is, the time span that contains the story's action. Ross proceeds in an anthropomorphic and expressionistic fashion, associating mental states with elemental phenomena in a deliberate pathetic fallacy: "A little before noon she lit the lamp. Demented wind fled keening past the house: a wail through the eaves" (13). The wind, "quak[ing] among the feeble eaves, as if in all this dust-mad wilderness it knew no other sanctuary," symbolically represents the anguish of Ellen, the wife, and foreshadows her mental breakdown. Her perceiving "two winds" suggests an imminent schizophrenia: "the wind in flight, and the wind that pursued. The one sought refuge in the eaves, whimpering, in fear; the other assailed it there, and shook the eaves apart to make it flee again" (14). The fleeing wind can be associated with Ellen, who wants to give up the farm after five years of drought; the pursuing wind would then be a trope for the husband's obstinacy, which hounds her into madness and into fleeing from the farm with her baby in the dust storm.

The text's imagistic plane involves a flexible handling of narrative perspective. As a third-person narrative, "The Lamp at Noon" commands a gamut of modes: authorial narration, neutral scenic presentation, and figural perspective (use of focalizing characters to convey thoughts, feelings, and perceptions) — modes susceptible to transitional use. All the "wind" passages quoted above employ an incipient figural perspective, approximating free indirect discourse and thus reflecting Ellen's sensations of fear and panic. In addition, she articulates her wish to leave the farm as a plea (only too understandable considering the story's dire outcome). As part of a critical minority (see McMullen 1979, 31–33), I strongly sympathize with Ross's heroine. However, the authorial voice points out Ellen's "plaintive indignation" and presents her as "a woman that had aged without maturing, that had loved the little vanities of life, and lost them wistfully" (15). This authorial comment (unlike her husband Paul's subjective view of Ellen) possesses implicit authority and radiates a reliability that the reader, short of criticizing the text, cannot easily reject (see Meindl 1999, 14). As we will see, a certain weakness of character on the part of the text's female protagonist makes its feminist implications in fact more intricate. Confronted with Ellen's peevishness, the reader will not flatly dismiss Paul's side of the argument, that is, his objection to living in town as a pauper and dependent on her relatives, with a lack of any prospects once he has left the land he dreams of reclaiming. Ambiguity also extends to the text's central symbol (announced by the title). The lamp warns of the coming catastrophe, the extinction of the light of Ellen's mind. Yet, metonymically, the lamp is also associated with home and hearth as emblems of peace and tranquility set against the outside turmoil. A momentary ceasefire in the couple's quarrel makes the farmhouse appear as a refuge: "There was silence now — a deep fastness of it enclosed by rushing wind and creaking walls. It seemed the yellow lamp-light cast a hush upon them" (17). The reader cannot side unconditionally with either one of the two opponents, even if our empathy (as well as the clarity of hindsight) would want Paul to take his anguished wife off the farm. The veil of dust coating Paul's land symbolically hints at his "clouded" perception of the seriousness of the situation as well as at mortality, that is, the death of the baby, who gets smothered by the dust and/or stifled by Ellen's protecting arms as she flees the farm.

Viewing the story's action as "a test of endurance in which only the very strong such as Paul" survive (Djwa 1973, 191) works toward exonerating its male protagonist. In the tradition of Western Canadian writing in general and Frederick Philip Grove in particular, "The Lamp at Noon" constitutes an example of "pioneer fiction" (Comeau 1984), with the bankrupt, "dusted-out" farmer being one of those unsung heroes who confront the great and lonely spaces of North America's last farming frontier, as evoked in Ross's first novel: "the prairie, the vacancy and stillness of it, the bare essentials of a landscape, sky and earth" (*As for Me and My House*, 59). Projected against the immense horizontal land, vertical man (see Ricou 1973) appears both grand and puny: "Man, the giant-conqueror, and man, the insignificant dwarf always threatened by defeat, form the two polarities of the state of mind produced by the sheer physical fact of the prairie" (Kreisel 1971, 256). This internalized geography makes for the tragic atmosphere already alluded to: a universe reigned by hostile Fate or (in more North American terms) an angry Puritan God. Paul would thus gain stature from a solitary fight against overwhelming odds which abrogate human responsibility by making defeat a foregone conclusion. "The hopelessness of striving to eke out an existence from the harsh, indifferent prairie environment pervades the stories of Sinclair Ross" (Fraser 1970, 72). This ring of fateful futility tempts many critics to give "The Lamp at Noon" a too constricted reading.

Contingency and the openness of the future are strong themes in the text. Ellen, an educated woman, believes in progress and reproaches her husband for having "plowed and harrowed [the soil] until there's not a root or fibre left to hold it down" (17) — an accurate observation in view of the fact that the Saskatchewan "dust bowl" (like the Oklahoma one) was caused by a convergence of inclement climate, economic situation, and soil erosion caused by monoculture. Paul seems finally willing to integrate his wife's knowledge (crop diversification) into his plans for the future and conjures up a vision of an estate that will support them all: "A new house — land for the boy — land and still more land — or education, whatever he might want" (20). Given the calamitous consequences of this dream, it cannot simply be called a necessary illusion constituting "a weapon against being defeated by reality" (Bowen 1979, 39). Another critic more equitably sees both husband and wife "waver between insight and delusion" and tends to equate Ross's "complex and ironic interweaving of reality and illusion" with his transcendence of realism — but is not Ross's "concern with the many ways we resist objective reality" an eminently realist feature (Esterhammer 1992, 17, 19, 22)? As Dennis Cooley argues: "Realist fiction, whether psychological or sociological, commonly observes as its ethos the stripping away of illusions that perpetuate stupidity and injustice"; Cooley further points out the "visual economy" of "The Lamp at Noon," which, in terms of what the couple sees and fails to see (in both senses of the term, perceive and realize), turns the story into "a quilt of illusion and revelation" (Cooley 1987, 139, 142). Another writer-critic also links illusionism to realist practice: "Nineteenth-century novels had characters playing out their dreams with each other against a static background" (Cohen 1984, 69). How then does Ross emerge as a modernist from a realist tradition?

In the final analysis, the quarrel between husband and wife in "The Lamp at Noon" evokes two different epistemological perspectives that affiliate the text with both realism and modernism. Paul's reasons for staying on the farm are not irrational: in fact, he is something of a logocentrist adhering to a typically North American combination of idealism (that is, the epistemological primacy of the subject) and materialism (the epistemological precedence given to the object world). Assailed by misgivings about his course, he nonetheless clings to his latter-day pioneering perspective and nourishes a vision of material gain which dispels reality: "And so vivid was the future of his planning, so real and constant, that often the actual present was but half felt, but half endured" (20). Here we touch upon what is perhaps the metanarrative of literary realism: a man, bent on rising in the world, tries to impose on it a dream that, whether resulting in success or failure, cannot but take a material form (see, for example, Rubempré's rise and fall in Balzac's *Illusions perdues*). This conjunction of visionary subject and material object corresponds to Cartesian subject/object dualism (which distinguishes between thinking substance, *res cogitans*, and "extended" substance, *res extensa*) and thus to the subject/object structure of the mind. Within this epistemological framework, woman easily becomes identified with her sex and hence objectified as mere deluded woman deviating from the rational masculine norm. Ross's text indicates that Ellen has to a certain degree internalized such patriarchal thinking as she tries to conceal "the fear and weakness of a woman" (14) from Paul, who, on his part, seeks "not to reveal a fear or weakness that she might think capitulation to her wishes" (20–21).

Ellen lives in a more modern universe than her husband, in which the latter's idealist/materialist mold of thought has already been undermined by life and existential philosophy, with epistemological priority now being conferred upon neither subject nor object, but on the flow of life, the all-encompassing existential dimension that grounds the mind, but can also do without it (see Meindl 2003, 34).[1] This decentering of the mind is enacted by Schopenhauer's blind "will of the world," Bergson's *élan vital*, Nietzsche's treatment of "the notion of the self as a unified and rational being [as] an illusion inimical to life itself" (McAfee 2004, 2), and Heidegger's *Sein* (Being). Clearly, life in its totality is impossible to render in narrative, which hinges on the presentation of concrete and specific events and situations. Nonetheless, "life as such" becomes a key concept in modernist literature given the crumbling of the West's metaphysical superstructure, Christian belief, whose demise resulted in the typical *fin-de-siècle* split of sensibility and the accompanying phenomena of, on the one hand, art supplanting religion and, on the other, the valorization of life in its totality (a dichotomy reflected in such antithetical turn-of-the-century writers as Henry James — an aesthete — and Jack London — a champion of raw life — or Thomas Mann and Rudyard Kipling).

[1] This philosophical matrix becomes explicit in Ross's story "Saturday Night" (1951), in which a young man bested in love by a rival has to perceive the insignificance of his disappointment, with the text signaling that "the rhythm of life [is] going on with or without him" (Mitchell, 25).

"In Ross's world, art replaces religion as a spiritual and creative force" (McMullen 1979, 139). Ellen is therefore typically modernist on account of her immediate desire and concern for life.

Ellen is "afraid" (15) of the dust storm, understandably. Yet "the intensity of her dread" (18) goes beyond fear of something specific and into the realm of existential anxiety, Heidegger's *Angst*, which is the manner in which *Dasein* (the human being) encounters the world as such:

> Anxiety does not "see" any definite "here" or "yonder" from which [something threatening] comes. That in the face of which one has anxiety is characterized by the fact that what threatens is nowhere. Anxiety "does not know" what that in the face of which it is anxious is. "Nowhere," however, does not signify nothing: this is where any region lies. . . . Therefore that which threatens cannot bring itself close from a definite direction within what is close by; it is already "there," and yet nowhere; it is so close that it is oppressive and stifles one's breath, and yet is nowhere. (Heidegger 1962, 231)

The dust-filled, choking air, which causes Ellen to feel "caged" (18) and makes her "throat so tight" (19) — a diluted enveloping world that is nowhere and everywhere, that is — constitutes the perfect "objective correlative" (T. S. Eliot) of Ellen's oppression. Her entrapment will eventually reduce and de-individualize her to the level of bare existence as she loses her reason and joins the ranks of mad modernist figures (in works by Gilman, Mann, Faulkner, Rhys, and many others).

Angst and insanity, in yielding access to the totality of bare life, are related to the grotesque, which undoes the logical separation of life into human, animal, plant, and inanimate realms and hints at totality by conjoining the antithetical literary modes of the comic and the terrifying. In Ross's story, Paul seeks mental relief in the stable, where he communicates with a horse: "At a whinny from the bay mare, Bess, he went forward and into her stall. She seemed grateful for his presence, and thrust the nose deep between his arm and body" (19). Ironically, Paul finds comfort with, and gives it to, a mare while denying his presence to Ellen, his longing wife. Even when he has a premonition of "her running, pulled and driven headlong by the wind" (20), he does not join her in the house. Long on reason and short on caring, he merely reassures himself by looking through the window from outside. The grotesque nature of the stable episode is not immediately apparent. As Bakhtin's investigation of medieval and Renaissance folk literature demonstrates, the grotesque affirms life as a whole by articulating a semantics of the body, its protrusions and orifices, which are expressive of those basic corporeal functions in which body and body, as well as body and earth, are involved with one another (see Bakhtin 1984, 26). In this sense, the displaced sexual union performed in the stable expresses existential well-being and connectedness. For Bakhtin, the least grotesque and hence most individual and expressive parts of the human body are the eyes. Aptly, Ellen's eyes become "fixed and wide with a curious immobility" (13), as her personality crumbles. Her "immobile stare" (23) is eventually supplemented by a fixed smile when Paul finds her with the dead baby at a (symbolic) drift of sand. The wind and Ellen's eyes and smile thus represent a grotesque animism and lifelessness, respectively. Like many texts in the wake of Romanticism, Ross's story demonstrates why the grotesque has come to veer toward its dark pole, all but abandoning its original joyful and carnivalesque mood. Total life is the mode of extinction of the individual mind; *Bewusstsein* (consciousness) yielding to *Sein* (being), of which going insane is an extreme version, could not but become terrifying in the increasingly individual-focused realm of fiction (see Meindl 1996, 19). Faulkner, perhaps the foremost North American modernist and a master of the grotesque, defined life *in toto* as "motion" and "fluidity" (Meriwether and Millgate 1968, 253). Given the specific nature of narrative reality, it makes sense that "life as such" is best conveyed indirectly, *ex negativo*, by an absence of motion and change in a static character like Paul. He stubbornly clings to his plan not to budge from the land and to cultivate only wheat; he ignores his wife's advice "to grow fibrous crops" (21) so as to hold down the thin prairie topsoil. The sand storm leaves a "naked" field (21), which, had the family survived the storm, would presumably have provided not "so much as an onion or potato" ("A Field of Wheat," 82). Hence, the male protagonist of "The Lamp at Noon" is associated with reason suppressing his emotions, but does not strike one as particularly sensible.

The idea of woman as closer to the motion of life, as more emotional and mentally less stable than man, is deeply ingrained in the history of Western thought. Is "The Lamp at Noon" thus merely a fine story adopting a traditional cultural pattern devoid of anthropological validity? Or is woman, in a gender-related, genuinely cultural sense, different from man? Here, I propose to skip socially-oriented, egalitarian feminism of (predominantly) American provenance and turn instead to French feminism, particularly to Julia Kristeva and her concept of maternity. Adopting Kristeva's line of thought means courting the charge of biological essentialism, but enables one to assign a crucial role to the third protagonist of Ross's story, the baby son. Thus, the consideration of love is brought to bear upon a text in which the only words of love (not counting the madwoman's flirtatious cooing at the end) are those Ellen whispers to her baby at the text's beginning: "Sleep. . . . It's too soon for you to be hungry. Daddy's coming for his dinner" (14). For Kristeva, "contrasted with the love that binds a mother to her son, all other 'human relationships' burst like blatant shams" (Kristeva 1986, 172).

Kristeva is best known for her concept of abjection, which focuses on the act — on the part of the child striving to become a subject — of abjecting, or rejecting what is "other" to it. Nonetheless, the abject never entirely disappears from consciousness; it always threatens at, and thus marks, the borders of the "I": "The abject is what does not respect boundaries. It beseeches and pulverizes the subject" (McAfee, 46). This notion is germane to a text about a de-individualized dust-storm victim, but need not long concern us. More importantly, Kristeva's work "unsettles the sex/gender dichotomy" (McAfee, 80) by stressing woman's embodiedness, which, instead of marginalizing her role in our culture's symbolic, logocentric order, actually enhances it. The maternal body — for Bakhtin (Kristeva's early model) neither strictly self nor other, neither one nor two bodies, and thus the paradigm of the life-affirming grotesque — folds nature and culture into one and engenders a new ethics that "seems to be about undoing the dualisms of mind/body, culture/nature, and word/flesh. . . . the mother does right for her child not just out of duty (law) but out of love, a love that is not just for an other but for what was once in her and for the species, for the singular other and for the universal" (McAfee, 86). As a philosopher, Kristeva takes up the worldly metaphysics of the philosophy of existential processes mentioned earlier in connection with the rise of literary modernism. In our text, Ellen exemplifies woman's broad nature/culture bond. Her arranging a tent of muslin over the crib to protect the baby from the dust strikes one as an instinctive and sensible action derived from the sheltering function of the womb: "[Maternal love], of which divine love is merely a not always convincing derivation, psychologically is perhaps a recall . . . of the primal shelter that ensured the survival of the newborn" (Kristeva, 176). Conjoining nature and culture, discourse and biology, Ellen also engages in a symbolic signifying practice superior to that of her husband when she stresses the necessity of diversifying the farm's crops. The end of the story depicts her as a victim of panic, but also supplies a parody of feminine gender roles as the madwoman goes through the motions of perfect mistress, mother, and wife all combined — preening herself, handling the dead child like a doll, quipping about her husband's clumsy hands as well as admiring his strength and meteorological foresight, and looking optimistically to the future: "tomorrow will be fine" (23).

Kristeva's philosophy distinguishes between the semiotic and the symbolic, with the latter designating "an expression of clear and orderly meaning" and the former "an evocation of feeling or, more pointedly, a discharge of the subject's energy and drives" (McAfee, 15–16). These are not separate domains, however; rather, the semiotic energizes the symbolic sphere, constituting what Kristeva calls a subject in process. Ellen, in responding immediately and emotionally to the situation on the farm, performs a more vivid and life-affirming signifying operation than Paul. What, then, about her authorially certified personal peevishness and frustrated love of pleasure, to which she admits: " 'I'm young still. I like pretty things' " (17)? In a general yet significant fashion, the couple can be viewed in the light of Hélène

Cixous's concern with "the mystery and continuity of life" (Cixous 1988, 14), which preserves a certain modernist aura. Cixous distinguishes between "'feminine' and 'masculine' [as] the relationship to pleasure," a relationship in principle not determined by the individual's anatomical sex, but by a gendered nature/culture nexus based "on the way society has used the body and on the fact that it is much easier to inflict on men than on women the horror of the inside. After all women do all virtually or in fact have an experience of the inside" (Cixous, 15, 18). Cixous contrasts Eve's daring to taste the inside of the apple with Adam's greater respect for the law. This gloss of the Eden myth strikes one as poetic (which is precisely Cixous's criterion for truth), but is certainly appropriate to Ross's text, remembering Paul's observance of the Protestant work ethic and his reproaching Ellen for craving "a better time" (17) off the farm.

Paul's denial of the affective dimensions to which Ellen so keenly responds disrupts her mental balance. To put it differently: he drives her crazy. She flees the farm seeking to shield the baby from danger, but does so too late — or too soon, before the dust storm abates. We may call hers hysterical action, using the blanket medical term associated with women since antiquity (hysteria being derived from *hystera*, the Greek word for uterus, and describing a female disorder including, among its symptoms, the sensation of choking; see Showalter 1998, 15). However, in calling Ellen a hysteric, one can usefully consult Luce Irigaray's "re-evaluation of hysteria as the unheard voice of the woman who can only speak through somatic functions" and heed what the French psychoanalyst and thinker calls "a revolutionary potential in hysteria" (Irigaray 1991, 26, 47). Ross's story — in which a woman, when her protest is of no avail, protests with her body by running away — uses gender stereotypes, but also includes a connotative potential enabling the reader to transcend them.

Works Cited

Bakhtin, Mikhail. *Rabelais and His World.* Trans. Hélène Iswolsky. Bloomington: Indiana University Press, 1984.

Bowen, Gail. "The Fiction of Sinclair Ross." *Canadian Literature* 80 (1979): 37–48.

Cixous, Hélène. "Extreme Fidelity." Trans. Ann Liddle and Susan Sellers. In *Writing Differences: Readings from the Seminar of Hélène Cixous*, ed. Susan Sellers. New York: St. Martin's Press, 1988. 9–36.

Cohen, Matt. "Notes on Realism in Modern English-Canadian Fiction." *Canadian Literature* 100 (1984): 65–71.

Comeau, Paul. "Sinclair Ross's Pioneer Fiction." *Canadian Literature* 103 (1984): 175–84.

Cooley, Dennis. "The Eye in Sinclair Ross's Short Stories." In Cooley, *The Vernacular Muse: The Eye and Ear in Contemporary Literature.* Winnipeg: Turnstone, 1987. 139–65.

Djwa, Sandra. "No Other Way: Sinclair Ross's Stories and Novels." In *Writers of the Prairies,* ed. Donald G. Stephens. Vancouver: University of British Columbia Press, 1973. 189–206.

Esterhammer, Angela. "'Can't See Life for Illusions': The Problematic Realism of Sinclair Ross." In *From the Heart of the Heartland: The Fiction of Sinclair Ross,* ed. John Moss. Ottawa: University of Ottawa Press, 1992. 14–23.

Fraser, Keath. *As for Me and My Body.* Toronto: ECW Press, 1997.

———. "Futility at the Pump: The Short Stories of Sinclair Ross." *Queen's Quarterly* 77.1 (1970): 72–80.

Heidegger, Martin. *Being and Time.* Trans. John Macquarrie and Edward Robinson. New York: Harper and Row, 1962.

Irigaray, Luce. *The Irigaray Reader,* ed. Margaret Whitford. Oxford: Basil Blackwell, 1991.

Kreisel, Henry. "The Prairie: A State of Mind." In *Contexts of Canadian Criticism,* ed. Eli Mandel. Chicago: University of Chicago Press, 1971. 254–66.

Kristeva, Julia. "Stabat Mater." In *The Kristeva Reader,* ed. Toril Moi. Oxford: Blackwell, 1986. 161–86.

Laurence, Margaret. "Introduction." In Ross, *The Lamp at Noon and Other Stories by Sinclair Ross.* New Canadian Library. Toronto: McClelland & Stewart, 1968. 7–12.

Lesk, Andrew. "Something Queer Going on Here: Desire in the Short Fiction of Sinclair Ross." *Essays on Canadian Writing* 61 (1997): 129–41.

McAfee, Noëlle. *Julia Kristeva.* New York: Routledge, 2004.

McMullen, Lorraine. "Introduction." In Ross, *The Race and Other Stories by Sinclair Ross.* Ottawa: University of Ottawa Press, 1982. 15–21.

———. *Sinclair Ross.* Boston: Twayne, 1979.

Meindl, Dieter. *American Fiction and the Metaphysics of the Grotesque.* Columbia: University of Missouri Press, 1996.

———. "Companions in Modernism: Comparing Faulkner, Hemingway, and Wolfe." In *Look Homeward and Forward: Thomas Wolfe, an American Voice across Modern and Contemporary Culture,* ed. Agostino Lombardo et al. Rome: Casa Editrice Università La Sapienza, 2003. 33–44.

———. "A Model of Narrative Discourse along Pronominal Lines." In *Recent Trends in Narratological Research,* ed. John Pier. GRAAT 21. Tours: Université de Tours, 1999. 11–29.

———. "Modernism and the English Canadian Short Story Cycle." *RANAM* 20 (1987): 17–22.

McMullen, Lorraine. *North American Encounters: Essays in U.S. and English and French Canadian Literature and Culture.* Münster: LIT Verlag, 2002.

Meriwether, James B., and Michael Millgate, eds. *Lion in the Garden: Interviews with William Faulkner 1926–1962.* New York: Random House, 1968.

Mitchell, Ken. *Sinclair Ross: A Reader's Guide.* Moose Jaw, Saskatchewan: Thunder Creek Publishing, 1981.

Ricou, Laurence. *Vertical Man/Horizontal World: Man and Landscape in Canadian Prairie Fiction.* Vancouver: University of British Columbia Press, 1973.

Ross, Sinclair. *As for Me and My House.* New Canadian Library. Toronto: McClelland & Stewart, 1957.

———. *The Lamp at Noon and Other Stories.* New Canadian Library. Toronto: McClelland & Stewart, 1968.

———. "The Lamp at Noon." In Ross, *The Lamp at Noon*, 13–23 [first published in *Queen's Quarterly* 45.1 (1938)].

———. *The Race and Other Stories*, ed. and introd. Lorraine McMullen. Ottawa: University of Ottawa Press, 1982.

Showalter, Elaine. *Hystories: Hysterical Epidemics and Modern Culture.* London: Picador, 1998.

7: "An Artful Artlessness": Ethel Wilson, "We Have to Sit Opposite" (1945)

Nina Kück (University of Constance)

ETHEL WILSON (1888–1981) OPENED HER FIRST NOVEL *Hetty Dorval* (1937) with an epigraph from John Donne's seventeenth "Devotion": "No man is an Iland, intire of it selfe" (Donne 1975, 87) — a conviction that would inform all her later writing. Displaying the theme of the individual embedded in society, this quotation has been interpreted by critics as an important clue to the oeuvre of a Canadian writer who has been variously and contradictorily described as "the most traditional, experimental, artless, and sophisticated" of Canada's writers (McPherson 1976, 219). Wilson's books were published at a time when Canadian literature was only beginning to achieve academic respectability, and her career ended just when the Canadian short story rose to prominence and became "the genre [through] which the explosive literary renaissance in Canada was probably made most apparent" (Nischik 1987, 233). Owing in part to the lack of interest in story collections among publishers at the time, Wilson's stories first appeared in periodicals; a collection of her short stories in book form — *Mrs. Golightly and Other Stories* — did not appear until 1961. In 1990, though, her works were reissued and canonized within the New Canadian Library Series.

Although Wilson's short stories have been anthologized relatively frequently, her published output — though of high quality — is relatively small, consisting of five short novels and only one short-story collection, as well as some essays and articles. *Hetty Dorval* was followed by the novels *The Innocent Traveller* (1949), *The Equations of Love* (1952), *Swamp Angel* (1954), *Love and Salt Water* (1956), as well as *Mrs. Golightly and Other Stories* (1961), all published by Macmillan. Two of her approximately thirty published stories have appeared since the publication of *Mrs Golightly*: "Simple Translation" and "A Visit to the Frontier." Wilson also wrote a serialized children's story between March and June 1919. Her last novel "The Vat and the Brew" (according to critics, not up to her "usual standards," see for example Mitchell 1993, 102, note 12) has never been published.[1] Most

[1] The largest Wilson archive exists at the University of British Columbia Library, Rare Books and Special Collections. UBC holds the copyright to her unpublished

of her stories were released in the 1940s and 1950s, when Canada was just beginning to find a (literary) identity of its own, and writers like Wilson tried to express the "Canadian experience." Wilson combined a descriptive realism, which dominated short-story writing at the time, with modernist techniques, such as a sophisticated style, irony, and a controlled narrative voice (and, on a few occasions, even a postmodernist tinge avant-la-lettre). Yet she also deviated from modernism by preserving what has been called an "Edwardian" sensibility (Gadpaille 1988, 26–27).

David Stouck has recently corrected Wilson's self-styled, persistent legend of a socially prominent doctor's wife with an amusing hobby, who allegedly began writing when she was almost sixty years old.[2] Stouck (1987, 2003) revealed that Wilson had worked on her novel *The Innocent Traveller*, an autobiographical combination of social history and fiction, as early as 1930, that is to say, nearly twenty years before its publication. Her career can be said to have truly started with the publication of the short story "I Just Love Dogs" in the British *New Statesman* in 1937. Reprinted in *O'Brien's Best British Short Stories* in 1938, its publication outside Canada is symptomatic of the situation of Canadian writing at the time, when literary magazines and periodicals were extremely rare in Canada.

Shorter forms of fiction, especially the genre of the short story, seem to have suited Wilson's talent best; even her novels — some sections of which were originally published in periodicals as short stories — often take an episodic approach. Wilson felt the most important thing in a story to be the design of the sentence, "a never-ceasing miracle and source of fascination" (Wilson in Stouck 2003, 239). Her simple and economical sentences are strikingly elegant, although critics have remarked on inconsistencies and idiosyncrasies such as frequent repetitions or over-stated symbolism, irritating changes of narrative pace, or unmotivated authorial intrusion (see for example New 1982, 144). Interspersed in her concise, economical diction are words or sentences in parentheses, which introduce, for example, the simultaneous existence of pleasure and sorrow, terror and happiness — in short, the ambiguities of life.

Although Wilson's stories have a distinctive Canadian orientation that goes beyond British Columbian history and setting, she did not primarily view her work in the larger context of Canadian literature. An outsider to the literary community of her generation, she once stated that "what

---

as well as her published literary works (see Stouck 2003, 329–38, for an updated account on archival materials; McComb 1984 gives a full account of primary and secondary sources up to 1982).

[2] Previous research on Wilson mostly referred to Desmond Pacey's 1967 biography or Mary McAlpine's 1988 biography. In 2003, Stouck published the most comprehensive and detailed critical study to date.

Canadians have to aim at is not to write something Canadian (they'll do that anyway) but to write *well*!" (Wilson in Stouck 2003, 168). Her carefully crafted style has prompted critics to link her to British writers (Stouck 1984, 81; New 1982, 142; Rimanelli 1966, xxi). Considering her slice-of-life stories, her characters' capacity for humor and self-criticism, her strong reverence for the English sentence, and a deceptively lucid style that hides the extensive polishing and revision applied to it, it comes as no surprise that reviewers singled out the "Jane Austenish" aspect of her writing, or perceived her as the "Katherine Mansfield of Canada" (see reviews in Stouck 2003, 109 and McComb, 475).

Autobiographical detail has a particular significance for Wilson's selection of topics. Her childhood in an environment "permeated with religious influence" (Mitchell 1979, 228), her move from England to Canada at the age of ten in 1898, her adoption of a world view that came straight out of mid-nineteenth century Burslem, Staffordshire (her mother's hometown), as well as her happy marriage of forty-five years (Stouck 2003, 63–78) all seem to have influenced her writing. Other autobiographical references can be found in her use of her own relatives as dramatis personae in *The Innocent Traveller* and some short stories, the recurrence of cherished Lac Le Jeune as setting (Whitaker 1980), her apologetic or self-deprecating remarks (Wild 1982, 36), and her various alter egos in her female protagonists (Pacey 1967, 31).[3]

Wilson's own life is essential in the configuration of her "capricious fictional world" (Comeau 1981, 34) and helps to explain much of her choice of material and the prominence of rather "traditional and bourgeois" values in her work (Smyth 1982, 88). Many of her characters are upper-middle-class (female) Canadians, in whose lives "nihilism and beliefs struggle for supremacy" (Gelfant 1982, 121), lives affected by British social propriety and dismissive of "Americanisms" (New 1982, 142). Wilson repeatedly portrays the tension between the individual's engagement with and responsibility for others, its struggle for independence and the dangers of isolation and alienation, particularly with regard to her female protagonists. Compared to Canadian writers like Margaret Atwood or Alice Munro, however, who more rigorously reflect the processes of repression, rebellion, and the urge for self-determination, Wilson's criticism and skepticism appear softer, her cynicism milder and rather apolitical.

The eighteen stories in *Mrs. Golightly* bring together Wilson's many narrative formats, ranging from non-fiction to fully-fledged fantasy, from science fiction to surrealist detective fiction. Embracing action stories, social comedies, comic dialogue, diary forms, didactic narratives and more,

[3] For more biographical details see Pacey 1967, McAlpine 1988, and Stouck 2003.

the collection does not contain a single "conventional short story" (Stouck 2003, 249). From the gentle mockery of the title story to the psychological fable of "Mr. Sleepwalker," Wilson's characters span the human spectrum as well, displaying shrewd and witty insights interwoven with obscure reflections. Highly symbolic and detailed, nature serves both as the background to and reflection of the characters' lives. What is striking in Wilson's stories is their characteristic voice, an "incandescence" from which "meaning emerges," deceptively simple on the surface, but in fact highly complex — an "artful artlessness" (Wilson 1959, 16). Another distinct characteristic of her prose is the unique point of view, Wilson's "innocent" (Pacey 1954, 43), "overviewing" (New 1968, 42) eye, swiftly shifting and moving from one protagonist to another.

The number of reviews published in Canada, as well as her numerous awards, might suggest, as Pacey claims, that Wilson was reviewed almost exclusively in Canada (Pacey 1967, 28), but McComb's bibliography (1984) indicates that critical response to her fiction has been widespread. Wilson's short stories have generally elicited favorable reviews in many English-speaking countries, including ones by renowned Canadian writers such as Alice Munro, Morley Callaghan, Joyce Marshall, and Gabrielle Roy. Not least because of Wilson's universal topics, a small but constant interest in her writing remains. Furthermore, an "Ethel Wilson Prize" was established in Canada in 1985 and is awarded annually to a British Columbian or Yukon, i.e. Western Canadian, author.

Originally planned as part of a novel[4] and first published in *Chatelaine* magazine in May 1945, "We Have to Sit Opposite" is one of Wilson's best known and most frequently anthologized short stories. Based on a personal experience from 1929, it depicts a disturbing encounter between two Canadian women and a German family in a train traveling from Salzburg, Austria, to Munich, Germany, in 1931. Set in a train compartment, thus in an anonymous, yet at the same time rather intimate atmosphere, the almost plotless story of Wilson's narrative, heavily reliant on dialogue, opens *in medias res*, presenting the main characters as well as the setting. The opening resembles the beginning of a detective story or murder mystery: "Even in the confusion of entering the carriage at Salzburg, Mrs. Montrose and her cousin Mrs. Forrester noticed the man with the blue tooth" (56). With Wilson's typical usage of suggestive names in her

[4] Wilson refers to this in an unprinted talk read on CBS in April 1956. During the 1940s she was working on an extended narrative about a character called Lucy Lovet Forrester. Three stories about Mrs. Forrester were published in *Mrs. Golightly*, and three more exist in manuscript form in the UBC library (for details see Stouck 2003, 254; Stouck 1987, 28).

fiction, "Forrester" and "Montrose" evoke the Canadian landscape with its abundance of forests and mountains, and at the same time hint at the English and French parts of Canada (French "mont" = mountain).

The first paragraphs of the story are ambiguous and offer two diverging perspectives. In contrast to the rigidity implied by the title, the beginning conveys a light-hearted mood but at the same time introduces the reader to an inescapable situation that will soon lead to confrontation. In a brisk, funny, unpretentious way, and combining short, comic sentences and more complex, hypotactic ones, the narrator introduces the social background and character traits of the two good-humored young Canadian ladies. "Clinging vines" (56) to their doctor husbands, the tall, slender, and elegant women represent the modern lifestyle of the New (Canadian) World, having just spent (as now recounted in retrospect) a wonderful time in Vienna, a capital of European culture ("Ah Vienna, they thought, Vienna, Vienna," 57). Although the narrative voice mostly reflects the view of Mrs. Forrester throughout the story, this does not preclude some highly ironic but affectionate remarks about the ladies. The reader can hardly suppress a smile, imagining the two ladies longing "almost passionately" (57) to participate in cultural events, but instead dawdling away the time by shopping and going to a café, thus establishing a comical contrast between education and leisure. The premonitory question of the intrusive narrator in a parenthetical aside, however, disrupts this pleasant narrative chatter: "They were fortunate. Were they too fortunate?" — another detective story-like harbinger that marks the transition from expository retrospection back to the situation in the train carriage.

In the train compartment the two young women have entered a confined space where their gaiety and naïveté is soon to be transformed into a feeling of intense unease (foreshadowed by words like "tyrannical," "occupy," "blue tooth," and "confusion," 56), a "cultural wilderness," as it will turn out, in stark contrast to their world of civilized and polite people and conversations. Wilson characteristically develops the story from marginal details. A small incident — the ladies' polite request to move a hamper placed on a seat — triggers a profound irritation. Two worlds collide when the smiling, panting, and apologetic Canadians meet their fellow travelers, a German family under the patriarchal command of a man with a particular physical mark: a blue tooth. The motif of the blue tooth will remain a mysterious element in this text: is this a reference to remote lexical connotations, with "blue" also meaning "low in spirits, tending to lower the spirits," and "tooth" meaning "something that injures, tortures, devours or destroys" (*Webster's New Encyclopedic Dictionary* 1994, 106, 1093)? Or is it an allusion to the Danish King Harald Blue Tooth, who in the tenth century forcibly united his people and sowed centuries of conflict between Denmark and Norway? The latter interpretation would support the picture of an idyllic journey from Austria to Germany — significantly, only a few years before the *Anschluss*, Nazi Germany's annexation of Austria.

Gradually, tension increases. The blunt, uncouth man denies the two Canadian women their polite and matter-of-course request. The stage is set: good humor, smiles, and courtesy on the one side, indecent gaping, raised voices, and a peremptory tone on the other. The members of the petit-bourgeois German family remain unnamed and are repetitively referred to in an enumerative or collective way, which creates an eerie air of impersonality ("the man" [thirty times], "the man with the blue tooth" [fourteen times], "the husband" [twice], "the man, his wife and his daughter," "these people," "the German family," etc.). Representing types rather than individuals, they mostly act collectively, too. The individuality of the female family members is further reduced as they are only mentioned in connection with the man ("his wife," "his daughter"). The *pater familias* is portrayed as an obsessional neurotic, insistent on his views and what he considers to be "logical." The conversation soon turns into an interrogation, especially on the nationality of the Canadian ladies. National identity is both his interest and his weapon; the ladies, in contrast, try to avoid this issue, not yielding to his attempt at categorization.

> "Are you English?" "Yes — well — no," says Mrs. Forrester. "No — well — yes," says Mrs. Montrose. "Americans?" "No." "You can't deceive me," says the German man, needing categories to classify them, "you must be something." (60)

That the text should play with the question of Canadian identity is an ironic sideswipe by Wilson; Marshall MacLuhan quips that Canadians "know how to live without identity, and this is one of [their] marvelous resources" (in Kilgallin 1971, 2).

At first, the intimidated ladies eagerly submit to the man's obstinate catechism, but soon enough they begin to develop a counterstrategy: they dissimulate, begin to switch the interrogation into a game of hare and hounds, and ironically deceive him. While the dialogue conveys an impression of directness, the oscillation of the narrative voice between a distinctively judgemental, omniscient point of view on the one hand and a subjective, figural one on the other hand encompasses both instances of flashback and the alternation between outer and inner perspectives. Even though the changes in perspective are indicated by slightly old-fashioned technical devices such as authorial comments or the use of direct thought or parentheses, the story is modernist in its multiple points of view (Wilson uses free indirect speech and even inner monologue once), and the handling of parataxis and focalization create a figural style that brings the story close to the women's consciousness and involves the reader in the narrative.

The Canadian ladies regain power over the conversation through a misunderstanding: while they use the term "bear" in the sense of "unbearable," the German man, conjuring clichés of the North American wilderness, presumes they are talking about the animal. The ladies, hitherto reacting rather passively, turn this misunderstanding to their advantage: recalcitrantly, they begin to fib about bears as Canadians' favorite pets and food. As frequently occurs in Wilson's work, there is a preoccupation with the question of truth in this story, with "falsifying life's simple or portentous truths and creating truths through falsehoods" (Gelfant 1995, 9). The women themselves cleverly introduce the clichés that they expect their counterpart to have in mind by playing on the stereotype of North American materialism and by boasting about the wilderness of Canadian life. This mimicry is part of a tug-of-war: the greater the indecency of their German interlocutor, the more elaborate the verbal games of the two Canadians become, up to a point where they even sabotage his idea of manhood by making the uncultured man (a manufacturer of trousers) believe that Canadians (like Scots) wear kilts. Their game of lies, exaggerations, and fake identities soon slips from the women's control, however, making them feel uncomfortable with themselves ("'how horrid of us . . . isn't it true that horridness just breeds horridness. We're getting horrider every minute,'" 62) and wavering between "distaste" and "pity" (62) towards the man.

In her subtle psychological style, Wilson configures the narrative structure as a kind of downward spiral. "The two liars" (64), as the narrator eventually calls the protagonists, seem to have become conscious of this destructive course of action, and, for a brief moment, it looks as if the conflict could be appeased. Feeling victorious ("the battle was going in [their] favour," 62), Mrs. Montrose at least physically turns away from the controversy and restores her appearance by arranging her hair and powdering herself, once again a Victorian lady. This retreat is useless, however, as her German opponent, in his attempt to make the women conform to his preconceptions, now turns from nationality to old-fashioned gender stereotypes: "'I do not allow my wife and daughter to paint their faces so. Good women do not do that'" (65). The text then progresses towards its final climax. For the first time in the story, Mrs. Forrester crosses the borderline of role play and becomes openly aggressive. The more infuriated she becomes, the more she resembles her adversary with regard to intonation, syntax, and content of speech. Speaking loudly herself ever since the misunderstanding over the "bear," using short and choppy sentences, and arguing illogically in a strangely mimicking fashion, Mrs. Forrester becomes tactless and offensive, too. The situation reaches a climax when she mentions the man's blue tooth and absurdly threatens him with what she thinks impresses Germans most: the police ("'In our country . . . anyone needing attention is taken straight to the State Dentist by the Police,'" 65). In a way, the entire conflict revolves around the problem of complying with social rules. Accordingly, for the second time, the women reflect upon respecting or breaking the rules of the game: "They felt," in the phrasing of the British idiom, "that they had gone a little bit too far" (65). Having been "properly brought up" (60) as true ladies, the two women eventually resort to a fitting strategy of resignation: they close their eyes and try to sleep.

But even though the conversation ends at this point, the story continues. Certainly, to shut one's eyes and fall asleep while traveling to Munich is highly significant here, bearing in mind that Munich was the capital of the Nazi movement and a symbol of the failure of British appeasement policy. While describing how the German mother and daughter wash and dress up the petit-bourgeois patriarch — a scene that lies somewhere between grotesqueness and cliché — the narrative voice becomes allegorical and didactic. The text turns towards political analysis, which contrasts with the humorous narrative tone of the opening. In an insightful, almost epiphanic moment, the German family is suddenly portrayed as embodying a menacing collective mentality: "What of a world in which this mentality might ever become dominant?" (101). At the end of the story, the implications are clear: the Canadians presumably return to their far-off country in the New World, while in the heart of Europe the greatest catastrophe of the twentieth century is looming on the horizon. "Many people slept until they reached Munich," Wilson concludes her story gnomically, "then they all began to wake up" (66).

"Depth must be hidden. Where? On the surface," writes *fin-de-siècle* poet Hugo von Hofmannsthal in his *Buch der Freunde* (1973, 47). Indeed, when reading Wilson's short story for the first time, lightness and humor — at times bordering on slap-stick comedy — dominate its tone, created by Wilson's wide range of irony, by the use of personification ("Beside them the hamper looked out of the window at the charming view," 58), morphological-rhetorical figures such as anaphora ("So did his wife. So did his daughter," 59) or epiphora ("Your bear? Have you a bear? But you cannot have a bear!" 61), and by syntactical-rhetorical figures such as the remarkably frequent use of parallelisms and repetitions ("'Shall we tell him?' . . . 'You tell him' . . . 'No, *you* tell him' . . . 'I do not like to tell him' . . . 'I'd rather you told him' . . . 'Very well. I shall tell him,'" 63–64). Decidedly modern — using narrative techniques like free indirect discourse, ironic and suggestive methods, featuring "ordinary people" as characters, presenting a "slice of life," starting *in medias res*, and reducing the plot — Wilson's story exposes the disparity between appearance and reality. The text generates situation comedy and character comedy, satirical, absurd, and grotesque elements; it amuses the reader, but also provokes compassionate smiles, ridicule, even malicious pleasure. The reader's sympathy is thus generally guided in favor of the Canadians, and only once, if at all, something like empathy with the German man's pride arises, a man who is more and more "tortured by curiosity" (63): "'How horrid of us, he was so pleased'" (62).

The underlying menace beneath the deceptively simple surface of the ordinary and comical is revealed early on in the story, conveying Wilson's general view that "civilisation is paper-thin," a "mere veneer over barbarism" (in Stouck 2003, 252). By anticipating the constellation of characters and the impending conflict, the title foreshadows the coercive circumstances of the story. The suggestive setting, the confinement of which mirrors the narrow-mindedness of the German family, contributes to the overall atmosphere of constriction. The train, moving ever forward, symbolizes the passing of time, as well as the fatality of historical events yet to come. The women caught in the compartment as in a trap have no possibility of escape. There are many oppositions: outer world versus inner worlds, spatial distances (Vienna, Salzburg, Munich) versus confinement (train compartment), well-kept appearance versus an unsightly blue tooth, open- versus narrow-mindedness, and well-educated polyglotism versus intercultural ignorance. Turning the tables on a typically Jamesian opposition, Wilson has the liberal, democratic New World clashing with a European patriarchal, pre-war one: Canadian civilization meets European "barbarism."

Though criticized for allegedly racist tendencies — Hilda Kirkwood, for instance, thought that the story should not have been published because of its anti-German sentiments (McComb, 473) — and although Wilson herself had severe doubts about publishing it because she herself feared being branded a racist (Stouck 2003, 75), her rather atypical political allegory has nevertheless been successful. More than fifty years after the publication of the story, the theme of dangerous narrow-mindedness and insular mediocrity as a substratum for the rise of the Nazi regime continues to provoke harsh und dismissive reactions. A typical example is Daniel Goldhagen's historical-sociological thesis *Hitler's Willing Executioners* (1996), which caused political and emotional turmoil by unmasking the Nazi perpetrators as average, petit-bourgeois citizens. In a country that in the past century has been guilty of the most devastating genocide in history, questions as to how such violence or terror can evolve at all are still of vital importance. Wilson delineates the dangerous dynamics of a vicious circle, which in her short story is reflected in Mrs. Forrester's alarming realization that "horridness breeds horridness" (62).

The motif of the journey suggests spatial, temporal, and also psychological development. But while the two Canadian ladies undergo a dynamic change of behavior and a development that takes them through a whole range of feelings, the behavior of the German man stays more or less the same. Neither the women's irony, "the key to Canadian identity" (Kröller 2004, 264), nor their pretending to fall asleep prove successful strategies for coping with the likes of him. Just as half the literary world would fall silent in the face of the Nazi regime, the women simply stop talking. Without a conciliatory end to the story, the gulf between the characters remains unbridgeable — spatially, mentally, and ideologically. The reader is left wondering: is this political allegory an example of too excessive a didactism? Is there too great a discrepancy between an — at first sight — comic fable and the allegorical weight it is then made to carry? Is the allegory too transparent or even taken ad absurdum by its exaggeration? The last point at least might well hold true. Nevertheless, Wilson correctly observed in this political allegory that Nazism did not grow out of a vacuum. And the story's last two words, an indirect call for a greater political consciousness, are applicable to today's world, too: "wake up."

Works Cited

Comeau, Paul. "Ethel Wilson's Characters." *Studies in Canadian Literature — Etudes en littérature canadienne* 6.1 (1981): 24–38.

Donne, John. *Devotions: Upon Emergent Occasions*, ed. Anthony Raspa. Montreal: McGill-Queen's University Press, 1975.

Gadpaille, Michelle. *The Canadian Short Story.* Toronto: Oxford University Press, 1988.

Gelfant, Blanche. "Ethel Wilson's Absent City: A Personal View of Vancouver." *Canadian Literature* 146 (Autumn 1995): 9–27.

———. "The Hidden Mines in Ethel Wilson's Landscape: Or, An American Cat Among Canadian Falcons." In McMullen 1982, 119–39.

Goldhagen, Daniel Jonah. *Hitler's Willing Executioners: Ordinary Germans and the Holocaust.* London: Little, Brown, 1996.

Kilgallin, Tony. *The Canadian Short Story.* Vancouver/Toronto: University of British Columbia Press/Holt, Rinehart and Winston, 1971.

Kröller, Eva-Marie, ed. *The Cambridge Companion to Canadian Literature.* Cambridge: Cambridge University Press, 2004.

McAlpine, Mary. *The Other Side of Silence: A Life of Ethel Wilson.* Madeira Park, BC: Harbour Publishing, 1988.

McComb, Bonnie Martyn. "Ethel Wilson: An Annotated Bibliography." In *The Annotated Bibliography of Canada's Major Authors*, ed. Robert Lecker and Jack David. Downsview, ON: ECW Press, 1984. 415–80.

McMullen, Lorraine, ed. *The Ethel Wilson Symposium.* Ottawa: University of Ottawa Press, 1982.

McPherson, Hugo. "Fiction 1940–1960." In *Literary History of Canada*, ed. Carl F. Klinck. 2nd ed., vol. 2. Toronto: University of Toronto Press, 1976. 205–33.

Mitchell, Beverly. "Ethel Wilson." In *ECW's Biographical Guide to Canadian Novelists*, ed. Robert Lecker, Jack David, and Ellen Quigley. Toronto: ECW Press, 1993. 98–102.

Mitchell, Beverly. "'On the Other Side of the Mountains': The Westering Experience in the Fiction of Ethel Wilson." In *Women, Women Writers, and the West*, ed. L. L. Lee and Lewis Merrill. Troy, NY: Whitston, 1979. 219–31.

New, W. H. "Critical Notes on Ethel Wilson: For a Concluding Panel." In McMullen 1982, 141–44.

———. "The 'Genius' of Time and Place: The Fiction of Ethel Wilson." *Journal of Canadian Studies* 3 (November 1968): 39–48.

Nischik, Reingard M. "The Short Story in Canada: Metcalf and Others Making It New." *Die Neueren Sprachen* 86.3/4 (1987): 232–46.

Pacey, Desmond. *Ethel Wilson*. New York: Twayne, 1967.

———. "The Innocent Eye: The Art of Ethel Wilson." *Queen's Quarterly* 61 (Spring 1954): 42–52.

Rimanelli, Giose, and Roberto Ruberto. "Introduction." In *Modern Canadian Stories*, ed. Rimanelli and Ruberto. Toronto: Ryerson, 1966. xiii–xxxi.

Smyth, Donna E. "Strong Women in the Web: Women's Work and Community in Ethel Wilson's Fiction." In McMullen 1982, 87–97.

Stouck, David. "Ethel Wilson." In *Major Canadian Authors: A Critical Introduction*, ed. David Stouck. Lincoln: University of Nebraska Press, 1984. 81–97.

———. *Ethel Wilson: A Critical Biography*. Toronto: University of Toronto Press, 2003.

———, ed. *Ethel Wilson: Stories, Essays, and Letters*. Vancouver: University of British Columbia Press, 1987.

von Hofmannsthal, Hugo. *Buch der Freunde*. Frankfurt: Suhrkamp, 1973.

Webster's New Encyclopedic Dictionary. Cologne: Könemann, 1994.

Whitaker, Muriel. "Ethel Wilson at Lac Le Jeune." *Canadian Literature* 86 (1980): 143–48.

Wild, Barbara. "Piety, Propriety, and the Shaping of the Writer." In McMullen 1982, 27–47.

Wilson, Ethel. "A Cat Among the Falcons." *Canadian Literature* 2 (Autumn 1959): 10–19.

———. *Mrs. Golightly and Other Stories*. Toronto: McClelland & Stewart, 1990 [1961].

———. "Simple Translation." *Saturday Night*, 23 December 1961, 19; abridged and reprinted as "Journal to a Fair Land" in *Reader's Digest*, April 1962, 143–44.

———. "A Visit to the Frontier." *Tamarack Review* 33 (Autumn 1964): 55–65.

———. "We Have to Sit Opposite." In Wilson, *Mrs. Golightly*, 56–66.

8: Social Realism and Compassion for the Underdog: Hugh Garner, "One-Two-Three Little Indians" (1950)

Stefan Ferguson (Meersburg, Germany)

HUGH GARNER (1913–79) IS ONE OF THE most prolific of Canadian writers. The five short-story collections (*The Yellow Sweater*, 1952; *Hugh Garner's Best Stories*, 1963; *Men and Women*, 1966; *Violation of the Virgins*, 1971; *The Legs of the Lame*, 1976) containing his best-known and most critically acclaimed works represent only one aspect of his literary oeuvre. In a career spanning five decades from the 1930s to the 1970s he published novels, around 100 short stories,[1] pieces of journalism, works of detective fiction and autobiography, and adaptations for television and radio. This productivity was a result both of Garner's provocatively anti-intellectual aesthetic credo, leading him to state that "the first duty of a writer is to entertain" (1952, n.p.), and of the necessity — emphasized by Garner himself — to earn a living as a writer. He was thus perfectly willing to produce hack-work, and to publish, re-publish, and adapt his writings as often as possible.

This attitude to creativity has proved to be a double-edged sword for Garner's reputation. While ensuring him a wide readership during his lifetime, as well as a certain amount of critical acclaim — his short-story collection *Hugh Garner's Best Stories* won the prestigious Governor General's Award in 1963 — it led the majority of critics to dismiss his work as uninspired and workmanlike. However, his best and most frequently anthologized pieces, such as "One-Two-Three Little Indians" or "The Yellow Sweater," transcend his limitations, and rank as classic examples of the Canadian short story. These are works of which Garner was justifiably proud; he describes them as being among his "favorite stories" (1952, n.p.), a judgment that has been echoed by critics, for example in Tracy Ware's statement that "One-Two-Three Little Indians" "has its place on

[1] Paul Stuewe gives the number as "an even 100 stories" (1986, 28), while Doug Fetherling talks of "between eighty and a hundred stories" (1972, 65). This emphasizes the difficulty of precisely quantifying Garner's prolific output.

the shortlist of Garner's best works and in the canon of Canadian short fiction" (1998, 72). If Garner's works are now more critically acclaimed than they were during his lifetime, it is thanks in large measure to the efforts of Paul Stuewe, a scholar and writer who has devoted considerable energies to the study of Garner. Not only did he complete Garner's unfinished police novel *Don't Deal with Five Deuces*, he has also written a biography of Garner (1988), as well as a study of the author and his work (1986).[2] It is nevertheless fair to claim that, apart from a few regularly anthologized short stories, Garner's work as a whole is still underrated today. At present, this is perhaps less due to the preferences of highbrow criticism than to Garner's being overtaken by the Canadian Renaissance in the 1960s, when new talents such as Margaret Atwood swept away the reputations of a somewhat older generation of writers like Morley Callaghan or Hugh MacLennan, drawing all critical attention inexorably to their own outstanding work.

Much of the content of Garner's work is inextricably linked to his childhood in the Toronto slum area of Cabbagetown, to which his family moved in 1919 (Garner was born in Yorkshire, England), as well as to his peregrinations as a young man, during which he not only traveled in Canada, but spent some time in a West Virginia jail,[3] fought in the Spanish Civil War, and served in the Canadian Navy in the Second World War. His interest in, and sympathy for, the underdog, his social realism, his depiction of working-class life, his deep-rooted Canadianness (his stories are almost all set in Canada, with Canadian protagonists whose names are lifted from Canadian telephone directories[4]) — all these central characteristics of his work are grounded in his experience of Cabbagetown. Garner's version of social realism, however, is at times colored by a tendency towards moralizing sentimentalism, a trait that — as we shall see — makes itself felt even in a story of the quality of "One-Two-Three Little Indians."

Stylistically and in his plot construction, Garner is no innovator, but nevertheless a master of his craft. His prose is pithy, concise, and straightforward. Sentences tend to be paratactic, and Garner avoids the use of extraneous adjectives. This prose style, devoid of superfluity, is well tailored to the requirements of the short-story genre, though it perhaps lacks the individuality that is the hallmark of the truly great writer. In their structure, too, Garner's stories reveal their author's familiarity with, and command of, the genre. His openings set the scene and draw the reader into

2 The importance of Stuewe's work to the study of Hugh Garner is underlined by the critic's own comment that "both the volume and the quality of this criticism [i.e. about Garner] are surprisingly low" (1986, 7).

3 He was imprisoned for vagrancy; see Stuewe 1988, 37.

4 For a discussion of this, see Stuewe 1986, 14.

the story in one or two sentences, the narrative is tautly constructed, and the endings suitably memorable and thought provoking, though generally without the often contrived sting in the tail that characterizes Maupassant's work, for example.

"One-Two-Three Little Indians," from the short-story collection *The Yellow Sweater* (1952), is a concise and well-crafted masterpiece of its genre. It is arguably Hugh Garner's best-known and most highly rated piece of work. In just over twelve densely written pages of text, Garner presents a tragic episode from the life of the Native Canadian Big Tom, his wife Mary, and their terminally ill baby, which by the end of the story is dead. As we will see, the story poses some important questions regarding central aspects of Garner's work, such as its social realism and its sympathy with the underdog. At the same time, in writing about Native Canadians, the author brings a new perspective to his central themes. These points will be examined in more detail below, following a close analysis of the short story.

The first three and a half pages of the story set the scene — a rather lengthy but highly effective opening section. We are introduced to Big Tom and the poverty of his home near a trailer camp in Northern Ontario, with its "cracked and dirty supper things" (225) and "mirrorless dressing table beside the stove" (226). We are perhaps surprised at this stage by unconventional gender roles when we see Tom looking after his baby boy alone. Tom is presented as a caring, sensitive man, feeding and talking to his baby, concerned with the traditions of his people, and responsive to the smells of nature around him. Indeed, a link is immediately set up between the baby and the history of the Native Canadians, with Tom telling it the "story of Po-chee-ah and the Lynx," and speaking to it in what the narrator calls "the old dialect" (225). Apart from the touch of condescension here, with Tom's speech being denied the status of a language, this passage is important in its juxtaposition of Native tradition and the child in whom the tradition is vested. In an elegiac passage that borders on the sentimental, we learn what this tradition means to Tom as he is comforted by "the knowledge that once his people had been strong and brave, men with a nation of their own" (226). One cannot help but feel that Tom sees his people nearing the end of their history, a pessimism reinforced by his own poor health, his lungs having been ruined by mining work, leaving him with a rasping cough.

These opening paragraphs also introduce the reader to Tom's wife, Mary, of whom the narrator somewhat disparagingly says that she had "learned to live in gaudy imitation of the boomtown life" (226). Indeed, the portrayal of Mary remains ambivalent. We first see her when she returns home, and her off-hand reaction to the child's sickness ("I guess it's his teeth," 227) stands in stark contrast to Tom's brooding, guilty meditation on the seriousness of the situation, "trying to diagnose the child's restlessness into something other than what he feared" (227). The reader is also struck by Mary's vanity and interest in gaudy clothes. On the other hand, her willingness to scrub trailers in exchange for a silk dress and the fact that her "silver dancing pumps" are "dirty" and have "broken-down heels" (227) introduce a touching note of pathos to her portrayal, as does the fact that, at only twenty-two years of age, she is described as "no longer pretty" (228). The impression of a young woman who would dearly love to enjoy life, but is prevented by circumstances from doing so, is heightened by Tom's gruff response to her suggestion that she might go dancing the following winter: "A lot of dancing you'll do. . . . You'd better learn to stay around and take care of the kid" (228).

At the end of this introductory section of scene setting, the reader is faced with the tragedy that will inevitably unfold: Tom says that the baby needs to be taken to the doctor for treatment; Mary replies that she cannot go, as she must work the next day. For the attentive reader it is now less a case of what is going to happen than how and when. This uneasy feeling is underlined by the narrator's effective, if slightly maudlin, image of a "moth beating its futile wings against the glass of the window" (228).

The next morning, Tom's attempts to make enough money to take the baby to the doctor's begin. He first takes baskets to the trailer camp to sell them to the tourists, equipping himself with "a bedraggled band of cloth, into which a large goose feather had been sown" (229). By thus becoming "a real Indian with a feather'n everything" (229) Tom hopes to improve his sales. How are we to interpret Tom's pandering to the expectations of the tourists? On one level, we see Tom as a victim of exploitation, forced out of desperation into a humiliating role. To characterize Tom as merely a passive victim, however, would be to miss the point that the exploitation is to a degree reciprocal. With resignation, but also with a degree of cunning, Tom turns the tourists' prejudices against them, tricking them into parting with their money for the fake experience of seeing a "real" Indian. Of course, Tom's situation is degrading in a way that the tourists' is not; he must endure being peered at like an exhibit ("They circled him warily"; "[they] approached and stared at Big Tom"; "an animal in a cage," 230). He does, however, retain a sense of dignity, a fact underlined by his polite — and not subservient — answer to a woman who, asking which tribe he belongs to, seems to expect a grunt in reply: "I belong to the Algonquins, Ma'am" (230).

In contrast, the tourists are portrayed as ignorant, prejudiced rednecks. The reader is immediately struck by their speech which, in contrast to Tom's — typographically represented as standard English — is laced with indicators of its low register: "picshus," "somep'n," "they was small," "Gawd" (231). The vulgarity of the speech underlines and heightens the rudeness of its content, as the people among other things talk about Tom as if he were not present ("I wish he'd look into the camera," 230).

Having sold a number of baskets, Tom attempts to supplement his income by rowing anglers out onto the lake. In an exchange with Mr. Cooper, the trailer camp owner, during which Tom asks if anyone is interested in going angling, he once more appears superficially "shy and deferential" (231). Again, however, Tom's behavior can be interpreted as an act, a part he is obliged to play, but which enables him at least to some extent to control his surroundings — even if, in this case, Mr. Cooper is mildly annoyed by "the overtone of servility in the Indian's attitude" (231). In contrast to the boorish vulgarity of the people Tom meets while selling baskets, Mr. Cooper displays a more subtle and thus more pernicious racism. On the surface, he treats Tom with civility and even some concern. However, this veneer of friendliness masks an attitude of unthinking condescension. This is nicely conveyed by the narrator's statement that Mr. Cooper's voice was "kind, with the amused kindness of a man talking to a child" (231); with his paternalistic attitudes, Mr. Cooper effectively denies Tom's status as an adult. Cooper's profound lack of empathy is subtly conveyed by his statement that Tom should stay at home to look after his baby — on the surface a sign of compassion, but in fact completely ignoring the Natives' precarious financial situation, which makes staying at home an impossibility. The reader's parting image of Mr. Cooper and his wife once more underlines the way they wash their hands of all responsibility, as they drive away, symbolically "leaving behind them a small cloud of dust" (232).

Before rowing out onto the lake, Tom takes over the baby from Mary, who has also been working for the Coopers. From this significant moment onwards, the little boy becomes Tom's sole responsibility. Almost as soon as he meets the man, Mr. Staynor, whom he is to accompany, Tom is greeted by more throwaway prejudice, as his baby is referred to as a "papoose" (232), a pejorative term for a Native infant. Tom "wince[s]" (233) at this, and though he retains his composure, it is clear that his attention is increasingly focused on the health of the child. The tension in Tom's situation becomes even clearer during the course of the boat trip, which Tom must see through to its conclusion in order to earn the money to treat the baby, but which at the same time exposes the child to the beating sun. This scene is narrated with the touch of an author who is a master at tugging at the heartstrings of the reader, and is not afraid to verge on the sentimental. When Garner writes, "The baby's skin was bone dry. . . . With the tips of his fingers he brushed some of the cold water across the baby's forehead. The child woke up, looked at the strange surroundings, and smiled up at him" (233), we can see that he is playing on our emotions, but we are moved all the same. On the other hand, the comparison made between a hooked fish caught by the angler and "the struggles . . . of the baby lying on the seat in the blanket" (233) may strike us as too banal to be successful. The attitude of the angler in this scene is initially characterized by the same condescending dismissiveness with which Big Tom has repeatedly been confronted. When Tom, worried by his child's condition, indicates that he would soon like to return to land, Staynor callously replies, "We've hardly started. . . . Don't worry, there's not much wrong with the papoose" (234). Staynor, however, subsequently shows genuine concern and sympathy when he realizes the state the baby is in, even cooling the child as Tom rows and paying him the full fee for the afternoon. The exchange between the two men, with its casual prejudice followed by real compassion, demonstrates how easily off-hand racism can creep into the discourse of even well-meaning people. It is thus, in the final analysis, such people's thoughtlessness rather than their active spite that makes the lives of those on the margins of society so difficult.

Back on land, Tom's first instinct is to look for his wife. She, however, has driven off minutes earlier, confirming once again in the reader's mind that the quest to save the child is to be Tom's alone. He immediately asks a group of tourists if they can drive him to the doctor's, and in their reaction we can see again that the true danger lies in a lack of respect and in disinterest. The driver agrees to help Tom (whom he refers to as "Chief"), but only after he has "take[n] the girls to the beach" (235). Of course, they do not return, and from this point onwards Tom becomes more and more a Sisyphus-like figure, struggling against all odds to perform an impossible task. He sets off "up the highway in the direction of the town" (235), like Sisyphus trudging up his mountain for the umpteenth time, and when we are told that "his long legs pounded on the loose gravel of the road, his anger and terror giving strength to his stride" (235), we might be reading a description of the mythological figure.

At this point, Tom performs what is undoubtedly the most symbolically charged act in the entire story. Seeing that the people in the cars driving past are laughing at him, he pulls off the feather he is still wearing and casts it down into a ditch. The gesture is ultimately futile and cannot keep the looming tragedy at bay, but it is still existentially powerful, constituting Tom's first explicit refusal to conform to the stereotypes imposed upon him by society.

Nevertheless, no car stops to give him a lift, and at this point the narrative homes in on Tom's thoughts and feelings as he trudges onwards in spite of the fact that "it had been hours since [the child] had cried or shown any other signs of consciousness" (236). Part of the effectiveness of this passage lies in the fact that it seems to take place in time-lapse. Within the space of two or three paragraphs the action turns from day to night; the sun sets rapidly (note the use of the word "fell"), and shortly afterwards comes "nightfall" (236). As a result, this section of the narrative has an almost hallucinatory quality to it, rendering palpable the turmoil in Tom's mind as he "stumbled along . . . while the hot tears ran from the corners of his eyes" (236). The rapid passing of time is punctuated by his attempts to revive the baby, and in these moments time slows down again, as if Tom is lurching temporarily back into harsh reality: "Making a crude cup with his hands, [he] tried to get the baby to drink. He succeeded only in making it cough, harshly," and "he waved his hand above the fevered face of the baby, keeping [the flies] off, while at the same time trying to waft a little air into the child's tortured lungs" (236). These remarkably rich paragraphs also contain moving musings on the injustice of Tom's situation. Knowing Garner's preoccupation with the underprivileged, and being aware of his social criticism, it is easy to hear his voice intersecting here with that of the narrator, which is in itself strongly focalized through Tom: "Babies did not die like this, in their father's arms, [when] there was a doctor and all the life-saving devices to prevent their deaths" (236).

Eventually, Tom must admit defeat. In a grand, if futile, gesture, he rails against existence itself: "He cursed [the stars], and cursed what made them possible" (236). As he turns and heads back home, the weather mirrors his sorrow, pouring rain beating down on him. The child is now reduced to nothing more than a "sodden bundle" (236). By the time Tom arrives back at the camp, the story has turned full circle. It is night once more and Tom is again alone with his child, waiting for his wife to get back home, though this time the circumstances are different. He goes back out into the rain to wait for Mary to return. The reader's attention is drawn to a trailer camp sign which reads "Hot And Cold Running Water, Rest Rooms. FISHING AND BOATING — INDIAN GUIDES" (237). The sign sums up with poignant irony the status of the Native Canadians. They are reduced to conveniences and commodities, sharing the status of toilets and showers. "One-Two-Three Little Indians" illustrates the possible consequences of this state of affairs.

By the time Mary gets home, evidently from a bout of drinking, Tom is beyond words and can only express his rage through violence. He pulls down his wife by her hair, but at the last moment refrains from hitting her. Realizing what has happened, and perhaps recognizing the consequences of her irresponsibility, Mary breaks down. One of her silver shoes remains stuck in the mud, symbolically representing the failure of her attempt to break free from the social constraints of her life. Tom is merely empty and numb, drained of all feeling, emotional or physical (his recurrent cough no longer bothers him). We leave the protagonists as they mourn their dead child.

This overview of "One-Two-Three Little Indians" has touched upon a number of important themes that are worth looking at in more detail. Most notable among them is the subject of race, so fundamental to this short story, yet unusual in the context of Garner's work as a whole. Garner's treatment of the topic is on a basic level straightforward and unambiguous: the story illustrates and unequivocally condemns the racism to which Native Canadians are routinely subjected. However, it can be argued that there are aspects of Garner's narrative that undermine the effectiveness of this condemnation. Firstly, it has to be admitted that there are moments in Garner's portrayal of Tom that descend to the level of sentimental cliché, reflecting stereotypical depictions of Natives, and thus detracting from the story's otherwise well-gauged treatment of race. A case in point is the passage near the start of the short story, in which Tom dreams that "once his people had been strong and brave, men with a nation of their own, encompassing a million miles of teeming forest, lake and tamarack swamp" (226). One can only agree with Paul Stuewe that this is "romantic in a way that detracts from an otherwise powerful tragedy" (1986, 30).

Then, and potentially more problematic, there is the portrayal of Mary, Tom's wife, in which, Tracy Ware maintains, Garner "lapses into what Janice Acoose calls the stereotype of the 'easy squaw'" (1998, 72). While such negative stereotyping would indeed undermine Garner's anti-racist message, I would argue that criticism in these terms is unjustified. First of all, automatically relating a flawed character to the appropriate racial stereotype is in itself a form of racism. Mary may be frivolous, but that does not make her an "easy squaw" — merely a frivolous person. Additionally, condemnations of Mary often have a misplaced censorious quality about them. Of course Mary is uncaring, but for those who live in drudgery and poverty, the small pleasures of owning a fancy dress take on an importance far greater than for those who can buy such things every week. This is not to exculpate Mary, whose behavior remains troubling. It should rather emphasize that Garner's portrayal, far from being a racist stereotype, is a psychologically plausible analysis of the effects poverty and despair can have on people.

Finally, a third criticism that could be leveled at Garner's treatment of race is that it panders to clichés of Native victimhood, both on an individual level and on the level of the race as a whole. As Tracy Ware puts it: "Has Canadian literature not seen enough dying Indians?" (1998, 74). Certainly, Tom and his family are victims both of racism and of a society that offers little hope for the poor, whatever their race. But that is not a racial stereotype, just a social fact. In addition, as we have already seen, Garner is at pains to point out that Tom, in particular, is not merely a passive sufferer, but a man who makes his own choices. This is seen most clearly at the end of the story, when Tom throws away his feather, casting off his sham identity; but we detect it too in the dignity with which, at the onset, he puts on his feather and faces up to prejudice. Though he ultimately does this out of obligation, one nevertheless gets the impression that it is a free gesture in an existentialist sense. An association with stereotypical views of Native victimhood can perhaps be argued for more strongly on the basis of the connection made in the story between the inevitability of the baby's death and the supposedly inevitable decline of the Native people (in spite of the fact that Mary is pregnant). In this context, Ware has rightly pointed out that the story's title is an allusion to an American counting song — and not to the British rhyme "Ten Little Niggers," whose title is used in Agatha Christie's eponymous novel (published in America as *Ten Little Indians*), which counts down the dead bodies until nobody is left standing. However, we must perhaps reconsider Ware's contention that this negates any suggestion of Garner's playing on the death of the Indian people, as personified by the dying child. The American rhyme may start off by counting the Indians up from one to ten, but it, too (at least in some versions) ends up by counting them back down again. An allusion to a growing, and then dying, people, thus does not seem too far-fetched, especially if we bear in mind the events of the story. Indeed, it may even be Garner's intention to make the link between the individual baby and the people as a whole explicit. We can see the connection, for instance, in the scene where Tom, singing to his son, dreams of his people's great past. And, interestingly, we can see the connection being made in the story's final words, "the vigil over their dead," where the final word seems to operate both as a singular — referring to the baby — and as a plural, thus conceivably referring to the Native people as a whole. Be that as it may, it is doubtful whether Garner's equation of the individual and the race should be a point of criticism. It should rather be taken at face value: he sees the death of an individual Native baby as a tragedy, and in the same way he bemoans the decline of the Native people and their culture. Given these attitudes, Garner should not be criticized too harshly for implying that the decline is inevitable.

What, then, can we surmise about Garner's treatment of race in "One-Two-Three Little Indians"? How can we explain the seemingly contradictory tendencies that the above analysis has unearthed, revealing as it does Garner's simultaneous sensitivity to issues of race and his tendency to cliché and sentimentality? Firstly, Garner is not concerned with what today would be referred to as "political correctness" (see also his use of the term "Indian"). This does not make his analysis of racial prejudice less effective, though it does leave it open to easy criticism. Secondly — and here we touch upon Garner's social realism and his preoccupation with the lower strata of society — the story should be read primarily as a tragedy related to poverty and the underprivileged in general, rather than to race alone. Tom and his family may thus be considered as poor people first and Native Canadians second; and they are individuals (though only superficially delineated) rather than representatives of a race. Interpreted in this way, some central aspects of the story become more convincing. We have seen, for instance, that the character of Mary can more profitably be seen against this background than reduced to the stereotype of the "easy squaw." Thirdly, we should bear in mind that Garner was a writer who was not afraid of writing for effect, even at the expense of artistic integrity. The yoking together of the baby's death and the death of an entire people may well be an example of this. Although at times this treatment seems sentimental, and though it, to some extent at least, reinforces clichéd visions of "dying Indians," it nevertheless serves to heighten the emotional impact of the story on an individual level.

Hugh Garner's "One-Two-Three Little Indians" is not only well crafted and soundly written, but genuinely moving. Although the characters are only roughly delineated, the simplicity of the characterization serves to underline the archetypal tragedy of the story. And "One-Two-Three Little Indians" does indeed come close to genuine tragedy in the Hegelian sense of a man caught between two paths, both of which can only lead to despair and catastrophe: Tom's attempts at raising enough money to treat the child effectively condemn it to death, but any attempt at finding treatment for the child without the necessary money would be equally futile.

If "One-Two-Three Little Indians" is one of Hugh Garner's finest works, it is not least because it encapsulates the themes that were at the heart of his work, at least that aspect of his work that was devoted to aesthetic achievement rather than financial gain. There is the social realism (at times tinged with sentiment), the empathy with the downtrodden, and the Canadian setting. If, however, one comes to look at the position of "One-Two-Three Little Indians," or indeed Garner's short stories in general, within the broader field of Canadian literature, it becomes clear — in spite of what has already been said — that they are somewhat outside the mainstream of Canadian literature and in some respects quite "un-Canadian." This perspective is strongly emphasized by Doug Fetherling, who states that "though he is personally Canadian to the bones, Garner is a writer whose traditions are nearly all American" (1972, 1), and by Paul Stuewe, who maintains that Garner's work "displays few signs of overt influence by any of his fellow countrymen" (1986, 4). This is not least a consequence of, as Stuewe puts it, the fact that "there simply was no popular tradition for Garner to follow" (1986, 5). Fetherling goes on to state that Garner's predecessors in terms of his social realism and style are to be found not in Canada, but in the group of American authors whose mindset was molded by the upheaval of the Great Depression: John Steinbeck, John O'Hara, John Dos Passos, Nelson Algren, and of course, Hemingway, whose characteristic style echoes through that of Garner. Indeed, Garner himself explicitly expressed his indebtedness to these authors for matters of style and technique (see Stuewe 1986, 4). Stuewe also stresses Garner's indebtedness to J. B. Priestley, suggesting that the sentimental side of Garner's work "stem[s] from a conservative, English tradition quite different from interwar American realism" (1986, 5). If Garner's predecessors are not to be found in Canadian literature, the same can be said for his followers. There seems to be little connection, for instance, between Garner and later exponents of the Canadian short story, such as Margaret Atwood or Alice Munro, whose work is fundamentally different from Garner's rough-hewn simplicity and solidity.

It is fair to say, then, that Hugh Garner, in spite of his Canadian settings and characters, is *sui generis*, a lone figure in the history of the Canadian short story and a writer who, through his explicit rejection of the trappings of literature as art, stands somewhat apart from the mainstream of literary fiction. At his best, however, as in "One-Two-Three Little Indians," he takes his place as one of the finest Canadian exponents of the short story.

Works Cited

Fetherling, Doug. *Hugh Garner.* Toronto: Forum House, 1972.

Garner, Hugh. *Hugh Garner's Best Stories.* Toronto: Ryerson, 1963.

———. *The Legs of the Lame and Other Stories.* Ottawa: Borealis, 1976.

———. *Men and Women.* Toronto: Ryerson, 1966.

———. "One-Two-Three Little Indians." In Garner, *The Yellow Sweater,* 225–38.

———. *Violation of the Virgins and Other Stories.* Toronto: McGraw-Hill Ryerson, 1971.

———. *The Yellow Sweater and Other Stories.* Toronto: Collins, 1952.

Stuewe, Paul. *Hugh Garner and His Works.* Toronto: ECW Press, 1986.

———. *The Storms Below: The Turbulent Life and Times of Hugh Garner.* Toronto: James Lorimer, 1988.

Ware, Tracy. "Race and Conflict in Garner's 'One-Two-Three Little Indians' and Laurence's 'The Loons.'" *Studies in Canadian Literature — Etudes en littérature canadienne* 23.2 (1998): 71–84.

9: The Perils of Human Relationships: Joyce Marshall, "The Old Woman" (1952)

Rudolf Bader (University of Applied Sciences, Zurich)

JOYCE MARSHALL WAS BORN in Montreal in 1913. After her education at McGill University in Montreal, she moved to Toronto where she remained throughout her life. She is well known for her translation work as well as for her contributions as a freelance editor to the Canadian Broadcasting Corporation (CBC). Her best-known translations are works of fiction by the French-Canadian writer Gabrielle Roy, for which she was awarded the Canada Council Translation Prize in 1976. Her own works comprise two novels and a number of short stories, plus many journalistic texts of non-fiction.

Her first novel, *Presently Tomorrow*, appeared in 1946, her second novel, *Lovers and Strangers*, in 1957. Both novels explore new and unusual, even delicate aspects of sexual relationships in subtle language that earned substantial critical praise: "The fine prose and the subtle exploration of character and motivations that distinguish *Presently Tomorrow* — which achieved some notoriety on publication because of its subject matter — are noticeable once again in *Lovers and Strangers*" (Weaver 1997, 745). What the relationships portrayed in both novels have in common is their precarious nature and the inherent danger of emotional misunderstandings. These aspects also appear again and again in her short stories, most pointedly in "The Old Woman," which appeared in her first short-story collection, *A Private Place* (1975), but was first published in 1952.

Throughout the 1950s and 1960s, Joyce Marshall was primarily associated with the Canadian Broadcasting Corporation's radio program "CBC Wednesday Night," which was developed by Robert Weaver in 1948 and which gave various short-story writers — among them Alice Munro and Mordecai Richler — what could be called "a listening audience" (New 2003, 173). Weaver's reputation as the patron of the Canadian short story, which he owed to his various editorships of anthologies and of the literary journal *Tamarack Review*, supported public recognition of the undisputed talents of these writers. Thus, when *A Private Place* appeared, Marshall was already a well-established Canadian fiction writer, and her collection of short stories was immediately well received.

Almost twenty years after her first success as a short-story writer, Marshall published two further collections of short fiction, *Any Time at All and Other Stories* in 1993 and *Blood and Bone / En chair et en os* in 1995. This latest collection contains seven stories in English along with their French translations, each of which was done by a different translator. During the last ten years, Marshall has also published texts of literary criticism.

Joyce Marshall's work can be seen in the tradition of well-known Canadian short-story authors and within the international mode of modernism, particularly in its exploration of human behavior based on multi-layered motivation. While the economy and subtlety of her prose are reminiscent of Ernest Hemingway and other American modernists, her probing into the human psyche appears to demonstrate more similarities with Canadian writers such as Morley Callaghan, Mavis Gallant, and Margaret Laurence. Some of her stories show a certain influence of American literary naturalism in their indications of psychological and social determinism. The story under discussion is such an example. Its connection with the Canadian variant of literary naturalism, its skilful psychological exploration, its use of specifically Canadian elements, its very fine and economical prose, and its near-perfect structure have earned it a prominent position as a Canadian masterpiece of short fiction.

"The Old Woman" can justifiably be seen as Marshall's best and perhaps her most typically Canadian story. It links its major themes with Canadian realities and mirrors its central developments against the Canadian landscape. The story deals with the basic human theme of life and death, with the dangers of fateful psychological inflexibility, and more specifically with an estrangement between husband and wife based on unequal positions in a gender conflict. The plot of the story is quite straightforward. Following the end of the Second World War, an English war bride joins her husband in remote northern Quebec, where she finds a new purpose in her life by helping French-Canadian women in childbirth, while her husband spends all his time at the power plant where he is in charge. The estrangement between the two escalates until he is killed in the turbines at the plant. But the psychological subtlety and the rich layers of meaning conveyed by the economy of the narrative discourse yield a wealth of nuances that take the reader's imagination far beyond the mere plot.

The mood of the entire story is determined by the subjective narrative voice and its closeness to the female protagonist. Both voices, narrative and figural, fall under the influence of a threatening and increasingly sinister atmosphere, heralded by the landscape and fostered by minor signposts in the shape of symbols or specific terms interspersed throughout the story. The metaphorical involvement of the Canadian landscape, which developed out of "the imaginative, but recognizable, depiction of man struggling against a vast and harsh country" (Dahlie 1985, 218) and which Marshall shares with Frederick Philip Grove, "derived from metaphysical as well as social and psychological reassessments of reality" (Dahlie, 219). In the case of a woman struggling not only against a harsh country but also against the restrictions of a narrow-minded, male-dominated society, initial illusions may quickly turn into disappointment and estrangement from her husband — a predicament depicted in this story as well as in, for example, Margaret Laurence's later novels, *The Stone Angel* (1964) and *The Diviners* (1974). Marshall's metaphysical reassessment of reality in view of the role of technology — particularly its inherent danger of corrupting the relationship between humanity and the machine — can be understood as a modernist writer's reaction to the philosophical mood of the first postwar generation, which detected a new antihumanist materialism in an age that allowed not only the nuclear bomb, but also ever more human subjugation under the dictatorship of the machine. In this mood, which was perhaps best expressed by the German philosopher Günther Anders, the story considered here illustrates the French philosopher Lamettrie's theory of "l'homme machine," in which humans gradually come to resemble the machines they originally controlled (Anders 2002, 112). The danger lies in the new determinism dictated by the age of the machine that is not based on man's fallacious control of technology but is inherent in the very nature of technology itself: the age of technology forces humanity into a certain attitude towards its achievements (Anders, 126–27).

The very first sentence of "The Old Woman" points to the estrangement between Molly and Toddy: "He has changed" (94) is Molly's first thought upon meeting him at the station. He has little to say to her, and the text repeats the adjective "strange" several times, linking Toddy's strangeness to the strangeness of the Canadian landscape in winter. He is no longer "the Toddy she had known" (94). In the first phase, the reasons for Molly's "uneasiness" (96) cannot be clearly divided between Toddy and the Canadian landscape. The loneliness and remoteness of their new home are conveyed by several observations — "more than 30 miles away" (95) and "cut off" (96) — made either by Molly in inner monologues or by the narrative voice, which, throughout the story, influences the reader to take Molly's side and to see the development through her eyes. These examples of indirect discourse mark Marshall as an avant-garde writer of the 1950s (New 2003, 167). When they arrive at their new home near the electric power plant, the close link between Toddy and the powerhouse is immediately established by his proud remark: " 'My old woman' " (95), and Molly's uneasiness is shifted from the landscape to the powerhouse, which she finds "sinister-looking" and "engulfing" (96). At the same time the growing estrangement between husband and wife is signaled by her detached reaction to "his habit of personalizing an electric generating plant" (95).

Another facet of Canadian reality is introduced when the French-Canadian operators and assistants who work for Toddy are mentioned. Toddy calls them "a lazy bunch of bums" (97), an observation that, in the course of the story, proves to be more than a boss's assessment of his employees, for it signifies Toddy's arrogant contempt for all French-Canadians based on his utter ignorance of their culture and their way of life. The relationship between Toddy and his men thus becomes an emblem of Canada's proverbial "Two Solitudes," reminiscent of Hugh MacLennan's portrayal of mutual ignorance and misunderstanding between Canada's two major cultures in his novel *Two Solitudes* (1945). While the French-Canadians mentioned in the story have well-sounding names like Louis-Paul, Lucienne, Marie-Claire, and Mariette, the names of Molly and Toddy in their ridiculous reduction to the simplicity of similar dullness (number of letters, distribution of vowels and consonants, concordance of vowels) rather suggest a pair of circus clowns. This aspect presents them as naïve and ignorant victims of a deterministic fate. At this level, the story can be seen in the tradition of North American literary naturalism and its engagement with determinism, as demonstrated in the works of such writers as Theodore Dreiser and Sinclair Lewis in the United States, or Frederick Philip Grove in Canada.

Once Molly and Toddy are settled in their home, the estrangement between them takes its unrelenting course. When they sit down to their first evening meal, he is presented in more coarse and brutish terms — "Toddy had wolfed his meal" (97) — and she realizes: "He *was* different" (97). He appears "more withdrawn than ever." The only thing that interests him, she learns, is his powerhouse with its turbines, his "old woman." Nothing else is of the slightest interest to him, not even the arrangements in their home or her activities during his long absences. Molly first tries friendly bantering, then sympathizing. "She tried constantly to build up some sort of closeness between herself and Toddy" (98–99), but all her efforts prove fruitless and futile; he has "no companionship to spare for her" (99). When Molly is so fortunate as to find a real and fulfilling task in her lonely life, he calls her activities "nonsensical" (104), and the estrangement between them reaches its climax when she visits him in the powerhouse on their last evening: "She felt he did not know who she was" (107). At this point Molly realizes that his obsession with the machine has grown into hopeless madness.

The marriage between Molly and Toddy is abortive from the outset. Their estrangement is predetermined: first by the fact that they hardly knew each other before they finally got together; secondly by the fact that the position of his wife and companion is already occupied by his "old woman," the powerhouse, and Molly is assigned the role of an unwelcome intruder in his life; and thirdly by his primitive mind being imprisoned in fixed role patterns. The rivalry between the powerhouse and Molly becomes evident when Toddy looks "elated and eager" (96) whenever he speaks of his "old woman," and at first Molly is so naïve as to allude to such a rivalry in her bantering: " 'Won't your old woman give you an evening off — even when your wife has just come from the old country?' " (97). But on the threshold of the final catastrophe she sees the bitter earnestness of this rivalry: "The struggle she had sensed without being able to give it a name had been between herself and the power-house" (107). The fixed role patterns that guide Toddy's primitive mental and emotional world may have had their basis in his long solitude before her arrival, in his being "bushed" (99). This is a typical danger for lonely people in countries with wide, open spaces like Canada. Toddy seems to have fallen into this mental state, as Molly soon detects in her efforts to build up the missing closeness between them. He believes she does not need an interest because there should be "interest enough" for her in simply being his wife (100). His wife's role is just to be present in the house and to have his meals ready for him when he gets home, while he is free to come and go as he pleases and to spend as much time as he likes with his turbines. He sees this pattern as an unalterable, God-given law, as becomes clear when he shouts at her: " 'By God — you will stay where you belong' " (105). Since he is already married to his "old woman," he has no need to adapt to that irksome intruder, Molly. At the same time, his inflexibility works as a protective shield against the truth. While Molly wonders if she should learn to ignore the truth — "She might even be able to ignore the thundering of the water" (96–97) — he withdraws from it and refuses to learn or to accept new situations. Molly ruminates: "He was a little — well, selfish about her. He would have to learn" (103). But he never even begins to take her seriously: " 'Molly, you're a fool' " (103).

The interest in life that Molly discovers for herself — her new role as an amateur midwife to poor French-Canadian women of the area — introduces the theme of life and death. The figurative language ensures that this fundamental aspect of existence accompanies the development throughout the story — for example, "the waterfall was going to live with them" (96), "this barren land" (103) — and the dividing line between life and death emerges as very precarious or even as "treacherous" as snow (96). Molly at first helps Lucienne to nurse her baby (101), then she is called to help another woman give birth, and eventually she accepts her role as a midwife, which gives her satisfaction and also social prestige among the French-Canadians. This role implies an acknowledgement, even a celebration, of life, in contrast to Toddy's denial or rejection of life, which is signaled when he comments on the birth of a baby: " 'Another French-Canadian brat' " (103). Thus, Molly and her midwifery become a symbol of life, while Toddy and his powerhouse turn into a symbol of death.

Living together cannot continue for Molly and Toddy, Toddy's inflexibility cannot hold, the conflict between Toddy's "old woman" and his wife cannot escalate any further, and neither can the estrangement between husband and wife. Toddy realizes that his wife will never succumb to the role he sees fit for her. The only "solution" to this conflict is death as foreshadowed by the numerous descriptions of a threatening nature in the story, such as the dangerous landscape, the steely coldness of the snow, the treacherous and sinister-looking waterfall, and the daunting aspect of the barren land. Finally, when the moment arrives in which Toddy falls into one of the turbines and is killed instantly, the economy of the discourse is supreme: after his movements have become "automatic," his face "empty except for a strange glitter," and his voice mute — a sort of de-humanizing process — what actually happens is only reflected by an "expression of sick shaking terror" on Louis-Paul's face and Molly's realization of "what the fear had been that she had never allowed herself to name" (107). The horrible accident is conveyed indirectly through the comments and reactions of the witnesses, and the story concludes with a brief but extremely detached exchange between Molly and Louis-Paul. She asks " 'But is he safe?' " and " 'Will he — damage the machines perhaps?' " And Louis-Paul answers: " 'Oh no. He would never hurt these machines. For years I watch him fall in love with her. Now she has him for herself' " (107). Thus, like a choric character in Greek drama, Louis-Paul gives us the final explanation: Toddy has been mystically united with the object of his great love, the machine. His obsession with an inanimate object at the expense of a real human relationship was incompatible with life, so death became inevitable. In this sense, he is now indeed quite "safe."

Toddy's mystical union with the machine is also the climax of his path to insanity, a development discernible quite early in the story when Molly first meets him at the station, and one that connects Marshall's text with the novels of Morley Callaghan and his treatment of madness (Conron 1975, 15). The fact that Toddy's departure from human companionship and from his role as a social being leads him to an insane quasi-marriage with a machine, an inanimate mechanical construction, clearly places the author in the modernist tradition, while the inevitability and the apparent self-centeredness of his path to self-destruction in a crazy fascination with technology are reminiscent of Grove's *The Master of the Mill* (1944), of Robert Stead's *Grain* (1926; see New 2003, 150), and even of Theodore Dreiser's *Trilogy of Desire* (1912–47). However, Toddy is even less fit for life than any of his literary predecessors.

It is obvious that this story — besides depicting an estrangement between husband and wife, following a road to insanity, and contrasting aspects of life and death — also offers a specific version of the gender conflict. Molly is shown repeatedly attempting to challenge Toddy's fixed gender pattern, in what W. H. New calls a more conventional system of gender encoding, by being "substantially referential in character" (New 2003, 251). This referential mode means that the male as well as the female individual each refers certain fixed activities, opinions, reactions or even ideologies to his or her ascribed role in the world. This reference then functions as a navigational tool or compass for everyday behavior. For Toddy this means sticking to his principles, asserting his seemingly God-given superiority, putting his work before domestic life; for Molly it means finding excuses for his faults and resorting to household chores. From the moment of Molly's arrival in Canada she conceives excuses for Toddy's strange behavior, adapting to her role as a good wife with a generous attitude of understanding: "She tried to soothe herself" and "he must have found it hard" (94). When she arrives at their new home and is left there alone, she first turns to her housewifely duties: "She found a pail and mop and began to clean the kitchen" (96). She keeps herself occupied for as long as she can find jobs around the house: "She would have to learn to keep busy" (97). Molly has accepted the fact that she has to adapt, while Toddy just continues with the same routines he had as a bachelor. This makes Molly wonder if he has realized that he is now a married man: "She had a curious sense that none of this was real to him" (97). But again, she finds that it is only she who is to be blamed, not he. When she eventually finds the courage to announce her need for an interest beyond the household chores, he fails to understand. Molly thus feels as if she is just another machine to him, "moving only when he tells me to move" (100), thereby reproducing the very essence of Toddy's relationship with his "old woman," which is based on male control of the female. This relationship is not guided by ethical or moral principles, but by the capacities and limitations of the machine, according to the philosophical imperative of our technological age.

The only hope for her not to lose her mind and get "bushed" in her own way is to grasp the first opportunity that comes. So when Louis-Paul appears with his request, and after him the other French-Canadians in their desperate situations, she regains a purpose in life, saving the lives of others. By accepting this challenge, Molly takes her destiny into her own hands, and her initiative must eventually lead her away from Toddy and his male arrogance, his blind obstinacy, his inability to see her needs as a human being.

This treatment of the gender theme, which may be compared to Margaret Laurence's purpose "to deal with the definition and liberation of the female" (Mathews 1978, 135) in her Manawaka novels, can be seen as a gender-specific version of the more general modernist theme of struggles against authority, of the affirmation of life in the face of a threatening, engulfing technology, and of psychic isolation. The latter theme is especially prevalent in Canadian fiction from the 1950s to the 1970s (New 1976, 233) and is accentuated in this story by the gloomy atmosphere of impending doom. Thus, Molly's situation reveals itself as the *condition humaine* of most individuals in the modern world.

Works Cited

Anders, G. *Die Antiquiertheit des Menschen. Band II: Über die Zerstörung des Lebens im Zeitalter der dritten industriellen Revolution.* 3rd ed. Munich: Beck, 2002.

Conron, B., ed. *Morley Callaghan.* Toronto: McGraw-Hill, 1975.

Dahlie, Hallvard. "Alice Munro." In *Canadian Writers and Their Works,* ed. Robert Lecker, Jack David, and Ellen Quigley. Toronto: ECW Press, 1985. 213–56.

Marshall, Joyce. *Any Time At All and Other Stories,* ed. Timothy Findley. Toronto: McClelland & Stewart, 1993.

———. *Blood and Bone / En chair et en os.* Oakville: Mosaic Press, 1995.

———. "The Old Woman." In *Any Time At All,* 94–107.

———. *A Private Place.* Ottawa: Oberon, 1975.

Mathews, Robin. *Canadian Literature: Surrender or Revolution.* Toronto: Steel Rail Educational Publishing, 1978.

New, W. H. *A History of Canadian Literature.* 2nd ed. Montreal & Kingston: McGill-Queen's University Press, 2003.

———. "Fiction." In *Literary History of Canada: Canadian Literature in English.* Vol. 3, 2nd ed., ed. Carl F. Klinck. Toronto: University of Toronto Press, 1976. 231–83.

Weaver, Robert. "Marshall, Joyce." In *The Oxford Companion to Canadian Literature,* ed. Eugene Benson and William Toye. 2nd ed. Toronto: Oxford University Press, 1997. 744–45.

10: The Social Critic at Work: Mordecai Richler, "Benny, the War in Europe, and Myerson's Daughter Bella" (1956)

Fabienne C. Quennet (University of Marburg)

WHEN MORDECAI RICHLER PASSED AWAY on July 3, 2001, Canada lost one of its most prolific and engaging writers. As a novelist and essayist, he played a prominent role in ushering Canada into the international scene of world literature. For his Canadian literary generation Richler was a pivotal figure. In several obituaries, his qualities as a trenchant satirist and keen observer of Canadian society and politics were hailed. For these qualities he has earned admiration and reaped dislike from critics, contemporaries, and readers alike. However, Richler never refrained from socially criticizing what he knew best: the Jewish community in Canada and Canadians in general.

Mordecai Richler, a third-generation Canadian Jew, was born at the beginning of the Depression in 1931 in Montreal, where his grandfather settled, having come to Canada in 1904 to escape the Eastern European pogroms. Growing up in the Jewish working-class area around St. Urbain Street, Richler attended a predominately Jewish public high school, often referred to in his work as "Fletcher's Field," run by the Protestant School Board. Later he went to Sir George Williams College, now a part of Concordia University, as an English major. In 1950, at the age of nineteen, Richler left for Europe, returning to Canada for a short period, and two years later in 1954 moved to England, where he lived for the next eighteen years. During this time he wrote five novels and a collection of short stories (Frank and Shatzky 1997, 314–15). In 1959, he wrote his first important and publicly acclaimed novel, *The Apprenticeship of Duddy Kravitz*, set in the neighborhood of St. Urbain, a place that also prominently features in his short-story collection *The Street* (1969) and in *St. Urbain's Horseman* (1971). In 1972, Richler returned to Canada and settled in Montreal, publishing a number of essay collections and three more novels, of which *Barney's Version* (1999) was to be the last before his death in 2001.

When Richler published *The Street* — a collection of stories and memoirs — in 1969, many of the pieces had already been published in magazines of the 1950s and early 1960s and subsequently anthologized. The collection was first published by the Canadian publisher McClelland & Stewart and included ten stories. The French edition, published by Éditions HMH, and the British edition by Panther came out in 1971, followed by another in 1972, published by Weidenfeld and Nicolson. An American edition was published in 1975 by New Republic Books, and two years later Penguin released another British edition. The latest edition dates from 1996 and was published again in Canada by McClelland & Stewart, with an afterword by William Weintraub.

The story "Benny, the War in Europe, and Myerson's Daughter Bella" was first published in *The Montrealer* in October 1956. This early newspaper version is only three pages long and differs in some respects from the story included in the 1969 edition of *The Street*, where it extends to almost seven pages. Michael Darling notes that most of Richler's short stories in *The Street* are "the early versions . . . published in *The Montrealer* and *New Statesman*" (Darling 1979, 157). As early as 1965, some of the stories later collected in *The Street* were broadcast on CBC Radio and read by Lewis Negin. This radio reading was released on tape by Scenario Productions in 2001 as "Stories by Mordecai Richler: 11 Autobiographical Sketches." It starts with a reading of "Bennie [*sic*], the War in Europe and Myersons [*sic*] Daughter Bella," as found in the 1956 version. Richler also wrote a television play based on this story, *The Trouble with Benny*, which was shown on ABC Weekend Television (a commercial television company which broadcast between 1956 and 1986 on Saturdays and Sundays in the Midlands and the North of England) as part of the drama series *Armchair Theatre* in April 1959. The story itself has been anthologized in various short-fiction collections.

Although Richler is best known for his novels, *The Street* established him as a writer of shorter fiction as well. Later in his career it was more in his essays than in his short stories that his talent for brevity showed; in fact, *The Street* can be considered his only short-story collection proper, although the stories' "fictional status is indeterminate" (Darling 1986, 6). The strong autobiographical element in *The Street*, which, as Michael Darling claims, "is discernible in the novels and the non-fiction as well" (Darling 1979, 156–57), is also an important characteristic of "Benny, the War in Europe, and Myerson's Daughter Bella."

The Street essentially pays homage to Richler's hometown Montreal and portrays the city at a certain moment in time, with the war in Europe and its impact on the Jewish community being one of the major concerns in the stories. Often praised as a brilliant introduction to Richler's life-long "love affair" with St. Urbain Street and its inhabitants, *The Street* captures "the local, rather than the national experience," a characteristic of the "resurgence of the [Canadian] short story" in the 1960s and 1970s (Kent 1979/80, 170). Since "regional attachments surpass national loyalties," there can hardly be a Canadian short story that can be considered representative of the country as a whole (Kent, 170). However, Richler's depiction of his hometown is not only an example of the regional short story but is an "ethnic" short story as well. Underlying both orientations is Richler's preoccupation with defining one's sense of identity — regional, ethnic, or even national. What it means to be Jewish in Canada and how the relationship between Jews and gentiles manifests itself are two of the most pertinent questions Richler poses in his work. For the author, who, according to Birbalsingh, possesses a double consciousness, "Canadianism and Jewishness, in fact, jointly form the main theme of his fiction and the chief concern of all his writing" (Birbalsingh 1972, 72). Correspondingly, the lives of the Jewish immigrants Richler presents in *The Street* are infused with a sense of finding one's place, of "constructing boundaries and assimilating territories" (Greenstein 1997, 184) within Canada.

Most of the stories in *The Street* were written during the 1950s and 1960s, at a time when Richler lived in England as an expatriate Jewish-Canadian writer (other well-known examples are Norman Levine and Leonard Cohen). His view of the past is accordingly characterized by nostalgia, humor, wisdom, and satire. He looks back at his childhood in Montreal and recaptures the vibrant community of St. Urbain Street and its surroundings, the area in which he grew up. The Montreal of the 1940s and 1950s haunts him, as Victor Ramraj writes in a critical essay. Richler himself admits in his essay, "Why I Write," published in the essay collection *Shovelling Trouble* in 1972, that he was "forever rooted in Montreal's St. Urbain Street. This was my time, my place, and I have elected myself to get it right" (Richler 1972, 19). His memoir and short-story collection form a successful attempt "to get it right" and are testament to George Woodcock's conviction that "Richler is always going back to his past" (Woodcock 1990, 34).

David Arnason claims that "the short story has been a popular literary genre in Canada, and it is the form of Canadian writing that has traditionally had the largest appeal to international audiences" (Arnason 1983, 159). Arnason further argues that Canadian writers who have been taken most seriously abroad are those who have mastered the short-story form. This is not so in the Richler's case: his literary reputation in Canada and internationally derives mostly from his acclaimed novels. But *The Street*, "so much less known than the novels, ranks . . . very high among the best of his works" (Weintraub 1996, 137). Jewish-Canadian writer Naïm Kattan wrote a passionate review for *Liberté*, while critic William French compared Richler's St. Urbain Street to Faulkner's Yoknapatawpha. In 1972 the Australian writer Peter Porter praised the British edition in *New Statesman*, and *The New York Times Book Review* celebrated the American edition as "lovely, irrepressibly alive, funny, mean, self-derisive" in 1975 (Darling 1986, 6). Although the short-story collection received excellent reviews, "it has attracted surprisingly little attention since" (Darling 1986, 6).

Within the tradition of Canadian short-story writing, Richler's stories have been regarded as extending "the urban tradition of Callaghan and Garner into the sidestreets of wartime Montreal's Jewish neighbourhood surrounding St. Urbain St." (Gadpaille 1988, 36). Morley Callaghan, whose career began as a representative of post-First World War Canadian literature of the 1920s, took modern urban life as the focus for his novels and short stories. W. H. New identifies his novels as "urban romances" in which "the moral innocents come into conflict with the streetwise and powerful" (New 1992, 165), and one can see a parallel in Richler's social and moral humanism, which leads him to satirize not only his own people but to attack all "men of uncertain ethics" (Woodcock 1990, 56). Hugh Garner's portrayal of urban settings, in his case, Toronto's Cabbagetown of the 1940s and 1950s, revealed life on the city streets in a realistic and, at times, sentimental mode. In 1949, Garner published *Storm Below*, a novel about the war at sea and the Canadians who crewed the war ships. Richler stands in the tradition of these realist writers, and within this tradition he portrays the conflicts between "Montreal's privileged insiders (Anglo-Saxon Westmount) and ethnic outsiders (the St. Urbain Street Jews, the Catholic labourers, the poor)" (New, 207). However, he also transcends conventional social realism by using satire and black comedy to great effect, particularly in his novels.

In his memoirs, the themes chronicled include events such as wars, political battles, and business ventures, and the subject is the role of the individual on the vast stage of history. In Richler's *The Street,* the one great event referred to — directly and indirectly — is the Second World War. The individual, however small he or she may be, is influenced by the events taking place in Europe and thus he or she becomes touched by world history, even on the pavements of St. Urbain Street. "Benny, the War in Europe, and Myerson's Daughter Bella" is an excellent example, as the effect of the war on the young and simple Benny Garber is one of the central topics of the story. Benny returns to Montreal having been injured in the war in Europe. Although he tries hard to lead a normal life, working in his older brother's garage, he regularly suffers from what would then have been regarded as shell-shock. This condition is characterized by a sense of dread and a fear of things falling from the sky, a condition that today would be diagnosed as "post-traumatic stress disorder," and to which Benny's family members seem insensitive. Constantly and unfavorably compared to a neighbor's son, "Shapiro's boy," Benny is regarded as a failure by his family. When he meets Bella Myerson, the unattractive daughter of the owner of Pop's Cigar & Soda on St. Urbain Street, he finds somebody who recognizes the change he has gone through during the war and who allows him to be himself. They get married and Benny's life seems to improve, but while Bella is pregnant and making plans for their future, he suffers a mental breakdown and commits suicide.

Of the ten short pieces in the collection, nine are written in the first-person singular and can be considered autobiographical sketches or memoirs rather than fiction. "Benny, the War in Europe, and Myerson's Daughter Bella" is the only example in this collection of a third-person narrative. The lack of a first-person narrator gives the impression of a non-autobiographical point of view; in fact, this story can be called the only short story proper in the collection. The autobiographical voice, so prominent in the other stories of the collection, disappears behind the narrator's; consequently, its fictional status seems to be less in question. However, in its essence it still appears to be an autobiographical piece of work. In this story the third-person narrator takes the sympathetic and ironic perspective of an interested observer who has intimate knowledge of the place and the people. Many of the narrator's comments have the feel of gossip passed among people who know the Garbers, Shapiros, and Myersons as one would know one's neighbors or acquaintances. In this regard, the names of the characters are symbolic and ironic, and characterize the narrative point of view. The narrator speaks of Benny's parents as Mr. and Mrs. Garber, denoting the hierarchy in his/her relationship to these people and revealing the distance between the generations as well. Another adult referred to as "Mister" is the class master Mr. Perkins, again a figure of authority. In contrast, the younger generation are referred to by their first names: Abe, Benny, and Bella. However, in Bella's case she is introduced, even in the title, as "Myerson's daughter Bella," which expresses the parents' authority over their children and shows that Bella, like Shapiro's boy, is defined in terms of patriarchal lineage. Bella's father is always called Myerson and is strongly identified as the proprietor of Pop's Cigar & Soda. Myerson, who has a glass eye, emanates the fatherly aura of "Pop" as he holds court in his store like Cyclops. In addition, the nickname "Pop" symbolizes the lower social standing he has within the community, especially in the eyes of Mr. and Mrs. Garber. "Shapiro's boy" is mentioned ten times in the story, which emphasizes the importance of this character for the other protagonists; at the same time he is not delineated as an individual but as a type, the son whose success brings his family a higher social standing. Equally, the narrator talks of "Huberman's boy," who is the counterpart to "Shapiro's boy" and Benny because he is said to be a crook; both boys' careers signify that one can either go up or down on St. Urbain Street. The narrator's familiarity with the characters is further revealed when he or she refers to the minor figures such as Shub, a frequent customer at Myerson's. Calling him just Shub and not offering anything further about this character adds to a sense of intimate knowledge. The narrator gives the impression of being familiar with the characters, and there is no need for further introduction of the nameless card players at Pop's Cigar & Soda, Garber's cronies who attend the wedding of Benny and Bella, and their neighbors, the Idelsohns.

The paratactic title of the short story suggests an equal amount of attention to all three parts; however, the focus of the story is clearly Benny and his family, Mr. and Mrs. Garber and their oldest son Abe. The story, like the title, begins with Benny but the war in Europe serves as a syntactic and thematic link between Benny and Myerson's daughter Bella. On the one hand it is Benny's war experience that brings them together in the first place, while on the other hand it is exactly this experience which serves as a wedge that drives them apart, leading to the tragic consequences that provide the ending. The role of the family and the effects of the war on the characters and their relationships are Richler's main concerns in this short story.

The narrator plunges into the story by introducing the protagonist Benny through the different attitudes his father and mother and his older brother Abe reveal when he is sent overseas to serve in the army. This narrative strategy, characterizing Benny through the perspectives of the other characters and talking about him from a third-person point of view, is continued throughout the story, and underlines Benny's passivity and suffering, as well as the inability of Benny and his family to communicate. The tone of the narrative point of view throughout the story is one of sympathy and irony: "When Benny was sent overseas in the autumn of 1941, his father, Garber, decided that if he had to yield one son to the army it might just as well be Benny, who was a dumbie and wouldn't push where he shouldn't" (77). Mrs. Garber has faith in Benny and believes that he will take care of himself and come back safely; his brother Abe proclaims that he will offer him a job in his garage after the war. That Benny is the son Mr. Garber can spare and has therefore given up on is nevertheless the bitter truth of Benny's life.

Seen from a historical perspective, having their sons serve in the Canadian Army during the Second World War was one of the ways in which many Canadian Jews expressed their loyalty to their new homeland. By the end of the war in 1945 almost 17,000 Jewish men and women — which at that time was ten percent of the total Jewish population of Canada — had participated in the war against fascism; more than 500 Canadian Jews died and hundreds more returned injured and wounded (Monson 2004, 185). In Richler's story, Benny is among the victims of the war, returning to Montreal with shrapnel in his leg before the war is over. He does not talk about the war and throughout the story his war experiences and the war itself remain rather abstract. Places such as Camp Borden, Aldershot, Normandy, and Holland are mentioned; and Benny, suffering from shell-shock, constantly seems to be afraid that something from above could fall on his head. Since none of his experiences, emotions, and thoughts are conveyed directly, however, the actual horrors witnessed and the pain suffered by Benny are transferred to the reader's imagination. One may surmise that Benny not only witnessed fighting, blood, and death, but also learned about the fate of the Jews in Europe. Whatever happened to Benny during the war is left unspoken, which renders it more powerful and haunting.

The fact that the Garbers are Jewish is also never mentioned directly but merely indicated in various ways. First and foremost is the mention of the street where the Garbers live, St. Urbain Street, which back in the 1950s was still the Jewish area of Montreal where the majority of first- and second-generation Jews had settled. The naming of the characters clearly denotes the ethnic and religious background of the family and is in itself highly symbolic. The first names of Garber's sons are typical Jewish names and have biblical references but are used in ironic reversals of the original meanings. The biblical Abraham (of which Abe is the short form) is the progenitor of the Jews, yet in the story Abe is unmarried and childless. Benny is short for Benjamin, Jacob's youngest and favorite son. However, in Richler's story he is clearly not the most beloved son. In addition, the various food items that the Garbers send to Benny in Europe, "parcels full of good things a St. Urbain boy should have" (77) such as herring, *shtrudel* and salami, make their religious affiliation clear, as well as the fact that Benny and Bella get married in a small synagogue.

What seems more importantly Jewish is Richler's description of the attitude of the parents to their children, and to Benny in particular. A crucial moment in Benny's school career is when his class master, Mr. Perkins, sends a note to his parents recommending that Benjamin learn a trade because he is not a promising student but could make a good and hard-working citizen. Mr. Garber does not accept this verdict and, even though he has a trade himself, he compares Benny to a boy from the same school and neighborhood, Shapiro's boy, who will be a doctor (79), a profession that, according to Richler, was "the ideal of our ghetto" (Richler 1981, 229). Although Mr. Perkins limits Benny's opportunities and degrades him to a second-class citizen (in a subtle act of anti-Semitism), Benny, putting the note in his pocket, seems to agree with Mr. Perkins' evaluation, in contrast to his father.

The Shapiros remain the touchstone against which Mr. Garber defines his family. Shapiro's boy, who seems to have everything Benny does not, also served in the army. "When Benny came home from the war in Europe, the Garbers didn't make an inordinate fuss, like the Shapiros did when their first-born son returned" (77). Obviously, the family enjoys a better social position, partly because of their son, and Mr. Garber has aspirations to rise up the social ladder by way of his children's achievements and careers. "One of the concerns of Mordecai Richler's work is describing the lives of Jewish families in their struggle for a better life" (Gadhi 1989, 99). "Better life" entails a commitment to Canadian society, in particular to Anglo-Canadian society. As ethnic outsiders, the Jews' wish to rise is the wish to find a place within mainstream society and in doing so to escape the stigma and discrimination that was the lot of most poor Jewish immigrants. During the mid-twentieth century the immigrants who inhabited St. Urbain Street "were determined [that] their children would become professionals. Kindergarten, in the eyes of their St. Urbain mothers, was the first step to the middle class, in their imagination the equivalent of pre-med school" (Grossman 2001, 3). This attitude has proven to be true and is reflected in some of the statements collected in Michael Posner's excellent biography of Richler, *The Last Honest Man*, in which, for example, Jack Rabinovitch, a life-long friend of Richler's, describes their high school as a school for aspiring kids whose parents were immigrants "who had decided that education is the avenue to prosperity" (Posner 2004, 31). Richler's classmate Sid Kastner puts it this way:

> You see, all of us were children of immigrants and we were given the opportunity to move into a world different than our predecessors. Jews before the Second World War were more closely guarded and they had fewer opportunities. . . . And Mordecai grew up in this generation, where to be a Jew was to be a second-class citizen, and therefore had to prove something. (Posner, 38)

In "Benny, the War in Europe, and Myerson's Daughter Bella" this struggle for a better and a more assimilated life is shown in the worst possible light. Human tragedy is the result when people forget their basic humanity and lose respect for the individual or sections of society. Richler's use of irony in this story is a means of criticizing a society that compels people like the Garbers, and other Jewish inhabitants of the area around St. Urbain, to prove themselves, no matter how individuals may suffer from it. He portrays the Jewish world of his childhood environment as "a confined world where people live by comfortable lies and adhere to parochial and biased notions of 'the other' " (Gadhi, 100), as a ghetto with "no real walls and no true dimensions" (Richler 1989, 10).

On returning to Montreal, the passive Benny, unable to put his experiences into words, is described as follows: "He didn't limp too badly and he wouldn't talk about his wound or the war, so at first nobody noticed that he had changed. Nobody, that is, except Myerson's daughter, Bella" (78). Benny does not seek company but, as he spends his days at Myerson's Pop's Cigar & Soda, he and Bella, who works in the store, start a silent courtship; while she is knitting, he smokes. Bella has a clubfoot, limps as Benny does, has mousey brown hair in her face, is twenty-six and destined to end up an old maid. Like Benny she is considered a failure in the eyes of her father and his customers. Yet bodily defects run in the family; Myerson himself has a glass eye, which he uses to threaten other people but which is also symbolic of his one-sided vision and the limited understanding he has of others. Their physical deficiencies mark all three as failures within the larger community. The description of Benny is just as unfavorable: he "was short and skinny with a long narrow face, a pulpy mouth that was somewhat crooked, and soft black eyes. He had big, conspicuous hands which he preferred to keep out of sight altogether" (78). That Benny prefers to be invisible has been one of his trademarks ever since his school days and is one of the reasons why, whenever Benny is asked if something is wrong with him, he answers "No. I'm all right." Benny's body and soul have suffered in the war, but he is unable to communicate his experiences, which isolates him from his family members and the other people he comes into contact with. His standard answer, "No, I'm all right," creates a parallel with his father's standard comparison of Benny to Shapiro's boy. Benny's inability to communicate his true feelings is caused by his father's materialism and hypocrisy and the pressure he imposes upon him.

The war, or rather the under-acknowledgement of the war, characterizes all of Benny's relationships. His brother Abe, happy to see him return, calls him throughout the evening "Atta boy" (77). He is pleased when Benny starts to work in his garage soon after his return and brags about Benny's war experiences, feeling fortunate not to have been in the war and proud of his younger brother: " 'That's my kid brother Benny,' Abe used to tell the taxi drivers. 'Four years in the infantry, two of them up front. A tough *hombre*, let me tell you' " (79). At the same time, Abe also belittles his war experiences: " 'Hey, when Artie Segal came back . . . he told me that in Italy there was nothing that a guy couldn't get for a couple of Sweet Caps' " (78). The situation soon deteriorates. Benny starts "to sit shivering in a dim corner, with his hands folded tight on his lap" (79), whenever there is not much to do. During rain and thunder showers, Benny locks himself in the toilet and buries his head in his knees, sweating. The only explanation he can give Abe is that it is raining. Traumatized by his war experience and the fear of destruction from above, Benny behaves in a manner neither Abe nor his parents can understand and cope with.

At first, Bella seems sensitive and understanding enough to leave Benny alone. When she asks him what is wrong with him and he answers that he is all right, she does not inquire further. Her father is not supportive of their relationship; his dismissive comment to Bella is "I need him here like I need a cancer" (80), yet after he gets used to it, he realizes that he "can't start picking and choosing" and "it's not as if [Benny] is a crook" (81). Later he even praises him: "I couldn't wish for a better one than Benny" (81), but Myerson's motives for assenting to the marriage are obviously selfish; he is glad that Bella has at last found someone to marry, even if it is just simple Benny Garber. His family's reactions are equally ambivalent. Abe again calls him "Atta boy" and wants him back at the garage; Mr. Garber is not pleased and compares him again to Shapiro's boy who married into a better family.

After his marriage to Bella, Benny seems to get better. He works hard at the garage and, with Bella's help, makes plans for the future. Only occasionally, when there is not much work to do, does he suffer from bouts of anxiety and depression, retreating into himself again. After approximately four months, pregnant Bella's planning for the future puts new pressure on him. Somebody else is planning a "better future," where he would have been content to follow Mr. Perkins' realistic evaluation of what he is able to do. Thus, Benny is not only a victim of the war but also of his parents' and Bella's ambition, and the fact that he is constantly defined by other people. Patriarchal ambition coupled with his war trauma leads to Benny's suicide, which, as Michelle Gadpaille notes, seems tragic because "he almost made it, . . . family pride (from his brother and mother), and love (from his wife and new son) could, and almost did, overcome Benny's great fear of destruction from above" (36). The obstacles to a happy ending lie in the unrealistic expectations other people have for him.

Each of the major characters fails Benny in different ways, yet their common failing is that none of them understands the impact the war has had on Benny. No one, not even his father, wants to know what the war in Europe was really like. Nobody asks Benny about it and nobody shows any interest in the fate of the Jewish people in Europe. Only Bella and his mother demonstrate some kind of genuine understanding and sympathy. By being overly ambitious and comparing him unfavorably to Shapiro's boy all the time, Mr. Garber makes simple and unambitious Benny feel inferior and a failure. He is portrayed as jealous, narrow-minded, pushy, and insensitive; his relationship towards his son is marked by tension, misunderstanding, and a lack of communication. The filial theme in Richler's short autobiographical pieces, as well as in novels such as *Son of a Smaller Hero* and *St. Urbain's Horseman*, is evident in "Benny, the War in Europe, and Myerson's Daughter Bella" as well. Whereas the father-son relationship in other stories of *The Street* is often informed by a "softening tone of fond remembrance" (Ramraj 1983, 132), especially when the father is dead, in Richler's short story "the patently strained and guarded relationship" (ibid.) between Mr. Garber and Benny is one that cannot be rebuilt; the die is cast.

Mrs. Garber is an ambivalent figure. She attempts to help Benny and to protect him from his father's constant harassment, but most of the time she comes across as a weak character who appears only to make token gestures towards defending her youngest. Repeating the phrase "Shapiro's boy" every time Mr. Garber mentions it has the effect (probably unintended by her) of emphasizing the comparison and adding to the disastrous consequences of it. His mother's behavior and failure to forcefully stand up for him against his father aggravate Benny's situation. She may love her son but can save neither him nor herself from the patriarchal authority Mr. Garber represents.

Bella at first accepts Benny the way he his, but later wants him to change and asks for the impossible. She too wants to have a better life: an apartment with a shower and a fridge, a car, and an operation on her club-foot. That Bella does not understand him becomes obvious when, on his last day, she finds him trembling on the floor. "'It's raining,' he says. 'There's thunder,'" to which she replies, "'A man who fought in the war can't be scared of a little rain'" (83). His proclamation "'Bella, Bella, Bella'" is full of resignation and the realization that Bella, after all, fails to understand him. He cannot bear Bella's expectations and he is aware that even in his marriage he cannot escape the specter of Shapiro's boy, who, as he then finds out, is Bella's doctor. The final blow is delivered when Benny asks whether Dr. Shapiro remembers that he was at the same school as Benny, and Bella tells him, "'No.'" That Benny is not present in Dr. Shapiro's memory or consciousness but, conversely, that "Shapiro's boy" has taken up such a large and overwhelming role in Benny's life is one of the final ironies. Bella wants to send for a doctor; Benny, on the verge of his breakdown and in sardonic manner, giggles and suggests it be Dr. Shapiro. While Bella calls the doctor, Benny leaves the apartment; in the morning Myerson and the Garbers tell Bella that he is dead, that he has killed himself by running in front of a car. Even after Benny is dead, Mr. and Mrs. Garber repeat their often repeated mantra, "Shapiro's boy," still ignorant of what really killed their son.

This poignant, ironic, and unexpected ending adds to the strength of Richler's short story, which has been called "a tightly packed meditation on the family unit, and on the failure of its solidarity to close the wounds of wartime service" (Gadpaille, 36). The story exhibits themes such as generational and familial conflicts, including the strained relationship between father and son, and the disastrous effects of the Second World War, not only on those who participated but also on those who were at home and did not know or want to know about what happened in Europe, particularly about what happened to the Jews.

In his writings, Richler's reminiscences of St. Urbain Street are a mixture of nostalgia and the "sharp, objective perception of his Jewish community" (Ramraj 1983, 129). In "Benny, the War in Europe, and Myerson's Daughter Bella" the portrayal of his people is informed by a perspective of detached sympathy combined with an "ambivalence and mingling of tolerance and censure" (Ramraj 1983, 129), a stance Richler takes in other of his works. The mordant treatment of his own community leads the author to take "the standpoint of the 'loser's advocate'" (Gadhi, 101–2), of which "Benny, the War in Europe, and Myerson's Daughter Bella" is an excellent example. To the extent that the story represents the satirical treatment of negative aspects of Jewish-Canadian life, even of his own life, it is typical of his other literary writings as well, since he often employs satire and irony to describe the Jewish community. In Richler's short story one detects "the angry voice of the moralist" (Brenner 1989, 153), whose social criticism is directed against the Jewish community, which often reacted toward this portrayal with resentment. Nevertheless, by criticizing the Garbers, Myerson, and Bella for their ignorance and hypocrisy, Richler fulfills his role as a social critic who aims at correcting social malaise within Jewish-Canadian society.

Works Cited

Arnason, David. "The Historical Development of the Canadian Short Story." *RANAM* 16 (1983): 159–64.

Birbalsingh, F. M. "Mordecai Richler and the Jewish-Canadian Novel." *Journal of Commonwealth Literature* 7.1 (June 1972): 72.

Brenner, Rachel Feldhay. *Assimilation and Assertion: The Response to the Holocaust in Mordecai Richler's Writing*. New York: Peter Lang, 1989.

Darling, Michael. "Mordecai Richler: An Annotated Bibliography." In *The Annotated Bibliography of Canada's Major Authors*, ed. Robert Lecker and Jack David. Vol. 1. Downsview, ON: ECW Press, 1979. 155–211.

———, ed. *Perspectives on Mordecai Richler*. Toronto: ECW Press, 1986.

Frank, Esther, and Joel Shatzky. "Mordecai Richler (1931–)." In *Contemporary Jewish-American Novelists: A Bio-Critical Sourcebook*, ed. Joel Shatzky and Michael Taub. Westport, CT: Greenwood, 1997. 314–20.

Gadhi, Abdelhafid. "A Heideggerian Evaluation of Humanism in Mordecai Richler's 'The Street.'" *RANAM* 22 (1989): 99–104.

Gadpaille, Michelle. *The Canadian Short Story*. Toronto: Oxford University Press, 1988.

Greenstein, Michael. "Third Solitudes: Tradition and Discontinuity in Jewish-Canadian Literature." In *Canadian Culture: An Introductory Reader*, ed. Elspeth Cameron. Toronto: Canadian Scholar's Press, 1997. 179–87.

Grossman, Ron. "The Us-and-Them Universe of Writer Mordecai Richler." *Chicago Tribune* 22 (July 2001): 3.

Kent, David A. "Two Attitudes: Canadian Short Stories." *Essays on Canadian Writing* 16 (Fall/Winter 1979/80): 168–78.

Monson, David. "'The Chosen People': Who Chose Canada." 19 August 2004. http://www.collections.ic.gc.ca/heirloom_series/volume 1/chapter 5/184–189.htm.

New, W. H. *A History of Canadian Literature*. 2nd ed. New York: New Amsterdam Books, 1992 [1989].

Posner, Michael. *The Last Honest Man: Mordecai Richler: An Oral Biography*. Toronto: McClelland & Stewart, 2004.

Ramraj, Victor J. *Mordecai Richler*. Boston: Hall, 1983.

Ramraj, Victor J. "Mordecai Richler: Biocritical Essay." 9 February 2004. http://www.ucalgary.ca/library/SpecColl/richlerbio.htm.

Richler, Mordecai. "Benny, the War in Europe, and Myerson's Daughter Bella." In Richler, *The Street*, 77–83.

———. *Shovelling Trouble.* Toronto: McClelland & Stewart, 1972.

———. *Son of a Smaller Hero.* Toronto: McClelland & Stewart, 1989.

———. *The Street.* With an Afterword by William Weintraub. Toronto: McClelland & Stewart, 1996.

———. "Their Canada and Mine." In *The Spice Box: An Anthology of Jewish Canadian Writing*, ed. Gerri Sinclair and Morris Wolfe. Toronto: Lester & Orpen Dennys, 1981. 224–36.

Weintraub, William. "Afterword." In Richler 1996, 133–37.

Woodcock, George. *George Woodcock's Introduction to Canadian Fiction.* Toronto: ECW Press, 1993.

———. *Introducing Mordecai Richler's "The Apprenticeship of Duddy Kravitz": A Reader's Guide.* Toronto: ECW Press, 1990.

11: Myth and the Postmodernist Turn in Canadian Short Fiction: Sheila Watson, "Antigone" (1959)

Martin Kuester (University of Marburg)

> How dimly the light filters through the broken fragments gathered carelessly, pieced together when the sharp edges set in motion the curious workings of the fancy. . . . (Watson 1992, 36)

ALTHOUGH HER LITERARY OEUVRE is relatively small, Sheila Watson (1909–98) has been recognized as one of the most important and influential writers in postwar Canada. Up until the early 1990s, she was known mainly for her novel *The Double Hook*, published in 1959. The scantness of her publications seems to apply to information about her life as well. In Stephen Scobie's words, "the major fact about Sheila Watson's biography is that she does not have one; or, rather, that she would regard it as irrelevant" (Scobie 1985, 259; see also Bessai and Jackel 1985). She was born into the family of the superintendent of the British Columbia Provincial Mental Hospital in New Westminster and was brought up in the Catholic faith — a background that is, despite Scobie's remark, of utmost importance in understanding her work. This is especially the case in relation to "Antigone," as Watson herself states that her father insisted on a humane treatment regime for his patients, creating in the process an "experimental farm" rather than an asylum (Meyer and O'Riordan 1984, 165). She attended the University of British Columbia, receiving a B.A., a Teaching Certificate, and an M.A. in the early 1930s. She then worked as a teacher at various schools in British Columbia, including some very remote parts of the province, which provided the settings for her novels. She married the poet Wilfred Watson and attended the University of Toronto, where she completed her dissertation on the modernist writer Wyndham Lewis under the direction of Marshall McLuhan. Afterwards she and her husband took up teaching positions in the English Department at the University of Alberta in Edmonton. Upon their retirement, the couple moved to the West Coast and settled on Vancouver Island, where Sheila Watson died in Nanaimo in 1998.

Only in 1992, when she was well into her eighties, did Sheila Watson finally publish a second novel, *Deep Hollow Creek*, which she had written much earlier, in the 1930s. Her first published novel *The Double Hook* has been hailed as a central text of literary modernism in Canada, and the second published novel resembles it as far as setting and style are concerned, even though the influence of the British literary tradition is much more obvious than in *The Double Hook.* Leading contemporary Canadian authors such as the novelists George Bowering and Robert Kroetsch — both writers from western Canada — have pointed out the enormous influence that Watson's austere modernist style has had on their work. Kroetsch refers to *The Double Hook* as one of the "classic modern novels in the English-Canadian tradition" (Kroetsch 1989, 109), but he also points to the relationship between Old World and New World belief systems in the novel: in *The Double Hook*, Kroetsch claims, "the Old World's beliefs come under pressure from the physical experience, and the gods, of the New World" (Kroetsch, 185); the New World gods are represented especially by the trickster figure of Coyote, looking down on the isolated valley in which the novel is set.

With only a handful of short stories — six sparse and taut texts, "Rough Answer" (1938), "Brother Oedipus" (1954), "The Black Farm" (1956), "Antigone" (1959), "The Rumble Seat" (1975), and "And the Four Animals" (1980) — Watson has also left her mark on the short-story genre. Although Michelle Gadpaille, in her otherwise very useful introduction to the Canadian short story, claims that "the dense mythical parables of Sheila Watson" lie "outside the main traditions" (Gadpaille 1988, viii) of the genre in Canada, there is no doubt that these stories deserve more than just a passing mention. They were published in Canadian journals years apart from each other before some were first collected under the title *Four Stories* in 1979, then five years later — with the inclusion of an additional story — as *Five Stories*, and finally — with the addition of an earlier story from the 1930s — as *A Father's Kingdom* in 2004. While the first story, "Rough Answer," is a realistic depiction of a young schoolteacher arriving in a remote area to practice her profession, three of the narratives — "Brother Oedipus," "The Black Farm," and "Antigone," all from the 1950s — can be interpreted as parodic versions of Greek mythology transplanted into the environment of a mental hospital in twentieth-century Canada. "The Rumble Seat," on the other hand, is a later addition that started off as a parody of the style of Canadian author and TV personality Pierre Berton. In the very short last story of the 1984 collection, "And the Four Animals," Watson seems to be returning to (or preparing, see Scobie, 276) a mythologically haunting setting reminiscent of but even sparser than that of *The Double Hook.*

The "kingdom" of the mental hospital around which the "mythic cycle" (Irvine 1999, 115, quoting Watson's essay on "Myth and Counter-Myth") of the first four stories revolves is of course autobiographically motivated. Early interpretations only use these stories in order to back up readings of *The Double Hook* (Morriss 1969) or insist that they "resist intelligence and rely heavily on symbol," thus emphasizing the disparity between signifier and signified (Marta 1980, 55). More recent studies pay closer attention to the mythological content. What these four stories have in common is that the names of the characters and part of the action are based on Greek mythology — especially Sophocles' Theban plays (Grady 1980, 8) — as the titles "Brother Oedipus" and "Antigone" indicate. The British author and scholar Robert Graves claimed in *The Greek Myths* — published around the time these stories were written — that even "an educated person is now no longer expected to know (for instance) who Deucalion, Pelops, Daedalus, Oenone, Laocoön, or Antigone may have been" (Graves 1960, 1: 11). By contrast, the Canadian critic Judith Miller assumes "that readers know the classic story of Antigone and her defiance of the King of Thebes, and will appreciate how the author changes it in giving it a contemporary setting" (Miller 1987, 213). Miller, like Valerie Legge in her later essay, elaborately and insightfully identifies the classical and biblical sources that Watson makes use of. But, of course, the identification of sources does not exhaust the significance of Watson's treatment of myth.

At the very beginning of the first story in the series, "Brother Oedipus," readers are implicitly warned by the narrator not to take the "typological" reading of the story, that is, the equation of Greek gods and twentieth-century characters, too far. The reason underlying the naming of the narrator's brother Oedipus by his parents remains something of a mystery and resists straightforward explanation. His father, a psychiatrist, may have chosen the name "in some moment of illumination as he snipped and sewed together fragments of human life." His mother "gave no reason for anything she did," but on the other hand, of all the children in the family, "Oedipus was most attached to our mother." His brothers and sisters (as opposed to Watson's readers) do not even seem to be aware of the connotations his name has acquired over time, as they rather "contented [themselves] with learning to pronounce the name" ("Brother Oedipus," 15). They also call Oedipus Puss-Puss or Boots, associating him with an English myth quite different from the classical one we would have expected in the context of a psychiatric hospital.

An analysis of "Antigone" is helped by a basic knowledge of Greek mythology. In an interview, Sheila Watson claims that the story is about "an essential question — what is madness?" (Meyer and O'Riordan, 165). It starts with a reference to the first-person narrator's father, who "ruled a kingdom on the right bank of the river" ("Antigone," 51). A psychiatrist in a mental hospital, he is a man who "ruled men who thought they were gods or the instrument of gods or, at the very least, god-afflicted and god-pursued" ("Antigone," 51). Among his patients are Atlas, Hermes, Helen, Pan, and Kallisto. Like the disinherited Titans of Greek mythology, these gods had to surrender all divine pretensions: sober, serious, and severe, the narrator's father "watched over them as the hundred-handed ones watched over the dethroned Titans so that they wouldn't bother Hellas again" (51).

The narrator of "Antigone" is the son of the nameless doctor-king (nonetheless identified as Creon by most critics) who reigns over the asylum. The narrator himself is often identified as Haemon (Miller, 213, for example), although he, too, remains unnamed throughout Watson's story. Glenn Willmott adds weight to the theory that he may be a reincarnation of Haemon by mentioning in the afterword to the 2004 edition of Watson's complete stories that Watson had considered "Haemon's Story" as an alternative title for "Antigone" (Willmott 2004a, 97). His role as narrator and possibly disappointed lover may well be seen as a certain improvement on Haemon's dismal fate in the Greek myth, where he ends up slain by his own hand (see Ventura 1996, 185). In Watson's story, he grows up with his two cousins, Antigone and Ismene, and repeatedly affirms that his close relationship with these girls on the grounds of the mental hospital is the beginning of all evil: "if my father had had all his wits about him he would have sent me to a boarding school" (52) to avoid any kind of incestuous entanglements, which are amply suggested by the mythological names chosen for the children. Instead, however, the narrator indeed falls in love with one of his cousins, "who, except for the accident of birth, might as well have been my sisters" (52). For some reason he even chooses the wilful and impetuous Antigone rather than the more rational (or less idealistic) Ismene, who is willing and able to accept the rules imposed by the doctor-king. Antigone, however, like her classical counterpart, cannot and will not accept the arbitrary order imposed by her uncle. In Valerie Legge's words, "extreme rationalism confronts unrestrained passion" (Legge 1992, 32; see also Ventura, 191).

Having introduced himself and the other main characters of the story, the narrator interpolates the description of the Fraser River that separates "the wilderness" on the left bank from "the kingdom which my father ruled" (53) on the right bank, representing civilization together with "the convent, the churches, and the penitentiary" (55). This interpolation gives him the opportunity to illustrate Antigone's way of thinking. The river that symbolizes a frontier is spanned here by not one but two bridges, which makes her wonder how often one can cross the same river. The narrator is annoyed at this question and insists that "Heraklitos made nonsense of her question years ago" (53). He also points out once again that the mythical and geographical nomenclature of ancient Greece is not to be fully recovered in the context of this story — contemporary Canada is not typologically related to classical Greece: "[Heraklitos] saw a river too — the Inachos, the Kephissos, the Lethaios. The name doesn't matter. He said: See how quickly the water flows. However agile a man is, however nimbly he swims, or runs, or flies, the water slips away before him" (53). But

Antigone is willing to qualify the philosopher's insight by stating that "one must admit that it is the same kind of water" that is crossed the second time; it is populated by the same kind of fish, the oolichan, and the same kind of birds. Antigone thus repudiates the orderly, "scientific," and rational structure of the world to which her sister Ismene has adapted (Miller, 220–21) by refusing to subscribe to logical, pre-ordained truths; Antigone points out, for example, that not everybody wants to cross the river: "Men have walked into the water, she says, or, impatient, have jumped from the bridge into the river below" (54). And she complains about "her own misery" in the life she has to bear, although the narrator insists that "only a god has the right to say: Look what I suffer. Only a god should say: What more ought I to have done for you that I have not done?" She accepts neither Heraklitos's paradox nor Ismene's philosophical "diagrams to live by, cut and fashioned after the eternal patterns spied out by Plato as he rummaged about in the sewing basket of the gods" (56). Ismene, who the narrator thinks he should have loved (but does not), "managed somehow to see [the world] round," although she, like everyone, "walked the flat world with us." Antigone, on the other hand, does not follow the rational and unfeeling rules imposed by science but feels and thinks like the patients (and her cousin) in the asylum. In the narrator's words,

> Antigone is different. She sees the world flat as I do and feels it tip beneath her feet. She has walked in the market and seen the living animals penned and the dead hanging stiff on their hooks. Yet she defies what she sees with a defiance which is almost denial. Like Atlas she tries to keep the vaulted sky from crushing the flat earth. Like Hermes she brings a message that there is life if one can escape to it in the brush and bulrushes in some dim Hades beyond the river. It is defiance not belief and I tell her that this time we walk the bridge to a walled cave where we can deny death no longer. (56–57)

Almost imperceptibly, after the narrator's oblique reference to the "walled cave" or grave that awaits all of us, the story then switches from this scene depicting Antigone's personality to that of her open defiance of her uncle's rules and regulations. It is probably the bust of the explorer Simon Fraser overlooking the valley of the river named after him that makes the children think of death and burial. While Ismene proves again to be a rationalist, stating that it is the head that counts, Antigone insists about the bust that "it's no better than an urn . . . one of the urns we see when we climb to the cemetery above" (55). The narrator's own wish for nothing but a green grave with a chain about it brings us back to the classical intertext of Antigone wanting to honor the body of her dead brother who, according to Creon's orders, is "to be left unburied, left to be eaten / By dogs and vultures" (Sophocles 1974, 131): "A chain won't keep out the dogs, Antigone said" (56).

While in Sophocles' play Antigone decides to bury her brother's corpse, against the king's interdiction, here we are also dealing with a burial, but apparently one of lesser importance: "Antigone has cut out a piece of sod and has scooped out a grave. The body lies in a coffin in the shade of the magnolia tree. Antigone and I are standing. Ismene is sitting between two low angled branches of the monkey puzzle tree" (58). Only on the next page do we realize that what she is going to bury is a sparrow, whose classical forebear is compared to an angry bird screaming "when it finds its nest left empty and little ones gone" (Sophocles, 137). This funeral — which is quite different from the classical Antigone's "funeral" of her brother and, of course, also from that of the classical Antigone herself — inspires apocalyptic "private poetry" and religious litanies in the narrator ("Between four trumpeting angels at the four corners of the earth a bride stands before the altar in a gown as white as snow," 58) and a carnivalistic, party-like atmosphere among the inmates, who bring pink fish sandwiches. Still, when the narrator's father, the doctor-king, appears and accuses Antigone of having used public property for her private burial ceremony, she challenges him: "Things have to be buried, she says. They can't be left lying around anyhow for people to see" (61), and "I've taken six inches, Antigone says. Will you dig the bird up again?" (63). While Creon had savagely punished her classical ancestor, his twentieth-century incarnation — who otherwise insists on discipline — remains surprisingly calm in the heated atmosphere, which carries apocalyptic overtones: "But, as I look, I see the buds falling like burning lamps and I hear the sparrow twittering in its box: Woe, woe, woe because of the three trumpets which are yet to sound" (62). The doctor-king keeps his temper. As the last sentence of the story tells us, "From Antigone he simply turned away" (63).

Even though Judith Miller argues that "in his dismissal of her, he pronounces Antigone dead, as Sophocles' Creon tried to pronounce Antigone dead when she defied him" (Miller, 216), Watson's Antigone remains unpunished for her act of defiance, the burial of a dead bird (rather than a dead brother) on public ground. Haemon (or rather, his unnamed counterpart) also lives on to tell the story. The modern Creon's kingdom is "but a demented inversion of Greek myths and Greek tragedies" so that, as Shirley Neuman states, "this modern parable provides no moral resolution of its dualities but leaves us with the irresolution of the question implicit in the final scene in which Creon turns his back on his defiant niece: what can a character like Antigone do, how can she rebel, with no figure to rebel against?" (Neuman 1982, 48). The motivation behind Watson's new version of old myths is that of demythologization (see Grady, 8) and of playful, parodic adaptation. It seems to tell us that Greek myths do and do not work in twentieth-century British Columbia, but Legge also draws our attention to the fact that Antigone's act "questions the distinction between madness and sanity, complacency and complicity" and that "through the antagonistic figures of the paternal Creon and his obstinate niece, Watson constructs a literary paradigm which deconstructs the commonly held assumption that community and government in Canada are peaceable and orderly" (Legge, 29).

In what context could we then see Watson's use of myth here? While in ancient Greece, mythology was "a system of hereditary stories which were once believed to be true by a particular cultural group, and which served to explain . . . why the world is as it is," more recently anthropologists such as Claude Lévi-Strauss have studied "the myths of a particular culture as signifying systems whose true meanings are unknown to their proponents" (Abrams 1988, 111). Lévi-Strauss also worked on Native North American mythology, a mythology that plays an important part in Watson's writing. This is especially true of her novels, about which Watson says in an interview, "I was concerned . . . with the problem of an indigenous population which had lost or was losing its own mythic structure, which had had its images destroyed, its myths interpreted for it by various missionary societies and later by anthropologists" (Watson in Meyer and O'Riordan, 159).

According to one of the best-known dichotomies underlying the Lévi-Straussean concept of myth, myths are produced not by the organized and organizing mind of an *engineer* but rather by the savage mind of the *bricoleur*. Myths often "look more or less like shreds and patches, if I may say so; disconnected stories are put one after the other without any clear relationship between them" (Lévi-Strauss 1978, 34). Mythical thinking, as with that of the Natives of Watson's British Columbia, thus builds narratives that are loosely structured around the "odds and ends" of history (see Lévi-Strauss 1962, 32) or, in Watson's own words, around its "broken fragments gathered carelessly" (Watson 1992, 36). Sheila Watson has thus built her own mythical story in a similar fashion to the way traditional North American Native myths were constructed, by re-assembling mythemes gathered from various myths and legends. Most of her short stories feature characters drawn from classical Greek mythology, while in her novels, references are more frequently made to Native North American mythology, including such characters as the trickster figure Coyote.

Several critics have pointed out the parallels between James Joyce's use of classical myth in *Ulysses* and that in Watson's stories. We might see Watson's "Antigone" as another example of Joyce's "mythical method," which T. S. Eliot found to underlie the structure of *Ulysses* in his famous review of the novel — alluded to by Glenn Willmott in the title of his paper "Antigone, Order, and Myth." But although Willmott is insightful in his reading of "Brother Oedipus" and "Antigone" in the light of Eliot's concept of classical and vegetation myths, there is a major difference between the traditional modernist use of myth and Watson's appropriation of it. Following Canadian theorists and writers such as Robert Kroetsch, we can distinguish between the use of myth by writers representing modern and postmodern views of the world. In Kroetsch's words, "the Modernist was tempted by the cohesive dimension of mythology, while the Postmodernist is more tempted by those momentary insights that spring up here and there" (Neuman and Wilson 1982, 112). According to Kroetsch, "we are entrapped in those mythic stories; we can surrender to them or tell our way out" (Neuman and Wilson, 96). Kroetsch states about his own use of Native mythology that "there was a sense of being free from its residue of meaning that was very exhilarating" (97). In this sense, Kroetsch and Watson share a postmodern sensibility.

This postmodern attitude towards Native mythology leads back, as Kroetsch himself indicates, to Lévi-Strauss. Watson also draws attention to the ways in which the French structuralists Lévi-Strauss and Roland Barthes have defined and used the concept of myth. In her essay "Myth and Counter-Myth," which for the most part focuses on Wyndham Lewis's use of myth, she starts out by mentioning Lévi-Strauss's study of the structure of myths and Barthes's investigation of myths as sign systems. She refers especially to Barthes's concept of myth as a "stolen language," in which stories and story elements are taken from their original contexts and used in new ones by later generations and other tribes. Thus, according to Barthes, "the best weapon against myth is perhaps to mythify it in its turn, and to produce an artificial myth" (Watson 1975, 130). In the same way as the doctor-king reassembles the identities of his patients from the bits and pieces of destroyed personalities, Watson herself uses mythical elements — Native North American ones in her novels and ancient Greek ones in her stories — in order to create a new, postmodern kind of mythology. We can agree with Glenn Willmott when he admits that "we may first believe the stories to be constructed of fragmentary puzzle pieces of dialogue, image and gesture" and that "the task of gluing such fragments together — as we might in Ezra Pound's *Cantos*, for instance — here defeats us" (Willmott 2004a, 91). While Pound himself became a sort of prophet of postmodernity by exclaiming in Canto CXVI, "I cannot make it cohere" (Pound 1970, 118), Willmott shows that Watson, although strongly influenced by Eliot's mythical method, "turns these foundations to existential rather than transcendental ends" by playing "freely with aboriginal heritage" and by "appropriat[ing] mythic figures and motifs, abstracting them out of their specific, social, and historical grounds of meaning." As a qualification to Willmott's statement that "she reproduces an important aspect of aboriginal heritage in her own modern context" (Willmott 2004b, 6), I would claim that Watson does so in a demythologizing and postmodern way, in which the aboriginal heritage shows especially in the structure of her mythological composition of a coherent whole from "odds and ends" or "broken fragments," whereas the fragments themselves are adopted from European mythology.

Héliane Ventura interprets Watson's "Canadian recasting" of Greek mythology as "a displacement of the tragic into the lunatic" (186) in the context of many modern Canadian instances "of the invention of tradition through the reinterpretation of mythic patterns or stories" (Ventura, 183). I would add that Watson's rather ludic use of classical mythology in her short stories — and of many other materials gathered from folklore as well as the Christian tradition — corresponds to a tendency in contemporary Canadian poetry that Walter Pache refers to as the creative use of mythology in the form of "playful 'appropriations' by contemporary writers who show themselves familiar with classical myth without being imprisoned by it" (Pache 1991, 155). So Stephen Scobie is right when on the one hand he praises Watson for having "placed the Canadian novel firmly within the modernist tradition," while on the other hand he insists on her having "anticipated much of what we are forced to call, for want of a better word, post-modernism" (Scobie, 269; see also New 1987, 106–7 and Willmott 2004b). Her postmodernity, I would claim, shows especially in her short stories and their structure. In whatever way we classify Watson's "Antigone," the reader will see beyond the "broken fragments gathered carelessly" a rich structure full of mythical allusions to established plots that are deconstructed and re-interpreted in a contemporary Canadian context.

Works Cited

Abrams, M. H. *A Glossary of Literary Terms.* Fifth edition. Fort Worth: Holt, Rinehart and Winston, 1988.

Bessai, Diane, and David Jackel. "Sheila Watson: A Biography." In *Sheila Watson and* The Double Hook, ed. George Bowering. Ottawa: Golden Dog, 1985. 3–5.

Gadpaille, Michelle. *The Canadian Short Story.* Toronto: Oxford University Press, 1988.

Grady, Wayne. "The Riddles of the Shrinks." Review of *Four Stories* by Sheila Watson. *Books in Canada* 9.2 (February 1980): 8.

Graves, Robert. *The Greek Myths.* 2 vols. 1955. Revised edition. Harmondsworth: Penguin, 1960.

Irvine, Dean. "Oedipus and Anti-Oedipus, Myth and Counter-Myth: Sheila Watson's Short Fiction." In *Dominant Impressions: Essays on the Canadian Short Story*, ed. Gerald Lynch and Angela Arnold Robbeson. Reappraisals: Canadian Writers 22. Ottawa: University of Ottawa Press, 1999. 115–25.

Kroetsch, Robert. *The Lovely Treachery of Words.* Toronto: Oxford University Press, 1989.

Kuester, Martin. "(Post-)Modern Bricolage: The Use of Classical Mythology in Sheila Watson's Short Stories." *Zeitschrift für Anglistik und Amerikanistik* 42.3 (1994): 225–34.

Legge, Valerie. "Sheila Watson's 'Antigone': Anguished Rituals and Public Disturbances." *Studies in Canadian Literature / Études en littérature canadienne* 17.2 (1992): 28–46.

Lévi-Strauss, Claude. *La pensée sauvage.* Paris: Plon, 1962.

———. *Myth and Meaning.* London: Routledge, 1978.

Marta, Jan. "Poetic Structures in the Prose Fiction of Sheila Watson." *Essays on Canadian Writing* 17 (1980): 44–56.

Meyer, Bruce, and Brian O'Riordan. *In Their Words: Interviews with Fourteen Canadian Writers.* Toronto: Anansi, 1984.

Miller, Judith. "Rummaging in the Sewing Basket of the Gods: Sheila Watson's 'Antigone.'" *Studies in Canadian Literature* 12.2 (1987): 212–21.

Morriss, Margaret. "The Elements Transcended." *Canadian Literature* 42 (1969): 56–71.

Neuman, Shirley. "Sheila Watson." In *Profiles in Canadian Literature 4*, ed. Jeffrey M. Heath. Toronto: Dundurn, 1982. 45–52.

Neuman, Shirley, and Robert Wilson. *Labyrinths of Voice: Conversations with Robert Kroetsch.* Edmonton: NeWest, 1982.

New, W. H. *Dreams of Speech and Violence: The Art of the Short Story in Canada and New Zealand.* Toronto: University of Toronto Press, 1987.

Pache, Walter. "Modern Canadian Poetry and the Classical Tradition." In *Probing Canadian Culture*, ed. Peter Easingwood, Konrad Groß, and Wolfgang Klooß. Augsburg: AV-Verlag, 1991. 141–56.

Pound, Ezra. *Selected Cantos.* New York: New Directions, 1970.

Scobie, Stephen. "Sheila Watson (1909–)." In *Canadian Writers and Their Work*, ed. Robert Lecker, Jack David, and Ellen Quigley. Fiction Series, vol. 7. Toronto: ECW Press, 1985. 259–312.

Sophocles. *Antigone.* In *The Theban Plays*, trans. E. F. Watling. 1947. Harmondsworth: Penguin, 1974. 126–62.

Ventura, Héliane. "'The Energy of Reiteration': Sheila Watson's 'Antigone.'" *RANAM* 29 (1996): 183–98.

Watson, Sheila. "And the Four Animals." In Watson, *A Father's Kingdom*, 81–86.

———. "Antigone." In Watson, *A Father's Kingdom*, 49–63.

———. "The Black Farm." In Watson, *A Father's Kingdom*, 29–48.

———. "Brother Oedipus." In Watson *A Father's Kingdom*, 13–27.

———. *Deep Hollow Creek.* Toronto: McClelland & Stewart, 1992.

———. *The Double Hook.* 1959. New Canadian Library. Toronto: McClelland & Stewart, 1989.

Watson, Sheila. *A Father's Kingdom: The Complete Short Stories.* Toronto: McClelland & Stewart, 2004.

———. *Five Stories.* Toronto: Coach House Press, 1984.

———. *Four Stories.* Toronto: Coach House Press, 1979.

———. "Myth and Counter-Myth." In *Sheila Watson: A Collection. Open Letter* 3.1 (1975): 119–36.

Willmott, Glenn. "Afterword." In Watson, *A Father's Kingdom*, 87–98. 2004a.

———. "Antigone, Order, and Myth." Unpubl. ms. of a paper given at the ACQL conference in Winnipeg, May 2004. 2004b.

12: The Modernist Aesthetic: Hugh Hood, "Flying a Red Kite" (1962)

Jutta Zimmermann (University of Jena)

IN SPITE OF CRITICAL CONTROVERSY over Hugh Hood's place in Canadian literary history, it is safe to say that his literary oeuvre occupies a unique position in the canon owing to the way in which he combines an overt Christian content with a decidedly modernist form. In a more immediate way than is perhaps the case with most writers, Hood's literary career seems to have been shaped by his family background and academic training. Born in 1928 to Catholic parents in Toronto, Hood went to a Catholic school, received a Ph.D. in English at the University of Toronto, and taught at a college in the United States before establishing himself as a professor of English in Montreal in 1961. He emerged as a writer in 1962 when his first short-story collection, *Flying a Red Kite*, was published. In his prolific literary career, which spanned four decades — Hood died in 2000 — he published nine more collections of short stories (*Around the Mountain: Scenes from Montreal Life*, 1967; *The Fruit Man, the Meat Man and the Manager*, 1971; *Dark Glasses*, 1976; *None Genuine without This Signature*, 1980; *August Nights*, 1985; *A Short Walk in the Rain*, 1989; *The Isolation Booth*, 1991; *You'll Catch Your Death*, 1992; and *After All!*, 2003) and seventeen novels — among them a series entitled The New Age, which tells the story of Canada's coming of age in the twentieth century and is modeled on Marcel Proust's *A la recherche du temps perdu*. Hood's entire oeuvre is marked by his religious belief and his concern with the spiritual dimension of human existence. Rather than conveying any dogmatic religious position, however, Hood explores the relation between the mundane and the spiritual, the "secular and sacred experience" (Lecker 1982, 99). "Canada's most learned, most intellectual writer" (Keith 1980, 28) has never been a popular writer, and critics are divided about his role in Canadian literature. Admirers praise his work as an exceptional literary achievement. While lauded "as one of Canada's most versatile, sophisticated, and aesthetically self-conscious fiction writers" (Lecker 1986, 226), he is also criticized for his "unfashionably exemplary fiction" (Gadpaille 1988, 101). Even a sympathetic critic concedes that Hood, who looks upon himself as "through and through a Catholic novelist" (Hood in Struthers 1978–79, 81) and whose literary works are "dedicated to the service of God" (Hood in Cloutier 1973, 50), is somehow "uncongenial to our time" (Mathews 1978–79, 228).

In 1962, however, when *Flying a Red Kite* was published, the book was part of "a flowering both in the sheer number of published short-story writers and in the variety of the forms employed" (Gadpaille, 99). Hood actively participated in promoting the short-story genre in Canada. Along with Clark Blaise, Ray Smith, and Ray Fraser, he was a member of the Montreal Storytellers established by John Metcalf in the early 1960s. Although the members shared an interest in narrative form and theory, and cooperated on anthologies and short-story collections, they never formed a unified artistic movement but went in different directions as far as their literary practice was concerned. Where Ray Smith and Ray Fraser turned to postmodernism and magic realism, Hugh Hood vehemently rejected these trends. Together with Clark Blaise, John Metcalf, Alice Munro, and Sheila Watson, he has been said to "represent the coming into Canadian fiction . . . of the tradition of modernism" (Woodcock 1993, 100). Useful as such broad labels are to indicate major trends, they fail to do justice to the enormous differences between individual authors thus grouped together. Hood himself, for example, repeatedly draws attention to Alice Munro's focus on the psychological motivation of her characters, which he sees as being diametrically opposed to his own artistic goals (Struthers 58; Hood 1984, 155).

Hood's indebtedness to modernism is of a specific kind. He shares the cultural assumptions of modernists such as T. S. Eliot, Ezra Pound, James Joyce, and the American New Critic Allen Tate, for whom art has taken over the role traditionally fulfilled by Christian religion. Like his modernist predecessors, Hood envisions an aesthetic universe that transcends national borders as well as any particularity of time and place. Religious and aesthetic convictions merge in the belief that art is the medium that "transforms 'things' in order to make a form divined in them shine" (Orange 1978–79, 119). Hood, who wrote his Ph.D. thesis on "Theories of Imagination in English Thinkers 1650–1790," expresses an idea that, according to Canadian philosopher Charles Taylor, "sprang up in the Romantic era" and "is still central to modern culture" (Taylor 1989, 419), namely that the work of art has taken over the role of religious ritual and has become "the locus of a manifestation which brings us into the presence of something which is otherwise inaccessible, and which is of the highest moral or spiritual significance; a manifestation, moreover, that also defines or completes something, even as it reveals" (Taylor, 419).

Following James Joyce, Taylor uses the term "epiphany" as shorthand for this notion of the work of art. In his seminal study *Sources of the Self: The Making of the Modern Identity*, Taylor points to an important shift which has taken place since the Romantic period:

> There are two different ways in which a work can bring about what I'm calling an epiphany, and the balance over the last century has shifted from one to the other. In the first, which dominated with the Romantics, the work does portray something — unspoilt nature, human emotion — but in such a way as to show some greater spiritual reality or significance shining through it. . . . In the second, which is dominant in the twentieth century, it may no longer be clear what the work portrays or whether it portrays anything at all; the locus of epiphany has shifted to within the work itself. (Taylor, 419)

As transcendence can no longer be taken for granted in the twentieth century, modernist authors search for and create literary forms that allow for a new and immediate experience of the world. Based on the conviction that "we only see the world through the forms we construct to grasp it" (Taylor, 472), form becomes central. In the 1960s, the rejuvenation of this idea was promoted by, for example, Susan Sontag: "What is needed, first, is more attention to form in art" (Sontag 1990, 12). Like Sontag, Hood compares art to ritual. Its function is to "exhibit . . . the transcendental element dwelling in living things" (Hood 1971, 30). For Hood, the original religious meaning of "epiphany" as a manifestation of the divine spirit, and the secular meaning as "that sudden flashing forth of intelligibility — aesthetic intelligibility, sometimes intellectual intelligibility" (Hood in Struthers, 71) converge. He often refers to the Holy Ghost in contexts in which secular writers would speak of the power of language "to impose some order on [the world]" (Taylor, 472).

In order to characterize his literary style, Hood has coined the term "super-realism" to indicate the seemingly contradictory impulses involved. Hood thinks of himself as "*both* a realist and a *transcendental allegorist*" (quoted in Mathews 1978–79, 211). In his works, he combines a realist focus on ordinary life and characters and close attention to detail with an antimimetic foregrounding of the formal organization of the literary text.

In the following analysis, the title story of Hood's first short-story collection will be read as a poetological story which puts into practice the theoretical issues involved in Hood's concept of super-realism. Like much of Hood's later fiction, "Flying a Red Kite" presents a protagonist who is partly modeled on the author himself. Fred Calvert, a young professional, has recently moved his family to Montreal. As Hood's own return to Canada in 1961 coincides with his emergence as a professional writer, I will read the story as a fictional account of his quest for a literary style (see Hood 1987a). In brief, the quest exemplifies the historical shift from a Romantic to a modernist conception of art.

In "Flying a Red Kite," the protagonist Fred Calvert first appears as a man somewhat disoriented by his recent move. After a shopping spree in downtown Montreal he finds himself in a state of physical and mental exhaustion, and, in his thoughts, relives the afternoon. Among other things, he has bought a kite as a present for his little daughter. Not only does the kite seem "a natural symbol" (186) of the human longing for transcendence, but the protagonist is also aware "that people treated kites and kite-flying as somehow holy," and attributes "curative moral values" (186) to kite-flying. For himself, however, Calvert doubts his ability to fly the kite, indicating a lack of faith. On his way home, the protagonist suffers a shock of recognition when he meets a Catholic priest who quite openly expresses his sexual desires, "examining the passing legs and skirts with the same impulse Fred had felt" (188). Sexual frustration has led to disillusionment and a loss of religious belief. Passing a cemetery, the priest says: " 'It's all a sham . . . they're in there for good' " (189). Calvert is deeply affected by the priest's disillusionment. However, once home and reunited with his wife and daughter, Fred slowly recovers from his crisis. In order to reassure Calvert, his wife reminds him of their active and satisfactory sex life and of his professional success. Partly reconciled with his life, Calvert promises to fly the kite with his daughter. On the following day, a Sunday, the two of them walk up the mountain and, after two failed attempts, Calvert succeeds in flying the kite. The story ends with father and daughter looking up in the sky, watching the kite. At this moment, the meaning of life is revealed to Calvert. Intuitively, he grasps the immanence of the Spirit in the world.

Concluding with this epiphany, "Flying a Red Kite" is usually read as a religious allegory. Keith Garebian in 1983 refutes earlier readings that had emphasized Hood's realist and documentary style by polemically stating that any "critic who does not read [Hood's] fiction as allegory is either inordinately perverse or helplessly naive" (Garebian 2001, 178). Following in this vein, critics have since claimed that the story "expresses the way Hood colours the articles of this world with intimations of the next" (Copoloff-Mechanic 1988, 8) or that it "combines elegant formal design with theological substance" (Tranquilla 1996, 79). Mathews emphasizes the protagonist's epiphanic experience: the "protagonist's success in making a kite fly for his daughter credibly symbolizes his own spiritual resurrection" (Mathews 2002, 508–9).

Such religious readings rely not only on the epiphany but also on the symbolic function of the kite, which is read as "an emblem of the human soul" (Gadpaille, 101), "a symbol . . . of the promise of resurrection" (Tranquilla, 73), and is said to "signif[y] the union of heaven and earth" (Copoloff-Mechanic, 12). Although these interpretations certainly capture an important aspect of the story, one should nevertheless take Hood's strong rejection of the symbolic mode seriously: "I hate symbols because they propose an other-worldly truth which they never deliver" (Hood in Struthers 1978–79, 14). John Mills, Hood's most sympathetic reader, characterizes Hood's method as "anagogical" rather than allegorical (Mills 1978–79, 99). Instead of having concrete objects refer to abstract ideas,

Hood, in Mills's view, "*asserts* the value of the physical world" (100). Whereas Mills emphasizes the religious dimension of the protagonist's experience,[1] I argue that the religious content is actually subordinate to the poetological dimension of the story. "Flying a Red Kite" focuses on an aesthetic experience that "makes us see things with a freshness and immediacy which our ordinary routine way of coping with the world occludes" (Taylor, 468). The ending of the story expressly disappoints expectations raised by the protagonist's reflections on the symbolic meaning of kites. The epiphany in the end is brought about by the unexpected juxtaposition of two images, the kite, and a second one which appears completely unexpectedly. Such a superimposition of images is well known from imagist poems such as Ezra Pound's "In a Station of the Metro" or T. E. Hulme's "Above the Dock." The declared intention of these poets was to "restore immediacy to language" (Taylor, 473). Exactly this effect is created when Hood superimposes images in his fiction. Immediacy results from a short-circuit in the narrative communication. The epiphany is not portrayed or represented as the protagonist's experience, but is brought about in the reader by means of a metaphorical linking of two images.

In what follows, I focus on the title, the epiphany at the end, the structure, and the handling of point of view in order to illustrate the poetological implications of "Flying a Red Kite." As these implications result, to a large degree, from Hood's conscious break with earlier literary uses of the kite motif, particular attention is given to this intertextual relationship.

The story's title seems to be meant as an illustration of Ezra Pound's dictum that "great literature is simply language charged with meaning to the utmost possible degree" (Pound 1966, 167). First, the title anticipates the concluding scene when the protagonist succeeds in flying the kite he has bought for his daughter. From the beginning, the reader's expectations are directed towards the act of kite-flying. Second, the title introduces the leitmotif, the kite, which links the three episodes that make up the story. In the first episode the kite has yet to take form: the protagonist has simply "two flimsy wooden sticks rolled up in red plastic film, and a ball of cheap thin string" (186). At this point, these objects represent no more than a theoretical potential. In the second episode, the focus is on the assembly of the kite, while in the third, the protagonist succeeds in flying the kite:

[1] See Mills's interpretation of the ending: "The red object in the sky is, of course, symbolically linked to the raspberry stain as though the little girl had partaken, eucharistically, of a Godhead which the kite 'naturally' represents" (Mills 1978–79, 97).

> This time he gave the kite plenty of string before he began to move; he ran as hard as he could, panting and handing the string out over his shoulders, burning his fingers as it slid through them. All at once he felt the line pull and pulse as if there were a living thing on the other end and he turned on his heel and watched while the kite danced into the upper air-currents above the treetops and began to soar up and up. He gave it more line and in an instant it pulled high up away from him across the fence, two hundred feet and more above him up over the cemetery where it steadied and hung, bright red in the sunshine. (195)

The title does more than anticipate the ending and provide the link between episodes. The decisive word in the title is "red." The color word turns the title into a word play on the metaphorical expression, "flying a kite," which means "to try 'how the wind blows,' i.e. in what direction affairs are tending" (*OED*, "kite," 3b.). By simply adding the color adjective "red," Hood restores the literal meaning of the phrase. Hood's title thus foregrounds the idea that meaning "inhere[s] not so much in the words but in the oppositions between them" (Taylor, 477). Adding the adjective completely changes the meaning of the phrase. Accordingly, in Hood's story, kite-flying does not serve any practical purpose but is, as the passage quoted above shows, represented as a source of aesthetic pleasure for the protagonist. This pleasure is expressed by carefully constructed sentences: by means of parallelism and alliteration, and the repetition of words with which the gradual extension of the string on which the kite ascends into the sky is imitated. Thus the title's self-conscious break with conventional language use from the beginning serves as a signal that language in this story is used first and foremost for aesthetic effect.

The passage quoted above builds towards the story's climax. Watching the kite in the sky over the cemetery, Fred Calvert intuitively rejects the priest's denial of immortality: "He thought flashingly of the priest saying 'it's all a sham,' and he knew all at once that the priest was wrong" (195). However, the story does not end with this narrative report of the character's thoughts, but culminates in the following scene:

> Deedee came running down to him, laughing with the excitement and pleasure and singing joyfully about the gingerbread man, and he knelt in the dusty roadway and put his arms around her, placing her hands on the line between his. They gazed, squinting in the sun, at the flying red thing, and he turned away and saw in the shadow of her cheek and on her lips and chin the dark rich red of the pulp and juice of the crushed raspberries. (195–96)

Calvert, who serves as the focalizer in this scene, shifts his attention from his daughter to the kite and back to his daughter so that the two images merge. The traces of the "dark rich red of pulp and juice of the crushed raspberries" on his daughter's face blend with the red kite flying in the sky.

The two images are related by "a form of super-position" (Pound in Sullivan 1970, 53). Ezra Pound, whose "one image poems" (ibid.) rely on this form, comments on the intended effect: "One is trying to record the precise instant when a thing outward and objective transforms itself, or darts into a thing inward and subjective" (in Sullivan, 54). The inner experience, however, is not represented directly; it is rather evoked. Hood's concluding paragraph seems to be a perfect realization of T. S. Eliot's conception of the "objective correlative": "The only way of expressing emotion in the form of art is by finding an 'objective correlative'; in other words, a set of objects, a situation, a chain of events which shall be the formula of that *particular* emotion; such that when the external facts, which must terminate in sensory experience, are given, the emotion is immediately evoked" (Eliot 1934, 145). The narrative action in the concluding paragraph is completely restricted to the protagonist's sensory perceptions. The near-simultaneity of the impressions is emphasized by the paratactic sentence structure. No reference is made to the inner experience of the protagonist. The emotional response evoked depends on the mental associations triggered, for example, by the color "red." The "passion, sentiment and the life-giving principle" (Cirlot 1971, 54) expressed symbolically by the color are embodied in the juice stains on Deedee's cheek. The red stains are the manifest traces of the sensuous pleasure derived from the consumption of wild raspberries. As kite and juice stains merge in the protagonist's mind, the spiritual and the sensual merge and bring about a synthesis of mind and matter.[2]

Hood's own comments on "Flying a Red Kite" — although they draw attention to the specifically Christian meaning attached to the kite symbol — support the poetological reading suggested here:

> "Flying a Red Kite" . . . is firmly based on observation, referring in its second sentence to its narrator's recent arrival in Montréal. But the picture of the "flying red thing" which I meant as a reference to the Pentecostal tongues of fire which descended on the Apostles, pulled the story into a very expressive formal design. It originally had an additional three paragraphs, a solemn coda which moralized the meaning of the narrative, but Jack Zilber of *Prism: International* gave me the most effective bit of advice an editor has ever given me. "Drop off that last page," he said, "because the story ends when Fred sees the red stain on Dedee's cheek." He was exactly right; the story was published with its present ending. (Hood 1987a, 23)

[2] What is represented by this "super-position" of images is Hood's conviction that "the spirit is totally in the flesh" (Hood 1971, 32).

By cutting out the original moralizing ending, the aesthetic effect takes precedence over the religious content, foregrounding the aesthetic nature of the epiphany. The subjective experience of the protagonist is transcended at the story's end. The spiritual transformation takes place in the reader, who is subjected to the imaginative linking of the two images. Charles Taylor in his comments on Ezra Pound's imagist poetry has characterized the modernist epiphany in terms that apply equally to Hood's short story: "[The epiphany] happens not so much in the work as in a space that the work sets up; not in the words or images or objects evoked, but between them. Instead of an epiphany of being, we have something like an epiphany of interspaces" (Taylor, 475–76). The unexpected juxtaposition of two images at the end of "Flying a Red Kite" provides an objective correlative for the spiritual and emotional processes taking place within the reader. Attention is drawn to the poetic language and its potential to reveal a "visionary pattern which transfigures the world as it usually appears" (Taylor, 474). The superimposition of images foregrounds the frame that is projected onto reality and thus self-reflectively points to the function fulfilled by art, namely the revelation of an order behind the surface of things.

In his essays, Hood often draws attention to the "physical form of stories" (Hood 1971, 29) and to his foregrounding of the formal organization of the literary text. The strategy most frequently used in this context is the play with numbers. Hood speaks of numerology as "a kind of scaffolding for the imagination" (ibid.). Numerical principles and symbols are representative of the abstract forms and structures through which reality is apprehended. Hood illustrates this abstract ordering principle with examples from his literary practice: "A novel might have seven main sections, one for each day of a specific week in a given year . . . Or the book might be divided in three main parts, each with a specific number of subdivisions" (ibid.).

In "Flying a Red Kite," the second pattern is used. The story consists of three episodes which are set off from each other by breaks in the text. The first episode consists of ten paragraphs and forms the first half of the story, while the remaining two episodes consist of five paragraphs each and make up the second half of the text. The story thus revolves symmetrically around a middle, with ten paragraphs before and after. The structural tension between the three-part structure (three thematic units) and the quantitative division in two parts corresponds to a thematic tension between a dualistic and a Trinitarian view of the world. In "Christian numerological symbolism" (Hood 1971, 29), the number three represents unity: "The only tolerable form of unity was a triad, a triadic structure or a trinity. . . . I'm arguing, as a Christian, that unity and trinity are built into existence" (Hood in Struthers, 40). The Trinity represents the reconciliation of opposites and thus the overcoming of dualism. The structural tension in "Flying a Red Kite" is resolved when, in the third part, a synthesis of the spiritual and the physical is brought about.

The dualism of body and soul is introduced in the first episode. Fred Calvert is preoccupied with thoughts of failure and guilt. His trip downtown had, as he remembers, been triggered by a sexual urge which he feels again as he gets onto the bus home: "He elbowed and wriggled his way along the aisle, feeling a momentary sliver of pleasure as his palm rubbed accidentally along the back of a girl's skirt" (186). In order to alleviate his feelings of guilt, Calvert has bought presents for his family. The kite, explicitly chosen for its symbolic significance, expresses the protagonist's wish to transcend his physical existence.

In the second episode, the dualism of body and soul is challenged by the protagonist's wife, who objects to her husband's identification with the priest. She reminds Fred of their satisfying sex life. Unlike her husband, she does not associate the body with sinfulness and guilt. In the concluding episode, the opposition of the physical and the spiritual is overcome by the superimposition of images that suggests that the physical world is permeated by the spirit.

The synthesis achieved in the end is represented by the ascent that underlies the plot structure. The three episodes are set downtown, in the protagonist's apartment halfway up the mountain, and on the mountaintop, sequentially. As Simone Vauthier has pointed out with reference to Hood's second short-story collection *Around the Mountain*, Hood consciously fuses "a referential city and its Mount Royal and the spiritual connotations of the word *mountain* — commonly a locus of revelation and theophany" (Vauthier 1993, 153). As Mount Royal is not explicitly mentioned — throughout the story it is referred to as "the mountain" — the "moral topography" (Cloutier, 51) is foregrounded.

On their way up the mountain, father and daughter pass university buildings, parking lots, ash barrels, and trash heaps until close to the top they enter a pastoral landscape. The weather — "nearly perfect, hot, clear, a firm steady breeze but not too much of it" (193) — the vegetation — "great clumps of wild flowers" (194) and "a wild raspberry bush" (195) — as well as the wind — "from the east, over the curved top of the mountain, the wind blew in a steady uneddying stream" (195) — and the majestic view — "he spied the wide intensely gray-white stripe of the river" (195) — evoke an Edenic atmosphere. Once they reach the top ridge of the mountain, the protagonist realizes that "he'd never been up this far before" (194).

Not only does the height — "about six hundred feet above the river" (194) — symbolically represent an "inner 'loftiness' of spirit," the idea of spiritual elevation is "further defined by a complementary figure surmounting it" (Cirlot, 219, 221), in this case the kite flying in the sky above. Yet the story takes a surprising turn in the final scene when the kite blends with the red stains on Deedee's cheek. The spiritual meaning embodied by the kite is revealed to be immanent in the physical world represented by the juice of wild berries. The three-part structure reflects the synthesis of the opposition set up in the first two episodes, and ultimately prevails.

In relation to earlier texts in which the kite motif appears, "Flying a Red Kite" marks a clear break with Romantic tradition. Hood can be said to engage in a critical dialogue with earlier texts in which kites are used as symbols of transcendence. The poetological dimension is made explicit by the reference to kites as "natural symbols." Among the precursor writings, with which Hood was certainly familiar, are Somerset Maugham's short story "The Kite" and Charles Dickens's *David Copperfield.*

In his 1976 introduction to the collection *Flying a Red Kite*, Hood claims to have borrowed important principles of fiction writing from Maugham:

> In every story I tried to incorporate an action or thrust, a movement towards a revelation of some sort, which would hold [the] reader's concentration right down to the last line, and perhaps for some time afterwards. I paid special attention to my closing paragraphs and above all to my titles. (17)

That Maugham is given credit for these artistic principles — which might just as well be attributed to Edgar Allan Poe or James Joyce — is no coincidence. Hood himself gives an important clue when he draws attention to the importance of short-story titles. Besides the functions already mentioned, the title "Flying a Red Kite" is an intertextual reference to Maugham's story, published in 1947, focusing on a mother-son relationship. The son's fascination with kites keeps him in an emotionally stifling relation with his mother, who takes advantage of her son's hobby-horse in order to keep him from becoming independent and setting himself up in marriage. By means of a framing narrator, Maugham suggests a Freudian reading of the embedded story (Maugham 1972, 1). The narrator obviously alludes to the Oedipal conflict that is latent in the mother-son relationship and is intuitively grasped by the young wife, who looks down at kite-flying as a "kid's game" (Maugham, 18). The Freudian reading, however, is countered by the Romantic interpretation preferred by the narrator. In his opinion, kite-flying allows "an escape from the monotony of life" and provides a "sense of power" and "mastery over the elements," and the kite stands for the "ideal of freedom and adventure" (Maugham, 32). Two opposing views on human nature are thus brought into play. Maugham's story ironically evokes what Hood has called the "desperate psychologism of the twentieth century" (Hood 1984, 153), namely the tendency to look upon human beings as driven by unconscious impulses and as determined by their physical nature, over which they have no control. Hood is adamant in his rejection of such a view: "I don't think the bulk of extra-conscious motivation is sub- or pre- or unconscious at all. I think it's superconscious in the Latin sense of coming from above, . . . in my terms, from the Holy Ghost — down from above and enlightening and illuminating, not a dark pall cast up from below" (Hood in Struthers, 76).

The use of the kite as a symbol of spiritual aspirations links Hood to another author he admires, Charles Dickens.[3] In *David Copperfield*, a minor character, Mr. Dick, is fascinated by kite-flying. Although, by common agreement, Mr. Dick is considered mad, David Copperfield recalls his intuitive understanding of Mr. Dick's fascination with kites:

> I used to fancy, as I sat by him of an evening, on a green slope, and saw him watch the kite high in the quiet air, that it lifted his mind out of its confusion, and bore it (such was my boyish thought) into the skies. As he wound the string in, and it came lower and lower down out of the beautiful light, until it fluttered to the ground, and lay there like a dead thing, he seemed to wake gradually out of a dream; and I remember to have seen him take it up, and look about him in a lost way, as if they had both come down together, so that I pitied him with all my heart. (Dickens 1948, 216)

David Copperfield's ability to feel empathy with Mr. Dick's desire to escape into an imaginary world of his own and transcend his sordid reality results from his innocence and indicates his moral integrity. From the perspective of the adult David Copperfield, however, the futility of Mr. Dick's attempts is obvious.

What both forerunners of Hood's story have in common is that kite-flying is practiced by mad characters. Their madness, however, is relativized as it is presented from the point of view of sympathetic narrators. These narrators interpret the fascination with kites as a manifestation of spiritual longings that remain unfulfilled in the real world. Whereas Dickens and Maugham establish an opposition between real and imaginary worlds and use the kite motif to point to deficits inherent in the real world, Hood takes up the motif in order to transcend the dichotomy of "real" and "imaginary." Hood's theoretical claim that "the wholly imaginary is what is most real" (Hood in Fulford 1977, 77) is realized at the end of his story when the boundary between the spiritual and the material world collapses as a result of the superimposition of images.

Where in both previous stories, kite-flying is presented from the point of view of sympathetic yet distanced narrators, in "Flying a Red Kite" the

[3] Hood considers Dickens "the greatest writer of comedy in Western literature, and the subtlest of religious allegory in the English tongue" (Hood 1984, 154).

protagonist serves as the focalizing agent. The story opens *in medias res*: "The ride home began badly" (185). Although no agent is mentioned, the adverb "home" as well as the verb "begin" imply the perspective of a character who defines his location in relation to a place he calls home and who thinks of home as the final destination of his trip. However, in contrast to spatial or temporal deictics that refer to either the character's or the narrator's speech situation, "home" and "begin" can also be taken for the narrator's discourse. This double focus of character and narrator prevails throughout the story. The character's subjectivity is emphasized while, at the same time, the character's perspective is objectified:

> Fred stood for ten minutes, shifting his parcels from arm to arm and his weight from one leg to the other, in a sweaty bath of shimmering glare from the sidewalk, next to a grimy yellow-and-black bus stop. To his left a line of murmuring would-be passengers lengthened until there were enough to fill any vehicle that might come for them. Finally an obese brown bus waddled up like an indecent old cow and stopped with an expiring moo at the head of the line. (185)

From an external view of Fred, the passage shifts to a representation of the character's thoughts. The comparison of the bus with a cow, the association with indecent behavior, and most of all the use of the onomatopoeic expression "moo" clearly mark the end of the passage as free indirect discourse. In spite of the subjectivity markers, however, there is no distance between narrator and character in this passage. As the sensual perception of the outside world dominates in the passage — colors, weight, sounds, temperature — the reality depicted is not meant to be taken for the distorted vision of the protagonist. The metaphors are meant to represent the mental processes by which sense perceptions are transformed into a conscious awareness of the outside world.

Whereas Dickens and Maugham focus on the other-worldliness and psychological deviation of their kite-flying characters, the psychological motivations of Hood's protagonist are of only minor interest: "In terms of narrative, Fred, the salesman of the short story, hardly exists" (Mills, 103). In accordance with Hood's conviction that human actions are inspired from "above" rather than controlled by the sub- or unconscious, the epiphany in the end is effected by an imaginative act that completely transcends the individual experience of the protagonist.

By breaking down the boundaries between the real and the imaginary and by foregrounding the role language plays in our perception of reality, Hood engages in an artistic project that is — in spite of his polemical rejection of postmodernism — not as radically different from postmodern self-reflexive language experiments as it might at first seem. If, according to Larry McCaffery, postmodernist fiction is fiction "that had rejected traditional notions of representation, mimesis, or realism, or that was attempting to redefine what realism is" (McCaffery 1986, xii), Hood's short story "Flying a Red Kite" certainly qualifies as such.

That Hood "stands in many ways outside the Canadian mainstream" (Mathews 2002, 508) is largely the result of cultural developments since the 1960s. Multiculturalism, regionalism, and feminism have all challenged and undermined the assumptions on which modernist art is founded. The autonomy of art, the existence of an aesthetic value that would be independent of political and institutional conditions, as well as the differentiation between "high" and "low" culture have come to be seen by many critics as gate-keeping mechanisms to exclude women, ethnic minorities, and other social groups from participation. In spite of and in response to such claims, Hood reaffirms the cultural achievements of the West: "I think it's obvious that the West has been more richly endowed in its spiritual insights than the East, and that Western culture is the greatest of human cultures, and I think that the incarnation of Christ is at the centre of it" (Hood in Struthers, 39). "Uncongenial to our time" as such statements might indeed be, Hood does not stand entirely alone. The Canadian philosopher Charles Taylor, who sheds light on the "epiphanic nature of much modern art" (Taylor, 493), agrees with Hood on the formative and beneficial effect which Christianity has had on Western civilization. Ironically, in spite of the intellectual affinities between the two authors, Hood's literary oeuvre goes unnoticed by Taylor, who, like Hood, lives and teaches in Montreal. In relation to the European and American modernists of the early decades of the twentieth century, Hood is, after all, an epigone.

Works Cited

Cirlot, J. E. *A Dictionary of Symbols.* 2nd ed. New York: Dorset, 1971.

Cloutier, Pierre. "An Interview with Hugh Hood." *Journal of Canadian Fiction* 2.1 (1973): 49–52.

Copoloff-Mechanic, Susan. *Pilgrim's Progress: A Study of the Short Stories of Hugh Hood.* Toronto: ECW Press, 1988.

Dickens, Charles. *The Personal History of David Copperfield.* Oxford: Oxford University Press, 1948.

Eliot, T. S. "Hamlet." In *Selected Essays.* 2nd ed. London: Faber and Faber, 1934. 141–46.

Fulford, Robert. "An Interview with Hugh Hood." *Tamarack Review* 66 (1977): 65–77.

Gadpaille, Michelle. *The Canadian Short Story.* Toronto: Oxford University Press, 1988.

Garebian, Keith. "Excerpt from *Hugh Hood.* Boston: Twayne, 1983." In *Short Story Criticism.* Vol. 42, ed. Jenny Cromie. Detroit: Gale, 2001. 177–95.

Hood, Hugh. *After All! The Collected Stories V.* Erin, ON: The Porcupine's Quill Press, 2003.

———. *Around the Mountain: Scenes from Montreal Life.* Toronto: Martin, 1967.

———. *August Nights.* Toronto: Stoddart, 1985.

———. "Author's Introduction" (1976). In Hood, *Flying a Red Kite*, vol. 1 of The Collected Stories. Erin, ON: The Porcupine's Quill Press, 1987 (1987a). 9–24.

———. *Dark Glasses.* Ottawa: Oberon, 1976.

———. "The End of Emma." *Canadian Literature* 100 (1984): 148–56.

———. *Flying a Red Kite.* Erin, ON: The Porcupine's Quill Press, 1987.

———. "Flying a Red Kite." In Hood, *Flying a Red Kite*, 185–96.

———. *The Fruit Man, the Meat Man & the Manager.* Ottawa: Oberon, 1971.

———. *The Isolation Booth: The Collected Stories III.* Erin, ON: The Porcupine's Quill Press, 1991.

———. *None Genuine without This Signature.* Downsview, ON: ECW Press, 1980.

———. *A Short Walk in the Rain: The Collected Stories II.* Erin, ON: The Porcupine's Quill Press, 1989.

———. "Sober Colouring: The Ontology of Super-Realism." *Canadian Literature* 49 (1971): 28–34.

———. *You'll Catch Your Death: New Stories.* Erin, ON: The Porcupine's Quill Press, 1992.

Keith, W. J. "The Case of Hugh Hood." Review of Hood, *None Genuine without This Signature. Canadian Forum* (Oct. 1980): 27–29.

Lecker, Robert. "Hugh Hood." In *Dictionary of Literary Biography.* Vol. 53: *Canadian Writers Since 1960. First Series*, ed. William H. New. Detroit: Gale, 1986. 226–32.

———. *On the Line: Readings in the Short Fiction of Clark Blaise, John Metcalf, and Hugh Hood.* Downsview, ON: ECW Press, 1982.

Mathews, Lawrence. "Hood, Hugh." In *Encyclopedia of Literature in Canada*, ed. William H. New. Toronto: University of Toronto Press, 2002. 508–10.

———. "The Secular and the Sacral: Notes on *A New Athens* and Three Stories by Hugh Hood." *Essays on Canadian Writing* 13–14 (1978–79): 211–29.

Maugham, W. Somerset. "The Kite." In *Classic English Short Stories 1930–1955*, selected and introduced by Derek Hudson. Oxford: Oxford University Press, 1972. 1–32.

McCaffery, Larry. *Postmodern Fiction: A Bio-Bibliographical Guide.* New York: Greenwood, 1986.

Mills, John. "Hugh Hood and the Anagogical Method." *Essays on Canadian Writing* 13–14 (1978–79): 94–112.

Orange, John. "Lines of Ascent: Hugh Hood's Place in Canadian Fiction." *Essays on Canadian Writing* 13–14 (1978–79): 113–30.

Pound, Ezra. "How to Read." In Pound, *Polite Essays.* Freeport, NY: Books for Libraries Press, 1966. 155–92.

Sontag, Susan. "Against Interpretation." In Sontag, *Against Interpretation.* New York: Anchor Books, 1990. 3–14.

Struthers, J. R. (Tim). "An Interview with Hugh Hood." *Essays on Canadian Writing* 13–14 (1978–79): 21–93.

Sullivan, J. P., ed. *Ezra Pound: A Critical Anthology.* Harmondsworth: Penguin, 1970.

Taylor, Charles. *Sources of the Self: The Making of the Modern Identity.* Cambridge: Cambridge University Press, 1989.

Tranquilla, Ronald. "John Updike's 'Toward Evening': Hoodwinked." *The American Review of Canadian Studies* 26.1 (1996): 67–82.

Vauthier, Simone. *Reverberations: Explorations in the Canadian Short Story.* Concord, ON: Anansi, 1993.

Woodcock, George. *George Woodcock's Introduction to Canadian Fiction.* Toronto: ECW Press, 1993.

13: Doing Well in the International Thing?: Mavis Gallant, "The Ice Wagon Going Down the Street" (1963)

Silvia Mergenthal (University of Constance)

MAVIS GALLANT WAS BORN Mavis Young in Montreal in 1922. She was educated initially — rather unusually, given her English-speaking family background — in a French-speaking convent school, after which she attended various schools in Canada and in the United States. Upon graduating from High School in Pine Plains, New York, she returned to Canada, where she held various clerical jobs in Montreal and Ottawa, and then worked as a journalist for the *Montreal Standard*. In 1950 she emigrated to Europe, where she spent extended periods of time in the South of France, Austria, Italy, and Spain, before eventually settling in Paris. She returned to Canada to a post as writer-in-residence at the University of Toronto from 1983 till 1984, but has lived in Paris since then (Schaub 1998, xiii–xiv, 1–7).

In 1950, *The New Yorker* accepted Gallant's first short story, and subsequently nearly all of her short fiction has appeared in this magazine. Her stories have been collected in *The Other Paris: Stories* (1956); *My Heart Is Broken: Eight Stories and a Short Novel* (1964); *The Pegnitz Junction: A Novella and Five Short Stories* (1973); *The End of the World and Other Stories* (1974); *From the Fifteenth District: A Novella and Eight Short Stories* (1979); *Home Truths: Selected Canadian Stories* (1981); *Overhead in a Balloon: Stories of Paris* (1985); *In Transit* (1988); *Across the Bridge: New Stories* (1993); *The Moslem Wife and Other Stories* (1994); and *The Selected Stories of Mavis Gallant* (1996).[1] Gallant has also published two novels, *Green Water, Green Sky: A Novel* (1959) and *A Fairly Good Time: A Novel* (1970), as well as a play, *What Is to Be Done?* (1983). Her nonfictional prose has been anthologized in *Paris Notebooks: Essays and Reviews* (1988), which includes one of her rare commentaries on her own writing, the essay "What Is Style?" Other autobiographical and autocritical

[1] *Selected Stories* is the title of the Canadian (1996) and British (1997) editions; the US edition is called, misleadingly, *The Collected Stories of Mavis Gallant*.

comments can be found in interviews, introductions, and prefaces, for instance to *Home Truths: Selected Canadian Stories* and to *Selected Stories.*

Numerous critics, most comprehensively Danielle Schaub in a book-length literary biography, have remarked on Gallant's "invisibility" in Canada before the 1980s (Schaub 1998, 6), attributing this variously to her physical absence from Canada and her *New Yorker* affiliations, her proclaimed indebtedness to European and North American (rather than Canadian) writers, and her seeming unwillingness to align herself with Canadian literary traditions. Schaub explains:

> At the outset, [Gallant] developed on the margins of the local tradition by keeping aloof from the counter-culture and nationalist writing of the sixties and seventies that evolved into the postmodernist revival. She has not shown interest in this kind of writing, and the critics and writers who have chosen the new modes of expression and subvert traditional forms openly (like George Bowering or Robert Kroetsch, for example) have reciprocated her lack of interest. To them, she seemed, and still seems, marginal, like a "modernist anachronism" . . . Even Canadian internationalists with a vested interest in defining Canadian literature as intertextually and politically interwoven with world literature, or at least with European and North American literature, did not respond to her work earlier. (Schaub 1998, 5–6)

However, the collection *Home Truths* (1981), significantly subtitled *Selected Canadian Stories* and containing in its introduction Gallant's most sustained meditations on the issue of "Canadianness" (see below), marked a turning point for the writer's Canadian reputation. It earned her the Governor General's Award for Fiction, which has since been followed by other prestigious awards and honorary doctorates from universities across Canada. Gallant has come to be seen as the foremost Canadian expatriate author, with her contributions to the Canadian short-story tradition coming close to, if not equaling in importance, those of Margaret Atwood and Alice Munro. As a result, her work has attracted a great deal of critical attention, which is reflected in a number of articles and several book-length studies. She has also begun to exert a perceptible influence on younger Canadian writers, among them, for instance, Janice Kulyk Keefer (Schaub 1998, 6).

"An Ice Wagon Going Down the Street," first published in *The New Yorker* in 1963, exhibits some of the hallmarks of Gallant's short stories: an abiding interest in the relationship between past and present, and hence in the workings of memory; the juxtaposition of settings, often "embodied" in conflicts between "native" and "non-native" or rooted and alienated characters; cyclical narrative structures; and the economical use of realistic detail to create multiple layers of meaning. Her language is habitually terse, almost laconic, thus discouraging the reader from identifying all too easily with her characters.

"An Ice Wagon Going Down the Street" opens in the narrative present: Peter Frazier and his wife Sheilah have returned with their two young daughters from Europe and the Far East, where they have spent the previous nine years. While abroad, Peter has worked in a variety of unsatisfactory jobs, signally failing to "[do] well in the international thing" (192). For the time being, Peter and his family are ensconced in Peter's sister's Toronto apartment, and are waiting for another job opportunity to arise.

The use of the present tense in the first section of the story already hints at the entrapment of a series of Sunday mornings spent by Peter and Sheilah in exactly the same fashion, reminiscing about their sojourn abroad. In its concluding section, the story recurs to this Sunday ritual. As Schaub points out:

> Most of Gallant's stories have a circular twist to them — looping the loop —, a circularity which only reinforces the isolation the characters are trapped in. Like lions in a cage, they are seen going round in circles with no hopes of ever escaping. Thus, through the very construction of her stories, Mavis Gallant conveys her theme. (Schaub 1993, 55)[2]

The end of the story returns its readers to their point of departure (Grant 1990, 19–21), but this small degree of linear temporal progression is, in "The Ice Wagon Going Down the Street," more than compensated for by its great temporal depth, which is the depth of memory. In particular, two temporal layers can be distinguished, the first of which — narrated in chronological order but through vividly realized scenes rather than coherently — is concerned with the Fraziers' experiences abroad.

Their first station abroad is Paris, from where they move to Geneva. In Geneva, Peter is employed in a subordinate administrative position in a United Nations office, under the supervision of another Canadian, a young woman called Agnes Brusen. In spite of her indigent Norwegian immigrant background, her drab appearance, and her social awkwardness, Agnes has been taken up by the glamorous expatriates Mike and Madge Burleigh, from whose guest lists the Fraziers have been dropped. Peter and Sheilah, feeling the need to cultivate Agnes's acquaintance in order to re-ingratiate themselves with the Burleighs', invite her to dinner, but she refuses the food they provide. The Fraziers are eventually asked to a costume party at the Burleighs', at which Agnes drinks too much, and Peter is delegated to take her home. In her apartment, Agnes makes what can be construed as sexual advances to Peter, which he rejects. A few days later they discuss this encounter, and manage to converse as friends. But then the Fraziers move on, and Peter and Agnes do not remain in touch. His

[2] See also Woodcock, who has labeled this type of construction Gallant's "helical patterning of memory" (Woodcock 1980, 94).

memory of her — and even her name — endures as the only memory which he does not share with Sheilah, and he believes that Agnes in turn still remembers him.

Peter not only remembers Agnes, he also appropriates — in what Smythe has called "transferential epiphany" (Smythe 1992a, 42) — one of the childhood memories that she has shared with him, that of the eponymous "ice wagon going down the street," which she used to watch as a child growing up in small-town Saskatchewan. It is the sharing of this memory that strikes her, and Peter, as ultimately more significant than any sexual affair they might or might not have had.

The image of the ice wagon recurs three times in the story, one of many triadic patterns: the first time during Peter's and Agnes's encounter in Agnes's apartment, and the second time during their subsequent analysis of this encounter, when Agnes explains:

> In a big family, if you want to be alone, you have to get up before the rest of them. You get up early in the morning in the summer and it's you, you, once in your life alone in the universe. You think you know everything that can happen . . . Nothing is ever like that again. (211)

The third mention of the ice wagon is in the concluding paragraph of the story:

> He thinks of the ice wagon going down the street. He sees something he has never seen in his life — a Western town that belongs to Agnes. Here is Agnes — small, mole-faced, round-shouldered because she has always carried a younger child. She watches the ice wagon and the trail of ice water in a morning invented for her: hers. He sees the weak prairie trees and the shadows on the sidewalk. Nothing moves except the shadows and the ice wagon and the changing amber of the child's eyes. The child is Peter. He has seen the grain of the cement sidewalk and the grass in the cracks, and the dust, and the dandelions at the edge of the road. He is there. He has taken the morning that belongs to Agnes, he is up before the others, and he knows everything. There is nothing he doesn't know. (212)

If one arranges the events of the story along a chronological line, the three earliest events are three childhood experiences which are juxtaposed with one another: Agnes's ice wagon, Sheilah's experience of growing up in dire poverty in a Liverpool slum, and Peter's hiding from the chaos of his parents' parties in his room, where his sister read to him from Beatrix Potter books. At the same time, as Smythe has argued, the story also juxtaposes "two different uses of memory in this allegory of grieving: distorting and disabling memory-as-symbol of the past — the Fraziers' model of escape — versus memory as truthful fiction — Agnes's model of meaning" (Smythe 1992a, 42).

A first reading of "An Ice Wagon Going Down the Street" reveals that it is, predominantly, a story about memory, that is, about the impact of the remote upon the more recent past, and of both upon the present; or conversely, about the way in which the changing demands of the present shape, and reshape, one's memories of the past. These "faultlines" (Besner 1986, 89) between history and fiction, memory and imagination, are deepened in "An Ice Wagon Going Down the Street" by frequent intrusions, not of the past upon the present, but of the present upon the past (Dvorak 2002, 64). The following passage describes how recollections, or rather reconstructions, of the past are inevitably colored by intervening events:

> [Agnes] put down her hand. There was an expression on her face. Now she sees me, [Peter] thought. She had never looked at him after the first day. (He has since tried to put a name to the look on her face; but how can he, now, after so many voyages, after Ceylon, and Hong Kong, and Sheilah's nearly leaving him and all their difficulties — the money owed, the rows with hotel managers, the lost and found steamer trunk, the children throwing up foreign food?) She sees me now, he thought. What does she see? (210)

In addition, the story possesses a markedly self-reflexive quality. Memory and its propensities — which are, of course, the propensities of language — become topics of conversation between characters, as in the play upon the phrase "Nothing happened," which Peter repeats three times to reassure Agnes, the third time putting an extra stress on "happened" (italicised in print) and conjoining it to "You'd remember if it had" (210). This is taken up later, pointedly, by the voice of the narrator, who sums up the Geneva episodes with "Anyway, nothing happened" (211).

After this preliminary survey of the story, it will now be situated within its respective contexts, that is within those of the three Gallant collections in which it has appeared to date, namely: *My Heart Is Broken: Eight Stories and a Short Novel* (1964), *Home Truths: Selected Canadian Stories* (1981), and *The Selected Stories of Mavis Gallant* (1996); the final section of this article will then focus on clusters of specific images in "The Ice Wagon Going Down the Street": mirrors, animals, and clothes.

The title of *My Heart Is Broken* indicates the dominant mood of loss and grief in Gallant's second collection of short stories. According to Smythe, the protagonists of these stories are invariably adults who have been "orphaned and abandoned," and who now seek "fictive consolations" (Smythe 1992a, 38). These adults live in a condition of alienation or exile from their (mythical) "true home," from others, and ultimately, from themselves. On occasion they are granted an understanding of their condition, an insight that they tend to reject, as they do any possibility of re-rootedness, re-connectedness, and identity: "The unlucky among Gallant's characters are cured of their yearning for connection and identity; they find a role and disappear into it. The lucky may be forced, for a moment, to see themselves in their full infirmity; in this moment, though fleetingly, they find home" (Simmons 1993, 29). In "The Ice Wagon Going Down the Street," Peter experiences three moments of recognition. In parentheses, one wonders whether Peter might be named for the Peter of St. Luke's gospel, who like him, thrice denies his potential savior, whose name, after all, is Agnes (from Latin "agnus," the lamb, i.e. Jesus). Peter first intuits the truth about her character, which is that she, rather than he, is the true heir of their immigrant ancestors, only to retreat behind the platitude of an "inferior girl of poor quality" (200). He next senses the truth about their kinship — "I'd be like Agnes if I didn't have Sheilah" (206) — but repeats, mantra-like, the formula of "poor quality, really — he remembered having thought that once" (209). In his third and final act of denial, he rejects Agnes's memory of the ice wagon, which he had just appropriated as his imaginative — and imaginary — "home," as, after all, *in*appropriate:

> He could keep the morning if he wanted to, but what can Peter do with the start of a summer day? Sheilah is here, it is a true Sunday morning, with its dimness and headache and remorse and regrets, and this is life. He says, "We have the Balenciaga." He touches Sheilah's hand. The children have their aunt now, and he and Sheilah have each other. Everything works out, somehow or other. Let Agnes have the start of the day. Let Agnes think it was invented for her. Who wants to be alone in the universe? No, begin at the beginning. Peter lost Agnes. Agnes says to herself somewhere, Peter is lost. (212)

In Simmons's classification of "unlucky" versus "lucky" Gallant characters, Peter is still one of the "lucky" as, "in cherishing Agnes and her morning, Peter . . . is able at least to know what has been lost" (Simmons, 38).

However, the passage just quoted, which is the ending of the story, is deliberately ambiguous, an ambiguity that results from Gallant's handling of narrative perspective: while Peter serves as a reflector figure, or focalizer, throughout the story, there are occasional comments by a narrator, as in the following paragraph, in which the narrative voice appears to assert its omniscience only to relinquish it so as to allow Agnes and Peter some privacy:

> But what were they talking about that day, so quietly, such old friends? They talked about dying, about being ambitious, about being religious, about different kinds of love. What did she see when she looked at him — taking her knuckle slowly away from her mouth, bringing her hand down to the desk, letting it rest there? They were both Canadians, so they had this much together — the knowledge of the little you dare admit. Death, near death, the best thing, the wrong thing — God knows what they were telling each other. Anyway, nothing happened. (211)

In other passages, including arguably the ending, it is not clear whether the voice is Peter's or that of an intruding narrator. The last three sentences — "No, begin at the beginning. Peter lost Agnes. Agnes says to herself somewhere, Peter is lost" (212) — could either be a report of Peter's reflections, so that he can then be seen as projecting his self-awareness onto Agnes, or a statement from the narrator, which would give Agnes the last word.

The context of *My Heart Is Broken* suggests that "The Ice Wagon Going Down the Street" should be read, like many modernist narratives, as a story about the universal condition of alienation and loss, and about the curative potential of memory. The title and subtitle of the second collection in which it was published, *Home Truths: Selected Canadian Stories*, more strongly foreground its "Canadianness." As has already been indicated, Gallant's position within the Canadian literary canon is a problematic one, an issue that she raises herself in her introduction to the volume. This introduction has been analyzed perceptively by Smythe (1992b; see also Blodgett 1990), who stresses its para-critical dimension and its determined resistance to both domestic, that is, narrowly "Canadian," and to autobiographical readings of the stories which it precedes. Smythe also comments on the title:

> The title itself, *Home Truths*, refers to an ironic type of idiom: "home truths" are painful facts, consisting of the contradiction between what *is* and what *should be*, between some kind of discomfort and the presumed comfort of "home." Gallant may have wanted this title to play against the subtitle ironically. The "truth" is that there is no consensus as to what constitutes, precisely, a "Canadian" story (much less a collection of stories). "Home" may be "Canada," but the only "Truths" are "Stories," Canadian or otherwise. (Smythe 1992b, 109)

Another eminent Gallant critic, Neil Besner, claims that the stories in *Home Truths* do not differ from any other Gallant stories except for their setting, in the narrow sense of time and place. He argues that their Canadian setting (which is, at any rate, only one of several in "An Ice Wagon Going Down the Street") is only of secondary importance here, subordinated to their preoccupation with the past as "time misapprehended" (Besner 1988, 117–18).

Even so, "An Ice Wagon Going Down the Street" does engage, on several levels and quite explicitly, with the question of "Canadianness." Thus, Peter and Sheilah's two daughters, who were very young when their parents took them abroad, immediately feel "home" upon their return to Canada, and start speaking with the kind of voice that seems to be identified as quintessentially Canadian, "nasal and flat" (193; Agnes, incidentally, has the same voice, 200). Physically, the two girls and their aunt are throwbacks to their first-generation immigrant forebears, which points to a minor but important theme in the story — the persistence of physical and mental family traits across generations — and hence the importance of nature (in Peter's phrase, of what is "in the blood," 193) over nurture. Peter is a fourth-generation Canadian of Scottish Presbyterian stock. His father has squandered the family fortune amassed by Peter's great-grandfather and consolidated by his grandfather's generation. Peter is convinced that this background and the Frazier name still endow him with a kind of aura, and that he is being watched over and groomed for his future career by impersonal forces; in his view, his first step up the career ladder has been sabotaged by a "French-Canadian combine" (194).

While Peter was born and raised in central, urban Canada, Agnes, who is immune to his supposed aura and misremembers his name, hails from the Canadian West. As a second-generation immigrant, she is the first of her large family to have been given an education. Yet whereas Peter and Sheilah's marriage is threatened by underlying differences beneath surface similarities — differences which emerge, for instance, when Sheilah (being English) is unable to appreciate "the importance of the first snow" (205) — Peter and Agnes's abortive relationship is based on underlying similarities beneath surface differences (Besner 1988, 124–27). Hence, Peter's assertion that "they had been put together because they were Canadians; but they were as strange to each other as if 'Canadian' meant any number of things, or had no real meaning" (198) is clearly untenable. But what *does* "Canadian" mean, if anything? In the passage quoted above — "They were both Canadians, so they had this much together — the knowledge of the little you dare admit" (211) — the narrative voice does seem to endorse the view that there may be character traits that can be regarded as "typically Canadian": here, a certain reticence, caused perhaps by repressive education. Of course, in holding back the contents of Peter and Agnes's conversation, the narrative voice is itself reticently "Canadian." While Gallant's own comments on her writing similarly tend towards the oblique, it may be helpful, in this context, to quote from her introduction to *Home Truths*:

> What I am calling, most clumsily, the national sense of self is quite separate from nationalism, which I distrust and reject absolutely, and even patriotism, so often used as a stick to beat people with. Canada is one of the few countries that confers citizenship by birth, and we are apt to think that a national character automatically attaches itself to a birth certificate. The accident of birth does not give rise to a national consciousness, but I think the first years of schooling are indelible. They provide our center of gravity, our initial view of the world, the seed of our sense of culture. A deeper culture is contained in memory. Memory is something that cannot be subsidized or ordained. It can, however, be destroyed; and it is inseparable from language. (*Home Truths*, xv)

The third Gallant volume in which "The Ice Wagon Going Down the Street" appears is *Selected Stories of Mavis Gallant,* in which stories are grouped according to the decades in which they are set. "The Ice Wagon Going Down the Street" appears in the "Fifties" section, alongside stories with a wide variety of *non*-Canadian settings: Paris in "The Other Paris" and "Across the Bridge," Germany in "The Latehomecomer," Spain in "Senor Piñero," "By the Sea" and "When We Were Nearly Young," and the French Riviera in "The Remission." In this environment, passing references to fortunes to be made from black-market racketeering and from the end of British imperial rule in the Far East (193 and 206, respectively) provide a tantalizing counterpoint to the Fraziers' failure to "[do] well in the international thing."

Of the two approaches to "The Ice Wagon Going Down the Street" proposed in this article so far, the first, linear, reading has concentrated on the structure of the story, particularly on its interlocking temporal layers. The second has situated the story within its respective contexts and foregrounded its most important themes. In a third and concluding approach to what has begun to emerge as a highly complex narrative, the focus will now be on some of its key images: mirrors, animals, and clothes. In the process, the argument will circle back, rather like the story itself, to the central image of the "ice wagon going down the street." All these images, or clusters of images, may serve as examples of Gallant's so-called realism, which, as Besner has shown, does not simply render a "slice of life" but, in the Barthesian sense of the term "realism," names things in order *not* to name their ultimate meaning. According to Besner,

> documentary realism is a form serving a purpose; it is a means and not an end. It poses the prospect of meticulously realized settings *against* characters' "memorials," or inventions of settings. And whether we call these creations reflexive, or self-referential, or impressionist, or aspects of the three, one conclusion that we might draw is that realism in Gallant's fiction reflects as much as it refers, pointing to words and worlds with a particular emphasis on the ways in which the past is either called into being or banished into exile. (Besner 1986, 93)

This is quite literally true for the mirror in "The Ice Wagon Going Down the Street," an object of minor relevance in this particular story, but which both contributes to its self-reflexive quality and links it to many other Gallant texts in which characters catch glimpses of themselves and, in this meeting between their inner and outer selves, see themselves as others see them (Grant, 27–29). In Grant's analysis of the story, Peter is precipitated into a moment of insight watching himself and Agnes in the mirror over the fireplace in her apartment. This moment of recognition cannot be named directly, but finds expression in a series of mental images that Peter believes suggest "disaster," but that also appear to have sexual connotations:

> He thought, This is how disasters happen. He saw floods of seawater moving with perfect punitive justice over reclaimed land; he saw lava

> covering vineyards and overtaking dogs and stragglers. A bridge over an abyss snapped in two and the long express train, suddenly V-shaped, floated like snow. He thought amiably of every kind of disaster and thought, This is how they occur. (208–9)

While the mirror in "The Ice Wagon Going Down the Street" is a physical object, the hidden meaning of which the reader is invited to explore, animals, in most instances in the story, are used metaphorically: Peter and Sheilah are compared to peacocks, their daughters and Peter's sister to wrens, Agnes to a mole. Wrens and moles, though obviously very different animals, do share size and coloring — "sandy-coloured, proudly plain" in the case of the wrens (193), "small and brown" in that of the mole (199). On the level of images, Gallant stresses very economically the surface differences between Peter and Sheilah on the one hand, and the children, their aunt, and Agnes on the other — while simultaneously indicating underlying similarities between Peter's and Agnes's families. However, the story does not confine itself to metaphorical peacocks, but also introduces real birds. In another passage that is difficult to attribute to either Peter or to a distinct narrative voice, these peacocks — on the lawn and in the parking-lot of Peter's workplace, the Geneva Palace de Nations — are characterized as follows: "The peacocks love no one. They wander about the parked cars looking elderly, bad-tempered, mournful, and lost" (199–200).

In a story about memory, readers are required, when encountering the actual bird, to remember the metaphor, and to re-evaluate it. They find themselves in the same position as the characters, in that they have to piece together the puzzle that is their fellow human being: "Agnes is the only secret Peter has from his wife, the only puzzle he pieces together without her help" (212; see Grant, 23–24). While the peacock metaphor has initially seemed to suggest that the resemblance between peacocks and Peter and Sheilah is one of splendor, as against the drabness of their surroundings, it is now extended to include shared inner rather than outer qualities. This transition from outer to inner qualities is completed — again taxing readers' memories — when the word "lost" recurs at the very end of the story.

Gallant explores several ways, not in themselves startlingly original, of using clothes as signifiers. Peter and Sheilah, in their silk dressing gowns bought in Hong Kong, refuse to adapt to their Toronto environment; their children, by contrast, immediately and gladly conform to its sartorial norms when they accompany their aunt to church in "their new hats and purses and gloves and coral bracelets and strings of pearls" (193). In the Geneva episodes, Peter and Sheilah feel too insecure regarding their social status to appear in fancy dress at the Burleighs' costume party, but Agnes, otherwise the soul of drab propriety, defiantly flaunts her very different social background by dressing as a "ragged hobo, half tramp, half clown"

(205). Most tellingly, in a particularly fine instance of Gallant's use of realistic detail, Peter and Sheilah's proudest possession, a soiled and slightly old-fashioned designer dress by Balenciaga, is balanced against Agnes's: her pristine memory of the ice wagon. In the story's economy of images, Peter eventually settles for the former, the sole trophy of his and Sheilah's exile, over the latter, the embodiment of "a child's sense of identity as inseparable from a familiar universe" (Besner 1988, 125).

"The Ice Wagon Going Down the Street" is the most frequently anthologized of Gallant's stories. Among the many hallmarks of her fiction that it exhibits the most predominant is, perhaps, her fascination with what she herself has referred to as "the tick of a watch." In "What Is Style?" she writes:

> Style is inseparable from structure, part of the confirmation of whatever the author has to say. What he says — this is what fiction is about — is that something is taking place and that nothing lasts. Against the sustained tick of the watch, fiction takes the measure of a life, a season, a look exchanged, the turning point, desire as brief as a dream, the grief and terror that after childhood we cease to express. The lie, the look, the grief are without permanence. The watch continues to tick when the story stops. (*Paris Notebooks*, 177)

Works Cited

Besner, Neil K. "A Broken Dialogue: History and Memory in Mavis Gallant's Short Fiction." *Essays on Canadian Writing* 33 (1986): 89–99.

———. *The Light of Imagination: Mavis Gallant's Fiction.* Vancouver: University of British Columbia Press, 1988.

Blodgett, E. D. "Heresy and Other Arts: A Measure of Mavis Gallant's Fiction." *Essays on Canadian Writing* 42 (1990): 1–8.

Dvorak, Marta. "Mavis Gallant's Fiction: Taking the (Rhetorical) Measure of the Turning Point." In *Varieties of Exile: New Essays on Mavis Gallant*, ed. Nicole Coté. New York: Peter Lang, 2002. 63–74.

Gallant, Mavis. *Across the Bridge: New Stories.* Toronto: McClelland & Stewart, 1993.

———. *The End of the World and Other Stories.* Toronto: McClelland & Stewart, 1974.

———. *From the Fifteenth District: A Novella and Eight Short Stories.* Toronto: Macmillan of Canada, 1979.

———. *Home Truths: Selected Canadian Stories.* Toronto: Macmillan, 1981.

———. "The Ice Wagon Going Down the Street." In Gallant, *The Selected Stories*, 192–212.

———. *In Transit.* Markam, ON: Viking, 1988.

Gallant, Mavis. *The Moslem Wife and Other Stories.* Toronto: McClelland & Stewart, 1994.

———. *My Heart Is Broken: Eight Stories and a Short Novel.* New York: Random House, 1964.

———. *The Other Paris: Stories.* Boston: Houghton Mifflin, 1959.

———. *Overhead in a Balloon: Stories of Paris.* Toronto: Macmillan of Canada, 1985.

———. *Paris Notebooks: Essays and Reviews.* London: Bloomsbury, 1988.

———. *The Pegnitz Junction: A Novella and Five Short Stories.* New York: Random House, 1973.

———. *The Selected Stories of Mavis Gallant.* Toronto: McClelland & Stewart, 1996.

Grant, Judith Skelton. *Mavis Gallant and Her Works.* Toronto: ECW Press, 1990.

Schaub, Danielle. *Mavis Gallant.* New York: Twayne, 1998.

———. "Structural Patterns of Alienation and Disjunction: Mavis Gallant's Firmly Structured Stories." *Canadian Literature* 136 (1993): 45–57.

Simmons, Diane. "Remittance Men: Exile and Identity in the Short Stories of Mavis Gallant." In *Canadian Women Writing Fiction*, ed. Mickey Pearlman. Jackson: University Press of Mississippi, 1993. 28–40.

Smythe, Karen E. *Figuring Grief: Gallant, Munro and the Poetics of Elegy.* Montreal: McGill-Queen's University Press, 1992 (1992a).

———. "The 'Home Truth' about Home Truths: Gallant's Ironic Introduction." In *Double Talking: Essays on Verbal and Visual Ironies in Contemporary Canadian Art and Literature*, ed. Linda Hutcheon. Toronto: ECW Press, 1992. 106–14.

Woodcock, George. *The World of Canadian Writing: Critiques and Recollections.* Vancouver: Douglas and McIntyre, 1980.

14: (Un-)Doing Gender: Alice Munro, "Boys and Girls" (1964)

Reingard M. Nischik (University of Constance)

> Re-vision — the act of looking back, of seeing with fresh eyes, of entering an old text from a new critical direction — is for women more than a chapter in cultural history: it is an act of survival.[1]
>
> — Adrienne Rich

"IS IT TRUE THAT IN ORDER TO APPRECIATE Alice Munro's stories we need to begin by looking at a map of Canada?" These are the opening words of Coral Ann Howells's excellent book on Munro's oeuvre.[2] The answer to that question might be that a map of Canada is not really necessary to appreciate Munro's fictional worlds, but that Munro in her writing prefers to "map" a certain Canadian region: southwestern Ontario (sometimes abbreviated as "sowesto"), more specifically the area around London, close to Lake Huron.

Munro's longtime preoccupation with that particular region and her interest in local history and topography in her writing are linked to her own life. She was born on 10 July 1931 on a farm on the outskirts of the small town of Wingham, Ontario (some thirty miles from London in Huron County), the eldest of three children of a former school teacher and a fox farmer with a family history going back to Scottish pioneers. After completing school in Wingham she attended the University of Western Ontario (1949–51) in London, where she studied English and had her first short stories published in the university magazine. She married James Munro, a fellow student, in 1951, and they moved west to Vancouver. After the first of her three daughters was born, she sold her first short story to the (now defunct) Canadian magazine *Mayfair* in 1953 and then "The Strangers" to the radio programme *CBC Anthology* whose director, Robert Weaver, was to play an important role in popularizing Munro's writing in

[1] Rich 1979, 35.

[2] Howells 1998, 1; see also Howells 2002 for a short survey of Munro's life and work.

Canada. It was in the 1950s, when her second daughter was born, that Munro started to write short fiction on a regular basis and first published her stories in Canadian magazines such as *Queen's Quarterly*, *The Tamarack Review*, and *Chatelaine*. When Munro was twenty-eight years old, her mother died from Parkinson's disease, a painful experience which led Munro to write "The Peace of Utrecht" that summer (one of the many Munro classics today). In the 1960s the Munro family moved yet further west to Victoria, British Columbia, on Vancouver Island, where they ran a bookshop called Munro's Books[3] and where their third daughter was born. It was at the end of the 1960s, after the publication of seventeen stories in Canadian magazines, that Munro had her breakthrough with her first story collection *Dance of the Happy Shades* (1968), which won Canada's most prestigious literary prize, the Governor General's Award for Fiction. In 1971 *Lives of Girls and Women* was published, a book of linked stories which brought Munro international recognition. Since then, all of her short-story collections have been national and international bestsellers: *Something I've Been Meaning to Tell You* (1974), *Who Do You Think You Are?* (1978, which won Munro another Governor General's Award; it was published under the title *The Beggar Maid: Stories of Flo and Rose* in England and the USA[4]), *The Moons of Jupiter* (1982), *The Progress of Love* (1986, winning a third Governor General's Award), *Friend of My Youth* (1990, Ontario Trillium Book Award, Commonwealth Writers' Prize), *Open Secrets* (1994, W. H. Smith Award in England), *The Love of a Good Woman* (1998, National Book Critics Circle Award from the United States), *Hateship, Friendship, Courtship, Loveship, Marriage* (2001), *Runaway* (2004, Giller Prize and Commonwealth Writers' Prize), *The View from Castle Rock* (2006), plus four volumes of selected stories: *Selected Stories* (1996), *No Love Lost* (2003), *Vintage Munro* (2004), and *Carried Away* (2006).

In 1973 Munro's first marriage broke up and after more than twenty years on the Canadian west coast she moved back to Ontario to teach at York University in Toronto and at her former university, the University of Western Ontario. In 1975 she returned to southwestern Ontario, to Clinton, a small town twenty miles from Wingham, where she has lived with her second husband ever since, dividing her time between Clinton and Comox on Vancouver Island. In 1976 began Munro's longtime affiliation with *The New Yorker*, which published many of her stories for the

[3] Still trading under that name in Victoria, British Columbia.

[4] Because the publishers thought that while the provocative original title would make sense to Canadian readers, it would not appeal to an American or British audience.

first time,[5] thus popularizing her writing among American readers in particular.

Both nationally and internationally Munro's tremendous success as a short-story writer has done much to raise the profile of the Canadian short story. She is without doubt Canada's leading short-fiction writer and has, over five decades, created an impressive oeuvre. Munro is by far the most frequently anthologized writer of Canadian short fiction, and there are critics who argue that she is the best living short-story writer. The many literary prizes she has received (see also the PEN Malamud Award for Excellence in Short Fiction and the Canadian Authors Association's Jubilee Award for Short Stories in 1997) and the fact that her fifth story collection, *The Moons of Jupiter*, drew the highest price for the paperback rights ever arranged for a book of Canadian fiction (novels included) together attest to her extraordinary success as a short-fiction writer with critics and academics as well as the general reading public.

Munro is also exceptional in that she has published only short fiction (apart from several essays, mostly on aspects of writing, and some interviews). The closest she has come to the genre of the novel are her two short-story cycles *Lives of Girls and Women* and *Who Do You Think You Are?* Both have a curious publication history since they are the two instances where Munro — urged by her publisher to write a novel, mainly for financial reasons, after the big success of her prize-winning first short-story collection — tried very hard to forge her episodic technique and individual story units into the form of a novel.[6] During the painful process of revision, Munro became aware that it was stories she wanted to write more than anything else and that it was this genre that best suited her talent and writing habits (considering her heavy revising technique and her intense preoccupation with style as well as her status as a mother of three small children during the budding stage of her writing career). "I think the most attractive kind of writing of all is just the single story. It satisfies me the way nothing else does. . . . It took me a long time to reconcile myself to being a short-story writer" (Munro in Hancock 1987, 190). And although the stories in her more recent story collections (*Friend, Open Secrets, Hateship,*

[5] On the potential influence of that sought-after magazine on her writing see Beran 1999. See also Munro's "Author's Note" to *Love*: "Stories included in this collection that were previously published in *The New Yorker* appeared there in very different form."

[6] See her sometimes hilarious reminiscences in Struthers, for example, when he asks her about the revision of *Who*: "Oh, it's the most confused revision in history" (Struthers 1983, 29 *passim*).

Runaway) have become substantially longer, Munro still keeps faith with her preferred literary format.[7]

The attraction of the short-story format for Munro is also directly linked to her particular writing aesthetics, which through explanatory gaps, supplementarity (Howells 1998, 10–11), the construction of "worlds alongside,"[8] the contrasting of disparate interpretations, multiple views on a given event (by the same or by various characters), juxtaposition of the past and present, and the constant deferral of fixed meaning all stress the fluidity, incompleteness, variability, and the ultimate inexplicability of human experience (see Nischik 1992). The short story as a format that privileges slice-of-life representations, episodic and condensed time structures, suggestive, deliberately fragmentary representations and open endings is thus the perfect literary form to transport Munro's "snapshot"[9] views of her fictional world.

Next to the generic choice and the aesthetics connected with it, the multifaceted Munrovian fictional world has been marked over the course of half a century by three main characteristics: her regional attachments, her preferred choice of female protagonists and her privileging of a female perspective and "female themes," and the autobiographical or, as she prefers to call it, the "personal"[10] dimension of her work.

Munro understandably shrinks away from her frequent classification as a "regional writer": "A lot of people think I'm a regional writer. And I use the region where I grew up a lot. But I don't have any idea of writing to show the kind of things that happen in a certain place. These things happen and the place is part of it. But in a way, it's incidental" (Munro in Hancock, 200). Although several of her stories have a varied, even international setting (for example, Australia, Scotland, Albania) and although her long stay on the Canadian west coast resulted in several stories with a western Canadian setting, it is her rural home region and the small-town

[7] Building on the fact that Munro had her say, of course, in the choice of stories for her *Selected Stories*, Howells comments: "Only *Lives of Girls and Women* was ever published as a 'novel' and its omission from her *Selected Stories* would indicate that she wishes it to be considered as a novel" (Howells 1998, 157, note 35).

[8] "So lying alongside our world was Uncle Benny's world like a troubling distorted reflection, the same but never at all the same" (Munro, "The Flats Road" in *Lives*, 26).

[9] For example: "I didn't stop there . . . because I wanted to find out more, remember more. I wanted to bring back all I could. Now I look at what I have done and it is like a series of snapshots" (Munro, "The Ottawa Valley" in *Something*, 197).

[10] Munro in Struthers, 17.

life of southwestern Ontario that have most frequently formed the backdrop to her writing.[11] Her frank, detailed, unsparing depiction of this region and its inhabitants, her way of looking beyond appearances, and her unflattering revelation of backward mentalities and crankiness of character have led inhabitants of Wingham to reject her writing.[12] Howells discovered that neither the local museum in Wingham nor the Huron County Museum in Goderich stock a single reference to their region's international celebrity author (Howells 1998, 3). Howells also rightly points out about Munro's favorite setting that "what she emphasises is not its familiarity but its strangeness" (Howells 1998, 13). Especially at the beginning of her writing career in the 1950s, Munro was influenced by the female writers of the American South, such as Flannery O'Connor, Carson McCullers, and particularly Eudora Welty, in whose writing she "felt . . . a country depicted that was like my own. . . . I mean, the part of the country I come from is absolutely Gothic. You can't get it all down" (Munro in Gibson 1973, 248). Munro's gender awareness and her focus on the female perspective have made her a favorite author with astute (female) readers and critics alike. As early as 1972 Munro stated that she was generally sympathetic to the Women's Liberation movement. Both her "regionalism" and her gender awareness combine in the often personal sources of her writing.[13] One important thematic strand is the significance of family relationships, especially of mother-daughter relationships, which in Munro's writing — somewhat in contrast to Atwood's[14] — are usually highly problematic and psychological "works-in-progress." Munro's mother's early death has been reworked in "The Peace of Utrecht" (*Dance*), "The Ottawa Valley" (*Something*), and "Friend of My Youth" (*Friend*). Other specifically female and partly autobiographical themes in Munro's stories are the restrictive socialization patterns, especially of girls, in rural or small-town settings, gendered professional issues — often in the context of artist/writer stories ("The Office" in *Dance*), emotional dependence in love relationships ("Dulse" in *Moons*), and problems of aging ("What Is Remembered" in *Hateship*). Yet Munro is also a "writer's writer," who, making use of postmodern techniques, integrates poetological problems into her fiction ("Epilogue: The Photographer" in *Lives*, for

[11] See Howells: "To return to that map of Canada, if we began by locating a group of small towns in southwestern Ontario (Wingham, Clinton and Goderich on Lake Huron) we would delineate Munro's geographical territory" (1998, 2).

[12] Note Munro's disclaimer on the bibliographical page of *Lives*: "This novel [*sic*] is autobiographical in form but not in fact. My family, neighbors and friends did not serve as models. — A.M."

[13] On the strong autobiographical dimension in Munro's works see Thacker 1988.

[14] See my article on Atwood in this book.

example), experiments with the short-story form in her non-linear, digressive, sometimes montage-like narrative style ("White Dump" in *Progress*), reworks Joycean multiperspective ("The Albanian Virgin" in *Open Secrets*) and epiphanic techniques, and blends the quotidian with the extraordinary ("Miles City, Montana" in *Progress*). The metafictional tendencies of several of Munro's stories have been memorably enshrined by Munro herself in self-reflexive renderings such as:

> And what happened, I asked myself, to Marion? . . . Such questions persist, in spite of novels. It is a shock, when you have dealt so cunningly, powerfully, with reality, to come back and find it still there. ("Epilogue: The Photographer" in *Lives*, 247)
>
> People's lives, in Jubilee as elsewhere, were dull, simple, amazing, and unfathomable — deep caves paved with kitchen linoleum. (*Lives*, 249)
>
> Those shifts of emphasis that throw the story line open to question, the disarrangements which demand new judgments and solutions, and throw the windows open on inappropriate unforgettable scenery. ("Simon's Luck" in *Who*, 177)
>
> I always had a feeling, with my mother's talk and stories, of something swelling out behind. Like a cloud you couldn't see through, or get to the end of. ("Progress of Love" in *Progress*, 13)

Commenting on developments in Munro's writing over several decades, Howells states that "her topics have not changed but her narrative methods have" (Howells 1998, 68). It is striking that in more recent collections, beginning with *Love,* the protagonists tend to be older, having grown older along with Munro herself,[15] "with an accompanying sense of individual lives scrolling out over many decades" (Howells 2003, 54). The crucial aspect is still, however, the question of controlling one's own life in negotiation with restrictive social norms. The technical turning point in Munro's writing career may be identified as the collection *The Moons of Jupiter* (1982). Although Munro has always adhered to indeterminacy in her stories, it is in this collection that this principle is amplified, structuring not only her verbal discourse but also her narrative method: "multiple and often contradictory meanings have room to circulate in structures of narrative indeterminacy . . ., unsettling the story at every stage of its telling . . ., as she allows more and more possible meanings to circulate in every story while refusing definite interpretations or plot resolutions" (Howells 1998, 11, 10).

15 "We can see that, from her earliest stories on, Munro's narrative perspective has grown gradually older with her, so that now many characters have personal histories — and thus perspectives of time and space — roughly equivalent to Munro's own" (Thacker, 154); see also Martin 1998.

"Boys and Girls" was first published in 1964 and included in Munro's first story collection *Dance of the Happy Shades* (1968). The first paragraph immediately maps out the Munrovian fictional territory, with the three distinguished general features of her writing noticeable right from the beginning:

> My father was a fox farmer. That is, he raised silver foxes, in pens; and in the fall and early winter . . . he killed them and skinned them and sold their pelts to the Hudson's Bay Company or the Montreal Fur Traders. These companies supplied us with heroic calendars to hang, one on each side of the kitchen door. Against a background of cold blue sky and black pine forests and treacherous northern rivers, plumed adventurers planted the flags of England or of France; magnificent savages bent their backs to the portage. (111)

Apart from the clearly Canadian setting with its postcolonial historical background, we notice the autobiographical dimension to this first-person narrative told by an eleven-year-old girl growing up on a fox farm near Jubilee — if a strong personal orientation is assumed, with Munro born in 1931, the story would be set at the beginning of the 1940s, when Munro's father was indeed still a fox farmer in Wingham.[16] The rural setting of the farm surrounded by fields is only scantily sketched: "This was the time of year when snowdrifts curled around our house like sleeping whales and the wind harassed us all night, coming up from the buried fields, the frozen swamps" (112). Relevant as such information concerning place and time may seem, it is rather the highly traditional gender mentality of the unnamed girl's parents and of other characters, like the hired man or the salesman (that is, representing inner family and external social attitudes and prejudices), that stresses the story's setting with respect to time and place.[17]

A further autobiographical aspect of the story is the girl's habit of creating stories that imaginatively mirror her own state of development, at the same time revealing a budding writer (though this potential further development is, characteristically, left open in the story). One could even argue that the child's fantasies are the prototypes of Munro's "linked stories":

[16] In her second book, *Lives*, the first-person narrator's father is also a fox farmer, and this book of linked stories is also set in Jubilee, the fictional homage to Wingham, as has often been argued. For a later autobiographically inspired story on the father-daughter relationship see "The Moons of Jupiter," which was first published two years after Munro's father's death during heart surgery.

[17] See Carrington, who speaks of a "closed rural society" (1989, 15).

> Laird [the narrator's brother] went straight from singing to sleep. . . . Now for the time that remained to me, the most perfectly private and perhaps the best time of the whole day, I arranged myself tightly under the covers and went on with one of the stories I was telling myself from night to night. These stories were about myself, when I had grown a little older; they took place in a world that was recognizably mine, yet one that presented opportunities for courage, boldness and self-sacrifice, as mine never did. I rescued people from a bombed building. . . . I shot two rabid wolves who were menacing the schoolyard (the teachers cowered terrified at my back). I rode a fine horse spiritedly down the main street of Jubilee, acknowledging the townspeople's gratitude for some yet-to-be-worked out piece of heroism. (113–14)

This is an apt example of the potentially compensatory function of literature in general, of the narrator's imaginative ability in particular (which sets her apart from the rest of her totally unimaginative family, who are stuck in conventional thought patterns), and of Munro's supplementary narrative constructions, her "worlds alongside."

The later reference to the narrator's story compositions shows the effect of her ongoing socialization into received gender patterns and thereby points to the central theme of this story, the constructivist aspect of gender identity — how male and female children are socialized according to different role patterns, forming them into two different species, "boys and girls":

> Even in these stories something different was happening, mysterious alterations took place. A story might start off in the old way, with a spectacular danger, a fire or wild animals, and for a while I might rescue people; then things would change around, and instead, somebody would be rescuing me. It might be . . . Mr. Campbell, our teacher, who tickled girls under the arms. And at this point the story concerned itself at great length with what I looked like — how long my hair was, and what kind of dress I had on; by the time I had these details worked out the real excitement of the story was lost. (126)

In this mise-en-abymic structure (a writer telling about a budding writer telling autobiographically based stories), we see the results of initiation into the female gender role as conceived at the time.[18] While the narrator is still very young, she is allowed to do as she pleases, and she much prefers her father's (money-earning) outdoor activities to her mother's domestic sphere and chores: "My father was tirelessly inventive and his favourite

[18] See also Goldman: "No longer the valiant hero, she becomes the victim in need of rescue" (1990, 65).

book in the world was Robinson Crusoe" (114).[19] Indeed, the whole story hinges on an inside/outside dichotomy linked to gendered spaces. The young daughter identifies with the male world and feels at ease with it; she even considers herself more appropriate for it than her younger brother Laird, whom she regards as a sissy for a large part of the story: "Laird came too, with his little cream and green gardening can, filled too full and knocking against his legs and slopping water on his canvas shoes. I had the real watering can, my father's, though I could only carry it three-quarters full" (114).

In contrast, the girl turns decisively not only against the maternal domestic sphere, but against the mother herself: "It seemed to me that work in the house was endless, dreary and peculiarly depressing; work done out of doors, and in my father's service, was ritualistically important" (117). The daughter enters into a domestic tug-of-war with her mother, even calling her an "enemy" (117) because she feels that "she was plotting now to get me to stay in the house more, although she knew I hated it (*because* she knew I hated it) and keep me from working for my father" (118). That the mother might be in need of some help and allegiance, too, is a thought that never crosses the girl's mind ("It did not occur to me that she could be lonely, or jealous," 118).[20] In turning against her mother and against her domestic confinement she symbolically rejects the traditional female gender role cut out for her as a girl. The story demonstrates how in her adolescence the girl is pushed by manifold social pressures into a role she would never have chosen herself: "One time a feed salesman came down into the pens . . . and my father said, 'Like to have you meet my new hired man.' I turned away and raked furiously, red in the face with pleasure. 'Could of fooled me,' said the salesman, 'I thought it was only a girl'" (116). This gender contrast implies, of course, an upgrading of "male" and a downgrading of "female" — an evaluation that the girl, "red in the face with pleasure," internalizes when her father masculinizes her because she is doing a good job for him. Being compared to a male worker is flattering in her mind because she does not yet realize the implications this has for her own gender. Professional work outside the house is a male domain; the father unwittingly robs his daughter of her sexual identity, whereas the salesman quite unashamedly brings her down to earth by

[19] On the significance of Robinson Crusoe in the context see Goldman 1990, for example: "Robinson Crusoe, the economic man *par excellence*, is an apt hero for the narrator's 'tirelessly inventive' capitalistic father" (73 note 1).

[20] See Hallvard Dahlie's statement on Munro's biographical mother: "Like many of the unfulfilled and despairing mothers of Munro's fiction, she expended her energies during the formative years of the three Laidlaw children in the nurturing of a family under conditions of deprivation and hardship" (Dahlie 1993, 188–89).

reducing her to her biological sex with derogatory gendered implications — "only a girl." Statements by her visiting grandmother rub in the fact that the female gender role is an utterly restrictive one at the time in which the story is set: " 'Girls don't slam doors like that.' 'Girls keep their knees together when they sit down.' And worse still, when I asked some questions, 'That's none of girls' business' " (119).

For a while the girl manages to resist such strict gender norms: "I continued to slam the doors and sit as awkwardly as possible, thinking that by such measures I kept myself free" (119). Her most spectacular opposition works on a more pronounced symbolic level of action. She purposefully keeps the gate open for the female horse Flora,[21] thus enabling her to postpone her fate of being slaughtered by the narrator's father for fox food. The girl intuitively identifies with the female horse because she, too, wants to escape a certain death — if not in the literal sense of the word, then in the sense of the end of her free-ranging activities and options when she is pressed into a fixed female role pattern. The symbolic act of letting Flora run wild also constitutes the protagonist's first rebellion against her father, who adheres to the authoritative gender patterning. Mainly, however, it is a silent outcry against her own domestication. In this opposition, the girl is similar to the mare Flora, who is clearly contrasted with the stallion Mack in that she, too, refuses to be fenced in:

> Mack was an old black workhorse, sooty and indifferent. Flora was a sorrel mare, a driver. . . . Mack was slow and easy to handle. Flora was given to fits of violent alarm. . . . Flora threw up her head, rolled her eyes, whinnied despairingly. . . . It was not safe to go into her stall; she would kick. (119)

The climax occurs at the end of the story when the family is gathered at the dinner table, that is, symptomatically in a scene that is the epitome of ordered (or, depending on one's perspective, regulated and individually restricting) family life. Here, the gender pendulum fully swings back: Laird, in a classical act of "male bonding," tells on his older sister by disclosing that she let Flora escape on purpose. For the first time in the story he sides with his father against her. The father, having overcome his immediate consternation about his daughter's apparently ill-advised act, reacts in a manner that is even more threatening to his daughter than either fury or

[21] On the significance of this name for the female horse see Heliane Ventura: "The name given to the mare reinforces her female status. Flora is one of the minor Greek goddesses of agriculture. Like Demeter, she represents the bounties of nature, its seasonal fertility. Her liberation inaugurated by her passing through the opened gate can be likened to a new birth which reiterates the primordial act through which the individual takes possession of the world" (1992, 86).

reproach: "'Never mind,' my father said. He spoke with resignation, even good humour, the words which absolved and dismissed me for good. 'She's only a girl,' he said" (127).[22]

This reaction represents her initiation into a female gender role, with the word "girl" becoming what Jacques Derrida calls a "conflictual site." The implications are disastrous for the narrator. Girls behave irrationally and — like the mentally handicapped — cannot be held responsible for their actions; in any case, in the domestic sphere cut out for them it will not matter much *what* they do because power is not on their side. The girl's reactions to such implications are even graver because they suggest the impact of socialization on the forming of mentalities: "I didn't protest that, even in my heart. Maybe it was true" (127). The girl has learned her gendered place in the social hierarchy the hard way. Humiliated by her younger brother's self-seeking act of betrayal and now domineering attitude, she has internalized not only to behave, but also to feel and think as a girl and thus to consider herself, as the ending suggests, rather insignificant. Adopting her father's belittling view of her act of letting Flora run, she betrays her own desire to rid herself of the restrictive role patterns forced upon her by the dominant gender system.

Nevertheless, even on the level of the narrated time there is some hope presented at the end of the story by the modal adverb "maybe" ("Maybe it was true") — the girl may manage eventually to distance herself from prescribed gender roles (see the narrator's critical reflections on the past events) which, as this story illustrates, work against the interests of women by drastically reducing their options for leading a suitable and fulfilling life according to their individual — and not predominantly categorical, gender-type — characteristics and desires. As the quotation by Adrienne Rich at the beginning of this article suggests, especially for women, re-visioning and then revising traditional gender roles is not only part of cultural and personal history but a step towards self-acceptance and, finally, an act of survival. "Until we can understand the assumptions in which we are drenched we cannot know ourselves," Rich states (35). Questions of gender identity and an autobiographical impulse combine, as often with Munro, in this story told in retrospect by a narrating "I" that has a higher level of awareness than the narrator/protagonist as a young girl. As Robert Thacker claims, "Munro's stories share the definition of the self — the primary urge in autobiography — as their central aim. . . . In fact,

[22] See also the film *Boys and Girls* (1982) based on the Munro story, which was produced by the National Film Board of Canada and won an Oscar in 1984 for Best Short Film and Live Action. It is advertised on the Internet as "the paramount short film on sexism."

autobiography lies at the very core of Munro's celebrated ability to offer stories of such precision, such haunting beauty, and finally, such verisimilitude" (Thacker, 155). That Munro deals at the same time with general role models and goes far beyond a potential autobiographical background of shedding internalized social patterns through the liberating experience of writing is suggested from the beginning by the story's generic title in the plural form, "Boys and Girls," which points to the social significance of the individual experience rendered. The socialization forces with regard to both girls and boys are also evoked by the fact that the narrator's brother is named and thereby individualized, significantly through a speaking name that suggests his empowered gender role ("laird" is the Scottish word for "landowner"[23]). The female narrator, in contrast, remains nameless, which helps to generalize her socialization experience to a larger extent while at the same time keeping her character more open to an autobiographical reading of the story, as Munro herself has supported in various interviews concerning this and other stories.

"Boys and Girls," written at the beginning of the "second wave" of feminist involvement with literature in North America, renders gender relations in a rather programmatic manner:[24] the almost stereotypical characterization of the father and the mother, the systematic, highly symbolic opposition between interior/female and outer/male space, the divergent character of the male and the female horses, the clear-cut socializing influences imposed on the girl both by family members and by the closed rural society, and the seemingly logical mirroring of the girl's ongoing socialization process in her different dreams. This early story does not feature Munro's later postmodernist technique of circulating indeterminacy but rather "the capsule summary conclusions — the 'false unity' — found so often in *Dance of the Happy Shades*" (Thacker, 157). The story demonstrates the restrictive, de-individualizing forces of an essentialist gender concept during the adolescent phase of development. At the same time, it also points out positively valued, liberating opportunities for women to rebel against dominant male codes of behavior. Thus the girl feels the first estrangement from her father when she surreptitiously watches him kill a horse, apparently without any emotions on his side: "Yet I felt a little ashamed, and there was a new wariness, a sense of holding-off, in my attitude to my father and his work" (124), an attitude which later climaxes

[23] "Laird is a potential laird, the male heir to the family who will by-pass the law of primo-geniture to occupy the whole territory, inside and outside, in keeping with male prerogatives on the farm" (Ventura, 82).

[24] See Munro's interesting — and highly self-critical — comments on this story; for instance, "I wrote it rather too purposefully perhaps, to show something" (Munro, "Author's Commentary," 185).

in her spontaneous rebellion against her father when she helps Flora escape. It is part of the female role that the narrator abhors the routine killing of animals, although an economic necessity on the fox farm. Her brother Laird, in contrast, is ritualistically initiated into the male role by being allowed to join his father in the hunt to capture Flora and also through having her blood on his body. He seems to be proud of symbolically having arrived at male adulthood: "Laird lifted his arm to show off a streak of blood. 'We shot old Flora,' he said, 'and cut her up in fifty pieces.' 'Well I don't want to hear about it,' my mother said" (126–27).[25]

Nevertheless, from the vantage point of the experiencing "I," the clear difference between the girl's and the boy's initiation into their respective gender roles seems to be to the girl's disadvantage: "Far from being a heroic aggrandizement, her initiation, by contrast to her brother's, is an ironic deflation of her status, which helps her understand that for a girl to grow up is to come down" (Ventura, 80). The family scene at the dinner table is supposed to be a lesson for life, making the adolescent girl aware that, just as foxes are raised on the farm in fenced pens, so the gender role she is supposed to identify with is a social "production,"[26] a construct: "A girl was not, as I had supposed, simply what I was; it was what I had to become. It was a definition, always touched with emphasis, with reproach and disappointment" (119). With even her younger brother and former pal eventually joining the forces socializing and suppressing her, every character and almost every act or speech rendered in the text functions as a socializing agent or agency, pushing her in a certain direction of behavior and stressing a highly differential view of the sexes and their strictly separate spheres of action and development. Even the two types of calendars mentioned in the story bluntly differentiate between men and women on a symbolic level of meaning. The historical calendar on the kitchen door showing scenes from nature and of Canada's colonial past (thus representing domestication on a national level) openly marks the mother's personal domestication, with the kitchen being the epitome of domestic existence.

[25] See also Goldman: "As they lift him [Laird] into the truck, the little boy becomes a man: he joins the hunting party. . . . The mark of blood and the domination of the Other continues to function as a crucial element in the rites of manhood. The boy cements his alliance with the father on the basis of their mutual triumph over nature" (71).

[26] See again Goldman: "The familial discourse — a discourse which is 'absolutely central to the perpetuation of the present, phallocentric order' — must also be fed . . .; it too requires bodies. . . . The construction of gendered subjects constitutes a form of production. Yet unlike other systems of production, the mechanisms which assist in the creation of gendered adults remain invisible; they seem natural, and for this reason they are taken for granted" (69, 62).

Henry Bailey's (the hired man's) calendars, in contrast, are stashed away in the male sphere of the barn — most likely pornographic pin-up calendars which "embody" another, more drastic and reifying form of domestication of the female, that is, through the representation of her naked body as an object for the male voyeuristic gaze and desire.

The painful, conflicting feelings that the gender instruction at the dinner table must instil in the girl silence her for the moment yet make her body speak: as her brother points out "matter-of-factly, 'she's crying'" (127). On the one hand, the experiencing "I" is given a ready-made explanation for her behavior with Flora that she did not understand at the time of her spontaneous decision. On the other hand, she seems to have lost the gender battle for the more attractive and dominant position in the family, being reduced to the description of "girl," which is used dismissingly twice in the story. The conflicting feelings that such fixing, derogatory attributions must provoke under the circumstances are captured in contradictory, oxymoronic formulations, a hallmark of Munro's earlier writing in particular (see Hoy 1980), for example: "He spoke with resignation, even good humour, the words which absolved and dismissed me for good" (127).

Correlating with the conflictual ending of the story, "Boys and Girls" shows competing gender concepts at work, thereby calling into question a strictly essentializing view of gender hierarchies. Already in this early story, Munro has shifted the emphasis to "throw the story line open to question" and thereby to "demand new judgements and solutions" (*Who*, 177), because the binary oppositions between male and female in which the story is drenched are constantly undercut (for example, by the father calling his competent daughter a "hired man" and by the daughter feeling ill at ease with the stereotypical role distribution). What the girl yearns for is not an "either/or" but, in an early postmodernist stance and a plea for multiplicity, an "and."[27] As Dell, the female protagonist of Munro's second book following upon *Dance of the Happy Shades* was to formulate in another context and in more pronounced metafictional terms: "And no list could hold what I wanted, for what I wanted was every last thing, every layer of speech and thought, stroke of light on bark or walls, every smell, pothole, pain, crack, delusion, held still and held together — radiant, everlasting" (*Lives*, 249).[28]

[27] See Ventura, 84.

[28] The American theorist Judith Butler has popularized the concept of gendered behavior as a learned pattern and subject to the workings of the social environment (see Butler 1990 and 2004). Munro's view is similar, but the human concerns of her story and her sympathy with the victims of gender roles complement Butler's otherwise highly abstract arguments and bring home even more clearly the emotional implications of socially instilled gender identities.

Works Cited

Beran, Carol L. "The Luxury of Excellence: Alice Munro in the *New Yorker*." In *The Rest of the Story: Critical Essays on Alice Munro*, ed. Robert Thacker. Toronto: ECW Press, 1999. 204–32.

Butler, Judith. *Gender Trouble: Feminism and the Subversion of Identity*. New York: Routledge, 1990.

———. *Undoing Gender*. New York: Routledge, 2004.

Carrington, Ildikó de Papp. *Controlling the Uncontrollable: The Fiction of Alice Munro*. De Kalb, IL: Northern Illinois University Press, 1989.

Dahlie, Hallvard. "Alice Munro (1931–)." In *ECW's Biographical Guide to Canadian Novelists*, ed. Robert Lecker, Jack David, and Ellen Quigley. Toronto: ECW Press, 1993. 188–91.

Gibson, Graeme. "Alice Munro." In Gibson, *Eleven Canadian Novelists*. Toronto: Anansi, 1973. 237–64.

Goldman, Marlene. "Penning in the Bodies: The Construction of Gendered Subjects in Alice Munro's *Boys and Girls*." *Studies in Canadian Literature* 15 (1990): 62–75.

Hancock, Geoff. "Alice Munro." *Canadian Writers at Work: Interviews with Geoff Hancock*. Toronto: Oxford University Press, 1987. 187–224.

Hoy, Helen. "'Dull, Simple, Amazing and Unfathomable': Paradox and Double Vision in Alice Munro's Fiction." *Studies in Canadian Literature* 5 (1980): 100–115.

Howells, Coral Ann. *Alice Munro*. Manchester: Manchester University Press, 1998.

———. "Intimate Dislocations: Alice Munro, *Hateship, Friendship, Courtship, Loveship, Marriage*." In Howells, *Contemporary Canadian Women's Fiction: Refiguring Identities*. New York: Palgrave Macmillan, 2003. 53–78.

———. "Munro, Alice." In *Encyclopedia of Literature in Canada*, ed. William H. New. Toronto: University of Toronto Press, 2002. 769–72.

Martin, Peggy. "'What a Pathetic Old Tart': Alice Munro's Older Women." *English Studies in Canada* 24.1 (1998): 83–92.

Munro, Alice. "Author's Commentary on 'An Ounce of Cure' and 'Boys and Girls'" (1970), repr. in *How Stories Mean*, ed. John Metcalf and J. R. (Tim) Struthers. Erin, ON: The Porcupine's Quill Press, 1993. 185–87.

———. "Boys and Girls." In Munro, *Dance of the Happy Shades*, 111–27.

———. *Carried Away: A Selection of Stories*. New York: Knopf, 2006.

———. *Dance of the Happy Shades*. Toronto: McGraw-Hill Ryerson, 1968.

———. *Friend of My Youth*. Toronto: McClelland & Stewart, 1990.

———. *Hateship, Friendship, Courtship, Loveship, Marriage*. Toronto: McClelland & Stewart, 2001.

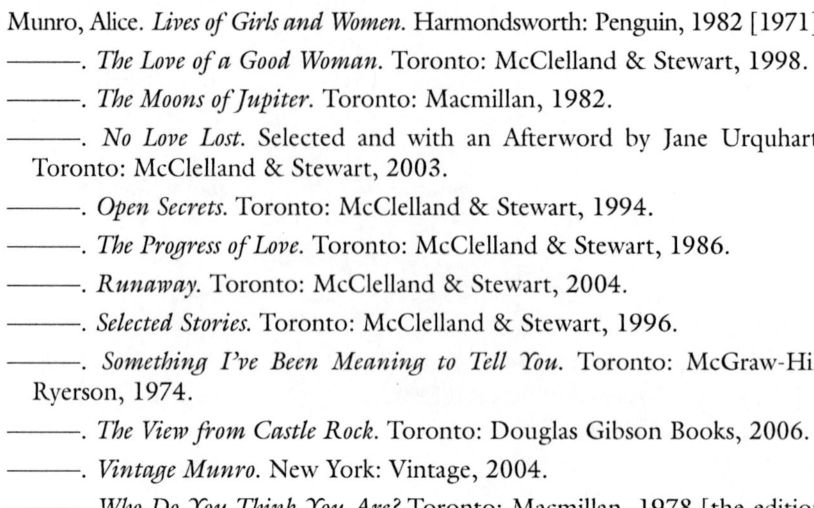

Munro, Alice. *Lives of Girls and Women.* Harmondsworth: Penguin, 1982 [1971].

———. *The Love of a Good Woman.* Toronto: McClelland & Stewart, 1998.

———. *The Moons of Jupiter.* Toronto: Macmillan, 1982.

———. *No Love Lost.* Selected and with an Afterword by Jane Urquhart. Toronto: McClelland & Stewart, 2003.

———. *Open Secrets.* Toronto: McClelland & Stewart, 1994.

———. *The Progress of Love.* Toronto: McClelland & Stewart, 1986.

———. *Runaway.* Toronto: McClelland & Stewart, 2004.

———. *Selected Stories.* Toronto: McClelland & Stewart, 1996.

———. *Something I've Been Meaning to Tell You.* Toronto: McGraw-Hill Ryerson, 1974.

———. *The View from Castle Rock.* Toronto: Douglas Gibson Books, 2006.

———. *Vintage Munro.* New York: Vintage, 2004.

———. *Who Do You Think You Are?* Toronto: Macmillan, 1978 [the edition used is the Penguin edition of 1980 under the title *The Beggar Maid*].

Nischik, Reingard M. "'Pen Photographs': Zum Phänomen des (kanadischen) Kurzgeschichtenzyklus." *Deutsche Vierteljahrsschrift für Literaturwissenschaft und Geistesgeschichte* 66.1 (1992): 192–204.

Rich, Adrienne. "When We Dead Awaken: Writing as Re-Vision (1971)." In Rich, *On Lies, Secrets, and Silence: Selected Prose 1966–1978.* New York: Norton, 1979. 33–49.

Struthers, J. R. (Tim). "The Real Material: An Interview with Alice Munro" (1981). In *Probable Fictions: Alice Munro's Narrative Acts*, ed. Louis K. Mackendrick. Downsview, ON: ECW Press, 1983. 5–36.

Thacker, Robert. "'So Shocking a Verdict in Real Life': Autobiography in Alice Munro's Stories." In *Reflections: Autobiography and Canadian Literature*, ed. K. P. Stich. Ottawa: University of Ottawa Press, 1988. 153–61.

Ventura, Heliane. "Alice Munro's 'Boys and Girls': Mapping out Boundaries." *Commonwealth Essays & Studies* 15 (1992): 80–87.

15: Collective Memory and Personal Identity in the Prairie Town of Manawaka: Margaret Laurence, "The Loons" (1966)

Caroline Rosenthal (University of Constance)

WHEN MARGARET LAURENCE DIED on 5 January 1987, taking her own life in the face of terminal cancer, she had become one of Canada's most prolific, highly acclaimed, and beloved authors. She contributed extensively to Canadian literature and cultural memory, and her innovations in narrative style and modes of representation earned her an international reputation in addition. Laurence published five novels (*This Side Jordan*, 1960; *The Stone Angel*, 1964; *A Jest of God*, 1966; *The Fire-Dwellers*, 1969; *The Diviners*, 1974), two short-story collections (*The Tomorrow-Tamer and Other Stories*, 1963; *A Bird in the House*, 1970), five books of non-fiction (*A Tree for Poverty*, 1954; *The Prophet's Camel Bell*, 1963; *Long Drums and Cannons*, 1968; *Heart of a Stranger*, 1976; *Dance on the Earth*, 1989), and four books for children (*Jason's Quest*, 1970; *Six Darn Cows*, 1979; *The Olden Days Coat*, 1979; *The Christmas Birthday Story*, 1980). Her oeuvre also comprises numerous poems, letters, addresses, reviews, and articles, some of which were collected and published in *Heart of a Stranger*. Laurence received the Governor General's Award twice (1967 for *A Jest of God*, 1975 for *The Diviners*) and in 1971 was made Companion of the Order of Canada, the highest award available to a Canadian citizen. Between 1970 and 1981 Laurence received eleven honorary degrees.

Laurence was born as Jean Margaret Wemyss on 18 July 1926 in Neepawa, Manitoba, where she was raised by her aunt, both of her parents having died before she was nine. The imaginary town of Manawaka, which features prominently in five of Laurence's books as the fictional epitome of any small Canadian prairie town, is closely modeled on her home town. "The Loons" is taken from Laurence's short-story cycle *A Bird in the House* (1970), which is set in Manawaka and which Laurence described as the only "semi-autobiographical fiction I have ever written" (Laurence in Woodcock 1983, 5).

Before returning to the Canadian prairies and writing about the region's myths and history, Laurence went abroad. From 1950 to 1957 she and her husband lived in Africa, in what are now Somalia and Ghana, and had two children. Upon her return from Africa in 1957, Laurence lived in Vancouver until she and her husband separated in 1962, after which she moved to England for several years. Laurence's detailed observations of religious, social, and narratological aspects of African culture resulted in five books. In 1954 Laurence published her first book, *A Tree for Poverty*, in which Somali oral folklore was translated into English for the first time. *This Side Jordan*, Laurence's first novel, is set in Ghana and — well before the advent of postcolonial studies — portrays clashes between British and African, between colonizing and colonized cultures. In 1963 *The Prophet's Camel Bell*, a travel memoir, and *The Tomorrow-Tamer and Other Stories*, her first collection of short stories, were published. Another product of her stay in Africa was *Long Drums and Cannons*, the first broad study of Nigerian writers in English, which, at the same time, also illustrates Laurence's own approach to writing. In the introduction she says that fiction "must be planted firmly in some soil. . . . The main concern of the writer remains that of somehow creating the individual on the printed page, of catching the tones and accents of human speech, of setting down the conflicts of people who are as real to him as himself" (Laurence 1968, 10). Laurence's fiction is deeply rooted in regionalism and in a realistic mode of representation; it also defies universal truths and master narratives by illustrating how reality always depends on cultural background and personal point of view.

Laurence's African writings prepared the ground for her famous "Manawaka cycle," which explores the regional identity of the Canadian prairies in the 1930s. It consists of four novels (*The Stone Angel*, *A Jest of God*, *The Fire-Dwellers*, and *The Diviners*) and the short-story collection *A Bird in the House*, which assembles stories previously published in Canadian magazines between 1962 and 1969. In her Manawaka fiction, Laurence picks up themes and techniques she had already investigated in her African books, for instance, the theme of multiculturalism, and the adaptation of oral storytelling techniques to written literature. The Manawaka cycle explores the conflicted cultural memory of the Canadian prairies by drawing on oral traditions of both Scottish-Canadians and the Métis, people of mixed Native-European descent, and demonstrates how deeply Canadian identity has been informed by multiculturalism. The Manawaka books also comprise "elements that can be recognized as parts of a Canadian tradition in fiction — the strong voices of women writers, the West, the Canadian Scottish mythology, the small town, the search for home and the language of home" (Thomas 1976, 1). They vividly portray the struggles, desires, and relationships of women in a small prairie town. In her rewriting of the West and of pioneer life from a female perspective, Laurence has often been compared to Willa Cather, while her fictional Manawaka has been likened to William Faulkner's Yoknapatawpha in Mississippi. Yet Laurence's rendition of a small Canadian town is also distinctively Canadian in the sense that it exemplifies the "garrison mentality," which Northrop Frye postulated as characteristic of Canadian identity. Frye defined "garrison" as "a closely knit and beleaguered society [whose] moral and social values are unquestionable" (Frye 1971, 225–26). The town of Manawaka imposes rigid moral and ethical standards on its inhabitants, standards which on the one hand confine people but which, on the other, supply them with a strong collective identity and a sense of home and community. The female protagonists of the Manawaka books all rebel against family duties and social norms in their attempt at self-realization. While they physically leave Manawaka, they carry the place with them in their hearts and minds. Laurence felt the same way about her home: as a young writer, she needed to distance herself from her place of origin, but she knew that "one day I would have to stop writing about Africa and go back to my own people, my own place of belonging" (Laurence 1976, 14).

This is echoed by Vanessa MacLeod, the first-person narrator and main protagonist of *A Bird in the House*, who begins her narrative, "That house in Manawaka is the one which, more than any other, I carry with me" (1). Regional identity and how we integrate this identity into ourselves is one of Laurence's primary concerns; yet, as *A Bird in the House* suggests, this identity is not static, but the ever-changing result of a complex process of becoming. Unlike the other Manawaka texts, *A Bird in the House* is not a novel but a short-story cycle that nonetheless bears the structure of a Bildungsroman or artist novel as it traces Vanessa's development from a naïve child to a mature woman writer. In her posthumously published memoir *Dance on the Earth*, Laurence relates how her editor at Knopf doggedly tried to persuade her to turn *A Bird in the House* into a novel like the other books of the Manawaka cycle, but she felt strongly that "I would rather not have the book published at all than to make the stories into a novel" (Laurence 1989, 198). Laurence had solid reasons for her decision: the more condensed and at the same time more open-ended style of the short story suits the subject matter of the book as much as its linguistic and narrative design. Each story is carefully crafted and self-contained, yet all the stories in *A Bird in the House* are related to each other by an array of recurring themes, images, and motifs (see Stovel 1996). The bird motif from the title, for instance, persists in each story, mostly as a metaphor for women's entrapment in gender expectations and social roles.

Laurence's greatest narrative achievement in the short-story cycle is her handling of point of view: Vanessa MacLeod tells the story of her childhood from an adult perspective, which splits the narrative subject into a reflecting, mature Vanessa and an experiencing and acting younger self (see Darling 1984; Capone 1985; Stovel). This bifurcated point of view doubles events and people in *A Bird in the House* as they are constantly portrayed through the eyes of the innocent younger child and from the perspective of the knowing older self. As Laurence explained, "the narrative voice had to speak as though from two points in time, simultaneously" (Laurence 1972, 128). Laurence masterfully accomplishes what Thomas calls "a technique of double exposure," in which the mature narrator assumes the voice of the child she once was and at the same time "remains her present self, far older in compassion and understanding" (Thomas, 104). While the young Vanessa escapes reality by adorning the world with romantic tales, the older writer uses writing as a way to come to terms with her past. By realistically portraying the Canadian prairies in the 1930s she cuts through her younger self's romantic notions of both cultural and personal history. Laurence's juxtaposition of jarring modes of representation thus makes us aware of the fact that reality changes within the lifetime of one and the same person because it always depends on standpoint, time, and cultural context:

> Laurence . . . can be seen as a committed realist, but deeply opposed to a form of realism which would appear to take for granted the conditions it describes. Her semi-autobiographical fiction takes so little for granted that it represents one of the strongest revisions of Western experience in contemporary Canadian writing. (Easingwood 1991, 28–29)

A Bird in the House describes the effects of the Depression on a small prairie town and touches upon themes found across the breadth of Laurence's fiction: the nature-culture paradigm, the acceptance of death, the complexity of human relationships, myths, and the constructed nature of both historiography and space. Laurence drew on her own background for the stories in *A Bird in the House*. Her paternal grandparents were of Scottish descent, while her maternal great-grandparents had immigrated to Canada from Northern Ireland. The depiction of Vanessa's grandparents illustrates how much the founding generation of white settlers was influenced by thoroughly protestant values. Because of financial problems, Vanessa and her parents had to move in with her father's mother, Grandmother MacLeod, a rigid and apparently unfeeling woman who runs a strict regime of order and propriety in her house. She looks down on the maternal side of Vanessa's family, the Connors, because they are descended from "famine Irish" ("The Mask of a Bear," 53), while Grandmother MacLeod's family derives from an old Scottish clan whose motto was "Pleasure Arises from Work," a slogan which pinpoints the protestant work ethic that dominates her life. It forbids her to show emotions even when her daughter-in-law almost dies in childbirth; and when her son, Vanessa's father, dies she does not allow herself to shed a tear. She reminds Vanessa of "the caught sparrow fluttering in the attic" ("To Set Our House in Order," 44), implicitly pointing to women's social entrapment. The bird motif also occurs in connection with Vanessa's maternal grandmother. Up to her death, Grandmother Connor is the only soothing influence in the Brick House, which is ruled menacingly by Grandfather Connor. After her father's death, Vanessa, her mother, and her brother have to move into the Brick House — another echo of Laurence's own biography (Laurence 1989, 63–65). While Grandfather Connor in *A Bird in the House* has a sharp tongue and demands effectiveness as well as discipline from everyone living under his roof, his wife is a very religious, quiet, and gentle woman, who is, however, petrified in the role of angel in the house, pretty to look at, like her caged canary, but rarely capable of singing. Vanessa says about the Brick House: "I felt . . . that my lungs were in danger of exploding, that the pressure of silence would become too great to be borne" ("The Mask of a Bear," 55).

The young Vanessa invents romantic adventure stories "of spectacular heroism" ("The Sound of the Singing," 4) to escape the dire reality of Manawaka, with its limited possibilities of self-realization for women, and also to gain some control over her life (see Buss 1985, 54–76). When Grandfather Connor tells her for the umpteenth time how he walked the hundred miles from Galloping Mountain to Manawaka and became one of the founders of the town, Vanessa is disappointed that "he had not met up with any slit-eyed and treacherous Indians or any mad trappers" (7) and makes up her own pioneer story, in which a man is dying in a log cabin "*with only the beautiful halfbreed lady* to look after him" (13, emphasis in the original). Vanessa's romantic tales reflect the sexist and racist clichés held by the society she is growing up in. She gets the material for her stories from the only sources available to her, the Bible and Eaton's catalogues, as well as from romantic tales about "Indians," which all have the effect of misinforming her about Native Canadians, a factor that becomes important in "The Loons." Tracing Vanessa's development into a writer, *A Bird in the House* shows her to increasingly turn away from romantic tales as she realizes that they are not grounded in reality. Inspired by "The Song of Solomon," for instance, she thinks up the tale of "some barbaric queen, beautiful and terrible" ("The Mask of a Bear," 54), but tears it up when she realizes that her romance does not measure up to the real women she encounters in everyday life — her beloved Aunt Edna, for example, who, as the unmarried daughter, keeps house for Grandfather Connor and has to endure his derogatory remarks. Vanessa destroys her story when it dawns on her that the imaginative "barbaric queen" has nothing to do with her real aunt's "sturdy laughter, the way she tore into housework" (65). While her aunt's heroism is less spectacular than that of some imaginary queen, it is grounded in reality, a quality that becomes more and more important to the aspiring writer.

Laurence convincingly conveys how much Vanessa but also her parents' generation suffered from the rigid social codes and morality which both the Connor and the MacLeod families forced onto them, yet she never portrays the grandparents' generation unsympathetically. Despite the restrictive and often tyrannical structures that confine both men and women in gender stereotypes and limit their individual development, Laurence stresses that family and a common place of origin bind people together and become the backbone of their individuality. This effect is again achieved by the split-narrative perspective: while the child is often hurt and confused by the rigidity of her grandparents, the older narrator understands that her grandparents were hard because they lived hard lives. What the innocent child feels only obscurely is revealed by the ordering narrative of the woman writer (Darling, 194). All of the Manawaka books deal with how individuals are informed by an ancestral past and by "the much much longer past which has become legend, the past of a collective memory" (Laurence 1972, 126).

"The Loons" is the fifth story in the collection and was first published under the title "Crying of the Loons" in the *Atlantic Advocate* in 1966. It follows upon the eponymous "A Bird in the House," in which Vanessa's father dies, and marks a pivotal point in the collection for various reasons. While up to then the stories proceed chronologically, "The Loons" is the first story that breaks this linear structure. It moves first back to and then beyond the time of Vanessa's father's death, which upsets the narrative order as well, and portrays Vanessa subsequently at the age of eleven, fifteen, and nineteen. Laurence skillfully changes the tone of narrative in the story according to Vanessa's age and point of view. While the eleven-year-old is caught up in romantic stereotypes, the teenager sees things in a more realistic way, and the grown Vanessa finally comprehends the events in their full complexity. "The Loons" thus highlights Laurence's narrative technique of a split subject. The story is also special because Vanessa veers from exploring her family story and Scottish-Irish ancestry and turns her attention to the Métis[1] population of Manawaka, specifically the Tonnerre family, and their history. Unlike the Brick House where Vanessa lives, the Tonnerre's dwelling is a wood cabin "chinked with mud" in the middle of the forest ("The Loons," 96). The Tonnerres are poor, uneducated, and

[1] The Métis are a nation within Canada whose people are of Cree or Ojibwa and European descent. They emerged as a group in the eighteenth century when trading companies explored the Western territory. They became a political force in the nineteenth century under the leadership of Louis Riel in the Red River Rebellion of 1869–70, a conflict over land ownership which led to battles at Batoche and Duck Lake.

at the bottom of the social scale in Manawaka. People refer to them as "French halfbreeds," who "did not belong among the Cree of the Galloping Mountain reservation, further north, and they did not belong among the Scots-Irish and Ukrainians of Manawaka, either" (96). In Laurence's Manawaka the Métis occupy a position between cultures, and historically they have had difficulties settling their land claims and attaining legal status as a nation in Canada because, unlike Native Canadians or the Inuit, they are not considered a "purely" indigenous group. The narrator of "The Loons" characterizes the Tonnerres as underdogs who speak a "patois" (a substandard regional dialect) and an English that "was broken and full of obscenities" (96), but at the same time she points out that they made prairie history before they settled on the margins of Manawaka fifty years ago. The narrator relates how the clan's ancestor Jules Tonnerre "came back from Batoche with a bullet in his thigh, the year that Riel was hung and the voices of the Métis entered their long silence" (96). By introducing Jules in the context of Batoche, an important place of battle in the Métis' first rebellion, and Louis Riel,[2] the legendary hero of the Métis resistance, Laurence places the Tonnerres side by side with the Scottish-Irish legendary figures of Manawaka.

"The Loons" concentrates on Piquette Tonnerre, one of Vanessa's classmates who has tuberculosis of the bone and is treated by Vanessa's father, a doctor.[3] In school, Vanessa recognizes her "as an embarrassing presence" because of her "hoarse voice and her clumsy limping walk and her grimy cotton dresses" (97). One night at dinner, Vanessa's father proposes to take Piquette with them to the family cabin at Diamond Lake, Ontario, for the summer vacation. He wants to give her a chance to recover from her tuberculosis and is afraid of releasing her from the hospital because once home she would have to work too much. The conversation at the MacLeod's dinner table is a subtle commentary on family

[2] Louis Riel (1844–85) played a pivotal role in two rebellions (1870 and 1885), in which the Métis fought for recognition and land settlement claims and were engaged in battles with the Canadian government. After a highly political trial, Riel was hanged in Regina in 1885. He has become a symbolic figure not only of the Métis but of "Aboriginal resistance to Canadian assimilation" in general and has turned into "a legendary figure — even a hero — of mythological proportions" (Bumsted in New 2002, 974).

[3] In his 1997 biography of Margaret Laurence, King quotes Wes McAmmond, one of Laurence's primary school teachers: "Neepawa didn't have any French or Métis. [However] there was a little girl . . . who came from Sandy Bar Reserve up on the lake [Lake Manitoba, north of Langruth] and was brought there with tuberculosis of the bone or something. . . . I think Margaret probably befriended her" (King 1997, 302–3).

dynamics as Vanessa's mother first rejects the idea but is all for it when Grandmother MacLeod announces that "'if that half-breed youngster comes along to Diamond Lake, I'm not going'" (98). As the lesser evil, Piquette, and not Grandmother MacLeod, accompanies Vanessa's family to the cottage. On the first day it becomes clear, however, that despite their closeness in age, a friendship between the two girls is impossible because of class and race barriers. After Vanessa has taken possession of her "kingdom," she asks Piquette whether she wants to come along and play, to which Piquette replies sullenly, "'I ain't a kid'" (100). Eleven-year-old Vanessa is hurt by Piquette's coarse response to her friendly advances and fails to understand the cultural abyss that lies between her world and that of Piquette. Unable to understand the reality of Piquette's life, Vanessa, the budding writer, reverts to romantic fantasies and pictures Piquette as a serene Indian who "sprang from the people of Big Bear and Poundmaker, of Tecumseh, of the Iroquois who had eaten Father Brebeuf's heart" (100).[4] While this testifies again to the naïvety of young Vanessa, Laurence enumerates leading Native Canadian chiefs to call upon a repressed part of prairie history and to criticize the misrepresentation of First Nations People in Canadian history. In her memoir *Dance on the Earth*, Laurence recalls her own history lessons in Neepawa:

> History was taught from the Anglophone point of view, the view that presented Louis Riel and Gabriel Dumont [another Métis leader], Big Bear and Poundmaker as rebel villains. It was the Upper Canadian, white Protestant interpretation of our history and it was dreadfully distorted. I had no idea that both Big Bear and Poundmaker, those proud and courageous men, virtually the last of the old independent Cree chieftains, had, after their defeat in 1885, been incarcerated, humiliatingly, in the Stony Mountain penitentiary in my own province. . . . When I think of what I learned of Canadian history, I feel cheated, not by my teachers but by the society in which I grew up. (Laurence 1989, 77)

"The Loons" reflects on the effects of such crucial misrepresentations as the young Vanessa's consciousness mirrors the stereotypes of her cultural surroundings. Vanessa is well meaning but naïvely turns Piquette into a "Hollywood Indian" or a "storybook character" (New 1987, 198); she

[4] Big Bear and Poundmaker were two important Cree chieftains, while Tecumseh, who was chief of the Shawnee Indians, became a Canadian national hero when he helped the British to defend the Canadian border against the USA in the war of 1812. Father Jean de Brébeuf was known to every Canadian child. As a Jesuit missionary, he came to Canada (or New France as it was called at the time) in 1625 and lived with the Hurons at various times. During one of the battles between the Hurons and the Iroquois, he was captured and tortured to death by the Iroquois.

appropriates her to fit her fantasies of what Indians are like. As her earlier versions of pioneer tales show, to Vanessa Indians are wild creatures with a secret knowledge of nature; she sees in Piquette "a daughter of the forest, a kind of junior prophetess of the wild" (100), and hopes that she will share some of her secret knowledge with her. Vanessa's clichéd notions of Indians derive from canonical texts that at the end of the nineteenth century romanticized and misrepresented First Nations People, works such as Pauline Johnson's *The White Wampum* and Longfellow's "The Song of Hiawatha."[5] In a tragicomic way these romantic notions clash with the reality in which Piquette lives. To the same extent that Vanessa misjudges the situation, Piquette is unable to see Vanessa's friendliness for what it is and instead consistently mistrusts her. When, for instance, Vanessa "respectfully" (101) says that Piquette must certainly know a lot about the woods, Piquette is offended because she thinks that Vanessa is making fun of where and how the Tonnerres live in Manawaka. While the other stories in the cycle illustrate how much Vanessa suffers from the protestant values of her grandparents, this story elucidates how much she herself is caught up in them.

The bird motif, which persists through the story cycle, occurs in "The Loons" as well, but where in other stories it signifies the wish for freedom, here it stands for freedom lost. Vanessa tries to share one of her treasures with Piquette when she tells her about the loons on the lake, which she and her father listen to at night. Ewan MacLeod predicts that they will soon be gone because more cottages will be built on the lake, to which Piquette frostily replies, " 'who gives a good goddamm' " (102), and refuses to come down to the lake just to listen to " 'a bunch of squawkin' birds' " (103). It is then that Vanessa realizes that "as an Indian, Piquette was a dead loss" (102). Her flippant assessment proves correct, as Piquette defies any of Vanessa's attempts to romantically position her either as the unflinching Indian warrior or the sage. When Vanessa listens to the loons that summer with her father, she little imagines that not only will the loons soon be gone but also that this will be her last time spent with him at the lake. At night the lake looks like "black glass with a streak of amber which

[5] Emily Pauline Johnson (1861–1913) was a writer of English and Mohawk ancestry who combined the oral traditions of the Iroquois with those of English Romanticism. Her renditions of Native culture were later criticized for being idealistic, theatrical, and inauthentic. One should also bear in mind, however, that she also had to cater to an audience with a very limited and clichéd knowledge of "Indians." Henry Wadsworth Longfellow (1807–82) wrote his long poem "The Song of Hiawatha" at a time when the fictional romanticizing of Indian culture had reached a climax and white authors appropriated Native culture to project their own visions, hopes, and images onto it.

was the path of the moon" (102); the atmosphere is described as tranquil, wild, and almost mythical:

> Then the loons began their calling. They rose like phantom birds from the nests on the shore, and flew out onto the dark still surface of the water. No one can ever describe that ululating sound, the crying of the loons, and no one who has heard it can ever forget it. Plaintive, and yet with a quality of chilling mockery, those voices belonged to a world separated by aeons from our neat world of summer cottages and the lighted lamps of home. (102)

The loons signify a realm before and beyond civilization, and their "plaintive" cry with its "chilling mockery" seems to carry a wisdom that lies beyond the settled and cultured sphere. Vanessa and Piquette remain distanced from each other all summer and afterwards lose touch; the following winter Vanessa's father dies of pneumonia after less than a week's illness and Piquette drops out of school.

When four years later the two girls meet by chance at the Regal Café in Manawaka, the differences between them have deepened and the now fifteen-year-old Vanessa is more aware of them. Piquette's hair, which had been long and straight, is now "frizzily permed" and she acts out a "gaiety that was almost violent" (104). When Piquette walks over to Vanessa she staggers, not now because of her tuberculosis but because she is inebriated. In a newly acquired "worldliness" Piquette tells Vanessa that she has " 'been all over the place — Winnipeg, Regina, Saskatoon' " and that she is not going to stay in this " 'jerkwater town' " (104). As Piquette boasts that she is engaged to " 'an English fella' " with " 'blond wavy hair' " Vanessa recognizes the "real" Piquette for the first time: "I really did see her, for the first and only time in all the years we had both lived in the same town. Her defiant face momentarily became unguarded and unmasked, and in her eyes there was a terrifying hope" (105). Piquette's hope is to rise socially and to win the respect of people in Manawaka. Even as the fifteen-year-old Vanessa grasps the tragedy of the Métis girl's life for the first time, she still envies Piquette, who is allowed to do all the things she herself is forbidden to do.

Laurence convincingly portrays first the voice of the eleven-year-old and then that of the teenaged Vanessa. This voice changes again when Vanessa leaves home to go to college. On her first summer back her mother tells the now nineteen-year-old Vanessa that Piquette and her two children have died in a fire at the Tonnerre shack when the woodstove on which her father Lazarus and her brothers made their homebrew exploded. Beth MacLeod further relates that Piquette, who had gotten divorced and returned to Manawaka to keep house for the Tonnerre men, had put on a lot of weight and had been arrested for being drunk and disorderly in public several times before her death. Vanessa now realizes for the first time that Piquette was "doomed to disaster" from the start (Kertzer 1992, 65) and never had a fair chance in a society that entirely marginalized her. She also comprehends that by being part of "white" Manawaka, she herself had inadvertently participated in this marginalization. The adult Vanessa then revisits Diamond Lake, where she had spent the summer with her family and Piquette, and finds the place much changed. The Cree reservation, Galloping Mountain, has been turned into a national park, and Diamond Lake has been renamed Lake Wapakata, "for it was felt that an Indian name would have a greater appeal to tourists" (107) — the name has been chosen purely for commercial reasons and not to acknowledge the fact that this is Natives' land. The formerly quiet lake has turned into "a flourishing resort" with "hotels, a dance-hall, cafés with neon signs"; it now has several dozen stores instead of just one and is permeated with the "odours of potato chips and hot dogs" (107). This commodification and commercialization of "natural" space exploits the same romantic notions of the wilderness and of the noble savage that Vanessa held when she was younger. As Ewan MacLeod had predicted, the loons are gone from the lake, as Vanessa muses, to "some far place of belonging" or because they "had simply died out, having ceased to care whether they lived or not" (106). Vanessa remembers how Piquette had been indifferent to the loons, and at the end of the story she wonders: "It seems to me now that in some unconscious and totally unrecognized way, Piquette might have been the only one, after all, who had heard the crying of the loons" (108). Laurence indicates that the older Vanessa has achieved a heightened sense of Piquette's ethnic background and personal dilemma.

Some critics read the ending as implying that "Piquette *does* turn out to have some secret knowledge of the wilds and *does* impart it in the end to Vanessa" (Stovel, 83) or that Piquette is rendered as "the true aristocrat of Diamond Lake" and as " 'the only one' to whom the former spirit of the place was perhaps still recognizable" (Easingwood, 23). Such readings run the risk of romanticizing Piquette and her people in the same way that the younger Vanessa saw Piquette as a fictitious noble savage instead of a real person. The older Vanessa, however, has learned a lesson in history. As Thomas points out, each story in *A Bird in the House* ends with "a recognition that is a step towards maturity" (Thomas, 105), and at the end of "The Loons" Vanessa has developed an understanding for the Métis' complex history and their mistreatment in Canadian culture. When the grown narrator concludes that Piquette was the only one who had heard the crying of the loons, she no longer thinks that Piquette is a "junior prophetess of the wild" (100). Quite to the contrary, Vanessa has come to understand that although they are the rightful heirs of the place and its ancestral history, the Métis have been alienated and disconnected from their origins and traditions. She finally accepts that Piquette could not have imparted any knowledge to her, because she and her people, like the loons, were driven off their land a long time ago. Vanessa MacLeod has matured because she realizes that her Scottish ancestors established a tradition in Canada at the cost of the indigenous people. Through the growth of her narrator-character Laurence makes the readers aware of "the underside of the pioneer myth" (Buss, 62), of the "other" side of prairie history.

While the other stories in the collection recall the heroic tales of the Scottish pioneers, "The Loons" fills in the gaps in these tales and stresses that historiography is always a narrative construct that renders one story by eclipsing various others. In all of her books in the Manawaka cycle, Laurence writes the Métis into the history of the Canadian prairies and blurs the boundary between historiography and literature.

Works Cited

Bumsted, J. M. "Riel, Louis." In New 2002, 972–75.

Buss, Helen M. "Vanessa, Morag and the Creative Spirit." In *Mother and Daughter Relationships in the Manawaka Works of Margaret Laurence*, ed. Helen M. Buss. Victoria: English Literary Studies, 1985. 54–76.

Capone, Giovanna. "A Bird in the House: Margaret Laurence on Order and the Artist." In *Gaining Ground: European Critics on Canadian Literature*, ed. Robert Kroetsch and Reingard M. Nischik. Edmonton: NeWest, 1985. 161–70.

Darling, Michael. "'Undecipherable Sings': Margaret Laurence's 'To Set Our House in Order.'" *Essays on Candian Writing* 29 (1984): 193–204.

Easingwood, Peter. "Semi-autobiographical Fiction and Revisionary Realism in *A Bird in the House*." In *Narrative Strategies in Canadian Literature*, ed. Coral Ann Howells and Lynette Hunter. Philadelphia: Open University Press, 1991. 19–29.

Frye, Northrop. *The Bush Garden: Essays on the Canadian Imagination*. Toronto: Anansi, 1971.

Kertzer, Jon. *"That House in Manawaka": Margaret Laurence's* A Bird in the House. Toronto: ECW Press, 1992.

King, James. *The Life of Margaret Laurence*. Toronto: Knopf, 1997.

Laurence, Margaret. *A Bird in the House*. Toronto: McClelland-Bantam, 1985.

———. *Dance on the Earth: A Memoir*. Toronto: McClelland & Stewart, 1989.

———. *Heart of a Stranger*. Toronto: McClelland & Stewart, 1976.

———. *Long Drums and Cannons*. Macmillan: London, 1968.

———. "The Loons." In Laurence, *A Bind in the House*, 96–108.

Laurence, Margaret. "Time and the Narrative Voice." In *The Narrative Voice: Short Stories and Reflections by Canadian Authors*, ed. John Metcalf. Toronto: McGraw-Hill Ryerson, 1972. 126–30.

———. *The Tomorrow-Tamer and Other Stories.* London: Macmillan, 1963.

New, W. H. *Dreams of Speech and Violence: The Art of the Short Story in Canada and New Zealand.* Toronto: University of Toronto Press, 1987.

———. *Encyclopedia of Literature in Canada.* Toronto: University of Toronto Press, 2002.

Stovel, Bruce. "Coherence in *A Bird in the House.*" In *New Perspectives on Margaret Laurence: Poetic Narrative, Multiculturalism and Feminism*, ed. Greta M. K. McCormick Coger. Westport: Greenwood, 1996. 81–96.

Thomas, Clara. *The Manawaka World of Margaret Laurence.* Toronto: McClelland & Stewart, 1976.

Woodcock, George, ed. *A Place to Stand On: Essays By and About Margaret Laurence.* Edmonton: NeWest, 1983.

16: "Out of Place": Clark Blaise, "A Class of New Canadians" (1970)

Wolfgang Klooß (University of Trier)

WHEN *OUT OF PLACE*, one of prairie writer and critic Eli Mandel's outstanding poetry collections, appeared in 1977, Clark Blaise's *A North American Education: A Book of Short Fiction* had already made an impressive impact on the short-story genre in Canada. Published in 1973, *A North American Education* comprises three groups of stories ("The Montreal Stories," "The Keeler Stories," "The Thibidault Stories") that, as in Mandel's ambivalent poetic treatment of home and place (see Cooley 1992), explore nomadic lives in North America. They investigate dreams of belonging, question notions of identity, and introduce characters who hanker for a meaningful existence, but are left in limbo — characters who in effect remain "out of place." Correspondingly, search, loss, and defeat, as well as alienation, dislocation, and a desperate urge for recognition, are recurrent motifs in a body of short-prose works marked by highly poetic features. As writer and critic John Metcalf has argued, the plot of a Blaise story unfolds against the background of an "unobtrusive chain of images much in the manner of poems" (Metcalf 1973, 79).

"A Class of New Canadians" is the first of the three "Montreal Stories" in Blaise's aforementioned first volume of short-prose writings. As the subtitle of the collection suggests, Blaise considers his stories to be "short fictions," in contrast to "short *stories.*" Short fictions are "imaginings, reminiscent of Jorge Luis Borges' *ficciones*, bound not by logical organization, nor by chronological sequence, nor by cause and motive. They are, in their own way, reflections of the pre-operational sensibility [see Piaget 1959], with the connections made more intuitively than rationally" (Ricou 1987, 41). Set in Quebec's metropolis, the "Montreal Stories" are not so much narratives with plots as they are arrangements of materials held together by a human voice or presence (for Blaise's understanding of the genre, see also Cameron 1982, 10–11). The stories are informed by Blaise's own experiences in this profoundly multicultural city, where he arrived in 1966 and remained until 1978, the longest time he has ever stayed in one place. "The parallels between the characters and events in his stories and the experience of Blaise himself have led some reviewers and critics to describe his fiction as autobiographical. Blaise has disagreed, saying that his writing is more 'created' than personal. The personal is, nevertheless, an important element" (Jackel 1990, 59).

Born on 10 April 1940 in Fargo, North Dakota, to an English-Canadian mother from Manitoba and a Quebecois father whose profession as an itinerant furniture salesman forced the family into an unstable life on the move, Clark Blaise spent part of his childhood in Alabama and Georgia, before central Florida became his temporary home. At the age of ten, the family left for Winnipeg, only to continue to Springfield, Missouri, and to Cincinnati, Ohio, before settling in Pittsburgh, Pennsylvania, in 1953. Four years later, Blaise enrolled at Denison University in Granville, Ohio. He abandoned his original major, geology, when he dropped out of university, and returned after eight months to study English instead. According to his own reminiscences, the next few years were an especially formative period as he became seriously engaged in writing and reading. Besides Theodore Dreiser, Sinclair Lewis, and Thomas Wolfe, he studied French novelists including Gustave Flaubert, Emile Zola, Louis-Ferdinand Céline, and Stendhal; Thomas Mann also came into play, yet it was D. H. Lawrence and, above all, William Faulkner whose works particularly attracted Blaise. In 1961 Blaise graduated from Denison with a B.A. in English. He then went to Harvard, where he participated in a creative writing class conducted by Bernard Malamud, who became Blaise's mentor and "closest and dearest friend in writing" (Cameron 1982, 12). The following selected entries in Blaise's "Chronology of Salience" cover the period until 1985 and provide an important inventory of dates and turning points in the life of an emerging writer and academic:

> **1962** February: entered Writers' Workshop, University of Iowa, with scholarship. Studied with Philip Roth. **1962** Summer: Europe. Mainly in Wuppertal, Germany. First story published: "A Fish Like a Buzzard." **1963** 19 September: married Bharati Mukherjee [the Bengali-Canadian novelist whom he had met at the Iowa writers' workshop]. Stories published in *Chrysalis* and *Carolina Quarterly*. . . . **1966–78** Montreal. Began as sessional lecturer at Sir George Williams University and TESL instructor at McGill. . . .**1968** *New Canadian Writing 1968* (with Dave Godfrey and David Lewis Stein). Four stories. . . . **1973** Became Canadian citizen. . . . **1974** *Tribal Justice*. . . . **1977** *Days and Nights in Calcutta* (with Bharati Mukherjee). **1978** Accepted position as professor of humanities, York University. . . . An excellent job, but Toronto proved inhospitable to us on racial grounds. . . . *Lunar Attractions*. . . . **1980** . . . emigrated to U.S. Visiting professor, Skidmore College, Saratoga Springs, New York. . . . **1983** *Lust*. . . . **1984–1986** Iowa City. . . . **1986** January: moved to Long Island city (Queens), New York. . . . Adjunct professor, Columbia University Graduate School of the Arts. **1986** *Resident Alien*. **1986–87** Writer-in-residence, Concordia University, Montreal. . . . **1987** *The Sorrow and the Terror*. . . . (from Blaise, "Chronology of Salience," 16–19)

Further stages in his busy career include the directorship of the International Writing Program (IWP) at the University of Iowa (1990–98), a teaching post at the University of California, Berkeley, and the presidency of the Society for the Study of the Short Story, which he has held since 2002. Currently, Blaise is Professor of Humanities and English at Southampton College of Long Island University in New York, and he lives in Southampton and San Francisco.

In addition to *Lunar Attractions* (1979), for which he received the *Books in Canada* First Novel Award, and *Lusts* (1983), Blaise has published two other novels, *If I Were Me* (1997) and *Time Lord: Sir Sandford Fleming and the Creation of Standard Time* (2001), which was awarded Canada's Pearson Prize. A piece of non-fiction, entitled *I Had a Father: A Post-Modern Autobiography* (1993), was written primarily during Blaise's around-the-world travels as director of the IWP and won the Book of the Year Award from the Canadian Booksellers Association. In 1992, the short-story collection *Man and His World* had appeared. Besides the President's Medal for Best Story in Canada, Blaise also received an American Academy of Arts and Sciences Award for his lifetime achievement.

With the exception of *The Sorrow and the Terror* (1987), Blaise's and Mukherjee's collaborative journalistic account *The Haunting Legacy of the Air India Tragedy* in 1985, and *Time Lord* (a dazzling meditation on social change and the cultural effects of technology caused by a unified standard for telling time), Blaise's works are primarily concerned with finding or inventing an identity which is then deconstructed. Blaise has returned repeatedly to the essential experiences of his life in his work, re-articulating and reshaping them. In "possibly his best" work (Ross 1991, n.p.), *Resident Alien*, a book in which short stories are framed by autobiographical fragments, Blaise has identified himself in the following manner: "Sociologically, I am an American. Psychologically, a Canadian. Sentimentally, a Québecois. By marriage, part of the Third World. My passport says Canadian, but I was born in America; my legal status says immigrant" (Blaise, *Resident Alien*, 1; see also MacLeod 2003).

The uneasiness expressed here may explain why Blaise is prompted "to question his motives, to doubt his values, to interrogate his fiction, his art, his life" (Lecker 1988, 9). Meandering between autobiography and fiction, *Resident Alien*, in the words of the author, "is a journey into my obsessions with self and place; not just the whoness and whatness of identity, but the whereness of who and what I am. I call it an autobiography in tales and essay, though it contains some of the most thoroughly invented stories I have ever written" (*Resident Alien*, 2). Illness, witnessed in his grandfather's and mother's suffering from Alzheimer's disease, serves him as a metaphor for the "provisional nature of our sense of self and sanity" (Ross, n.p.). Family disease becomes "emblematic of a twentieth century experience of wiping out memory and identity, the progressive loss of both personal and cultural memory" (ibid.).

Subsequently, Blaise's "fiction, on a thematic level," can be seen "as a sustained inquiry into the nature and meaning of identity" (Lecker 1988, 9), which, according to Blaise, cannot be taken for granted but must be strenuously sought:

> Anyone who led a life as tenuous as I did, fraught with almost daily evidence of evanescence, is obviously going to be concerned with establishing a place and a name and an identity for himself that he could not have established in life. I did not ever have a sense of place, or belonging, in my life. So I had to create it, fabricate it, in my art. That's why my stories and novels have such a strong genealogical impulse. I don't think I have ever written anything in which I did not in some way say, "I was born in this place or that place." Or, "My mother or father or grandparents were born in this place." This is all a kind of fraud. I was born in a town that I've never seen. I moved from Fargo, North Dakota, when I was six months old, and I've never been back. (Hancock 1979, 31)

Similarly, in one of his critical essays he talks about the "border as fiction" (see Blaise, "The Border as Fiction"), not only describing the floating space between fiction and autobiography and the role of the border in the definition of identity, but also directly referring to his own transient life in North America. This life also comes significantly to bear on his most recent works of short fiction. In *Southern Stories* (2000), *Pittsburgh Stories* (2001), and *Montreal Stories* (2003), new and previously published stories are grouped according to geographic and cultural regions that have played a dominant role in Blaise's writing life, namely, Florida, where he grew up, Pittsburgh, where he lived and worked, and Montreal, where he was active as one of the legendary Montreal Story Tellers.

The Montreal Story Teller Fiction Performance Group (1970–76), founded by John Metcalf and counting among its members Hugh Hood, Ray Smith, and Raymond Fraser, exercised a considerable influence on the development of the short story in Canada. As indicated by the group's name, Metcalf and his fellow writers strongly emphasized the performative character of their work. They introduced short fiction to college and university students, high school pupils, and bookstore audiences alike. Hugh Hood recalls: "All five of us appeared at the first reading, at Rosemere High School, just off the island of Montreal to the north, on a fearsomely cold afternoon in February, 1971. I do believe that we were the first persons to produce a performance of just this kind in Canada, perhaps anywhere" (Hood 1985, 12). One of the group's objectives was to read stories their hearers could identify with. Clark Blaise's "Eyes," the second piece of "The Montreal Stories" in *A North American Education*,

> used to fascinate audiences in such settings, especially the menacing closing lines concluding, "and then your neighbours would turn upon you." These listeners obviously appreciated the contrast between what Clark was describing, and his quiet, neat, self-contained personal appearance. It may have surprised them that this unobtrusive gentleman knew so many of the same things they knew, better than they did themselves. (Hood, 19–20)

According to Hood, Blaise was successful with his presentations because he managed to give his readings a highly persuasive quality: "He would stand there in dark, unobtrusive clothes, looking what he is, a grave, supernally intelligent artist, and enthral the audience by some recital of a series of terrific disasters, never raising his voice, but managing to chill everybody's imagination very sufficiently" (Hood, 16).

Apparently, life in the multi-faceted and culturally inspiring metropolis of Montreal, as well as the fact that he had become an acknowledged and much-respected member of an innovative artists' collective, evoked a new sense of writing in Blaise. Montreal as an urban space — like the South as a region — became for him a place "where setting is not merely an excuse, but where setting is in fact the mystery and the manner" (Metcalf, 78). Looking back on these years, Blaise said later, "I'd never been so open to story, so avid for context" (*Resident Alien*, 32). Subsequently, Blaise made himself a name as one of Canada's most accomplished writers of short fiction, with the result that his mastery of form and technique, rather than his skillful treatment of theme and plot, has received special recognition (see, for example, Lecker 1982). Blaise himself employs the term "personal fiction," thereby pointing at a narrative stance which privileges his two major concerns in fiction, texture and voice: "Texture is detail arranged and selected and enhanced. . . . By voice I am referring to the control, what is commonly referred to when we mention the 'world' of a certain author, the limits of probability and chance in his construction, the sanctions he leaves us for our own variations, what we sense of his own final concerns and bafflements" (Metcalf, 78).

Although four of Blaise's stories — "The Fabulous Eddie Brewster," "How I Became a Jew," "The Examination," and "Notes Beyond a History" — together with works by Dave Godfrey and David Lewis Stein, had already been included in the anthology *New Canadian Writing* (1968), it was the stories in *A North American Education* and in *Tribal Justice* that initiated Blaise's growing reputation as a distinguished writer of short prose in Canada. Despite the fact that a manuscript containing many of the stories in the above volumes was rejected by several American and Canadian publishers because the stories' high literary standards made commercial success unlikely (see Metcalf, 79), the two collections were eventually released by Doubleday Canada.

Originally written in 1967 (see Lecker 1988, 36), "A Class of New Canadians," the first of "The Montreal Stories" and thus the opening piece of the collection, has received special attention. Blaise, who had been writing for almost fifteen years by the time he published *A North American Education*, reintroduces protagonist Norman Dyer in this particular story, a character he had established several years earlier in the short story "Grids and Doglegs" (1965), where Dyer, as Blaise did himself, attends a high school in Pittsburgh. Dyer is also at the center of the other two "Montreal Stories," "Eyes" and "Words for the Winter."

Like so many of Blaise's works, the opening sentences of "A Class of New Canadians" position the main character not only in a clearly defined spatial and temporal setting, but hint at the protagonist's mental and emotional condition as well:

> Norman Dyer hurried down Sherbrooke Street, collar turned against the snow. "Superb!" he muttered, passing a basement gallery next to a French bookstore. Bleached and tanned women in furs dashed from hotel lobbies into waiting cabs. Even the neon clutter of the side streets and the honks of slithering taxis seemed remote tonight through the peaceful snow. *Superb*, he thought again, waiting for a light and backing from a slushy curb: a word reserved for wines, cigars, and delicate sauces; he was feeling superb this evening. (3)

In stressing such details, the author catches the reader's immediate attention. For Blaise, "the first paragraph [of a short story] is a microcosm of the whole, but in a way that only the whole can reveal. . . . The [first] line doesn't have to 'grab' or 'hook' but it should be striking" (Blaise, "To Begin, to Begin," 22). He is even more explicit when he offers three uses of the idea of beginnings "as a means of understanding fiction, *his* fiction" (Ricou, 42):

> Lesson One: as in poetry, a good first sentence of prose implies its opposite. . . .
>
> Lesson Two: art wishes to begin, even more than end. . . . the ending is a contrivance . . . ; the beginning, however, is always a mystery. . . .
>
> Lesson Three: art wishes to begin *again*. The impulse is not only to finish, it is to capture. In the stories I admire, there is a sense of continuum disrupted, then re-established, and both the disruption and reordering are part of the *beginning* of a story. (Blaise, "To Begin, to Begin," 23–24)

After eighteen months in search of Montreal, its people, and his own place in the metropolis, Blaise's third-person narrator — Dyer speaks in the first person in "Eyes" and "Words for the Winter" — follows the author's example and "lectures at one university," teaching "English as a Foreign Language at McGill" (5). For him there is "something fiercely elemental, almost existential, about teaching both his language and his literature in a foreign country" (5). Teaching about one's own culture in an alien environment becomes absolutely vital for Dyer in his attempt to start anew in

French Canada. The students enrolled in his evening course represent a wide range of nationalities. They have either recently moved to Canada — like the elegant and vain Miguel Mayor from Madrid, or Mr. Weinrot, the Israeli, who, after working for years in Italy and Denmark, now holds a job with the Canadian government — or, like Gilles Carrier, Claude Veilleux, and Miss Parizeau ("a jolly French-Canadian girl that Dyer had been thinking of asking out," 10), come from Francophone families.

Among the other members of the class are a "sultry Armenian girl with . . . bewitching half-glasses," who has difficulties comprehending "that 'put on' is not the same as 'take on,'" Mr. Vassilopoulos from Greece, and Mrs. David, who "speaks with a nifty British accent" (6), and who, Dyer claims, loves him.

> In the halls of McGill they broke into the usual groups. French-Canadians and South Americans into two large circles, then the Greeks, Germans, Spanish, and French into smaller groups. The patterns interested Dyer. Madrid Spaniards and Parisian French always spoke English with their New World co-linguals. The Middle Europeans spoke German together, not Russian, preferring one occupier to the other. (7)

Thus Blaise exposes the reader to a broad spectrum of ethnic voices which, similar to Mordecai Richler's Jewish and immigrant voices in *The Street* (1969) (a collection of autobiographical stories from the same period; see the article by Fabienne Quennet in this volume), echo the polyphonic city life of Montreal. As Richler points out in his title story, Montreal's Main was

> also a dividing line. Below, the French Canadians. Above . . . the dreaded WASPS. On the Main itself there were some Italians, Yugoslavs, and Ukrainians, but they did not count as true Gentiles. Even the French Canadians, who were our enemies, were not entirely unloved. Like us, they were poor and coarse with large families and spoke English badly. . . . Actually, it was only the WASPS who were truly hated and feared. . . . We were convinced that we gained from dissension between Canada's two cultures, the English and the French, and we looked neither to England nor France for guidance. We turned to the United States. The real America. (Richler 1990, 36, 37–38)

Norman Dyer has found his current bearings near a "colony of *émigré* Russians just off Park Avenue," where he keeps a "small but elegant apartment" (4). (In the following two stories he will move with his German wife and small child to "French, then Jewish, then Italian and [eventually] Greek" neighborhoods ("Words for the Winter," 26), scanning the city, section by section.) Although the job is "beneath him, a recent Ph.D." (5), he is flattered to be hired as a language instructor. He has left the United States for Canada and has no intention of returning to the country of his birth. Instead, he constructs himself as a "semi-permanent, semi-political exile" (4), wishing to follow in the tradition of "Joyce in Trieste, Isherwood and Nabokov in Berlin, Beckett in Paris" (5). As becomes evident from the very beginning of this short story, Dyer tries hard to get rid of his past, to suppress what he *was*, and to raise himself into august literary company. Without a history, however, he also falls short on the present and suppresses what he *is*. As he dives into the "cosmopolitan surface of Montreal, there is a strong suggestion that he has never known who he is" (Cameron 1985, 18).

In desperately trying to immerse himself in the cultural and linguistic environment of Montreal, Dyer implicitly acknowledges "the fact that language, and language variety — dialect or sociolect — is one of the overt signs of cultural identity which people meet daily in their lives" (Byram 1989, 40). Consequently, the language teacher and literature expert from south of the border uses accented English or French — preferably the local dialect (4) — in street conversations. At the same time, Dr. Dyer does not refrain from poking fun at the French-Canadians in the classroom, who are "like children learning the language" (10). Two evenings a week, his own mastery of English as the esteemed language makes him feel like an "omniscient, benevolent god," who demonstrates his linguistic skills in front of "silent, ignorant" students "dedicated to learning English. No discussions, no demonstrations, no dialogue" (5). Language means power — the lack of it means vulnerability.

Viewed against the background of the 1960s and the "Quiet Revolution" (1960–66), "A Class of New Canadians" gains additional momentum as a literary comment on multiculturalism within the framework of bilingualism. The Quiet Revolution meant the modernization of and major social and economic changes in Quebec, as well as the awakening of a cultural self-awareness, which, for instance, found its expression in the Official Languages Act of 1969 (see Durocher 1988). The text indirectly reflects some aspects of the political climate in a turbulent decade of rising separatism (the terrorist Front de Libération du Québec began to operate in 1963, and the Parti Québecois was founded in 1968); in the year in which Blaise drafted the story, Canada not only celebrated her centennial, hosting the Expo in Montreal, but heard Charles de Gaulle proclaim his famous "Vive le Québec libre" from the balcony of Montreal's town hall. Interestingly, Dyer sides with the Quebec cause and tweaks "his colleagues for not sympathizing enough with Quebec separatism" (4).

Dyer's conceited bearing and his arrogance towards the students (for example, when he exposes his class to lines from Faulkner's *Absalom, Absalom!* in elaborate Latin) are directly connected to his rootlessness. A newcomer to the country himself, he is not only an immigrant surrounded by immigrants, but poses deliberately as an exile who continuously shifts homes so that dislocation and new beginnings strongly impact on his personality. "Physical dislocation results in emotional and psychic dislocation. Starting over implies plunging again into confusion and bewilderment: never feeling at home, never learning, never building" (Ricou, 36). Subsequently, Dyer's unsettled mindscape leads him into a number of traps. Confusing his own objectives with those of his students, he feels almost personally attacked by Mr. Weinrot's decision to choose Canada over South Africa and Australia: " 'Canada says come right away, so I go. Should have waited for South Africa.' 'How could you?' Dyer cried. 'What's wrong with you anyway? South Africa is fascist. Australia is racist' " (9). Similarly, Dyer is surprised to hear that the *lingua franca* at Weinrot's job is not French but "Hebrew, sometimes German, sometimes little Polish" (7) and that Weinrot has not been "truck-driving, perhaps of beer, maybe in Germany" (7), but was trained as an engineer. With only a passing knowledge of French, he is now eager to acquire a proper command of English in order to find work in the United States:

> "What I was wondering, then [Weinrot says, ignoring Dyer's outburst], was if my English is good enough to be working in the United States. You're American, aren't you?"
>
> It was a question Dyer had often avoided in Europe, but had rarely been asked in Montreal. "Yes," he admitted, "your English is probably good enough for the States or South Africa, whichever one wants you first." (9)

Strongly resenting the uncultured materialism which his students seek in the USA, Dyer is only too keen to show them what is dear to him — and fails. His idealism makes him sympathetic to the reader and accounts for his partially tragic stature. Guided largely by idealist misreadings and deceptions, he feels betrayed by Weinrot and his kind, since in Dyer's eyes Montreal is "the greatest city on the continent, if only they knew it as well as he did. If they'd just break out of their little ghettos" (10). Ironically, he does not realize how much he is caught in his own ghetto. Enshrined by a set of self-constructed values, essentially differentiating only between "the authority of simple good taste" (4) and "simple bad taste" (3), Dyer's "North American education" fosters a self-understanding which also "implies the cultural distinctions in which Dyer and his students are involved" (Lecker 1982, 20). This is in keeping with the attitude he has developed towards his job, as he shows right at the beginning of the narrative: "He was proud of himself for having steered his life north, even for jobs that were menial by standards he could have demanded" (3). He refuses to be seen as an immigrant as such, and instead uses his authority in the classroom to deliberately set himself apart from his students. Moreover, as becomes more and more obvious during the course of the narrative, Dyer's normative codes are, in the end, informed by the same notions of materialism and vanity as those of Weinrot and Mayor.

Like most of Blaise's North Americans, who are "uneasy in their occupation of space" (Ricou, 38), Dyer in effect lacks a sense of understanding for place and people. He remains an outsider throughout the story, a voyeur collecting impressions and "respond[ing] only to the surfaces of Montreal" (Cameron 1985, 17). The true native, in contrast, as Robert Lecker claims, "is not the man who knows the bistros, the bookstores, and where to find the finest clothes; he is the man who stands faceless, a non-entity at the corner of the street" (Lecker 1982, 22). Dyer, however, is primarily concerned with cultivating his exquisite taste. He walks the streets of Montreal and simply feels "*superb* . . . a word reserved for wines, cigars, and delicate sauces" (3). Overwhelmed by the city's cultural mosaic, he has "sampled every ethnic restaurant downtown and in the old city, plus a few Levantine places out in Outremont" (4). Likewise, he wants his two students from Israel to supply him with "the name of a good Israeli restaurant" (7) but, upon second thoughts, decides that neither of them can be of any help to him. He is equally disappointed when Mr. Mayor tells him that "there are not any good Spanish restaurants in Montreal" (11). Evidently, Dyer's cultural interests do not extend far beyond a liking of exotic cuisine.

Dyer's lack of connection is further evident when the "vain and impeccable Spaniard" (11) asks him to check a letter of application for its proper English. Mayor is dressed in just the kind of "checkered sports-coat . . ., blue shirt and matching ascot-handkerchief" (11) that Dyer had studied on the dummy in the window of "Holt-Renfrew's exclusive men's shop" (4) before he went to class. Dyer feels mocked by the stylish fashion plate from Madrid, "somehow pitting [Mayor's] astounding confidence and wardrobe, sharp chin and matador's bearing against his command of English and mastery of the side streets, bistros, and ethnic restaurants" (13). Despite his better understanding, and ignoring Mayor's remark that the "letters in Spanish are not the same to English ones" (13), Dyer does not correct any of the obvious flaws in the application, but assures the student that his letter will do. It will not, of course, since Mayor, who "looks so prosperous, so confident, like a male model off a page of *Playboy*" (13), is unfamiliar with the kind of matter-of-fact business discourse that distinguishes North American from Spanish business letters with their explicit references to personal connections. In his own "new Canadianness" Dyer feels "abused by the very people he wants so much to help" (14), being deeply distressed by his students who are "always leaving Montreal" (11) in search of the "real America." As Mayor puts it: " 'Montreal is big port like Barcelona. Everybody mixed together and having no money. It is just a place to land, no?' " (13). Offended by Mayor's indifference to Montreal, Dyer practices a linguistic segregationalism which keeps the Spaniard uninformed about the fact that his letter lacks the necessary intercultural competence, thereby intentionally jeopardizing his economic prospects in the United States.

Inasmuch as Dyer is a different kind of exile at the university, his self-imposed superiority gradually vanishes outside the classroom. As the story unfolds, he shrinks to being just another new Canadian foreigner in Montreal, struggling and uprooted. Revelation and recognition of his own preposterous self-image and less flattering true status come to him when later in the evening he returns to the window of "Holt-Renfrew's exclusive men's shop" (4). Earlier on in the story, Dyer had supposed that "unlike food, drink, cinema, and literature, clothing has never really involved him" (4), and as a result he remains "a walking violation of American law, clad shoes to scarf in Egyptian cottons, Polish leathers, and woolens from the People's Republic of China" (4–5). Dyer comes back to stare at the expensive clothes on the mannequin — this lifeless, fashion-bound imitation of a human being, who had been Dyer's alter ego at the beginning of the story, Dyer's "ironic *Doppelgänger* in the flesh . . ., an image of what Dyer would like to be" (Cameron 1985, 19, 21). Now Dyer pictures himself in the store with three hundred dollars to spend on Mayor's expensive outfit, but discovers that the tanned mannequins behind the windows are "legless dummies" (14) — a moment of revelation to finally spur some self-recognition in the rootless American.

> "Absurd man!" Dyer whispered. There had been a moment of fear, as though the naked body would leap from the window, and legless, chase him down Sherbrooke Street. But the moment was passing. Dyer realized now that it was comic, even touching. Miguel Mayor had simply tried too hard, too fast, and it would be good for him to stay in Montreal until he deserved those clothes, that touching vanity and confidence. With one last look at the window, he turned sharply, before the clothes could speak again. (15)

Norman Dyer, like Paul Keeler in "The Keeler Stories," or Frankie Thibidault in "The Thibidault Stories," personifies the "dilemmas caused by conflicting cultures" (Davey 1974, 55; see also Davey 1983). Dyer's voice of authority in front of his students becomes strangely eroded by the limited third-person narrative by which Blaise operates his protagonist, which eventually "suggests that the central character is disembodied, and despite his ardent claims to the contrary, voiceless" (Lecker 1982, 21). This gives the story a certain tragic undercurrent. The more Dyer believes in his own cultural achievements, the less successful he is in his attempts to acculturate himself as a "new Canadian." Like most of his students, he is a recent immigrant to a city "made only for fresh men" (Lecker 1988, 62). Furthermore, as his name indicates, Dyer is so withdrawn from life that he is on the verge of non-existence. Yet he moves on in a constant search for assurance. This is in keeping with Blaise Pascal's epigraphic statement from *Pensées* (1670) — "So we never live, but we hope to live; and, as we are always preparing to be happy, it is inevitable we should never be so."

(*A North American Education*, 1) — which introduces the three "Montreal Stories" and points towards Blaise's affinity with what he has called the French "discursive tradition, . . . literature compounded of cold observation and subjective passion" (Blaise, "Author's Introduction," 67).

As in many of Blaise's short fictions, "A Class of New Canadians" features a tone of mourning. Dyer perpetuates his self-delusions "because this perpetuation is the very substance and subject of the only story Dyer will ever know. To find identity is to lose it; to name everything is to die" (Lecker 1987, 72–73). This paradox suggests a self-reflexive, postmodern stance (see Lane 1992). And yet, "A Class of New Canadians," like the other stories, "is still more traditional than experimental in form" (Brown 1973, 115), and, as Blaise has repeatedly argued, he is not even "quite modern and combatively at odds with the meta-literatures and strenuous fabulations of an exhausted imagination" (*Resident Alien*, 13). On the contrary, he conceives of himself rather as a writer whose (fictionalized) geographical regions and urban spaces turn into moral landscapes. In the end, it is Dyer's self-irony that leads not only to a moment of self-recognition, but might also be read as a possibility, at least temporarily, for his world and himself to "fall into place."

Works Cited

Blaise, Clark. "Author's Introduction." In *New Canadian Writing, 1968: Stories by David Lewis Stein, Clark Blaise and Dave Godfrey*. Toronto: Clarke, Irwin, 1968. 67–68.

———. *The Border as Fiction*. Borderland Monograph Series 4. Orono, Maine: University of Maine, 1990.

———. "Chronology of Salience." In Lecker 1988, 13–20.

———. "A Class of New Canadians." In Blaise, *A North American Education*, 3–15.

———. "Eyes." In Blaise, *A North American Education*, 16–24.

———. "Grids and Doglegs." In Blaise, *Pittsburgh Stories*, 51–64.

———. *I Had a Father: A Postmodern Autobiography*. Reading, MA: Addison-Wesley, 1993.

———. *Man and His World*. Erin, ON: The Porcupine's Quill Press, 1992.

———. *Montreal Stories*. Erin, ON: The Porcupine's Quill Press, 2003.

———. *A North American Education: A Book of Short Fiction*. Toronto: Doubleday, 1973; repr. Don Mills, ON: PaperJacks, 1974. 3–15.

———. *Pittsburgh Stories*. Erin, ON: The Porcupine's Quill Press, 2001.

———. *Resident Alien*. Toronto: Penguin, 1986.

Blaise, Clark. *Southern Stories.* Erin, ON: The Porcupine's Quill Press, 2000.

———. "To Begin, to Begin." In *The Narrative Voice: Short Stories and Reflections by Canadian Authors*, ed. John Metcalf. Toronto: McGraw-Hill Ryerson, 1972. 22–26.

———. *Tribal Justice.* Toronto: Doubleday, 1974.

———. "Words for the Winter." In Blaise, *A North American Education,* 25–37.

Brown, Russell M. "The Insolent Infinity: Clark Blaise, *A North American Education.*" *Canadian Literature* 58 (Spring 1973): 114–16.

Byram, Michael. *Cultural Studies in Foreign Language Education.* Clevedon/Philadelphia: Multilingual Matters, 1989.

Cameron, Barry. *Clark Blaise and His Works.* Toronto: ECW Press, 1985.

———. "A Conversation with Clark Blaise." *Essays on Canadian Writing* 23 (Spring 1982): 5–25.

Cooley, Dennis. *Eli Mandel and His Works.* Downsview, ON: ECW Press, 1992.

Davey, Frank. "Clark Blaise." In Davey, *From There to Here: A Guide to English-Canadian Literature Since 1960.* Our Nature-Our Voices II. Erin, ON: Press Porcépic, 1974. 55–57.

———. "Impressionable Realism: The Stories of Clark Blaise" (1976). In Davey, *Surviving the Paraphrase: Eleven Essays on Canadian Literature.* Winnipeg: Turnstone, 1983. 73–85.

Durocher, René. "Quiet Revolution (Révolution tranquille)." In *The Canadian Encyclopedia.* Vol. 3, 2nd ed., ed. James H. Marsh. Edmonton: Hurtig, 1988. 1813–14.

Hancock, Geoff. "Clark Blaise on Artful Autobiography: 'I Who Live in Dreams Am Touched by Reality.'" *Books in Canada* (March 1979): 30–31.

Hood, Hugh. "Trusting the Tale." In *The Montreal Story Tellers: Memoirs, Photographs, Critical Essays*, ed. J. R. (Tim) Struthers. Montreal: Véhicule Press, 1985. 7–22.

Jackel, David. "Short Fiction." In *Literary History of Canada: Canadian Literature in English.* Vol. 4, 2nd ed., ed. W. H. New. Toronto: University of Toronto Press, 1990. 46–72.

Lane, Richard. "Clark Blaise and the Discourse of Modernity." *Canadian Literature* 132 (Spring 1992): 126–35.

Lecker, Robert. "Clark Blaise: Murals Deep in Nature." In Lecker, *On the Line: Readings in the Short Fiction of Clark Blaise, John Metcalf, and Hugh Hood.* Toronto: ECW Press, 1982. 17–58.

———. *An Other I: The Fictions of Clark Blaise.* Downsview, ON: ECW Press, 1988.

———. "Self-Reflexive Elements in Stories of Clark Blaise." *RANAM* 20 (1987): 71–75.

MacLeod, Alexander. " 'Too Canadian for the Americans and too American for the Canadians': An Interview with Clark Blaise." *Essays on Canadian Writing* 79 (Spring 2003): 178–90.

Metcalf, John. "Interview: Clark Blaise." *Journal of Canadian Fiction* 2.4 (Fall 1973): 77–79.

Piaget, Jean. *The Language and Thought of the Child.* 3rd ed. London: Routledge and Kegan Paul, 1959.

Richler, Mordecai. *The Street.* Toronto: McClelland & Stewart, 2002.

———. "The Street." In *Other Solitudes: Canadian Multicultural Fictions*, ed. Linda Hutcheon and Marion Richmond. Toronto: University of Toronto Press, 1990. 33–48.

Ricou, Laurie. "Perpetual Rebeginnings: The Short Fiction of Clark Blaise." In Ricou, *Everyday Magic: Child Languages in Canadian Literature.* Vancouver: University of British Columbia Press, 1987. 35–47.

Ross, Catherine Sheldrick. "Clark Blaise: Biocritical Essay." In *The Clark Blaise Papers.* First Accession and Second Accession, ed. Jean F. Tener and Apollonia Steele. Calgary: University of Calgary Press, 1991. Online version under www.ucalgary.ca/library/SpecColl/blaisbioc.htm.

17: Realism and Parodic Postmodernism: Audrey Thomas, "Aquarius" (1971)

Lothar Hönnighausen (University of Bonn)

AUDREY THOMAS, BORN IN 1935, is one of the leading short-story writers in a period that may well come to be called the Golden Age of the Canadian short story. Like Alice Munro and Mavis Gallant, with whom she is often grouped, Thomas has been influenced not only by great international forerunners such as Henry James, Joseph Conrad, James Joyce, and Ernest Hemingway, but also by other Canadian writers and literary activists including Frederick Philip Grove, Sinclair Ross, and Ethel Wilson, who prepared the reading public for the international breakthrough of Canadian literature in the 1960s. Earlier, Morley Callaghan (*A Native Argosy*, 1929; *Now That April's Here*, 1936) had introduced the Canadian public to the modernist style in the short story (Thacker 2004, 184), while Robert Weaver and John Metcalf had created — through CBC programs such as *Anthology* (1953–85) — a literary milieu in which short stories were regarded not merely as merchandise and entertainment but were also appreciated as a serious art form. Since 1983 some 600 short-story collections by individual writers have been published (Thacker, 190), and the range of short stories presented in anthologies, for example Margaret Atwood and Robert Weaver's *The New Oxford Book of Canadian Short Stories in English* (1995) is impressive. With this abundance of competitors, among them Alice Munro, Mavis Gallant, and Margaret Atwood, Audrey Thomas's success is well-earned. Today her novels and short stories, in which realistic and parodic elements interact in subtle ways, are highly regarded as sophisticated fiction (Davey 1986, 5; Gillam 1996, 2; Kleiman 2000, 660).

Unlike the early Atwood, for instance, Thomas is not a cultural nationalist but belongs to the large group of Canadian writers who, having non-Canadian roots, add an international dimension to the nation's culture. Born in Binghampton, New York, and educated at Smith College, Massachusetts, and the University of St. Andrews in Scotland, she undertook a Grand Tour of Europe, lived in Ghana, Greece, France, and England, and traveled to French West Africa, Senegal, and Mali before buying a house on Galiano Island, in the Gulf of Georgia, British Columbia. Like Alice Munro and other female authors of her generation, she had to reconcile her profession with her role as housewife and mother (Munro 1998, x).

Thomas continued to write fiction, completed an M.A. thesis on Henry James, and started on a Ph.D. dissertation (Godard 1989, 2). After her divorce, she held several teaching positions in creative writing, while at the same time pursuing her career as a professional writer. The impact of her literary studies as well as that of her contacts with George Bowering and other members of the avant-garde West Coast Tish group (Godard, 5) manifests itself in her strategies of parody and pastiche, and her numerous literary allusions in both novels and short stories (Kleiman, 660–61). Like the members of the Tish group, Thomas is not a regionalist writer, although she often draws on West Coast scenery. In "Aquarius," for instance, she uses Vancouver locations (Aquarium, Stanley Park, Horseshoe Bay), but without insisting upon regionalist aesthetics. What she shares with the postmodernists and the George Bowering of *Burning Water* (1980) is an interest in parodying old stories and old histories (Kuester 1992). This is evident in Thomas's two interrelated portrait-of-the-artist novellas, *Munchmeyer and Prospero on the Island* (1971), in the retelling of the fairy tale "Rapunzel" in the short-story collection *Ladies and Escorts* (1977), and in *The Ballad of Isabel Gunn* (1987), a revisionist version of a Hudson Bay Company story about a young Orkney woman who disguises herself as a man.

Thomas employs literary devices and historical material to create the distance that enables her to artistically integrate her autobiography. The parodic reformulating of these texts provides a necessary element of stylization that counterbalances the realism of her "life stories." What makes her writing particularly interesting is that it subtly explores and convincingly embodies hitherto neglected aspects of femininity. While Thomas is hardly a radical or theorizing feminist (Godard, 8, 17, 20), she shares Daphne Marlatt's preoccupation with volatile female identities (Hales 1987, 77; Rosenthal 2003, 40–45 and 66–70), adumbrated in a rich assortment of intertextual references ranging from Christopher Marlowe's *Doctor Faustus* to Lewis Carroll's *Alice in Wonderland*. However, in contrast to Marlatt's lesbian commitment, Thomas focuses on heterosexual gender relations. More specifically, she dismantles clichés in dealing with marriage problems, mother-daughter relations, the lost-child motif, and the exploratory lives of single women in the Africa of Conrad and Jung (Godard, 6; Vice 1989, 121), in a tourist's Mexico, or in an everyday West Coast environment. In some of her works, for instance in the short stories "Rapunzel" and "Initram" and in the novel *Latakia* (1979), she uses the situation of a woman writer to present new forms of female consciousness, in the manner of Alice Munro (*Lives of Girls and Women*, 1976), Margaret Laurence (*The Diviners*, 1974), Margaret Atwood (*Lady Oracle*, 1976), and Carol Shields (*Small Ceremonies*, 1976) (Howells 2004, 196–97).

In addition to her ten novels, among them such acclaimed works as *Mrs. Blood* (1975), *Latakia* (1979), and *Intertidal Life* (1984), Thomas has published four very rich short-story collections: *Ten Green Bottles* (1967), *Ladies and Escorts* (1977), *Real Mothers* (1981), and *Goodbye Harold, Good Luck* (1986), supplemented by the two short-story selections *Two in the Bush and Other Stories* (1982) and *The Path of Totality* (2001). The range of these collections is too wide to be easily summarized, but Pauline Butling, skillfully using the cover designs of Thomas's first three short-story volumes, provides some thematic orientation:

> *Ten Green Bottles* (1967), for instance, has Jack and Jill on the cover. The stories then deal with the loss of innocence, but not the traditional loss of physical innocence. . . . Innocence is a mental/emotional condition; the fall is into the self. . . . In *Ladies and Escorts* (1977), the cover illustration of Little Red Riding Hood introduces the subject of women's encounters with the "wicked wolf." . . . But Thomas then de-constructs the images of women as helpless, passive, and in need of escorts. . . . In *Real Mothers* (1981), she parodies the image of the super Mom, that post-war ideal of domesticity implied by the book's title, and by the cover illustration of mother and daughter happily rolling out pastry, smiling at each other . . . [the] daughter apprenticing to become cook, love object, wife and mother, happy in the role of domestic servant. (Butling 1984, 197)

The cover illustration of Thomas's fourth short-story collection *Goodbye Harold, Good Luck* refers to the volume's title story, which incorporates some of its major thematic concerns. Little Emily and her mother Francine — about to separate from her husband — stare at the mirror in the bathroom of a seedy hotel and the farewell message "Goodbye Harold, Good Luck" brought out by the steam, evidently written by "somebody who got up and left while Harold was still sleeping." The motif of the script on the mirror stirs up a host of connotations reflecting the female predicament and the sad state of gender relations, the major theme of Thomas's novels as well as her short stories.

In her introduction to *Goodbye Harold, Good Luck* — where Thomas explains her method of composition through association, what she calls "correspondences" (Godard, 18) — she speaks of herself as a novelist. While acknowledging the fact that her readers tend to regard her primarily as a writer of short fiction, she points out the origins of several of her novels as short stories and refers to the different kinds of tension in the two genres that fascinate her (Thomas 1986, xviii). The example of "Aquarius" will not only show that Thomas is a skillful writer, masterfully using all the tricks of the trade — judicious choice of point of view, effective structuring, and clever positioning of punch lines — but will also demonstrate that she is a subtle artist who "moves into thought through her senses"

(Thomas 1986, xvi) and who, through her fusion of realism and postmodern pastiche (Kleiman, 660), reveals new sides of women and men.

Thomas gave her 1977 collection of short stories the title *Ladies and Escorts*, thus foregrounding gender roles and major aspects of femininity. It indicates the direction and the tone of the author's explorations of love relations, in which men are cut down to size and mainly serve as foils for critical portraits of women. A good example is the opening story, "Aquarius," in which the nameless husband of a seemingly powerful woman named Erica functions as the central intelligence, but where, right from the beginning, the parodic reference to the mythical figure of Aquarius from the zodiac casts an ironic light on the man's encounter with the whale in the aquarium — the more so as his stream of consciousness focuses on his wife's dominance and his own feeling of inferiority. Resembling the antihero of T. S. Eliot's "The Love Song of J. Alfred Prufrock" (1917), who "[has] heard the mermaids singing each to each," but says "I do not think that they will sing to me" (Eliot 1959, 15), the Aquarius of Thomas's story is an "escort" in the sense of being a weak hanger-on to his wife. The story opens with his experience of the whale's power, but ends with his degrading return to his wife.

Thomas's achievement lies in her narrative and stylistic handling of the relationship between the whale episode and the story of a failed marriage. The husband provides the point of view but, as we soon come to realize, the wife dominates the narrative. In view of Thomas's ironic rendering of animal metaphors and gender stereotypes, traditional approaches to her story are hardly applicable here (Dorscht 1987, 18). Instead, the interplay between the treatment of nature and gender suggests an ecofeminist reading. However, as ecofeminism is "a constantly changing field" (Armbruster 1998, 97) and "not a single master theory" (Gaard and Murphy 1998, 2), some methodological observances are in order.

Against the background of intense and wide-ranging debates between essentialist and constructionist ecofeminists, the study of nature and gender in Thomas's "Aquarius" demands a modified version of a constructionist ecofeminism, which sees language as essentially mediating our experiences of "reality." In contrast to the Romanticists of the past, who regarded nature, mind, and soul as spiritually attuned to each other and in a symbolic relationship, contemporary ecofeminists tend to see nonhuman and human nature as regulated by power relations. Such a view rejects both essentialist concepts of nature and woman/man and the assumption of their culturally constructed character (Slicer 1998, 57; Armbruster, 100). No less important in ecofeminism is the emphasis on the body as "mediated by social constructs" (Slicer, 57), not as an ontological reality. In the case of Thomas's "Aquarius," the striking concreteness of both the descriptions and the stream of consciousness suggests a reading of the story informed by a constructionist understanding of literary realism and postmodern parody.

> They had been warned what to expect; yet the explosion — what else could you call it? — and the quantities of water which leapt at them — for as the whale descended the water did, indeed, seem to leap, as though it had almost taken on the shape, or at least the strength, of the great beast which had violated its calm — there was a collective "aaahh" from the little group of spectators, and a band of elementary-school children drew in closer to their teacher and shrieked in fearful delight.
>
> "Brian, Daniel," called out the honeyed, public voice of the teacher, "Settle down now; come away from the side." ("Aquarius," 5)

The reader's perception of the story as "realistic" arises from its narrative jump-start and its *in-medias-res* rhetoric ("They had been warned what to expect"), as well as from the "naturalness" with which the male protagonist establishes his viewpoint and voice, while stressing the extraordinary character of the event ("the explosion — what else could you call it?"). This impression of immediacy is enhanced by the narrator first registering the displacement of the water and only then telling us of the whale that caused it. Also contributing to the "realism" of the scene are such closely observed details as the school children who "shrieked in fearful delight" and their teacher's "honeyed, public voice." However, if we take the metaphors into account, we quickly get beyond this "realistic" surface to the story's deep structure.

In the second paragraph, the central consciousness reflects on what has happened, and his imagery reveals his mental state: "like the water, he, too, had felt the shape and thrust of all that energy and had been strangely thrilled by it and strangely envious" (5). The repetition of the word "strangely" stresses the peculiarity of the emotions with which he observes the whale displace the water. We understand that he is "thrilled" by the powerful splash, but why "strangely" and why would he be "strangely envious" of the displaced water? We find a clue by returning to the first paragraph and by examining the two metaphoric references to the whale and the water together ("the water did, indeed, seem to leap, as though it had almost taken on the shape, or at least the strength, of the great beast which had violated its calm," 5). In both instances, the depiction of the whale and the water has anthropomorphic, sexual overtones, the whale representing the stereotypical male and the water the female part: "violated its calm" (5); "thrust of all that energy" (5); "plunged deeper and deeper into the heaving water" (6). However, there is an important variation of the conventional gender pattern in that the male protagonist on the one hand identifies himself with the female role of the water — "like the water, he, too, had felt the shape and thrust of all that energy" (6) — and on the other hand imagines himself riding the whale, waving superciliously to Erica and, in a further escalation, ascending on the whale's back into heaven:

> He riding the slippery back as though it was the easiest thing in the world, waving his hand to Erica as he passed, casually, . . . then up and up with the whale, out away from the blue water of the pool, which burned upward after them like transparent, ice-blue fire. A triumph against gravity, captivity, everything. "O Ile leape up to my God." (6)

This ecstasy and the bonding with the whale are carefully prepared for, being an imaginatively heightened version of the original encounter with the whale in the first paragraph. The first experience is epiphanic, leaving the hero overwhelmed ("as if he had heard a voice calling to him from a dream," 5) and, as the text says, doubly "disoriented." His first disorientation is physical, causing claustrophobia: "as though he were looking out from the lower port-holes of the whale pool" (5). His second disorientation is more profound ("And disoriented in another way as well, for something had happened to him as the whale leapt up," 5), caused by his imaginative exposure to the whale's vital power ("like the water, he, too had felt the shape and thrust of all that energy," 5). As a lover after the act, or a devotee following religious ecstasy, he feels "abandoned, cast down from some unimaginable height of strength and brute beauty and thrust" (5–6).

In the ensuing depression, he submits to a fancy that is both regressive and self-protective ("Wished, for a moment, to be one of the children who could close up, like delicate petals, around the tight bud of their teacher's serenity," 6), the rarefied quality of this nature simile contrasting with the sublime metaphor of the whale. Both these nature images are strongly anthropomorphic, characterizing the protagonist who in the union with the whale assumes a stereotypical female role and, in their painful "separation," a childlike posture. In addition, an unidentified quotation — "'*O Ile leape up to my God*,' he remembered, '*who pulls me downe*?'" (6, italics added), repeated in the visionary transformation of the original scene ("then up and up with the whale . . . '*O Ile leape up to my God*,'" 6) — suggests by its thematic and stylistic difference that the reader view both the *unio* with the whale and their separation (6, 9) as events transcending the "realistic" surface. The quotation, from Christopher Marlowe's play *Doctor Faustus* (V.ii. 77), does indeed have metaphysical implications, concerning as it does the protagonist's vain attempt to escape the devil's claws. Even the presence of the children and their teacher, which had initially seemed to be a neutral detail in a realistic setting, turns out to be a contrastive symbol and, because of its escapist implications, relevant to the psychoanalytic deep structure of the story.

In a later scene, the zoo attendant identifies the whale as female: "Now I'll get Skana to give me a kiss," the boy said. . . . The whale stopped circling immediately and sped over toward her master, lifting her great blunt head up toward his inclining cheek. They touched and the spectators 'aaahhed' again" (7–8). This bit of information has a significant and demonstrable bearing on both the thematics of nature and gender because most readers, guided by traditional stereotypes, will probably take the whale in the opening scene to be the embodiment of the male principle, with the water representing the female element. To counteract this stereotypical response, Thomas sets a complex parodic process in motion, with the male protagonist assuming the conventional female posture and the powerful female whale metaphorically reflecting the new female self-confidence of the 1970s that we find in Audrey Thomas, Margaret Atwood, and others.

The parody of gender stereotypes does not stop here. In his afterthoughts, the antihero not only comes to regard the whale as a superfemale but to identify it with his formidable wife: "And the creature was powerful and female, sleek and strangely beautiful — like the woman herself" (9). In other words, we see the protagonist creating another of those metaphorical animals (like the snake or the tiger) associated with the *femme fatale*. From an ecofeminist viewpoint it is important to emphasize that the whale, who to the protagonist had seemed an embodiment of natural power, soon shows herself to be a mere circus animal. She does not appear in her natural habitat but in the artificial environment of a sea-water aquarium. Her amazing leap is made for one of the raw herrings that the zoo attendant rewards her obedience with. Apparently giving the zoo attendant a "kiss," the whale in fact performs a grotesque and demeaning anthropomorphism. Moreover, the whale is turned into the object of a popular zoology lesson for school children: "The boy explained that the teeth were used only for holding and grasping" (8).

However, this zoological demonstration of the whale's teeth is interrupted first by the grotesque association with George Washington's notoriously ill-fitting dentures, and then, in an equally surprising turn, by the memory of a forgotten detail from the protagonist's love story with Erica that foreshadows their final alienation: "And suddenly he remembered the feel of Erica's teeth that first time, and how something had willed him, just for a moment, to set his teeth against her determined seeking" (8). As it turns out, these surprising associations are quite characteristic of Thomas, who, for all her realistic description, shares with the postmodernists a predilection for parody and pastiche as a means of curtailing any naïve realism. The ironic inversions in the first part of "Aquarius" warrant a detailed study of the intertextual ruptures in the second part, which presents a devastating double-portrait of husband and wife. From the narrator's self-indulging account we come to realize that he is a failed poet, hibernating in the safe haven of academia and in awe of his more vigorous and robust wife. If he had once been impressed by her pretentious pronouncement, "I am terrified only of the mediocre" (10), he now sarcastically notes her "extraordinary talent for seeming to know more than she really did" (7) and for asking "one or two extremely intelligent questions" (7). Thomas uses her antihero's bitter reflections to reveal that Erica is the more powerful personality and the natural leader in their marriage: "She had taught him all he ever knew of sex . . . and cooked for him thick homemade soups. . . . And she it was, too, who willed him to be a poet" (10). This marriage is in fact a caricature of that of many young academics and would-be artists of the 1970s, "with bare floors and tipsy, mismatched chairs," and "cheap wine and crusty bread" (10). Thomas shows a special genius for caustically handling ostensibly casual realistic details: "They were poetic about their poverty too, acting out the romantic role of the artist and his barefoot wife, for she had given up shoes (at least indoors) long before it was fashionable to do so. And had named their first child Darius" (14). For a while his poetic ambitions and her sexual drive carry them through, but, as Thomas in her sarcastic rhetoric puts it, eventually "she took a lover and he a full-time job" (15).

Thomas's great gift for close observation enables her to produce a kind of photographic realism that makes both the Prufrock-like narrator and his wife appear as "authentic" characters. ("He knew the shape of her neck as it rose from the cardigan, and the texture of that neck, with its tiny orange mole, like a rust spot, and the texture of her pale, coarse hair," 6–7). This insistent realism is in line with the new emphasis on the body in ecofeminism, in turn making us pay special attention to Erica's bodily superiority. While Thomas's Aquarius figure shares with Eliot's Prufrock a peculiar, anxious awareness of his bodily weakness ("blinking as he rubbed his glasses clean, terribly conscious of his thin body and his pale, scholar's hands," 5; "They will say: But how his arms and legs are thin," Eliot, 12), Erica appears to him "the ultimate in womanhood, the very essence of female with her full, Northern figure and her incredible self-assurance and practicality, so different from the flat-bosomed, delicate foolishness of his own well-bred female relatives" (10). However, in the terminal stage of their relationship, he turns in revulsion from Erica's body and she in threatening disgust from his: "Three nights before she had unexpectedly thrown her heavy, blue-veined thigh over his as she was getting into bed and had cried out in triumph, 'Look how thin you are getting! I could crush you!'" (16).

Interacting with an ecofeminist emphasis on the body is the tendency towards postmodern parody and pastiche. A good example is the following intertextual allusion to Herman Melville's *Moby Dick*. The narrator, jealously watching his wife engage the young zoo attendant in a conversation about the whale, remarks with malicious glee that "he had watched her leaf quickly through the paperback on whales which had been on display in the souvenir shop as they came in" and that "the boy was not to know this, or to know that years before she had typed for him an article *on the reality factor in Moby Dick*" (7, italics added). The comic effect of this allusion is intensified when the protagonist, in his frustration, imagines how Erica will turn his own encounter with the whale before the children into a burlesque, with herself starring as the comic victim: " 'My dears, I was nearly *swallowed up*, like a female Jonah or Pinocchio' " (9).

The parodic coupling of the biblical whale story with Carlo Collodi's popular children's book *Le avventure di Pinocchio* (1883) indicates how we are to take the narrator's story of Skana, the circus animal. Erica's travesty of the male prophet ("like a female Jonah") caricatures her husband's sublime encounter with the whale. As a consequence, we come to understand that Aquarius is not only one of the mythical figures of the zodiac but also somebody whose wife has taken him to the Vancouver Aquarium — although he would have preferred an idyllic picnic beside the water of Horseshoe Bay (17), another popular British Columbia location. Aquarius is also somebody who, in his youthful idealism, had associated his beloved with the sea. Above all, Aquarius is the parodic reference point of the ingenious water imagery running through and structuring the whole story.

While Joyce's and Eliot's modernist art of quotation, even in works where its purpose is ironic inversion, is characterized by a certain air of self-consciousness and seriousness, Thomas and other writers of the postmodern era seem to use literary references much more casually and with a peculiar nonchalance and farcical abandon. An example of this occurs when she lets her Aquarius "*dryly* mock himself" (italics added) and slip into the congenial role of the forsaken merman: "He could only *dryly* mock himself, forsaken merman, and mocking, failed again" (13, italics added). The failed poet-turned-full-time-academic probably knew Matthew Arnold's poem "The Forsaken Merman" (1847) from Victorian Poetry courses. Mermen and mermaids belong to the arsenal of popular literary motifs and stereotypes with which writers, composers, and artists embodied socially unacceptable emotions from the era of Romanticism to Eliot's "Love Song of J. Alfred Prufrock." Thomas, like Eliot, makes satirical use of the old literary motif of the merman/mermaid to caricature her antihero.

As a consequence of this and other parodic intertexts through which the author hints at the "literariness" of her characters, readers begin to view them and their story, "realistic" though they appear, with ironic detachment. This process is subtle and varied, beginning when the protagonist's literary consciousness makes him "remember" and twice repeat the quotation "*O Ile leape up to my God who pulls me downe?*" from Marlowe's *Doctor Faustus.* The ironic attitude increases when Thomas exposes her readers to the leitmotif complex "Sea — Siegfried — Northern woman — Vikings":

> He had always associated her, too, with the sea — because of her name and her pale blond hair and cold blue eyes. When he first loved her he even saw himself as something Scandinavian, a Siegfried, and exulted in her restrained, voluptuous power and her ice-blue eyes. . . . Later, because the Siegfried role was not his true self-idealization, he allowed

> himself to be mothered by her . . . and cooked for him thick home-made soups. . . . She had seemed the ultimate in womanhood, the very essence of female with her full, Northern figure and her incredible self-assurance and practicality. (9–10)
>
> Had it all been a trick, her violent lovemaking which somehow was in keeping with her Nordic looks — a love like waterfalls and mountain torrents. . . . He entered her as Siegfried leaping through a wall of fire. (12)

Thomas ironically reveals how her male protagonist and narrator mythicizes his love story and idealizes Erica extravagantly by associating her name with the great early northern seafarers Erik the Red and his son Leif Erikson. The imagery ("a love like waterfalls and mountain torrents") calls up the world of Nordic sagas and the mythic spirit of Wagner's tetralogy of musical dramas *The Ring of the Nibelung*, with the metaphor "Siegfried leaping through a wall of fire" clearly pointing to the third and fourth operas of the cycle, *Siegfried* and *The Twilight of the Gods*. However, at the same time that the pathos of these mythicizing metaphors affects us, we are humorously reminded that they refer only to the couple's long-gone early phase, that the would-be Siegfried was not driven by his own passion but was inspired by hers, and that it was only their little apartment he had turned into a pseudo-mythic arena.

The story's setting inside the aquarium building gives it a sense of unity and compactness that acts as a counterweight to the narrator's many flashbacks. While the first part of the story (5–11) is clearly dominated by the encounter with the whale, the second part (11–18) has the narrator look at some of the other animals in the aquarium: iguana, octopus, alligators, wolf-eel, and Mozambique Mouth-Breeder. Not only the female whale but all animals in the story are presented from an anthropocentric, not from an ecocentric viewpoint. In fact, the narrator endows all his perceptions with a subjective and emotionalizing quality that says more about him than the animals: "The octopus flattened his *disgusting* suckers against the *harsh reality* of glass" (11, italics added). In the case of the iguana, who "observed him wipe his forehead with a cynical, prehistoric eye" (11), the anthropomorphic imagery has a humorous effect. In contrast, "the alligators . . . with tourists' pennies clinging to their heads and backs" (11) show us the trivializing impact of humans on animals. Thanks to these verbal strategies, the animals, although appearing as part of the protagonist's realistically portrayed world, function as if they were literary allusions, quotations, scientific intertexts. This has a distancing effect on the reader, the more so because the protagonist has become so exhausted by the visit to the aquarium and his reflections on his unhappy marriage that he loses interest in the animals ("And he was bored with all these strange, slippery creatures that surrounded him, lost in their own dream-like, antiseptic coffins," 15).

The aquarium, serving in the first part as the scene of his thrilling encounter with the whale, in the second part makes him feel claustrophobic, eventually leading to a reversal of his position and that of the animals: "Yet he felt cold and claustrophobic in the aquarium, as though it were he who was shut in, not the fish and other specimens" (11). This reversal is of interest from an ecofeminist standpoint because it corresponds to a reversal of gender roles: "her strength and his incredible, female, weakness" (17). The reversal, or rather his perception of it, takes place in several stages. First, the protagonist loses interest in his "old preoccupations with beauty and order and truth" (13), that is, in the kind of "old-fashioned" aesthetics promulgated by the New Criticism which, in Thomas's time, was replaced by those of postmodernism. Later, Thomas's subtle irony shows him overcome by a fascist-cum-Manichaean disgust, a "physical revulsion now for anything that smacked of foreigness or dirt or unclean, hidden things" (16).

In ironically casting a man in the traditionally female role of the complaining victim (see, for example, Charlotte Perkins Gilman's "The Yellow Wall-paper") and a woman in that of the aggressor, Thomas reverses established gender stereotypes. Her configuration "weak man — powerful woman" reflects the crisis of the patriarchal system since the 1960s and the newly won self-confidence of women of her generation. This shift in social values is effectively dramatized by Thomas's original idea of presenting the superior woman indirectly, from the self-destructive viewpoint of the resentful and self-pitying man. By making the male protagonist enter into imaginary relationships with the female whale Skana and the other anthropomorphized animals in the "un-natural" environment of an aquarium, Thomas widens her theme, giving it an ecofeminist dimension. She achieves a convincing combination of realistic portrayal and postmodern parody because her language is both richly concrete and playfully intertextual, her title "Aquarius" and the leitmotif-complex "Sea — Siegfried — Northern woman — Vikings" being only the most prominent instances.

Judging from the example of "Aquarius," it would seem that the demands of the short-story genre, with its tightly controlled structure and language and its special regard for brevity, kept Thomas from giving in to the exuberant self-referentiality and intertextuality that make her novels so rich but also so much less popular than her short stories. With its profound psychological insight and its subtle fusion of realistic depiction and postmodern parody, "Aquarius" is a masterpiece by an author who is one of Canada's best short-story writers. Although the narrator's confession in "Aquarius" is accompanied by growing irony, Thomas — thanks to her shaping power and verbal wit — still manages to keep her characters and their situation interesting, from the whale's first splash to the final calmness of the pool: "He inclined his cheek, waiting. 'Skana,' he whispered, 'Skana.' But the surface of the pool remained a calm, indifferent blue. The whale did not hear or did not choose to answer. He got up, slowly, awkwardly, and went to join his wife" (18).

Works Cited

Armbruster, Karla. "'Buffalo Gals, Won't You Come Out Tonight': A Call for Boundary-Crossing in Ecofeminist Literary Criticism." In Gaard and Murphy 1998, 97–122.

Butling, Pauline. "Thomas and Her Rag Bag." *Canadian Literature* 102 (1984): 195–99.

Davey, Frank. "Alternate Stories: The Short Fiction of Audrey Thomas and Margaret Atwood." *Canadian Literature* 109 (1986): 5–14.

Eliot, T. S. *Collected Poems 1909–1935.* London: Faber and Faber, 1959.

Gaard, Greta, and Patrick D. Murphy, eds. *Ecofeminist Literary Criticism: Theory, Interpretation, Pedagogy.* Urbana: University of Illinois Press, 1998.

Gillam, Robyn. "Ideals and Lost Children: An Interview with Audrey Thomas." *Paragraph: The Fiction Magazine* 18.1 (Summer 1996): 2–6.

Godard, Barbara. *Audrey Thomas and Her Works.* Toronto: ECW Press, 1989.

Hales, Leslie-Ann. "Meddling with the Medium: Language and Identity in Audrey Thomas' *Intertidal Life.*" *Canadian Woman Studies / Les Cahiers de la Femme* 8.3 (Fall 1987): 77–79.

Howells, Coral Ann. "Writing by Women." In *The Cambridge Companion to Canadian Literature*, ed. Eva-Marie Kröller. Cambridge: Cambridge University Press, 2004. 196–206.

Kleiman, Ed. "'If One Green Bottle . . .': Audrey Thomas Looks Back on the Cauldron of History." *University of Toronto Quarterly* 69.3 (Summer 2000): 660–69.

Kuester, Martin. *Framing Truths: Parodic Structures in Contemporary English-Canadian Historical Novels.* Toronto: University of Toronto Press, 1992.

Munro, Alice. *Selected Stories.* Toronto: Penguin, 1998.

Rosenthal, Caroline. *Narrative Deconstructions of Gender in Works by Audrey Thomas, Daphne Marlatt, and Louise Erdrich.* Rochester, NY: Camden House, 2003.

Rudy Dorscht, Susan Arlene. *Blown Figures and Blood: Toward a Feminist/Post-Structuralist Reading of Audrey Thomas' Writing.* Ottawa: University of Ottawa Press, 1987.

Slicer, Deborah. "Toward an Ecofeminist Standpoint Theory: Bodies as Grounds." In Gaard and Murphy 1998, 49–73.

Thacker, Robert. "Short Fiction." In *The Cambridge Companion to Canadian Literature*, ed. Eva-Marie Kröller. Cambridge: Cambridge University Press, 2004. 177–93.

Thomas, Audrey. "Aquarius." In Thomas, *Ladies and Escorts*, 5–18.

———. *Goodbye Harold, Good Luck*. Markham: Penguin, 1986.

———. *Ladies and Escorts*. Ottawa: Oberon, 1977.

———. *The Path of Totality: New and Selected Stories*. Toronto: Viking, 2001.

———. *Real Mothers*. Vancouver: Talonbooks, 1981.

———. *Ten Green Bottles*. Ottawa: Oberon, 1977.

———. *Two in the Bush and Other Stories*. Toronto: McClelland & Stewart, 1981.

Vice, Sue. "Real Mothers: Feminity, Motherhood and Fiction: The Short Stories of Audrey Thomas." *RANAM* 22 (1989): 121–26.

18: "The Problem Is to Make the Story": Rudy Wiebe, "Where Is the Voice Coming from?" (1971)

Heinz Ickstadt (Free University of Berlin)

RUDY WIEBE'S NATIONAL AND INTERNATIONAL reputation is largely based on his novels, but short stories have formed a substantial part of his literary production from the very beginning. Although he often used them as an experimental ground for his longer narratives — those "great black steel lines of fiction" required "to touch this land with words" (Wiebe 1995, 4) — he also "touched" his country's history and physical enormity in the shorter genre. As the Canadian short story boomed in the 1960s and afterwards, Wiebe came to represent a distinctly regional voice (that of Alberta and its northern frontier) within a national literary tradition that has characteristically defined itself in regional terms. Wiebe's stories — like those of Frederick Philip Grove, one of his acknowledged influences — deal with the immensity of the western prairies, but also with the sublime vastness of the Arctic North, whose forbidding grandeur of ice, snow, and solitude has been a constant object of fascination for Wiebe.

Born to Mennonite immigrants in Northern Saskatchewan in 1934, Wiebe's mother tongue was Low German, and a religiously anchored social consciousness became a crucial part of his cultural heritage. The family had left the Soviet Union in the early 1930s in order to find a safer home in Canada. In his early novels *Peace Shall Destroy Many* (1962), *First and Vital Candle* (1966), and *The Blue Mountains of China* (1970) as well as in his first short stories, Wiebe dealt critically with the life of his brethren in faith and with their diasporic communities in Canada and South America.

His early story "Where Is the Voice Coming from?," first published in 1971,[1] may usefully be considered alongside his two novels, *The*

[1] It first appeared in a collection edited by David Helwig and Tom Marshall, *Fourteen Stories High* (1971); then in Wiebe's own collection of short stories, *Where Is the Voice Coming from?* (1974), again in another collection, *The Angel of the Tar Sands and Other Stories* (1982), and finally in *River of Stone: Fictions and*

Temptations of Big Bear (1974) and *The Scorched-Wood People* (1978), that went beyond the experiential horizon of the author's Mennonite upbringing and, during the 1970s, brought him the reputation of a regional writer of national importance. In these novels as well as in the story, he deals with the life and beliefs of other marginalized groups — the repressed or forgotten history and culture of the Prairie Cree and the Métis — whose mythological bond to nature and to the land as "a gift from God" may have seemed familiar to him from the cultural tradition of his own religious community (Wiebe in Keith 1981, 207).

In both novels Wiebe merges the role of the storyteller with that of the historian, or, as Robert Kroetsch puts it, with that of the archaeologist determined to "unearth" (to use one of Wiebe's favorite words) the remnants of a buried past in order to reconstruct a lost history in the collective memory of those who now possess the land. The established history of his own region, as taught at school, was that of the Anglo-Saxon colonizers who had created "their" Canada in the Northwest by wresting it from its former owners, that is to say, the Cree or the Métis, who had ruled and administered the land, if only for a short time, following the Red River Rebellion of 1870. To give them voice, to inscribe their history into Canada's cultural memory, and to redraw "the imaginative map of our country" thus became the goal of Wiebe's writing.

The question forming the title of the short story that Wiebe once called "a kind of try-out for some of the things that happen in *Big Bear*" (Keith, 241) is therefore as crucial as it is ambivalent. Where indeed does the voice come from — a voice only heard at the end of the story yet prefigured in the very name of its protagonist, the historically documented Almighty Voice? To this question Wiebe gives a historiographical, a poetological, and a religious dimension: how can a buried history come back to life? To what extent can historical facts be used by the literary imagination? How is literary insight legitimized, and what are the limits of its inventiveness?

"Where Is the Voice Coming from?" is a story about the making of (hi)stories. It gradually translates theoretical reflection into event and action, and constructs from the fragments of historical evidence a coherent narrative (the "story") without ever abandoning the reflective distance towards its own narrative making. In the story's very first sentence, the neutral voice of the narrator raises the theoretical problem of historical narration: "The problem is to make the story" (Wiebe 1982, 78). One should

---

Memories (1995). Together with "The Naming of Albert Johnson" (1974), one of Wiebe's fictions on the Arctic North, "Where Is the Voice Coming from?" has been the most frequently anthologized of his short stories.

note that he does not speak of "*a* story," but of "*the* story," implying that the story — the "plot" — has yet to be discovered and constructed in order to make the historical facts cohere. Since facts never speak for themselves, they need an interpreter to give them voice and meaning; at the same time, the interpreter himself is caught in this story, even if (as the narrator points out by quoting Teilhard de Chardin) "we are continually inclined to isolate ourselves from the things and events which surround us" (78). Whether hidden within this "story" there lies a still deeper truth (Arnold Toynbee's "undifferentiated unity of the mystical experience," 78), that is, a truth beyond the constructed narrative coherence of historical facts, is an idea left open by the narrator.

The events his story is meant to bring back to life happened seventy-five years before the time of writing, between 1895 and 1897. They are thus not only deeply buried in the past but have also been sifted through the discriminating filter of the established historical tradition. Therefore the narrator/historian first concentrates on collecting and describing the remnants of the past, the "bits and pieces" from which he has to understand the hidden story by reconstructing it. The historical material available to him, however, is not only of varied origin and quality (names of the participants, newspaper reports, photographs, official announcements and proclamations, skull fragments, rusty rifles, a polished canon in a local museum), but is itself already the product of interpretation, part of a version of history and therefore ambivalent and inviting further interpretation. The names of the protagonists with whom the narrator acquaints the reader mark the cultural difference and the oppositional structure that shaped the events of the past: "Sometimes it would seem that it would be enough — perhaps more than enough — to hear the names only" (78). The names of the Indians are suggestive and related to their specific qualities and skills, or are derived from a mythological or cosmological understanding of the world. Those of the whites, in contrast, are abstract and unspecific, relating to military rank or bureaucratic function, stiff as the language of the warrant promising a large reward for information about the Indian cattle thieves. The historical context of what happened still remains sketchy. We are given an exact date, however — the official document is from 20 April 1896.

The reader is gradually able to situate the narrator in time as well as in space. The narrator is obviously visiting a museum (the Royal Canadian Mounted Police Museum in Regina, as we are told later), slowly walking from one exhibit to another. Whereas the language of names and proclamations resonates in his inner ear (even if "such hearing cannot be enough"), he subsequently emphasizes exact observation and minutely describes several of the exhibits, such as a piece of skull to which hair is still attached (or perhaps not; he cannot quite be sure because of the thick glass of the showcase). The carefully polished "seven-pounder canon" placed next to the showcase is said to have once been used in the suppression of the rebellion of 1885 and then again, twelve years later, on that Saturday evening of 29 May 1897, which saw the death of Almighty Voice. In another showcase lies the rusty, dust-covered rifle (model 1866) apparently found next to his body.

The narrator now intensifies his local and historical contextualization: the little house that functioned as a police station at Duck Lake in 1895 has also become an exhibition piece, renovated, disinfected, made visitor-friendly, "smoothed" and "white-washed" for a contemporary audience largely unconscious of the repressed history. This particular space of colonial law and order seems insulated from the world surrounding it: "not a sound can be heard from the streets of the, probably dead, town" (81). The guard's song mocking the "Injun" cattle thieves which the narrator presumably hears at this moment is documented nowhere (as we are told later) and yet is real in his imagination.

The imagined song of the guard (whose identity is revealed only towards the end of the story) marks a first break in the narrative, since the narrator virtually leaves the closed rooms of historical evidence stored in museums and offers a wider range of information instead — his general knowledge of the nature of Canadian prairies, but also his more specific awareness of the region and its past. To "make the story" of what happened on those late May days of the year 1897, he increasingly draws on other historical sources. He turns to the gravestones on the English cemetery, "six miles east, thirty miles north in Prince Albert" (81), where the four Anglo-Canadians shot by Almighty Voice and his band are buried. The scanty data the grave-stones provide allow the construction of the temporal frame of those past events: Sergeant Colin Campbell Colebrook of the North West Mounted Police, shot by Indians who escaped from a prison near Prince Albert on 29 October 1895; the other three killed almost two years later, on 28 May 1897, "shot by Indians at Min-etch-inass Hills, Prince Albert District" (81). While the names, dates, and graves of the white victims are part of a known regional history, those of the Indians are invisible — their graves unknown, their names extinguished in collective anonymity.

The last source the narrator consults challenges his reflective observation most intensely: the photographs of the policemen and of some of the Indians, especially that of Almighty Voice. To the picture of Sergeant Colebrook he pays only passing attention — the large ears, short haircut, and bushy eyebrows seem merely to mark the stereotypical military man, the rigorous guardian of white laws. In contrast, the pictures of the Indians, their attitudes and gestures, are described and tentatively interpreted in great detail; for example, the facial expression of Spotted Calf (Almighty Voice's mother) when she turns her wrinkled face questioningly toward her husband, Sounding Sky.

But the narrator gives his greatest attention to the photograph of Almighty Voice. It is placed next to the piece of skull, and although both exhibits are unequivocally ascribed to Almighty Voice, the narrator nevertheless speaks in this context of the "ultimate problem in making the story." For the photograph does not seem to concur with the official descriptions of Almighty Voice. One of them mentions a scar on the left side of his face, while the other — strangely enough, the most official of all, his warrant — does not mention the scar at all but emphasizes Almighty Voice's "feminine appearance." Neither description can the narrator reconcile with the photographic representation of the Indian, leaving the reader with only two possible interpretations: either text and image do not refer to the same person (which would make the authenticity of both sources highly dubious), or neither of the two official documents is able to represent the person and the figure of the Indian without turning the latter into a racial stereotype.

At this point the narrator leaves the assumed position of detached observer/historian. His tone of neutral and quasi-scientific description gives way to one of passionate engagement, for despite "this watered-down reproduction of unending reproductions of that original," the image's expressive power reveals to him a character and not a type: "no believed face is more *man* than this face" (84). The phrase "believed face" once again points to the uncertain identity of the person photographed, but also suggests a face that can be believed and trusted, "that the world acknowledges as *man*" (84). In explicit contrast to the official document ascribing feminine traits to Almighty Voice (even though, as the narrator suggests, the predicate of the feminine applies more to the seal of the Queen "and all the heaped detail of her 'Right Trusty and Right Well-beloved Cousin,'" 84), this emphasis on "man" is surely meant to insist on the manhood and manliness of the Indian. Yet "man" obviously also has universalist implications, allowing the narrator to name Almighty Voice with the "great" figures of human history (he mentions Socrates, Jesus, and Ghandi but also Genghis Khan, Attila, and Stalin): "a steady look into those eyes cannot be endured. It is a face like an axe" (84).

After this moment of passionate revelation, the story returns to the metahistorical reflection of its beginning. Teilhard de Chardin's opening dictum that "we are continually inclined to isolate ourselves from the things and events which surround us . . . as though we were spectators, not elements, in what goes on" is repeated in emphatic denial of the possibility of either objective historiography or narrative. It is evident that the narrator's attempt to "make" the story from the evidence of historical facts has been an impossible exercise in quasi-scholarly "disinterestedness." It collapses at the moment when the ambivalence of the documented facts can no longer be ignored, and he has to recognize that his effort to perceive historical truth through the eyes of the impartial observer has failed: "Despite the most rigid application of impersonal investigation, the elements of the story have now run me aground. If ever I could, I can no longer pretend to objective, omnipotent disinterestedness. I am no longer *spectator* of what *has* happened or what *may* happen: I am [*sic*] become *element* in what is happening at this very moment" (85). The ambivalence of the last sentence is striking. "I am become *element* in what is happening at this very moment" refers as much to the temporal level of a present that is now past as to the participation of the narrator in his present telling. (The archaic "I *am* become" could be understood as an accentuation of this double sense of the present.) Such a "re-presentation" of a past event cannot, by definition, be disinterested. By uncovering forgotten, discarded, or repressed knowledge of the past, the "making" of the story as well as the making of history become an intervention in, and an attack on, established historical knowledge. In other words, it becomes a form of counter-history.

Over the last three pages, the narrator therefore reconstructs his story once again, but now from the position of a participant, that is, someone who, on the basis of handed-down evidence, "makes" his story but also reinvents it as an empathetic representation. The mocking of the proud Indian warriors by Constable Dickson (now an agent with a name), the Crees' experience of 350 years of expulsion from their homelands in Eastern Canada ("a war already lost the day the Cree watch Cartier hoist his guns ashore at Hochelaga," 85), their helplessness in the face of an incomprehensible ideology of Law — all this enters into the staging of the last and decisive encounter: the dramatic confrontation between three Indians and an overwhelming white power of police, military, and Indian-hating civilians. The narrator from now on asserts his subjectivity either directly by changing into a narrative "I," or indirectly by disappearing within his narrative and betraying his presence only in the vivid rendering of the historical event. Not only does he relate the last moments before the assault on the bluff (where Almighty Voice and his group have retreated) in the present tense but also in cinematic slow motion, minutely, and in sensuously concrete detail:

> The first gun and the second gun are in position, the beginning and end of the bristling surround of thirty-five Prince Albert Volunteers, thirteen civilians and fifty-six policemen in position relative to the bluff and relative to the unnumbered whites astride their horses, standing up in their carts, staring and pointing across the valley, in position relative to the bluff and the unnumbered Indians squatting silent along the higher ridges of the Hills, motionless mounds, faceless against the Sunday morning sunlight edging between and over them down along the tree tips, down into the shadows of the bluff. Nothing moves. Beside the second gun the red-coated officer has flung a handful of grass into the motionless air, almost to the rim of the red sun. (86)

It is in this singular moment when time seems suspended that Almighty Voice begins his death chant. Just as his "believed face" exalts him into the ranks of those "that the world acknowledges as *man*," his becoming the Almighty Voice prefigured in his name makes him give voice to more than an individual's dying. His voice survives its extinction in the very story that brings it back to life; as much as it is still present in the history that the story reveals:

> And there is a voice. It is an incredible voice that rises from among the young poplars ripped of their spring bark, from among the dead somewhere lying there, out of the arm-deep pit shorter than a man; a voice rises over the exploding smoke and thunder of guns that reel back in their positions, worked over, serviced by the grimed motionless men in bright coats and glinting buttons, a voice so high and clear, so unbelievably high and strong in its unending wordless cry. (86)

The interpretation/translation of the Indian name "'Gitchie-Manitou Wayo' — *interpreted* as 'voice of the Great Spirit'" (86) allows the participating narrator (and reader) to hear in the "almighty voice" of Almighty Voice the sublime Voice of the Almighty — "no less incredible in its beauty than in its incomprehensible happiness" — as a revelation of the divine presence in a history that rather seems to demonstrate His absence from it.

In his concluding reflection on the narrative process, the narrator who had first been a neutrally observing eye now becomes openly subjective as he reflects on the limits of his mediation between past and present as well as that between cultures. Commenting on the Indian's final chant, he notes in the last three sentences of the story, "I say 'wordless cry' because that is the way it sounds to me. I could be more accurate if I had a reliable interpreter who would make a reliable interpretation. For I do not, of course, understand the Cree myself" (86–87).

J. M. Kertzer argued that with this statement of resignation the narrator admits his defeat and recognizes that he does not qualify as a "true storyteller" (Kertzer 1986, 4). This interpretation, however, misses the point of a story that, on the contrary, uncovers and transcends the limits of what is translatable in the very act of translation — those gaps, walls, and ditches obstructing the possibility of historical, cultural, and linguistic understanding. To comprehend the different existence of the "other" also means to discover the beauty that is hidden in that difference. The "wordless cry" of Almighty Voice does not *need* exact translation: it is Wiebe's story that gives word and translation to the "wordless cry." The "of course" in the last sentence ("For I do not, of course, understand the Cree myself") is a recurring phrase throughout the story. It ironically marks as natural the acceptance of mis- or non-understanding, the all-too-easy arrangement with the limits of language and the limited evidence offered by known facts. But the voice "speaks" to the narrator even without the certainty of exact translation. For Wiebe, writing is an act of translation and translation a metaphor of an imaginative comprehension that transcends literal meanings and thus acts against the constant failure of communication. It rests — against all historical evidence — on an instinctive "trust" in the possibility of understanding not only between human beings of different cultures but also between man and nature, the one inseparably connected with the other:

> Through the smoke and darkness and piled up factuality of a hundred years to see a face; to hear and comprehend, a voice whose verbal language he will never understand; and then to risk himself beyond such seeing, such hearing as he discovers possible, and venture into the finer labyrinths opened by those other senses: touch, to learn the texture of leather, of earth; smell, the tinct of sweetgrass and urine; taste, the golden poplar sap or the hot, raw buffalo liver dipped in gall.
>
> This trust of the wayward though beloved senses: that is the problem of the storyteller. (Wiebe in Keith, 132)

The world of Big Bear that Wiebe evokes here is also that of Almighty Voice, even if the latter ("a petty human being," as Wiebe remarked in an interview with Eli Mandel [Wiebe in Keith, 154]) reaches greatness only in his heroic death chant. It is a world as far apart from contemporary culture and the spirit of progressive civilization as is the world of the Mennonites. Although it appears to be a world lost and destroyed, what seems hopelessly past becomes a living presence through the ability of the writer to "dig up" and reinvent. To this extent, Wiebe's narrative expresses as well as postulates faith in a continuity that exists beyond all knowledge of the limits of communication (beyond historical collapses and seemingly irreversible changes) — a continuity inscribed in history as its indelible and essentially religious subtext where the truth of the Bible and the nature religion of the Indians meet and overlap. Wiebe states in his interview with Mandel on *The Temptations of Big Bear*:

> [The book] is my way of looking at the world, and that's why I call it a novel and I don't pretend it's a history which is written impartially. It's written in a very biased way. But I do think that, say, the Biblical prophets and Big Bear had a great deal in common, the sense of a heritage that has been sold out, that through ignorance or neglect has simply been left: and the voice very clearly says that you cannot neglect your inheritance like this, the gifts of — the Cree call it "the Main One," the Jews "Jehovah"; you cannot do that and expect to get away with it.

And again in the same conversation:

> You began this with the prophets. And that's the reason why they had such great voices, right? Because they felt they spoke directly from God. They didn't speak out of the smallness of man but out of the greatness of all that man can comprehend . . . and . . . not only in connection with themselves but also with the spirit that made them . . . and that I think is important. For me as a writer anyway. (Wiebe in Keith, 152, 155)

The "truth" that Wiebe tries to comprehend in the process of writing is therefore as absolute and indubitable as it is approximate and hypothetical — at once beyond language and mediated through language. It issues from the "trust of the wayward and beloved senses" in a linguistically and sensuously understandable reality that nevertheless escapes the grasp of language and the senses time and again. The narrator recognized such a trust in Almighty Voice's death chant, even though he does not know the exact meaning of the words. The question "Where Is the Voice Coming from?" therefore also refers to the origin of this trust that allows Wiebe at least subjectively (and beyond the possible reproach of his inappropriately appropriating the voice of the "other") to rediscover a voice by inventing it — a voice that is a stranger's as much as it is his own. In the last instance, it is the voice of a creative agency revealing itself to him in the process of writing as it has revealed itself to the prophets and mystics of all religions of the past and present.

It comes as no surprise, then, that Robert Kroetsch, the postmodern skeptic, and Rudy Wiebe, the confessing Mennonite, talk to each other at cross-purposes in their amiable (and often-quoted) conversation. Reality, for Wiebe, is by no means mere surface or material for verbal play resulting from what Kroetsch calls a "profound distrust of meaning" (Kroetsch in Neuman 1981, 233). Although Wiebe aims at the deconstruction of established certainties as much as the conventions of narrative form, he attempts, at the same time, to rediscover — hypothetically and tentatively — lost or forgotten depth by a careful search for fact and document on the one hand, and by intuitive and sensuous empathy on the other. Thus, Arnold Toynbee's belief in the hidden meaning of history (the "undifferentiated unity of the mystical experience") — which is nevertheless based on the conscientiousness and the factual knowledge of the historian — finds an echo in Wiebe's own narrative strategy. Aritha van Herk, writing in 1982, called it a kind of fictional cartography ("mapping") by which it is possible to cope with, and to communicate about, a reality whose "truth" is absent and yet latently present. Wiebe illustrates his method by referring to Michelangelo's "wonderful" (if apocryphal) statement "that he studied the rock for the shape that was inside it and then used his chisels not to create that shape out of the rock but rather to release the shape from all encumbering rock around it — that has always seemed to me profoundly true to the storymaker's art also" (Wiebe in Keith, 133).

To give shape and reality to the hidden, buried, or forgotten inner "form" of the material world, is, however — as in Aristotle's classic definition of mimesis — not only the affair of the artist but also that of a potential audience willing to actively join him in this creative process. That Aritha van Herk rediscovered Big Bear's final speech, invented by Wiebe but now presented as an "authentic" historical document in a regional museum only a few years after the publication of the novel, seems to point both towards a communal embeddedness of the literary discourse and to the social function of the writer as a shaper of collective memory and a communal sense of belonging (van Herk 1982, 83). In any case, Wiebe's belief in such embeddedness forms the basis of his historical narration as well as of his aesthetic convictions: "The stories we tell of our past are by no means merely words: they are meaning and life to us as *people*, as a *particular* people; the stories are there, and if we do not know of them we are simply, like animals, memory ignorant, and the less are we people" (Wiebe in Keith, 134). In a time of crisis, when "Canada's larger society now appears on the verge of breaking apart" (Wiebe in Keith, 211), it is the communal function of the "story" (whose making is the author's "problem") to sustain the nation, to create coherence. If the larger public (the "people") recognized its own life in that of its marginalized groups and accepted the story of Almighty Voice as part of its own history, Canada might indeed prove itself to be "a particular people" and a country in which the still-present agency of the Almighty Voice could find expression in the multiplicity of its languages and cultures — beyond the gaps of the untranslatable and despite its historically documented failures of communication.

Works Cited

Keith, W. J., ed. *A Voice in the Land: Essays by and about Rudy Wiebe.* Edmonton: NeWest, 1981.

Kertzer, J. M. "Rudy Wiebe: Biocritical Essays." The University of Calgary Library Special Collections (1986), http://www.ucalgary.ca/lib-old/SpecColl/wiebebioc.htm: 4, 12 December 2005.

Mandel, Eli, and Rudy Wiebe. "Where the Voice Comes from." In Keith 1981, 150–55.

Neuman, Shirley. "Unearthing Language: An Interview with Rudy Wiebe and Robert Kroetsch." In Keith 1981, 226–47.

van Herk, Aritha. "Mapping as Metaphor." *Zeitschrift der Gesellschaft für Kanada-Studien* 2 (1982): 75–86.

Wiebe, Rudy. *The Angels of the Tar Sands and Other Stories.* New Canadian Library. Toronto: McClelland & Stewart, 1982.

———. "On the Trail of Big Bear." In Keith 1981, 132–41.

———. *River of Stone: Fictions and Memories.* Toronto: Vintage Canada, 1995.

———. "Where Is the Voice Coming from?" In Wiebe, *Where Is the Voice*, 78–87.

———. *Where Is the Voice Coming from? Stories by Rudy Wiebe.* Toronto: McClelland & Stewart, 1974.

19: The Canadian Writer as Expatriate: Norman Levine, "We All Begin in a Little Magazine" (1972)

Gordon Bölling (University of Cologne)

AT THE CLOSE OF HIS autobiographical essay "The Girl in the Drugstore" (1969), Norman Levine defines his dilemma as a Jewish Canadian writer as follows: "I had to recognize that one of the conditions of my being a writer is of living in exile. I felt it in Canada, as the son of orthodox Jewish parents in Ottawa; then as the poor boy among the rich at McGill. And now I feel it as a Canadian living in England" (Levine 1993b, 140). In June 1949, the need to distance himself from his Jewish as well as his Canadian heritage caused Levine to leave his native Canada and to settle permanently in Europe. Over the course of the next three decades, this self-imposed exile in England allowed Levine to thoroughly examine the origins of his alienation in both fictional and autobiographical writings. Although long exiled from Canada, Levine has never severed the strong ties to his homeland and is recognized today as a Canadian writer of international standing, particularly for his short fiction. In fact, Levine's well-crafted stories have been favorably compared to the works of such masters of the short-story genre as Anton Chekhov and Ernest Hemingway.

In his writings, produced over a period of more than half a century, Levine frequently draws on personal experiences, which he then incorporates into his fictional worlds. As he writes in his introduction to the short-story collection *Champagne Barn* (1984), "the stories form a kind of autobiography. But . . . it is autobiography written as fiction" (Levine 1984b, xv). Born in October 1923, Norman Albert Levine grew up in Ottawa's Lower Town as the son of orthodox Jewish immigrants from Poland. Because his first language was Yiddish, he did not speak a word of English when he began at public school at the age of five. Levine later attended the High School of Commerce but soon left to become an office boy at the Department of National Defense. During the Second World War, he served as a pilot officer with a Lancaster squadron of the RCAF based at Leeming in Yorkshire. Returning to Canada after the war, Levine studied English language and literature at McGill University and graduated with an M.A. in 1949. Although he received a well-paid fellowship for a Ph.D. at King's College, London, Levine showed little interest in pursuing an academic career and his dissertation, tentatively entitled "The Decay of Absolute Values in Modern Society," was never finished. By this time, Levine had already decided to become a writer and to leave Canada for Europe: "All I wanted to do was write. And I knew that this would be easier, at the beginning, away from home. Writing, in the immediate circle of relatives and friends, was resented; even though they paid lip service to it" (Levine 1960, 53). England, mainly St. Ives, Cornwall, became Levine's home for more than three decades from 1949 onward. In 1965/66, he returned to Canada to spend a year as the first writer-in-residence at the University of New Brunswick in Fredericton. In the early 1980s, Levine moved to Toronto, but in later years he lived in Europe again, in France and in the north of England. Levine died in June 2005.

Although he is primarily known as a writer of short fiction and as the author of the controversial travelogue *Canada Made Me* (1958), Levine began his literary career as a poet. At the age of twenty-four he published his first volume of poetry, *Myssium* (1948), followed by two more verse collections in 1950 and 1976 respectively. In 1990, *The Beat and the Still* was published. This richly illustrated book is a collaborative effort between Levine and the Canadian painter Ron Bolt, in which the latter's work on St. Ives is framed by excerpts from Levine's verse and prose. In addition, Levine is the author of two autobiographically inspired novels, *The Angled Road* (1952) and *From a Seaside Town* (1970). Chapters of his second novel were later republished as short stories in Levine's *Selected Stories* (1975).

His early poetry as well as his first novel mark important stages in Levine's development as an artist. However, he did not achieve artistic maturity until the late 1950s with the writing of his travelogue *Canada Made Me*, which records his extensive travels through Canada in 1956. The expatriate Levine combines the critical reassessment of his native Canada with a more personal objective: "I felt the need to make a reconciliation. I didn't want to run away from the country as I had originally when I sailed in that freighter on that hot June day in 1949 from Montreal" (Levine 1993a, 11, Author's Note). A highly controversial portrayal of the underside of Canadian society, Levine's travelogue was first published in England in 1958, with the first Canadian edition not appearing until 1979. Today, *Canada Made Me* is rightfully considered a classic of Canadian autobiographical writing (see Nadel 1984).

Levine is known mainly, however, as a prolific writer of short fiction. A number of his stories were first published in renowned periodicals such as *Harper's Bazaar, Saturday Night*, and *Vogue*. Others were broadcast by the CBC and the BBC. Levine's stories also found a wide European readership and were translated into German, French, and Dutch. In Germany, the recipient of the 1972 Nobel Prize for Literature, Heinrich Böll, and his wife, Annemarie Böll, were Levine's translators. Levine also edited an anthology of short fiction, *Canadian Winter's Tales* (1968). It is remarkable that this volume features an exceptionally high number of Canadian expatriates. At the time of publication, just three of the nine contributors lived in Canada. The others, including Brian Moore, Mavis Gallant, Margaret Laurence, Mordecai Richler, and Levine himself, lived either in the United States or in Europe.

One Way Ticket, Levine's first book of short fiction, was published in 1961. In the early 1970s, this debut collection was followed by *I Don't Want to Know Anyone Too Well* (1971) and *Selected Stories* (1975). The latter comprises eight previously published works and one new short story, "In Lower Town." As one of his best stories, "In Lower Town" was also included in Levine's next volume, *Thin Ice* (1979). In 1984, Levine published two collections of short fiction, *Why Do You Live So Far Away?* and *Champagne Barn*. However, of the seven stories collected in *Why Do You Live So Far Away?*, only two had not appeared in book form before. Published in the Penguin Short Fiction series, *Champagne Barn* features a selection of twenty-three stories from Levine's earlier books. The collection *Something Happened Here* was published in 1991.

All of Levine's short fiction is characterized by a sparse style with a deceptively simple surface. Michelle Gadpaille points out that the "sophisticated leanness of his work suggests a poet's respect for the depths of language" (Gadpaille 1988, 101). Levine's writing might best be considered in the context of a broader modernist tradition. In an interview, he cites Anton Chekhov, Ernest Hemingway, George Orwell, and Graham Greene as important influences on his style (Levine 1970, 66). Elegantly written in short and, at times, elliptical sentences, Levine's stories capture the intricacies of human relationships precisely. In his realistic and minimalist prose, he closely examines the psychological conditions of his first-person narrators. His distinctive narrative voice is often detached and allows him to convey the subjective perceptions of an outsider. As John Metcalf notes, "Levine refuses to explain or interpret his scenes for us; requiring us, in a sense, to *compose* the story for ourselves. It is that act of composition that turns these stories into such powerful emotional experiences" (Metcalf 2000, 9). In many cases, the acute observation of his surroundings permits Levine to create a strong sense of place and region. Among the places his writing keeps returning to are Ottawa's Lower Town, Montreal, Quebec City, and, in Europe, London and Cornwall. Over the decades Levine's writing has remained remarkably consistent in theme. Much of his short fiction deals with the complex figure of the writer. His protagonists are often artists who are trying to come to terms with either the past or the present. In "In Lower Town," the first-person narrator, a successful writer, returns to the places of his youth in Ottawa. His need to remember stands in direct opposition to the advice of his elderly mother: " 'That's the old life — it's finished' " (*The Ability to Forget*, 174). Reminded of the humble beginnings of his literary career, the narrator of "Class of 1949" asks his wife: " 'And how can you be a writer if you reject your past?' " (*By a Frozen River*, 125). However, not all of Levine's protagonists are well-established writers engaged in an artistic struggle with their pasts. The central figures in such stories as "I'll Bring You Back Something Nice," "Ringa Ringa Rosie," and "Feast Days and Others" are unsuccessful writers who are unable to support their families. For them the daily struggle for survival has taken precedence over the pursuit of their artistic goals.

Another central theme in Levine's short stories is the Canadian writer as expatriate. The protagonist is often a solitary figure who has rejected Canada in order to fulfill his literary ambitions in Europe. In "A Canadian Upbringing," the hero is fascinated by the expatriate writer Alexander Marsden and his novel *A Canadian Upbringing*. As a young and aspiring writer, Levine's Jewish protagonist decides to follow Marsden's example:

> Although I was brought up in Ottawa — and Ottawa has, compared to Montreal, a small Jewish community — the kind of upbringing I had wasn't much different from the one Marsden describes in Montreal. He pinned down that warm, lively, ghetto atmosphere; the strong family and religious ties — as well as its prejudices and limitations. And when, at the end of the book [*A Canadian Upbringing*], Marsden decides to leave Canada for England, not because he wants to deny his background but because he feels the need to accept a wider view of life, I knew that was the way I would go as well. (*By a Frozen River*, 48)

However, when he finally meets Marsden in Cornwall, the narrator is utterly disappointed. Having lost all interest in writing, Marsden makes a living manufacturing toy roundabouts for children. He advises the by now well-established writer to return to Canada: " 'Go home while you are still young' " (51). The figure of the exiled Canadian writer and his experiences of dislocation and detachment are also at the center of such stories as "I Like Chekhov," "Class of 1949," "A Visit," and "Because of the War." The latter story explores the exile's return to his native Canada. Here, Levine links the homecoming of the expatriate writer to the diverse experiences of immigration of several minor characters.

In the history of the Canadian short story, Levine's writing is of particular importance also because it transcends narrow definitions of Canadian literature. Levine's chosen fictional territory very often lies outside of Canada and his cultural references are not restricted to Canadian culture. Like John Glassco, the early Mordecai Richler, and, most importantly, Mavis Gallant, Levine belongs to a larger tradition of Canadian expatriate writers (see Dahlie 1986). In their works, these expatriates not only redefine the central preoccupations of Canadian literature but offer new and original perspectives on Canada. In addition, Levine's writing is a substantial contribution to Canadian Jewish literature. Although he does not always foreground his Jewishness, Levine has repeatedly explored aspects of Jewish culture (see Greenstein 1989, 68–83). In a greater number of his stories, the hero is a Jewish writer who confronts and problematizes the meanings of his Jewish identity. The story "Continuity" probably represents Levine's most sophisticated treatment of this theme. In this short story, an expatriate writer's sense of dislocation and insecurity is contrasted with the continuity of a long Jewish tradition. In 1990, Miriam Waddington selected Levine's "By a Frozen River" for inclusion in her anthology *Canadian Jewish Short Stories.*

"We All Begin in a Little Magazine," published in the collection *Thin Ice* in 1979, was written in the fall of 1971. At this point, Levine had just published his collection *I Don't Want to Know Anyone Too Well*, and the previous year had finally seen the publication of his second novel, *From a Seaside Town*, which he had been writing and revising for four years. In his informative afterword to "We All Begin in a Little Magazine," Levine comments on the curious circumstances that led to the writing of this story (Levine 1982, 135–36). In late 1971, his poor financial situation prompted him to submit various stories to Robert Weaver at the CBC, who, to Levine's dismay, kept returning them. However, Weaver then commissioned him to write a new story for the radio series *Anthology*. According to Levine, this was the first time the CBC had ever commissioned anyone to write a story. Although Weaver regarded "We All Begin in a Little Magazine" as a "sad" story, he accepted Levine's submission and promptly arranged for a new commission. Weaver then aired Levine's short story as part of his CBC program *Anthology* on 13 November 1971. The following year, the story was first printed in the magazine *Encounter* (October 1972: 13–17).

In a number of ways, "We All Begin in a Little Magazine" is representative of Levine's oeuvre. The story's protagonist is an unnamed Canadian writer who has lived abroad for two decades. Although the story is set in England, this time the setting is not the idyllic St. Ives in Cornwall but rather central London. The expatriate writer, his wife, and their children come to London for their annual holiday. Their home is in a small, unnamed seaside town, which in summer is overrun by tourists, and the family has therefore made a habit of spending the vacation in a rented house in London. As the narrator outlines in the story's brief exposition, over the years they have rented a number of houses from very different people. This particular summer the wife responds to an advertisement in *The Times*, in which a doctor's house is offered for a reasonable rent. The story proper begins with the family's arrival at London's Paddington Station. Following a circular structure, "We All Begin in a Little Magazine" ends with the family's departure from London after a period of three weeks. As Simone Vauthier convincingly argues, Levine's symmetrical structure achieves an effect of closure (Vauthier 1991, 91). However, this effect is undermined by a chain of unexpected events during the family's vacation, which in turn trigger off a series of memories for Levine's Canadian protagonist. It is the resulting confrontation of the past with the present that dominates the story (see Levine 1982, 136).

While they were both living in England, Mordecai Richler regularly allowed Levine the use of his house on Kingston Hill in Surrey while he and his family went away on holidays. Thus it may be tempting to read "We All Begin in a Little Magazine" as autobiographical and to regard the anonymous narrator as a persona for the thinly disguised Levine. Such a straightforward reading would, however, belittle the merits of Levine's story. Told by a homodiegetic narrator, "We All Begin in a Little Magazine" works on various levels of time. In the narrative present, the Canadian expatriate not only recounts the events that took place in the more recent past, that is, events that occurred during the family's most recent summer vacation in London; he also remembers the time twenty years before, when he first came over to postwar England as a young and aspiring writer (see Vauthier, 91–94). Through the juxtaposition of the recent with the more distant past, "We All Begin in a Little Magazine" traces the protagonist's development from an ambitious and idealistic writer to a celebrated professional author of international standing.

For the central character the unexpected confrontation with his past begins very shortly after his arrival in London. From the moment the family steps into the rented house, the phone starts to ring. To his surprise, the protagonist finds himself faced with numerous callers asking for the house's owner and enquiring about manuscripts they have submitted to the doctor. Only gradually does the narrator realize that the absent Doctor Jones edits a literary periodical entitled *ABC.* Taking the doctor's mail up to the office at the top of the house, the Canadian writer is suddenly reminded of the humble beginnings of his own literary career in postwar England:

> As I put the envelopes and parcels on the chair in the office and saw the copies of *Horizon* and *New Writing*, the runs of *Encounter, London Magazine*, and a fine collection of contemporary books on the shelves right around the room — it brought back a time twenty years ago when I first came over. ("We All Begin in a Little Magazine," 85)

With the following paragraph, the story moves on to a longer section in which the first-person narrator gives an account of his early days in London. This second part of the story takes up just under one third of the text. The final third then returns to the more recent past and resumes the narrative from where the first part left off. This tripartite structure permits Levine to frame the narrator's memories of his more distant past with two sequences set in the more recent past of present-day London. He thereby effectively heightens the contrast between the various stages in the protagonist's literary career.

Although the beginnings of this career in postwar England are overshadowed by the hardships of poverty, the narrator remembers these years as one of the happiest periods in his life. As an expatriate, he belongs to a larger group of enthusiastic young people who have come to London to pursue their artistic careers. Spending a lot of time in pubs and restaurants, he frequently meets other aspiring writers to discuss aesthetic theories and poetic practices. In the early stages of their careers, the lives of these young writers revolve exclusively around their art. Only little magazines offer them the opportunity to present their works to the reading public: "We used to send our stories, optimistically, to the *name* magazines. But that was like taking a ticket in a lottery. It was the little magazines who published us, who gave encouragement and kept us going" (86). Remembering his early years in London, the unnamed protagonist recalls Miss Waters in particular, who edits a little magazine founded by her great-grandfather. In his fairly detailed account of a typical visit to Miss Waters, the narrator emphasizes the respect he meets with: "I was treated as a writer by this woman when I had very little published. And that did more than anything to keep up morale" (86). In addition to strengthening his self-esteem, Miss Waters offers financial help to the young writer. She gives him books she does not want to have reviewed and suggests that he sell these to a bookseller in the Strand. Miss Waters also asks him to write reviews for which she always pays in advance. However, at the end of the second part of the story, Levine's narrator expresses his belief that little-magazine publishing has now all but disappeared. The flashback ends with the writer's lament about the past:

> They [the editors of various literary magazines] are all gone — like their magazines.
>
> And something has gone with them.
>
> Those carefree days when you wrote when you felt like it. And slept in when you wanted to. And would be sure of seeing others like yourself at noon in certain places. (87)

Thus for the unnamed protagonist the days of little-magazine publishing are inextricably linked to a rather bohemian existence. This unsteady and unrestricted way of life stands in strong contrast to the daily routine of the established writer that is at the center of the concluding third of the short story. Describing the writer's present attitudes towards his life as well as his art in great detail, Levine reveals a dramatic change in the artist's construction of personal identity.

Despite his enviable status as a widely celebrated writer, the protagonist experiences a sense of loss. Since the beginnings of his career, he has gradually abandoned his bohemian lifestyle, and now works regular hours. Often commissioned by well-paying periodicals to submit a short story or an article, the narrator regards writing solely as a profession: "I feel reasonably certain now that what I have written will be published. Writing has become my living" (88). While in London, he is interviewed for Canadian television, meets his American publisher for an expensive dinner, and sees his agent over a meal. However, the conversations no longer focus on the aesthetics of writing. For Levine's narrator and for those associated with him, writing has become a business in which a lot of money is to be made. Even the private lives of other authors have become more important than art itself:

> He [my agent] took me out for a meal. And we talked about the size of advances, the sort of money paperback publishers were paying these days, the way non-fiction was selling better than fiction. I met other writers in expensive clubs and restaurants. We gossiped about what middle-aged writer was leaving his middle-aged wife to live with a young girl. And what publisher was leaving his firm to form his own house. I was told what magazines were starting — who paid the best. (90)

Although his writing permits him to lead a comfortable life, the Canadian expatriate is no longer enthusiastic about his art. Very rarely is he satisfied with his work. In contrast to those vividly remembered postwar years, his writing and his life in the present seem to be disconnected: "Of course there are still the occasional days when things are going right and the excitement comes back from the work. Not like in those early days when writing and the life we were leading seemed so much to belong together" (88). For Levine's protagonist the current separation of art and life reduces writing from a calling to a mere means of living.

The narrator's complacency is challenged, however, when in the third part of the story a number of aspiring writers not only try to reach Doctor Jones on the phone but also appear frequently on the doorstep of his London house: "There was, it seemed, a whole world that depended on the little magazine" (90). In the face of these repeated intrusions on his summer vacation, the Canadian expatriate begins to feel uncomfortable and attempts to evade the visitors: "I tried to be out of the house as much as possible" (90). The protagonist's efforts to circumvent a direct confrontation with these reminiscences of his personal past are, however, largely unsuccessful. As becomes clear from his encounters with various aspiring writers, the protagonist is increasingly troubled: "I didn't mind the young. But it was the men and women who were around my age or older who made me uncomfortable. I didn't like the feeling of superiority I had when I was with them. Or was it guilt? I didn't know" (90). Unsure about how to react and uncertain about his feelings, the narrator, in contrast to his wife and children, is more than happy when the three-week stay in London comes to an end. Leaving Doctor Jones's house finally gives him the opportunity to escape the disturbing confrontation with his past:

> I had passed through my *ABC* days. And I wanted to get away. Was it because it was a reminder of one's youth? Or of a time which promised more than it turned out to be? I told myself that there was an unreality about it all — that our lives then had no economic base — that it was a time of limbo. But despite knowing these things, I carry it with me. It represents a sort of innocence that has gone. (91)

The protagonist's attempt to relegate his former outlook on art as well as his bohemian lifestyle to the realm of illusions is a strategy for avoiding a thorough and potentially painful questioning of his present existence as a well-established professional writer. The insurmountable gap between past and present and the gradual disillusionment with his aspirations as an artist are also evident in the final telephone conversation between the protagonist and an anonymous "girl." On the morning the writer's family is to leave London, a young girl phones and enquires about a short story she has submitted for publication in Doctor Jones's periodical. Only halfway through the conversation does she realize that her interlocutor has nothing to do with *ABC*. In her surprise she asks the Canadian writer a very straightforward question: " 'Oh,' she said. 'You're not one of us?' " (91). Replying in the negative, Levine's protagonist firmly raises a barrier between himself as an established writer and those younger writers who rely on little magazines for publication. Furthermore, by answering with a decisive " 'no' " (91), the narrator is quick to distance himself from his past and seemingly shrinks from a critical reassessment of his current attitudes towards his art. However, the short story's title, "We All Begin in a Little Magazine," subverts such clear-cut readings and instead points to an element of ambiguity. In fact, Levine's use of the first-person plural pronoun emphasizes the shared experience of all writers of fiction and thereby links the protagonist's outstanding career to the efforts of a great number of aspiring writers. The narrator, then, is one of the very few who succeed in building a long career out of such humble but necessary beginnings as publication in a little magazine.

In recent years there has been a renewed interest in Levine's writing. Both his autobiographical travelogue *Canada Made Me* and his second novel, *From a Seaside Town*, were reissued by John Metcalf and John Newlove for the series Sherbrooke Street: A Collection of Reprints of Modern Canadian Classics. Twenty-seven of Levine's short stories were recently collected in *By a Frozen River: The Short Stories of Norman Levine* (2000). This book comes with a foreword by Metcalf and offers a very good overview of Levine's accomplishments as a writer of short fiction. In 2003, this collection was supplemented by the publication of *The Ability to Forget: Short Stories*. In addition to a selection of fourteen previously published stories, Levine's latest collection includes the new story "The Ability to Forget." Set in a small town in northeast England, the title story explores acts of remembering and forgetting. In 2002, Norman Levine's great achievements as a Canadian writer — despite his somewhat problematic relationship with Canada — were recognized when the Writers' Trust of Canada presented him with the newly established Matt Cohen Award, following Mavis Gallant to become the second author to receive this prestigious prize in honor of a lifetime of distinguished work.

Despite the rediscovery of Levine's writing by a more general reading public, Canadian literary criticism has so far paid little attention to Levine's oeuvre. With the exception of Lawrence Mathews' thin book (1986), only a handful of articles on Levine's work have been published. An in-depth study of the writings of this powerful storyteller has yet to be written. Norman Levine's manuscripts, his correspondence, and other papers are collected in the York University Archives and Special Collections and are available for use by researchers.

Works Cited

Dahlie, Hallvard. *Varieties of Exile: The Canadian Experience.* Vancouver: University of British Columbia Press, 1986.

Gadpaille, Michelle. *The Canadian Short Story.* Toronto: Oxford University Press, 1988.

Greenstein, Michael. *Third Solitudes: Tradition and Discontinuity in Jewish-Canadian Literature.* Montreal/Kingston: McGill-Queen's University Press, 1989.

Levine, Norman. *The Ability to Forget: Short Stories.* Toronto: Key Porter Books, 2003.

———. "Afterword." In *Making It New: Contemporary Canadian Stories*, ed. John Metcalf. Toronto: Methuen, 1982. 134–36.

———. *By a Frozen River: The Short Stories of Norman Levine.* Toronto: Key Porter Books, 2000.

———. *Canada Made Me.* 1958. Erin, ON: The Porcupine's Quill Press, 1993 (1993a).

———, ed. *Canadian Winter's Tales.* Toronto: Macmillan of Canada, 1968.

———. *Champagne Barn*, ed. Wayne Grady. Harmondsworth: Penguin, 1984 (1984a).

———. "The Girl in the Drugstore." 1969. In *How Stories Mean*, ed. John Metcalf and J. R. (Tim) Struthers. Erin, ON: The Porcupine's Quill Press, 1993 (1993b). 136–40.

———. *I Don't Want to Know Anyone Too Well.* London: Macmillan, 1971.

———. Interview with John D. Cox. *Canadian Literature* 45 (Summer 1970): 61–67.

Levine, Norman. "Introduction." In Levine, *Champagne Barn*, 1984 (1984b). xiii–xv.

———. *One Way Ticket*. London: Secker and Warburg, 1961.

———. *Selected Stories*, ed. Michael Macklem. Ottawa: Oberon, 1975.

———. *Something Happened Here*. Toronto: Penguin, 1991.

———. *Thin Ice*. Ottawa: Deneau and Greenberg, 1979.

———. "We All Begin in a Little Magazine." In Levine, *By a Frozen River*, 183–91.

———. *Why Do You Live So Far Away?* Ottawa: Deneau, 1984.

———. "Why I Am an Expatriate." *Canadian Literature* 5 (Summer 1960): 49–54.

Mathews, Lawrence. *Norman Levine and His Works*. Toronto: ECW Press, 1986.

Metcalf, John. "Foreword." In Levine, *By A Frozen River: The Short Stories of Norman Levine*. Toronto: Key Porter Books, 2000. 9–11.

Nadel, Ira Bruce. "*Canada Made Me* and Canadian Autobiography." *Canadian Literature* 101 (Summer 1984): 69–81.

Vauthier, Simone. "Portrait of the Artist as a (No Longer) Young Man: Norman Levine's 'We All Begin in a Little Magazine.'" In *New Directions From Old*. Canadian Storytellers 7, ed. J. R. (Tim) Struthers. Guelph: Red Kite Press, 1991. 87–106.

Waddington, Miriam, ed. *Canadian Jewish Short Stories*. Toronto: Oxford University Press, 1990.

20: Canadian Artist Stories: John Metcalf, "The Strange Aberration of Mr. Ken Smythe" (1973)

Reingard M. Nischik (University of Constance)

IN AN INTERVIEW WITH Geoff Hancock in 1981, John Metcalf stated:

> We now have *sophisticated* writers who make considerable demands on readers.
>
> Compare this with what we had before. When I arrived in Canada in 1962, the Canadian story was more tale or yarn. . . . Heavy on plot and light on brains, style, and elegance. . . . Callaghan may have *known* Hemingway but I can't see any evidence that he learned from him. It was Hugh Hood with *Flying a Red Kite* who signalled that we were joining the rest of the 20th century. (Metcalf 1982a, 13)

Asked by Hancock whether anything had changed concerning the short story in Canada in the previous decade, Metcalf replied: "It's changed out of recognition" (Metcalf 1982a, 12).

This brief extract from an interview may serve to indicate, if indirectly, that John Metcalf has been the most important supporter and mentor of short fiction in Canada (even surpassing Robert Weaver from CBC Radio in this respect).[1] For almost five decades now Metcalf has worked devotedly to this purpose, in several ways and with unflinching determination: as a cultural critic, literary critic, anthologizer, editor of short fiction, and also as a short-fiction writer himself.

As suggested in the quotation above, Metcalf started out as an immigrant to Canada in 1962. He was born in Carlisle, England, in 1938 to a schoolteacher and a Methodist minister (for biographical information see Rollins 1985). Metcalf was a voracious reader at school and university, which he completed with a B.A. in 1960 and a Certificate in Education in 1961 (Rollins, 155). After several teaching jobs in England, he went to Canada to teach English and Canadian history at a high school in

[1] See my introductory chapter to this volume.

Montreal. He soon became aware of the relative dearth of Canadian literature and Canadian literary studies at the time and, after settling in Canada in 1966 for good (and becoming a Canadian citizen in 1970), he developed into one of the most outspoken and severe critics of Canadian culture, cultural policy, and of Canadian literature, with a special dedication to Canadian short fiction (see Nischik 1987).

Metcalf's main goal at the time was to make Canadians conscious of and interested in their own literature, that is, to make Canadians *read* Canadian literature (he claimed in 1986 that "one out of every five Canadians is functionally illiterate," see Metcalf 1986b, 4). This strong focus on the author/work-reader relationship was complemented by his endeavors to support particular writers (and praise very few critics) and harshly criticize others in order to steer the emergent Canadian literature away from a parochial interest in the (preferably "Canadian") themes of writing (see his critical stance towards the "thematic criticism" which ruled "CanLitCrit" in the 1960s and 1970s) and towards an emphasis on style and the technique of writing (see statements such as "I regard writing not as investigation of character but as an exercise in the use of language," Metcalf 1982a, 6; in the same interview he also uses the expression "CanLitCrit," 8). His preoccupation with the craft rather than the themes of fiction contributed considerably to bringing Canadian literature up to world literary standards. In his many essays, books of cultural and literary criticism, and in his interviews, Metcalf formulated his views drastically, clearly taking sides and not shrinking from exaggerations or even harsh personal attacks on writers, critics, or journalists (see, for example, Metcalf 1982a; 1986b; 1994). He thus developed into a controversial figure, an *enfant terrible* of Canadian literary and cultural criticism. Particularly in retrospect, however, it is obvious that although the tone of his criticism often seemed inappropriately offensive, Metcalf's self-proclaimed "missionary" attempts (Metcalf 1982a, 10) contributed significantly to the "Canadian Renaissance" in the 1960s[2] and especially to the rapid increase in the quality of Canadian short fiction and (to a lesser extent) short-fiction criticism.

The central tenet of Metcalf's cultural and literary criticism is that the quality of writing should be the only valid criterion for judging a work of literature — not its themes, motifs, or settings, nor whether the writing appeals to the masses ("You cannot write well for the mass because the mass can't read," Metcalf 1982a, 1). His is clearly and unashamedly an elitist, demanding view of literature: "I want to write elitist art. It's the austere that appeals to me more than anything else in art" (Metcalf in

[2] See my introductory chapter to this volume.

Cameron 1975, 411). Metcalf thus firmly argued against the cultural policy of the Canada Council at the time, which supported Canadian literature simply because it was Canadian and preferred Canadian themes and settings. Metcalf, with his international outlook, countered: "The pervasive identification of art with nationalism is one of our central problems. It stands in the way of artistic maturity" (Metcalf 1986b, 4).

A teacher of English at Canadian high schools, Metcalf soon turned to anthologizing Canadian short fiction for teaching purposes and thereby developed into the most active and influential supporter, "popularizer," and talent scout of Canadian short fiction (see his involvement in practically all the series of Canadian short fiction over the decades, such as — partly under another name — *Best Canadian Stories* 1971–82 or *New Canadian Stories* 1972–76; see Nischik 1987). One of his earliest short-fiction anthologies, *Sixteen by Twelve* (1970), was the first anthology of Canadian texts for teaching purposes in Canada; his later anthology *Making It New: Contemporary Canadian Stories* (1982b) was one of the first Canadian short-story anthologies explicitly addressing an international market. To date, Metcalf has some forty short-fiction anthologies to his credit (edited either for a general readership or for schools and universities), all of which have been instrumental in forging a Canadian short-fiction canon.

In 1970 Metcalf, still living in Montreal (he later moved to Ottawa), initiated the Montreal Story Teller Fiction Performance Group, together with Hugh Hood, Clark Blaise, Ray Smith, and Ray Fraser. All group members apart from Fraser were or developed into important short-fiction writers. The intention of this group, which officially disbanded in 1976, was again a "missionary" one: if poetry could be read "live" to audiences, so could short fiction. The group toured mainly in the Montreal area, reading out their short stories to audiences at schools, universities, community colleges, and bookshops, educating young people in particular towards literature, especially the short story (see Struthers 1985).

The Montreal Story Tellers were united by their shared reader-oriented outlook, but they were not a homogeneous group of writers, with Ray Smith and Ray Fraser in particular belonging to the "postmoderns," against whose writing style Metcalf repeatedly argued. This in itself shows that Metcalf has not been such a partial critic as he may sometimes seem at first sight owing to his often drastic outspokenness. His literary activities and his own writing style, however, clearly underline his preference for the modernist-realist tradition of writing over the antimimetic, postmodernist style (which, as he repeatedly argued, sometimes covers up bad writing). In his critical articles and especially his anthologies he has thus particularly (but not exclusively) supported those writers who conform to this tradition — writers such as Clark Blaise, Hugh Hood, Alice Munro, and Mavis Gallant.

Not the least of Metcalf's achievements concerning the Canadian short story is that he is an excellent writer of short fiction himself. Although both his anthologies and his books of nonfiction outnumber his fiction volumes, he has nevertheless created a noteworthy fiction oeuvre over the years: three novels between 1972 and 1988, and seven collections of short fiction (short stories and novellas) between 1970 and 2004. Even though the three volumes *Selected Stories* (1982c), *Shooting the Stars* (1993), and *Standing Stones: The Best Stories of John Metcalf* (2004) reprint stories from his earlier collections or anthologies, Metcalf must be regarded as a fairly productive short-fiction writer, who has produced not only several novellas[3] — a rather neglected genre in Canada — but also critically well-received short stories such as "The Teeth of My Father," "Gentle as Flowers Make the Stones," "The Years in Exile," "Keys and Watercress," and "The Strange Aberration of Mr. Ken Smythe" (all in the New Canadian Library edition of his *Selected Stories*). Metcalf's first story, "Early Morning Rabbits" (collected in *The Lady Who Sold Furniture*, 1970), won him first prize in a CBC short-story competition in 1963 and reinforced his decision to become a writer.

Although Metcalf once stated that he does not regard himself as a traditional writer,[4] he writes in the modernist-realist tradition (a pronounced example of a modernist writing style is his frequently anthologized artist story "Gentle as Flowers Make the Stones"[5]). Metcalf explains that he likes writing "factually," carefully focusing on the object, the particular as such, irrespective of its potential symbolic values (compare American writer William Carlos Williams's modernist-imagist credo "No idea but in things"); yet it is obvious that, for instance, the keys in Metcalf's artist story "Keys and Watercress" have a resonating symbolic significance. Metcalf has stated repeatedly that he is a slow writer whose first responsibility — as with many writers of short fiction — is to style, not theme, that is, to the discourse level. He heavily revises his writing ("I write each page 20 times over," Metcalf 1982a, 22) to come up to his own critical standards, as postulated again and again in connection with other writers. Because of his often self-reflexive, "elitist" themes (about one third of his collected stories are explicitly about artists, with many others related to questions of

[3] See "The Lady Who Sold Furniture," "Girl in Gingham," "Private Parts: A Memoir Call" (in *Shooting the Stars*); "Polly Ongle" and "Travelling Northward" (in *Adult Entertainment*).

[4] "Most critics seem to have me pegged as a very traditional writer. I'm not sure why. . . . I don't follow any school or manner. . . . I just *discover* the right shape" (Metcalf 1982a, 22).

[5] In *The Teeth of My Father* (1975) and *Selected Stories*; for an interpretation of this story and a survey of Metcalf's artist stories see Nischik 1988.

art or writing), unusual set-ups, and demanding writing style, he has remained largely a "writer's writer," unknown to a wider audience. Thus, the American magazine *Harper's Bazaar* once referred to John Metcalf as "one of Canada's best-kept literary secrets."[6] Metcalf's concern with art, the artist, and the craft of writing in his fiction is not surprising in view of his intensive and long-term efforts to raise the standard of Canadian writing. Although he has also dealt with such topics in his satirical novels (*General Ludd*, 1980 or *Going Down Slow*, 1972), Metcalf has claimed that his particular style of writing (a focus on episodes and objects, on suggestive rather than explicatory writing, with intensive dedication to structure and to verbal style) is more suited to the genre of the short story than to the novel (which he admits to having tried his hand at, as with Alice Munro, mainly because his publisher wanted him to, that is, for financial reasons). His short fiction — more than fifty published pieces altogether, several of them novellas — may be classified into three groups according to the status of the protagonist: first, initiation stories, featuring boys or adolescents growing in awareness and experience; second, stories with protagonists who have reached a certain educational and professional status, such as students or teachers; third, stories whose protagonists are actively involved with art.[7]

The story selected for interpretation here belongs to the third type. "The Strange Aberration of Mr. Ken Smythe," the opening story of Metcalf's second short-story collection *The Teeth of My Father* (1975), was first published in *73: New Canadian Stories* (ed. David Helwig and Joan Harcourt). The story is situated in the Pleasure Gardens of Edinburgh and deals with a performance of popular culture in front of an international, entertainment-seeking audience — it is thus a somewhat unusual Canadian artist story (especially for the 1970s), displaced in location and motif because it is not at all concerned with Canadian "highbrow art" or writing at first sight. Nevertheless, this story ingeniously reflects Metcalf's preoccupation with the Canadian artist and the artist-audience relationship. The story's didactic potential also shows at several removes, since this easily accessible, engaging text on art in the context of entertainment may be read as a weighty allegory about the status of the artist in society and what "true" art is all about. To make his critical implications more palatable to a Canadian readership, perhaps, Metcalf chooses a decisively international setting: the third-person narrator, a traveler to Edinburgh, Scotland, visits one of the city's most frequented tourist spots, the Pleasure Gardens, to see the evening show of a local vaudeville group and the performance of a German brass band.

[6] Printed on the back cover of Metcalf, *Shooting the Stars*.

[7] Nischik 1988, 164.

The third-person narrator is introduced at the very beginning of the story: "The traveller strolled up the incline of the station approach."[8] He remains unnamed and hardly characterized, apart from the fact that he is only traveling through Edinburgh and has decided to spend the time waiting for his connecting train to London at the Pleasure Gardens. The manner in which the narrator — or, rather, focalizer — is introduced proves important for the reader's overall reception of the text. We are aware of a focalizer only during the first one and a half pages of the story, where his approach and entry to the Pleasure Gardens are reported in a simple, factual style: "He glanced at his watch and then strolled around the curve of the paling fence to the entrance. He paid his one shilling and sixpence and sat in the corner of an empty row. He finished the ice-cream. Rolling and unrolling the blue ticket, he stared down into the cave of the bandshell. The shouting startled him" (162). The last sentence is the only overt comment about the focalizer throughout the whole story. After that, the focalizer functions purely as an unintrusive, seemingly neutral "camera-eye," through which the events unfold as if speaking for themselves; the readers are left to form their own opinions and conclusions about them.

The way space is handled in the exposition subtly hints at what is in store for us. Establishing a contrast between "up" and "down," the exposition also partly suggests a decline in action, behavior, character, and values: in the very first paragraph of the story, the traveler "strolled *up* the incline of the station approach," and sees "*high above* the city, Edinburgh Castle . . . just beginning to lose detail in the evening light. . . . He stopped to look at a statue of Robert Burns" (161; italics added). In view of what is to follow, a symbolic meaning arises. The monuments, which belong to an elevated level of culture and are probably perceived by an educated character (see his looking at the statue of one of Scotland's best-known writers, "poet of brotherhood and the common man," Rollins, 185), indeed "lose detail" to black-and-white contrasts in an increasingly gloomy atmosphere after sunset when the expected entertainment begins. After this reference to the statue of Robert Burns, the story's movement turns in a downward direction,[9] both spatially and culturally. The traveler gazes "*down* in the Pleasure Gardens," comes, during his strolling through the city, to "a flight of steps leading *down* into the Gardens" (161), and stares "*down* into the cave of the bandshell"; "leaves drifted *down*" (162;

[8] "The Strange Aberration of Mr. Ken Smythe," 161; the text quoted from is that of the *Selected Stories* edition (1982c).

[9] Some of the arguments in the following analysis were first presented, though in much briefer form, in my article "Contrastive Structures in John Metcalf's Artist Stories" (Nischik 1988, 172–75 on "The Strange Aberration").

italics added). This spatial descent is paralleled by a cultural descent: having viewed Edinburgh Castle "*high above* the city" (161; italics added), approaching the Pleasure Gardens he sees "tourists mill[ing] along the gravel paths between the fragrant rose-beds photograph[ing] each other" (161), "family groups of Americans" (161) in "plastic mac[s]" (162), "a mob of soldiers . . . running across the lawn booting a football in long passes, with the boys chasing after yelling" (162). The focalizer also perceives the potentially destructive force of such mass activities: "One of the soldiers turned and punted the ball black into the sky. It *crashed* through the branches of the oak tree . . . ; leaves drifted *down* (162; italics added).[10]

We can thus trace in the short overture to the events proper a subtly transmitted outlining of a factual and symbolic descent from "high" to "low" or from highbrow to lowbrow. Just as spatial and cultural descents coincide, the earlier reference to the reaction of the focalizer ("the shouting startled him," 162), too, is a foreshadowing of how he is bound to react to the gruesome ensuing events. In this brief exposition we see Metcalf's modernist craft at work, for although he seems to merely report factually, focusing strictly on objects, human figures, and visual matters, the exposition, when read in the context of the story as a whole, is a densely structured, subtly symbolic foreshadowing of events in concrete and increasingly drastic terms.

While the exposition introduces us to the make-up of the show's audience, it also, quite factually again, announces the performers in printed capital letters on "the large notice-board": "MUNICIPAL ENTERTAINMENTS . . . THE GLASGOW VARIETY SHOW AND THE ESSEN INTERNATIONAL AMITY BOYS BRASS BAND" (162). The reader awaits a vaudeville show by a Scottish group followed by a German youth brass band performing German folk songs, a genuine event of popular culture designed to give pleasure, as the venue's name suggests, to a varied audience, but also to raise intercultural understanding and friendship ("International Amity") through the exchange of popular national art forms.

[10] This particular reading of the story corresponds with Jurij M. Lotman's conception of space in fiction as not only pertaining to topographical locales, but also to the totality of homogenous objects (phenomena, conditions, functions, figures, variables, etc.) between which there are relationships similar to those of common spatial relationships. Lotman concludes that it thus becomes possible for designations of spatial relationships to structure reality in and via narrative. Concepts such as "high–low," "right–left," "close–distant," "open–closed" serve to establish cultural models with not just spatial content, acquiring meanings such as "good–bad," "valuable–valueless," "advantageous–disadvantageous," "recommendable–not recommendable" in fiction (Lotman 1972).

The Glasgow Variety Show Company starts off the evening with typical vaudeville acts: "Vladimir produced playing cards, ping-pong balls, handkerchiefs, flags, rabbits, and doves from tubes, hats, pockets, and his nose. He ended by sawing Wanda in half" (164). The matter-of-fact-style reporting on supposedly surreal vaudeville tricks of the trade exposes the banality, if not the ridiculousness of the show. Also performing are "two great stars . . . Scotland's pride" (164) of the Scottish National Opera Company, who sing songs from various popular musicals, such as *Oklahoma* and *The Sound of Music*. Though the crowd is later said to become "restive" about "lengthy selections" (164) from these musicals, thus indicating their short attention span, the first part of the evening is all in all a success with the audience: "The entire company bowed; the audience broke into unrestrained applause; . . . the light inside the bandshell died. Whistling and stomping continued for some time in the darkness" (164).

The very positive reception given to the Scottish actors and singers, singing songs in English and performing in their home country, obviously serves not only to "warm up" the audience for the subsequent performance of the German boy band, but also to indicate that the disastrous way in which the performance by the German musicians develops is due to a large extent to intercultural ignorance, intolerance, prejudice, and, finally, downright nationalistic hostility.

Ironically, the German band is visiting Scotland for just the opposite reason, namely to foster international exchange and understanding. As the Scottish compere, the Mr. Ken Smythe of the story's title, explains to the audience, "these young German lads are the guests of Rotary International" (165), the "worldwide organization of business and professional leaders that provides humanitarian services, encourages high ethical standards in all vocations, and helps build goodwill and peace" (quoted from the homepage of Rotary International); their exchange with "a Temperance Band from Leicester, . . . touring Germany" indeed intends to "foster international goodwill" (165). That these enlightened words are spoken by Ken Smythe, of all people, proves a stark irony in light of the subsequent events, for it is the Scottish compere, a Second World War veteran with an RAF (Royal Air Force) badge pinned to his blazer, who will incite the audience first to restlessness, then to a slanted reception, and eventually to downright hostility towards the German band. It is through his interference that the "amity" event will eventually result in sexist and nationalistic obscenity, aggression, and chaos.

Smythe at first appears to give himself a sophisticated air with his "sleek hair gleam[ing] in the lights" (165) and suave language marked by a strained politeness — the very spelling of his surname ("Smythe" rather than "Smith") looks pretentious. Yet right from the beginning his cultured middle-class mannerisms strike a false note, as his first utterance on stage, which he thinks is not overheard, betrays his lower-class origins: " 'What, mate?' boomed over the sound system" (165). As the events unfold, Smythe shows his true colors more and more. Although in his announcements he repeatedly tries to pass himself off as putting a lot of idealistic effort into youth work, it soon becomes obvious — actions speaking louder than words — that he is a most unsuitable model for young people or anyone interested in respectful personal and intercultural relationships. For one thing, he is revealed to be a drinker, covertly drinking alcohol even during the performance ("As the section sat and the trombones dipped to rest position, Ken Smythe's tilted face was revealed for a second, a square bottle at his lips," 167; note that the face is tilted while drinking only when the fluid level of the bottle is rather low). Throughout the concert, Smythe gets increasingly inebriated and soon becomes a nuisance and eventually a disaster for the music performance (barging into Herr Kunst, the conductor; losing his balance, "falling sideways into the trumpet section, knocking over two music stands," 169).

His actions and speeches become increasingly unrestrained and vulgar. This is first noticed in his behavior towards "Fräulein Hohenstaufen," his German female co-host, dressed in a clichéd (Bavarian) "native costume" ("Plump and pretty in yoke blouse and dirndl skirt, rosy cheeks and hair in coiled braids, Fräulein Hohenstaufen blushed and curtsied to the cheers and piercing whistles," 166). Smythe's increasingly sexist advances towards her on stage climax when his assault turns into nationalistic antagonism: "He put his arm around her shoulders again and pulled her close. . . . 'Like dumplings,' he said, looking down" (170). The fact that he chooses a Bavarian food speciality ("dumpling") to refer to the woman's breasts, and publically so, is indicative of his combined sexist and racist mind-set.

These developments are carefully foreshadowed earlier in the story. If one sequences the titles of the German folk songs as Ken Smythe announces them, they unmask the chauvinistic behavior of the Scottish compere in leading the masses towards first sexist and eventually nationalistic aggression: "*Auf, auf zum fröhlichen Jagen . . . Happy Hunting Song*" (167). To the translation of "*Das Wandern ist des Müller's Lust,*" "*The Millers Like to Wander,*" he adds a lewd translation of his own, which plays on the ambivalent meaning of "Lust" in German: "*The Millers' Lust.*" "*Ein Jäger aus Kurpfalz,*" for which the translation on his card correctly reads "*A Palatinate Hunter,*" is first falsely rendered by him as "*A Passionate Hunter,*" again with sexual innuendo. Further German songs like "*Ich hab' mein Herz in Heidelberg verloren*" ("I Lost My Heart in Heidelberg") or "*Auf der Lüneburger Heide*" ("On the Lüneburg Heath," all 167) lead to the titles "*Wenn alle Brünnlein fliessen*" (168, "When All the Fountains Flow") and "*Ein Vogel wollte Hochzeit machen*" ("*A Bird's Wedding,*" 168), which are clearly given a sexual interpretation by Mr. Smythe. During the performance of "*Wenn alle Brünnlein fliessen,*" Fräulein

Hohenstaufen, apparently being sexually molested by Smythe, "rose from behind the trombone section with a sudden screech"; and to his announcement of "*A Bird's Wedding*" he insinuatingly adds: " 'And with a bird like our Miss Hohenstaufen here we shouldn't have long to wait, should we?' " (168).

The turning point in the story occurs when the drunken host falls into the trumpet section, finally making a fully-fledged slapstick performance out of an earnest "amity" event:

> Herr Kunst [the band's conductor] extricated him [Smythe]. Hauling him to his feet, gripping him by the upper arm, Herr Kunst guided him to the farther side of the microphone. Above the stamping and applause of the crowd, any exchange of words was inaudible. . . .
>
> Ken Smythe shook himself free and stood glaring at Herr Kunst's back as the boys in the trumpet section righted the stands and finished sorting the sheet music. (169)

Characteristic of Metcalf's art of omission, the reader does not get to know what exactly the conductor has said to Mr. Smythe; a highly disciplined character, Herr Kunst has probably simply tried to bring Smythe to his senses and to moderate his inappropriate behavior. However, Smythe's behavior ("glaring" at Herr Kunst) only changes from sexist to nationalistic, with his primary target now no longer Fräulein Hohenstaufen but Herr Kunst. After his — unwittingly self-revealing — announcement of the song "*Trink, trink, Brüderlein trink . . . Drink, my Brothers, Drink*" (170), he uses the first opportunity to twist the mood towards nationalistic hostility, by indirectly referring to the Germans' role in the Second World War:

> " . . . a most typical German song named *Warum ist es am Rhein so schön.*"
>
> "And we all know what's typically German, don't we?" said Ken Smythe, jerking his thumb backwards at Herr Kunst. . . . "It wasn't so beautiful the last time *I* was there, Herr Kunst or no Herr Kunst. . . . Last time *I* saw the Rhine — last time I saw *Essen* . . . , it was through my bomb-sights. . . . RAF, mates." (170)

The inebriated Scottish compere and Second World War veteran, parodying Herr Kunst's highly controlled, even stiff conducting motions, eventually drifts into a military posturing ("Ken Smythe lurched out to the edge of the stage and, pulling himself erect, saluted," 172). He now quite purposefully directs the audience to turn against the German brass band. The innocent performance of a German youth band metamorphoses horribly into modern-day warfare on the battlefield of "popular culture" (see the foreboding juxtaposition of the Pleasure Gardens with the War Memorial at the beginning of the story, 161):

> Ken Smythe launched the crowd into yet another chorus.
> HITLER HAD ONLY GOT ONE BALL
> GOERING TWO BUT VERY SMALL
> HIMMLER WAS VERY SIMLAR
> BUT POOR OLD GOBALLS HAD NO BALLS AT ALL
> . . .
> BOLLOCKS! roared the crowd THEY MAKE A TASTY STEW!
> BOLLOCKS! (173)

With Smythe's primitive sexual and nationalistic leanings fully unleashed, his revolting song reduces the most hated Germans ever (Hitler, Goering, Himmler, Goebbels)[11] to their sexual organs in a barbarian, cannibalistic context ("they make a tasty stew").

Smythe is thus depicted as an extremely unlikeable character: lower-class, ignorant, sexist, vulgar, and racist. The story also makes clear that this behavior is not really (in ironic negation of the understated title) a "strange aberration" at all, but an authentic expression of his character and mind-set. Smythe's influence on the ignorant and gullible masses which eventually turn against the German brass band under his direction delivers a gloomy message: "Smythe emerges as a kind of everyman who is both a member of and a voice for the mob" (Rollins, 186).

The reader's sympathy in this story lies with the members of the German music band, who become innocent and rather arbitrary victims of nationalistic aggression. Against this background of popular culture turning into vulgarity and obscenity, the Germans are marked positively from the outset by their names: "Heine" recalls one of the most important German writers,[12] while Fräulein Hohenstaufen's name is reminiscent of

[11] These names of course signify the inner circle of power of the Nazi regime: Adolf Hitler (1889–1945) of the National Socialist German Workers Party (NSDAP or Nazi Party) became leader ("Führer") and chancellor of Germany in 1934 and started the Second World War in 1939. Hitler's racial policies culminated in the Holocaust, that is, the genocide of at least eleven million people, including more than six million Jews. Hermann Wilhelm Goering (1893–1946), one of the main leaders of Nazi Germany, was the founder of the Gestapo (the Nazi's secret state police), who helped to keep Hitler in power by brutally executing opponents. Heinrich Himmler (1900–45) was the commander of the German Schutzstaffel (SS) and controlled the Gestapo. He was also founder and officer-in-charge of the Nazi concentration camps. Joseph Goebbels (1897–1945) was Hitler's Propaganda Minister, known for his zealous and energetic speeches, his virulent anti-semitism, and his efficient use of the mass media.

[12] Heinrich Heine (1797–1856), poet and politically active journalist and essayist, represents German (post-)Romanticism. He is one of the most translated of German authors.

German aristocracy and tradition.[13] The most obvious reference to the allegorical meaning of this artist story is the name of the disciplined director and conductor, Herr Kunst ("Mr. Art"). Indeed, his band, though performing in the context of mass entertainment, is dedicated to its *art* rather than its audience, displaying the utmost discipline of appearance and behavior:

> A small boy [Hans] wearing a black suit and black bow-tie ran out to the microphone. He bowed, a sharp jerk forward of his head and shoulders, and went back to sit behind his drums. . . . A tall blond boy [Heine] came out and gave a stiff bow; he cradled a trumpet in his arms. The other boys, black-suited, filed onto the stage and to their section places. . . . Suddenly onto the stage strode a man in a black suit, halted, faced the silent band. The arm of Herr Kunst rose; the arm of Herr Kunst descended.
>
> The burst of sound was crisp and perfect, the sections rising and sitting as one man, the soloists flawless. Herr Kunst stood rigid except for the metronome pump of his elbows.
>
> During the applause, Ken Smythe and the Fräulein came forward. Herr Kunst remained motionless facing the band who were turning over the sheet music on their stands. (166)

To further stress the value of their performance, the instruments of the band members are described using bright and precious colors. The cymbals are said to be "glittering"; "light shone in the trombone bells, glanced off the slides" (167); and blond Heine's trumpet is twice referred to as "golden": "Light flashed golden on his trumpet" (172).

The spatial contrast introduced in the exposition of the story runs throughout the text. Of Heine's performance we read: "Heine's golden trumpet tones *soared* round and sweet *above* them" (167; italics added); at the end of the story, we read in horrible contrast how

> Heine suddenly staggered, *dropping* his trumpet and half-*falling* against the boy next to him. His hands covered his face. Herr Kunst was at his side in two strides. A stone, a bottle, something thrown from the darkness. Blood was shining, trickling *down* the backs of his hands. (173, italics added)[14]

[13] The Hohenstaufen family brought forth several kings and emperors of the twelfth and thirteenth centuries, including Friedrich I, "Barbarossa." The name Hohenstaufen derives from the castle Stauf near Göppingen in southwestern Germany.

[14] This spatial orientation also applies to Smythe to a certain extent. His movements are, not surprisingly, mainly downward: the deterioration in his state is indicated by his *dropping* his file cards during an announcement (167); he is then seen "*falling* . . . into the trumpet section" (169); later the drunk man "*sinks* from view" (171; italics added).

The earlier up-and-down movements of the conductor's arm and the band's exact response to it strikingly show the concentration and precision of their performance (though also, in their rigor of appearance and movements, that is, their stereotypical Germanness, the band members are also satirized to some extent). Herr Kunst's conducting initially even seems capable of imposing some order on the increasingly noisy audience: "The arm of Herr Kunst remained raised until the noise had stopped and then descended" (167). At the end of the story, by contrast, the movements of the conductor's arms are no longer mentioned. Although the band, despite an increasingly disorderly and eventually hostile audience, keeps an admirable discipline, Herr Kunst is as powerless to control the hostile masses as the rest of the band: "The louder the stamping, the louder played the band" (172) changes into: "The roaring voices and the pounding feet had drowned the band although the boys still played" (173). The masses seem to prevail over the elitist artist.

It is in the ending that the allegorical meaning of this artist story becomes particularly clear, as the absolute dedication of the artists to their art clashes with an audience that is not, to put it mildly, interested in a "serious" music performance. This is also stressed in interspersed episodes showing the reactions of an American family to the evening show. Shooting several rolls of film, peeling oranges, and eating potato chips, the Americans, like the rest of the audience, disrespect the performance of the brass band, which is obviously the result of a lot of talent and intensive practice. When the trumpet player Heine is physically assaulted by someone from the audience, the Americans are only interested in getting a good picture of the blood running down the boy's face: " 'The color!' screamed the mother, tugging at the edge of the father's plastic mac. 'Use the color film!' " (173). On this sensationalist outburst, enhancing the shock of the violent ending, horrible enough in itself, the story ends.

"The Strange Aberration of Mr. Ken Smythe" is the most dismal of Metcalf's artist stories, which are generally concerned with the precarious state of the artist in a social context that does not particularly value art or artists. The development of the action on stage and the reactions of the audience may thus be understood as an allegory illuminating this strained relationship between the artist and society, if pushed to extremes here (see also Metcalf's treatment of national clichés: Germany is associated with "highbrow" culture — Heine, Herr Kunst — yet also with the Second World War and the Nazi regime; the Scots, through Mr. Smythe, are associated with drinking, and the Americans with superficiality and a sensationalist tourist stance). The social context, the audience, appears as a backdrop against which art goes on *in spite* of the antagonism presented between the artist and society. The artists must carry on no matter what the hindrances, and according to their own demanding standards, not catering merely for an uneducated mass audience. Although in constant friction with their surroundings, Metcalf's artists never give up but keep striving to give the best they can. The story also demonstrates that Metcalf, no matter how involved with the craft of writing, does not take a purely aestheticist stance, but regards himself as a political writer in the final analysis ("all writing is political, all great writing subversive," Metcalf 1972, 154). It is interesting to keep in mind that this story was first published at the beginning of the 1970s, during the period that came to be called the "Canadian Renaissance," when Canadian culture was in a crucial formative stage. Clearly the story makes a highly negative statement about the relationship between artist and audience. Yet it also insists on high, if not elitist, standards of art, irrespective of what an uneducated audience finds palatable. One would hope that Metcalf, having clamored for a suitable reception of Canadian literature by an educated audience for decades, would not see quite as much necessity to write such a story nowadays. In any event, "The Strange Aberrration of Mr. Ken Smythe" demonstrates that John Metcalf, apart from having been the foremost mentor of Canadian short fiction, is also an excellent writer himself, for whom the craft of writing short fiction is definitely not a "strange aberration," but another important means to the end of fostering nothing short of excellence in Canadian short fiction.

Works Cited

Cameron, Barry. "The Practice of the Craft: A Conversation with John Metcalf." *Queen's Quarterly* 182 (Autumn 1975): 402–24.

Lotman, Jurij M. *Die Struktur literarischer Texte.* Transl. Rolf-Dietrich Keil. Munich: Fink, 1972.

Metcalf, John. *Adult Entertainment.* Toronto: Macmillan, 1986 (1986a).

———, ed. *The Bumper Book.* Toronto: ECW Press, 1986 (1986b).

———. *Freedom from Culture: Selected Essays 1982–92.* Toronto: ECW Press, 1994.

———. *General Ludd.* Downsview, ON: ECW Press, 1980.

———. *Girl in Gingham.* Ottawa: Oberon, 1978.

———. *Going Down Slow.* Don Mills, ON: Paperjacks, 1975.

———. *Kicking Against the Pricks.* Downsview, ON: ECW Press, 1982 (1982a).

———. *The Lady Who Sold Furniture.* Toronto: Clarke, Irwin, 1970.

———, ed. *Making It New: Contemporary Canadian Stories.* Toronto: Methuen, 1982 (1982b).

Metcalf, John. *Selected Stories.* New Canadian Library. Toronto: McClelland & Stewart, 1982 (1982c).

Metcalf, John. *Shooting the Stars.* Erin Mills, ON: The Porcupine's Quill Press, 1993.

———, ed. *Sixteen by Twelve.* Toronto: McGraw-Hill Canada, 1970.

———. "Soaping a Meditative Foot (Notes for a Young Writer)." In *The Narrative Voice: Short Stories and Reflections by Canadian Authors*, ed. John Metcalf. Toronto: McGraw-Hill Ryerson, 1972. 154–59.

———. *Standing Stones: The Best Stories of John Metcalf.* Toronto: Thomas Allen, 2004.

———. "The Strange Aberration of Mr. Ken Smythe." In Metcalf, *Selected Stories*, 161–73.

———. *The Teeth of My Father.* Ottawa: Oberon, 1975.

Nischik, Reingard M. "Contrastive Structures in John Metcalf's Artist Stories." *Critique* 29.3 (Spring 1988): 163–78.

———. "The Short Story in Canada: Metcalf and Others Making It New." *Die Neueren Sprachen* 86.3/4 (1987): 232–46.

Rollins, Douglas. "John Metcalf (1938–)." In *Canadian Writers and Their Works*, ed. Robert Lecker, Jack David, and Ellen Quigley. Fiction Series, vol. 7. Toronto: ECW Press, 1985. 155–211.

Struthers, J. R. (Tim). *The Montreal Storytellers: Memoirs, Photographs, Critical Essays.* Montreal: Véhicule Press, 1985.

21: "A Literature of a Whole World and of a Real World": Jane Rule, "Lilian" (1977)

Christina Strobel (Munich)

JANE RULE OPENS THE FILM *Fiction and Other Truths* (*FOT*)[1] with a statement that captures one of her central concerns: "The literature I create, I hope, is a literature of a whole world and of a real world. I am a realist." Rule says she decided to be a writer "because I wanted to speak the truth as I saw it. . . . No political or moral ideal can supersede my commitment to portray people as they really are" (*A Hot-Eyed Moderate*, 43). In Rule's aesthetics, "real" is not a naïve concept. First of all, Rule's interest is in telling a truth she did not find in the literature of "the great liars" (*FOT*) she studied at college. While regarding sexuality as an integral part of the human experience and not as *the* single feature defining a person, she bemoans the lack of representations of men and women loving someone of their own sex. Rule describes the realities she lives in as a "very mixed world, a world of old and young people, of heterosexuals and homosexuals" (*FOT*). She portrays a wide range of people and voices, whom she may not always admire or love but always accepts for themselves, and a variety of social, political, and moral positions which she may or may not share but which are all part of the world she lives in.

Clearly, being a realist for Rule is not an affirmation of an existing consensus — unless readers share an understanding of what is "real." More likely, since particular perspectives from different points of view exist, realism invites a negotiation of conflicting concepts of reality (Fluck 1992, 27). Rule is very much aware that there are various other ways of seeing the world, or other "truths" about reality. To her, it is important to offer her own truth as an active involvement with power structures and to negotiate between her version of the world and the versions of others. Rule writes:

[1] This film about Jane Rule and her work was released on video in 1995. It won the Canadian "Genie" award in 1996.

> By a willing suspension of disbelief, we allow ourselves to experience another's idea of reality. We must always be willing to risk that if we are to gain insight into who we are as individuals in our culture. Misogynists are not necessarily telling lies about women when they express their genuine dislike. The same is true of racists and snobs. We'll not cure them of biases we don't approve of by silencing them, but we can help to cure the world of their power by expressing world views that are different from theirs. We must, however, claim the world as our own to do so. (Rule 1990, 228)

By calling herself a realist, Rule makes a claim to authority. She posits herself as a subject authorized to make culturally valid decisions about what is a useful concept of the real, about how the real can be seen and described. This claim is founded in moral and political beliefs, and continually structures her desire to influence and shape reality. Rule belongs among the realists "for whom social, political and moral questions are paramount" (*A Hot-Eyed Moderate*, 5). In this sense, realism is a form of politics, whose aim is to change reality (Heath 1986, 119). This begins by telling "real" stories.

On the occasion of being awarded an honorary doctorate from the University of British Columbia in 1994, Rule appealed to her audience to take responsibility for the location they speak from:

> I think the thing that is most important to me to say to you today is that each of us is made up of a number of minorities, some of them privileged, some of them problematic. I am white, I am well educated, and I am well-off. Those privileges could teach me to be smug, judgmental and condescending, or they could teach me to take responsibility for the gifts I have and compassion for those who have not been not so blessed. I am also a woman, a lesbian and an arthritic. Any of these could have taught me to be a bitter victim. I hope they have taught me instead courage and humor. (*FOT*)

Jane Rule was born into a white, middle-class family in Plainfield, New Jersey, on 28 March 1931. She grew up as the middle child in a nurturing environment. Her family moved frequently all over the USA, following her father, a businessman. Rule appreciates how frequent relocation helped her to recognize the variety of human manners and how they are usually naturalized and spoken of as "values":

> I think the moving around was very good in one sense. I learned very early that what a great many people thought of as "values" were really "manners," and that "manners" shifted radically from community to community. . . . the sense of how you behaved in somebody's house, what kind of language you used, what kind of *accent* you used, all seemed to the people who had always been there the way you always did it. For me, it was being a foreigner and figuring out what the rules of the game were. (Rule in Hancock 1976, 60–61)

Her understanding of the world was also shaped by seemingly minor experiences: she learned to read and do math only after she got her first pair of glasses at ten; she realized that she was left-handed; at sixteen she was six feet tall and had a very deep voice. Charm school (an institution that taught young women manners and poise), especially learning to walk in high heels, was wasted on her, and Rule was quite aware that she did not conform to contemporary ideals of womanhood. In 1952 she earned a B.A. in English from Mills College and then studied for a year at University College, London, taking courses in seventeenth-century literature as an occasional student. Back in California she found it difficult to bear what she regarded as the intellectual narrowness of the USA and its fierce nationalism. Teaching English at Concord Academy from 1954 to 1956, she met Helen Sonthoff, who was to become her life partner. In 1956, she moved to Vancouver, adopting Canadian citizenship after several years before moving further west to Galiano Island in the Gulf of Georgia in 1976.

Jane Rule calls herself both a lesbian and a feminist, thereby taking a double stand. Today, it may be hard to imagine what it must have meant to be coming of age in the McCarthy era when "homosexual" and "communist" were synonyms and could mean the loss of job and friends. Rule likes to tell the story about risking her job at UBC with the publication of *Desert of the Heart*: "When my reappointment as a university lecturer was challenged because of the book, my more liberal colleagues defended me with the argument that writers of murder mysteries were not necessarily themselves murderers; therefore it followed that a writer of a lesbian novel was not necessarily a lesbian. I was reappointed" (Rule 1982a, 1). A lesbian or feminist movement had yet to exist when Jane Rule wrote this first novel, which was finally published in 1964. Out of her own sense of what was possible, Rule invented a story of a love between two women, a relationship that — unlike the only models at the time — did not focus on self-loathing and did not end in either death or heterosexual marriage. Rule's book meant a lot to large numbers of readers and has now acquired cult status. Today, the book and the film version by Donna Deitch, *Desert Hearts*, are modern classics.

Between 1964 and 1989 Rule published seven novels, three short-story collections, and a volume of essays, as well as a pioneering study of lesbian literary history, *Lesbian Images* (1975).[2] In 1959, *Klanak Islands* accepted her story "A Walk by Himself"; in the same year, she bought her first house with a federal housing mortgage (which for the first time was granted to two women). "If There Is No Gate," written in 1959, was printed by *The San Francisco Review* in 1960. Rule included both stories

[2] Rule has retired from writing. For reasons, see her statement in the film *Fiction and Other Truths.*

in her first collection, *Theme for Diverse Instruments*, published by Talonbooks in Canada in 1975. It consists of thirteen stories, ten previously published. The stories vary between six and twenty-nine pages in length, and adopt male and female or children's perspectives by means of experimental and straightforward storytelling approaches. In 1963 Rule sold "No More Bargains" to *Redbook*, the first of many stories she would sell to women's magazines. "My Country Wrong" was the first story accepted by *The Ladder*, the publication of the lesbian homophile organization The Daughters of Bilitis, in 1968. Between 1968 and 1972 Rule contributed seven stories and numerous letters and essays to *The Ladder*. *Chatelaine*, a Canadian women's magazine, also bought several stories. In 1981 *Outlander: Short Stories and Essays*, a hybrid collection of thirteen stories (nine of these reprinted) and twelve essays, was published by Naiad. Most of the essays had first appeared in *The Body Politic*, a Toronto-based gay liberationist newspaper where Rule took a stand in public debates on sexuality, gender, censorship, children's sexuality, and pornography. The third and final collection, *Inland Passage and Other Stories* (1985), comprises twenty-one stories, only nine of them previously published.

Rule's desire to portray and address "a whole world" is reflected in both the range of media disseminating her work — mainstream women's magazines, lesbian feminist magazines, lesbian, feminist, and general literary publishers — and in the range of voices and themes in her stories. Nearly half of the forty-seven stories collected in *Theme for Diverse Instruments*, *Outlander*, and *Inland Passage* are focalized through or feature heterosexual protagonists. Less than half focus on lesbian protagonists. Well over ten percent are written from a male perspective, with one from a child's. A few stories feature a first-person narrator, in one case a first-person plural perspective. All stories deal with ordinary questions of daily life, such as how to negotiate a working balance between a couple (with one four-and-a-half-page story comprising almost exclusively dialogue), or how to adapt to various stages of life and make sense of changes (for example, a thirty-two-page account of the life of a muse). A subset of "heterosexual" stories are the five "Anna and Harry" stories in *Inland Passage* (with the characters first appearing in *Theme for Diverse Instruments*), which portray a married couple raising two children. With a laconic sense of humor and the vision of a world in which things can turn out for the best, these stories make us believe that an ordinary life can be both nonconformist and extraordinarily enjoyable. Some of the "lesbian" stories take up lesbian issues (loving women and what that implies in social terms), while others address questions of daily life (coming to terms with a friend dying, for example) with protagonists who only happen to be lesbians.

The short story "Lilian" first appeared in *Conditions II* in 1977. It was reprinted in the 1981 collection of short stories and essays, *Outlander*. Only five pages long, it is one of Rule's shortest stories. It was reprinted in a number of anthologies and thereby found its way into university curricula.

The story begins with an analogy: "Like the pages of a pop-up book, the scenes of love remain" (89). With these first words, the reader learns what the focus of the story is: love, and how it is remembered. This image readily evokes memories ("pop-up") that are neither fully welcome nor a full representation of the real love. The whole quotation reads: "Like the pages of a pop-up book, the scenes of love remain, three-dimensional, the furniture asking more attention than the flat doll who is more like wallpaper, a bedspread, a detail rather than the focus of memory." Despite the picture's three-dimensionality and its richness of detail, the human figure remains out of focus. With the "woman standing by a small gas stove" (89) it is difficult to fill in her face. Detail is available for her clothes: "a suede jacket, a gray skirt with two pleats down the front nearly to the ankles. She has a purple and gray scarf, a pale lavender twin set" (90). Remembering is possible for some aspects of the past, while others defy capture. The paradoxical conclusion is that what "might have been a way of dealing with pain instead is the source of it" (89).

The first paragraph explores the metaphor of the pop-up book. The book has a title, *Lilian*, and the memory can be put away for a while like a book on a shelf. While the pain of that memory is an old one and has come to inhabit the body "like the ache of a bone broken twenty-five years ago" (89), it can flare up any time and will need to be explored like a sore that will not heal. The painful memory is usually triggered by a new lover's questions, inquiring into her past.

The first paragraph introduces the central themes: the story is about an old love, the pain its memory brings, and how a new love reflects on this old one and vice versa. It also introduces the revealing metaphor of the pop-up book, with a fake three-dimensionality, and its representation of everything in smaller-than-life form. Uniquely in a short story by Rule, the voice of the narrator is a consistent second-person "you" who directly addresses and intimately involves the reader: "and you, like a huge, old child, poke a finger as large as your old self once was into the flimsy trap of a very old beginning" (89). We all recognize the urge to scratch a sore that is healing and can empathize with the narrator.

Time and place are very precisely specified. The year is 1977, the love remembered was lost twenty-five years ago, when the narrator was not quite twenty and Lilian, the woman remembered, thirty. As the story progresses, the reader learns that the two shared a small and very cold flat in England. The setting of the memories of love contained in the pop-up book is the interior of an apartment. A private scene with a bedroom, a desk, a kitchen, and a hall. Similarly, the present-day setting of the story is the interior of an apartment, with a bedroom, a study, and a kitchen. The narrator's young lover in 1977 is the same age as Lilian was in 1952, but is married with two children. Concrete detail is provided that lets the reader "feel" the place and time beyond factual knowing ("How long has it been since anyone wore that sort of bra?" [90]; " 'a pair of gloves with the tips cut out of the fingers' " [89], so as to be able to work in the cold apartment).

The three female characters and their relationships are presented from a single point of view, that of the narrator; the new lover and Lilian have their own direct voice only in sparse dialogue. The reader meets the new lover through her actions, questions, and concerns. She escapes as often as she can from her husband and children to make love with the narrator. She will return to her family full-time soon, when the guilt about neglecting her responsibilities becomes too strong. The reader has no reason to doubt the narrator's view of the situation. No negative judgment is voiced by the narrator when she expects this course of events — to her, it is a welcome fact. The new lover does not have a name. She is one of a string of about a dozen lovers, nearly all of them thirty, as Lilian was, indicating the pain of loss the narrator feels. A name would give presence and identity, which the narrator cannot afford. She likes to keep her lovers at a calculated distance. That this one has a husband and children is almost a convenience.

There is limited factual information about the narrator. By the middle of the second page, the reader knows that it is a female voice. Describing the pleasures of making love, the narrator says, "you can both finally lie naked in a long feasting pleasure, where she can make no comparisons because her husband never does that, because you and Lilian had never even heard of it. When you came upon it in a novel written by a man, she was long since gone" (90). The narrator gives no physical description of herself. She neither looks in a mirror nor finds it necessary to report what others might see or have seen when they looked at her. At one point, she slips on a kimono to gain distance from her lover. The one piece of information that she tells us about her physical appearance is given repeatedly: she feels like or turns into a "huge, old child." She obliterates traces of her physical presence except for the anger and pain that have been internalized. We meet her as she has been shaped emotionally, and as her memories still shape her present feelings and actions.

As much as the use of the second-person narrator may draw the readers into the story, inviting them to measure and compare their experiences, actions, and feelings with those of the narrator, it is also a device that distances the narrator from herself. By not using a first-person voice when speaking of herself ("you've grown twenty-five years older," 90), she separates herself from her body and, implicitly, from experience and pain. She cannot be called, or addressed, or held responsible, because she does not give her own name.

The narrator's words and actions, which she comments upon in advance or retrospectively, also characterize her as someone who stays at a distance from her own feelings and, in consequence, from other people.

Her lover to her is "a face . . . which you don't have to struggle to remember or forget" (90). She thinks of herself as the controlling agent in the relationship and she acts accordingly. Very coolly she reflects: "you are slower now to encourage the break, though you know that to extend the strain on her for too long is a matter of diminishing returns. It's not that you'd have any difficulty replacing her" (92).

The narrator is a successful author, permitting herself an "expression of tolerant indulgence for her [lover's] admiration of your work, your success" (92). She has always lived alone, except for the time with Lilian. She has loved women for most of her life, but in the beginning did not fully know what she desired ("the ten minutes of touching which was all it ever occurred to either of you to do," 90). Her sole interest in her lover is, precisely, as a lover, whose "fully realized body" she appreciates (91). What the narrator notes as individual about this particular bed companion as one in a succession of many is the particular way in which she likes to make love. For Rule, sexuality is a language, and as a form of communication, sexuality can take on various forms and have different meanings. In her own words, it "can be as casual as a game of tennis, as friendly as a long correspondence, as important as one of the languages of a lifelong living with" (*A Hot-Eyed Moderate*, 91). Enjoying the "feasting pleasure" of leisurely sex, the narrator expresses a kind of indifferent respect, neither love nor hate nor connectedness beyond the physical act. She uses words from the language of sexuality, that is, sexual gestures to which the lover cannot afford to respond if she does not want to be late going home. This both honors the desire of her lover to be desirable, and in a conveniently predictable way determines her actions. The narrator is quite aware that she is managing this affair as she has handled those before. The present is shaped by the memories of the past. She controls, and needs to be in control. When her lover enjoys her sexual attention and compliments her, " 'You're so beautifully unlike a man' " (92), the narrator knows better: "So unbeautifully like one" (93). She takes on behavior generally considered appropriate for the male gender role — being a man means being in control, and being dominant — and she transgresses her position by assuming a gender-role identity[3] that puts her on the dominant side of power.

[3] I use the definitions of "gender identity," "gender-role identity," and "gender role" as given in Kessler and McKenna 1985. "Gender identity refers to an individual's feeling of whether she or he is a woman or a man, a girl or a boy" (8). "A gender role . . . is a set of expectations about what behaviors are appropriate for people of one gender" (11). "Gender-role identity refers to how much a person approves of and participates in feelings and behaviors, which are seen as 'appropriate' for his/her gender" (10).

Finally, there is Lilian. She comes alive in the details about her clothes, and memories of how she came home "on those dark, English afternoons . . . , her hair smelling of the tube, her face and hands cold, wanting a bath first to get warm, wanting her tea" (90). The little that we learn addresses all of the senses. Comparing her to her present lover, the narrator notes:

> Lilian at that age had none of the vestiges of childishness you notice increasingly now. She had not been raising children, of course, and was not absorbed, as all the others have been, with the ways of children and therefore inclined to tip into baby talk or take delight in small surprises. She had been as absorbed in her work as you were in yours. (92–93)

We do not learn what this work was, but we realize the importance of this point, which the narrator brings up repeatedly: "Lilian always believed in your work. Success wouldn't increase or diminish that, and it would never bring her back" (92). Clearly, believing in the other person's work and being grown up are features that are seen as related here. Since we learn so little else about Lilian, the information acquires weight. Does it provide a clue to the question of why the memory is so painful? And why did Lilian leave the narrator? The new lover wants to know:

> "Why did she leave you?"
> "Because I am not a man," you answer, as you have answered the same question a dozen times before.
> "She married then?"
> "No. Eventually she found a woman to live with." (91)

The lover cannot make sense of this exchange, and the reader may be confused too. The narrator obviously tells some things, yet leaves out others; she is not quite reliable. She acts "so unbeautifully" like a man, she has noted before, not really with pleasure. The narrator's distorted telling becomes evident when she remembers how she once tried to explain further. Her memories are more than she can bear and she transfers her anger to the questioner (91).

In the crucial final scene, after the lover has left, the narrator is drawn into the old scene of love. She shrinks to a size to fit the cardboard pop-up book, and feels compelled to sit at her old desk and re-live with dread what (might have) happened twenty-five years ago. We read a dialogue between the narrator and Lilian that might be remembered or, more likely, that presents a present-day reflection of past events and of the narrator's insight. Lilian addresses the narrator:

> "Look at me," she says, and you do, surprised by the clarity of her face, afraid.
> "You don't want a lover and a friend; you want a wife or a mistress."
> "What's the difference?" you ask.

"You're not a man. You have to grow up to be a woman, caring as much about my work as I care about yours."
"I can't." (93)

And Lilian begins to fade and flatten into a cardboard figure. In the only scene when she can see Lilian's face, the narrator is afraid of hearing a demand she cannot meet. What Lilian wants is clear: to be treated as an equal, as someone whose work is respected. The narrator finds herself incapable of doing so, and she grows "into that huge, old child again" (93). The female gender role and being grown up stand for an equal relationship with mutual respect. The narrator opts for the male gender role and for control at the price of feeling not fully grown up or smaller than life, and being alone. She is aware of her dilemma and feels the old anger and pain.

Gender roles seem to have changed very little between 1950 and 1975, certainly for the narrator. What has changed considerably in those twenty-five years is knowledge about sexuality and the definition of sexual identity. The narrator has become a knowledgeable lover and words can name what before were only vague longings. However, learning about sexuality has not changed views on gender roles. Rather, gender roles reflect on sexuality. Rule considers gender roles, or the ways in which men and women are supposed to act, as socially determined conventions, or, in her terms, as "manners." In England in 1950, a typical man might have expected to have a supporting and dependent wife (or mistress), as would have the majority of men in North America in the 1970s. It is a role that not every man would have filled. But it is the one chosen by the female narrator; "not being a man" was not the problem, acting like one was. She rejects the female gender-role identity when she loves a woman. Since in the hegemonic heterosexual economy, someone loving a woman can only be a man, and since a man is expected to be dominant, this can be read as an unsuccessful effort to find a consistent place in the social order.

As Lilian's position shows, there is no need to follow this unfulfilling logic. Lilian proposes a different construction of female gender identity: as a grown-up and as equal to an "Other." In the final analysis, the story is not about love between women, but about power relationships in love and about how identity is conferred. We depend on the other's affirmation of how we perceive both our own gender and gender-role identity (or our sexual identity). When it is denied in the encounter between the narrator and Lilian, the former is not "recognized" or accepted in her love. Failing Lilian/the Other, she cannot realize her full (adult) identity and hence lives with the need to repeat the encounter, both in memory and in real life.

Jessica Benjamin has proposed a concept of the relationship between self and other that she calls "the intersubjective view."[4] Intersubjective

[4] For more on what I call "Rule's ethics of difference" see Strobel 1999.

theory explores "the representation of self and other as distinct but interrelated beings" (Benjamin 1988, 20), a self meeting another self, or a subject another subject that is "different and yet alike" (20). Benjamin describes the ideal relationship between self and other as one that upholds the "necessary tension between self-assertion and mutual recognition that allows self and other to meet as sovereign equals" (12). Assertion and recognition, says Benjamin, are poles of a delicate balance; they are integral to "differentiation," that is, the individual's development as a self that is aware of its distinctness from others. The human need for recognition gives rise to a paradox:

> Recognition is that response from the other which makes meaningful the feelings, intentions, and actions of the self. It allows the self to realize its agency and authorship in a tangible way. But such recognition can only come from an other whom we, in turn, recognize as a person in his or her own right. (Benjamin, 12)

Mutuality must be sustained as a constant tension in this concept, not be "resolved" as in the Hegelian drama of master and slave. In Benjamin's terms, "sameness and difference exist simultaneously in mutual recognition" (47). Rule makes the same point using different words when she demands: "We have got to be peers, respecting each other's strengths without dependent envy, sympathetic with each other's weaknesses without cherishing or encouraging them, interdependent by choice, not by terrified necessity" (*Outlander*, 185).

Harking back to my introductory remarks about Rule's understanding of herself as a realist writer, what is realist about this story? Stories are, by way of their status as literary texts and as fictions, a field in which a writer can experiment. Fiction offers the potential for a symbolic intervention into cultural constructions of reality. Winfried Fluck speaks of "literature as symbolic action" to refer to this negotiating process. Fictions "respond to reality by inventing stories" (Fluck 1983, 364). Finding herself in disagreement with concepts or the experience of reality around her, a writer may react by fictionally re-arranging, reconstructing, and correcting reality (Fluck 1983, 365). In this way, literary writing is the test of given models of reality, not their reflection; it is heuristic work with the materials of a culture, not a mirror (Fluck 1992, 14; Fluck 1983, 361).

At the same time that Rule describes pre-existing gender roles in an accurate representation of things "as they really are," she is actively shaping social and cultural material in relation to conventions of reality, whether conforming, modifying, or dissenting. Here she breaks with conventions about what a male or a female role is and how identity is conferred for gendered individuals. It is not the question of a really existing reference that determines a text's realism, but rather its agreement with generally accepted linguistic and social conventions. Any divergent versions must establish themselves as being in agreement with a community, emerging from and creating that community. It is the reader, or a community of readers, who decides about the realism of the text — for example, whether one believes that a woman loving women can assume a male gender-role identity as portrayed in this story — and it is the reader who makes a decision about the morality of that fact. Is it a role that enriches or that narrows the narrator's life? Is the price to be paid acceptable? Will they refuse consent and turn to Lilian's definition of gender roles — a definition that finally transcends gender and posits the mutual recognition of sovereign equals?

Jane Rule, "authorized" to make culturally valid decisions about what is real on the grounds of her moral and political beliefs, certainly suggests that the narrator's life is narrower, lonelier, and more burdened with anger and pain without the mutual recognition gained from an Other. The narrator, interestingly, is also an author, that is, someone who invents fictions. However, there are subjects that resist her authority — the book *Lilian* is one she will never write. The memories remain personal images which can neither be turned into written language nor serve as the grounds for dialogue.

Rule is a pioneer of lesbian literature in North America. Marilyn Schuster writes: "From the beginning, readers have found in Rule's fictions a social landscape in which to reimagine themselves and their relation to the world. Her readers form invisible but passionate communities linked by texts that challenge as much as they confirm" (Schuster 1999, 257–58). As a writer who had to find her own territory before the feminist movement and lesbian recognition appeared on the horizon, and as one of her generation who did not know of the sparse literary tradition in this field, Rule at times felt like a "homesteader" who lives "a fair distance from other writers in the territory" (*A Hot-Eyed Moderate*, 60).

At the same time, Rule has much in common with other Canadian women writers such as Margaret Atwood, Alice Munro, or Nicole Brossard who look into the social construction of gender and sexuality. Rule's stories illustrate the constituting influence of social practices and institutions and describe how these are re-established in human interactions. Even — or especially — stories set in the interior of a private home show how social institutions such as gender inform private lives. Rule focuses on human interactions in daily lives with much attention to detail, an interest she shares with many women writers. While acknowledging normative identity formation, Rule never sees humans as passive agents, acting under more or less complete constraint. She, like other women writers, has never subscribed to a form of sociological determinism that credits individuals with neither initiative nor sense. Rule demands explanations which have a "place for the subjective experience of individuals willing and choosing" (Douglas 1987, 32). "But we do also have some capacity to resist our educations, to influence the world we live in, to change our perceptions of ourselves and other people. If this were not so, those in authority would have no fear of dissenters" (*A Hot-Eyed Moderate*, 129). Rule chooses to write about her themes in an unspectacular way, downplaying drama and action or patterns of conflict and resolution. Her focus is not on dramatic effects of plot or sudden revelation but on how individual people can negotiate their lives with others. Rule's writing is distinguished by an interest in communication, in dialogue, in human interaction.

In an essay about writing and the women's movement, Rule says: "In Canada we have a remarkable number of gifted and articulate women. . . . They will be our voices if we live up to their intent, severe, humane visions" (*A Hot-Eyed Moderate*, 24). What she appreciates most about these writers is also what she aims at in her own writing:

> For our women writers . . . have developed voices which do accurately describe for us the climate in which we live. They are being our historians, sociologists, psychologists. With their testimony we have an opportunity to make more informed political judgments because we have an understanding of our complex and particular culture only a real literature can give. (*A Hot-Eyed Moderate*, 23)

Works Cited

Benjamin, Jessica. *The Bonds of Love: Psychoanalysis, Feminism, and the Problem of Domination.* New York: Pantheon, 1988.

Desert Hearts, dir. Donna Deitch. With Helen Shaver, Patricia Charbonneau, and Audra Lindley. Samuel Goldwyn, 1985.

Douglas, Mary. *How Institutions Think.* London: Routledge & Kegan Paul, 1987.

Fiction and Other Truths: A Film About Jane Rule, dir. Lynne Fernie and Aerlyn Weissman. Toronto: Great Jane Productions, 1994.

Fluck, Winfried. *Inszenierte Wirklichkeit: Der amerikanische Realismus 1865–1900.* Munich: Fink, 1992.

———. "Literature as Symbolic Action." *Amerikastudien / American Studies* 28.3 (1983): 361–71.

Hancock, Geoff. "An Interview with Jane Rule." *Canadian Fiction Magazine* 23 (Autumn 1976): 57–112.

Heath, Stephen. "Realism, Modernism, and 'Language-Consciousness.'" In *Realism in European Literature*, ed. Nicholas Boyle and Martin Swales. Cambridge: Cambridge University Press, 1986. 103–22.

Kessler, Suzanne J., and Wendy McKenna. *Gender: An Ethnomethodological Approach.* Chicago: The University of Chicago Press, 1985 [1978].

Rule, Jane. 1964. "Deception in Search of the Truth." Reprinted in *Language in Her Eye: Views on Writing and Gender by Canadian Women Writing in English*, ed. Libby Scheier, Sarah Sheard, and Eleanor Wachtel. Toronto: Coach House Press, 1990. 225–28.

———. *Desert of the Heart.* London: Pandora, 1986 [1964].

———. *A Hot-Eyed Moderate.* Tallahassee, FL: Naiad Press, 1985.

———. *Inland Passage and Other Stories.* Tallahassee, FL: Naiad Press, 1985.

———. *Lesbian Images.* Trumansburg, NY: The Crossing Press, 1982 (1982a) [1975].

———. "Lilian." In Rule, *Outlander*, 89–93.

———. *Outlander: Short Stories and Essays.* Tallahassee, FL: Naiad Press, 1982 (1982b) [1981].

———. *Theme for Diverse Instruments.* Vancouver: Talonbooks, 1982c [1975].

Schuster, Marilyn R. *Passionate Communities: Reading Lesbian Resistance in Jane Rule's Fiction.* New York: New York University Press, 1999.

Strobel, Christina. *Reconsidering Conventions: Jane Rule's Writing and Sexual Identity in North American Feminist Theory and Fiction.* Augsburg: Wissner, 1999.

22: Failure as Liberation: Jack Hodgins, "The Concert Stages of Europe" (1978)

Waldemar Zacharasiewicz (University of Vienna)

UNLIKE MOST OF JACK HODGINS'S early stories, "The Concert Stages of Europe," which opens his second collection of short stories, *The Barclay Family Theatre* (1981), employs a first-person narrator and seemingly fictionalizes episodes from the author's own life. In this respect it differs from the narrative mode preferred by Hodgins. Gaining critical recognition in 1976 with his first collection, *Spit Delaney's Island*, he had originally written about characters very different from himself[1] and avoided the autobiographical impulse that inspired many stories by major Canadian writers like Alice Munro and Clark Blaise. Apart from the story "Earthquake" (later included in an adapted form in *The Macken Charm*, 1995, the first volume of Hodgins's trilogy, followed by *Broken Ground*, 1998, and *Distance*, 2003), which drew on the memories and experiences of Hodgins's parental generation and his extended family, only the two framing stories of *The Barclay Family Theatre* use first-person narration and focus on the activities of the author's alter ego, Barclay Philip Desmond. Here and elsewhere, the feats of his kin, such as the histrionic and humorous talents and adventures of the narrator's six maternal aunts, provide the touch of situational comedy that is the hallmark of Hodgins's art in his stories and early novels. He characteristically evokes a vivid and often humorous picture of life in the hitherto literally unmapped region of northern Vancouver Island, a territory populated by loggers, veterans, settlers on stump farms, and workers in pulp mills.

In an early interview, the author stated that he had overcome a sense of marginalization and insignificance by choosing to depict the sometimes freakish characters inhabiting his "own little postage stamp of native soil . . . worth writing about" (Faulkner in Cowley 1959, 141). William

[1] In various interviews Hodgins refers to his early habit of watching other people and being "supersensitive to the way they might feel" (see Twigg 1981, 188). In the same context, Hodgins maintained that he was not writing about himself.

Faulkner's famous phrase seems to be particularly apt in an analysis of Hodgins's fiction; the latter admitted to an intense admiration for the American writer, one that had initially prevented him from finding his own voice.[2] The precision of his depiction of landscape and of social structures in his early stories quickly earned him the label "realist" and "regionalist" (Pritchard 1984; 1985). But it was through American masters of fiction such as Faulkner, Eudora Welty, and Flannery O'Connor (see Zacharasiewicz 1986) that Hodgins learned to invoke the universal aspects of a seemingly restricted, rural existence, remote from the centers of culture. In various essays William Keith has suggested that Hodgins manages to transform "his local backyard into an image of the whole creative universe" (Keith 1981, 31; 1989, 195–213).

While concentrating on his own native region, Hodgins did not forget the wider world. Even as early as in *Spit Delaney's Island*, he recounted the confrontation of people from the Pacific Rim with, for example, the experiences they garnered on a Grand Tour through the Old World, as in the case of recently retired Spit Delaney on a journey to Egypt and Stratford-upon-Avon in the company of his family. Like the author himself — whose career as a writer and teacher of creative writing has taken him not only to Ottawa, but also to Asia, Australia, and various European countries — several of Hodgins's characters interact with individuals in foreign countries, be it in Japan with Kabuki actors and sumo wrestlers, or in Ireland with an amorous novelist. The desire to escape the narrow confines of Vancouver Island also prompts Rusty Macken's dreams of a career as a filmmaker on the mainland in Hodgins's fifth novel *The Macken Charm*. Similarly, Sonny Aalto in the novel *Distance* abandons his well-meaning but negligent father in the backwater of Vancouver Island and moves to Ottawa and on to other distant destinations.

It is this desire to break out that also motivates the mother of the protagonist, the first-person narrator of "The Concert Stages of Europe," to launch her son Barclay on an international career. Dissatisfied with the lowly role of her logger husband, she feels obliged to push at least one of her three children towards wider horizons. Her pleasure in the anticipated success (that she herself had been denied) and the failure of her son Barclay Desmond to fulfill her expectations lie at the heart of the story. Probably also because of the story's humor, "The Concert Stages of Europe" has frequently been included in anthologies and was also adapted into a film.[3]

[2] Note the story "Galleries" in his third collection *Damage Done by the Storm* (2004), where Hodgins introduces a Faulkner scholar and her son who visit "Faulkner country" in Mississippi.

[3] The film adaptation, which cast Angus MacKay in the role of Clay (as Barclay is affectionately called by his father in the story, and often in the film version) and

The title of the story suggests both the marginal position of which many characters in Hodgins's oeuvre are keenly aware, and the postcolonial stance often ascribed to the writer (Lawson and Slemon 1987; Slemon 1988). The "concert stages" are the focal points of the metropolises whose atmosphere the distant colonial (Barclay's mother) hopes to be able to enjoy. To perform on Europe's concert stages must appear as the ultimate dream for a kid from the frontier, "the stump ranches of Waterville" (*The Barclay Family Theatre*, 2). The mother's resolve to find her son a good teacher is strengthened when the parents of a girl (Cornelia Horncastle) in the same community decide to give their daughter piano lessons. That Barclay's father has other plans and is skeptical about the boy's musical training and the mother's eventual goal for their son (he would rather see him following in his own footsteps and becoming a logger) complicates the mother's ambitious plan only slightly. But when three years later Barclay displays excessive shyness and embarrassment in a talent competition and fails to win any of the prizes, her dream is cut short for good.

The author's choice of first-person narrative and the coverage of a lengthy time span (thirty years) is of crucial importance for the story. His experiences of training for great international success are told by Barclay himself in retrospect as a middle-aged man. The first-person narrator claims that the humiliation he suffered in this competition has overshadowed his entire existence ("I . . . ruined my life in the process," 1). The absence of any more specific details about the consequences of his failure allows one to read this claim as a deliberate exaggeration, which humorously undermines Barclay's somber assertion.[4] This omission also distinguishes Hodgins's text from the semi-autobiographical stories of Alice Munro or Margaret Laurence, who often trace the difficulties of budding writers (see also Isabel Huggan and Sandra Birdsell).

The story's comic episodes permit the reader to perceive the complications of young Barclay's protracted ordeal as humorously diverting, for example, his abortive piano lessons with Aunt Jessie, and his somewhat

---

Patricia Phillips as Mom (Lenora Barclay), was produced and released by the National Film Board of Canada in 1985. It offers a streamlined, restrospetive narrative of Barclay's youthful experiences and eclipses Barclay's two siblings and any references to the formidable aunts, the Barclay sisters. The film version, which was available through the National Film Board of Canada until 2003, remains closer to the original publication of the story in *Saturday Night Fiction* (1978) than to the story version expanded for the collection; see note 7 of this article.

[4] For the paradoxical connection between Barclay Philip Desmond and his namesake, altogether of a more optimistic disposition, see the comments below on "The Lepers' Squint," a story which uses a figural narrative situation.

ludicrous problems when, on his weekly treks to his second teacher, Mrs. Greensborough, he has to fight off various dogs. The reader's sympathies with the boy's general awkwardness with regard to social contacts do not preclude an awareness of the broad situational comedy, with even sympathetic observers like his father or the family's Finnish neighbors punctuating the narrative with teasing comments, such as: "That boy lookit like a drowny rat" (7). In retrospect, Barclay himself describes his embarrassing rate of growth at the onset of puberty with hyperbolic similes that create comic effects:

> I'd wakened one morning that year and found myself six feet two inches tall and as narrow as a fence stake. My feet were so far away they seemed to have nothing to do with me. My hands flopped around on the ends of those lanky arms like fish, something alive. (11)

While the narrator provides a frame in which Cornelia Horncastle is blamed for his still-unsolved problems, the story focuses on the exaggerated hopes of the mother and the resulting troubles of her son. The narrator describes in detail his initial uncertainty about what trade to learn, in the face of military propaganda during his early childhood on the one hand and his fascination with his Finnish neighbors — their strength, endurance, loyalty, and cleanliness — on the other. The conflict with his ambitious mother, whose firm opinions about his artistic potential are partly given in "narrated monologues" (Cohn 1978), involves him in regular debates and prompts lively and comic situations while he himself has only a vague sense of identity. The story also dwells on the boy's susceptibility to female charm, his fascination with the blue eyes of Lilja Korhonen, the beautiful Finnish girl, but also the "delicate femininity" of "Aunt Jessie" (7) and the aura surrounding his second teacher, Mrs. Greensborough. A reader of Hodgins's trilogy may relate Barclay's sexual awakening to the spell that glamorous Aunt Glory — also a passionate piano player and totally out of place in the derelict world of her rash and reckless husband Toby — casts on her devoted nephew Rusty in *The Macken Charm*.

The events before the contest take up half of the narrative time. The pace of the narrative varies considerably and progresses episodically. The crucial episode of the contest, for instance, is depicted as if in slow motion (with the narrative time exceeding the narrated time). There is a detailed and humorous description of the different performances of Barclay's three rivals: a girl completely bungles her act and hastily retreats in shame, a boy blasts out on his saxophone a song that should be played "piano," and a "smart-aleck" who plays several instruments wins "tremendous applause," especially as he is "physically challenged" (17). While this sequence provides ample evidence for the exuberance of Hodgins's comic imagination, the ensuing episode with Barclay on the stage catches the excitement and tension of the situation. His nervousness after becoming the butt of Richy

Rider's jokes ruins his performance. He is afterwards deeply ashamed of his discomfiture, temporarily choosing self-immurement, but eventually resigns himself to the end of his aspirations and those of his mother.

While Barclay's vision of success has vaporized under the impact of his encounter with the public, Cornelia Horncastle, by contrast, is unaffected by stage fright and performs like a professional. She wins both applause and a holiday in Hawaii, but what appears as an auspicious beginning does not usher in the career of a famous pianist either, for she afterwards abandons the instrument. It appears as if neither Cornelia nor Barclay have the energy and devotion necessary for artistic careers. (In Hodgins's new collection of short stories, *Damage Done by the Storm*, there is a story entitled "Astonishing the Blind," in which the first-person narrator Meg, a concert pianist, describes her success in Europe, where she has settled. But she admits that her private life has not been equally successful.)

Barclay's seeming withdrawal from the artistic sphere is strangely at odds with the attitude and actions of the character sharing his name in "The Lepers' Squint," the fifth story in *The Barclay Family Theatre* (160–80). There can be no doubt that Barclay Philip Desmond in the latter story is a relatively self-confident professional writer, whose sojourn in Ireland in the company of his family corresponds to Hodgins's own experiences when researching for his first novel *The Invention of the World* (1977), which explores the mythic antecedents of a failed utopian foundation on Vancouver Island and the fates of various characters in its aftermath. Assuming that fictional characters bearing the same name and featuring in different stories are indeed identical,[5] one perceives an artistic development here, namely from intimidated Clay to confident Barclay Philip Desmond. Certain of his own "postage stamp of his native ground" on Vancouver Island, the latter sticks resolutely to his writing despite various distractions, such as a female fellow-writer who implies that Desmond might borrow material from her sometime mentor, a prominent Irish writer, and also invites him to a writers' picnic and *soirée* with a possible *tête-à-tête* in mind. Barclay Philip Desmond's dedication to his role as a fiction writer contributes to the overall impression that *The Barclay Family Theatre* deals increasingly with the problems of artists already established or at the beginning of their careers.

There remains the question of whether Hodgins's stories are experimental in terms of structure and language. Although, like "The Concert Stages," they are for the most part written in a realist manner, some have also fused realism and parable and thus have helped to earn Hodgins's

[5] See my discussion of the return of characters in subsequent texts and of the phenomenon of "revenants" in fiction (Zacharasiewicz 1993).

writing the label of "magic realism" (see Delbaere-Garant 1987; Hancock 1979–80). The term was applied to Hodgins primarily on account of his first two novels, *The Invention of the World* and *The Resurrection of Joseph Bourne* (1979), as well as the two Spit Delaney stories from the first collection and "The Plague Children" from the second. There are, indeed, some links to the experimental features of avant-garde fiction. Yet "The Lepers' Squint" also contains passages that through the use of architectural metaphors seem to suggest less of the "fluidity" often maintained by advocates of postmodernism and poststructuralism; in fact, Frank Davey's hesitation to grant the same quality to Hodgins's stories as to his more "adventurous" long fiction implies Davey's preference for avant-garde fluidity (Davey 1983, 361). It remains to be seen whether *Damage Done by the Storm* will be regarded as innovative and fully successful.[6]

The open-endedness of many avant-garde stories is not emulated in "The Concert Stages." Cornelia Horncastle's desertion of her seeming road to success, for instance, is stressed in the concluding paragraph of the story, while in the film version she disappears much earlier. As mentioned above, the seven redoubtable Barclay Sisters do not appear at all in the film,[7] and were only introduced in the expanded story version revised for the collection. Barclay apparently has no siblings in the film and only one piano teacher, thus eclipsing the turbulent episode with Aunt Jessie. What is highlighted is Clay's desired integration into the lifestyle of the Korhonen family: "the only goal that ever really mattered to me [was] becoming a Finn" (23). Clay's peculiar wish presumably mirrors the author's own fascination with this national group (a fascination that does not correspond to the general perception and stereotype of Finns in North American culture[8]). Instead of the somewhat melancholy frame of the story there is an upbeat ending to the film, which shows Barclay sharing in

[6] In this new collection of nine stories, Hodgins again chooses settings on Vancouver Island as well as in Ottawa, Australia, and Europe.

[7] This emerges when one examines the two versions of the story, which had first appeared in *Saturday Night Fiction* in 1980 and was then revised to fit into the collection, originally entitled "Allied Invasions," but later published under the title *The Barclay Family Theatre.* The Jack Hodgins Funds in the National Library of Canada contain the text of the original publication with holograph and typescript alterations and a revised typescript intended to integrate the story better in the collection. References to the maternal aunts and their entourage as well as their histrionic talents and habits are added; moreover, Hodgins in the revision changed the constellation and names of Barclay's siblings, giving him both a brother (Kenny) and a sister (Laurel).

[8] Though the number of Finns who settled in Canada is relatively limited, their presence in the logging communities of British Columbia was certainly noticeable.

the sauna and swimming activities of his Finnish neighbors. His burgeoning affection for the charming Lilja Korhonen is clearly given more emphasis than in the story, a fact that is compatible with the casting of Clay, who in the film is probably a youth of about fifteen years, rather than a ten- to thirteen-year-old boy. Clay's individual tribulations and his development are thus the focus of the film, and the wider range of additional characters, including his antagonist, fades into the background.

One wonders whether the film version would have been different and whether Cornelia Horncastle's role more central if it had been shot some years later. For, curiously enough, a girl from Jack Hodgins's backyard (on northern Vancouver Island, the periphery of the continent), a schoolmate of his children in Nanaimo while her mother was temporarily a fellow-teacher of Hodgins's wife Dianne, has gained an international reputation as a singer after very intense training on the piano: Diana Krall.[9] Sometimes reality does seem to surpass the imagined achievements and careers of fledgling artists and the hopes of parents, after all.

Works Cited

Canell, Marrin, et al. *The Concert Stages of Europe.* VHS. Dir. Giles Walker. Ottawa: National Filmboard of Canada, 1985.

Cohn, Dorrit. *Transparent Minds: Narrative Modes for Presenting Consciousness in Fiction.* Princeton: Princeton University Press, 1978.

Cowley, Malcolm, ed. *Writers at Work: The* Paris Review *Interviews.* New York: Viking, 1959.

Davey, Frank. "Hodgins." In *The Oxford Companion to Canadian Literature,* ed. William Toye. Toronto: Oxford University Press, 1983. 360–61.

Delbaere-Garant, Jeanne. "Magic Realism in Jack Hodgins' Stories." *RANAM* 20 (1987): 41–49.

Hodgins's interest in Finns is evident in the painter Eli Warnamoinen in the story "More Than Conquerors" (*The Barclay Family Theatre*), and his preoccupation with Finnish families shows most clearly in Sonny Aalto and his father Timo from the novel *Distance.*

[9] Diana Krall's homepage reports that the jazz singer and pianist, born in Nanaimo in 1964, began studying the piano when she was four years old. Her father encouraged her interest in music and she won scholarships when still a teenager; since 1993 she has released several albums, some of which have won Grammies. She has been extremely successful in the United States, Canada, and in Europe, filling concert halls in London, Berlin, and Cologne.

Hancock, Geoff. "An Interview with Jack Hodgins." *Canadian Fiction Magazine* 32–33 (1979–80): 33–63.

Hodgins, Jack. *The Barclay Family Theatre.* Toronto: Macmillan, 1981; rpt. Toronto: Laurentian Library, 1983.

———. "The Concert Stages of Europe." In Hodgins, *The Barclay Family Theatre*, 1–23 [originally published in *Saturday Night* (July/August 1978): 37–49].

———. *Damage Done by the Storm.* Toronto: McClelland & Stewart, 2004.

———. *Spit Delaney's Island: Selected Stories.* Toronto: Macmillan, 1976.

Keith, William. "Jack Hodgins' Island World." Rev. of *The Barclay Family Theatre. The Canadian Forum* (September/October 1981): 30–31.

———. *A Sense of Style: Studies in the Art of Fiction in English-Speaking Canada.* Toronto: ECW Press, 1989.

Lawson, Alan, and Stephen Slemon. "Out on the Verandah: A Conversation with Jack Hodgins." *Australian-Canadian Studies* 5.1 (1987): 31–47.

Pritchard, Allan. "Jack Hodgins' Island: A Big Enough Country." *University of Toronto Quarterly* 55.1 (Fall 1985): 21–44.

———. "West of the Great Divide: Man & Nature in the Literature of British Columbia." *Canadian Literature* 102 (1984): 36–53.

Slemon, Stephen. "Magic Realism as Postcolonial Discourse." *Canadian Literature* 116 (Spring 1988): 9–24.

Twigg, Alan. "Interview with Jack Hodgins." In *For Openers: Conversations with 24 Canadian Writers*, ed. Alan Twigg. Madiera Park, BC: Harbour Publishing, 1981. 185–95.

Zacharasiewicz, Waldemar. "The Development of Jack Hodgins' Narrative Art in His Short Fiction." In *Encounters and Explorations: Canadian Writers and European Critics*, ed. Franz K. Stanzel and Waldemar Zacharasiewicz. Würzburg: Königshausen und Neumann, 1986. 94–109.

———. "The Resurrection of Characters: Aspects of Interconnected Narratives in North American Fiction." In *Tales and "Their Telling Difference": Festschrift für Franz K. Stanzel*, ed. Herbert Foltinek, Wolfgang Riehle, and Waldemar Zacharasiewicz. Heidelberg: Winter, 1993. 295–317.

23: Figures in a Landscape: William Dempsey Valgardson, "A Matter of Balance" (1982)

Maria and Martin Löschnigg (University of Graz)

As a writer who is at home in many genres, William Dempsey Valgardson has published two volumes of poetry (*In the Gutting Shed*, 1976; *The Carpenter of Dreams*, 1986), two novels (*Gentle Sinners*, 1980; *The Girl with the Botticelli Face*, 1992), several plays for radio and television as well as three highly acclaimed children's books (*Thor*, 1994; *Sarah and the People of Sand River*, 1996; *The Divorced Kids Club and Other Stories*, 1999). He is best known, however, as a writer of short stories. Born in Winnipeg in 1939, Valgardson spent most of his childhood in Gimli, Manitoba, an area that had been settled by Icelandic immigrants in 1873–74 and was therefore once known as "New Iceland." It is this Interlake region between Lakes Winnipeg and Manitoba whose harsh physical landscape provides the setting of most of Valgardson's short stories and of his first novel. Educated in Winnipeg and at the University of Iowa, Valgardson taught English and creative writing at various high schools and colleges in Manitoba, Iowa, and Missouri, before moving to Vancouver Island in 1974 to teach creative writing at the University of Victoria. Valgardson's life in Victoria is reflected in the urban setting of his second novel and in the West Coast scenery of some of his later stories, including "A Matter of Balance."

Valgardson's portrayals of Manitoba's Interlake area and its Icelandic community in his early collections of short stories (*Bloodflowers*, 1973; *God Is Not a Fish Inspector*, 1975; *Red Dust*, 1978) draw upon the author's own experience of the land and its people. Valgardson, whose family background is in fact mixed Irish and Icelandic, has been influenced most deeply by his Icelandic heritage. In an interview with fellow Icelandic-Canadian writer Kristjana Gunnars, Valgardson accepted the designation of "Icelandic mystic" (Gunnars 1989, 16). Indeed, the Icelandic farmers, fishermen, and pulp-cutters who people what Margaret Atwood has called "Valgardsonland" (Atwood 1982, 321) are reminiscent of the archetypal figures in Icelandic sagas. By the time Valgardson was born, however, New Iceland had become a multi-ethnic region, with Anglo-Saxon, Cree,

Scottish, and Ukrainian settlers joining the Icelandic population, and in some of Valgardson's stories this ethnic diversity forms the background of the conflict.

The stark realism and laconic style of Valgardson's early stories reflect the hostility of their setting as well as the harsh fates of many of the central characters. In accordance with the author's belief that "environment creates mentality" (Valgardson in Hancock 1979/80, 130), these stories depict characters whose emotional limitations are shown to be the result of their isolated lives in extremely inhospitable surroundings. Frequently, the severity of the land and its climate functions as a test that divides those who are able to adapt from those who are not. Valgardson's early stories thus take up one of the most prominent themes of Canadian literature, that of survival (see Margaret Atwood's famous *Survival* of 1972). Because of his emphasis on locale, Valgardson fits into the regional tradition, which is prominent in Canadian literature, including the genre of the short story. Moreover, he is a regional author in the best sense, in that his local microcosms clearly transcend the regional to imply the universal: "I do not fear the regional because I realize that the creation of the particular does not preclude the universal; rather, it makes it possible to communicate" (Valgardson in Sweet 1986, 102). Valgardson's telescoping of universal themes into a restricted regional setting contributes to a parabolic or even mythic quality in his stories that makes them comparable — differences in mimetic structure apart — to those of Jack Hodgins.

Most of Valgardson's short stories belong to the traditional type of the plot story rather than to the Chekhovian type that concentrates on the analysis of the characters' inner lives. They are marked by action, intensity of conflict (often involving matters of life and death), and suspense, focusing on characters who are forced to take decisive action in a dramatically intense situation, especially one that is set in an unforgiving landscape. Frequently, there are "breathtaking twists and plummets and sudden dark gaps in understanding that open like crevasses" (Atwood, 324). Valgardson views himself as a social realist, whose stories often "resemble documentaries" (Hancock, 124). His characters have been shaped by their physical surroundings, a theme that he shares, for example, with Alistair MacLeod among other contemporary short story writers in Canada. Margaret Atwood regards Valgardson as an "uncompromising" and even "unrelenting" writer, who adopts the role "of a meticulous chronicler of an implacably hostile and nasty world" (Atwood, 321). As such, he may be said to carry on the prairie realist tradition of Frederick Philip Grove and Sinclair Ross (see Neijmann 1999, 248), whom he resembles especially in his accurate descriptions of local settings. Rather than following trends towards a modernist or even postmodernist style, Valgardson has long set himself apart from experimental writers "[who] play all kinds of games with fiction," since he believes that "by doing that, the author sacrifices the chance of writing stories that have universality" (Valgardson in Gunnars, 15). In particular, Valgardson seems to be of the opinion that formal experiment weakens "the bond of understanding" that must exist between the text and the reader (Jackel 1990, 60), and that stories will then fail to touch the reader's "reality." The price Valgardson has had to pay for remaining a social realist has been to be neglected by many Canadian critics, who have increasingly favored those authors following international developments towards postmodernism and postcolonialism (see Neijmann, 248). This neglect has not yet been remedied, unfortunately, even though the formal innovations in Valgardson's fourth and latest collection of stories, *What Can't Be Changed Shouldn't Be Mourned* (1990), actually heralded a change in Valgardson's writing towards a (moderately) modernist style. Notwithstanding current trends in literary criticism, Valgardson's position as one of the most important contemporary Canadian short-story writers cannot be disputed.

"A Matter of Balance," like many of Valgardson's previous stories, centers upon a struggle for survival in a harsh landscape, and its emphasis on conflict is characteristic of Valgardson's writing in general. The characters in the story, however, are no longer the rural characters of most of the earlier stories, and what we see portrayed here is not just conflict but also unmotivated aggression and violence. "A Matter of Balance" was written in 1980, when it won the annual short-story competition of the Canadian Broadcasting Corporation (CBC). The story was first printed in Wayne Grady's *Penguin Book of Modern Canadian Short Stories* (1982) and was later included in *What Can't Be Changed Shouldn't Be Mourned.* Unlike most of Valgardson's works, which usually undergo protracted periods of revision, "A Matter of Balance" was apparently written in only three days. The story is based, however, on Valgardson's impressions gathered during more than a year's regular hiking in Vancouver Island's Goldstream Provincial Park (see Gunnars, 17); it thus conforms to the author's belief that "[a] writer should write about the things he knows and understands" (Valgardson in Hancock, 122).

"A Matter of Balance" is rendered in third-person form, which the author prefers to the subjectivity engendered by first-person narration (see Hancock, 124). Interestingly, he explains this preference by alluding to his Lutheran background, which for him entails a lack of doubt "about reality or about the self" (Gunnars, 17). In contrast to many of the earlier stories, however, which present the point of view of an omniscient, authoritative narrator, "A Matter of Balance" is clearly in the figural mode, providing immediate access to the protagonist's thoughts and feelings. The correspondence between the inner life of the protagonist and outside reality that is foregrounded in this story is again characteristic of some of Valgardson's earlier stories, and there are further parallels in the moral dilemma that the central character has to face (see, for example, "An Act of Mercy" in

Bloodflowers) and the reversal of the roles of victim and perpetrator that has taken place by the end (see "On Lake Therese" in *Bloodflowers*; "In Manitoba" in *God Is Not a Fish Inspector*).

In "A Matter of Balance," Harold, the protagonist, is pursued by two members of a motorcycle gang on one of his weekly hikes in a British Columbia provincial park. From occasional flashbacks it emerges that Harold has taken up hiking for therapeutic reasons. He is trying to overcome the death of his wife, who was gang-raped, it seems, and brutally murdered about a year previous to the events portrayed in the story. In the course of his weekly hikes, Harold has also been panning for gold in the river gorge that runs through the park. Looking forward to a good day's "sniping" (504; page references are to the first printing of the story in the *Penguin Book of Modern Canadian Short Stories*), he is disturbed, as the story opens, by the presence of the two bikers at the park entrance, and begins to be afraid when they appear to be following him. At first Harold cannot be certain whether their intentions are actually evil, and he reasons with himself, trying not to succumb to paranoia. As they continue to follow him, however, he becomes convinced that they really mean to assault him. Tension increases when Harold decides to climb down the river gorge in order to escape from his pursuers, and the story reaches its climax when the bikers, who lack the equipment as well as the experience to move in such difficult terrain, slide to the brink of an abyss. Harold, who is torn between the moral imperative to come to their rescue and his instincts for self-preservation, finally decides to leave the bikers to their certain fate.

As indicated before, "A Matter of Balance" is presented mainly in the figural mode, with Harold acting as reflector. The story opens in a manner that is typical of figural narration, namely by using the referentless pronouns that indicate an internal perspective: "He was sitting on a cedar log, resting, absentmindedly plucking pieces from its thick layer of moss, when he first saw them. They were standing on the narrow bridge above the waterfall" (503). In the following sentence, however, there is already a change in perspective, unless one takes "When they realized he had noticed them" (503) to express Harold's conjectures rather than the external point of view of the narrator. Insignificant as it may appear, this possible ambiguity points to the importance of perspective for an understanding of Valgardson's story. Since the events in "A Matter of Balance" are rendered exclusively from Harold's point of view, the reader cannot be certain, at least for some time, whether the bikers actually intend to attack Harold or whether the protagonist's imagination is merely constructing dangers out of nothing. The latter assumption seems to be supported by references to Harold's nervous instability as a result of the shock caused by his wife's tragic death: the reader learns that he was "in hospital for depression" (512), that he was "ill for over a year" (504), and that he is still seeing a psychiatrist once a week (see 504, 512). Also, it is implied at the end of the story that the murder, which took place "on a dark parking lot" (513), may have been committed by gang-members similar to the ones Harold is now confronted with. This suggests that Harold's feelings of "fear" (503) when he becomes aware of the bikers transcend the usual degree of uneasiness that Hell's Angels are apt to inspire, especially if met in lonely places. In addition, Harold is anxious anyway since he knows that panning for gold in provincial parks is illegal, and he must therefore take care not to attract anyone's attention. (The panning, one notes, also serves to explain why Harold has brought the equipment — including friction boots and ropes — which will finally enable him to gain a decisive advantage over his opponents.) As the bikers appear to be pursuing him, he makes an effort not to panic, yet the narrator's comment that "[Harold's] panic fluttered like dry leaves in a rising wind" (507) makes it clear that the effort has failed. (This sentence, with its pretentious image, stands out as a conspicuous breach of style in Valgardson's otherwise taut prose.) In spite of the author's vivid rendering and convincing psychological motivation of his protagonist's fear, however, it becomes evident that the story is not to be understood as a study in paranoia. For once, Harold's thoughts and actions (trying not to panic, considering ways of escape, looking for weapons to defend himself with, etc.) are perfectly reasonable. Also, there can be little doubt as the story progresses that the bikers really mean business. They split up in order to prevent Harold from circling back, and when they finally discover him on a steep slab of rock, they try to get at him in spite of the danger to themselves. Finally, the detailed descriptions of Harold's movements in the dramatic "showdown" on the rock present the external perspective of the narrator, thus precluding an understanding of this episode as springing entirely from the protagonist's imagination.

Important as it is, however, the psychological element in Valgardson's story does not become an end in itself. Indeed, its main function is to build up suspense. The protagonist's growing fear and simultaneous attempts to calm himself create a dynamic pattern that underlies the structure of the first part of the narrative. Harold's feelings of uneasiness and fear are conveyed by subtle means. In the light of what we come to know about his past, for instance, a sentence like "He was sorry that they were there but he considered their presence only a momentary annoyance" (503) clearly appears, in retrospect, to be an instance of self-deception, the more so since he immediately interprets the bikers' way of looking at him as staring (503). Very soon, he thinks of them as his "pursuers" (505), while at the same time he tells himself "not to be foolish, not to be paranoid" (505). And the more his fear seems to be justified by the behavior of the bikers, the more anxiously Harold tries to prove to himself that it is indeed unfounded. The dynamics of fear seem to be matched by the dynamics of aggression and (latent) violence in the story. What the bikers may have intended as a practical joke at the beginning (one of them points two fingers at Harold as if he were shooting a pistol, 503), escalates into a serious pursuit and, eventually, a life-or-death struggle. That the bikers have indeed transgressed mental boundaries is reflected by the fact that they continue the chase beyond certain thresholds along the path (a "series of switchbacks," a "railway trestle," 505–6) at which someone merely bent on giving Harold a good scare or maybe even robbing him would have given up. Like many of Valgardson's stories, "A Matter of Balance" explores the workings of unmotivated violence. It is significant, in this respect, that Harold remembers an incident from his schooldays, when he was bullied and beaten up, for no obvious reason, by a group of youngsters. His mother had no answer to his question as to why this had happened: "Only later, when he was much older, had he understood that their anger was not personal and, so, could not be reasoned with" (504). Young Harold's question to his mother is echoed by the frantic " 'Why?' " (511) which he hurls at his assailants on the rock, and once again receives no answer.

At the end of "A Matter of Balance" a reversal of roles, which is frequent in Valgardson's stories, has taken place: Harold has turned from the bikers' victim to the one who holds their fate in his hands. Like other characters in "Valgardsonland" he is faced with a dilemma. Naturally, he does not want to deliver himself into the hands of the bikers by pulling them up to safety. If he were to inform the park wardens, Harold thinks, the chances are that his story might not be believed and even if the bikers were convicted, he (and his children) would eventually have to fear their retribution. All things considered, Harold concludes that his only choice is to leave the bikers to die — and die they most certainly will, for it is made clear that there is no help to be expected from third parties, and with the cold of the night about to set in, the two will not be able to hold on to the rock for long. All the same, Harold seems to be struggling with himself before he answers the bikers' frantic pleas for help with a peremptory " 'No' " (513). He has reached his decision, as it turns out, because of a sudden vision he has had of his wife's desperate struggle for life during her last moments. This final twist in the story entails a shift in the moral balance which is unfavorable to Harold: while readers understand the pragmatic reasons for refusing to rescue the bikers, his decision now appears to have been motivated mainly by a desire for revenge.

"I think there's a real moral quality to my work, but I'm not a moralistic writer. . . . I'm very concerned in many of my stories with Christian and un-Christian behaviour" (Valgardson in Gunnars, 18). This statement made by Valgardson in an interview is highly significant with regard to the themes of "A Matter of Balance." If Harold gives way to a desire for revenge, this is clearly immoral, especially since the two bikers cannot be assumed to be the actual killers of his wife. His decision to leave the bikers is "un-Christian" in the sense that it contradicts Christ's teaching to love one's enemies, which would oblige Harold at least to raise the alarm, regardless of the consequences. Instead, Harold seems to be taking justice into his own hands, thereby putting himself in the wrong. He may have passed the physical "test of balance" (508) on the rock, yet in a moral sense he seems to have lost his balance and fallen. However, the tenor of Valgardson's portrayal of events is far from being "moralistic." Not only does he imply that, in the face of the "force of circumstance" (indeed, this title of the well-known story by W. Somerset Maugham would have suited Valgardson's, too), considerations of survival may legitimately prevail over moral principles, he also suggests that Harold's desire for revenge may be understandable if not pardonable. The reader is thus asked to view with some understanding an act which would have to be condemned by strict moral standards. A memorable example of this also occurs at the end of "Granite Point" (in *God Is Not a Fish Inspector*), in which a woman who has suffered from living at an isolated Hudson's Bay Company station leaves her husband to be ravaged by a pack of huskies because she knows that, out of petty jealousy alone, he has contrived to bring about the death of the man who has shown her some sympathy. Similar to "Granite Point," where the muskeg setting suggests that a one-sidedly "moralistic" view of the protagonist's act may be based on treacherous ground, "A Matter of Balance" employs scenery to underline the ambiguity of Harold's situation: "The moss that covered the rock and soil, the moss that clung thickly to the tree trunks, the moss that hung in long strands from the branches, deadened everything, muted it, until there were no sharp lines, no certainties" (512). As the dim West Coast rainforest acquires mystic dimensions, clear-cut distinctions between right and wrong, between moral and immoral, seem to blur.

In line with the author's preference for open endings, which he considers to be "much more intriguing than closed stories" (Valgardson in Hancock, 125), the ending to "A Matter of Balance" seems to be open, as the reader is left to balance Harold's reasons for acting in the way he does against the moral implications of his decision. Regarding its plot, however, "A Matter of Balance" rather conforms to the closed type of short story, since there can be no doubt that the bikers will not survive. In its ambiguity, the ending of the story thus keeps a certain balance between openness and closure, a balance that seems to have been demanded by the story's theme: the problem of passing moral judgement. Yet the impression of closure is enhanced by the very last sentence, whose summing up of Harold's dilemma anticipates the title of the collection in which "A Matter of Balance" was eventually included (*What Can't Be Changed Shouldn't Be Mourned*): "Then, with real regret for the way things were but which couldn't be changed, he hefted his pack so that it settled firmly between his shoulders and returned the way he had come" (513).

This concluding sentence, which strikes the reader as somewhat ironic or even flippant in tone, tends to spoil the effects of a style which works by implication rather than by the explicit formulation of moral questions. Also, the notion of Harold figuratively shrugging his shoulders provides an unfortunate anticlimax to the tension that has built up inside him, and destroys some of the suspense that has been engendered by the pursuit as well as by the portrayal of Harold's dilemma. In contrast, Valgardson's narrative skills, especially his ability to create suspense, are demonstrated most impressively in the rock-climbing scene — a "cliffhanger" in the true sense of the word. Here, the detailed account of the characters' movements, which is evidently based on some knowledge of the technicalities involved (as evident, too, in the subsequent story in the collection, "Saturday Climbing"), produces a high degree of dramatic intensity. The bikers, whose inexperience provides a foil to Harold's skilled performance, are now fully revealed in their role of antagonists. While they are described, throughout the story, in a stereotypical manner — a manner reminiscent, incidentally, of the description of the gangsters in Hemingway's short story "The Killers" — they acquire symbolic overtones. They come to represent the return of the traumatic past from which Harold has tried to distance himself by quite literally trying to walk away from it on his hikes.

As the extensive descriptions of scenery in the story suggest, it is not so much the bikers who play the most important role in the story besides the protagonist, but the landscape. In the climbing scene in particular, landscape becomes functional, providing the test of skills that the characters will either pass or fail. As in many of Valgardson's stories scenery serves as a mirror that reflects and intensifies the conflict as well as the emotional states of the characters. In the case of "A Matter of Balance," this scenery is an intimidating one of primeval forest and of rock: "Large cedars pressed close to the path, blocking out the light. Old man's beard hung from the branches. The ground was a tangle of sword fern, salal, and Oregon grape" (505). The scenery seems to be devoid of wildlife ("It was old forest and, in all the times he had come, he had never seen a bird or animal," 506), and therefore pervaded by a gloomy silence: "Around them, the forest was silent. Not a bird called, not an animal moved" (512). When Harold enters the rocky area that drops to the river gorge, the rugged terrain reflects the growing tension and (in the case of the bikers) the aggression within the characters. Most importantly, however, the dominant connotation of the landscape becomes that of a trap: "Harold felt the forest close around him like a trap" (506); when he gets near to the end of the trail, with his pursuers closing in upon him, he does indeed seem to be trapped (507). As Margaret Atwood has noted, "the physical surface upon which [Valgardson's] characters move is packed with traps. . . . Such a world does not demand goodness as the price of survival, merely knowledge, vigilance, and luck; and for some even these aren't enough" (Atwood, 321–22).

Harold survives because he knows how to move upon rock, while the bikers in their turn are entrapped.

In a few instances, details of the physical landscape are charged with symbolic meaning. When Harold becomes aware of an arbutus (a typical West Coast tree) shedding its bark, for instance, we learn that on his hikes he has indeed felt "like a snake or an arbutus shedding his old skin for a new, better one" (505). When he first notices the bikers, he is squeezing a handful of rotting cedar, the reddish water that runs through his fingers symbolizing the blood of his enemies, which will be on Harold's hands (503). Images of decay and of lichen and moss growing over everything recur throughout the story. Towards the end, Harold has a vision of himself and of the bikers disintegrating into the landscape: "Harold had, for a moment, a mad image of all three of them staying exactly as they were, growing slowly covered in moss and small ferns until they were indistinguishable from the logs and rocks except for their glittering eyes" (512). This image of stasis, which strongly contrasts with the dynamic action prevailing in the story, underlines the land's indifference to the fates of the characters, along with the archetypal nature of their struggle.

The title of Valgardson's short story is aptly chosen, working as it does on several levels. On a first, physical level "A Matter of Balance" refers to the characters' efforts to keep their balance on the rock; on a second level, that of the plot, it indicates the balance of power that has been established by the reversal of the roles of victim and perpetrators; on a third, psychological level, it points to the precarious mental balance that Harold has regained on his hikes, and to his attempts at balancing reason against fear when the bikers seem to be bent on attacking him; on a fourth level, the title anticipates Harold's dilemma at the end of the story, when he weighs his reasons for not helping the bikers against the moral duty to save their lives; and on yet another level, "A Matter of Balance" refers to the dubious moral balance that Harold establishes by avenging himself on his pursuers for the death of his wife. Finally, with the story's ending keeping a fine "balance" between openness and closure, it is left to the reader to weigh the protagonist's motifs against his or her own notions of right or wrong. In the text itself, the moral questions raised by Harold's decision remain unresolved: there are indeed "no sharp lines, no certainties" in what must remain a highly disturbing story about conflicting claims.

Works Cited

Atwood, Margaret. "Valgardsonland: *Red Dust*." In Atwood, *Second Words: Selected Critical Prose*. Toronto: Anansi, 1982. 320–24.

Gunnars, Kristjana. "'Voyage on a Dark Ocean': Interview with W. D. Valgardson." *The Icelandic Canadian Magazine* (Spring 1989): 14–19.

Hancock, Geoff. "An Interview with W. D. Valgardson." *Canadian Fiction Magazine* 32/33 (1979/80): 120–34.

Jackel, David. "Short Fiction." In *Literary History of Canada: Canadian Literature in English.* Vol. 4, ed. William H. New. Toronto: University of Toronto Press, 1990. 46–72.

Neijmann, Daisy. "Icelandic-Canadian Literature and Anglophone Minority Writing in Canada." *World Literature Today: A Literary Quarterly of the University of Oklahoma* 73.2 (1999): 245–55.

Sweet, Frederick D. "W. D. Valgardson." In *Profiles in Canadian Literature.* Vol. 6, ed. Jeffrey M. Heath. Toronto: Dundurn, 1986. 97–103.

Valgardson. W. D. (William Dempsey). *Bloodflowers.* Ottawa: Oberon, 1973.

———. *God Is Not a Fishing Inspector.* Ottawa: Oberon, 1975.

———. "A Matter of Balance." In *The Penguin Book of Modern Canadian Short Stories,* ed. Wayne Grady. Harmondsworth: Penguin, 1982. 503–13.

———. *Red Dust.* Ottawa: Oberon, 1978.

———. *What Can't Be Changed Shouldn't Be Mourned: Short Stories.* Vancouver: Douglas & McIntyre, 1990.

24: "The Translation of the World into Words" and the Female Tradition: Margaret Atwood, "Significant Moments in the Life of My Mother" (1983)

Reingard M. Nischik (University of Constance)

For we think back through our mothers if we are women.[1]
—Virginia Woolf

MARGARET ATWOOD IS, BY MANY A COUNT, Canada's most important writer. To begin with, she is an extremely versatile, imaginative, and, in the best sense of the word, productive writer, having published twelve volumes of poetry, twelve novels, seven short-fiction collections, six volumes of literary criticism, numerous reviews and critical articles, and even a history book, children's books, and comic strips.[2] Her fiction and to a lesser extent her poetry have been translated into more than thirty languages. Atwood won the prestigious Booker Prize in 2000 for her novel *The Blind Assassin* and has repeatedly been shortlisted for the Nobel Prize for Literature. On an international scale, she has become *the* voice of Canadian literature, not only an excellent and renowned writer, but also an intellectual and social critic who reflects upon literary as well as political and social issues in a global framework, and upon Canadian literature and culture in particular. Atwood, who is also one of the most frequently interviewed contemporary writers, has thus developed into an international celebrity and a literary icon.

Margaret Eleanor Atwood was born in Ottawa in 1939 to Margaret Dorothy and Carl Edmund Atwood. Her mother was a former schoolteacher, her father a professor of entomology. A large part of her childhood

[1] Woolf 2001, 91. Woolf's *A Room of One's Own* "was the first literary history of women writers and the first theory of literary inheritance in which gender was the central category" (Rosenman 1995, 11).
[2] See the comprehensive bibliography of books published by and about Atwood in Nischik, ed., 2000/2002, 319–23.

was spent in the northern bush regions of Quebec (see her novel *Surfacing*, 1972) where her father did his research. She received private lessons from her mother and went to a regular school only when she was twelve years old, after her family had moved to Toronto (see her novel *Cat's Eye*, 1988). Between 1957 and 1961 she studied at the University of Toronto under Jay Macpherson and Northrop Frye, whose mythopoetical approach to literature influenced the young Atwood considerably, resulting in her groundbreaking and bestselling book of literary criticism *Survival: A Thematic Guide to Canadian Literature* (1972), which identified the motif of survival as central to Canadian literature. *Survival* was published by House of Anansi Press in Toronto, which Atwood had co-founded in the 1960s in her endeavors to raise the profile of Canadian literature. From 1961 to 1963 Atwood studied at Harvard University (Radcliffe College) under Perry Miller, an expert on Puritanism (see her novel *The Handmaid's Tale*, 1987). She gave up her Ph.D. project on the English gothic novel (see her novel *Lady Oracle*, 1976), which she had begun in Harvard in 1962, when she won the Governor General's Award in 1966 for her second volume of poetry, *The Circle Game* (1966), and then decided to become a full-time writer.

Atwood started out as a poet (her first volume of poetry, *Double Persephone*, was published in Toronto in 1961), but she soon turned to fiction as well. Her debut novel, *The Edible Woman* (1969), appeared with Canada's most prestigious literary publisher, McClelland & Stewart in Toronto, and the same publishing house also released her first collection of short stories, *Dancing Girls and Other Stories*, in 1977.

Although Atwood — by virtue of her utter versatility — is definitely not a writer focusing on the short story like Alice Munro and Mavis Gallant, she joins those authors in making up the group of the three leading short-story writers of Canadian literature. Atwood has published short fiction for four decades (*Dancing Girls*, 1977; *Bluebeard's Egg*, 1983; *Murder in the Dark*, 1983; *Wilderness Tips*, 1991; *Good Bones*, 1992; *Bottle*, 2004[3]; *The Tent*, 2006; *Moral Disorder*, 2006, a short-story cycle), and has produced some of the modern classics of Canadian short fiction with stories such as "Polarities," "The Man from Mars," "Death by Landscape," "Bluebeard's Egg," "The Age of Lead," and "The Little Red Hen Tells All" (the first three of which were adapted for the screen in "The Atwood Stories," 2003).

Atwood's short stories and shorter fiction have undergone significant developments (see Nischik 2006). Atwood's short-fiction oeuvre may be formally divided into short stories proper (published in *Dancing Girls*,

[3] *Bottle* was printed in a limited edition of 1,000 copies (published for a worthy cause), all the stories of which were integrated into Atwood's next "regular" collection of short fiction, *The Tent*.

Bluebeard's Egg, *Wilderness Tips*, and *Moral Disorders*) and short prose pieces — of variable forms and styles but mostly of very short length — which are hard to classify, being partly prose poems, sketches, dramatic monologues, short dialogues, mini-essays, or "reflections." These pieces of "short short fiction," which explore and extend the received generic borderlines of the short story, have made up three of her seven short-fiction collections published up to 2006 (*Murder in the Dark, Good Bones, The Tent*). With respect both to form, contents and theme, Atwood is indisputably the most variable, innovative, and challenging Canadian short-story writer. As part of this range, the stories of *Dancing Girls* (the individual stories of which were first published between 1964 and 1977) often show borderline characters on the brink of or having already entered the realm of madness ("Under Glass" and "Polarities," for example). Individuals and partnerships in crisis and relationships in their terminal stages are other important themes of her first short-story collection, which are also to be found in her second collection, *Bluebeard's Egg*. In these latter stories, written in the 1970s and early 1980s, there is a move away from individual psychological problems towards sociopsychological themes. Individual characters are now rather shown not as loners but as members of specific groups, often within their family context. The collection *Wilderness Tips*, in turn, leaves behind the family-oriented stories of *Bluebeard's Egg*, often placing its protagonists in a work context instead.[4]

"Significant Moments in the Life of My Mother" is one of Atwood's formally more traditional short stories. It was first published in, and is the prominent opening to, her second collection *Bluebeard's Egg*. The story is indeed, as suggested above in connection with the entire volume *Bluebeard's Egg*, a "family story," but it is much more than that. The story has autobiographical generic traces,[5] not the only reason why it may also be regarded as a disguised artist story. It is an ingenious fictional demonstration of what it takes to "translate the world into words,"[6] that is, to be artistically creative, to develop into or to be a writer. Last but not least, it shows Atwood's focus on female characters, on female influences and on the long-neglected "female tradition" in literature.

The story is rendered in a retrospective set-up by a female first-person narrator, who focuses mainly on the representation of her mother, either

[4] Atwood's first short-story cycle, *Moral Disorder*, was published while this book was in its proofreading stage. For a treatment of Atwood's collections of shorter fictions see Nischik 2003.

[5] On autobiography in connection with Atwood's oeuvre see Grace 2006.

[6] "Perhaps it was then that I began the translation of the world into words. It was something you could do without moving," Atwood, "Unearthing Suite," in *Bluebeard's Egg* (275).

directly or, mostly, indirectly by what the mother transmits to her children and how. The mother's stories and remarks are either vividly rendered in direct speech, contextualized with comments by the narrator, or are summarized by the narrator. In either case, the narrator enters into a sort of indirect retrospective dialogue with her mother, whose apparently cheerful mentality colors the writing. The text, taking its cue from the mother's stories, is structured episodically and rather impressionistically, though in a largely chronological manner (starting with the mother as a child and ending with her daughter having grown into the role of the adult narrator). By telling stories to her children (to the narrator and to her brother and sister, usually referred to as "we") and others, the mother is characterized as a highly expressive and communicative person, observant, caring, mentally alert, not taking herself too seriously, and generally demonstrating a pronounced sense of humor.

The episodes, which are added to each other apparently at random, at first seem to belie their classification by the title as "significant moments" in the life of the mother. In fact, the "events" appear altogether rather insignificant; they mainly belong to the quotidian family and domestic sphere,[7] and are thus all in the realm of the mother's personal experience: baby chickens dying because as a child she had unwittingly fondled them too much ("'I'd loved them to death,'" 11); her appendix operation ("'Never get sick,' she says," 12); the mother tricking her father into allowing her to cut her hair; the preacher at Sunday service temporarily losing control over his false teeth; a cat transported in a car, "wet[ting] itself copiously" (19) on the mother's lap; the family driving along in the car and barely escaping a collision with a hay wagon, and other episodes.

These events as such are perhaps not particularly remarkable. Nevertheless, they are obviously "worth a story" — and on different levels of reception — because of the manner in which the narrator's mother tells these episodes, and how their telling characterizes her; because of her daughter's interpretation of the stories (attaching further significance to them); and because of the effects and influence this particular mother may have had on the narrator — a budding writer, as the story as a whole and in particular the ending carefully suggest.

In several respects, the narrator's mother seems to be a born storyteller. To begin with, she obviously loves telling stories. She does so graphically and entertainingly, in a fluent, witty, colloquial style. And she does so with an eye towards the addressees, those who listen to her stories. Thus she consciously tells certain stories only to a female audience, as the narrator remarks. The narrator also suggests that the mother may have told her

[7] Significantly, Atwood once called her mother's stories "kitchen stories" (quoted in Sullivan 1998, 36).

stories for an effect beyond a merely expressive, informative, or entertaining purpose, that is, with a particular "message," an educating intention, in mind. This is presumed right at the beginning of the story in the narrator's comments following upon the very first "significant moment," the chicken episode:

> Possibly this story is meant by my mother to illustrate her own stupidity, and also her sentimentality. We are to understand she wouldn't do such a thing now.
>
> Possibly it's a commentary on the nature of love; though, knowing my mother, this is unlikely. (11)

This beginning — a story told by the mother, contextualized by the daughter's evaluating comments — sets the stage for what is to follow. The mother relates events she finds noteworthy and largely refrains from commenting upon them. Whether or not the mother pursues effects beyond informative, expressive, or entertaining ones remains open. In the perspective of the daughter/narrator who analyzes and evaluates these stories in retrospect and thereby draws her own conclusions (the most effective method of learning), the mother seems not only to have been an active oral storyteller, but at the same time an educator as well (the mother's profession in the story is indeed that of a school teacher).

The narrator's mother also exerts an influence on her daughter in the art of storytelling. That domestic storytelling in this text is related to artistic storytelling, to writing, is suggested by reflective passages such as the following (if here perhaps *ex negativo*): "There is, however, a difference between symbolism and anecdote. Listening to my mother, I sometimes remember this" (27).[8] In the framework of the short story, it is the narrator/daughter who attaches significance to the partly hilarious, always entertaining and apparently rather harmless "events" her mother tells the children in a cheerful, jaunty, even chatty manner. It is the meaningful characterization and contextualization by the daughter in hindsight that attach to the storytelling a weightier cognitive significance and that at the same time, in the writing process, transfer an aesthetic value to the stories, thereby transforming the episodes and anecdotes indeed into "significant moments." In this step from oral to written storytelling, from the mother as storyteller to the daughter as narrator/ writer, lies the metafictional gist of "Significant Moments" and its Chinese-box-like set-up. The two types of storytelling — which share the sequencing of a meaningful series of events — are obviously related to each other. But whereas the mother's

[8] See Atwood's biographical comment on her mother: "Unlike the stories in books, my mother's stories did not have clear morals" (Atwood quoted in Cooke 1998, 45).

narrations, though nicely expressed for ready reception, stick factually and apparently as closely as possible to "real events," the daughter/ narrator makes use of her imaginative (" . . . which I pictured as . . ., " 17), analytical, and aesthetic capacities to make sense of these events not only as a daughter but also as a writer. By writing a short story about her mother's stories — and hereby we approach an autobiographical reading of the story — she "translates the world into words."

Atwood's short story is related in its poetological aspects to William Carlos Williams's equally deceptively simple poem "The Red Wheelbarrow." This imagist poem transforms everyday objects into art — through the perceiving, selecting, arranging, and representing perspective of the artist, on whom "so much depends" (as Williams's poem begins). In the Atwood story, this transforming power of art is suggested by a mise-en-abymic rendering of a mundane object turned into something marvelously extraordinary:

> It was in this house that I first saw a stalk of oats in a vase, each oat wrapped in the precious silver paper which had been carefully saved from a chocolate box. I thought it was the most wonderful thing I had ever seen, and began saving silver paper myself. (14)

This fascinating image of the metamorphosing capacity of art links the story's involvement with storytelling, its metafictional impact, with its autobiographical aspects and the female line of influences which this story sketches. For the wonderful image of the wrapped stalk of oats — which results in the first-person narrator's beginning to save silver paper, too (in order to be able to effect such metamorphosis herself) — is, significantly, situated in her *mother's* family house, where "its secret life . . . was female" (13). In connection with her mother's oral storytelling, we can see the coordinates of a female line of tradition.

The family context in this story is presented in harmonious, warm, well-meaning terms relating to mother and father, brother and sister, that is, irrespective of gender differences:

> I was in the back seat, making bagpipe music, oblivious. The scenery was the same as it always was on car trips: my parents' heads, seen from behind, sticking up above the front seat. My father had his hat on, the one he wore to keep things from falling off the trees into his hair. My mother's hand was placed lightly on the back of his neck. (23)

But it is the female connection which seems to influence the daughter most. The world in which the girl grows up is a gendered world, in her parents' as well as her own perception, with the female sphere appearing more exciting to her, definitely inspiring her to a greater extent:

> The structure of the house was hierarchical, with my grandfather at the top, but its secret life . . . was female. (13)
>
> My mother and her younger sister would loiter near the closed office door until shooed away. From behind it would come groans, muffled screams, cries for help. (12)
>
> "Your father was upset about it," says my mother, with an air of collusion. She doesn't say this when my father is present. We smile, over the odd reactions of men to hair. (15)
>
> Here my father looks modestly down at his plate. For him, there are two worlds: one containing ladies, in which you do not use certain expressions, and another one — consisting of logging camps . . . — in which you do. (21)
>
> Some of these stories, it is understood, are not to be passed on to my father, because they would upset him. It is well known that women can deal with this sort of thing better than men can. . . . My father enters the kitchen, wondering when the tea will be ready, and the women close ranks, turning to him their deceptively blankly smiling faces. (21–22)

Such gender differences and allegiances which her parents seem to adhere to are reported by the narrator in a friendly, tongue-in-cheek manner, brimming with mild irony in both gender directions ("Not everyone shares this belief about men; nevertheless, it has its uses," 22). Atwood is one of the few contemporary authors to occasionally set a female bonding against an overwhelming (literary) tradition of male bonding. She indirectly questions restricting gender definitions, conventions, and oppositions and implicitly argues for a more individual and less categorical approach, the "third eye" (see "The Third Eye" in *Murder in the Dark*), particularly in gender matters. Although even in an "autobiographical age" (Sherrill Grace) we should pay heed to the danger of the "biographical fallacy" and avoid mixing up literary and biographical characters and people, it is safe to say that Atwood's manifold references in this particular story will invite it to be read in an autobiographical context: the narrator's maternal grandfather was a country doctor, her mother a schoolteacher; the family originates from Nova Scotia; the narrator's parents have an affectionate relationship; the narrator has a brother and a sister; she has curly, intractable ("next-to-impossible," 27) hair which was eventually cut short when she was a child; the narrator went to university and is in her mid-thirties when she becomes a mother herself; the mother's fantasy of being reincarnated as an archaeologist and her ice-skating; the narrator's father wearing a hat to keep things from falling onto his head[9] — these and other details correlate the narrator's and Atwood's lives, thus inviting us to read this "family story" also for autobiographical reasons as an artist story, too.

[9] See Saline 1997, 63 and Sullivan, 31.

It is towards the end of the text that the mother's stories start to focus on her daughter. The text thus symbolically passes from the life and times of the mother on to the daughter (and her relationship to her mother), for example, "'You always kept yourself busy. . . . You always had something cooking. Some project or other,'" 28, but only relatively briefly so. The more the daughter develops into an intellectual ("I read modern poetry and histories of Nazi atrocities, and took to drinking coffee," 28), the more a silent gap seems to develop between mother and daughter:

> My mother has few stories to tell about these times. What I remember from them is the odd look I would sometimes catch in her eyes. It struck me, for the first time in my life, that my mother might be afraid of me . . .: at any time I might open my mouth and out would come a language she had never heard before. I had become a visitant from outer space, a time-traveller come back from the future, bearing news of great disaster. (29)

Thus the story ends. It may be considered ironic (or even tragic) that the mother's legacy to her daughter, the joy in and disposition towards storytelling, eventually seems to estrange them from each other, as if they originated not from the same family but from different worlds (see also: "Off in the distance, my mother vacuumed around my feet while I sat in chairs, studying," 28–29) — after all, as Atwood herself admits, her mother was an inspiring "raconteur" and a "deadly mimic," but not a writer.[10] But, ultimately, the story is not to be understood entirely in the light of this final turn towards mutual estrangement. Rather, what sticks in mind and what makes up the most substantial part of this text is the loveable mother and her engaged and vivid storytelling to her daughter, through which she plays a decisive role in the daughter's development. What the daughter could (and, in an autobiographical reading, apparently did) learn from her mother is, among other things, that the art of storytelling partly consists of the right selection and arrangement of material and encompasses the art of omission ("I realized that she never put in the long stretches of uneventful time that must have made up much of her life: the stories were just the punctuation," 16); that a good storyteller is a good listener and perceptive observer ("In gatherings of unknown people, she merely listens intently, her head tilted a little. . . . The

[10] Quoted in Cooke, 41–42; originally in Atwood 1989, 4. See also: "She was not particularly literary; she preferred dancing and ice-skating, or any other form of rapid motion that offered escapes from domestic duties. My mother had only written one poem in her life, when she was eight or nine; it began: 'I had some wings, / They were lovely things,' and went on, typically for her, to describe the speed of the subsequent flight. The beauty of this was that whatever I came out with in the way of artistic production, my mother would say, more or less truthfully, that it was much better than she could do herself" (Atwood quoted in Cooke, 44).

secret is to wait and see what she will say afterwards," 17); that storytelling may (or perhaps *should*) be connected with fun and delight ("my mother's eyes shine with delight while she tells this story," 21; "Having fun has always been high on my mother's agenda," 18); and that being a good performer is conducive to effective storytelling ("When she tells them [the stories], my mother's face turns to rubber. She takes all the parts, adds the sound effects, waves her hands around in the air. Her eyes gleam," 17).

"Significant Moments in the Life of My Mother" is a clever metafictional treatment of the "translation of the world into words." It is a celebration of the art of storytelling that also demonstrates Atwood's anti-Romantic, rather pragmatic view of artistic creativity. At the same time, it is a wonderful, moving homage by a daughter to her mother; an intellectual writer to a domestic oral storyteller; Margaret Atwood to her mother (who died on 31 December 2006 at the age of 97 in Toronto). In fiction as in life, Mrs. Atwood provided the model for her daughter's muse, in that she supplied the first female voice. Asked once whether her muse was male or female, Atwood replied: "Oh, she's a woman."[11] This story demonstrates — with both the author and narrator clearly having a lot of fun along the way — how high-quality literature may be born from the traditionally female sphere of the domestic[12] and how well aware the leading Canadian writer has been of the female constellation of influences,[13] the female tradition in which she firmly places herself with this wonderful story, "saving silver paper myself" (14).[14]

Works Cited

Atwood, Margaret. *Bluebeard's Egg*. Toronto: McClelland & Stewart, 1983.

———. *Bottle*. Hay: Hay Festival Press, 2004 [limited edition of 1,000 copies].

[11] Atwood in Sullivan, 37. On the mother's early gender influencing see also: "Margaret Killam Atwood was in the bush with her two small children providing Margaret with her first and strongest role model and defying her era's firmly established gender stereotypes" (Cooke, 49). "Because of her, I didn't grow up feeling that being female needed to mean having your feet bound. . . . When I was younger, say 10 or 11, I had fits of wishing that my mother was more average or at least looked better in hats. But I've since concluded that life doled out to me the perfect mother, although being the perfect mother was, I suspect, never one of her goals" (Atwood quoted in Cooke, 50–51).

[12] Successful fellow-writers like Alice Munro or Carol Shields stress a similar point.

[13] See also her stories "Death by Landscape" and "Weight" in *Wilderness Tips*.

[14] This article is dedicated to my mother, who turned 86 in October 2005, the month in which this article was written. Although she suffers from aphasia after a severe stroke in June 2002, she still tells me — or wants to tell me — stories all the time.

Atwood, Margaret. *Dancing Girls and Other Stories.* Toronto: McClelland & Stewart, 1977.

———. *Good Bones.* Toronto: Coach House Press, 1992.

———. "Great Aunts." In *Family Portraits: Remembrances by Twenty Distinguished Writers*, ed. Carolyn Anthony. New York: Doubleday, 1989. 1–16.

———. *Moral Disorder.* Toronto: McClelland & Stewart, 2006.

———. *Murder in the Dark: Short Fictions and Prose Poems.* Toronto: Coach House Press, 1983.

———. "Significant Moments in the Life of My Mother." In Atwood, *Bluebeard's Egg*, 11–29.

———. *Survival: A Thematic Guide to Canadian Literature.* Toronto: Anansi, 1972.

———. *The Tent.* Toronto/London/New York: McClelland & Stewart/ Bloomsbury/Nan A. Talese/Doubleday, 2006.

———. *Wilderness Tips.* London: Bloomsbury, 1991.

Cooke, Nathalie. *Margaret Atwood: A Biography.* Toronto: ECW Press, 1998.

Grace, Sherrill. "Atwood and the 'Autobiographical Pact.'" In *Margaret Atwood: The Open Eye*, ed. John Moss and Tobi Kozakewich. Ottawa: University of Ottawa Press, 2006. 121–34.

Nischik, Reingard M., ed. *Margaret Atwood: Works and Impact.* Rochester, NY/Toronto: Camden House/Anansi, 2000/2002.

———. "Margaret Atwood's Short Stories and Shorter Fictions." In *The Cambridge Companion to Margaret Atwood*, ed. Coral Ann Howells. Cambridge: Cambridge University Press, 2006. 145–60.

———. "Murder in the Dark: Margaret Atwood's Inverse Poetics of Intertextual Minuteness." In *Margaret Atwood's Textual Assassinations*, ed. Sharon Rose Wilson. Columbus: Ohio State University Press, 2003. 1–17.

Rosenman, Ellen Bayuk. A Room of One's Own: *Women Writers and the Politics of Creativity.* New York: Twayne, 1995.

Saline, Carol. "Margaret Atwood and Her Daughter, Margaret Atwood." In *Mothers and Daughters*, ed. Carol Saline and Sharon J. Wohlmuth. Toronto: Doubleday, 1997. 62–66.

Sullivan, Rosemary. *The Red Shoes: Margaret Atwood Starting Out.* Toronto: Harper Flamingo, 1998.

Williams, William Carlos. "The Red Wheelbarrow." In *The Norton Anthology of American Literature.* Vol. D, ed. Nina Baym. 6th ed. New York: Norton, 2003. 1271.

Woolf, Virginia. 1929. *A Room of One's Own.* Peterborough: Broadview, 2001.

25: "Southern Preacher": Leon Rooke, "The Woman Who Talked to Horses" (1984)

Nadja Gernalzick (University of Mainz)

LEON ROOKE WAS BORN in Roanoke Rapids, North Carolina, in 1934 and attended the University of North Carolina in the late 1950s and early 1960s. His Southern background as well as the similarities regarding the themes and techniques of his writing to, for instance, the work of Flannery O'Connor have led critics to count Rooke among the Southern writers of the United States. Yet while Rooke considers O'Connor's and other Southern writers' oeuvres part of his stylistic training (see Rooke in Hancock 1981, 116, 120), he refuses to be identified as a writer in this particular tradition because he does not want to be associated with Southern racial politics: "Then came the sixties. Martin Luther King singing 'We Shall Overcome' and a strong sense of too many in the older order singing 'You Shall Not.' And that did something to my sense of loyalty to the region. It took away some of the ghost's power" (Rooke in Hancock, 120).

Thus, having moved from the United States to Victoria, British Columbia, in 1969, Rooke has been more aptly described as "an American who has adopted the Canadian West Coast as his home" (Gadpaille 1988, 111); in 1981 he called himself "now Canadian" (Rooke in Hancock, 146). Rooke has since lived at various places in Canada. Nonetheless, when his writing is appropriated by a national literary tradition, Rooke — as a member of the large group of authors who have emigrated to Canada from all over the world since the 1960s — claims allegiance with an international standard: "The only tradition I dimly perceive is that one where we find the writer attempting to write well and knowing from the start the likelihood of failure. . . . And it is a territory without boundaries or borders, which is to say that it can be found anywhere" (Rooke in Hancock, 109). In accord also with recent redefinitions of Canadian identity, Rooke's literary work is therefore considered to have played "a crucial role in anticipating . . . a shift away from the nationalist paradigm of representation, based on recognizably Canadian themes and voices, to the current post-nationalist view of Canada as a pluralistic, multicultural and multiracial society" (Gorjup 1999, 269). This shift to a Canadian postnational or transnational cultural sensibility, frequently associated with the publication of Frank Davey's *Post-National Arguments: The Politics of the Anglophone-Canadian Novel since 1967* in 1993, was prefigured in 1985 in an observation by John Metcalf:

> You may be baffled by my insistence on the obvious but the obvious is not obvious to literary critics in Canada. Bear in mind that the most widely circulated anthology of Canadian stories — the *Penguin* book I mentioned earlier [Wayne Grady, ed. *The Penguin Book of Canadian Short Stories*, Harmondsworth: Penguin, 1980] — attempts to link Canadian stories with a tradition of Letters to the Editor of the *Pioneer Times and Daily Stump-Remover*. There are few critics in CanLit circles who could write perceptively on the texture of the stories of Hemingway, Lardner, Eudora Welty, Caroline Gordon, or Flannery O'Connor — and it is precisely these writers who are our influences. (Metcalf 1985, 49–50)

Rooke's writing career started in drama; he has written stage plays — for instance *Krokodile* (1973), *Sword/Play* (1974), and *The Coming* (1991) — as well as radio plays and screenplays. He has also written several novels, including *Fat Woman* (1982) and *The Fall of Gravity* (2000). Among the many awards he has received are the 1981 Canada-Australia Prize, the Pushcart Prize (1988), the North Carolina Award for Literature (1990), and the CBC Literary Prize (2003). *Shakespeare's Dog* (1985), his second novel, won the Governor General's Award, and *The Fall of Gravity* won the W. O. Mitchell Literary Prize of the Writers' Trust of Canada.

Rooke is mainly perceived as a "writer who has made an important contribution to the short-story tradition in Canada" (Gadpaille, 111). To date, he has published more than 300 short stories in magazines and in more than a dozen short-story collections, since 1977 mainly with Canadian publishing houses: *Last One Home Sleeps in the Yellow Bed* (1968), *Vault* (1973), *The Love Parlour* (1977), *The Broad Back of the Angel* (1977), *Cry Evil* (1980), *Death Suite* (1981), *The Birth Control King of the Upper Volta* (1982), *Sing Me No Love Songs I'll Say You No Prayers* (1984), *A Bolt of White Cloth* (1984), *How I Saved the Province* (1989), *The Happiness of Others* (1992), *Who Do You Love* (1992), *Muffins* (1995), *Oh! Twenty-seven Stories* (1997), *Painting the Dog: The Best Stories of Leon Rooke* (2001). In the 1970s, Rooke was also associated with the Montreal Story Tellers Fiction Performance Group, which was founded at the end of the 1960s. The Montreal Story Tellers feature John Metcalf, Clark Blaise, Hugh Hood, Ray Fraser, and Ray Smith and "are credited with helping to create an informed and appreciative audience for Canadian writing, and for making the Canada Council aware of the value of events involving visiting writers. Their fiction and performances had an exemplary effect on short fiction writing in the 1970s" (Whalen 2002,

752). Rooke's association with Metcalf also resulted in their joint editorship of many Canadian short-story anthologies since 1981, for example, *Best Canadian Short Stories 1981* (1981), *New Press Anthology* (1984), and the *Macmillan Anthology 1* (1988) through to the *Third Macmillan Anthology* (1990).

In her overview of the writers and traditions of the Canadian short story, Michelle Gadpaille locates the generative phase of Rooke's short fiction writing in his immensely creative period in Canada in the 1960s. "In the rush of new writing," Canada at that time saw the formation of "a new tradition that was widening out to include American post-modernist influences and other international trends" (Gadpaille, 99). Rooke's short-story oeuvre has been ranked among postmodernist works and is considered progressive rather than part of a Canadian realistic short-story tradition that was "largely regional and essentially conservative" (Gadpaille, 99). His metafictional pieces such as "Art" (1992) or "How to Write a Successful Short Story" (2002) are frequently quoted in support of his affirmation in 2003 that "Sure, I'm postmodern" (Rooke in Gorjup 2003, 54).

In particular, Rooke's style and technique are praised for a masterful use of voice and limited point of view. Rooke accounts for his use of voice as follows:

> I take the old-fashioned notion that one of the writer's jobs is to project a multitude of voices, of identities, and not simply to write of the self. . . . My conception of what a fiction writer ought to be is one who can move into and occupy all sorts of human frames — and take on all sorts of vastly opposed human voices. I find it peculiar that many writers are only willing to write out of one voice. (Rooke in Hancock, 108, 128)

There is usually no narrator with a third-person perspective or authorial omniscience in Rooke's stories, with the result that his characters often resemble characters on stage (see Gorjup 1999, 270). Fittingly, for Metcalf "Rooke's stories are essentially *performances.* He's an improviser, a jazz musician in prose" (Metcalf 1993, 147). In order to find short-fiction forms characteristic of manifold first-person narrators from the most varied social and ethnic backgrounds, Rooke occasionally draws on "bizarre vocabulary" and provides "unplaceable regional traits" when "enter[ing] fully into the persona of a character" (Gadpaille, 111). Since the authorial voice is dispensed with, however, Rooke's writing moves beyond localities and particularities into a postmodern, magic realism:

> While his characters embody life-styles and mind-sets that appear distinctively North American, they are less the product of specific historical, cultural, and social components than of the salient characteristics common to all human beings. Rooke's characters move effortlessly across vast spatial and temporal landscapes. They are . . . contemporary and ancient at the same time; they are both real and magical, existing in a world where

> there is no distinguishable demarcation between actuality and dreaming. (Gorjup 1999, 270)

Rooke's strong interest in moral issues and in the precariousness of distinctions between good and evil is aligned with his commitment to Gothicism. "Rooke's writing reveals discernible Gothic strains, mostly through its topography, which evokes the supernatural, the magical, the mysterious, the spectral, and the horrific, and through its characters, whose function is often formulaic, embodying the binary world of good and evil in a state of continuous crisis, riddled with obstacles" (Gorjup 1999, 270; see also Garebian, 41). Despite the appearance of demonic characters and the threat of damnation lending the stories their "fairy-tale motifs and structures" (Gadpaille, 111), the possibility of spiritual communion, love, and positive transformation always remains the implied horizon of Rooke's texts. These possibilities are supported by a sense of humor, as for instance in a recent project for which Rooke, as guest editor of *The New Quarterly* 86 (2003), invited submissions that all bore the title "Bad Men Who Love Jesus."

Regarding thematic dualities, the psychology of gender relations is also in the foreground of Rooke's interest: "Male writers such as Leon Rooke . . ., contemporary with feminism's second wave, are concerned with the possibilities for male identity and heterosexuality after feminism and after the decline of certain myths about what should be possible for men or with the exposure of those myths as damaging to both women and men" (Pennee 2002, 429). Rather than his male figures, however, Rooke's characterizations of women have been particularly noted. He explains the gender difference in his writing and his interest in women's voices as follows:

> It has seemed funny to me that I am interested more in my women characters than in my men. Most male writers are interested in writing about male characters. I may be wrong; I may have a total misreading of my own work, but I am also better at women characters. They simply interest me more. I don't really know why. I think I *understand* them better. I am attracted more to the female personality than I am to the male.
>
> There's one simple explanation for this. I grew up without a father. I just know women better. Or think I do. (Rooke in Hancock, 130)

In a later interview, however, Rooke answered the question about whether there was a difference between a male and a female voice negatively: "No, not a whit, where it matters. . . . The human heart in conflict with itself, to use Faulkner's phrase, is not exclusively one or the other" (Rooke in O'Brien, 302).

With "The Woman Who Talked to Horses" Rooke created a further variation on the theme of reciprocal and interdependent relations between the sexes. In this story, a male narrator eventually comes to know himself better through his conversation with a woman. Set on a horse farm in an unspecified place or country, the story may be generally associated with the

Canadian tradition of prairie writing (by Sinclair Ross or Frederick Philip Grove, for example). Themes typical of prairie fiction such as the indifference of nature, existential isolation, repressed emotions, alienation between husband and wife, and closeness of death do indeed feature in the story, yet they are conjugated and universalized from the point of view of a postmodern sensibility, including fantastic elements and solutions. Fusing neorealist and postmodernist elements, but also aligned with the tradition of the fantastic, "The Woman Who Talked to Horses" may well be considered a prime example of the contemporary Canadian short story as part of stylistic "crossover fiction" (Nischik in Groß/Klooß/Nischik 2005, 280).

"The Woman Who Talked to Horses" was first published in 1984 in Rooke's collection *Sing Me No Love Songs I'll Say You No Prayers: Selected Stories.*[1] The first-person narrator of "The Woman Who Talked to Horses" is George Gaddis, an owner of race horses, who has consulted an unnamed professional horse talker or "horse whisperer." He has called her to his ranch to help him with his horses, which, in his words, "[ha]ve been acting funny lately," "standoffish," and like "zombies" (106). The horse talker and Gaddis, however, eventually part in anger: Gaddis neither accepts the woman's professional authority nor is he willing to pay the fee she charges.

While they are speaking, Gaddis sees his wife Sarah at their nearby house angrily throwing a pot into the yard, followed by a bed pillow and a blanket. When they are alone again, Sarah eventually tells her husband to "stay away" and not to touch her (113). For the horse talker it is clear that Gaddis is "a distrusting person, a bullying one," and she suggests that his horses as well as his wife "have picked up these traits or are responding to them" (110). It is even implied that Gaddis physically abuses his wife when reference is made to a "little scratch on her forehead," which "had swollen some" since "last night" (112). At the end of the story, after the horse talker has left, the first-person narrator wonders what went wrong with his life and how he became "this bad person" (113). Hence, as a result of his confrontation with the horse talker, Gaddis experiences a sudden revelation

[1] Coral Ann Howells notes that the stories in the collection were all published before (Howells 1985, 165), yet the acknowledgements in the book do not credit a previous source for "The Woman Who Talked to Horses" nor does the bibliography of Rooke's works up to 1981 by J. R. (Tim) Struthers. The story was anthologized in 1990 in *Black Water 2: More Tales from the Fantastic*, edited by Alberto Manguel, as well as in both *The Oxford Book of Canadian Short Stories* of 1986 and *The New Oxford Book of Canadian Short Stories in English* of 1995, edited by Margaret Atwood and Robert Weaver; the latest collection in which "The Woman Who Talked to Horses" appeared is *Painting the Dog: The Best Stories of Leon Rooke* of 2001. The story, however, has not yet been discussed critically; in her review of *Sing Me No Love Songs I'll Say You No Prayers* Howells does not even mention the story.

of his own character, and the ending of the story suggests the possibility of a transformation for the better for him and his wife, as well as for his horses.

This ending comes as a surprise to the reader since throughout the conversation with the horse talker, Gaddis shows neither signs of doubts about the righteousness of his views nor any readiness for self-criticism. The horse talker — "all very feminine" — appears to him as "another one of those . . . who knew nothing about the real world but like to think they could tell you about horses. One of those grim, pitiful creatures who was forever saying to themselves and to each other, *I can relate to horses*" (105). He believes that the horse talker carries "some sort of chip around on her shoulder" and that she has "no use for men. One of *those* . . . " (109). The more clearly he sees that he is not going to win the discussion about her fee, the more aggressive he becomes. To him the horse talker is "one of those sanctified, scrubbed-out bitches who puts the dollar sign first" (111) and he is "tempted to step on her hand" (108). Eventually, after he cannot hold his own in the conversation, he is, as a last resort, even ready to fight her physically: "Go for the throat, I thought. Get them in the old jugular" (111).

The narrator's prejudices about women who refuse to act deferentially are further expressed through his limited point of view and subjective interpretation of the situation. In the narrator's perception, the horse talker bears Mephistophelian characteristics — a female demon bringing strife and misfortune to his home. He describes her as a she-devil or a witch bargaining for his soul. Throughout the story, statements such as "I didn't invite myself, Mr. Gaddis. You invited me" (107) seem to point to a demonic subtext. It is suggested that Gaddis feels as if he cannot rid himself of the devil upon whom he has called.

Many details support this subtext. The woman wears black britches (106), paws the ground with her foot (104, 105), and is "emaciated" (105), evoking medieval depictions of Satan as a scrawny figure with a horseshoe; she drives "a low convertible, red and shining and new" (111), "throwing up dust behind her and over the white fence" (112), calling up the image of hellfire. Her mocking laughter eerily resounds, and Gaddis believes he hears her "cackling, giving full rein to her pleasure" (112). Moreover, she communicates with the horses by "ESP," by extra-sensory perception, or "something like that" (110). The devil in the shape of a woman confounds Gaddis and also, in his view, tempts him sexually:

> For no reason at all this woman suddenly squatted down on her legs and began rooting through the thin grass with her long fingers. I couldn't make it out. I couldn't tell whether she was searching for rock or flower or clover, or for nothing at all. Maybe she had dropped a nickel. I had no idea what the hell she was doing. I moved a little closer. I was tempted to step on her hand. Her blouse ballooned out and I could see down her neckline to her breasts. She wasn't wearing any brassiere.
>
> Maybe that's why she was kneeling there. (108)

Another instance when the horse talker is associated with a devil is the moment in the story when she loses her self-control: Gaddis involuntarily demonstrates a lack of respect for mortality, so that by implication he would also have no fear of the devil. He mocks the horse talker about a young horse from Quebec which he expects to "talk French":

> "That filly I got from Quebec," I said, "she'd be speaking French, I suppose? *J'ai la mort dans mon â[me], j'ai la mort dans mon â[me], mon cœur se tend comme un lourd fardeau.*"
>
> She [the horse talker] spun and stared directly at me, her face burning. (110)

Gaddis sings the refrain of a French-Canadian folk song, and the apparent overreaction of the horse talker to this provocation indicates that rather than to the sarcasm about the French-talking horse, she is reacting sensitively to the meaning of the lyrics. The lyrics tell of a poor, grieving soul (French "â[me]" — the text only spells "â" since Gaddis apparently cannot pronounce the word "soul" in the presence of the devil), by implication Gaddis himself, and the horse talker responds to them as the devil might be expected to react when mocked about his practice of buying souls and of consorting with dead souls.

Finally, the narrator's vocabulary aligns both his wife and the horse talker with hell and death. The house, identified with Sarah, appears lifeless and like a tomb:

> Up at the house Sarah had all the doors and windows shut up tight and outside not a hint of wind was stirring. Even the grass wasn't growing. It seemed to me all the life had gone out of that house. It looked dumb and impenetrable and cold. . . . Sarah had closed the screen door, then she'd closed the cedar door behind it. It was quiet as a tomb in there. (106, 109)

In addition, Gaddis describes the horses and Sarah as "zombielike" (108): he feels surrounded by the living dead. His anger that his horses are "not producing" (106), in the sense of not making money on the race track, is paralleled by the fact that there are no children around; the couple apparently does not have any offspring. Therefore, the coldness and death Gaddis associate with Sarah suggests that he attributes frigidity and infertility to her, again aligning her with supernatural beings such as witches, who in traditional lore are held to be sterile.[2]

[2] In several respects, the story's theme of fertility as well as its figure of the ambiguously demonic intruder into a marriage are a reversal of the same theme and figure in Rooke's story "Sing Me No Love Songs I'll Say You No Prayers," published in the same collection of 1984.

The horse talker, in a scene that marks the turning point in the conversation and in the story, attributes a lack of manhood and virility, perhaps even impotence, to Gaddis when she negatively compares him to his stallion:

> "Go on," I said. "Get out of here."
>
> She wasn't listening to me. She seemed, for the moment, unaware of my presence. She was attuned to something else. Her jaw dropped open — not prettily . . . she *was* a pretty woman — her brows went up, she grinned, and a second later her face broke out into a full-fledged smile. Then a good solid laugh.
>
> She had a nice laugh. It was the only time since her arrival that I had liked her.
>
> "What is it?" I asked.
>
> "Your stallion," she said. "Egorinski, is that his name? He was telling me a joke. Not very flattering to you."
>
> Her eyes sparkled. She was genuinely enjoying herself. I looked over at Egor. The damned beast had his rear end turned to me. His head, too. He seemed to be laughing.
>
> She got her car started again and slapped it up into first gear. "I shall send you a bill for my time," she said. "Good-bye, Mr. Gaddis." (112)

The horse talker infers from the way Gaddis responds to her and from what she observes about the relationship between Gaddis and Sarah that his rude behavior might keep the marriage from being happy as well as reproductive. The name of the stallion — Egorinski — may be read as a play on "ego" and as a hint that Gaddis's selfishness and his insecurity about his manhood and about the productivity of both his horses and his wife are at the root of his problems. He represses his self-doubts and instead turns aggressively against the women in whose presence his insecurities surface. The power of the irrational — such as in talking to horses — and of the repressed, when it confronts him in the shape of the horse talker, is then rationalized in Gaddis's mind by identifying her with the devil; in this way, he also avoids acknowledgement of his own responsibility for the situation. By means of the descriptions from the first-person narrator's limited perspective, the reader begins to see Gaddis as unable to relate to the other sex, to admit the force of feelings and of the irrational, to acknowledge his insecurity, or — as a sort of "Hemingway Man" — to take a self-critical and humorous approach to the values stipulated by codes of manhood. Moreover, he apparently needs to compensate for a lack of education — marked by his faulty grammar — when face-to-face with the very eloquent horse talker. Yet because in the scene with the stallion he can neither ignore the horse talker's laugh nor the implied truth of the joke, he at last seems baffled and shaken in his self-complacency: " 'I'll have to think about this,' I said. 'I don't know if any of it makes any sense' " (111). His belief in a system of male superiority has been challenged.

At the center of the story's gender conflict and power struggles between the sexes is the question of distribution and allotment of time. The issue not only surfaces with respect to the theme of death and procreation, but also in the basic economics of the horse talker's "fee structures" and of the money Gaddis is asked to pay. In response to Gaddis's concern about his expenses and his feeling that he is wasting his time (105), the horse talker, too, concludes: " 'We are getting nowhere, . . . and my time is valuable' " (110). Her last words again refer to the question of value and temporality: " 'I shall send you a bill for my time' " (112). The relation between the sexes is constructed here as a fundamentally antagonistic one, with the implication that both experience their interaction as a loss of personal time rather than as rewarding. If Gaddis and his wife had a more harmonious relationship, the story suggests, time would work *for* them rather than appear scarce and empty. Moreover, Gaddis's reflections before his final insight into his personality paradoxically turn on time of waiting and time of fulfillment: "I could see now wasn't the time. That the time hadn't come. That maybe it would be a long time before it did" (113). The optimistic stance the story eventually takes towards gender relations and heterosexual desire is contained in the suggestion that a time of fulfillment of desire and of harmony between the sexes is promised, that this fulfillment is worth waiting for, and that the way to reach it is through self-investigation, self-improvement, and patience. As such, the story is also strongly supportive of Christian ethics, and, hence, an instance of what according to Metcalf has become characteristic of Rooke's short fiction: "structures that tend toward the parable or exemplum" (Metcalf 1993, 148).

In the final analysis, however, because of the restricted, first-person narrative perspective, the seemingly positive ending of the story remains ambiguous and its gender critique hard to pin down. When Gaddis admits his shortcomings by calling himself a "bad person," this self-designation and evaluation is strongly relativized by the structure of the story and its narrative technique. On the one hand, the horse talker has made it clear to Gaddis that he is to blame for the behavior of his horses and his wife, and that he is a "bad person" in the moral sense of being prejudiced and aggressive. On the other hand, in Gaddis's limited view that associates the horse talker with evil, the devil herself has made him recognize his badness, so that he may still consider himself deceived and disregard his insight as the devil's insinuation of self-doubt. The reader is left to choose: if the reader takes the horse talker's and Sarah's side, Gaddis's bullying behavior might be seen as responsible for the deterioration of his relations with his wife and his horses. If the reader, however, takes the narrator's side, Gaddis might be pitied for being confronted with the women's and horses' antagonistic attitudes, and the women might be considered the ones who act in an uncooperative way, thus inciting Gaddis's anger. By its potential for ambiguity the story exemplifies what Rooke has declared his goal in composing short stories: "a dramatic, uplifting conclusion for those who require reaffirmation of life's essential qualities — essential possibilities, hope, affection's penny's worth — while providing for others sobering suspicion that *life — the story!* — may not be quite what it seems" (Rooke 1982, 261). It is up to the individual reader to decide whether the first-person narrator of the story is reliable or unreliable and which position to take in the spectrum of possible gender codes and gender politics.

Rooke has repeatedly declared his preference for such a narrative structure: "I don't like resolving situations because most situations are not resolved. I like the open ending. I like the reader to say, 'This is the ending,' and the other reader to say, 'No, this is the ending.' I like to leave a situation poised like that" (Rooke in Hancock, 133). His use of a voice that effects the reader's participation and a deferral of closure has led critics to count Rooke as a postmodern author. The extension and subversion of realism through the characters of the talking horses and through the Mephistophelian subtext and its rewriting of Christian mythology are also postmodern features of this story. Yet clearly, and in contrast to frequent criticism of postmodernist texts, the relativism of the narrative structure and the lack of closure is not to be confused with a moral relativism of the author or even of the text. Similar to, for instance, Mordecai Richler in this respect, Rooke sees his task as an author in preparing and offering stories that confront readers with moral issues and allow them to refine their ethics: "One of the functions of literature is to change society. To change the way people think. To redress grievances. To mould society, to pace out, confirm, and secure certain desired directions. I'm a stoop-shouldered moralist" (Rooke in Hancock, 114). Or, in Metcalf's words: "Rooke is a southern preacher, the Rev. Jesse Jackson or Martin Luther King of stories" (Metcalf 1993, 147).

Works Cited

Davey, Frank. *Post-National Arguments: The Politics of the Anglophone-Canadian Novel since 1967.* Toronto: University of Toronto Press, 1993.

Gadpaille, Michelle. *The Canadian Short Story.* Toronto: Oxford University Press, 1988.

Garebian, Keith. *Leon Rooke and His Works.* Toronto: ECW Press, n.y. [after 1987].

Gorjup, Branko. "Lingering on Posted Land: An Interview with Leon Rooke." *World Literature Today* 77.1 (April/June 2003): 49–56.

Gorjup, Branko. "Perseus and the Mirror: Leon Rooke's Imaginary Worlds." *World Literature Today* 73.2 (Spring 1999): 269–74.

Groß, Konrad, Wolfgang Klooß, and Reingard M. Nischik, eds. *Kanadische Literaturgeschichte.* Stuttgart: Metzler, 2005.

Hancock, Geoff. "An Interview with Leon Rooke." *Canadian Fiction Magazine* 38 (1981): 107–33 [special issue on Leon Rooke].

Howells, Coral Ann. "The Gaiety of Dread: Review of *Sing Me No Love Songs I'll Say You No Prayers.*" *Canadian Literature* 105 (Summer 1985): 165–66.

Metcalf, John. "The Curate's Egg." *Zeitschrift für Kanada-Studien* 5.1 (1985): 43–59.

———. "Leon Rooke." In *Canadian Classics: An Anthology of Short Stories*, ed. John Metcalf and J. R. (Tim) Struthers. Toronto: McGraw-Hill Ryerson, 1993. 147–49.

O'Brien, Peter. "Leon Rooke." *So to Speak: Interviews with Contemporary Canadian Writers.* Montreal: Véhicule Press, 1987. 285–308.

Pennee, Donna Palmateer. "Gender and Gender Relations." In *Encyclopedia of Literature in Canada*, ed. William H. New. Toronto: University of Toronto Press, 2002. 425–30.

Rooke, Leon. "Art." In Rooke, *Painting the Dog*, 115–20.

———. *The Birth Control King of the Upper Volta.* Downsview, ON: ECW Press, 1982.

———. *A Bolt of White Cloth.* Don Mills, ON: Stoddart, 1984.

———. *The Broad Back of the Angel.* New York: Fiction Collective, 1977.

———. *Cry Evil.* Ottawa: Oberon, 1980.

———. *Death Suite.* Downsview, ON: ECW Press, 1981.

———. "Early Obscenities in the Life of the World's Foremost Authority on Heidegger." In Rooke, *Painting the Dog*, 53–64.

———. *The Happiness of Others.* Erin, ON: The Porcupine's Quill Press, 1991.

———. *How I Saved the Province.* Lantzville, BC: Oolichan, 1989.

———. "How to Write a Successful Short Story." *The Antioch Review* 60.3 (Summer 2002): 367–76.

———. *Last One Home Sleeps in the Yellow Bed: Stories by Leon Rooke.* Baton Rouge: Louisiana State University Press, 1968.

———. *The Love Parlour.* Ottawa: Oberon, 1977.

———. *Muffins.* Erin, ON: The Porcupine's Quill Press, 1995.

———. *Oh! Twenty-seven Stories.* n.p.: Exile Editions, 1997.

———. *Painting the Dog: The Best Stories of Leon Rooke.* Toronto: Thomas Allen, 2001.

———. *Sing Me No Love Songs I'll Say You No Prayers: Selected Stories.* New York: Echo, 1984.

———. "Sing Me No Love Songs I'll Say You No Prayers." In Rooke, *Sing Me No Love Songs*, 193–226.

———. *Vault.* Chapel Hill, NC: Lillabulero, 1973.

Rooke, Leon. "Voices." In *Making It New: Contemporary Canadian Short Stories*, ed. John Metcalf. Toronto: Methuen, 1982. 257–61.

———. *Who Do You Love*. Toronto: McClelland & Stewart, 1992.

———. "The Woman Who Talked to Horses." In Rooke, *Sing Me No Love Songs*, 104–13.

Struthers, J. R. (Tim). "A Preliminary Bibliography of Works by Leon Rooke." *Canadian Fiction Magazine* 38 (1981): 148–64 [special issue on Leon Rooke].

Whalen, Terry. "Montreal Story Tellers Fiction Performance Group." In *Encyclopedia of Literature in Canada*, ed. William H. New. Toronto: University of Toronto Press, 2002. 751–52.

26: Nativeness as Third Space: Thomas King, "Borders" (1991)

Eva Gruber (University of Constance)

THOMAS KING'S LIFE IS as multifaceted as his oeuvre, reflecting mythic and postmodern, classic and popular, Native oral and Western literary influences. Born in Sacramento, California, in 1943 to a Cherokee father and a Greek-German mother, King held various jobs (as a photojournalist in Australia and New Zealand, bank teller, ambulance driver, and tool designer for Boeing Aircraft) before pursuing a career as an academic and writer. After graduating from Chico State College he joined the doctoral program and later worked at the University of Utah, but then moved to Canada, where he taught at the University of Lethbridge between 1980 and 1989. It was during this time that King had his most extensive contacts with Native people (Cree and Blackfoot on the surrounding reserves), experiences that influenced much of his writing. He returned to the United States for a position as an associate professor of American and Native Studies at the University of Minnesota (1989–95), but eventually settled in Canada. King currently teaches English and Creative Writing at the University of Guelph, Ontario, and is a senior fellow of Massey College at the University of Toronto.

King's works to date comprise two volumes of short fiction (*One Good Story, That One*, 1993, and *A Short History of Indians in Canada*, 2005), five novels (*Medicine River*, 1989; *Green Grass, Running Water*, 1993, nominated for the prestigious Governor General's Award for Fiction and winner of the Canadian Authors' Award for Fiction; *Truth and Bright Water*, 1999; under the pen name of Hartley GoodWeather: *DreadfulWater Shows Up*, 2002, and *The Red Power Murders: A DreadfulWater Mystery*, 2006, two Native detective stories), and, finally, two children's books. In addition, King, who is considered to be Canada's foremost Native writer, edited one of the first collections of short fiction by Canadian Native writers, *All My Relations: An Anthology of Contemporary Canadian Native Fiction* in 1990. He also collaborated closely with the CBC, providing a number of film and radio scripts (for the most part based on his own fictional works) and designing and participating in the widely popular CBC radio show *The Dead Dog Café Comedy Hour* (1996–2001). King's critical essays and scholarly work on Native writing appeared in journals such as *World Literature Written in*

English (*WLWE*), *Multi-Ethnic Literature of the United States (MELUS)*, *Hungry Mind Review*, and *Western American Literature*, and together with Helen Hoy and Cheryl Calver he edited *The Native in Literature: Canadian and Comparative Perspectives* (1987). In 2003, King was selected as the first Massey lecturer of Native descent. The published version of his lectures, *The Truth About Stories: A Native Narrative*, was awarded the 2003 Ontario Trillium Book Award for English language prose.

"Borders" was first published in *Saturday Night* in 1991 and was later included in *One Good Story, That One* (1993). In addition to the pieces in his two story collections, King's stories and poems have appeared in various magazines and have been widely anthologized — "Borders" alone has been reprinted in twelve anthologies to date. His talents work across various media, and many of his stories have been produced as film or radio dramas, with King providing the scripts ("Borders" was the basis for a CBC radio drama in 1993 and a teleplay directed by Gil Cardinal, aired in 1996 in the CBC "Four Directions" series, on which King served as story editor).

King's short-story oeuvre ranges from stories in a predominantly realistic style about contemporary Native everyday life to wildly fantastic, mythic tales with a strong traditional foundation and a timeless setting. While "Borders" and the father-and-son story "Trap Lines," for example, are clearly located at the realistic end of the spectrum, others of King's stories mix contemporary settings with fantastic, surrealistic, or supernatural elements ("Totem" features a singing, re-growing totem pole, "A Short History of Indians in Canada" presents readers with flying Indians), or make extended use of intertextuality ("A Seat in the Garden" parodies the novel and film *A Field of Dreams*) and elements from science fiction ("How Corporal Colin Sterling Saved Blossom, Alberta, and Most of the Rest of the World" includes blue alien coyotes in space ships, and "Where the Borg Are" amalgamates commentary on Canadian Indian policy with elements from *Star Trek*. Furthermore, his stories rework traditional Native tales ("The One About Coyote Going West") or Western master narratives ("One Good Story, That One," a witty, indigenized retelling of the Book of Genesis). King's style too covers a wide spectrum. While some of the stories are told in a conventional narrative mode with an authorial or a first-person narrator, others — markedly those which refer to traditional ideas and materials — display a distinctly "oral" style (what King calls "interfusional" writing, 1990). Inspired by Okanagan storyteller Harry Robinson (see King in Canton 1998, 94–95), King in these "voice pieces" manages to recreate an oral storytelling mode by "rendering the rhythms and syntax of spoken Native English on the page, complete with pauses for breath and dramatic impact" (van Toorn 2004, 36).

Just like Coyote, the Native trickster par excellence — illustrations of whom King's first short-story collection uses to separate the different stories from each other on the page, and who also dances through several of

King's stories and the novel *Green Grass, Running Water* as a character — King both as a person and as a writer blurs boundaries, crosses borders, and defies categorizations (see Davidson/Walton/Andrews 2003, "Introduction: Whose Borders?"), both literally and figuratively. Of mixed Native and European descent, moving in Western and Native spheres, and a citizen of both the USA and Canada, King transcends racial, cultural, and national/territorial categorizations as he blurs the lines between the disciplines in his creative work in writing, photography, film, and radio. Questioned about the problematic description "Canadian Native author" (the Cherokee are not a Canadian tribe), he explains that "that becomes a problem only if you recognize the particular political line which runs between Canada and the US, and if you agree with the assumptions that that line makes" (King in Lutz 1991, 107).

This liminal, in-between position occupied by King in various respects leaves a clear imprint on his work, simultaneously affording him a view from the inside and the outside of otherwise clearly delineated spheres. He crosses between the realm of the empirically sound and that of wild imagination, between the natural and the supernatural, between Western written and Native oral modes of telling, but also between "reality" and fiction in general by incorporating historical personages and events into imaginary plots and settings. King's stories, like their author, do not always remain within conventional confines and delineations, but in some cases defy not only most readers' expectations about Native writing, but also those about the short-story's formal cohesion and consistency. Interweaving and combining various narrative strands and subplots into more complex (sometimes mise-en-abymic and metafictional) patterns, King's writing challenges genre conventions and subverts and deconstructs canonical narratives by alluding to or intertextually integrating them into a new, Native-centered context. Yet King's stories manage to create a specific impact and "tend to concentrate powerfully on a single effect," leading Teresa Gibert to conclude that "short fiction is particularly well suited to [King's] gifts and needs alike. . . . Its brevity does not constitute a limitation for him, since it helps him to enhance the deep impression he wants to make on his readers" (Gibert 2001, 76).

Finally, King continuously transcends customary demarcations between the serious and hilarious, considering himself a serious writer who uses humor as a strategy, a "subversive weapon" to ambush his readers (Atwood 1990, 244), to "get them laughing so they really don't feel how hard you hit them" (King in Canton, 96). In the best trickster tradition, truth enters laughing when King smashes racist notions and addresses past and contemporary injustices and discrimination with Native humor, wittily subverting Western assumptions of White superiority. He parodies, questions, and disrupts established master narratives, Eurocentric epistemologies, and conventional historiography, and instead creates complex First Nations characters and plots, that is true "alterNatives" (Drew Hayden Taylor) to the well-established literary and popular stereotypes of "the Indian" and to one-dimensional Western romances. With stories like "Borders," King therefore does what the storyteller in "One Good Story, That One," the collection's title story, likes best but is never asked to do: avoiding the cliché-laden, tragic, and mythologically over-determined nineteenth-century images so firmly lodged in the non-Native (and sometimes also in the Native) imagination, he tells stories that focus on "ordinary" contemporary Native life, on today's "comic survivors" (Gerald Vizenor's description of the trickster in Coltelli 1990, 164).

"Borders" tells the story of a Blackfoot mother and son from Alberta who set out to visit family across the border in Salt Lake City, Utah. They get trapped in Western nationalistic concepts of identity at the border when the mother proclaims her citizenship as Blackfoot rather than Canadian or American. Thus caught in the no-man's land between the American and the Canadian border stations because neither country accepts Blackfoot as a nationality (the Blackfoot nation is split by the US–Canadian border, with part of them living on either side), she refuses to give in to White domination and tenaciously clings to her Blackfoot identity. It is only when Mel, the owner of a convenience store situated between the borders, calls in the media, which start to exert pressure on the authorities, that mother and son are eventually allowed to continue on their way.

The story is presented in retrospect as a first-person narration by the woman's son, who mainly describes events at the border, but also on several occasions recalls the time when his sister Laetitia was still living with the family on the reserve. Within this narrative framework, established in the initial sentence, "When I was twelve, maybe thirteen . . ." (132), the narrator restricts himself to recollecting his perceptions of the time without adding comments or explanations that would exceed his adolescent perspective, his former self thus acting as the sole focalizer. This mode of telling, in addition to its inherently comic aspects — such as the narrator's marked fixation on food, his willingness to consider being stuck in no-man's land "as much an adventure as an inconvenience" (141), the deliberately unpretentious language, and his familiar way of addressing the reader with tags like "I can tell you that" (136) or "you know" (140) — conveys the narrator's limited insight into and lack of understanding for his mother's and sister's motivations at the time. He would have readily declared Canadian citizenship (137), he tells us, and cannot understand his sister Laetitia's anger when their mother finds out about her plans to move to Salt Lake City (141). The resulting uninvolved, almost detached narrative style for the most part naïvely reports rather than interprets, intentionally leaving the latter task to the readers. These, consequently, have to infer things from the bits of information they are presented with, and draw their own connections and conclusions rather than being told explicitly, especially so since much of the story unmediatedly renders dialogue between the characters (whom we get to know almost exclusively through this device, descriptions being scarce).

Dialogue and communication in general — especially communication gone awry — play a substantial role within the story. This is most obvious among the family members, whose contrapuntal conversations sometimes read more like alternately juxtaposed monologues, as in the following conversation between mother and daughter:

> "This is real lousy coffee."
> "You're just angry because I want to see the world."
> "It's the water. From here on down, they got lousy water."
> "I can catch the bus from Sweetgrass. You don't have to lift a finger."
> "You're going to have to buy your water in bottles if you want good coffee." (132)

The apparent lack of effort towards understanding, at one point accentuated by the mother's use of Blackfoot while her daughter answers in English (133), also shows when the mother attempts to pass on stories from the oral tradition to her son. He obviously does not quite understand the stories or the purpose of their telling, but he does not really seem to care, either (142). King's depiction of the scenario amalgamates a universal teenage disinterest in traditional values with the more specifically Native issue of the precarious nature of the oral tradition. Finally, the narrator's sparsely naïve rendering of the Native characters' conversations — be it Laetitia's boyfriend Lester telling her tall tales about Salt Lake City, Laetitia claiming that she will leave for the United States, or the mother recounting her daughter's American success story to her neighbor — sheds a questionable light on the reliability of the information gained from and the intentions stated by the characters.

Even more important than among the Native characters, though, is the role communication plays between the protagonist's Native mother and the white people she encounters, especially the border authorities. The border guards on both sides first try to ignore the woman's assertion of Blackfoot citizenship and start the conversation anew, pretending that the previous declaration never happened (135, 138). Realizing her tenacity, however, the American border guard calls it "a little misunderstanding" (136) and launches into an explanation about legal matters, whereas the Canadian official, in an attempt at political correctness and diplomacy, patronizingly signals understanding, but nevertheless does not accommodate the woman's cultural needs:

> "Citizenship?"
> "Blackfoot."
> "I know," said the woman, "and I'd be proud of being Blackfoot if I were Blackfoot. But you have to be American or Canadian." (138–39)

As in his novel *Green Grass, Running Water*, King plays with stereotypes about all the groups involved, Americans, Canadians, and Native North Americans. In the brief exchange just quoted, it is Canada's proverbial politeness and supposedly more liberal attitude towards its Native population — often depicted in official representations as just another happy fragment in Canada's idealized multicultural mosaic — that is being mocked. The narrator tells us that Carol, the Canadian officer, actually "seemed happy to see [them]," and engages them in "a nice conversation" (138). Still, the outcome remains the same as at the US border — they are not allowed to pass, the incident blatantly exposing the narrow limits of Canada's alleged liberalism and multicultural tolerance. Further highlighting Canada's hypocrisy concerning its past and present Native policy, King symbolically replaces the hard wooden bench on which the travelers are made to wait for an hour in the American border station (136) with a comfortable couch and magazines to pass the time in the Canadian border station (139, 140) — but eventually has them sent back, nonetheless, when they are not willing to comply with Canadian law. King thus on the one hand draws attention to how both countries have participated in the destruction of and ongoing discrimination against Native cultures; on the other hand, this alludes to the fact that in both nations Native people are still waiting for outstanding land claims, settlements, and rights to self-government. In particular, King subverts Canada's tendency to conceptualize itself as a "post-colonial" state, that is, "as historically vulnerable to the controlling whims of Britain and the United States, reinforcing the perception that Canada is not responsible for its own imperialising actions" (Davidson/Walton/ Andrews, 156) but merely an innocent participant.

Still, avoiding the trap of simplistic or polemic depictions, and underlining the omnipresent universal tendency to rely on stereotypical conceptualizations, King's tongue-in-cheek narrative shows to what extent Canada's image of itself as "the nicer nation" is internalized even by the story's Native characters. The young protagonist comments on the Alberta/Montana border towns' names:

> Just hearing the names of these towns, you would expect that Sweetgrass, which is *a nice name* and sounds like it is related to other places such as Medicine Hat and Moose Jaw and Kicking Horse Pass, would be on the Canadian side, and that Coutts, *which sounds abrupt and rude*, would be on the American side. But this was not the case. (134, italics added)

While this opinionated attitude might be expected from the young and impressionable narrator, the internalization becomes even more obvious by the fact that the narrator's mother, who unyieldingly insists on her Blackfoot identity, nonetheless displays a strong (and rather typically Canadian) aversion towards America and Americans. Not only does she complain about the allegedly "lousy water" (132) in the States, she actually dresses up for her trip across the border because she does not want herself and the boy "crossing the border looking like Americans" (133). And even though her strong dislike for Canada's southern neighbor could also be a projection originating from the failed relationship to the children's (absent) American father, who is mentioned only once at the beginning of the story, one can detect a certain pride in Canada when she highlights the country's positive features to counter her daughter's enthusiasm about Salt Lake City (137). King thus draws attention to the reductive and polemic nature of clichés and stereotypes in general, regardless of their orientation or subject matter.

This also becomes apparent in King's allusions to America's most potent machinery of self-conceptualization, Hollywood, the importance of which in creating the image of "the Indian" can hardly be overestimated. Questioned by the Canadian border guard about where she comes from and where she is headed for, the mother answers both questions with "Standoff" (138), referring, literally, to Stand Off, Alberta (also spelled Standoff), a small town near the Blood reserve close to Lethbridge; at the same time, however, her answer alludes to the confrontation between Native and white cultures going on at both of the border stations, the double entendre parodically evoking the "Cowboys vs. Indians" imagery of Hollywood Westerns. Intensifying this impression, the American border guards are described as "swaying back and forth like two *cowboys* headed for a bar *or a gunfight*" (135, italics added) as they walk towards the Native travelers' car. The repeated mention of the guards' weapons completes this picture — the guard who eventually has to let them pass does so with "his thumbs [jammed] into his gun belt . . ., his fingers patting the butt of the revolver" (144; the fact that only the American guards' weapons are mentioned may allude to Canada's far more restrictive weapon laws and the American gun craze).

Through his protagonist's observations, King provides his readers with a sharp and witty view on how the two countries that divide the North American continent among themselves see and represent themselves. It is particularly the Native characters' position of being "in between" that affords the reader this unusual perspective. They are part of both countries through their ties to the historical Blackfoot territory extending to both sides of the border, and part of neither, since they consider themselves neither American nor Canadian in terms of nationality. Their situation of being caught in no-man's land between two countries thus can be read as a "literalization of liminality" (Wyile 1999, 120), epitomizing Victor Turner's concept of a transitional space or phase that exists at the interface or intersection between, but at the same time outside of, two cultures or stages, a space where established paradigms become meaningless and hierarchies are leveled. As Davidson/ Walton/ Andrews propose, "being inside/outside the borders allows for an understanding of what the borders are delineating, at the same time that it allows for a critique of their seeming stability" (17), an effect that the readers experience when they take on the Native perspective on the 49th parallel which is offered in the story. Simultaneously, however, the incident most graphically exemplifies the marginalization that Native people experience at the fringes of the two major North American societies, since it is only within the narrowly defined space between the borders that the Blackfoot woman can identify exclusively as Blackfoot without being sanctioned.

The border between Canada and the USA is a recurring subject in King's and other Native authors' writing, appearing, in addition to the story discussed here, in *Green Grass, Running Water* and most prominently in *Truth and Bright Water*, a novel set in two border towns in Canada and the United States that are separated only by a river and the 49th parallel. Echoing Ambrose Bierce's definition of boundary — "in political geography, [it is] an imaginary line between two nations, separating the imaginary rights of one from the imaginary rights of the other" (quoted in New 1998, 6) — King explains his view of the border in an interview:

> I guess I'm supposed to say that I believe in the line that exists between the US and Canada, but for me it's an imaginary line. It's a line from someone else's imagination; it's not my imagination. It divided people like the Mohawk into Canadian Mohawks and US Mohawks. They're the same people. It divided the Blackfoot who live in Browning from the Blackfoot who live at Standoff, for example. So the line is a political line, that border line. It wasn't there before the Europeans came. It was a line that was inscribed across the country after that. (King in Rooke 1990, 72)

Even while calling the border an imaginary line, however, King is nevertheless aware of and frequently describes the very real effects this demarcation has on the lives of contemporary Native people. And while in "Borders" the degrading experience is to some extent "sugarcoated" by King's use of humor, others of his fictional accounts — that concerning the racism experienced by Amos Frank and his family at the hands of USA customs in *Green Grass, Running Water*, for example — deny the reader such comic relief. The declaration of citizenship, which for one side involved in the exchange is a mere "legal technicality," a measure that according to the border guards' euphemistic explanation simply "helps [them] keep track of the visitors [they] get from the various countries" (136), means much more for the "Other" side. Thus, despite its humorous tone, King's story underlines the fact that all interaction at this border takes place in a climate of asymmetrical power relations and often involves discriminating and degrading practices.

Consequently, regardless of the mother's inclination towards Canada and her obvious aversion to the USA, her unwillingness to accept the border that today divides what North America's Native people refer to as "Turtle Island" into separate states is clear from the very beginning, finding expression even in her body language. She "stiffen[s] up" (133) whenever her son mentions that they could visit his sister Laetitia in the United States; and when she finally makes up her mind to do so, she approaches the border in a most telling manner: "My mother straightened the dress across her thighs, leaned against the wheel, and drove all the way to the border in first gear, slowly, as if she were trying to see through a bad storm or riding high on black ice" (134). Her almost tangible reluctance makes it obvious that she foresees problems of the kind she will encounter, and that for her much more than a formality to "keep [their] records straight" (135) is at stake. To gain entrance into either territory beyond, she is required to submit herself to the system of mapping and categorization dictated by today's Western nation states that impose imperialist demarcations on previously Native territory; consequently, to comply with the border guards' request for her will mean implicitly acknowledging and accepting White dominance.

This story about a woman's refusal to compromise her Blackfoot identity takes place at the border between two countries that have vastly different concepts of their respective national identity, which gives the story a particularly sardonic twist. Whereas Canadians in general are terrified of being mistaken for Americans, and therefore eagerly assert their fragile Canadian identity, the Blackfoot mother shares neither this Canadian urge to emphasize and define one's identity nor the American self-assured leisurely neglect of the subject, signaled within the story, for example, by the American border guard's remark that "everyone who crosses our border has to declare their citizenship. *Even Americans*" (136, italics added). For her, being Blackfoot is "all she understands herself as — and it's the outside world that is unwilling and unable to see her as that" (King in Canton, 91), a position also expressed in her son's reaction to being questioned "about how it felt to be an Indian without a country. I told them we had a nice house on the reserve and that my cousins had a couple of horses we rode when we went fishing" (142–43). As this unobtrusive claim to both Blackfoot territory and identity illustrates, King, in addition to his use of allusion, imagery, and humorous subversion, introduces some of the story's central issues rather obliquely by instrumentalizing the narrator's presumed naïvety in the manner outlined at the beginning of this analysis. The boy's clumsy account of his mother's attempt to pass on stories from the oral tradition — "She was serious about it, too. She'd tell [the stories] slow, repeating parts as she went, as if she expected me to remember each one" (142) — on the surface reveals as little insight into her motivations as his assessment of Mel's emotional compliment to his mother upon receiving a hat she brought back for him as a souvenir from Salt Lake City: "Mel was a funny guy. He took the hat and blew his nose and told my mother that she was an inspiration to us all" (144). The narrator gives himself away, however — and with it one of the story's core issues, namely the importance of pride in Native identity and traditions — when upon realizing that his mother will not give in and declare her citizenship according to either country's rules, he abruptly declares that "Pride is a good thing to have, you know. Laetitia had a lot of pride, and so did my mother. I figured that someday, I'd have it, too" (140).

This strength inherent in the continuance of Native traditions, imagination, and identity is closely linked to King's understanding of and emphasis on story, spelled out in all of his writing but most clearly in *The Truth About Stories*, where he repeatedly maintains that "the truth about stories is that that's all we are" (King 2003, 2). Echoing N. Scott Momaday's assertion that "we have no being beyond our stories" (1997, 169), this statement expresses King's conviction about the indispensable role stories play in Native cultural survival, both individual and communal. In "Borders," this surfaces in various, rather dissimilar ways. Firstly, in the emphasis on the continued importance of traditional stories in Native cultures, exemplified in the mother's storytelling under the stars; secondly, in a contemporary context, when the stories Laetitia's boyfriend tells her turn Salt Lake City into a kind of personal "promised land" for her; thirdly in the fact that it is only when the woman and her son become a "story" on the news that they are allowed to pass the border identifying themselves as Blackfoot; and finally, in relativizing the concept of nation itself to the level of story — a powerful story with real consequences, but merely a story, a "narrative of nation," nonetheless.

That national borders are an imposed socio-cultural construct, delineating "imagined communities" (Benedict Anderson), becomes most visible in the woman's reclamation of a "third space."[1] When the American border guard asks "'Canadian or American side?,'" she answers "'Blackfoot side'" (136), thus subverting his implicit pronouncement that the US–Canadian border is a line that leaves only an either/or choice between the binary oppositions of American or Canadian identity. The assertion of a "Blackfoot side" that overlaps with but *precedes* both the American and the Canadian territory introduces an alternative, contesting concept into the territorial and colonial discourse on the North American continent. It exposes the postulated rigidity of national borders as artificially constructed,

[1] This is not meant in terms of Homi K. Bhabha's concept of the "third space" as it is not the result of a hybridization of existing binary oppositions, but designates a previously existing space.

their institutionalization, "naturalization," and self-perpetuation in discourse being merely one more consequence and marker of power based on racial oppression. In this context, it is important to note that "Borders" was written right after the 1990 Oka crisis, an extended and at times violent confrontation between Mohawks, protesting the expansion of a golf course onto Mohawk lands, and provincial police and Canadian military at Oka, Quebec. Extensive media coverage of the conflict (paralleling the story under discussion) brought Native presence and the disregard of Native rights in Canada to wider attention in an unprecedented way, the Canadian public for the first time becoming more aware of the debate surrounding First Nations self-government and what was referred to as "the Native problem." The woman's insistence on her Blackfoot identity, like the designation "First Nations," which Canada's indigenous population adopted for itself, is therefore a manifestation of the Native struggle for sovereignty, constituting a major challenge not only to American and Canadian nationalistic categories but also to the legitimate presence and primacy (in terms of power) of Western societies on the North American continent in general. Against this background, the fact that neither the protagonist nor his mother are given a name can be taken as an indication of the universality of the border problem for North America's entire indigenous population.

The title's plurality, "Borders," suggests both that there *are* alternative "lines" to the one that is presently perceived as crucial in terms of conceptualizing space in North America, and questions the validity of borders in general — not only in territorial and national but also in other respects. The story asks its readers to transcend the thresholds of established paradigms, the boundaries between the known and the unknown, and their familiar frames of reference and perception. Rounding off this account of the naturalization of hierarchies in the coexistence of cultures, the story's ending thus once more emphasizes that how we conceive of things is always a matter of perspective. The narrator tells the readers in a final sentence that as they were driving away from the border he "watched the border through the rear window until all you could see were the tops of the flagpoles and the blue water tower, and then *they* rolled over a hill and disappeared" (145, italics added). It is the narrator who is moving, but by putting things into (his) perspective he describes the flagpoles that mark the border as "roll[ing] over the hill." As Native-Mexican stand-up comedian Abel Silvas remarks, "Since we were here before the border, we didn't cross the border — we were crossed by the border" (in Price 1998). King in this parable on cultural relativity trickster-like parades familiar images, mutual stereotypes, and national and cultural self-conceptualizations in order to reveal the paradigm of the US–Canadian border to be but a White fiction, simultaneously asserting the continued Native presence in North America.

Works Cited

Atwood, Margaret. "A Double-Bladed Knife: Subversive Laughter in Two Stories by Thomas King." *Canadian Literature* 124/125 (Spring/Summer 1990): 243–53.

Canton, Jeffrey. "Coyote Lives: Thomas King." In *The Power to Bend Spoons: Interviews with Canadian Novelists*, ed. Beverly Daurio. Toronto: Mercury, 1998. 90–97.

Coltelli, Laura. *Winged Words: American Indian Writers Speak.* Lincoln: University of Nebraska Press, 1990.

Davidson, Arnold E., Priscilla L. Walton, and Jennifer Andrews. *Border Crossings: Thomas King's Cultural Inversions.* Toronto: University of Toronto Press, 2003.

Gibert, Teresa. "Narrative Strategies in Thomas King's Short Stories." In *Telling Stories: Postcolonial Short Fiction in English*, ed. Jacqueline Bardolph. Amsterdam: Rodopi, 2001. 67–76.

King, Thomas. "Borders." In King, *One Good Story*, 131–45.

———. "Godzilla vs. Post-Colonial." *World Literature Written in English* 30.2 (1990): 10–16.

———. *One Good Story, That One.* Toronto: HarperCollins, 1993.

———. *A Short History of Indians in Canada.* Toronto: Harper Collins, 2005.

———. *The Truth About Stories: A Native Narrative.* Toronto: Anansi, 2003.

Lutz, Hartmut. *Contemporary Challenges: Conversations with Canadian Native Authors.* Saskatoon: Fifth House, 1991.

Momaday, N. Scott. *The Man Made of Words: Essays, Stories, Passages.* New York: St. Martin's, 1997.

New, William H. *Borderlands: How We Talk About Canada.* Vancouver: University of British Columbia Press, 1998.

Price, Darby Li Po. "Laughing Without Reservation: Indian Standup Comedians." *American Indian Culture and Research Journal* 22.4 (1998): 255–71.

Rooke, Constance. "Interview with Tom King." *World Literature Written in English* 30.2 (1990): 62–76.

Turner, Victor. *The Ritual Process.* Ithaca, NY: Cornell University Press, 1969.

van Toorn, Penny. "Aboriginal Writing." In *The Cambridge Companion to Canadian Literature*, ed. Eva-Marie Kröller. Cambridge: Cambridge University Press, 2004. 22–48.

Wyile, Herb. "'Trust Tonto': Thomas King's Subversive Fictions and the Politics of Cultural Literacy." *Canadian Literature* 161/162 (Summer/Autumn 1999): 105–24.

27: Digressing to Inner Worlds: Carol Shields, "Our Men and Women" (1999)

Brigitte Glaser (University of Göttingen)

BORN IN OAK PARK, ILLINOIS, in 1935, Carol Shields, neé Warner, immigrated to Canada in 1957 having married the Canadian engineering professor Donald Shields. Prior to her immigration she had earned a B.A. and a Master's degree in Arts from Hanover College, Indiana. In 1975 she graduated with an M.A. from the University of Ottawa. It was only in her forties, after she had raised her five children, that she launched her literary career. Over the years Shields has also traveled and lived in Europe. While working as a writer, she also held the positions of Professor of English at the University of Manitoba and Chancellor of the University of Winnipeg. She died in Victoria, British Columbia, in 2003 after a long battle with cancer.

Carol Shields is one of those exceptional writers who publish in almost all genres. Not only did she produce three collections of poetry and three plays, she also wrote literary criticism as well as literary biographies and edited an anthology of woman's writing. Shields is best known, however, for her fiction. The latter includes eleven novels — among them *Small Ceremonies* (1976), *Swann: A Mystery* (1987), *The Stone Diaries* (1993), and *Larry's Party* (1997) — as well as three collections of short stories. In 1993 she received the Governor General's Award for her novel *The Stone Diaries* (which had also been shortlisted for the Booker Prize in the same year), and, being of American nationality as well, Shields was also awarded the Pulitzer Prize for this book in 1995.

In the course of fifteen years, Shields published three collections of short stories, *Various Miracles* (1985), *The Orange Fish* (1989), and *Dressing Up for the Carnival* (2000). Several of the pieces compiled in these collections had appeared earlier in journals and magazines, some of them winning awards. In scholarly analyses of Shields's work, greater emphasis has been given to the novels; moreover, when short fiction is considered, it is often explored in relation to the novels. Hence it does not come as a surprise that the same or similar aspects are addressed with regard to both genres. Among the aspects relevant for Shields's short fiction in particular are the author's vision of the relationship between art and audience; her particular use of point of view and narrative consciousness; her choice of polyphonic texts, in the sense of juxtaposing different discursive spheres, such as masculine and feminine, intellectual and popular, specialized and clichéd; her working with postmodern aspects of synchronicity and coincidence; as well as her texts' recurring celebration of the extraordinary behind the ordinary, the reliability and actual beauty of the daily, and the — often surprising — connectedness and coincidence of daily events. A repeated return by scholars to these aspects may suggest that Shields abides by her approaches and methods, prominent among which are the disappointment of readers' expectations through a subversion of linearity, causality, and traditional plotting as well as her apparent privileging of everyday details over supposedly more significant topics.

Shields's particular use of language is evident throughout her work and is frequently commented on. In an analysis of one of the stories from *Dressing Up for the Carnival*, Marta Dvorak explores in great detail the ways in which Shields employs language to move from the ordinary and familiar to another level, inducing in readers a state of contemplation that makes them aware of "numinous moments" (Dvorak 2003, 135). Shields achieves this transition using a number of techniques (also to be found in other stories, including "Our Men and Women") such as seriation, inner focalization, as well as an implied author evident through irony and gentle mocking. Other devices include, for instance, vignettes which present variations of the initial situation; flat characters functioning as universal, even allegorical characters; enumeration as a rhetorical device that draws attention to the artificiality of the text, as well as an evocation, despite one's awareness of the text's artificiality, of real life in the form of sensual impressions, material objects, daily occurrences, and the sense of one's own existence (Dvorak, 136–43).

An important and recurring element in Shields's fiction is her emphasis on ordinary aspects of apparently insignificant lives, which she renders extraordinary and exceptional. Unconcerned about repeated accusations of dwelling on domesticity, and frequently linked with marital compromise and happy endings, Shields continued to highlight the need of individuals to be connected — to a family, to friends, to a community. Yet the author's preoccupation with seemingly simple sensations, trivial details, and common events may be misleading, as below the surface of conventionality readers often encounter subtle ironies as well as sophisticated speculations about the nature of human identity and desire. Shields commented in a 1993 interview on the gradual revival and revaluation of domestic fiction in contemporary writing:

> My earlier books were very much considered women's books, but that was in a very curious time in our history when the kind of books I wrote were described as domestic. We all now agree that everyone has a domestic

> life. We used to just pretend we didn't. I never thought for a minute that the domestic life wasn't important to write about. I never doubted its validity but, I must say, other people did. Of course now that men are writing so-called domestic novels they are not called that at all; they are called sensitive, contemporary reflections of modern life. (Shields in Anderson 2003, 60)

Over the years, Shields has become a more gender- and politically minded writer, although her convictions only occasionally emerge, at times only at a second reading. Probably to counter the assumption that she prefers to concern herself with women's lives, she has deliberately taken the male's perspective in two longer fictional texts, *Happenstance* (1980) and *Larry's Party* (1997), successfully showing her flexibility in capturing life experiences of both sexes. In the short story to be discussed here she adopts the same approach in miniature.

Among the recurring themes of Shields's fiction and non-fiction are those of human identity and relationships. Citing Roland Barthes's rhetorical question, "Isn't storytelling always a way of searching for one's origin?," Shields draws attention to the close relationship between narration and lived experience in her essay "Narrative Hunger and the Overflowing Cupboard" (2003, 22). Her characters tend to be upper-middle class contemplative types living in stable environments and politically uninvolved. Yet the imagery the author uses to present them is often of an opposite nature — violent, dynamic, and body-related. Shields employs indirectness as an artistic means to convey her message in subtle and unobtrusive ways.

The short story "Our Men and Women" was first published in 1999 and included in Shields's third and last collection of short fiction, *Dressing Up for the Carnival* (2000). The story is subdivided into five sections, four of which focus on two men and two women, with the final section presenting the conclusion. The narrated events are set in an unspecified university environment: all the central characters hold faculty positions, do research, teach seminars, and meet in the staff room at lunchtime. All of them are concerned about the environment, more precisely about unpredictable weather- and climate-related events in nature. Researching natural disasters in the daytime, they are haunted by them in their dreams at night. As the story unfolds, it becomes clear — especially through imagery and metaphor — that there is a connection between their professional experiences and their private lives. The conflict between and connectedness of the external world and the individuals' private concerns are subtly commented on. The story is narrated for the most part from a limited third-person perspective, with the focalization shifting from section to section depending on the individual at its center.

The first professional introduced to us, "the Earthquake man," is a seismologist whose daily work — the observation of the movements of tectonic plates and the subsequent prediction of earthquakes — seems to resonate in his private life as well. We learn that, despite his present happiness with his new wife Patricia, fifteen years his junior, he is concerned about the possibility of sudden upheavals like those he experienced in his thirty-five-year marriage to his first wife: "Those years with Marguerite taught him that making projections is like doing push-ups in water. The world spewed and shifted. There was nothing to lean against" (84). As a result of his recurrent worries, which usually manifest themselves in "night dreams . . . of molten lava, and the crunch and grind of tectonic plates" (84), he displays fear and uncertainty in his new relationship with Patricia. Thus he misinterprets her gesture of giving him a hug as an attack on him, imagining a great wave of water coming towards him and wiping him out. Likewise, Patricia misunderstands his whispered response of "tsunami"[1] as a term of endearment and replies, "I love you." This brief scene illustrates Shields's method of indirectness, in this case subtly situating the two lovers in different spheres. The initial celebration of marital happiness is gradually replaced by the Earthquake man's emerging insecurities and his extreme overreactions.

A meteorologist's daily preoccupations, professional and psychological, constitute the focus of the next section. Obsessed both by the difficulty of forecasting the weather and of keeping in check the influence of her domineering father, the woman ("Rainfall woman") is burdened by dreams of drowning amidst waves of water as well as torrents of her father's admonitions, both of which she attempts to cope with by attending a course on visualization. Shields takes up the topic of randomness again, not only through references to climate variability and chaos theory, but also through the sudden announcing at the end of the section that the father had unexpectedly passed away one day: "The space in between was so tightly packed that there wasn't room to squeeze in one word" (87). A hint of irony is noticeable in the observation that "there's no way people can protect themselves against surprise" (86), suggesting that the "surprise" was not just the daughter's but the father's too and thus perhaps allowing her a little defiant satisfaction towards the seemingly powerful parent. Again, Shields closely connects professional and private life, depicting her character as viewing the world through the prism of her professional interests.

The exact field of research and teaching of the third scholar, "the Fire fellow," remains vague. While he lectures on "reality" (88), which could

[1] *Tsunamis* are "large water waves, typically generated by seismic activity, that have historically caused significant damage to coastal communities throughout the world" (http://www.geophys.washington.edu/tsunami/welcome.html, accessed 9 December 2004).

probably be done by individuals of almost any field of study, it is his character rather than his scientific pursuit that is associated with fire. Overly ambitious and convinced of his own brilliance, he strikes one as being like a firecracker or a rocket ready to explode or take off at any moment. Shields renders the intricacies of his personality through her choice of words, characterizing the man with a certain ornamental rhetoric: he is "presenting arguments that are bejewelled with crafty irrelevance, covering the blackboard with many-branched equations that establish and illuminate his careful, random proofs" (88). Shields endows him with an explosive energy when she describes him as concluding his lectures "steaming with his own heat, panting, rejoicing" (88). This emotional immediacy, which exposes him in all his arrogance and self-importance, is furthermore presented through a passage of interior monologue which, through the Fire fellow's condescending thoughts about the Earthquake man ("old What's-His-Name and his new wife!," 87) and the Rainfall woman ("that lachrymose young Rainfall woman," 88), connects this section to the previous ones. Yet, just like his colleagues, he too suffers from nightly dreams, in his case from childhood memories focusing on his apparently inferior position in his family. These memories undermine his notion of superiority and often leave him with a feeling of inadequacy.

The mind of the fourth person, "the Plague and Pestilence woman," presumably a biologist, is dominated by the factors of chance, of being lucky in life and escaping deadly, infectious diseases, of experiencing unexpected moments of happiness, and of meeting congenial individuals. The topic of good fortune is already addressed in the first paragraph when she is reported to have won the "staff-room World Series pool" (89), one of those little details already mentioned in the earlier parts of the short story. Good fortune appears to have been a substantial ingredient in her life, including her mother's accidental yet welcome pregnancy with her, her husband's unforeseen change of character for the better, as well as her children's continued good health, especially since they are surrounded by germs, bacteria, and viruses. Although she, too, is regularly haunted by nightmares, again connected with her professional life — that is, dreams of multiplying microbiological substances and progressive poisoning and decay — her overall nature is a cheerful and positive one. This is evident from her joy in having brought about the match between the Earthquake man and his young wife and from her implicit hope that a similar connection will arise out of the previous night's meeting of the Rainfall woman and the Fire fellow.

In the concluding section Shields has the narrative voice summarize the four scientists' achievements, undoubtedly with a considerable degree of irony. While praising their purely rational approach to life in her appeal that "we" should be proud of their constant effort "to understand the topography of the real" (90), the narrator simultaneously draws attention to their "limitations" (91), that is, to their possibly futile attempts to evade that inner reality which they suppress and which nevertheless continues to surface in their dreams at night. Thus their work-related theories, despite being ingenious stratagems to lift them above their fellow human beings, may turn out to be "fragile, speculative, and foolish" (91). Particularly ironic is the final paragraph's reference to the scientists' indeterminate condition in possibly doing *nothing* while doing *all* they can. The implication is either that their work is an irrelevant, unprofitable endeavor (the "act of extraordinary courage" [91] for which we are supposed to admire them is nowhere specified) or that they do indeed deserve our genuine admiration simply for carrying on with their lives, of which their work is such a significant part. Despite this final emphasis on their occasional display of "extraordinary courage," the human beings presented in the story are conspicuous for their ordinariness and the common everyday situations they are involved in. In progressing from one individual to the next, the author employs a number of recurring themes, which upon close examination shed light on Shields's central interests (also to be found in her other works), namely the exploration of the everyday and the juxtaposition of fact and fiction, or real life and art.

Stressing the connectedness of professional and private lives, the simultaneous presence of external reality and internal sensations in individuals, as well as the occasional intrusion of randomness into a person's daily existence, Shields draws attention to the complexity of even the most ordinary episodes of human life. Furthermore, she adds yet another layer to this complexity by subtly pointing to the aspect of human relationships. Thus, the four scientists are depicted with regard to their professional activities, but at the same time other influences on their lives — such as their pasts, their individual unconscious, their families, and their friends — are pointed out. Although each of them may seem to be grounded in him- or herself, they are always, as Shields shows, part of a network of human relationships, in which sudden changes may have a considerable impact on their life. Some of them, such as the Fire fellow, would like to place themselves above others and are proud of what they perceive to be their elevated and unique status but, as the match-making activities of the Plague and Pestilence woman imply, they may quickly be caught up in relationships that go against their wishes and plans.

Much of the short story "Our Men and Women" is characteristic of Shields's fiction in general, especially in its display of the extraordinary in the ordinary, or the metaphorical dimension in the unspectacular everyday. The author's notion of her aesthetics of the everyday is commented on in her novel *Swann*: "The mythic heavings of the universe, so baffling, so incomprehensible, but when squeezed into digestible day-shaped bytes, made swimmingly transparent. Dailiness. The diurnal unit, cloudless and soluble" (*Swann*, 21–22). It is possible, this passage suggests, to attain privileged knowledge, that is, access to a heightened layer of being, through our encounter with the ordinary in everyday situations. There are dimensions of existence that reveal themselves gradually and through indirect means. At the center of the story, we find the correspondence between the visible and the invisible. It is no coincidence that the four segments introduce individuals professionally concerned with elemental upheavals, that is, the sudden outbreak of the invisible, and that this particular preoccupation is then also shown to emerge in their unconscious, their dreams and fears. Nightmares of earthquakes and flooding, or visions of spreading mould and multiplying bacteria and viruses, take us from the ordinary, everyday existence of these individuals into their respective private worlds. Shields makes this transition possible through her use of narrative perspective, leading us from an initial objective point of view toward different levels of subjectivity via indirect or direct interior monologue. With the help of focalization, we are able to transcend the layer of outward appearance, which is often only a mere act on the part of the character (for example, the Fire fellow's bravura lecture), and have access to his or her inner reality, which then raises more questions than it answers.

Despite her clear preference for domestic realism, Shields the short-story writer can also be aligned with the experimental strand of the genre. Her texts are not in the tradition of the plot story, which is marked by linearity, the gradual building-up of suspense, and the use of surprise endings. Rather, her stories, as is often found in women's writing, are characterized by episodic structures, seeming digressions which then turn out to be of central importance, and a "deliberately squinting view" (Howells 2001, 145). The digressions frequently produce gaps of understanding to be filled in by readers' assumptions and interpretations. In "Our Men and Women" these digressions are presented in the form of those inner processes that are related to dreaded possibilities rather than actual occurrences. Shields's predilection for potentialities in *Dressing Up for the Carnival* has been noted by Coral Ann Howells, who speaks of the author's employment of the "subjunctive mode," that is, her "looking at what human beings may do or might have done or would do" (Howells, 144). Shields's evocation of these parallel realities — in the present story in the form of nightmares indicating suppressed emotions — is suffused with a particular kind of imagery related to weather, climate, natural disaster, and the elements in general, and points to her interest in extending the geography of nature to that of the mind.

Through her constant foregrounding of language as the primary medium for narrating lives, Shields subtly draws attention to the gap between fact and fiction, reality and the work of art. Language constitutes for Shields not only a mediating but also a limiting force. She therefore rejects "realism," which she regards as highly artificial and certainly not mimetic. "[A] life does not unfold in chapters," she writes in "Narrative

Hunger" (28). Referring to John Barth's claim that the central question posed by fiction is not "What happens?" but "Who am I?" (Barth, quoted in Shields 2003, 29–30), Shields places her emphasis on self and self-identity, which in present-day writing are often interrogated through narrative experiments focusing on human thought and which are evoked through new forms of narrative strategy "opening [people's] lives to the kind of digressions that build to narrative form" (Shields 2003, 35). Shields thus defines herself as a postmodern writer, confirming this position especially through her playful construction of fictional worlds suffused with various forms of irony, such as the intrusion of the factor of randomness in individuals' lives (and in the narrative) or the unexpected associative links established between them. At first glance, Shields's short story "Our Men and Women" is a highly readable and approachable text that gradually, however, reveals itself to be an intricately designed and poignantly multilayered construct. The text's complexity invites readers to embark on a journey of discovery, leading to new dimensions of meaning through the chance encounter with the seemingly familiar.

Simone Vauthier, commenting on *Various Miracles*, describes the impression readers of Shields's subsequent stories are left with:

> When we finally stop negotiating between discontinuity and continuity, fiction and reality, our universe has been expanded by the quiet, luminous, upbeat art of Carol Shields: we understand more about miracles, about stories, about our lives and ourselves. . . . by offering us miracles in everydayness, showing the extraordinary in the ordinary, it [*Various Miracles*] wonderfully restores trust in a life which is less determined and less chaotic than it may appear, where improvisation therefore has a place, and it restores faith in language, too, since it allows us to talk, however obliquely, of mystery. (Vauthier 2003, 205–6)

In "Our Men and Women" Carol Shields has incorporated many of the writing techniques and approaches to fiction developed earlier, and has created a text at once appealing and mysterious.

Works Cited

Anderson, Marjorie. "Interview with Carol Shields." In Besner 2003, 55–71.

Besner, Neil, ed. *Carol Shields: The Arts of a Writing Life*. Winnipeg: Prairie Fire Press, 2003.

Dvorak, Marta. "An Aesthetics of the Ordinary in *Dressing Up for the Carnival*." In Besner 2003, 133–44.

Howells, Coral Ann. "In the Subjunctive Mood: Carol Shields's *Dressing Up for the Carnival*." *Yearbook of English Studies* 31 (2001): 144–54.

Shields, Carol. *Dressing Up for the Carnival.* London: Fourth Estate, 2000.

———. "Narrative Hunger and the Overflowing Cupboard." In *Carol Shields, Narrative Hunger, and the Possibilities of Fiction*, ed. Edward Eden and Dee Goertz. Toronto: University of Toronto Press, 2003. 19–36.

———. *The Orange Fish.* Toronto: Random House, 1989.

———. "Our Men and Women." In Shields, *Dressing Up*, 83–91.

———. *Swann: A Literary Mystery.* Toronto: Stoddart, 1993 [1987].

———. *Various Miracles.* Don Mills, ON: Stoddart, 1985.

Vauthier, Simone. "'They Say Miracles Are Past' but They Are Wrong." In Besner 2003, 183–208.

28: A Sentimental Journey: Janice Kulyk Keefer, "Dreams:Storms:Dogs" (1999)

Georgiana Banita (University of Constance)

As a second-generation Ukrainian immigrant to Canada, long-time resident of Europe, and literary heir to English Modernism, Janice Kulyk Keefer situates herself on the margins of several groups. For one thing, her relationship to the Ukrainian community in Canada is ambivalent. Born in suburban Toronto in 1952 to parents who were neither pioneer immigrants from Ukraine nor postwar DPs (displaced persons),[1] Keefer has long repressed her ethnic origins by striving to conform to the English environment, on both a linguistic and a personal level (she married an Englishman). She majored in English Literature and did not express an interest in the Ukrainian language and culture until very late. Having attended the University of Toronto as an undergraduate, she studied in Europe — in England and France — for eight years and returned to Canada, more precisely to Ottawa, where she picked up a copy of Mavis Gallant's *From the Fifteenth District*, which turned out to be her first encounter with contemporary Canadian literature. After a stay in Europe that had left indelible marks, Keefer could relate to Gallant's experience and referred to her book as a "revelation." Ever since then, she has addressed the question of how we construct personal and collective identities through narratives, which she recounts in a lyrical style that is more commonly seen in poetic novelists such as Anne Michaels than in social fiction. Like Myrna Kostash, Dionne Brand, and Rohinton Mistry, Keefer exploits and at the same time yearns to dissolve ethnic and cultural boundaries by ignoring the secluding ring that the words "immigrant" or "hyphenated" writer convey and opening up to a larger audience.

Her ethnic background — part Ukrainian, part Polish on her mother's side — has played a large part in Keefer's explorations of Canadian encounters with Eastern Europe and her forays into the hybrid genre of "creative

[1] "I was born into a family that occupied if not a marginal then a distinctly off-centre position in the Ukrainian Canadian community in Toronto" (Keefer 1995, 85).

non-fiction." This only occurred, however, after 1991, when she could gain first-hand experience of the Ukrainian culture and investigate "the true site" (Keefer 1995, 89) of her ethnic heritage. Her conversion could not have been timelier: the stigmatizing trend of "writing ethnicity," which emerged in the 1970s, had begun to die down, while Keefer had already made a name for herself through other writings that did not emphasize her personal background. There is no doubt, however, that questions of identity interference, ethnic or otherwise, are the trademark of her oeuvre. Her novel *The Green Library* (1996) and the family-memoir-cum-travel narrative *Honey and Ashes: A Story of Family* (1998) attempt to rescue narratives of the past and bridge traumatic gaps between imagined and actual worlds. These overlapping realms are often in conflict, as in Keefer's other novels *Constellations* (1988) and *Rest Harrow* (1992), conveying a sense of cultural rupture. Against overarching paradigms such as those proposed by Margaret Atwood, Keefer's characters act as "correctives to the victimized figure" (Clayton 1999, 193), in that they rise above their inherited communities towards an understanding of their own and other people's "otherness" as both obstructive and profitable. Keefer herself seems to have reached the same conclusion:

> Ethnicity — that lived experience of otherness, of difference from the "given" or imposed sociocultural norm — has been for me both positive and negative: otherness can be a matter of addition as well as subtraction — a gift rather than a theft. Likewise, difference can be a source of imaginative richness, as well as of anxiety and humiliation. And ethnicity . . . can become a complementary sphere of identity and belonging that confers meaning and dignity upon who and what and why one is. (Keefer 2000, 5)

What emanates from Keefer's texts is not only the otherness of cultures (be they Ukrainian, British, or French), but also the fluidity of any given cultural artifact. Anna English (in *Rest Harrow*) follows her fascination with Virginia Woolf and proceeds to write a book on the Bloomsbury author, only to discover that Woolf herself can never be located, embedded as she is in a cultural context that is always subject to change.[2] Like Katherine Mansfield,[3] her impressionist forerunner, whose life she recounted in the recent biographical novel *Thieves* (2004), Keefer is also a poet (*White of the*

[2] Keefer wrote her M.A. thesis on Virginia Woolf, whom she often references in her writings. Her doctoral thesis dealt with Joseph Conrad and Henry James. She currently teaches Modern British Fiction at the University of Guelph.

[3] Mansfield returns in many stories and novels under various guises. As the subject of Rosalind's doctoral thesis in *Rest Harrow*, she acts as a counterfoil to Anna's absorption in the work of Virginia Woolf.

Lesser Angels, 1986; *Fields*, 1989; *Marrying the Sea*, 1998), and her understanding of poems as "the eyes of stories" (Clayton, 189) shows in the poetic structures that her narrative work is steeped in. Figments of an inward-looking, imaginative frame of mind (taking the form of poems, dreams, reveries, and iconic images) are interspersed in her texts, sewing up fragments of selves into a hybrid patchwork.

There is a continuing tradition of relocated identities in Keefer's oeuvre so far. Not only has she written about the immigrant condition, she has also acknowledged the implications of this "flexible, capacious, ramiferous" (Keefer 1998: 99) experience on the literary choices that a writer makes and the politics of difference at work in every text. One of her aims, especially in her study of maritime fiction *Under Eastern Eyes* (1987), has been to dispel all illusions that flashpoint statements on *the* Canadian culture or *the* immigrant experience are possible. The "transcultural aesthetics" that Keefer is careful to delineate in connection with multiculturalism are quite radical, but justify on the other hand the play on translation, linguistic and cultural, that pervades her own work, and her academic interest in Mavis Gallant, who was just as convinced of the "sacredness" of transnational bridges (Keefer, *Reading Mavis Gallant*, 1989).

Divisions abound in Janice Kulyk Keefer's work, particularly in her short-story collections (*The Paris-Napoli Express*, 1986; *Transfigurations*, 1987; *Travelling Ladies*, 1990). The latest of these weaves together the fragmentary experiences of a handful of characters, while teasing out — both lyrically and dramatically — the friction between their multiple, displaced selves. Keefer thus bases her writing on two coordinates: on the one hand, the nostalgic, idealistic narratives that memory impels, on the other, the burden of a less-than-satisfying present, while the tension between them results in a ravaging "sense of the present as infinite loss" (Keefer 1992, 234). The intimate connection with the irrecoverable past comes under the guise of the journey, by which layers of identity are shed and others recovered or discerned for the first time. Geographical and inner distances are traversed, while the stories meander around events happening *with* and *to* the characters. Their frequent emotional deprivation is illuminated by unexpected changes of heart and insights spurred by chance encounters. A little girl becomes aware of the duplicitous and corporeal nature of love relationships through her mother's promiscuous behavior and Ovid's *Amores* ("The *Amores*"); a young bride abandons her husband during their honeymoon in France, giving in to a local charmer, whose wife and gardener she then becomes ("The Gardens of the Loire"); an elderly, childless Englishwoman, who offers English lessons in France, strengthens her contact with her only sister after a distressing encounter with a backward pupil ("The Lesson").

From the point of view of theme and narrative method, Keefer's short story "Dreams:Storms:Dogs," written for a special short-story collection celebrating the Canadian short story at the turn of the millennium (*The Turn of the Story*, 1999), is closely related to *Travelling Ladies*, reiterating to some extent the connubial plot in "The Gardens of the Loire," in that both stories depict couples reaching foreign territory in the thick of a personal crisis. While the earlier story delivers an unsurprising ending, almost in the vein of a Harlequin romance, "Dreams:Storms:Dogs" performs a balancing act between a relatively trite matrimonial crisis and an epiphanic reunion, a precarious shift that is carried out on several levels. An even more apparent forerunner to "Dreams:Storms:Dogs" is the considerably shorter and more schematic "Somewhere in Italy" (from *The Paris-Napoli Express*), which shares not only the Italian setting, but also the main plot trajectory, with a couple blundering through a resourceless relationship towards an uplifting reunion. "Dreams:Storms:Dogs" does not reflect its author's recent interest in unraveling the roots of her ethnic identity, but still illustrates her general interest in those fleeting moments when "the root of the self pushes up through a weight of earth and dead leaves to achieve a momentary flowering" (Keefer 2001, 16–17). In the vein of Keefer's more autobiographical stories, "Dreams:Storms:Dogs" offers a kaleidoscopic view of the self, reflected in a non-linear narrative sprawling over several levels of perception and consciousness.

The title prefigures the multi-layered structure of the story. Only in retrospect are the apparently random nouns comprehensible, and even then their interconnectedness is not fully revealed. Their sequencing points to a regressive level of abstraction, from indefinite dreams to palpable storms and finally the somewhat annoying animals that turn up at the end of the story. The striking punctuation of the title anticipates the structure of the text, which contains four clearly marked sections. The first of these is marked by dream visions, the third by a pictorial storm, the fourth brings the realization of the storm and the short but arresting appearance of the dogs, while the second section works as an expository hinge for the other three. This careful arrangement is further enhanced by the parallel structure of the narrative: the text juxtaposes two stories told by different characters in the form of interior monologue, thus creating two adversarial identities that communicate only at the end, in the grip of momentary communion.

What the reader is not privy to at the very start of the story is that the narrator, whom we later identify as Leah, is spending her forty-fifth wedding anniversary together with her husband in Venice, in the very same hotel room in which they spent their honeymoon. The narrator of the first section is undoubtedly the wife, whose account begins with a description of Carpaccio's painting *The Dream of Saint Ursula*, not as art history would have it, but adapted to the fantasies and frustrations of the female protagonist. Leah hides from her husband — who drags her through Venetian museums — and pines for the repose and rest promised by Saint

Ursula's bed. The discrepancy between her passive fantasies and the athletic dominance of the husband is sharpened by the mise-en-abymic construction of this ekphrastic scene.[4] Leah speaks of "the bed of my dreams" (199), but Saint Ursula herself, as the legend goes, is also dreaming. For a short moment, Leah seems beguiled by the artistry of the painting and its dreamlike imagery, only to redirect her gaze towards a highly Woolfian reading of the large, imposing bed as "a bed of one's own," one that would not allow for any male company and the prosaic familiarity it entails: "No husband's body beside you, hairy-chested or sleek, feet like fish on a marble slab or two warm piglets rooting up to you" (200). The color of the bed — its raw, reddish tint — holds, however, a deeper significance, which Leah does not seem to be aware of. It is not "the colour of the heart" that suffuses this image, but the aura of death, announced by the figure of an angel entering Ursula's dream, whom Leah interprets as an androgynous lover. The harmonic symmetry and peacefulness of Carpaccio's painting are far less benign than Leah imagines them to be. The depth and dignity of the woman's pose point to her tense anticipation of death. The well-lit space seems to be leaking through open doors and windows, leaving behind an other-worldly stillness and clarity. One is tempted to believe that Leah taps her own unconscious sources rather than grasp the poetic morbidity of the painting (see Serres 1975).

There is something of her own sense of alienation in this identification with the strange woman listening to her dreams — haunted by death as they may be — since life itself is hardly worth listening to anymore. Not even her husband seems to seek or attract Leah's attention. For the entire length of the story, they do not exchange a single word, although they are both busily speculating on the topic of the "other." The narrator takes in every single detail of the "ambassadorial" (200) bed, including the little white Cerberus at its foot. The columns, the canopy, the tassels, and the pillow prompt memories of bygone days, when dreams were expected to function as correctives to reality, but failed to change even trivial matters such as the color of one's hair, which "stayed black as coal and poker straight" (201). Sprinkled between descriptions of the painting are details of the couple's plight in Venice. Through an agglomeration of negative words ("no," "not," "none," "nothing"), the dream bed of Leah's vision becomes the perfect foil to connubial frustration. Humorous details of married life, such as the husband's habit of dropping items of clothing on the floor for his wife to pick up, are even more unbearable against the romantic backdrop of Venice, from which both protagonists try to take

[4] In the same vein, the earlier story "Somewhere in Italy" also begins and ends with an ekphrastic moment. In this case, it is a holiday snapshot and not a painting.

shelter: the wife in her dreams, the husband in the paintings of Venetian museums. In the resulting visual collage, the characters revolve around each other like mute somnambulists, unable to connect or communicate in any way ("All the time he's lying beside you staring at the ceiling and won't say a single word," 203). While Leah longs for pleasantly ambiguous dream images, her husband turns towards the past: the past of the city and his own. Just as the wife seeks sexual wish-fulfilment in her dreams, the husband develops an ambivalent romance with the city, watching it "comb its hair" as it used to, dressing "in the old, familiar style" (203). Both are tucked up in a set of illusions, grieving for their lost selves. Leah's resentment reaches its peak in her resolution to start saving once she returns home, so that she can order her own dream bed. It is not exactly Katherine Mansfield's triad "power, wealth, and freedom" that Leah longs for, but a temporary seclusion, whose tomblike finality she understands for the first time: "And when it's done, I'll just lie myself down, and never get up again" (204).

The second section of the story marks the transition to the husband's point of view, which is not the return to the bedrock of common sense that one might expect. His letter to the hotel owners, wrapped as it is in formal clichés, does reveal a kinder and certainly a more romantic nature than Leah's account has suggested. The episode revolves around another Venetian masterpiece, this time Giorgione's *The Tempest.* The contrasts with his wife's artwork of choice are quite clear. The husband, who remains unnamed, takes more interest in the characters than in the objects depicted; in his eyes, the image is a human drama rather than a still life. He wonders who these figures are, "what's between them; whether they even know one another" (204). It is an outdoor scene, whose ambiguity is enforced by the threat of an approaching storm. From this point on, the story gathers momentum and becomes more ominous, both in tone and imagery. The main question, both in the picture and in the husband's mind, is how to find "a place of safety" from "the rain and cold and dark" (205). The secret of Giorgione's characters — an apparently detached onlooker who resembles a soldier, and a naked young woman, perhaps a gypsy, with a child — reflects the crisis of the couple. It is no accident that Keefer selects a painting that remains one of the most impenetrable mysteries of art history. Puzzled by the strange detachment of the figures, who seem unaware of each other's existence, one of Giorgione's contemporaries confessed, "I myself do not understand it, nor have I found anyone who did" (Wind 1969, 2). Just like Giorgione's figures, Leah and her husband gravitate around one another, without being able to read each other's minds. The husband seems to feel that the fault lies entirely with him: "Like me, he is one of those men who can never come out with a single thing to say when it matters most" (205). He balks from speaking, even when asked, closing in upon himself "as if language were a sealed room and I'd used up all the oxygen" (205). He is just as mute in his relationship with Leah and thus unable to heal the rift between them. Their silence is as poisonous as the mosquitoes that they try to exterminate every night by burning a mosquito lamp. Five days after his wife's disappearance, he hopes to find her under this lamp again, shining with light, as when they first met. The tension of a relationship haunted by routine, coupled with a strong emotional release, is best expressed by the motif of the storm with its dual connotations, referring to the storm that occasioned their chance encounter (the Italian "tempesta" is close in meaning to "fortuna") and to love at first sight many years before. Also, there is a sudden break when the other has "changed past knowing" (206), requiring a re-evaluation of what has and what should have happened:

> I could tell her none of this, I made no mention of her beauty, though it lapped against everything I thought or felt, then and ever since. Night after night I've lain awake wondering what I could have done, how I could have kept her from turning away as she did; from walking into the rift opened by a storm, and vanishing. (206)

Although the sequence of events threatens at times to vanish as well, certain recurring objects or parallelisms hold the narrative together in an intricate manner. A small white dog — such as the one curled at the foot of Saint Ursula's bed — struts through the fish market as if with a purpose; the husband wants to follow the dog and the plastic bottle it is carrying, full of an invisible, precious elixir, or so he thinks. In the end, he imagines Leah waiting in their room, "listening hard to whatever it is she dreams: lightning, silence, the open sky" (207), just like the expectant Saint Ursula, only more alive.

When they find each other, in the fourth section of the story, the husband and wife realize that their respective hiding places are also great discoveries. "Footsore and forlorn," they are as tired of their nightly, imaginary ramblings as they are hungry for the familiarity of "the way it's always been" (207). The husband gives in first, allowing her to choose a restaurant and putting up with the overpriced food and condescending waiters. Beyond the façade, however, little has changed: "As always, he says nothing, pulling the bread to pieces, rolling them between his fingers, making eggs or stones, she can't tell which and it doesn't much matter" (208). In a few hours, she will be collecting the clothes he has scattered on the floor, as she has done for almost half a century. In the meantime she stares apprehensively at the Venetian canals, still waiting for the romantic miracle that she has come such a long way in search of. But the stranger of her fantasy, the one with a ruffled bouquet, the stranger walking in on the sleeping Ursula, turns out to be her husband. He is, in other words, a highly ambivalent character: both a harbinger of death and an endearing, comic figure, with "his glasses like a slide trombone on the end of his nose" (208). In a further mise-en-abymic twist, he recalls an anecdote about a husband who is pushed into despair and the green waters of the Venetian lagoon by his ill-matched wife. Marriage, Venice, pictorial visions of bliss, all seem to lure and betray. Like Leah's golden hair, they are all "products of a false elixir" (209). It is through the sudden discharge of a storm that they reveal their true colors. As Joseph Conrad's character says at the end of *Victory*, an explosion can be the most liberating thing in the world (Clayton, 187). Indeed, many of Keefer's finales are modeled upon this natural and psychological release of tension. In "Dreams: Storms: Dogs," a piece of street theater prepares the way for the sudden reconciliation between the two protagonists. Two ridiculously mismatched dogs proceed to copulate in the middle of the street, defying their owners, only to be flung into the canal by a waiter; cooled down in the water, they forget their seizure as if it had never happened, and go their separate ways. Coupled with the storm, this absurd incident releases a tension that both characters have unsuccessfully tried to overcome.

> The suddenness of this storm, the abruptness of its resolution, the possibilities opened and extinguished before their very eyes have entered them like electricity, singeing each branch of their blood. Without a word, they shoot their hands across the table, grabbing one another, holding fast. So fast they can never shake free, no matter how many mazy streets they must turn down to get to their hotel, no matter how many cues for vanishing they give to one another. (209)

Just as imperceptible as their initial fall-out, the reunion may be a sign of regained strength in dealing with the spaces that unavoidably stretch between them, or the symptom of a weakness so numbing that they cannot even manage to pull away from one another, as they had done through their dream visions and escapes. Keefer does not pronounce a clear verdict on the outcome of this sentimental journey.

The entire story is threaded around ambiguities and apparent contradictions. The characters in "Dreams:Storms:Dogs" attempt to forge a sense of security by creating narrative and visual fictions. Despite appearances, these fictions do not distance the protagonists, but connect them. Through the intimate relation they re-establish with their imagined or dreamed selves, they mobilize enough courage to bridge their own disconnectedness. No doubt, something is shattered by their acknowledgment of failure, regarding marriage in general and their ability to communicate in particular. The sensations of the mind — be they dreams, memories, reveries, or pictures — give voice to an inarticulate inner self, disturbing and at the same time prescriptive: "In dreams begin responsibilities," wrote Yeats, whom Keefer is fond of quoting (Clayton, 190). The dream sequences of the story are involuntarily poetic. In fact, the entire text displays a dreamlike quality, in that it employs compression of narrative and imagery, and proceeds by leaps rather than by conventional logic. The account of the characters' thoughts is associative and based on the reiteration of several images, from which three have been selected to form the title. Keefer writes at the speed — or rather, leisure — of dreams, using various forms of juxtaposition and leaving out the connections, as dreams do.[5] From the general welter emerge scraps of conversation, childhood memories, and stray thoughts: praying for her hair to turn gold, names of girlfriends, Angelo's Carpentry. Unexplained particulars, such as a lamp, a small white dog, or a bed, are fraught with meaning. The story progresses along a sinuous line, not at all chronological, with sudden flashbacks, some of which occur twice (the first meeting in the rain, for example) and differ according to who reminisces, the husband or the wife. In addition, the motions of the characters' minds are not at all identical, even when they are doing the same thing, such as looking at a painting. Keefer develops a gender contrast between their different perceptions: the wife settling on color, the absent space of the image, and the way she herself relates to the objects and persons depicted; the husband analyzing the complex relationship and the tension between the figures. What Norman Bryson writes of the difference between "glancing" and "gazing" applies with very little adjustment to the two characters' habits of looking at a painting (see Bryson 1983). The husband "glances" at *The Tempest*, searching for a rational answer that would explain the alchemy between its component parts. Leah, however, "gazes" at a painting which calls forth a myriad of temporary impressions of the details that she picks up individually, as her eye travels across the field of the painting.

The pictorial excursions do not dislodge the narrative, but become enmeshed with the characters' thoughts, thus creating a unique lyrical fluency. The lyricism of this story is not the counterfoil of prose, but a form of liminal discourse — on a par with dreams and visions — the subtle means by which narratives (especially alternative ones) can be negotiated and interchanged. The narrative perspective is also permanently shifting

[5] Keefer seems to have been well aware of dreams' ability to form, in John Berryman's words, a panorama of the whole mental life. In an interview she goes so far as to suggest that she intended her prose to mime actual dream logic and narrative: "What fascinates me about narrativity in dreaming is the jumps, the leaps one makes. . . . When I'm teaching creative writing to students both in poetry and fiction I tell them to think of how you dream, think of the narrative of dreams. . . . This notion is of juxtaposition and what Freud called condensation, where things that in ordinary waking life would never appear connected or interdependent in dreamwork are sewn up together. That's what can be so disconcerting, but also so revealing" (Clayton, 190).

between the two first-person "focalizers" — to use Gérard Genette's term — and an extra-diegetic or omniscient narrator, who hovers between the two protagonists and comes to the fore more clearly in the last section, where he pulls together the diverse threads of the story.

It is not by chance that the text pivots on an ekphrastic technique and on the paradox of the verbal expression of a visual representation. The impossibility of fully grasping the meaning of a painting mirrors the characters' difficulty in coming to terms with and verbalizing their emotional dilemmas. The husband associates the lightning that cuts through the inscrutable distance between Giorgione's soldier and gypsy with the void between himself and Leah, which he cannot fill, at least not verbally: " 'What are you thinking?' An impossible question; not a question at all, I can see that now. And all I had to do was open my mouth and say something, anything, just to reach across that split she'd opened in the sky" (205). Although the paintings described are real works of art, they are enveloped by the characters — who are by no means art connoisseurs — in a poetic atmosphere and infused with a very personal lyrical mood, so that in the end they become "notional" descriptions (Hollander 1988, 209), conveying an imaginary rather than a verifiable impression.

Even Venice is depicted derisively as a clichéd photograph ("foggy shots of gondolas," 203) or a canvas, not as a real city. Venice appears as a fabric or a quality of the mind, a free-floating space where the self is not moored by circumstances, where it can explore itself and improvise, even when this entails an upsurge of negative impulses, such as marital conflict or a crisis of identity. More of an afterthought than a clear setting, Venice is only mentioned in the titles of the two paintings, and does not appear at all in the text. Even more than Keefer's earlier story "Somewhere in Italy," which still displayed an architectural interest in Venice and its slummy aspects, "Dreams:Storms:Dogs" limits the description to a few fleeting impressions, which point to the city as an empty signifier, a simulacrum that cannot deliver on its romantic promises: "The city of love, romance thicker than the letters in alphabet soup" (202); "the city itself, which has only tantalized them, giving them nothing at all to keep for their own" (208).

If we accept, as is commonly assumed, that ekphrasis is a descriptive detour from the main road of epic narrative, or a detachable fragment thereof, then it becomes understandable why a short story, with its usual focus on a tight, homogeneous plot rather than ornamental digressions, is challenged by this technique.[6] However, Keefer does not make a point of

[6] Ekphrasis appears prominently in Keefer's novel *Rest Harrow*, as it does in other novels by Canadian authors (Margaret Atwood, *Cat's Eye*, *The Blind Assassin*; Robertson Davies, *What's Bred in the Bone*, which feature paintings, and many more that deal with photographs: Michael Ignatieff, *Scar Tissue*; Thomas King,

keeping narration and description apart. The two paintings supply alternative — not rival — plots, which do not decelerate the narrative's progression. This lyrical intent of the short story also accounts for the insertion of actual verse and a highly poetic descriptive style. Keefer's images are created by evoking a concatenated mood, in that her metaphors and comparisons come together by means of a fusion between different aspects of the object described. Her figures of speech often appear in strings, adding to the effect of a single image and requiring a constant shift of attention, for example, in the depiction of Saint Ursula's bed: "It has a canopy, like I said: nothing flim-flam flighty, but dignified — ambassadorial, you might even say. Red like blood; deep, not dark. The colour of the heart/that pulpy bridge where all/the rivers end and start" (200). Or in connection with *The Tempest*: "the storm breaking over their heads: sky bruised by cloud and split by lightning; sky green as grass and deep as drowning" (204). The most typical form of coordination is the asyndetic one, as in: "*Everything's gone, changed, spoiled*" (203); or: "her hair, under the mosquito lamp: a cloud, a sun, red-golden" (206). Very often these chains of imagery are linked through long hyphens as a form of enjambment in order to keep the unit within the space of one breath and create a sense of expectancy without breaking the flow — a method more frequent in poetry than in prose.

It is a rare moment when a text can straddle the line between poetry and prose with the wayward elegance that "Dreams:Storms:Dogs" displays. Keefer's ability to mingle dream visions, fantasies, memories, and pictorial images adds to her stylistic achievement and reinforces the intertextual (and intermedial) concerns of her work, as well as her awareness of the conflict between fantasies and realities that lie disturbingly far apart. Hers is a story of inner, almost unhoped-for resilience in the face of this tension, allowing Keefer to emerge as — to borrow a phrase by Katherine Mansfield — "a writer about the submerged world" (Mansfield 1981, 89).

Works Cited

Bryson, Norman. *Vision and Painting: The Logic of the Gaze.* New Haven: Yale University Press, 1983.

Clayton, Cherry. "Janice Kulyk Keefer Interviewed by Cherry Clayton." *Journal of Commonwealth Literature* 34.1 (1999): 183–97.

Medicine River; Daphne Marlatt, *Taken*, etc.). Only rarely is this device used in short stories. An example of an interesting use of ekphrasis is Alice Munro's short story "Tilting Fields."

Hollander, John. "The Poetics of *Ekphrasis*." *Word and Image* 4 (1988): 209–19.

Kulyk Keefer, Janice. "'Coming Across Bones': Historiographic Ethnofiction." *Essays on Canadian Writing* 57 (Winter 1995): 84–104.

———. "Dreams:Storms:Dogs." In *The Turn of the Story: Canadian Short Fiction on the Eve of the Millennium*, ed. Joan Thomas and Heidi Harms. Toronto: Anansi, 1999. 199–210.

———. "The Gardens of the Loire." In Keefer, *Travelling Ladies*, 99–137.

———. "Limitations and Possibilities: On the Writing of Autobiographical Short Fictions." In *Telling Stories: Postcolonial Short Fiction in English*, ed. Jacqueline Bardolph. Amsterdam: Rodopi, 2001. 13–22.

———. *The Paris-Napoli Express.* Toronto: HarperCollins, 1990.

———. "Personal and Public Records: Story and History in the Narration of Ethnicity." In *Tricks with a Glass: Writing Ethnicity in Canada*, ed. Rocío G. Davis and Rosalía Baena. Amsterdam: Rodopi, 2000. 1–18.

———. "'The Sacredness of Bridges': Writing Immigrant Experience." In *Literary Pluralities*, ed. Christl Verduyn. Peterborough, ON: Broadview Press, 1998. 97–110.

———. "Somewhere in Italy." In Keefer, *The Paris-Napoli Express*, 66–72.

———. *Transfigurations.* Charlottetown: Ragweed Press, 1987.

———. *Travelling Ladies.* Toronto: HarperPerennial, 1992.

Mansfield, Katherine. *Selected Stories.* Oxford: Oxford University Press, 1981.

Serres, Michel. *Esthétiques sur Carpaccio.* Paris: Hermann, 1975.

Wind, Edgar. *Giorgione's* Tempesta*: With Comments on Giorgione's Poetic Allegories.* Oxford: Clarendon, 1969.

Further Reading on the Canadian Short Story

Abley, Mark. "Bob's Our Uncle." *Books in Canada* 8.5 (May 1979): 4–9 [on Robert Weaver].

Arnason, David. "The Historical Development of the Canadian Short Story." *RANAM* 16 (1983): 159–64.

Davey, Frank. "Genre Subversion and the Canadian Short Story." *RANAM* 20 (1987): 7–15.

Fetherling, Doug. "Anthology: The Secret Radio Programme that May Last Forever." *Saturday Night* (November 1979): 68–70.

Gadpaille, Michelle. "Canadian Short Fiction." In *Critical Survey of Short Fiction*. Vol. 7, 2nd rev. ed. Pasadena, CA: Salem Press, 2001. 2898–2907.

———. *The Canadian Short Story*. Toronto: Oxford University Press, 1988.

Hancock, Geoff. "Here and Now: Innovation and Change in the Canadian Short Story." *Canadian Fiction Magazine* 17 (1977): 4–22.

Jackel, David. "Short Fiction." In *Literary History of Canada: Canadian Literature in English*. Vol. 4, 2nd ed., ed. W. H. New. Toronto: University of Toronto Press, 1990. 46–72.

Kent, David A. "Two Attitudes: Canadian Short Stories." *Essays on Canadian Writing* 16 (Fall/Winter 1979/80): 168–78.

Lucas, Alec. "Canadian Short Story Anthologies: Notes on Their Function and Form." *World Literature Written in English* 11.1 (1972): 53–59.

Lynch, Gerald. *The One and the Many: English-Canadian Short Story Cycles*. Toronto: University of Toronto Press, 2001.

Lynch, Gerald, and Angela Arnold Robbeson, eds. *Dominant Impressions: Essays on the Canadian Short Story*. Reappraisals: Canadian Writers 22. Ottawa: University of Ottawa Press, 1999.

Meindl, Dieter. "Modernism and the English Canadian Short Story Cycle." *RANAM* 20 (1987): 17–22.

New, W. H. "Back to the Future: The Short Story in Canada and the Writing of Literary History." *Australian-Canadian Studies: A Journal for the Humanities & Social Sciences* 4 (1986): 15–27.

———. *Dreams of Speech and Violence: The Art of the Short Story in Canada and New Zealand*. Toronto: University of Toronto Press, 1987.

New, W. H. "Tense/Present/Narrative: Reflections on English-Language Short Fiction in Canada." In *Studies on Canadian Literature: Introductory and Critical Essays*, ed. David E. Arnoldson. New York: MLA, 1990. 34–53.

Nischik, Reingard M. "'Pen Photographs': Zum Phänomen des (kanadischen) Kurzgeschichtenzyklus." *Deutsche Vierteljahrsschrift für Literaturwissenschaft und Geistesgeschichte* 66.1 (1992): 192–204.

———. "The Short Story in Canada: Metcalf and Others Making It New." *Die Neueren Sprachen* 86.3/4 (1987): 232–46.

Regan, Stephen. "'The Presence of the Past': Modernism and Postmodernism in Canadian Short Fiction." In *Narrative Strategies in Canadian Literature: Feminism and Postcolonialism*, ed. Coral Ann Howells, Lynette Hunter, and Armando Jannetta. Milton Keynes: Open University Press, 1991. 108–33.

Struthers, J. R. (Tim). *The Montreal Storytellers: Memoirs, Photographs, Critical Essays.* Montreal: Véhicule Press, 1985.

———. "Myth and Reality: A Regional Approach to the Canadian Short Story." *Laurentian University Review* 8 (Nov. 1975): 28–48.

Thacker, Robert. "Short Fiction." In *The Cambridge Companion to Canadian Literature*, ed. Eva-Marie Kröller. Cambridge: Cambridge University Press, 2004. 177–93.

Thompson, Kent. "The Canadian Short Story in English and the Little Magazines: 1971." *World Literature Written in English* 11.1 (1972): 15–24.

van Herk, Aritha. "Scant Articulations of Time." *University of Toronto Quarterly* 68.4 (Fall 1999): 925–38.

Vauthier, Simone, ed. *Espaces de la Nouvelle Canadienne Anglophone.* Special issue of *RANAM* 20 (1987).

———. *Reverberations: Explorations in the Canadian Short Story.* Concord, ON: Anansi, 1993.

Weiss, Allan. "Beyond Genre: Canadian Surrealist Short Fiction." In *The Postmodern Short Story: Forms and Issues*, ed. Farhat Iftekharrudin, Joseph Boyden, Mary Rohrberger, and Jaie Claudet. London: Greenwood, 2003. 233–45.

———. *A Comprehensive Bibliography of English-Canadian Short Stories: 1950–1983.* Toronto: ECW Press, 1988.

Time Chart: The Short Story in the USA, Canada, and Great Britain

Great Britain		USA		Canada	
		Washington Irving (1783–1859)			
		– "Rip van Winkle"	(1819)		
		– "The Legend of Sleepy Hollow"	(1820)		
		Nathaniel Hawthorne (1804–64)			
		– "My Kinsman, Major Molineux"	(1832)		
		– "Young Goodman Brown"	(1835)		
		Edgar Allan Poe (1809–49)			
		– "Ligeia"	(1838)		
		– "The Fall of the House of Usher"	(1839)		
		– "The Murders in the Rue Morgue"	(1841)		
		– "The Masque of the Red Death"	(1842)		
		– "The Tell–Tale Heart"	(1843)		
		Herman Melville (1819–91)			
		– "Bartleby, the Scrivener"	(1853)		
		Mark Twain (1835–1910)			
		– "The Notorious Jumping Frog of Calaveras County"	(1865)		
		– "The Man That Corrupted Hadleyburg"	(1899)		
		Bret Harte (1836–1902)			
		– "The Luck of Roaring Camp"	(1868)		
		– "The Outcasts of Poker Flat"	(1869)		
Thomas Hardy (1840–1928)					
– "The Three Strangers"	(1883)	Sarah Orne Jewett (1849–1909)		Isabella Valancy Crawford (1850–87)	
		– "A White Heron"	(1886)	– "Extradited"	(1886)

Time Chart (*continued*)

Great Britain	USA	Canada
		Susan Frances Harrison (1859–1935) – "The Idyl of the Island" (1886)
Oscar Wilde (1854–1900) – "The Canterville Ghost" (1887) – "The Happy Prince" (1888)	Ambrose Bierce (1842–1914?) – "An Occurrence at Owl Creek Bridge" (1890)	Duncan Campbell Scott (1862–1947) – "The Desjardins" (1887)
Rudyard Kipling (1865–1936) – "The Man Who Would Be King" (1891)	Mary E. Wilkins Freeman (1852–1930) – "A New England Nun" (1891)	
Robert Louis Stevenson (1850–94) – "The Beach at Falesa" (1892)	Charlotte Perkins Gilman (1860–1935) – "The Yellow Wall-paper" (1892)	Charles G. D. Roberts (1860–1943) – "Do Seek Their Meat from God" (1892)
Arthur Conan Doyle (1859–1930) – "The Speckled Band" (1892)	Henry James (1843–1916) – "The Real Thing" (1892)	
		Ernest Thompson Seton (1860–1946) – "Lobo, the King of Currumpaw" (1894)
	Stephen Crane (1871–1900) – "The Open Boat" (1897) – "The Bride Comes to Yellow Sky" (1898)	
	Kate Chopin (1851–1904) – "The Storm" (wr. 1898/ 1969)	
	Theodore Dreiser (1871–1945) – "Old Rogaum and His Theresa" (1901/ 1918)	
Joseph Conrad (1857–1924) – "Typhoon" (1902) – "The Secret Sharer" (1909)	Jack London (1876–1916) – "To Build a Fire" (1902/ 1908)	Sara Jeannette Duncan (1861–1922) – "A Mother in India" (1903)

Time Chart (*continued*)

Great Britain		USA		Canada	
Saki (H. H. Munro) (1870–1916) – "Reginald" – "Esmé"	 (1904) (1911)				
H. G. Wells (1866–1946) – "The Country of the Blind" – "The Door in the Wall"	 (1904) (1911)				
E. M. Forster (1879–1970) – "The Celestial Omnibus"	 (1908)	O. Henry (1862–1920) – "A Municipal Report"	 (1910)		
D. H. Lawrence (1885–1930) – "Odour of Chrysanthemums" – "England, My England"	 (1911) (1915)	Edith Wharton (1862–1937) – "Autres temps"	 (1911)	Stephen Leacock (1869–1944) – "The Marine Excursion of the Knights of Pythias"	 (1912)
James Joyce (1882–1941) –"The Dead" – "Eveline"	 (1914) (1914)				
Virginia Woolf (1882–1941) – "The Mark on the Wall" – "An Unfinished Novel"	 (1917) (1920)	F. Scott Fitzgerald (1896–1940) – "Tarquin of Cheapside" – "Babylon Revisited"	 (1917) (1931)		
W. Somerset Maugham (1874–1965) – "Rain" – "Louise"	 (1919) (1936)	Sherwood Anderson (1876–1941) – "I Want to Know Why" – "Death in the Woods"	 (1919) (1926)		
Katherine Mansfield (1888–1923) – "The Garden Party"	 (1922)				
Aldous Huxley (1894–1963) – "The Giaconda Smile"	 (1922)				

Time Chart (*continued*)

Great Britain		USA		Canada	
Liam O'Flaherty (1897–1984) – "Going into Exile"	 (1924)	Ernest Hemingway (1899–1961) – "Big Two-Hearted River" – "Hills Like White Elephants" – "The Snows of Kilimanjaro"	 (1925) (1927) (1936/1938)	Raymond Knister (1899–1932) – "The First Day of Spring"	 (wr. 1924/25)
				Frederick Philip Grove (1879–1948) – "Snow"	 (1926/1932)
				Morley Callaghan (1903–90) – "Last Spring They Came Over"	 (1927)
		Willa Cather (1873–1947) – "Neighbor Rosicky"	 (1928/1932)		
		Katherine Anne Porter (1890–1980) – "Flowering Judas"	 (1929/30)		
Graham Greene (1904–91) – "The Basement Room" – "The Invisible Japanese Gentlemen"	 (1935) (1965)				
Evelyn Waugh (1903–66) – "Mr. Loveday's Little Outing"	 (1936)				
				Sinclair Ross (1908–96) – "The Lamp at Noon" – "The Painted Door"	 (1938) (1939)
Elizabeth Bowen (1899–1973) – "The Demon Lover"	 (1941)	Eudora Welty (1909–2001) – "Petrified Man"	 (1941)		
		William Faulkner (1897–1962) –"The Bear"	 (1942)		
				Ethel Wilson (1888–1980) –"We Have to Sit Opposite" – "Mrs. Golightly and the First Convention"	 (1945) (1945)
Samuel Beckett (1906–89) – "The Expelled" – "Ping"	 (1946) (1974)				

Time Chart (*continued*)

Great Britain		USA		Canada	
		J. D. Salinger (1919–) – "For Esmé – With Love and Squalor"	(1950)	Hugh Garner (1913–79) – "One–Two–Three Little Indians"	(1950)
				Joyce Marshall (1913–) – "The Old Woman"	(1952)
Angus Wilson (1913–91) – "Higher Standards"	(1953)	Flannery O'Connor (1925–64) – "A Good Man Is Hard to Find"	(1953)		
Kingsley Amis (1922–95) – "My Enemy's Enemy"	(1955)	Bernard Malamud (1914–86) – "The Magic Barrel"	(1954)	Mordecai Richler (1931–2001) – "Benny, the War in Europe, and Myerson's Daughter Bella"	(1956)
		James Baldwin (1924–87) – "Sonny's Blues" – "Going to Meet the Man"	(1957) (1965)		
Allan Sillitoe (1928–) – "The Loneliness of the Long-Distance Runner"	(1959)	Philip Roth (1933–) – "The Conversion of the Jews"	(1958)	Sheila Watson (1909–98) – "Antigone"	(1959)
V. S. Pritchett (1900–97) – "When My Girl Comes Home"	(1961)			Alice Munro (1931–) – "The Peace of Utrecht" – "Boys and Girls" – "Dulse" – "Miles City, Montana" – "Powers"	(1960) (1964) (1980) (1985) (2004)
				Hugh Hood (1928–2000) – "Flying a Red Kite"	(1962)
Doris Lessing (1919–) – "To Room Nineteen" – "The Old Chief Mshlanga"	(1963) (1988)	John Cheever (1912–82) – "The Swimmer"	(1964)	Mavis Gallant (1922–) – "The Ice Wagon Going Down the Street" – "The Moslem Wife"	(1963) (1976)

Time Chart (*continued*)

Great Britain		USA		Canada	
Muriel Spark (1918–)		John Barth (1930–)		Margaret Laurence (1926–87)	
– "House of the Famous Poet"	(1966)	– "Lost in the Funhouse"	(1967)	– "The Loons"	(1966)
		Donald Barthelme (1931–89)			
		– "The Balloon"	(1968)		
		– "At the Tolstoy Museum"	(1969)		
		Joyce Carol Oates (1938–)		Ray Smith (1941–)	
		– "How I Contemplated the World from the Detroit House of Correction and Began My Life Over Again"	(1969)	– "Cape Breton Is the Thought Control Centre of Canada"	(1969)
		– "Ghost Girls"	(1995)	Clark Blaise (1940–)	
				– "A Class of New Canadians"	(1970)
				– "A North American Education"	(1971)
				Audrey Thomas (1935–)	
				– "Aquarius"	(1971)
				– "Kill Day on the Government Wharf"	(1977)
				Rudy Wiebe (1934–)	
				– "Where Is the Voice Coming from?"	(1971)
				Norman Levine (1923–2005)	
				– "We All Begin in a Little Magazine"	(1972)
				– "Something Happened Here"	(1982)
B. S. Johnson (1933–73)		Alice Walker (1944–)		John Metcalf (1938–)	
– "A Few Selected Sentences"	(1973)	– "Everyday Use"	(1973)	– "The Strange Aberration of Mr. Ken Smythe"	(1973)
				– "Gentle as Flowers Make the Stones"	(1975)

Time Chart (*continued*)

Great Britain		USA		Canada	
Angela Carter (1940–92)		Grace Paley (1922–)			
– "Flesh and the Mirror"	(1974)	– "A Conversation with My Father"	(1974)		
– "The Bloody Chamber"	(1979)	– "The Expensive Moment"	(1985)		
		John Updike (1932–)			
		– "Separating"	(1975)		
		Robert Coover (1932–)			
		– "The Elevator"	(1975)		
Graham Swift (1949–)				Jane Rule (1931–)	
– "Seraglio"	(1977)			– "Lilian"	(1977)
Sylvia Townsend Warner (1893–1978)					
– "A Widow's Quilt"	(1977)				
Edna O'Brien (1930–)		Ann Beattie (1947–)		Jack Hodgins (1938–)	
– "Mrs. Reinhardt"	(1978)	– "Weekend"	(1978)	– "The Concert Stages of Europe"	(1978)
		– "The Last Odd Day in L.A."	(2001)		
		Cynthia Ozick (1928–)		George Bowering (1935–)	
		– "The Shawl"	(1980)	– "A Short Story"	(1980)
				Sandra Birdsell (1942–)	
				– "Flowers for Weddings and Funerals"	(1980)
		Raymond Carver (1938–88)			
		–"What We Talk About When We Talk About Love"	(1981)		
		– "Cathedral"	(1983)		
		Leslie Marmon Silko (1948–)			
		– "Lullaby"	(1981)		
Kazuo Ishiguro (1954–)		Bobbie Ann Mason (1940–)		Matt Cohen (1942–99)	
– "A Family Supper"	(1982)	– "Shiloh"	(1982)	– "The Sins of Tomas Benares"	(1982)
				– "The Eiffel Tower in Three Parts"	(1987)

Time Chart (*continued*)

Great Britain	USA	Canada
		W. D. Valgardson (1939–) – "A Matter of Balance" (1982)
	Paule Marshall (1929–) – "Reena" (1983)	Margaret Atwood (1939–) – "Significant Moments in the Life of My Mother" (1983) – "Death by Landscape" (1989) – "The Age of Lead" (1989) – "The Little Red Hen Tells All" (1992)
	Thomas Pynchon (1937–) – "Entropy" (1984)	Timothy Findley (1930–2002) – "Dinner Along the Amazon" (1984)
		Leon Rooke (1934–) – "The Woman Who Talked to Horses" (1984)
		Marian Engel (1933–85) – "Anita's Dance" (1985)
		Alistair MacLeod (1936–) – "As Birds Bring Forth the Sun" (1985)
		Rohinton Mistry (1952–) – "Condolence Visit" (1986)
	Richard Ford (1944–) – "Sweethearts" (1987) – "Puppy" (2002)	Jane Urquhart (1949–) – "The Death of Robert Browning" (1987)
	Louise Erdrich (1954–) – "Fleur" (1988)	Dionne Brand (1953–) – "Photograph" (1988)
	Gerald Vizenor (1934–) – "Almost Browne" (1988)	
	Sandra Cisneros (1954–) – "The House on Mango Street" (1989)	

Time Chart (*continued*)

Great Britain		USA		Canada	
J. G. Ballard (1930–) – "Dream Cargoes"	(1990)	Amy Tan (1952–) – "Two Kinds"	(1989)		
				Thomas King (1943–) – "Borders"	(1991)
Salman Rushdie (1947–) – "The Prophet's Hair"	(1993)	Joy Williams (1944–) – "Honored Guest" – "The Girls"	(1994) (2004)		
		Jane Smiley (1949–) – "The Life of the Body"	(1994)		
Alison Kennedy (1965–) – "Awaiting an Adverse Reaction"	(1997)	Annie Proulx (1935–) – "Brokeback Mountain"	(1997)		
		Lorrie Moore (1957–) – "People Like That Are the Only People Here"	(1997)		
				Carol Shields (1935–2003) – "Our Men and Women"	(1999)
				Janice Kulyk Keefer (1952–) – "Dreams: Storms:Dogs"	(1999)
		T. Coraghessan Boyle (1948–) – "The Love of My Life"	(2000)	Lisa Moore (1964–) – "Mouths, Open"	(2000)
		Sherman Alexie (1966–) – "What You Pawn I Will Redeem"	(2003)	Elisabeth Harvor (1936–) – "One Whole Hour (Or Even More) with Proust and Novocaine"	(2003)
		John Edgar Wideman (1941–) – "What We Cannot Speak About We Must Pass Over in Silence"	(2003)		
Julian Barnes (1946–) – "The Revival"	(2004)				

Contributors

DR. HEINZ ANTOR is Professor of English Literatures at the University of Cologne. Among his recent publications are *Refractions of Canada in European Literature and Culture* (co-ed., 2005), *Refractions of Germany in Canadian Literature and Culture* (co-ed., 2003), and *English Literatures in International Contexts* (co-ed., 2000).

DR. RUDOLF BADER is Professor of English at Zurich University of Applied Sciences, School of Education. Among his works are a bi-lingual (English-German) edition of Shakespeare's comedy *The Merry Wives of Windsor* (2000) and an interdisciplinary introduction to Australian studies in German (2000).

GEORGIANA BANITA, M.A. is a Ph.D. student at the University of Constance. Among her forthcoming publications is "Translated or Traduced? Canadian Literary and Political Theory in a German Context: Northrop Frye, Michael Ignatieff, and Charles Taylor" in *Translating Canada: Charting the Institutions and Influence of Cultural Transfer: Canadian Writing in German/y*, ed. von Flotow and Nischik (2007).

DR. GORDON BÖLLING is Assistant Professor of English at the University of Cologne. His most recent publication is *History in the Making* (2006), a study of contemporary Canadian historical fiction. He is co-editor of *Refractions of Canada in European Literature and Culture* (2005) and author of "Acts of (Re-)Construction: Traces of Germany in Jane Urquhart's *The Stone Carvers*" (2003).

JULIA BREITBACH, M.A. is a research assistant at the University of Constance. She has worked on the short-story oeuvre of American minimalist writer Raymond Carver and is currently preparing a Ph.D. thesis on the role of photographic discourses in neorealist literature from the United States, Canada, and Great Britain.

DR. STEFAN FERGUSON is a teacher of English and French in Markdorf, Germany. His doctoral dissertation (available on microfiche) is entitled *Translating Margaret Atwood into German: A Study of Translation as Cultural Transfer* (2005). His article "Margaret Atwood in German/y: A Case Study" is forthcoming in *Translating Canada: Charting the*

Institutions and Influence of Cultural Transfer: Canadian Writing in German/y, ed. von Flotow and Nischik (2007).

DR. NADJA GERNALZICK is Assistant Professor of American Studies at the University of Mainz. Among her recent publications are "From Classical Dichotomy to Differantial Contract: The Derridean Integration of Monetary Theory" in *Metaphors of Economy* (ed. Bracker and Herbrechter, 2005) and "To Act or to Perform: Distinguishing Filmic Autobiography" (2006). An article on John Augustus Stone's *Metamora; or, the Last of the Wampanoags* in a volume on melodrama is forthcoming (ed. Kelleter and Mayer, 2007).

DR. BRIGITTE GLASER is Professor of British Literature and Cultural Studies at the University of Göttingen. She is the author of two monographs, *The Body in Samuel Richardson's* Clarissa (1994) and *The Creation of the Self in Autobiographical Forms of Writing in Seventeenth-Century England* (2001), and has recently co-edited the study *Europa interdisziplinär: Probleme und Perspektiven heutiger Europastudien* (2005).

DR. PAUL GOETSCH is Professor Emeritus of English Literature at the University of Freiburg. Among his book publications are *The Oral and the Written in Nineteenth-Century British Fiction* (2003), *Monsters in English Literature: From the Romantic Age to the First World War* (2002), and *Important Speeches by American Presidents after 1945* (ed., 1994).

DR. KONRAD GROSS was Professor of American and Canadian Literature at the University of Kiel until his retirement in 2005. Among his publications are *Probing Canadian Culture* (co-ed., 1991), "America and Canada: Continentalist Approaches" (2000), and "From Space to Place: Constructing Manitoba in Frederick Philip Grove's *Settlers of the Marsh* and *Fruits of the Earth*" (2000).

EVA GRUBER is Assistant Professor of American Literature at the University of Constance. Among her publications are "Humour in Contemporary Native Canadian Literature" (2005) and the forthcoming "Native Canadian Literature in German/y" (in *Translating Canada: Charting the Institutions and Influence of Cultural Transfer: Canadian Writing in German/y*, ed. von Flotow and Nischik, 2007). Her completed Ph.D. thesis with the working title "Reimagining Nativeness: Humour in Contemporary Native American Literature" is scheduled to appear in 2007.

DR. LOTHAR HÖNNIGHAUSEN is Professor Emeritus of North American Studies at the University of Bonn. Among his recent publications are *William Faulkner: Masks and Metaphors* (1997), *Space — Place — Environment* (co-ed., 2004), and "Defining Regionalism in North American Studies," in *Regionalism in the Age of Globalism*, 2 vols. (co-ed., 2005).

DR. HEINZ ICKSTADT is Professor Emeritus of American Literature at the John F. Kennedy Institute of North American Studies, FU Berlin. Among his publications are "Myth and History — Symbolizations of the Frontier in US-American and Canadian Fiction" and "The City in English-Canadian and US-American Literature," both published in a collection of his essays, *Faces of Fiction* (2001).

DR. WOLFGANG KLOOSS is Professor of English at the University of Trier. He has edited *Narratives of Exploration and Discovery: Essays in Honour of Konrad Groß* (2005), *Across the Lines: Intertextuality and Transcultural Communication in the New Literatures in English* (1998), and *Giving Voice: Canadian and German Perspectives* (co-ed., 2001).

NINA KÜCK, M.A. works as a postgraduate research associate at the University of Constance and is coordinator of the Network Transatlantic Cooperation. She is currently preparing a Ph.D. thesis on the sociological and political role of the semantics of love in Margaret Atwood's novels.

DR. MARTIN KUESTER is Professor of English Literature at the University of Marburg and Director of the Marburg Centre for Canadian Studies. Among his publications are *Framing Truths: Parodic Structures in Contemporary English-Canadian Historical Novels* (1992), *Reflections of Canada: The Reception of Canadian Literature in Germany* (co-ed., 2000), and *Writing Canadians: The Literary Construction of Ethnic Identities* (co-ed., 2002).

DR. MARIA LÖSCHNIGG is Assistant Professor of English and Canadian Literature at the University of Graz. She has published, together with Martin Löschnigg, the first history of English-Canadian literature in German (*Kurze Geschichte der kanadischen Literatur*, 2001). Other recent publications include the articles "Mavis Gallant's Dramas of Displacement" (in *Canada in the Sign of Migration and Trans-Culturalism*, ed. K-D. Ertler and Martin Löschnigg, 2004) and "Di Brandt's Poetic Work" (2004).

DR. MARTIN LÖSCHNIGG is Associate Professor of English at the University of Graz and Vice Director of the Graz Centre for Canadian Studies. He is co-author of *Kurze Geschichte der kanadischen Literatur* (2001) and co-editor of *Canada 2000: Identity and Transformation* (2000) and of *Canada in the Sign of Migration and Trans-Culturalism* (2004).

DR. DIETER MEINDL was Professor of American Literature at the University of Erlangen-Nürnberg until his retirement in 2006. His *North American Encounters: Essays in U.S. and English and French Canadian Literature and Culture* (2002) features treatments of "Modernism and the English Canadian Short Story Cycle" and "Gender and Narrative

Perspective in Margaret Atwood's Stories." He has also dealt with "(Un-) Reliable Narration from a Pronominal Perspective" (2005).

DR. SILVIA MERGENTHAL is Professor of English Literature at the University of Constance. Among her recent publications are *A Fast-Forward Version of England: Englishness in Contemporary Fiction* (2003) and *Autorinnen der viktorianischen Epoche* (2003). She also contributed the article on Katherine Mansfield and Virginia Woolf to *Geschichte der englischen Kurzgeschichte* (ed. Löffler and Späth, 2005).

DR. REINGARD M. NISCHIK is Professor of American Literature at the University of Constance. Among her recent publications are the award-winning *Margaret Atwood: Works and Impact* (ed., 2000; paperback 2002) and the chapter "Margaret Atwood's Short Stories and Shorter Fictions" in *The Cambridge Companion to Margaret Atwood* (ed. Howells, 2006). She is currently co-editing the forthcoming volume *Translating Canada: Charting the Institutions and Influence of Cultural Transfer: Canadian Writing in German/y*, to appear in 2007.

DR. FABIENNE QUENNET is an academic assistant at the University of Marburg. Among her recent publications are *Where Indians Fear to Tread: A Postmodern Reading of Louise Erdrich's North Dakota Quartet* (2001), "Jewish Food and Jewish Women's Identity in Tova Mirvis' *The Ladies Auxiliary*" (2004), and "Mordecai Richler, Montreal and the War: Reading *The Street*" (2005).

DR. CAROLINE ROSENTHAL is Assistant Professor of American Literature at the University of Constance. Her publications include *Narrative Deconstructions of Gender in Works by Audrey Thomas, Daphne Marlatt, and Louise Erdrich* (2003), "Canonizing Atwood: Her Impact on Teaching in the US, Canada, and Europe" in *Margaret Atwood: Works and Impact* (ed. Nischik, 2000/2002), and "Comparing Mythologies: The Canadian North versus the American West" in *Regionalism in the Age of Globalism* (ed. Hönnighausen et al. 2005).

MARTINA SEIFERT is DAAD-Lecturer in German Studies at Queen's University Belfast. She has published *Rewriting Newfoundland Mythology: The Works of Tom Dawe* (2000), "The Image Trap: The Translation of English-Canadian Children's Literature into German" (2005), and is co-author of *Ent-Fernungen: Fremdwahrnehmung und Kulturtransfer in der deutschsprachigen Kinder- und Jugendliteratur seit 1945* (2006).

DR. CHRISTINA STROBEL (Munich) is the author of *Reconsidering Conventions: Jane Rule's Writing and Sexual Identity in North American Feminist Theory and Fiction* (1999) and "Reconsidering Conventions:

Fictions of the Lesbian" (in *International Journal of Canadian Studies*, 1995), and the co-editor of *Selbst und Andere-s: Von Begegnungen und Grenzziehungen: Feministische Arbeiten im Rahmen der Kanada-Studien* (1998).

DR. WALDEMAR ZACHARASIEWICZ is Professor of American Literature and Director of the Centre for Canadian Studies at the University of Vienna. Among his publications are *Canadian Interculturality and the Transatlantic Heritage/Interculturalité canadienne et héritage transatlantique* (co-ed., 2005) and *Möglichkeiten und Grenzen des Multikulturalismus: Der Schutz sprachlich-kultureller Vielfalt in Kanada und Europa/The Protection of Cultural and Linguistic Diversity in Canada and in Europe: Chances and Obstacles of Multiculturalism* (ed., 2004). His book *Images of Germany in American Literature* is forthcoming.

DR. JUTTA ZIMMERMANN is Assistant Professor of American Studies at the University of Jena. She has written a monograph on Canadian metafiction (*Metafiktion im anglokanadischen Roman der Gegenwart*, 1996). Other publications include "'My Canada Includes the North': Literary Representations of the Canadian North in the 1990s" (2005) and "The Recreation of History on the Prairie: Rudy Wiebe" (1994).

Index